Best Editorial Cartoons of the Year

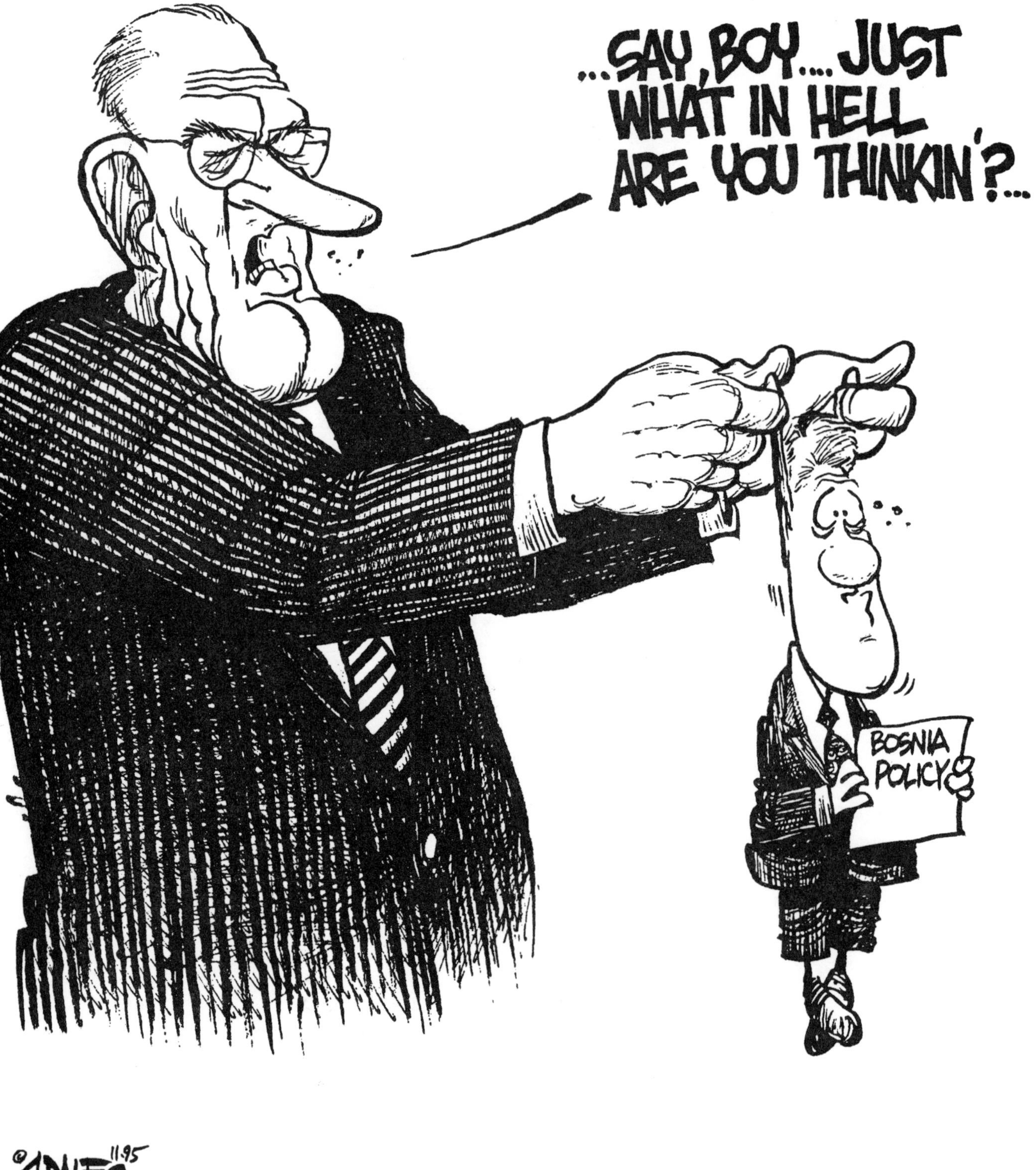
...SAY, BOY.... JUST WHAT IN HELL ARE YOU THINKIN'?...
BOSNIA POLICY

DALE STEPHANOS
Courtesy Haverhill Gazette (Mass.)

BEST EDITORIAL CARTOONS OF THE YEAR

1996 EDITION

Edited by
CHARLES BROOKS

PELICAN PUBLISHING COMPANY
Gretna 1996

Library of Congress Serial Catalog Data

Best editorial cartoons. 1972-
  Gretna [La.] Pelican Pub. Co,
  v. 29 cm annual-
  "A pictorial history of the year."

  1. United States—Politics and government—
1969—Caricatures and Cartoons—Periodicals.
E839.5.B45   320.9'7309240207   73-643645
ISSN 0091-2220   MARC-S

Manufactured in the United States of America
Published by Pelican Publishing Company, Inc,
1101 Monroe Street, Gretna, Louisiana 70053

Contents

Award-Winning Cartoons

1995 PULITZER PRIZE

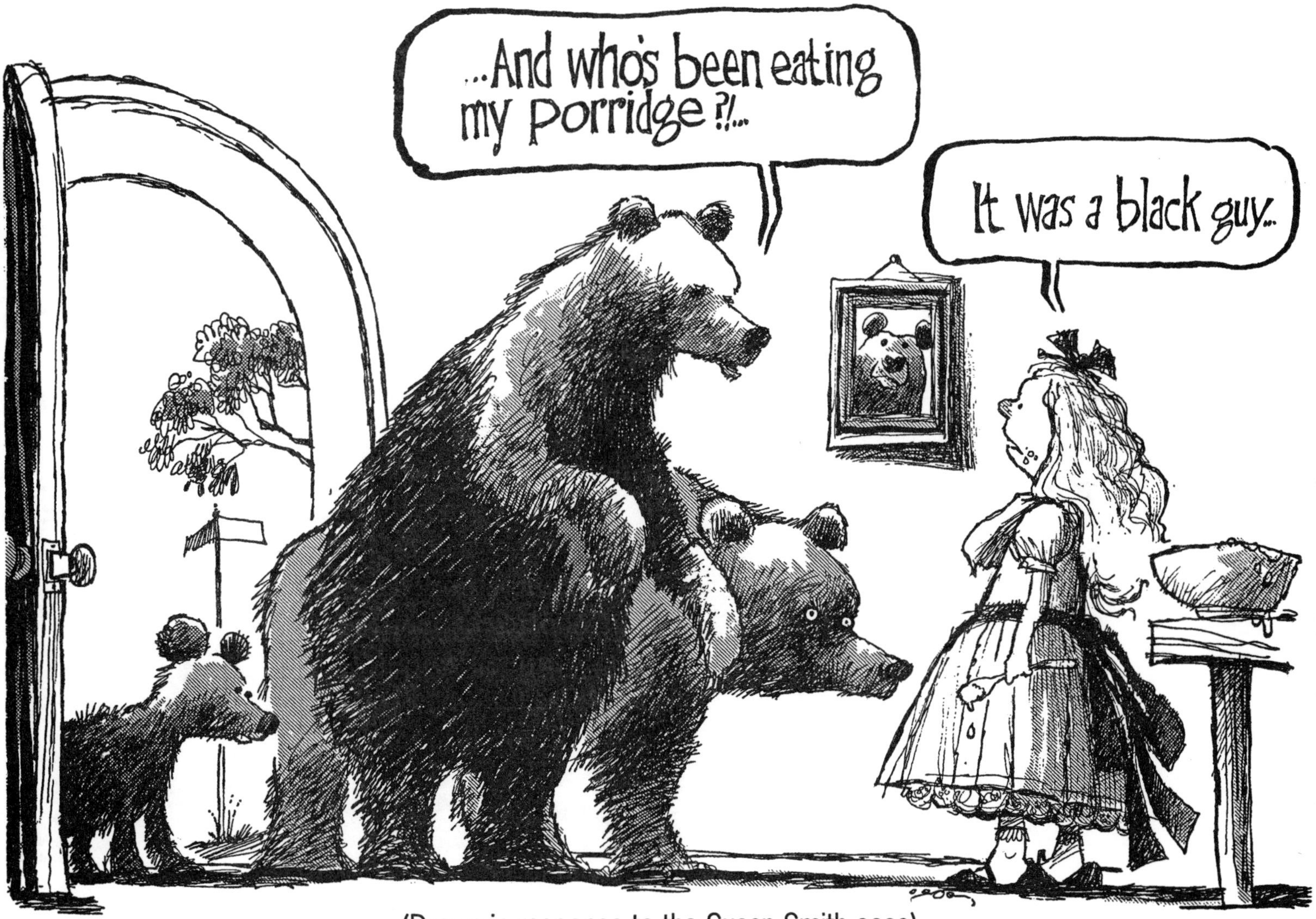
...And who's been eating my porridge ?!...
It was a black guy..

(Drawn in response to the Susan Smith case)

MIKE LUCKOVICH

Editorial Cartoonist
Atlanta Constitution

Born January 28, 1960; editorial cartoonist for the *Greenville News,* 1984-85, the *New Orleans Times-Picayune,* 1985-89, and the *Atlanta Constitution,* 1989 to the present; winner of the Overseas Press Club Award, 1990 and 1994, the National Headliners Club Award, 1992, and the Robert F. Kennedy Award, 1994; syndicated in 150 newspapers.

1994 NATIONAL SOCIETY OF PROFESSIONAL JOURNALISTS AWARD
(Selected in 1995)

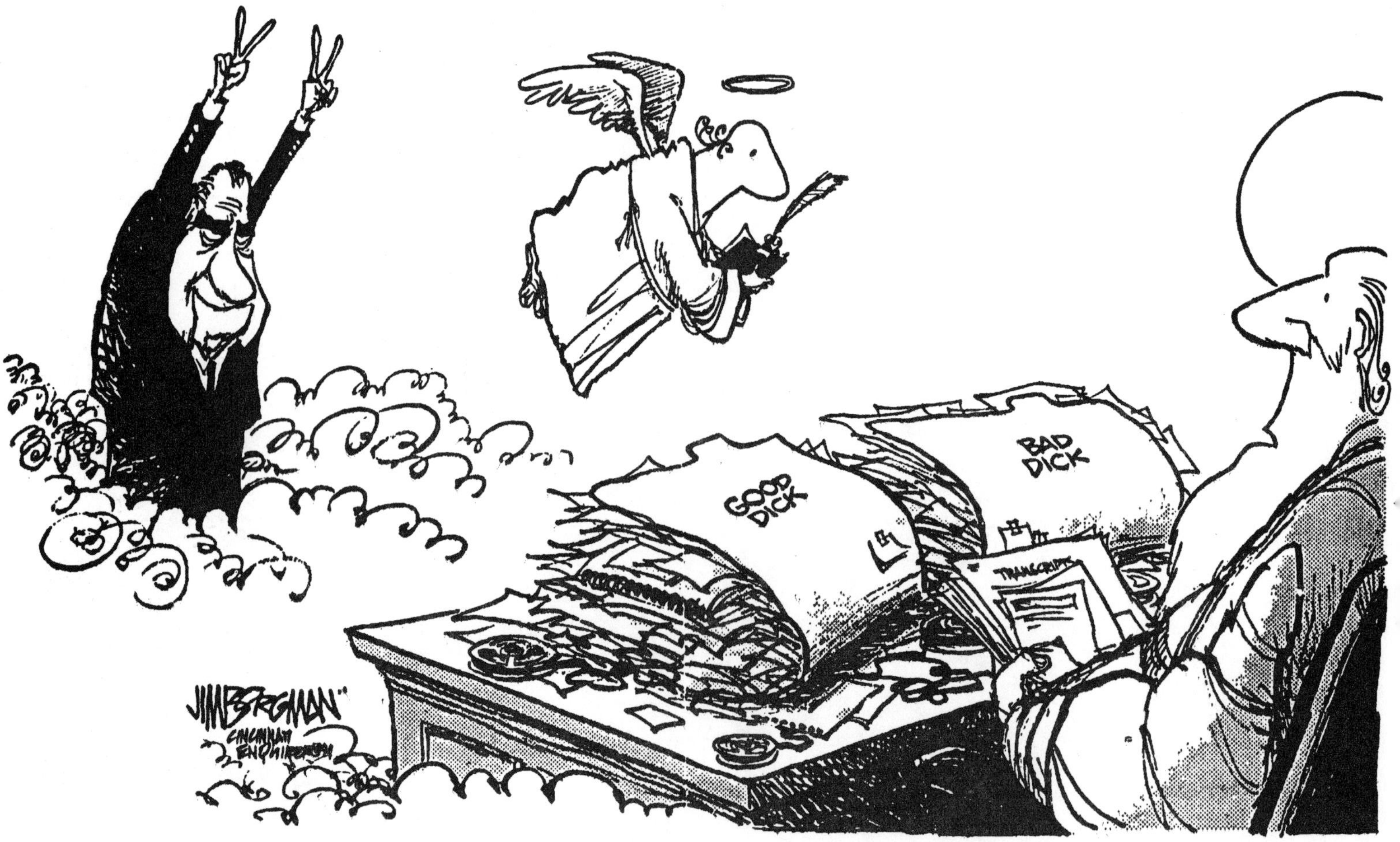
GOOD DICK
BAD DICK
JIMBORGMAN

"CANCEL MY APPOINTMENTS..... THIS ONE MAY TAKE AWHILE."

JIM BORGMAN

Editorial Cartoonist
Cincinnati Enquirer

Born in Cincinnati, February 24, 1954; graduated summa cum laude with Phi Beta Kappa honors from Kenyon College, 1976; editorial cartoonist for the *Cincinnati Enquirer,* 1976 to the present; cartoons syndicated by King Features to some two hundred newspapers; winner of the Sigma Delta Chi Award, 1978, the National Headliners Club Award, 1991, and the Reuben Award, 1993; author or coauthor of four cartoon books.

1995 NATIONAL HEADLINERS CLUB AWARD

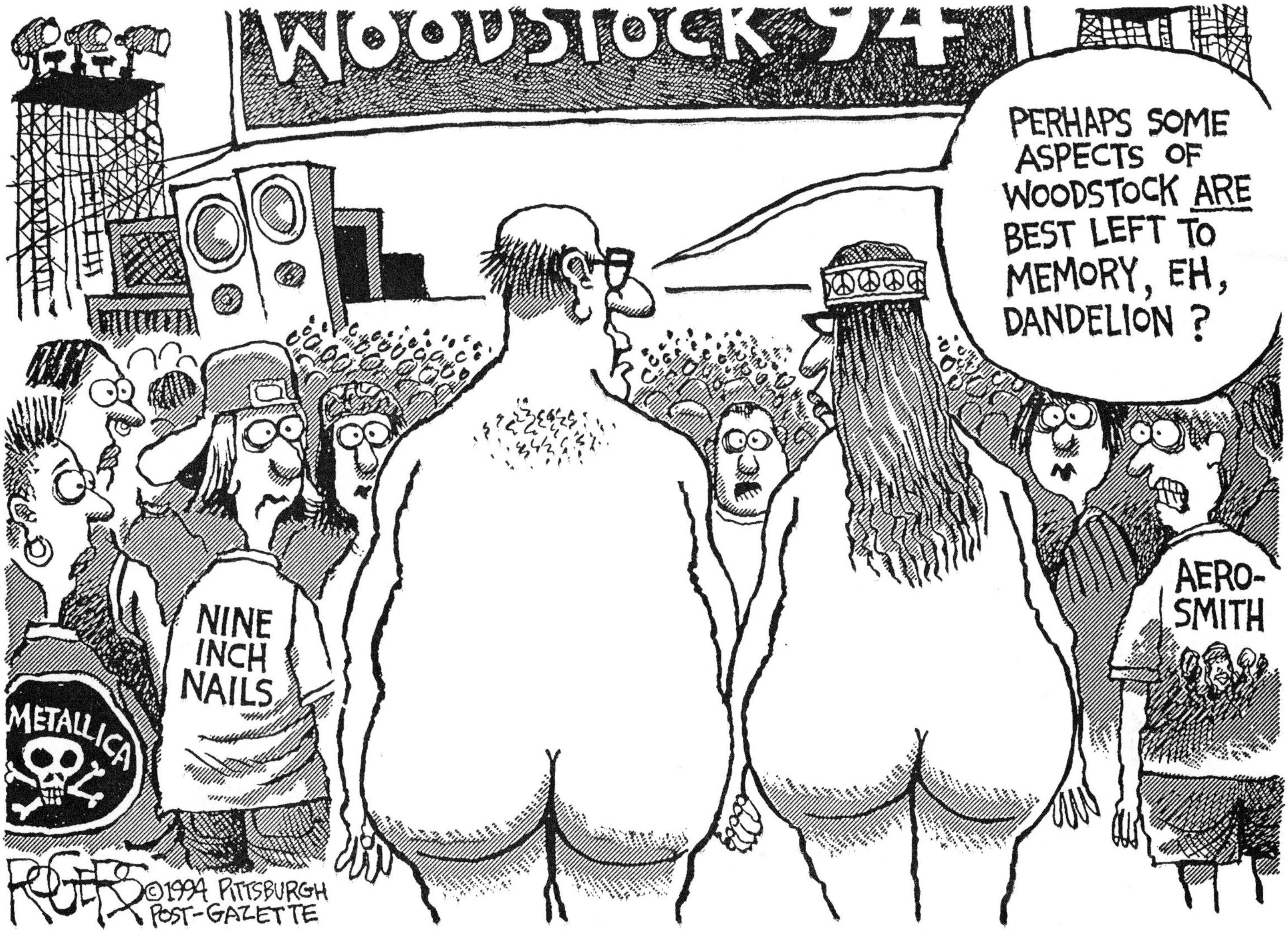
WOODSTOCK 94
PERHAPS SOME ASPECTS OF WOODSTOCK ARE BEST LEFT TO MEMORY, EH, DANDELION ?
NINE INCH NAILS
METALLICA
AERO-SMITH
ROGERS ©1994 PITTSBURGH POST-GAZETTE

ROB ROGERS

Editorial Cartoonist
Pittsburgh Post-Gazette

Born in Philadelphia; attended Oklahoma State University and holds degrees from Central State University and Carnegie Mellon University; editorial cartoonist for the *Pittsburgh Press,* 1984-92, and the *Pittsburgh Post-Gazette,* 1992 to the present; cartoons syndicated by United Features Syndicate since 1988; winner of the Golden Quill Award, 1987, 1989, 1990, and 1993.

1995 FISCHETTI AWARD

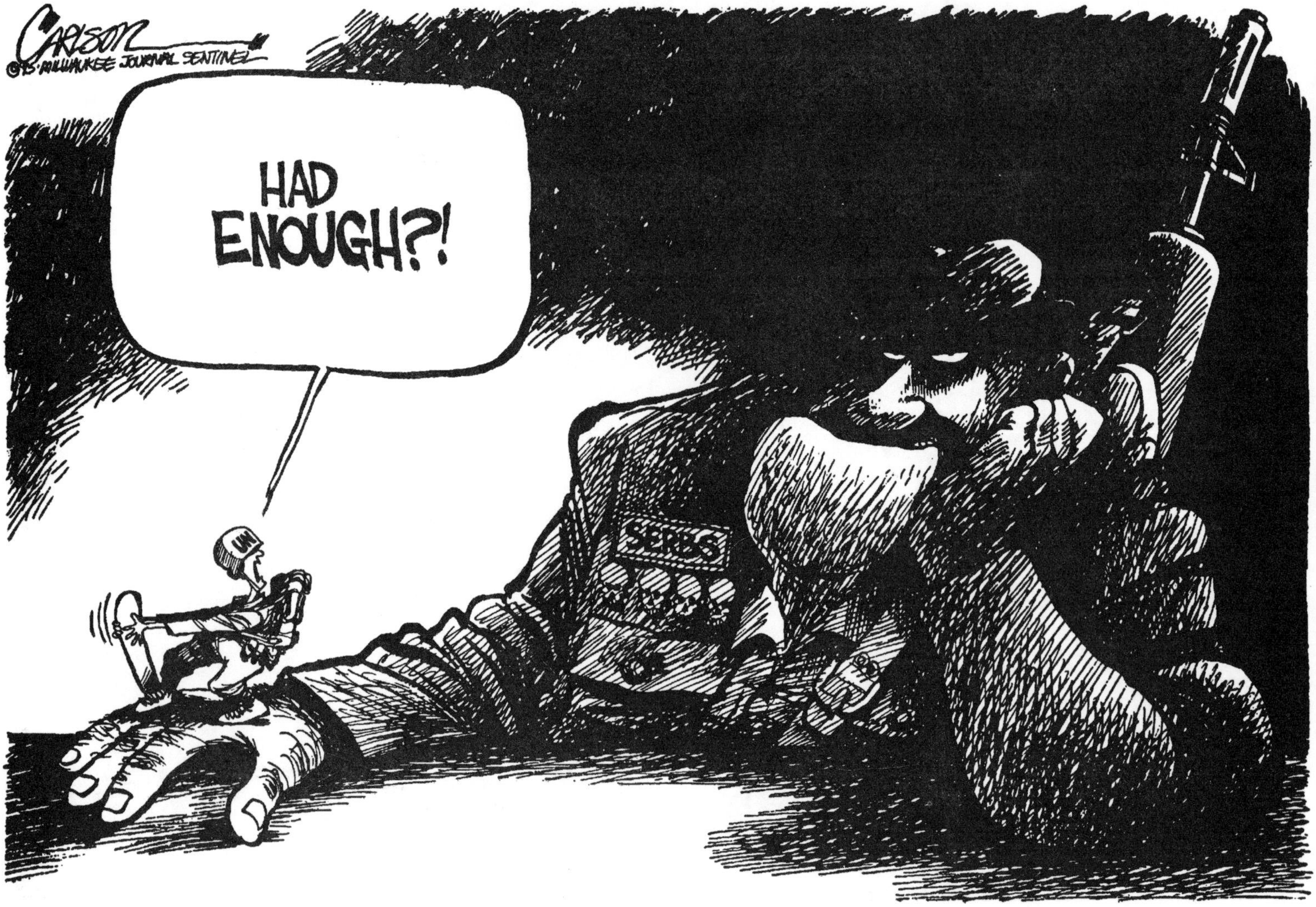
CARLSON
©'95 MILWAUKEE JOURNAL SENTINEL
HAD ENOUGH?!
SERBS

STUART CARLSON

Editorial Cartoonist
Milwaukee Journal Sentinel

Native of West Bend, Wisconsin; reporter, cartoonist, and editor for weekly and daily newspapers in Wisconsin; winner of various honors for his work, including the National Press Foundation Award for cartooning, 1991; editorial cartoonist for the *Milwaukee Journal Sentinel,* 1983 to the present.

1994 NATIONAL NEWSPAPER AWARD/CANADA
(Awarded in 1995)

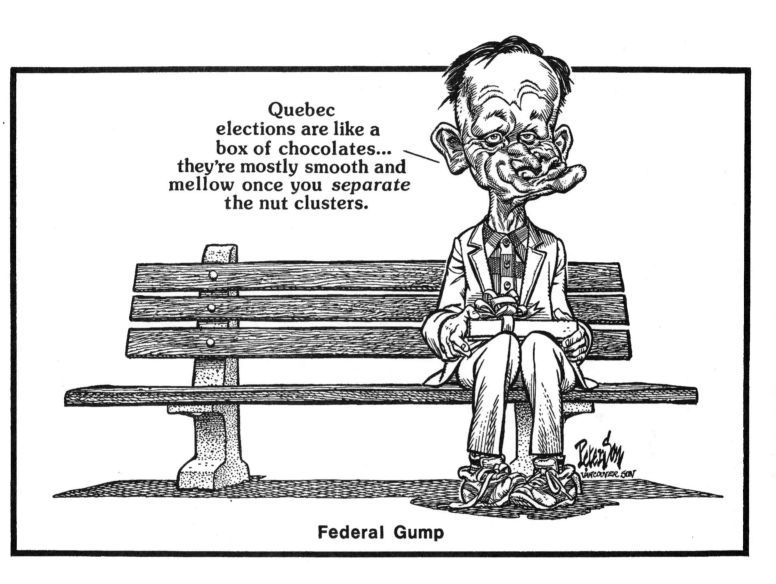

Quebec elections are like a box of chocolates... they're mostly smooth and mellow once you *separate* the nut clusters.

Federal Gump

ROY PETERSON

Editorial Cartoonist
Vancouver Sun

Born in Winnipeg, Manitoba, 1936; editorial cartoonist for the *Vancouver Sun,* 1962 to the present; cartoonist/illustrator for *Maclean's* newsmagazine, 1962 to the present; winner of five national Canadian newspaper awards; winner of the International Salon of Cartoons Grand Prize, 1973; syndicated by Torstar of Canada and Cartoonists & Writers of New York; past president of the Association of Canadian Editorial Cartoonists and of the Association of American Editorial Cartoonists.

1995 NATIONAL PRESS FOUNDATION AWARD

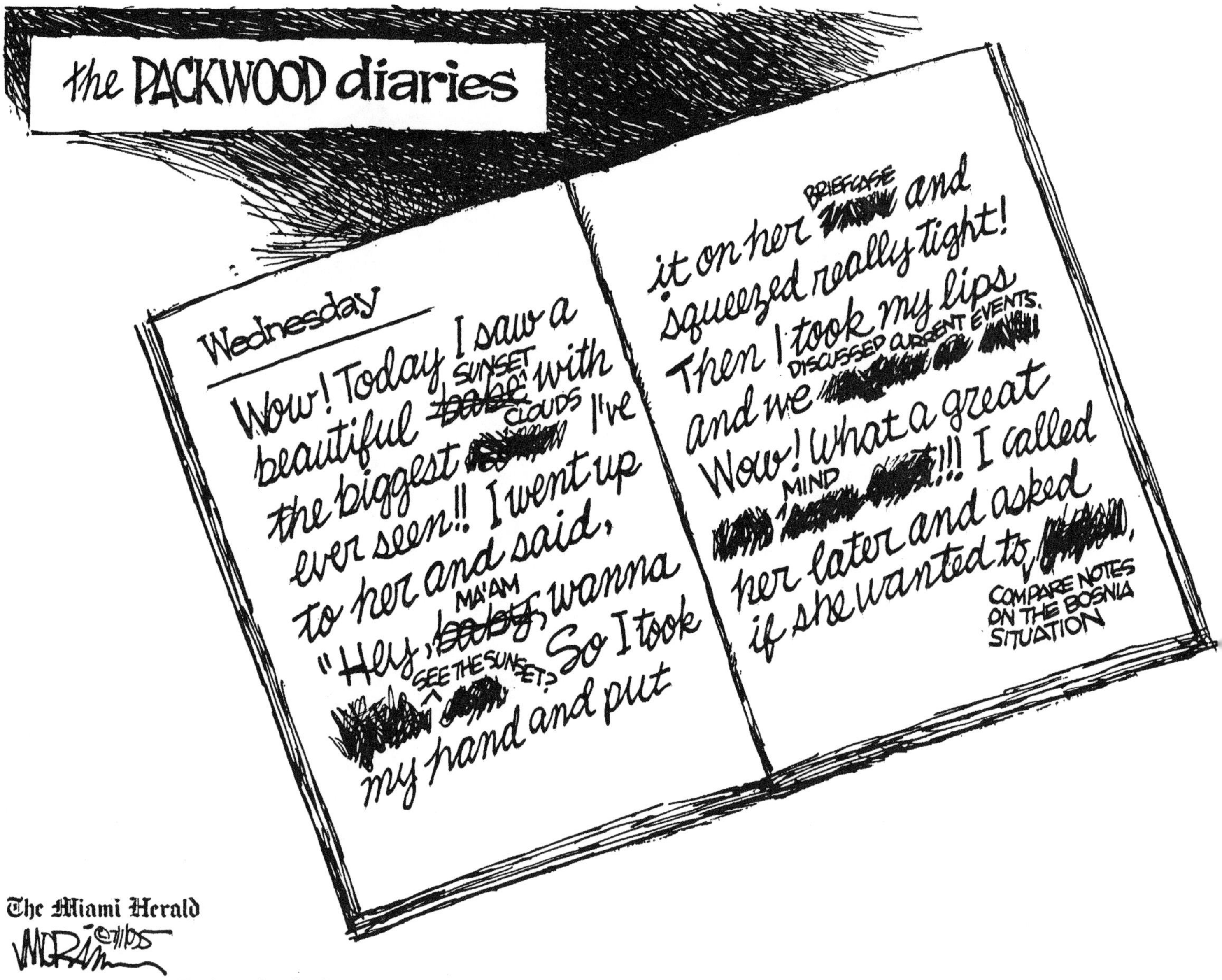
the PACKWOOD diaries
Wednesday
Wow! Today I saw a beautiful babe SUNSET with the biggest CLOUDS I've ever seen!! I went up to her and said, "Hey, baby MA'AM, wanna SEE THE SUNSET?" So I took my hand and put
it on her BRIEFCASE and squeezed really tight! Then I took my lips and we DISCUSSED CURRENT EVENTS. Wow! What a great MIND!!! I called her later and asked if she wanted to COMPARE NOTES ON THE BOSNIA SITUATION
The Miami Herald
MORIN ©7/95

Distributed by King Features Syndicate

JIM MORIN

Editorial Cartoonist
Miami Herald

Born in Washington, D.C., January 30, 1953; graduated from Syracuse University, 1976; editorial cartoonist for the *Beaumont Enterprise and Journal,* 1976-77, the *Richmond Times-Dispatch,* 1977-78, and the *Miami Herald,* 1978 to the present; syndicated internationally by King Features Syndicate; received the Overseas Press Club Award in 1979 and 1990, the Mencken Award in 1990, the Fischetti Award in 1991, and the National Cartoonist Society Award in 1992; author of three books.

Best Editorial Cartoons of the Year

Presidential Portraits

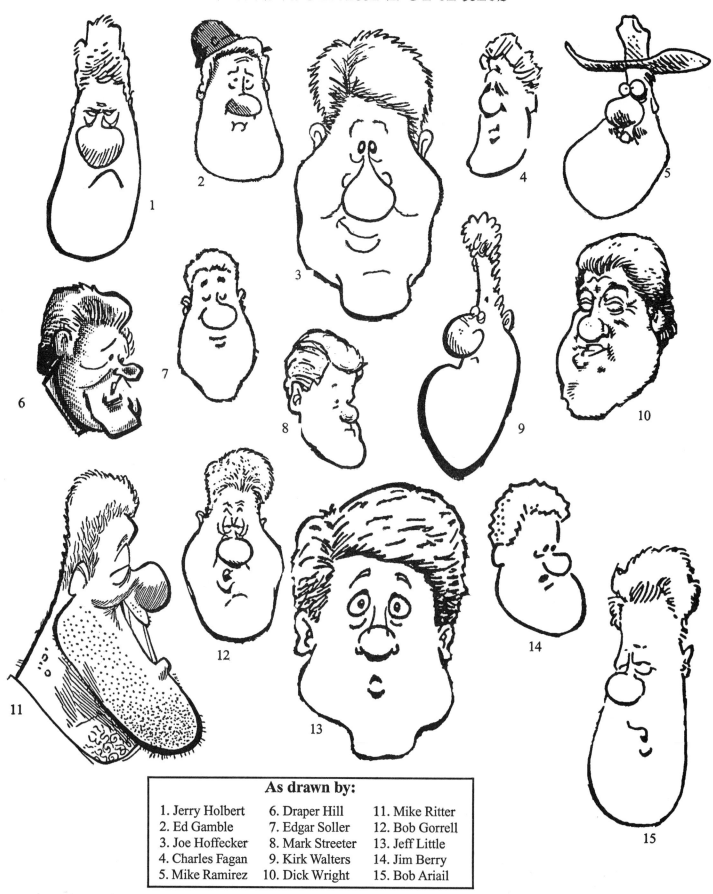

As drawn by:		
1. Jerry Holbert	6. Draper Hill	11. Mike Ritter
2. Ed Gamble	7. Edgar Soller	12. Bob Gorrell
3. Joe Hoffecker	8. Mark Streeter	13. Jeff Little
4. Charles Fagan	9. Kirk Walters	14. Jim Berry
5. Mike Ramirez	10. Dick Wright	15. Bob Ariail

The Clinton Administration

After months of acrimonious debate, the Republican-led Congress voted to overhaul Medicare and reduce spending, and was challenging President Clinton head on to balance the budget as 1995 ended. Although Clinton had campaigned on much the same program in 1992, he and his party charged that the GOP program was callous and cruel to the poor, to children, and to the elderly. Although he acknowledged he had raised taxes too high, he promised to veto any budget cuts he considered too extreme.

Surgeon Gen. Joycelyn Elders was fired by Clinton, who then nominated Dr. Henry Foster for the post. After Foster admitted to having performed "about thirty-nine abortions," a Senate filibuster killed his bid for the post.

In the long-running Whitewater investigation, three Arkansas cronies of the Clintons were indicted. At year's end, Senate investigators were still trying to locate billing reports detailing Mrs. Clinton's legal work in connection with Whitewater matters.

Clinton orchestrated a $40-billion bailout of the Mexican economy, despite heated opposition. He also extended formal diplomatic recognition to Vietnam.

MICHAEL RAMIREZ
Courtesy Memphis Commercial Appeal

RAMIREZ
FIRST, THE REPUBLICANS ACTED TO CUT THE SIZE OF GOVERNMENT, ITS ENTITLEMENTS, SPENDING AND THE DEFICIT...
THEN THEY MOVED TO SAVE MEDICARE FROM BANKRUPTCY...
NOW THEY WANT TO BALANCE THE BUDGET...
THERE'S NO WAY I CAN GO ALONG WITH THAT KIND OF EXTREMISM.

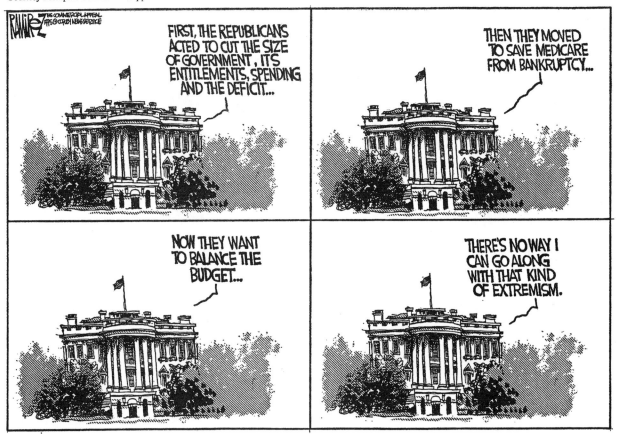

MICHAEL RAMIREZ
Courtesy Memphis Commercial Appeal

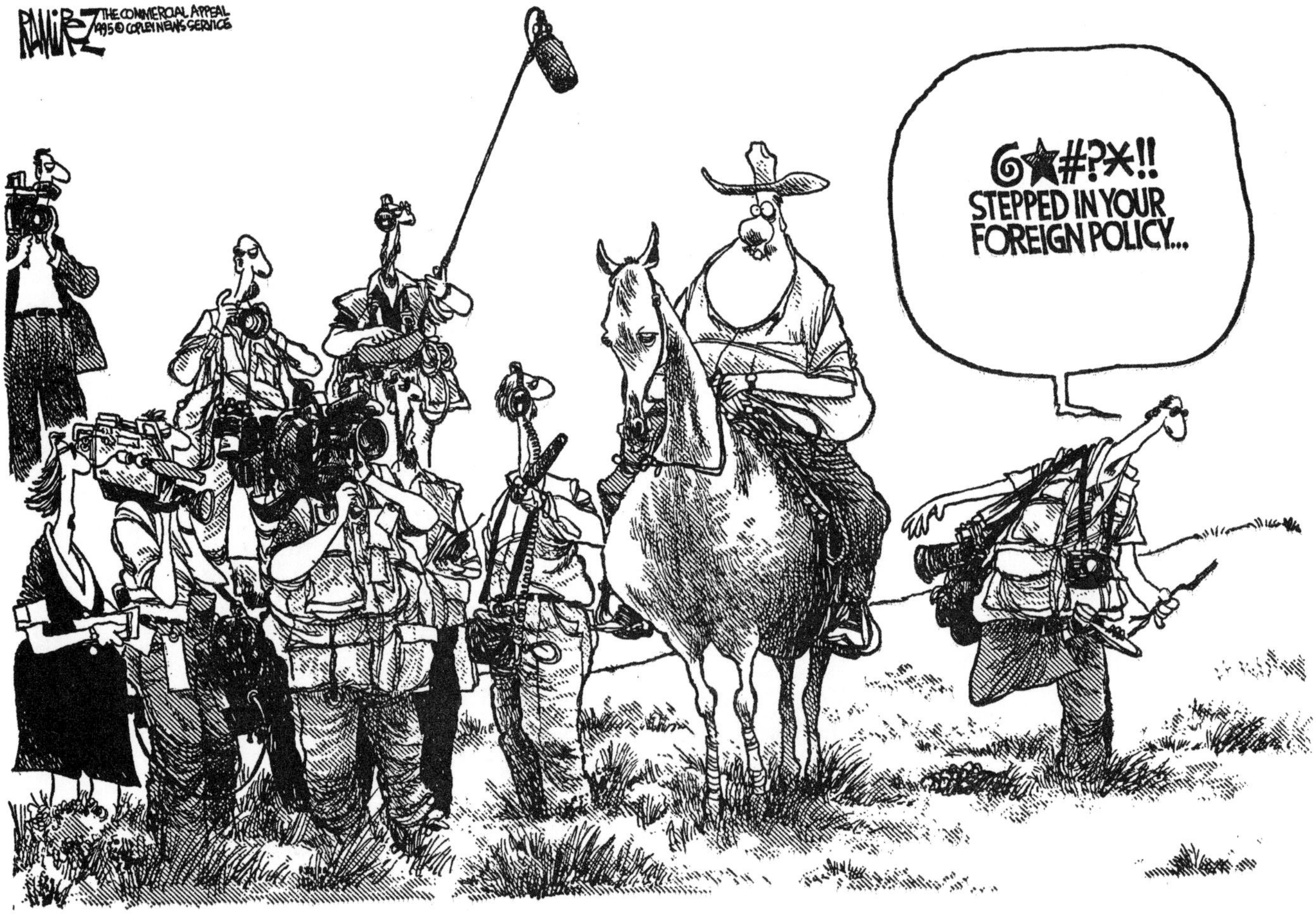
RAMIREZ THE COMMERCIAL APPEAL 1995 © COPLEY NEWS SERVICE
6★#?*!!
STEPPED IN YOUR
FOREIGN POLICY...

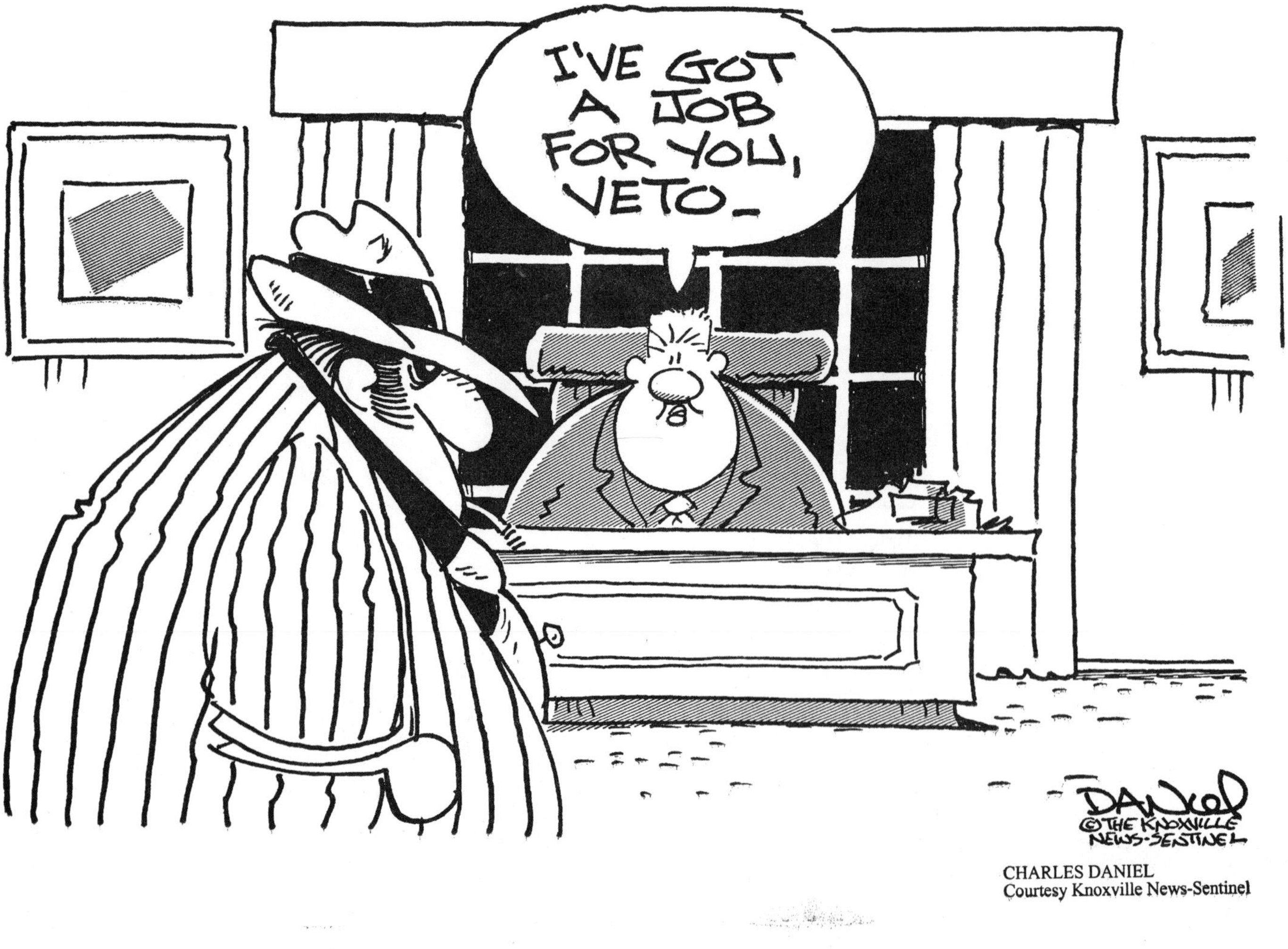
I'VE GOT
A JOB
FOR YOU,
VETO_
DANIEL
© THE KNOXVILLE
NEWS-SENTINEL

CHARLES DANIEL
Courtesy Knoxville News-Sentinel

STEVE KELLEY
Courtesy San Diego Union

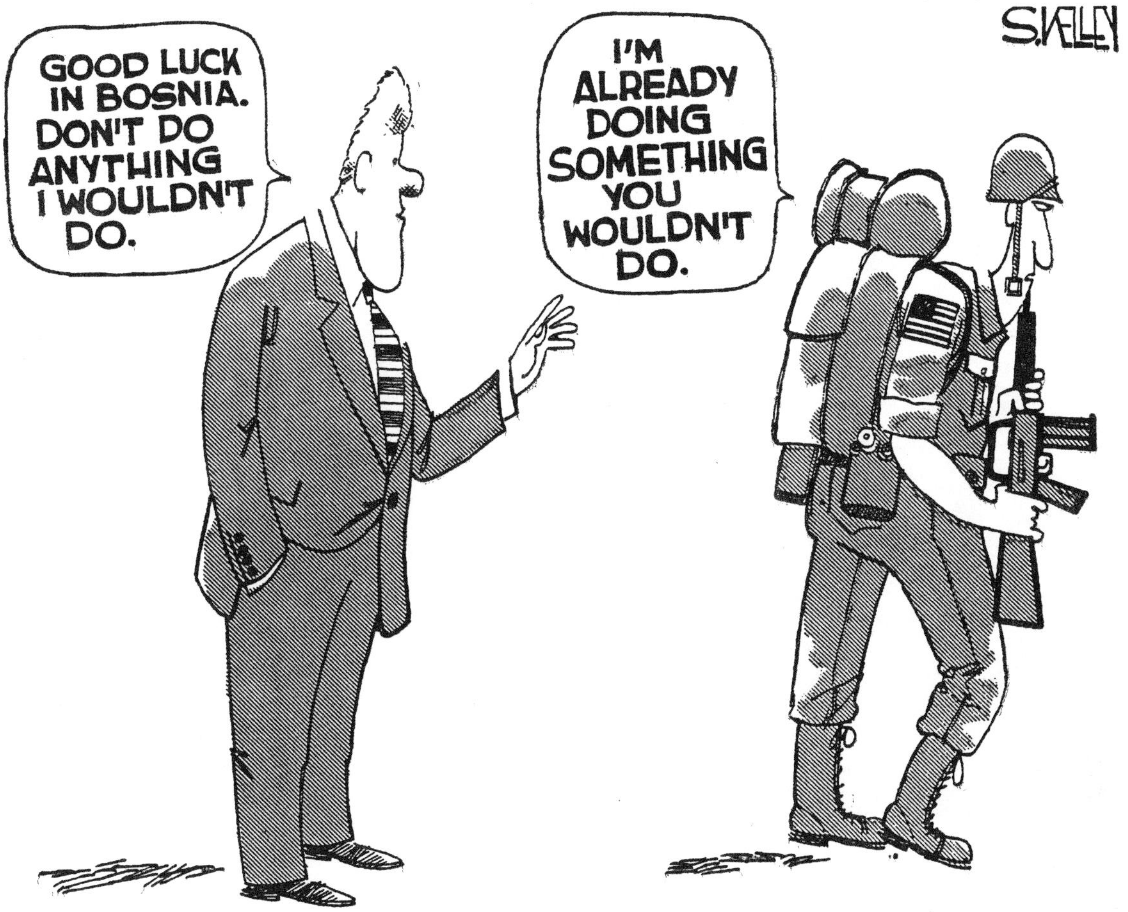
GOOD LUCK IN BOSNIA. DON'T DO ANYTHING I WOULDN'T DO.
I'M ALREADY DOING SOMETHING YOU WOULDN'T DO.
S.KELLEY

ROBERT ARIAIL
Courtesy The State (S.C.)

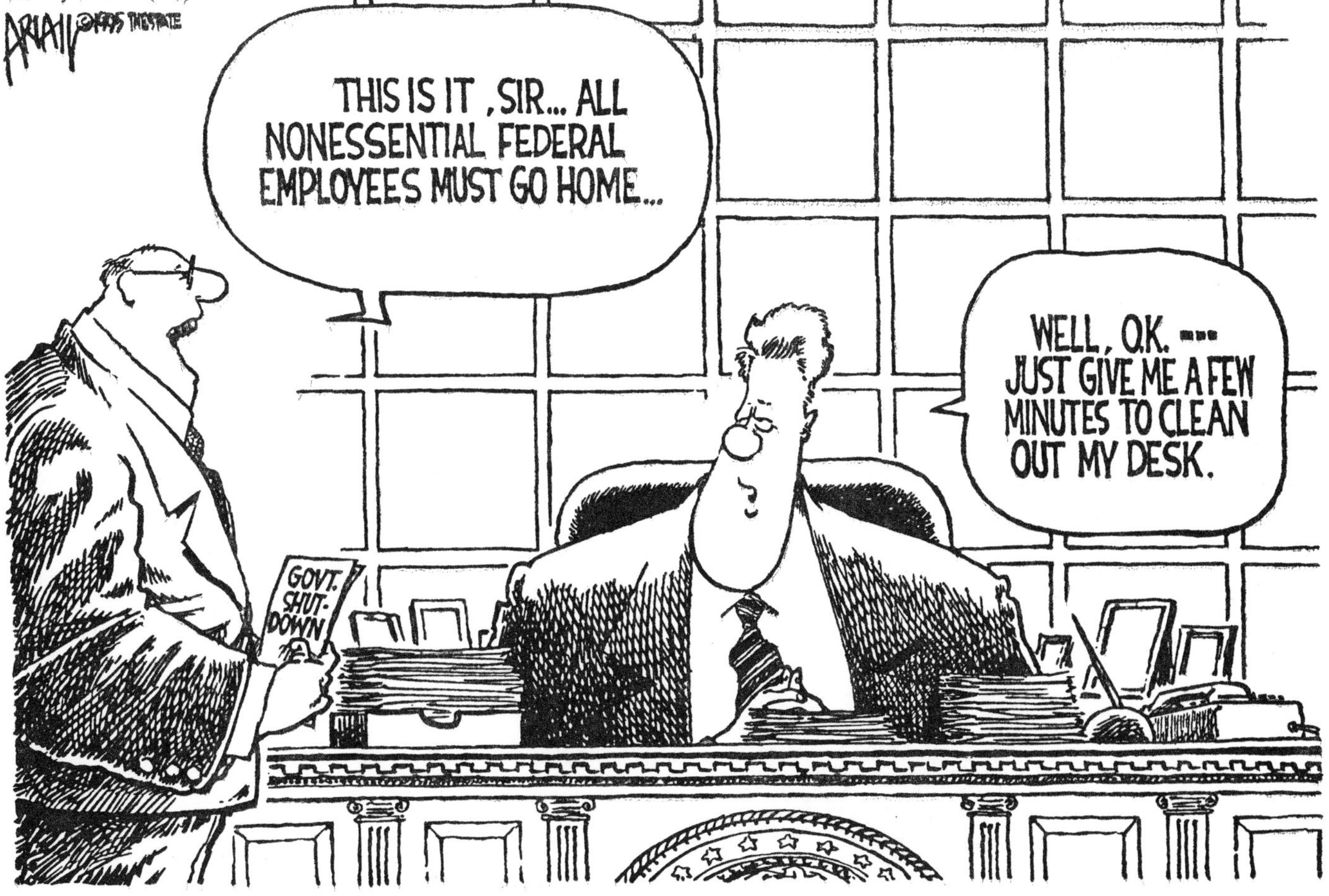
ARIAIL ©1995 THE STATE
THIS IS IT, SIR... ALL NONESSENTIAL FEDERAL EMPLOYEES MUST GO HOME...
WELL, O.K. --- JUST GIVE ME A FEW MINUTES TO CLEAN OUT MY DESK.
GOVT. SHUT-DOWN

JOE HOFFECKER
Courtesy Cincinnati Business Courier

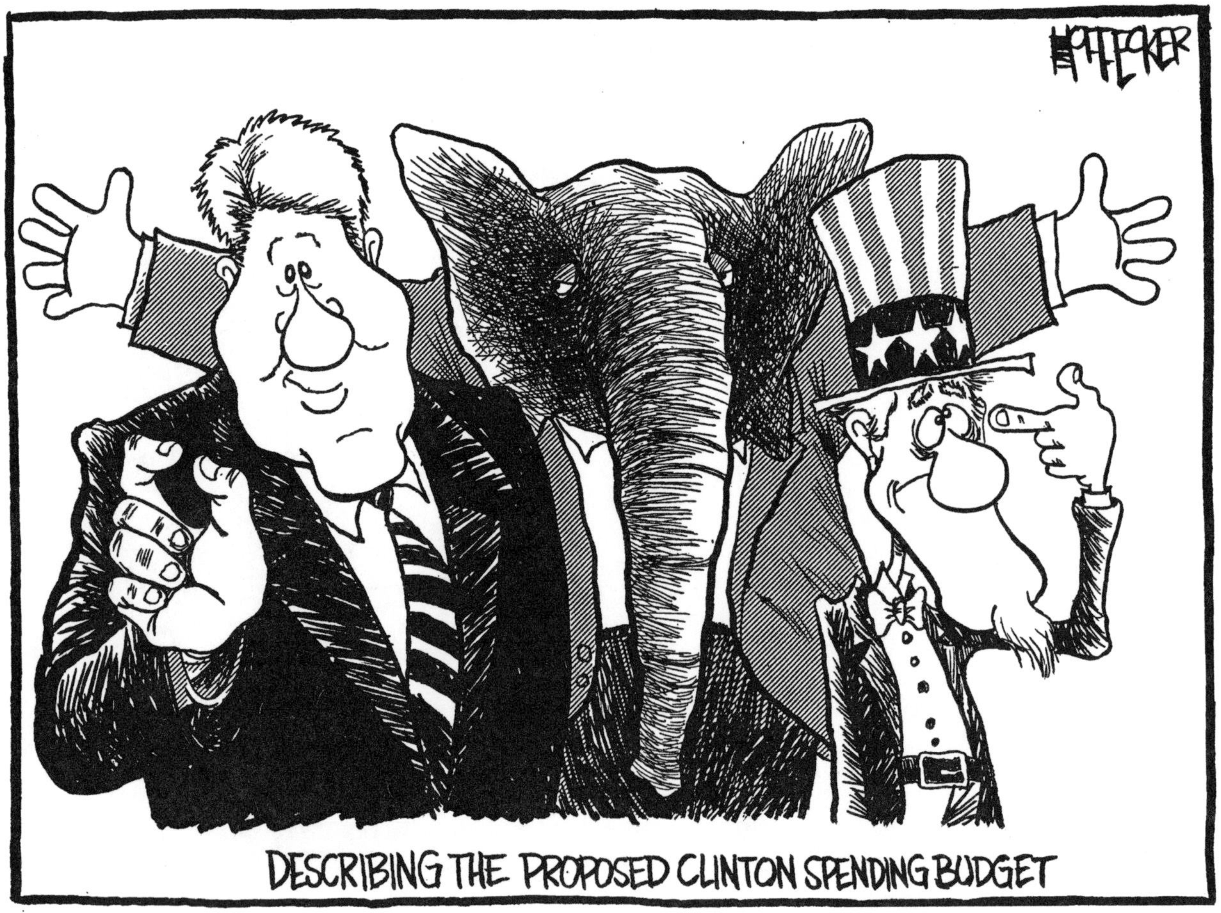
HOFFECKER
DESCRIBING THE PROPOSED CLINTON SPENDING BUDGET

CHARLES FAGAN
Courtesy Associated Features Syndicate

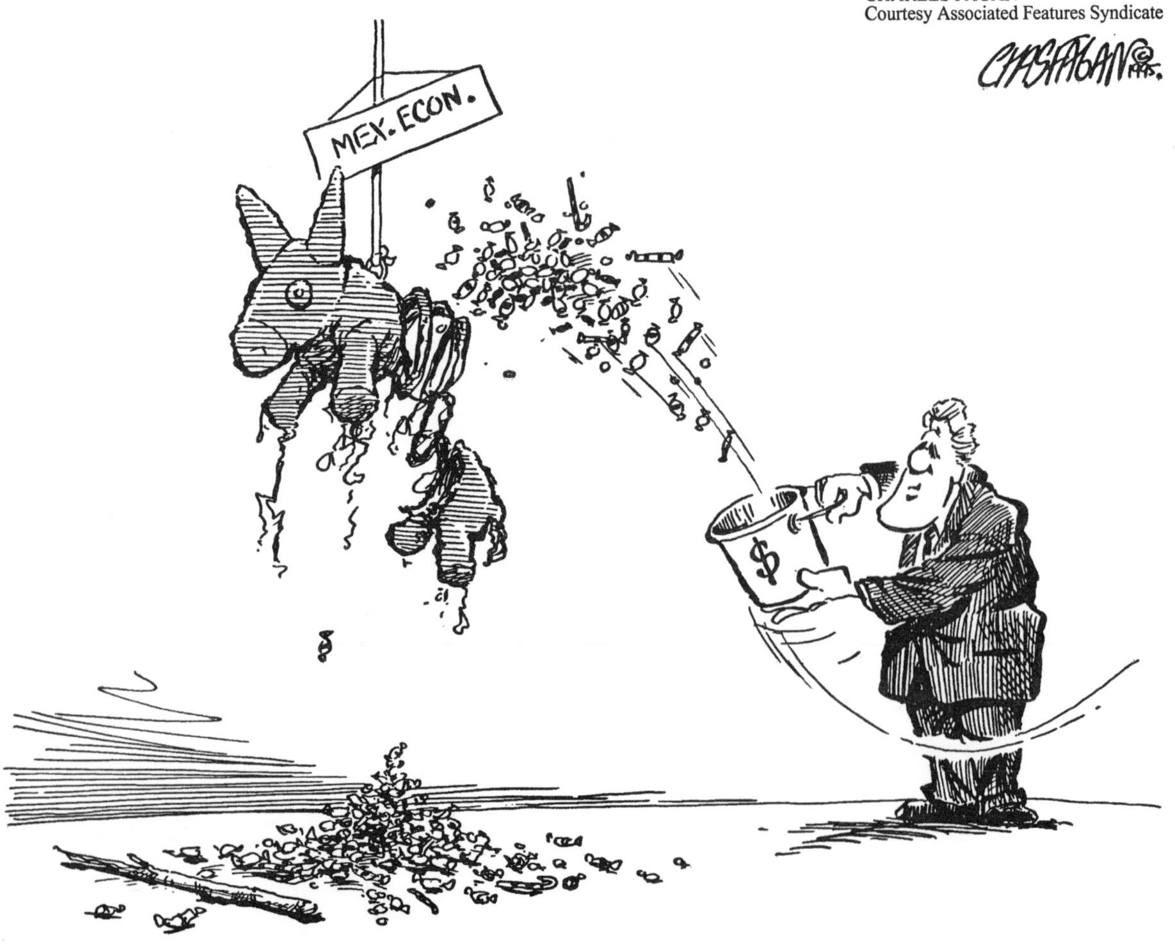
CHAS FAGAN © 1995.
MEX. ECON.
$

VIC HARVILLE
Courtesy Arkansas Democrat-Gazette

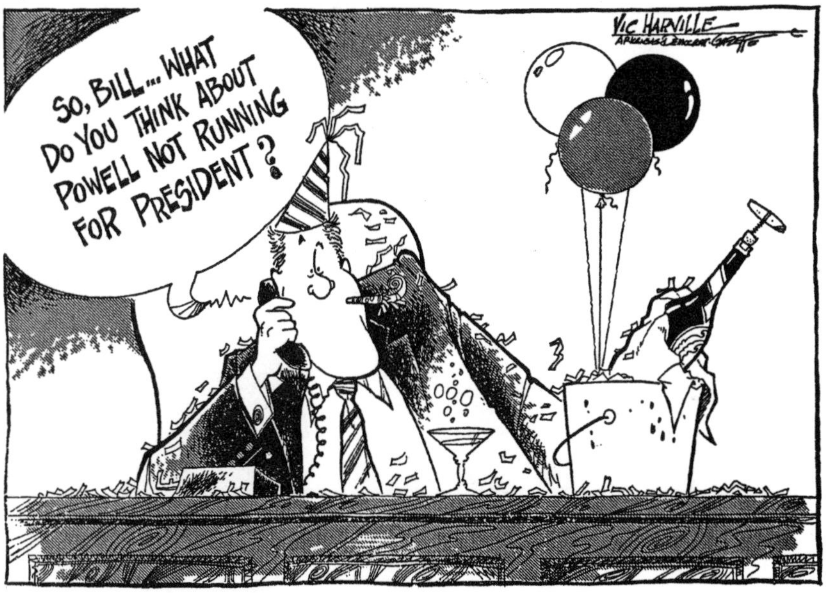
So, Bill... What do you think about Powell not running for President?
Vic Harville

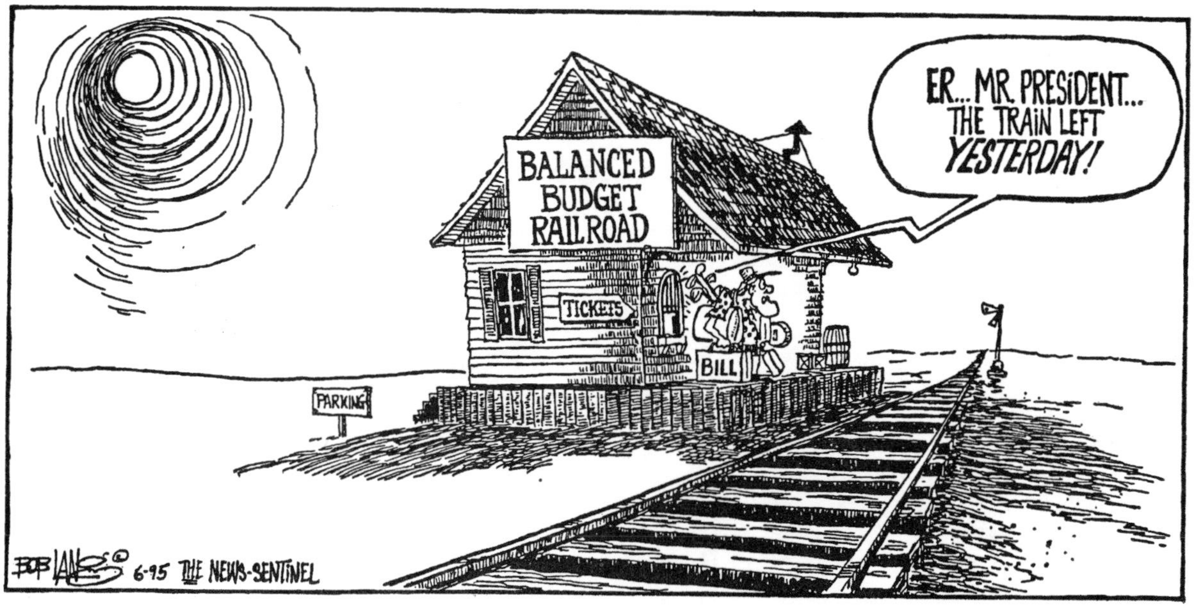
Er... Mr. President... the train left *yesterday!*
Balanced Budget Railroad
Tickets
Bill
Parking
Bob Lang 6-95 The News-Sentinel

BOB LANG
Courtesy News-Sentinel (Ind.)

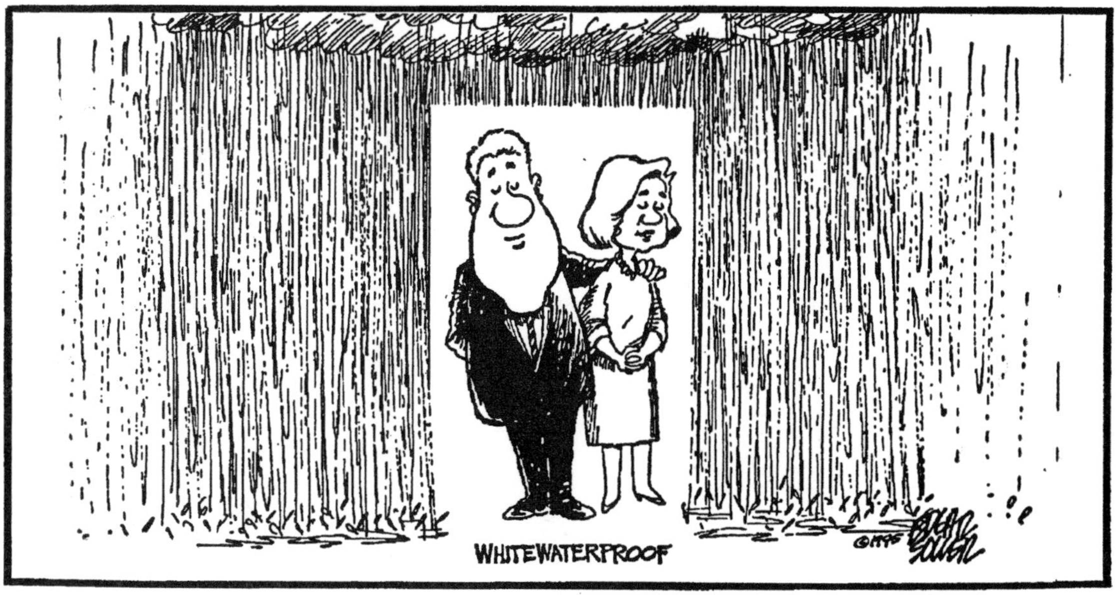
Whitewaterproof
©1995 Edgar Soller

EDGAR SOLLER
Courtesy California Examiner

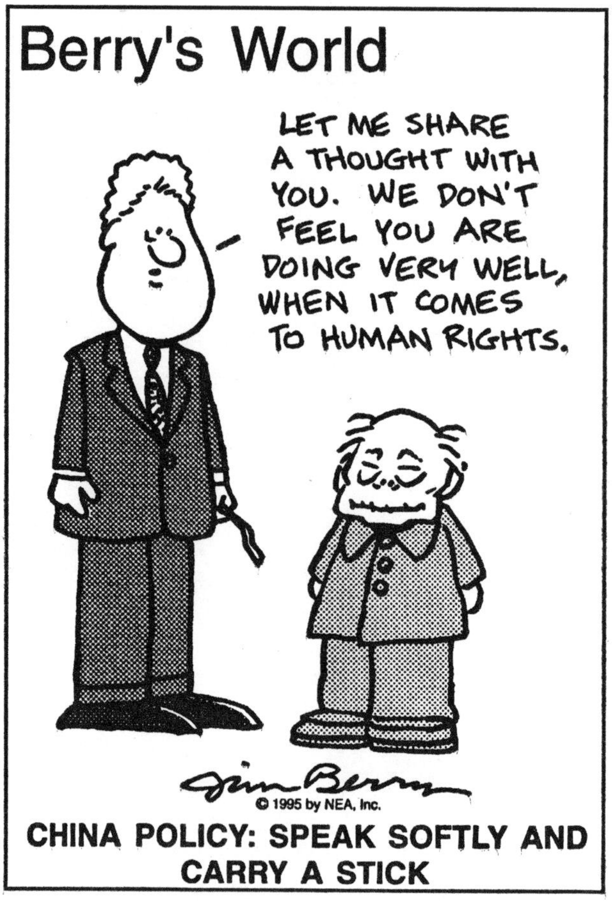
Berry's World
LET ME SHARE A THOUGHT WITH YOU. WE DON'T FEEL YOU ARE DOING VERY WELL, WHEN IT COMES TO HUMAN RIGHTS.
© 1995 by NEA, Inc.
CHINA POLICY: SPEAK SOFTLY AND CARRY A STICK

JIM BERRY
Courtesy NEA

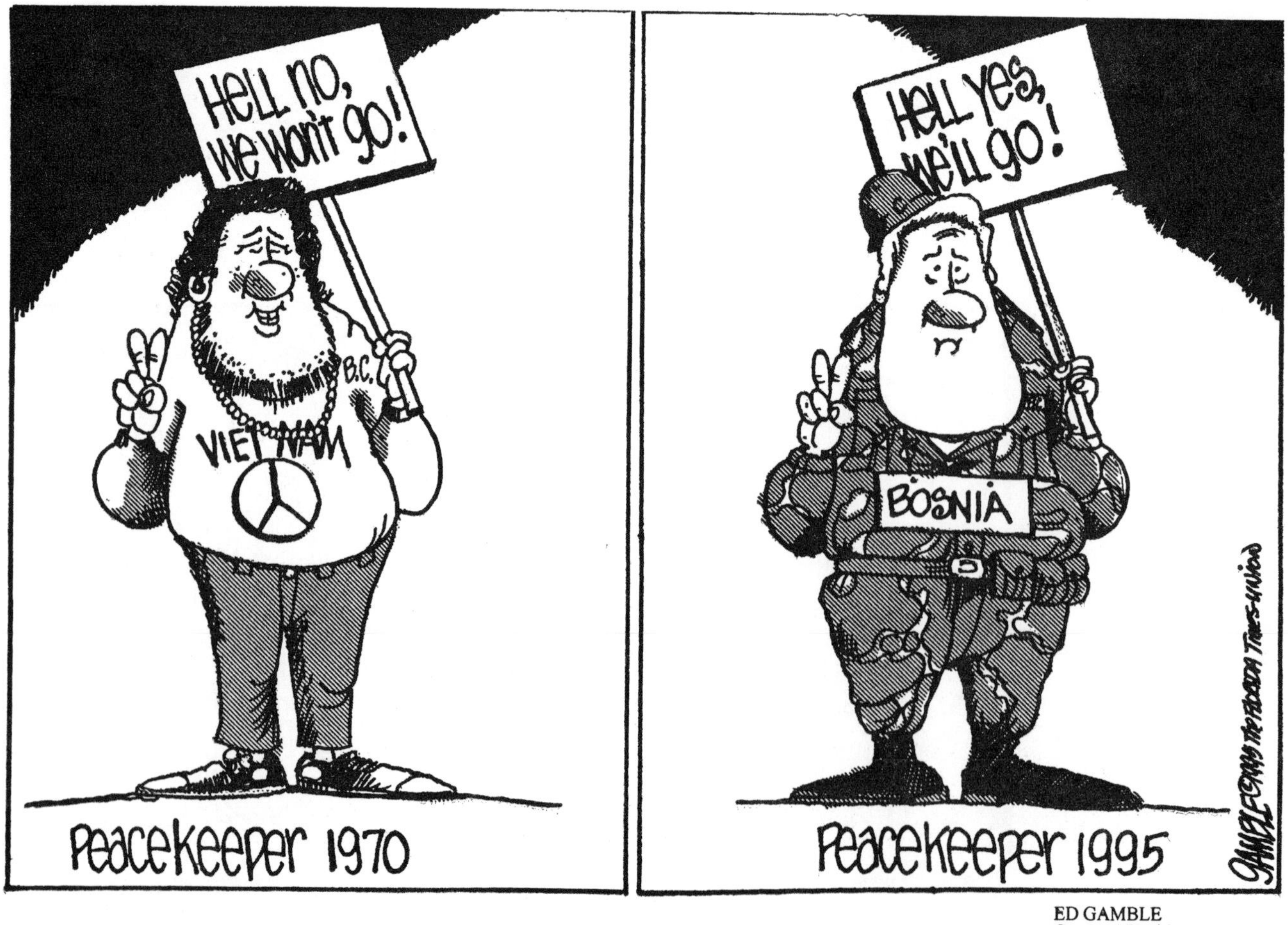
Hell no, we won't go!
B.C.
VIETNAM
Peacekeeper 1970
Hell yes, we'll go!
BOSNIA
Peacekeeper 1995
GAMBLE

ED GAMBLE
Courtesy Florida Times-Union

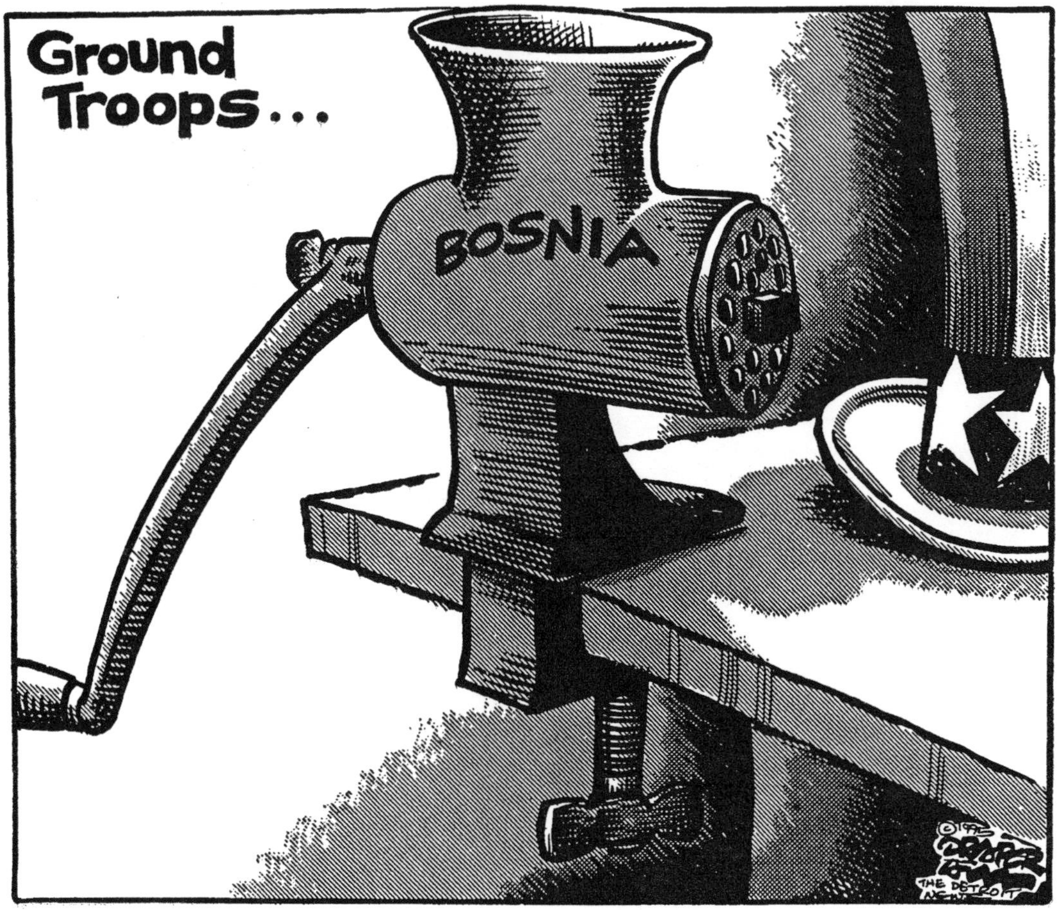
Ground Troops...
BOSNIA

DRAPER HILL
Courtesy Detroit News

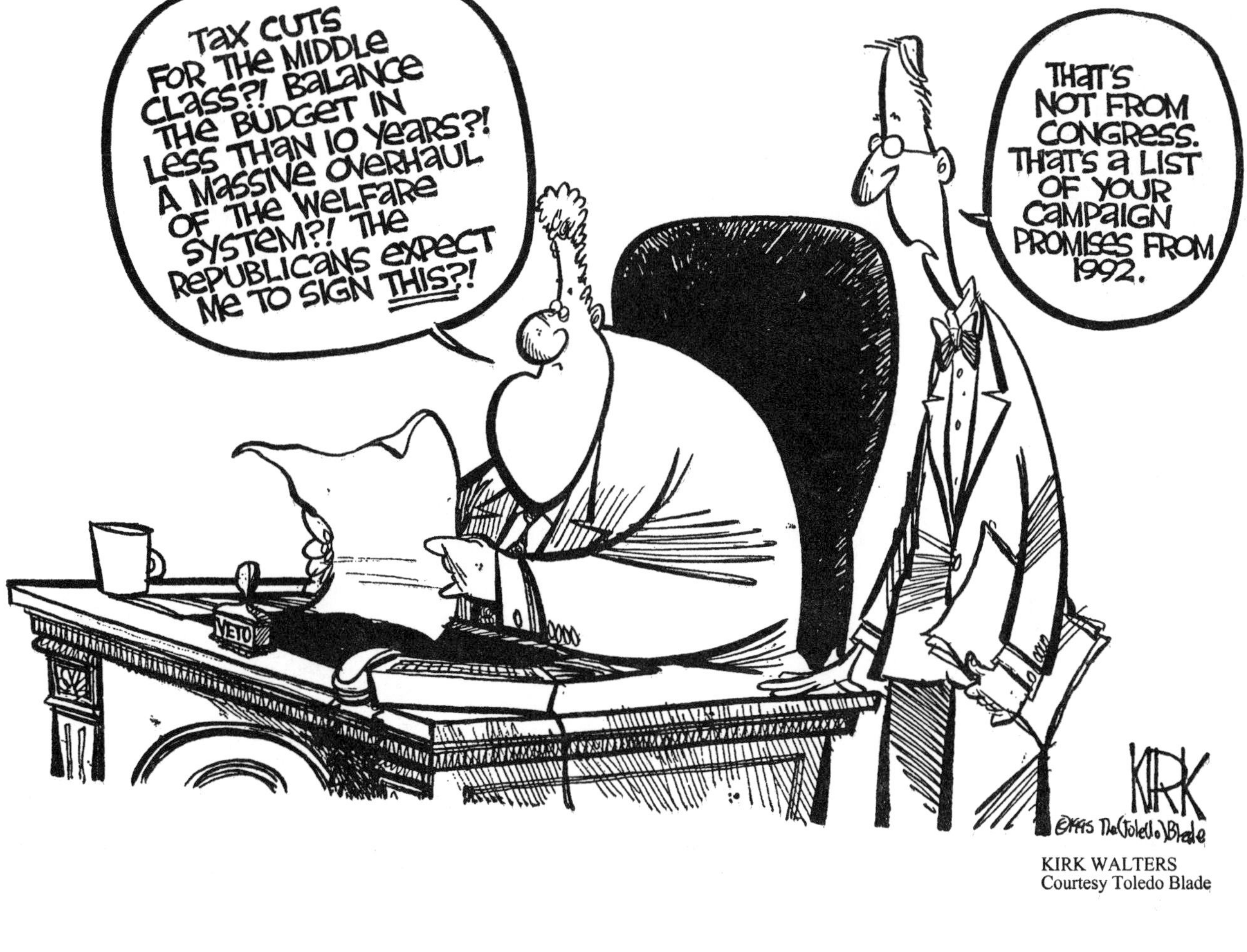
TAX CUTS FOR THE MIDDLE CLASS?! BALANCE THE BUDGET IN LESS THAN 10 YEARS?! A MASSIVE OVERHAUL OF THE WELFARE SYSTEM?! THE REPUBLICANS EXPECT ME TO SIGN THIS?!
THAT'S NOT FROM CONGRESS. THAT'S A LIST OF YOUR CAMPAIGN PROMISES FROM 1992.
VETO
KIRK

KIRK WALTERS
Courtesy Toledo Blade

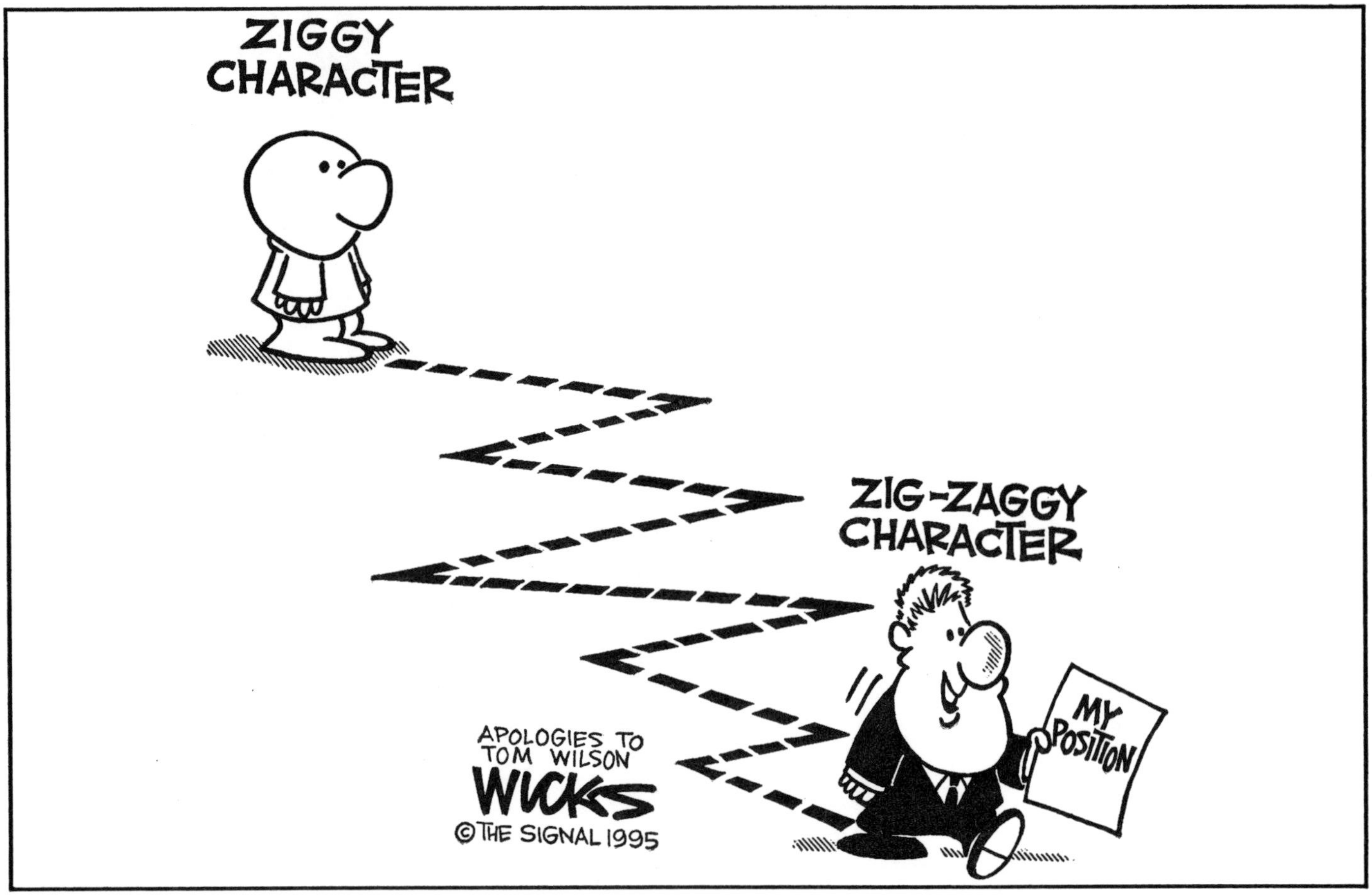
ZIGGY
CHARACTER
ZIG-ZAGGY
CHARACTER
MY
POSITION
APOLOGIES TO
TOM WILSON
WICKS
©THE SIGNAL 1995

RANDY WICKS
Courtesy Valencia Signal (Calif.)

RANAN LURIE
Courtesy Cartoonews International

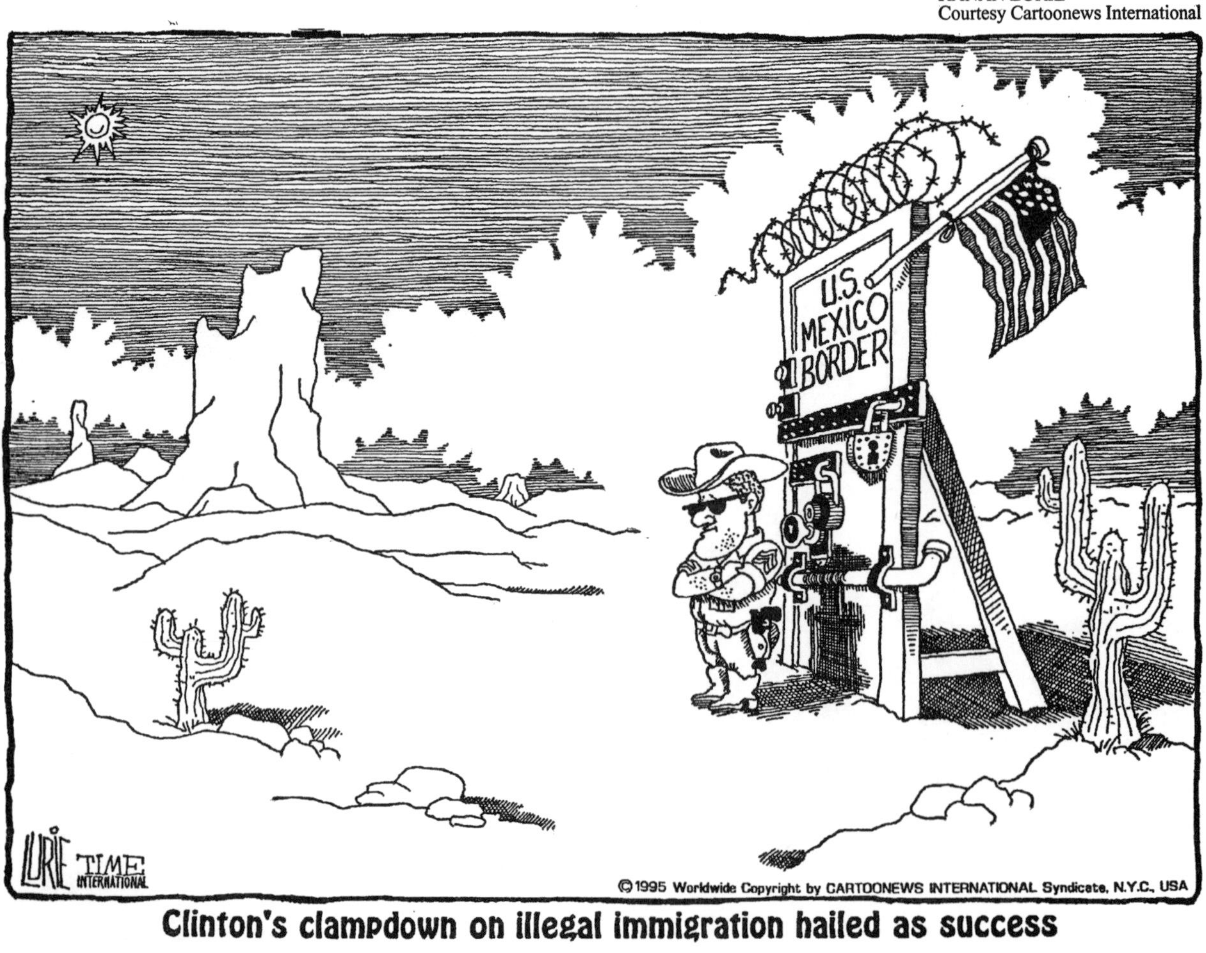
U.S.
MEXICO
BORDER
LURIE
TIME
INTERNATIONAL
©1995 Worldwide Copyright by CARTOONEWS INTERNATIONAL Syndicate, N.Y.C., USA

Clinton's clampdown on illegal immigration hailed as success

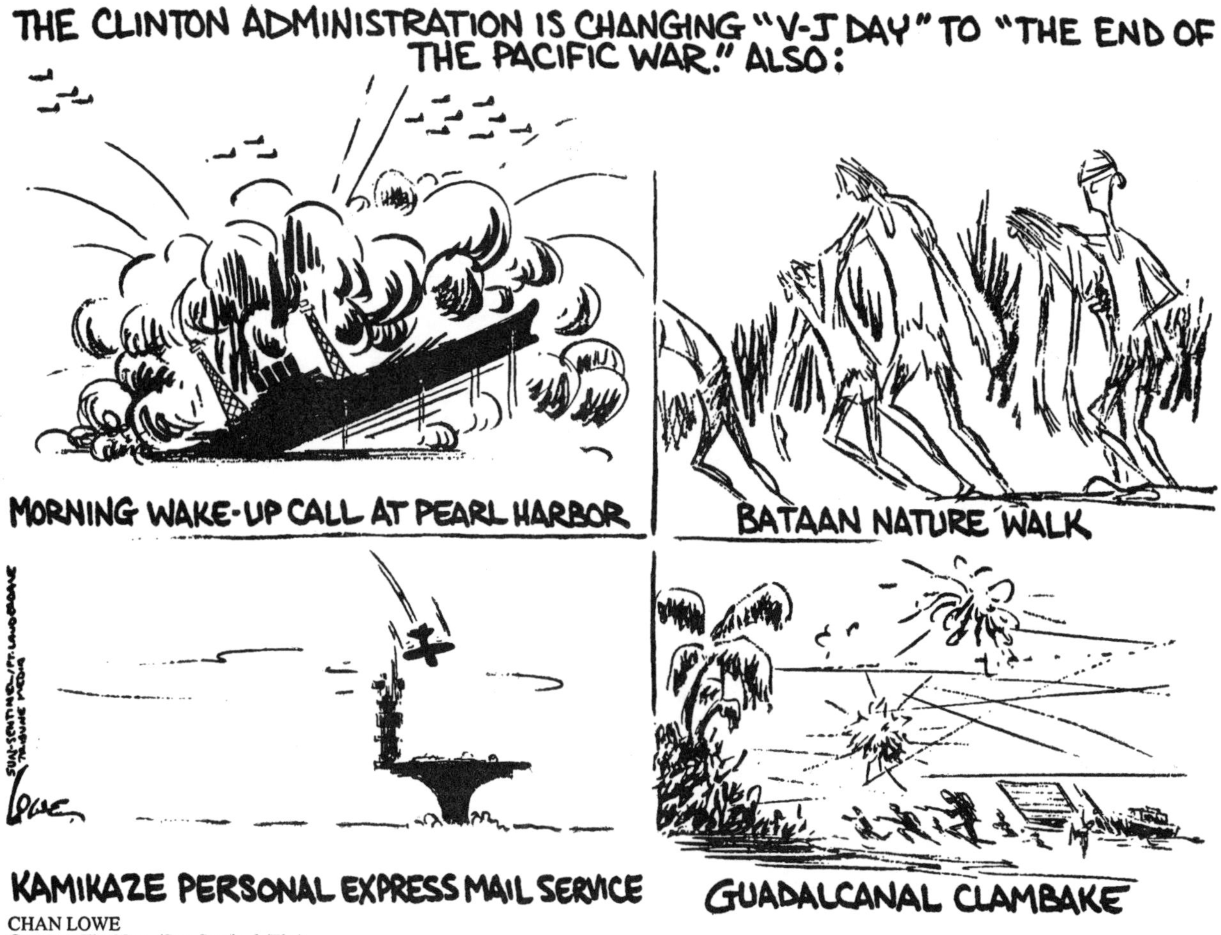
THE CLINTON ADMINISTRATION IS CHANGING "V-J DAY" TO "THE END OF THE PACIFIC WAR." ALSO:
MORNING WAKE-UP CALL AT PEARL HARBOR
BATAAN NATURE WALK
LOWE
KAMIKAZE PERSONAL EXPRESS MAIL SERVICE
GUADALCANAL CLAMBAKE

CHAN LOWE
Courtesy The News/Sun-Sentinel (Fla.)

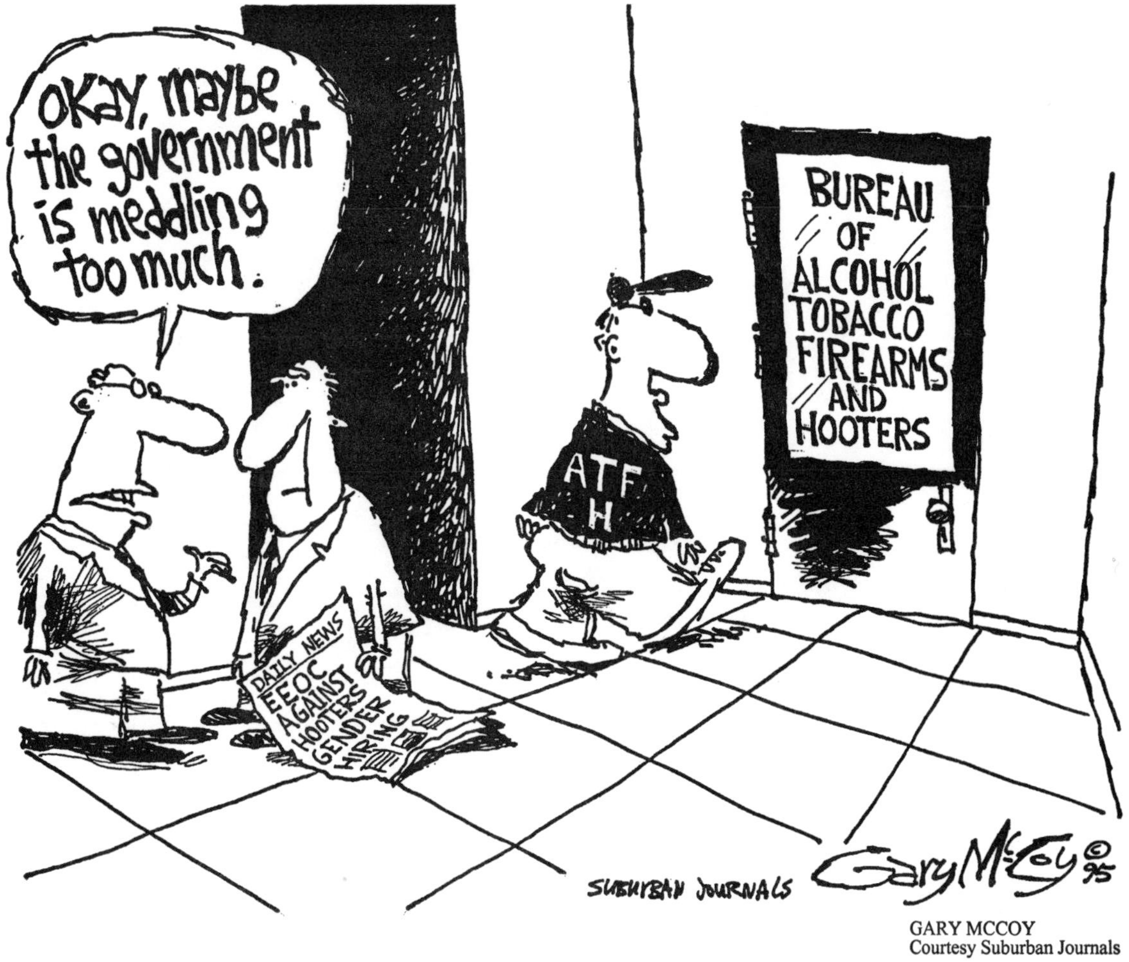
Okay, maybe the government is meddling too much.
BUREAU OF ALCOHOL TOBACCO FIREARMS AND HOOTERS
ATF H
DAILY NEWS
EEOC AGAINST HOOTERS GENDER HIRING
SUBURBAN JOURNALS
Gary McCoy © 95

GARY MCCOY
Courtesy Suburban Journals

RANAN LURIE
Courtesy Cartoonews International

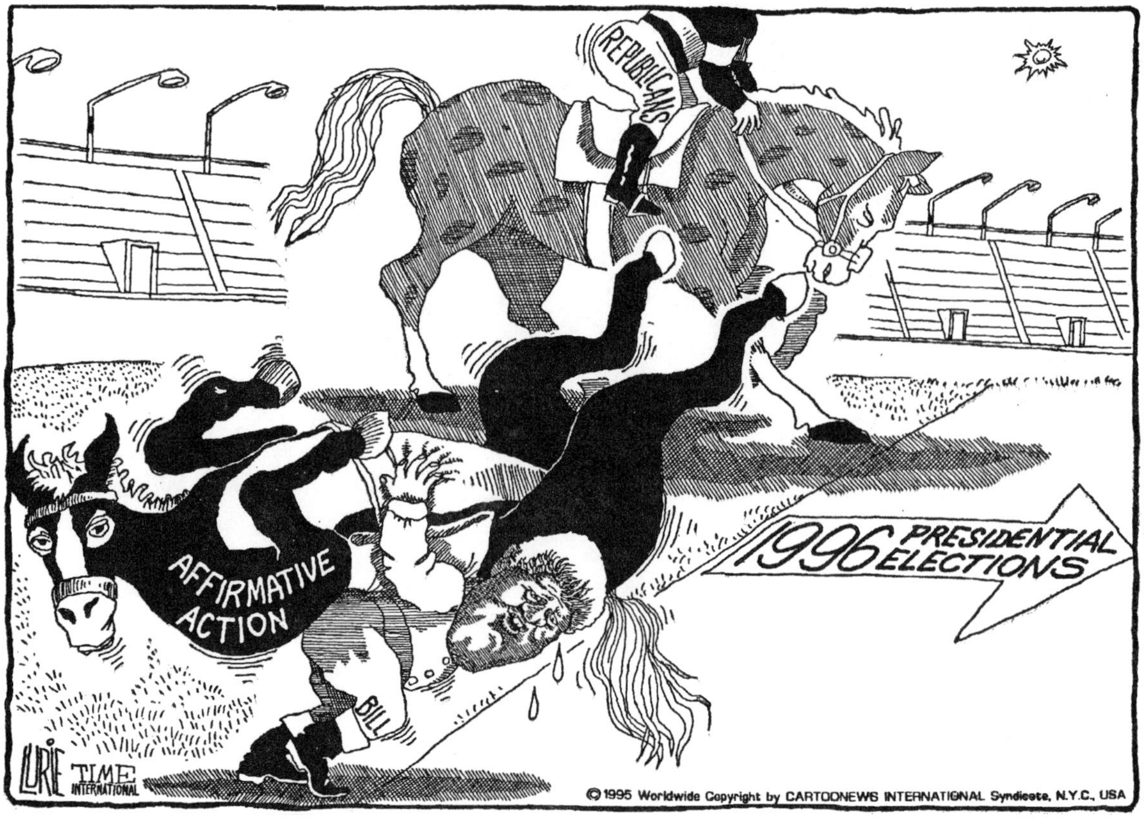
REPUBLICANS
AFFIRMATIVE ACTION
BILL
1996 PRESIDENTIAL ELECTIONS
LURIE
TIME INTERNATIONAL
© 1995 Worldwide Copyright by CARTOONEWS INTERNATIONAL Syndicate, N.Y.C., USA

"On your mark... Get set..."

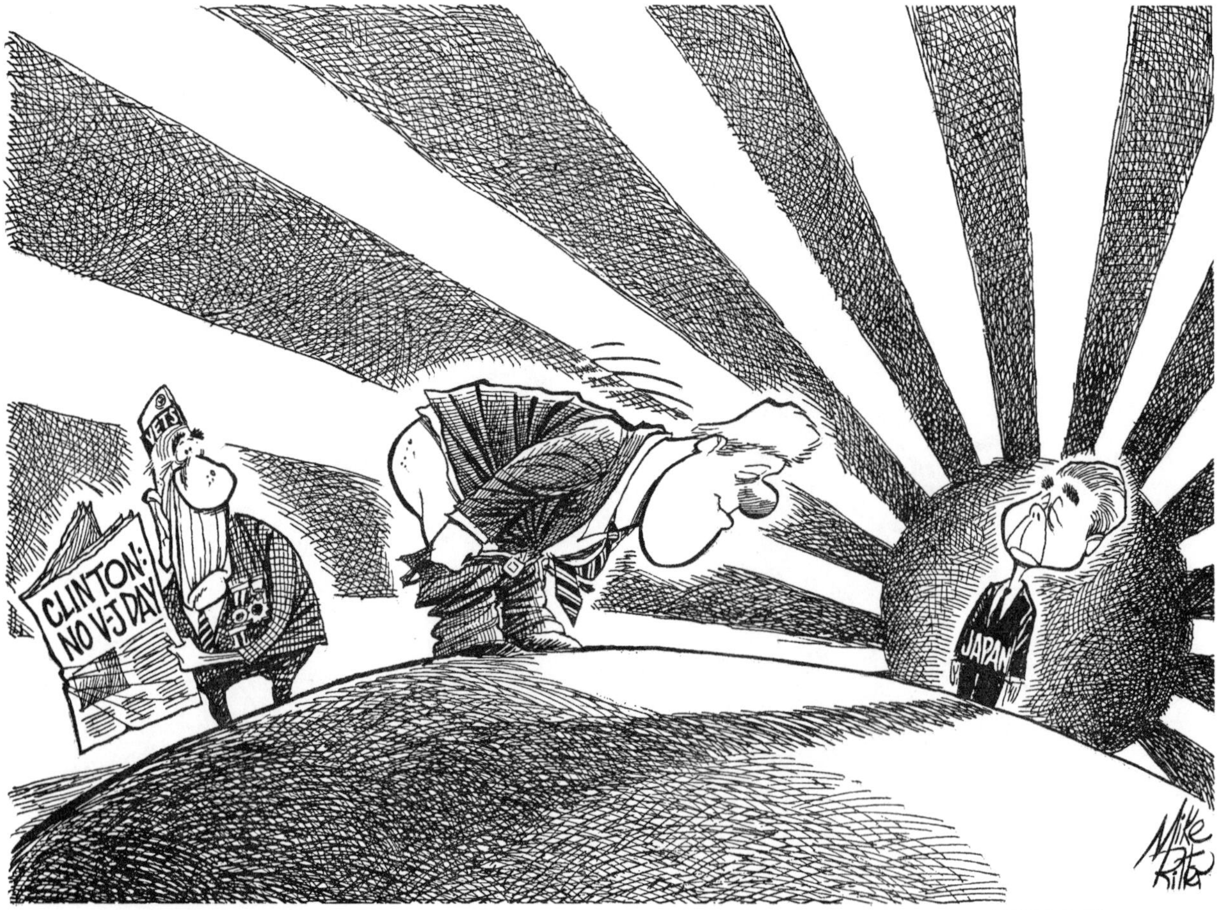
VETS
CLINTON: NO V-J DAY
JAPAN
Mike Ritter

MIKE RITTER
Courtesy Tribune Newspapers

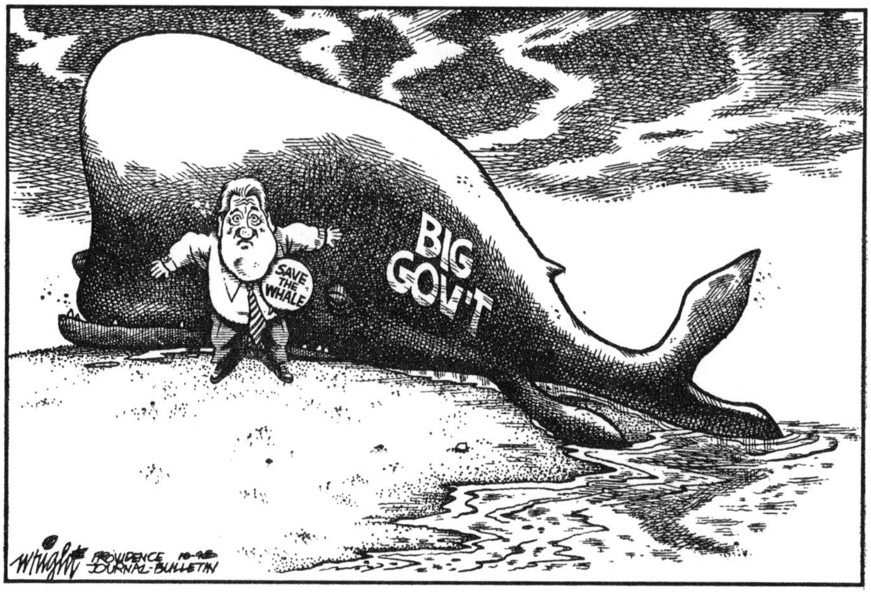
SAVE THE WHALE
BIG GOV'T
Wright PROVIDENCE JOURNAL-BULLETIN

DICK WRIGHT
Courtesy Providence Journal-Bulletin

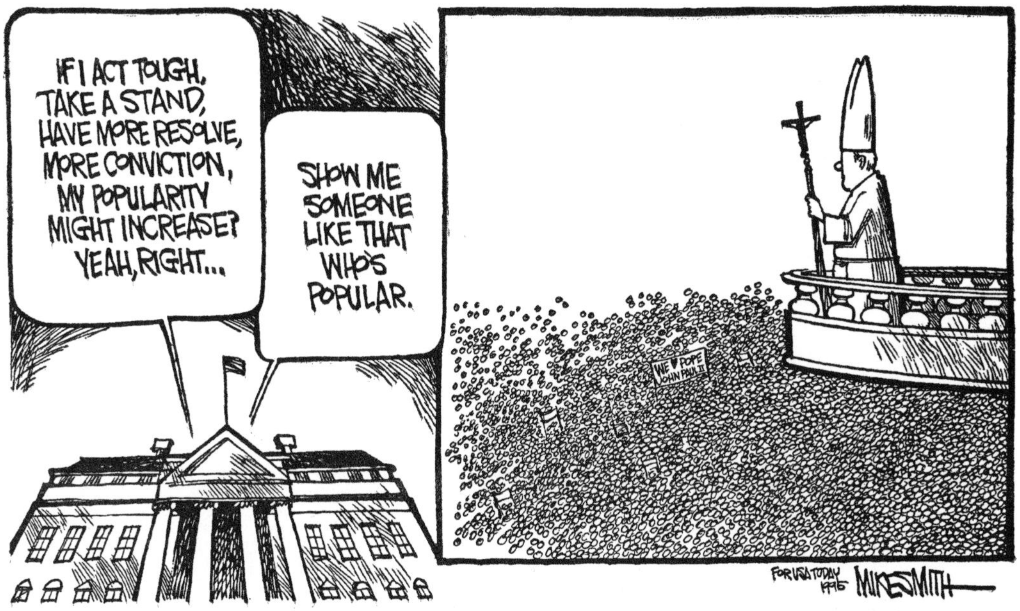
IF I ACT TOUGH, TAKE A STAND, HAVE MORE RESOLVE, MORE CONVICTION, MY POPULARITY MIGHT INCREASE? YEAH, RIGHT...
SHOW ME SOMEONE LIKE THAT WHO'S POPULAR.
FOR USA TODAY 1995 MIKE SMITH

MIKE SMITH
Courtesy Las Vegas Sun

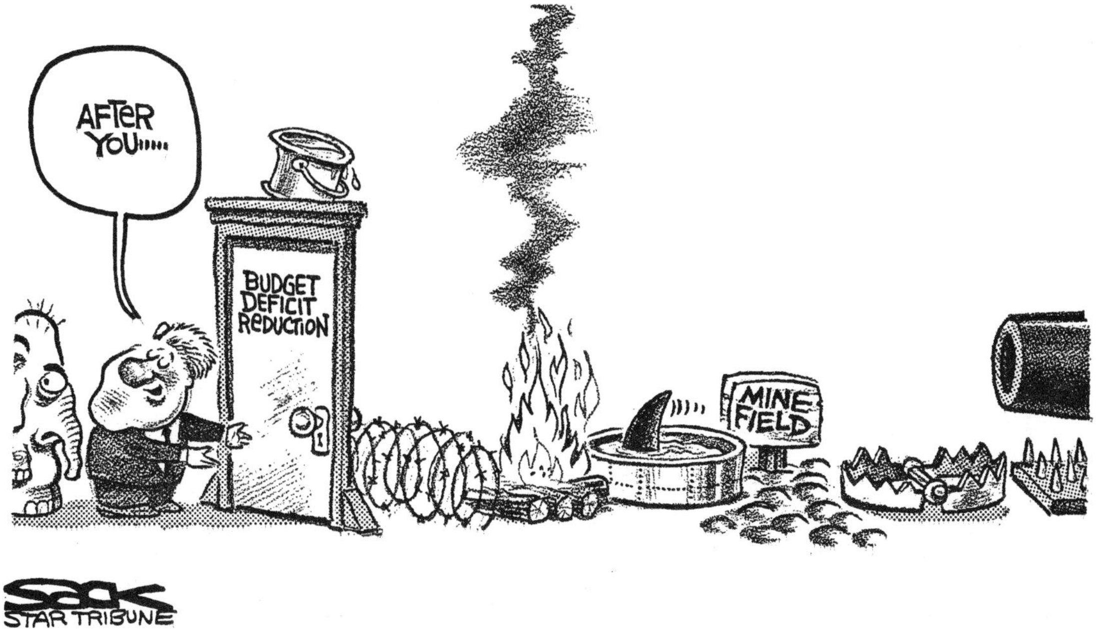
AFTER YOU.....
BUDGET DEFICIT REDUCTION
MINE FIELD
SACK STAR TRIBUNE

STEVE SACK
Courtesy Minneapolis Star-Tribune

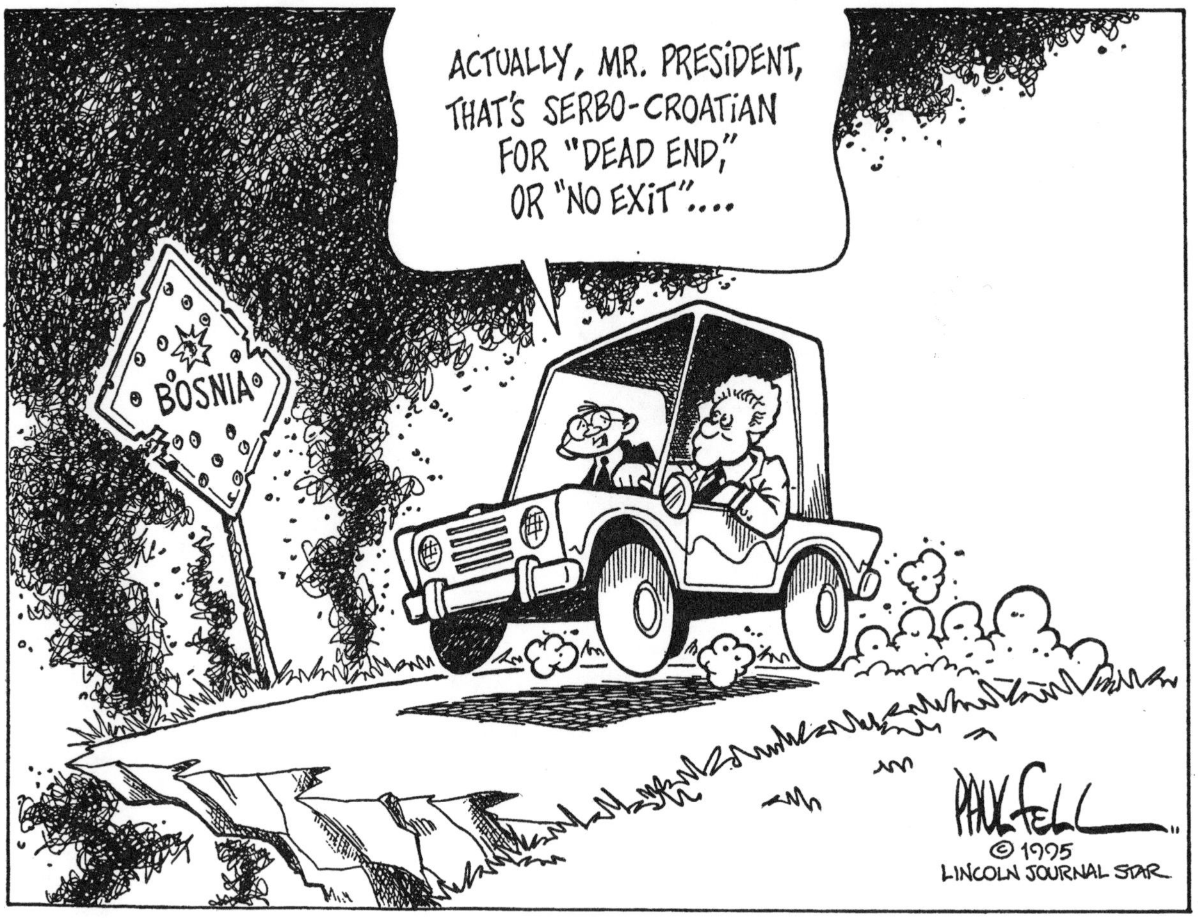
ACTUALLY, MR. PRESIDENT, THAT'S SERBO-CROATIAN FOR "DEAD END," OR "NO EXIT"....
BOSNIA
PAUL FELL
© 1995
LINCOLN JOURNAL STAR

PAUL FELL
Courtesy Lincoln Journal

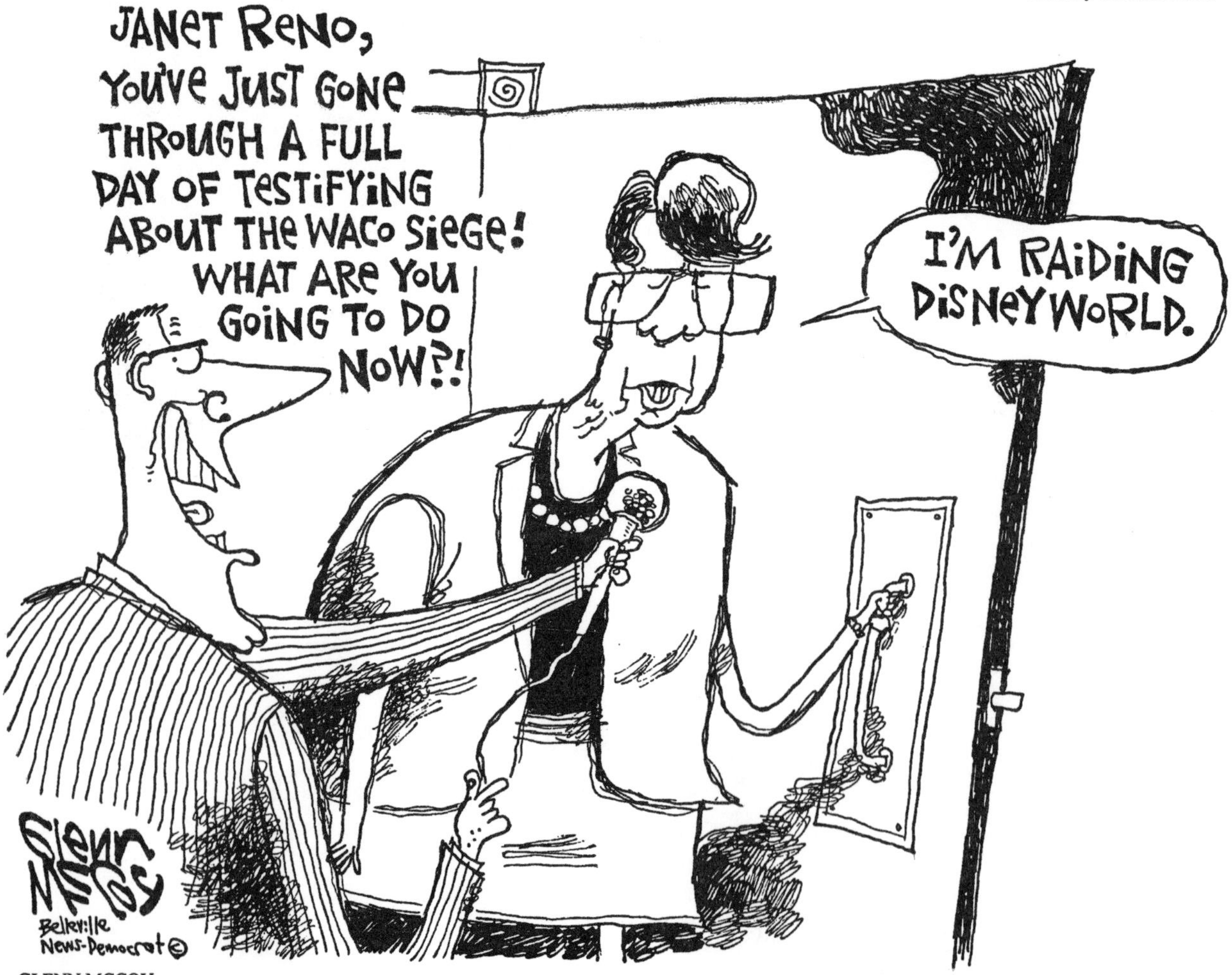
JANET RENO, YOU'VE JUST GONE THROUGH A FULL DAY OF TESTIFYING ABOUT THE WACO SIEGE! WHAT ARE YOU GOING TO DO NOW?!
I'M RAIDING DISNEYWORLD.
Glenn McCoy
Belleville News-Democrat ©

GLENN MCCOY
Courtesy Belleville News-Democrat (Ill.)

STEVE MCBRIDE
Courtesy Independence Daily Reporter (Kans.)

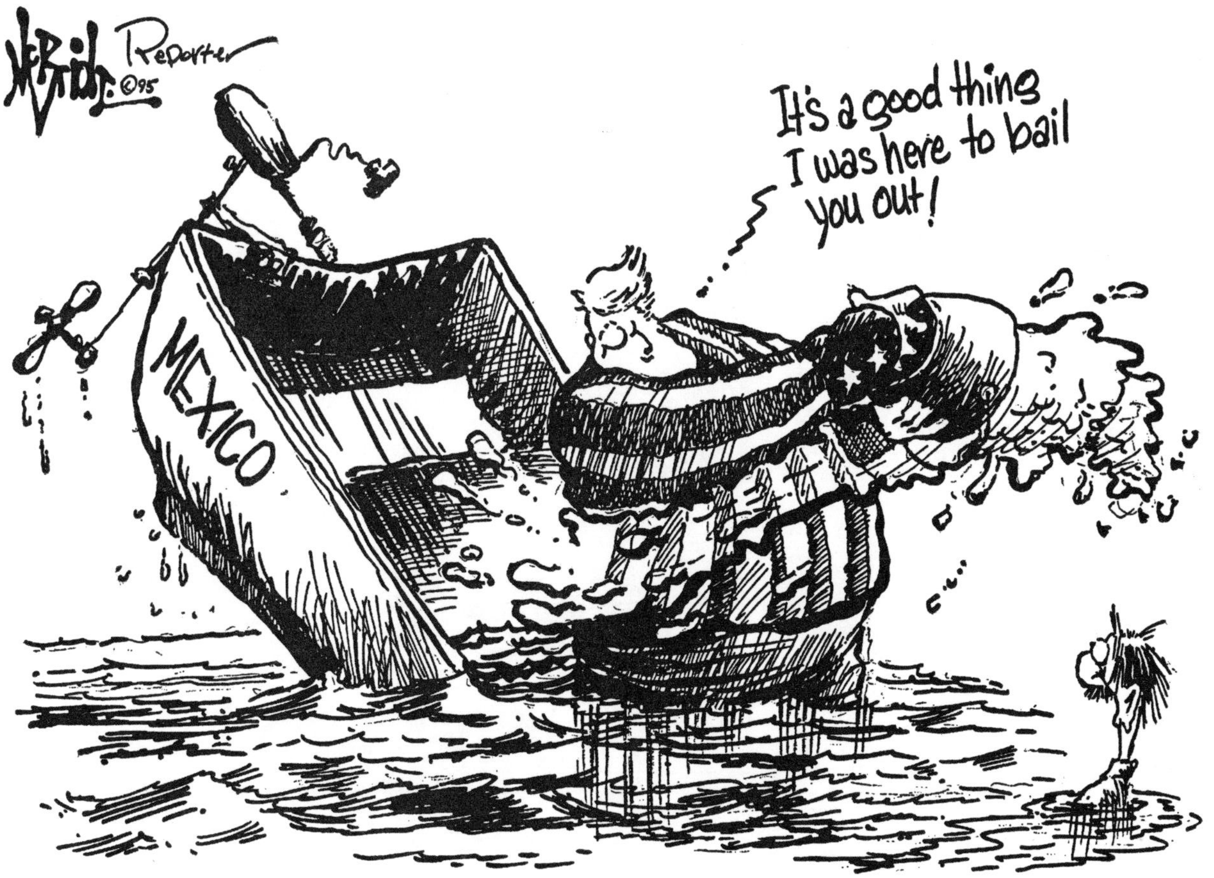
McBride Reporter ©95
It's a good thing I was here to bail you out!
MEXICO

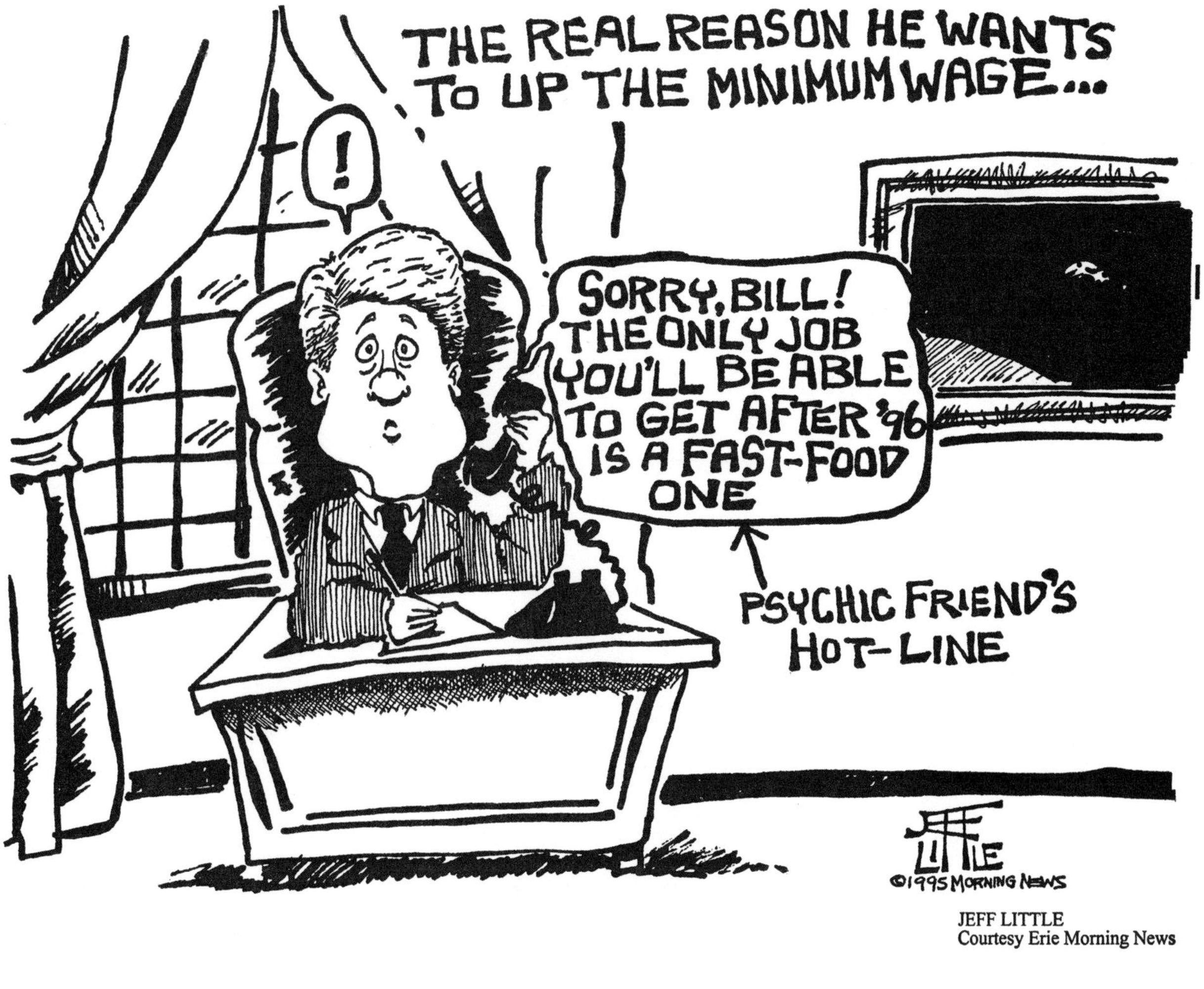
THE REAL REASON HE WANTS TO UP THE MINIMUM WAGE...
!
SORRY, BILL! THE ONLY JOB YOU'LL BE ABLE TO GET AFTER '96 IS A FAST-FOOD ONE
PSYCHIC FRIEND'S HOT-LINE
JEFF LITTLE
©1995 MORNING NEWS

JEFF LITTLE
Courtesy Erie Morning News

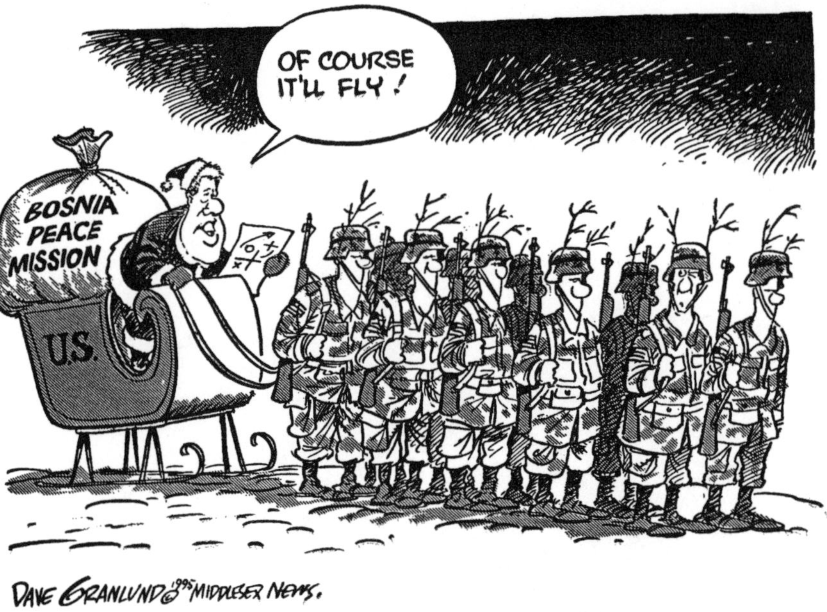
OF COURSE IT'LL FLY!
BOSNIA PEACE MISSION
U.S.
DAVE GRANLUND©1995 MIDDLESEX NEWS.

DAVID GRANLUND
Courtesy Middlesex News

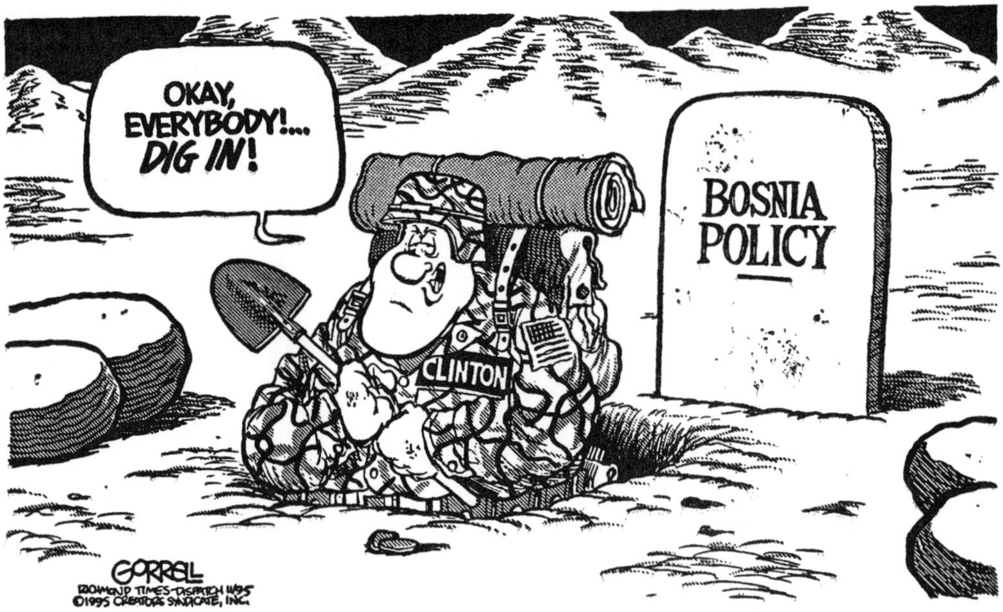
OKAY, EVERYBODY!... DIG IN!
BOSNIA POLICY
CLINTON
GORRELL
RICHMOND TIMES-DISPATCH 11/95
©1995 CREATORS SYNDICATE, INC.

BOB GORRELL
Courtesy Richmond Times-Dispatch/
Copley News Service

CHIP BOK
Courtesy Akron Beacon Journal

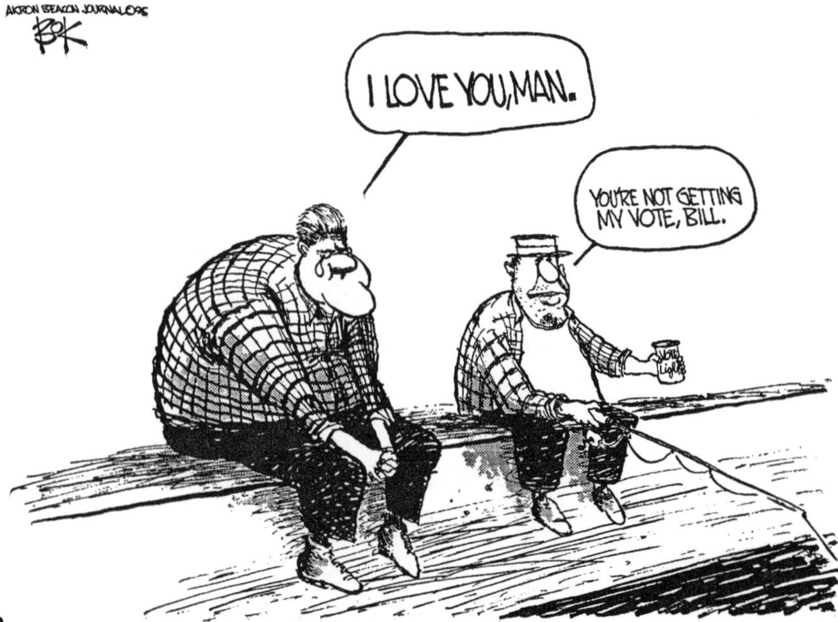
AKRON BEACON JOURNAL©95
BOK
I LOVE YOU, MAN.
YOU'RE NOT GETTING MY VOTE, BILL.

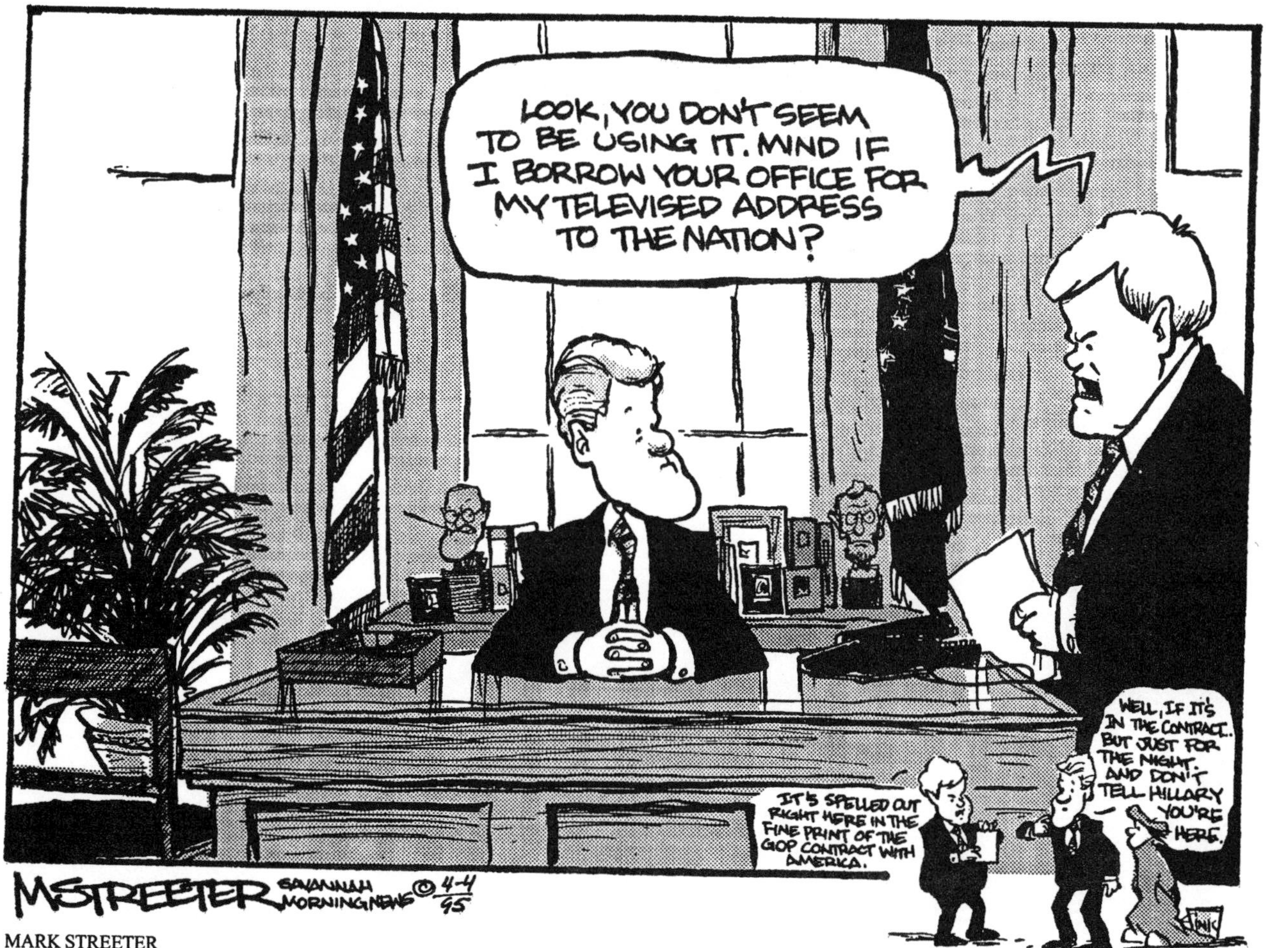
LOOK, YOU DON'T SEEM TO BE USING IT. MIND IF I BORROW YOUR OFFICE FOR MY TELEVISED ADDRESS TO THE NATION?
IT'S SPELLED OUT RIGHT HERE IN THE FINE PRINT OF THE GOP CONTRACT WITH AMERICA.
WELL, IF IT'S IN THE CONTRACT. BUT JUST FOR THE NIGHT. AND DON'T TELL HILLARY YOU'RE HERE.
MSTREETER SAVANNAH MORNING NEWS © 4-4 95

MARK STREETER
Courtesy Savannah Morning News

JIM JORDAN
Courtesy Press Publications

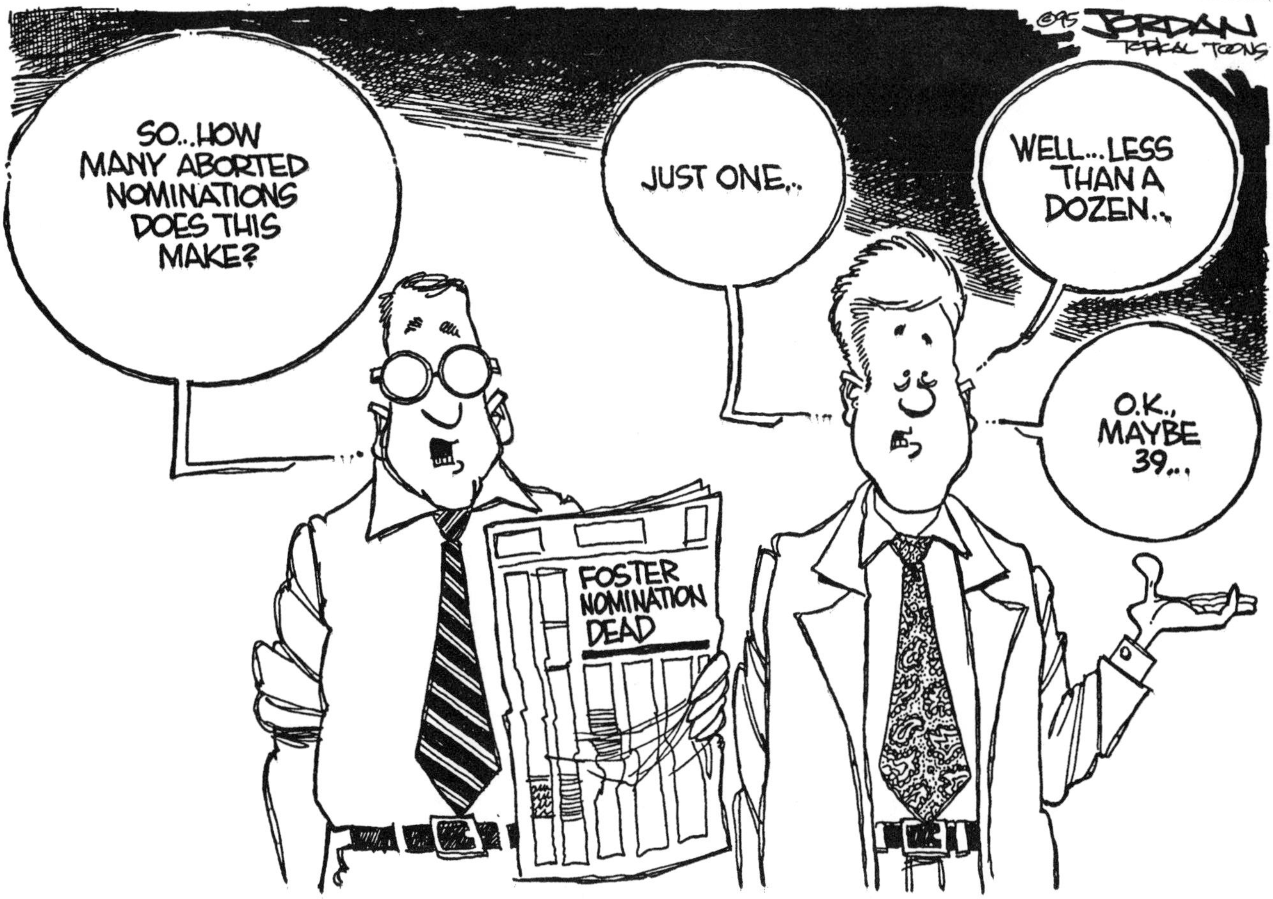
©95 JORDAN TOPICAL TOONS
SO...HOW MANY ABORTED NOMINATIONS DOES THIS MAKE?
JUST ONE..
WELL...LESS THAN A DOZEN..
O.K., MAYBE 39...
FOSTER NOMINATION DEAD

STEVE MCBRIDE
Courtesy Independence Daily Reporter (Kans.)

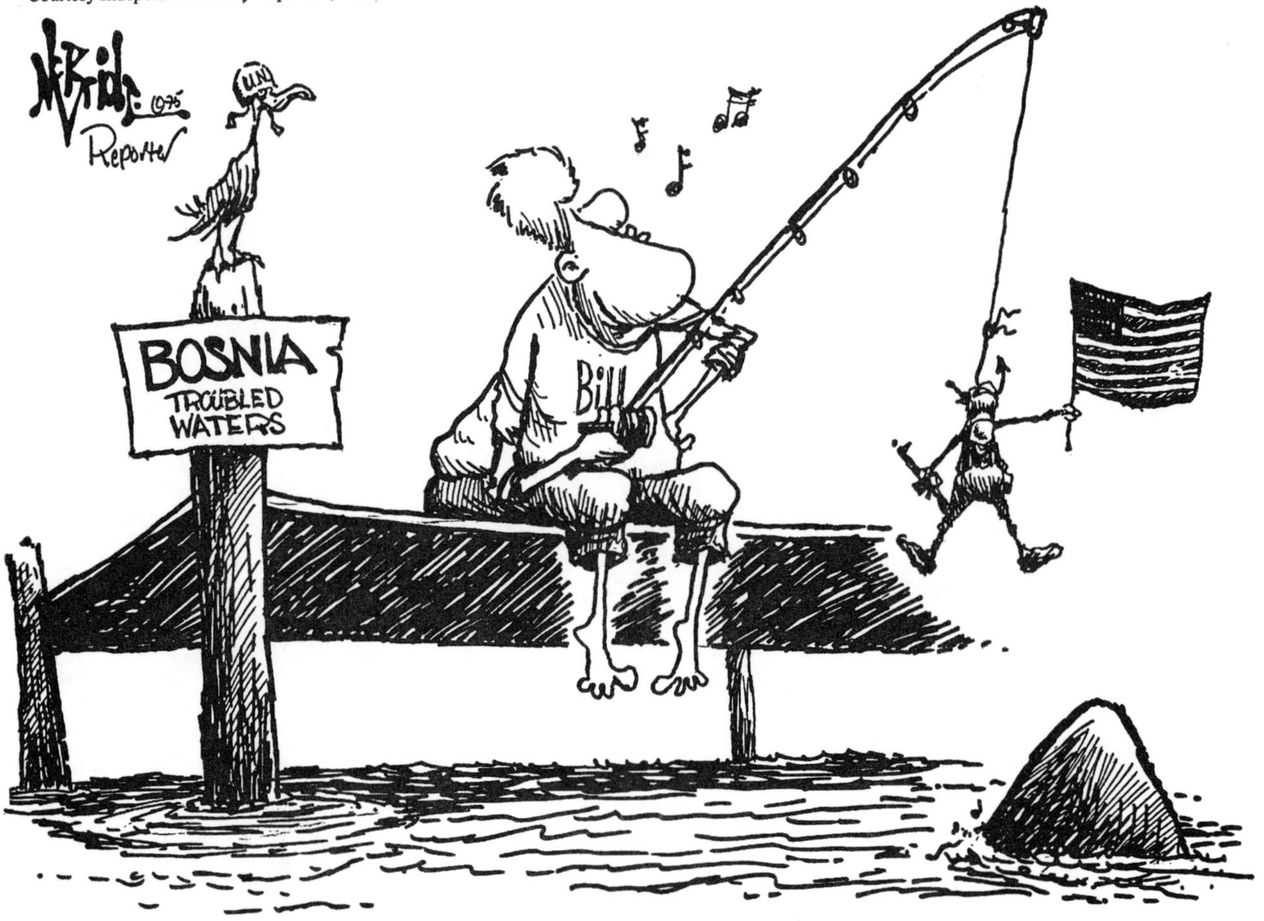

McBride ©95 Reporter
U.N.
BOSNIA
TROUBLED WATERS
Bill

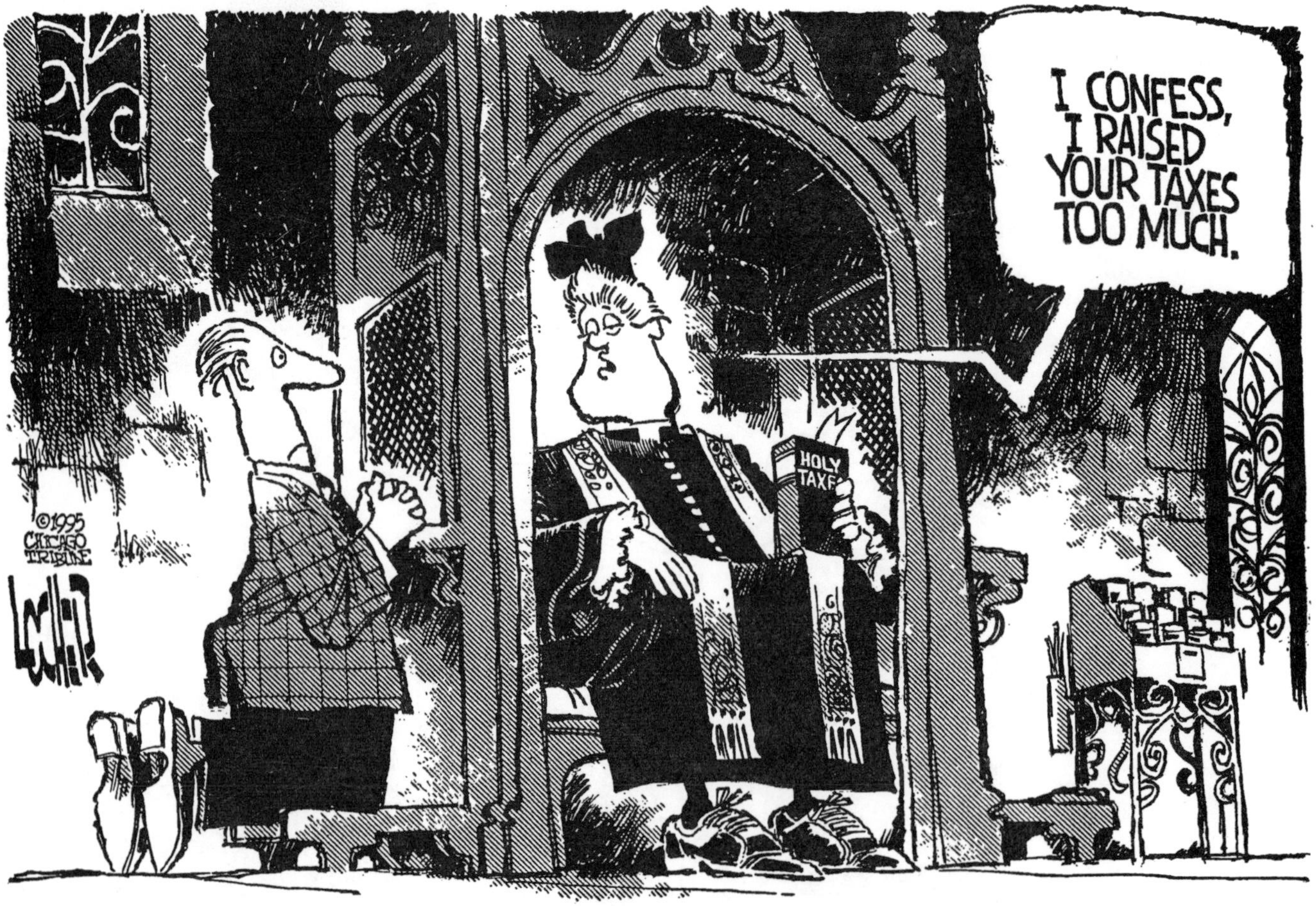

I CONFESS, I RAISED YOUR TAXES TOO MUCH.
HOLY TAXES
©1995 CHICAGO TRIBUNE
LOCHER

DICK LOCHER
Courtesy Chicago Tribune

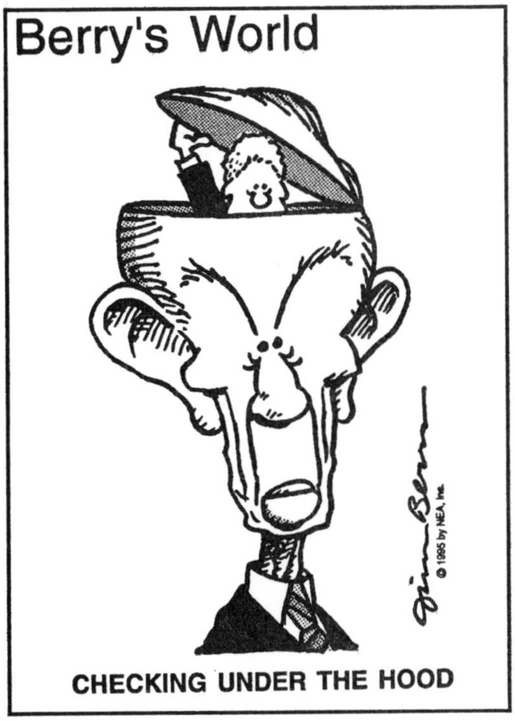
Berry's World
© 1995 by NEA, Inc.
CHECKING UNDER THE HOOD

JIM BERRY
Courtesy NEA

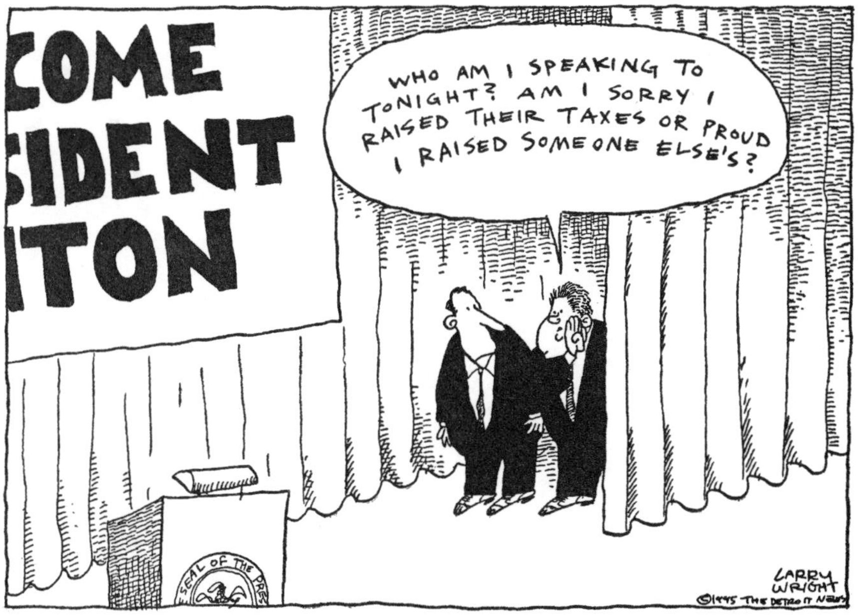
COME
SIDENT
TON
WHO AM I SPEAKING TO TONIGHT? AM I SORRY I RAISED THEIR TAXES OR PROUD I RAISED SOMEONE ELSE'S?
LARRY WRIGHT
©1995 THE DETROIT NEWS

LARRY WRIGHT
Courtesy Detroit News

BOB ENGLEHART
Courtesy Hartford Courant

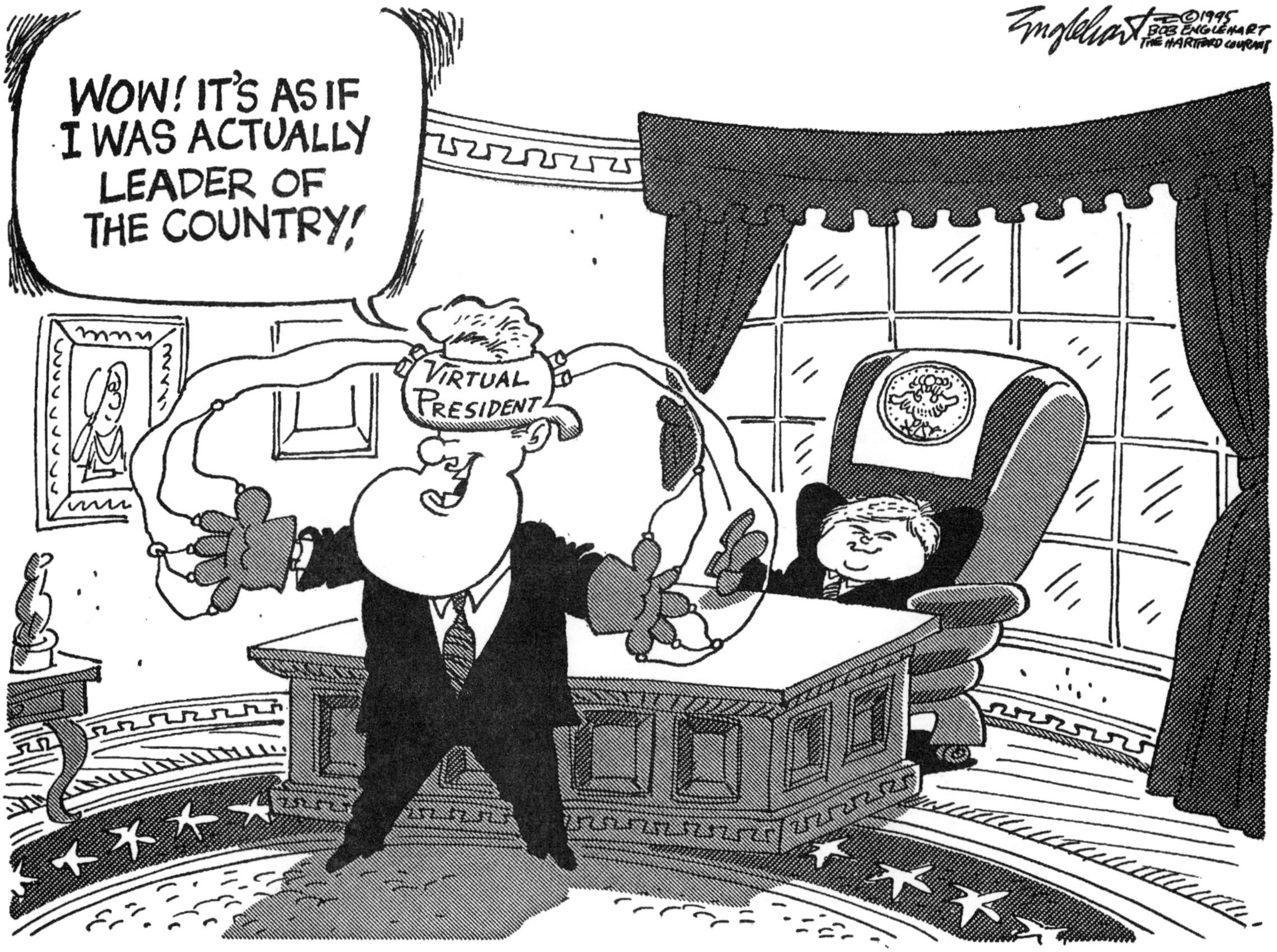
©1995 BOB ENGLEHART THE HARTFORD COURANT
WOW! IT'S AS IF I WAS ACTUALLY LEADER OF THE COUNTRY!
VIRTUAL PRESIDENT

J. R. ROSE
Courtesy Byrd Newspapers

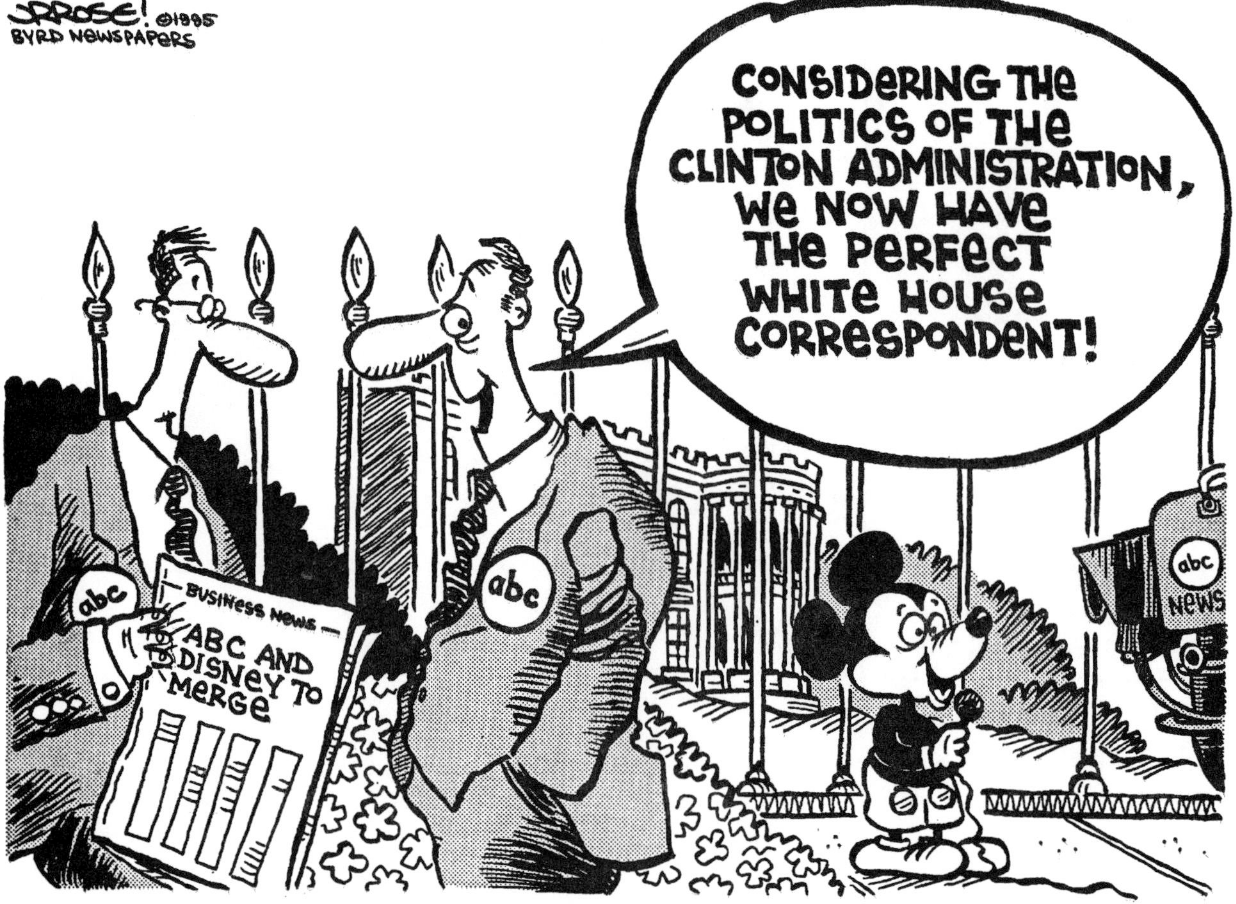
JRROSE! ©1995
BYRD NEWSPAPERS
CONSIDERING THE POLITICS OF THE CLINTON ADMINISTRATION, WE NOW HAVE THE PERFECT WHITE HOUSE CORRESPONDENT!
BUSINESS NEWS
ABC AND DISNEY TO MERGE
abc
abc
abc
abc NEWS

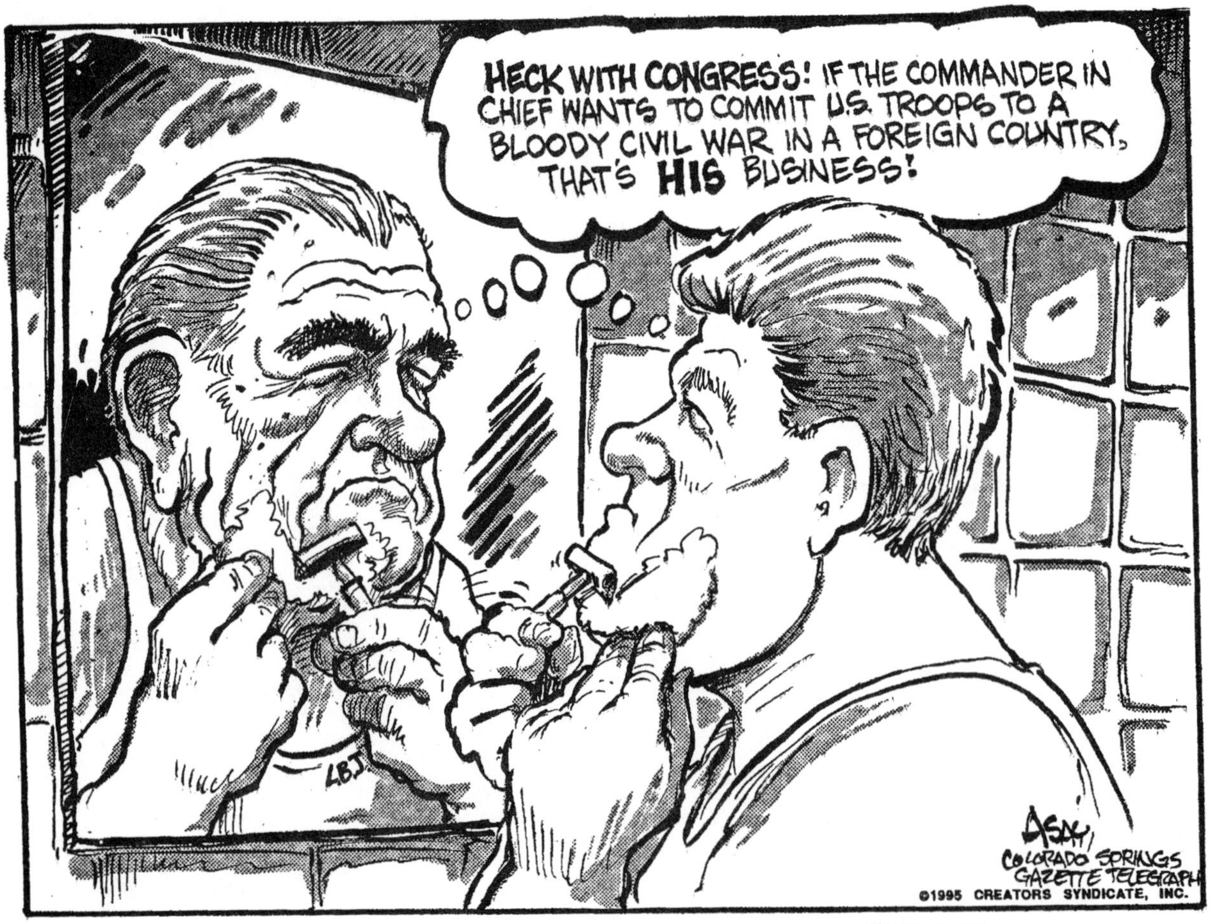
HECK WITH CONGRESS! IF THE COMMANDER IN CHIEF WANTS TO COMMIT U.S. TROOPS TO A BLOODY CIVIL WAR IN A FOREIGN COUNTRY, THAT'S HIS BUSINESS!
LBJ
ASAY
COLORADO SPRINGS GAZETTE TELEGRAPH
©1995 CREATORS SYNDICATE, INC.

CHUCK ASAY
Courtesy Colorado Springs Gazette Telegraph

LARRY WRIGHT
Courtesy Detroit News

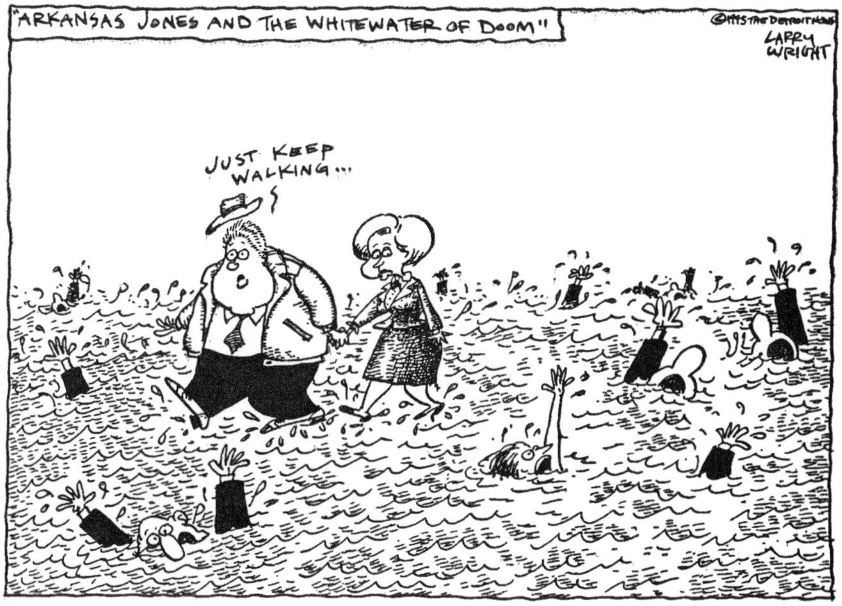

"ARKANSAS JONES AND THE WHITEWATER OF DOOM"
LARRY WRIGHT
JUST KEEP WALKING...

J. R. ROSE
Courtesy Byrd Newspapers

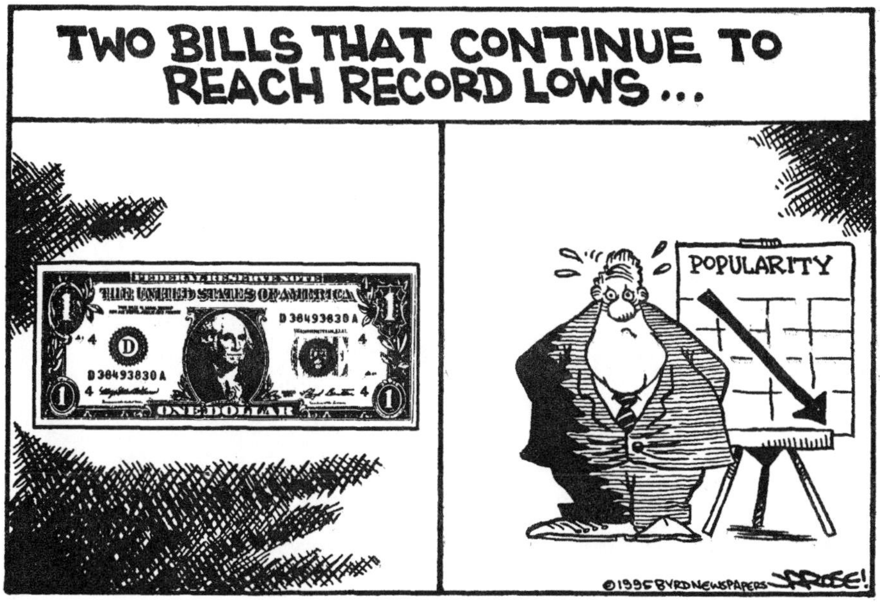

TWO BILLS THAT CONTINUE TO REACH RECORD LOWS...
FEDERAL RESERVE NOTE
THE UNITED STATES OF AMERICA
ONE DOLLAR
POPULARITY
©1995 BYRD NEWSPAPERS ROSE!

BOB GORRELL
Courtesy Richmond Times-Dispatch/
Copley News Service

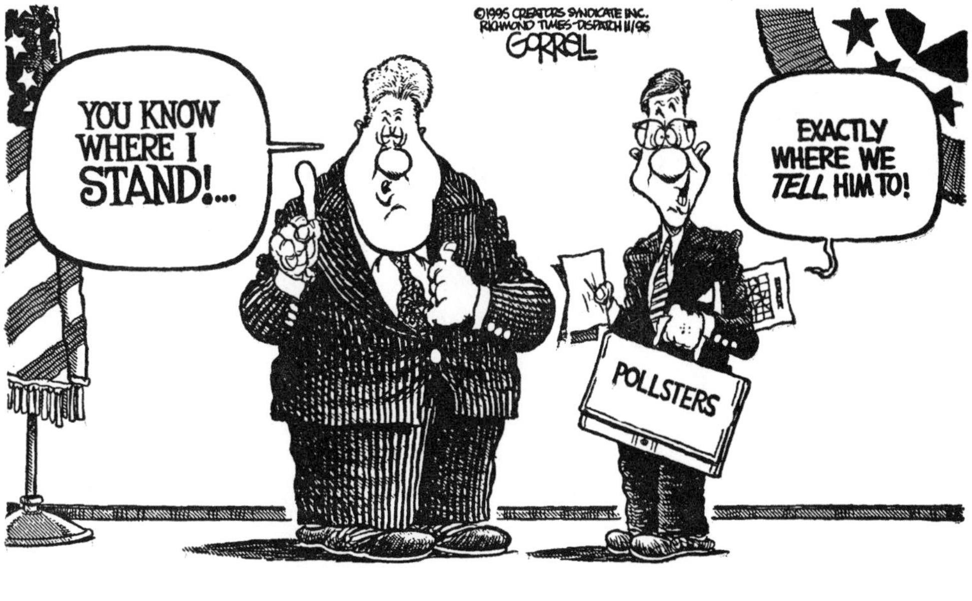

©1995 CREATORS SYNDICATE INC. RICHMOND TIMES-DISPATCH 11/95
GORRELL
YOU KNOW WHERE I STAND!...
EXACTLY WHERE WE TELL HIM TO!
POLLSTERS

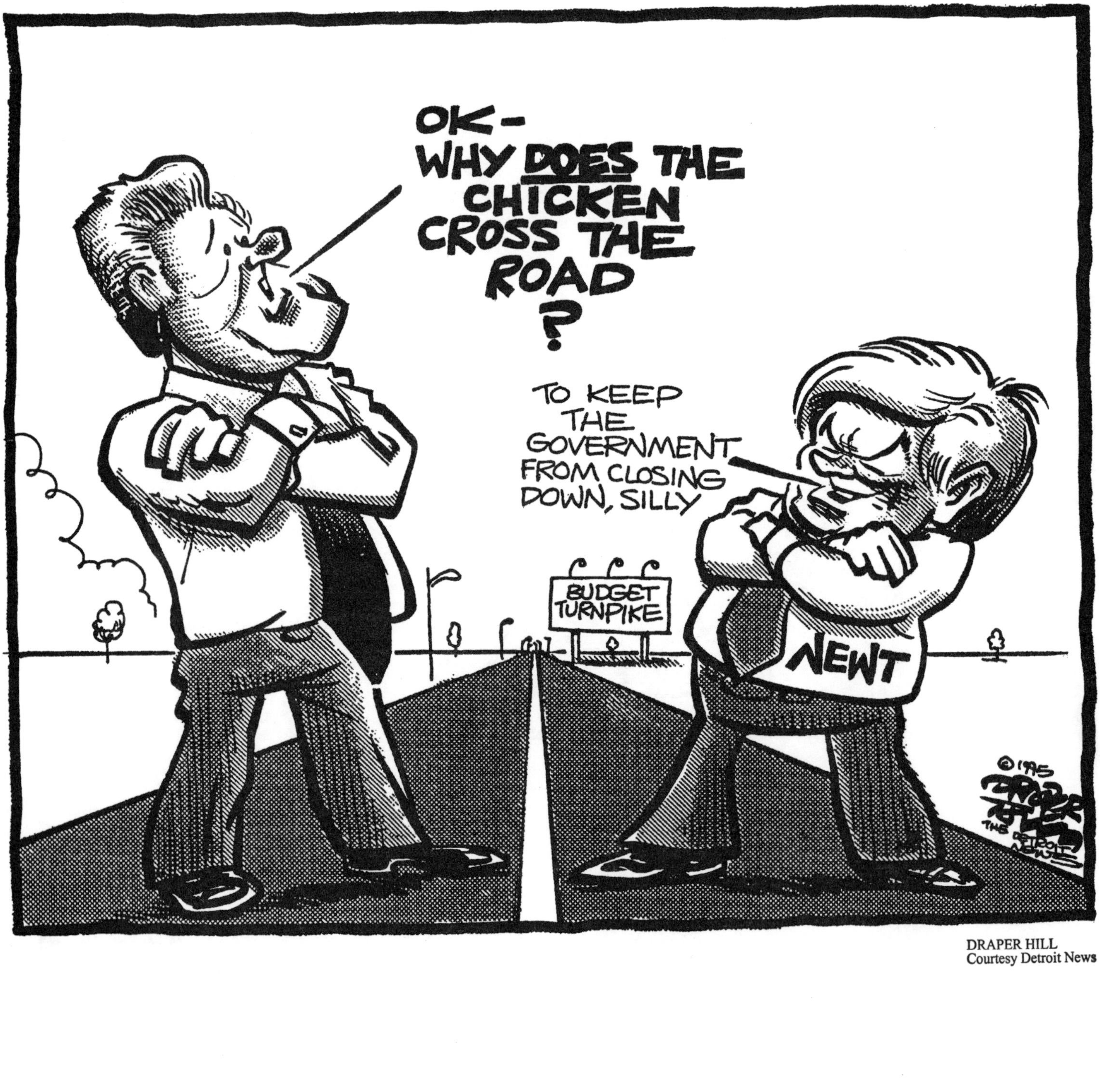
OK-
WHY DOES THE CHICKEN CROSS THE ROAD ?
TO KEEP THE GOVERNMENT FROM CLOSING DOWN, SILLY
BUDGET TURNPIKE
NEWT
©1995

DRAPER HILL
Courtesy Detroit News

Politics

Gen. Colin Powell, long rumored to be eyeing the presidency but never stating his position on major issues, finally spoke out. The former head of the Joint Chiefs of Staff announced that, among other things, he favored abortion rights but was opposed to quotas and the death penalty. He appeared to be ready to contend for the Republican nomination but, after a much-ballyhooed tour promoting his new book, declared he would not run.

Christian conservatives let it be known that they expect a voice in Republican political decision making, but some party members feel that their influence is already too strong. The Christian Coalition, founded by Pat Robertson, seems to give the GOP what organized labor once gave the Democrats—money, votes, and manpower.

Squabbling over a balanced budget led to two government shutdowns near the end of 1995. The seventy-three Republican freshmen in the House declined to compromise on the budget with President Clinton, who seemed to be restrained from compromise by the liberal wing of his party.

Texas billionaire Ross Perot announced the formation of the Independence party and said it will attempt to qualify its presidential candidate in every state. The GOP pushed through spending cuts for the arts, and Clinton made hay with scare talk about welfare spending.

MATT DAVIES
Courtesy Gannett Suburban Newspapers

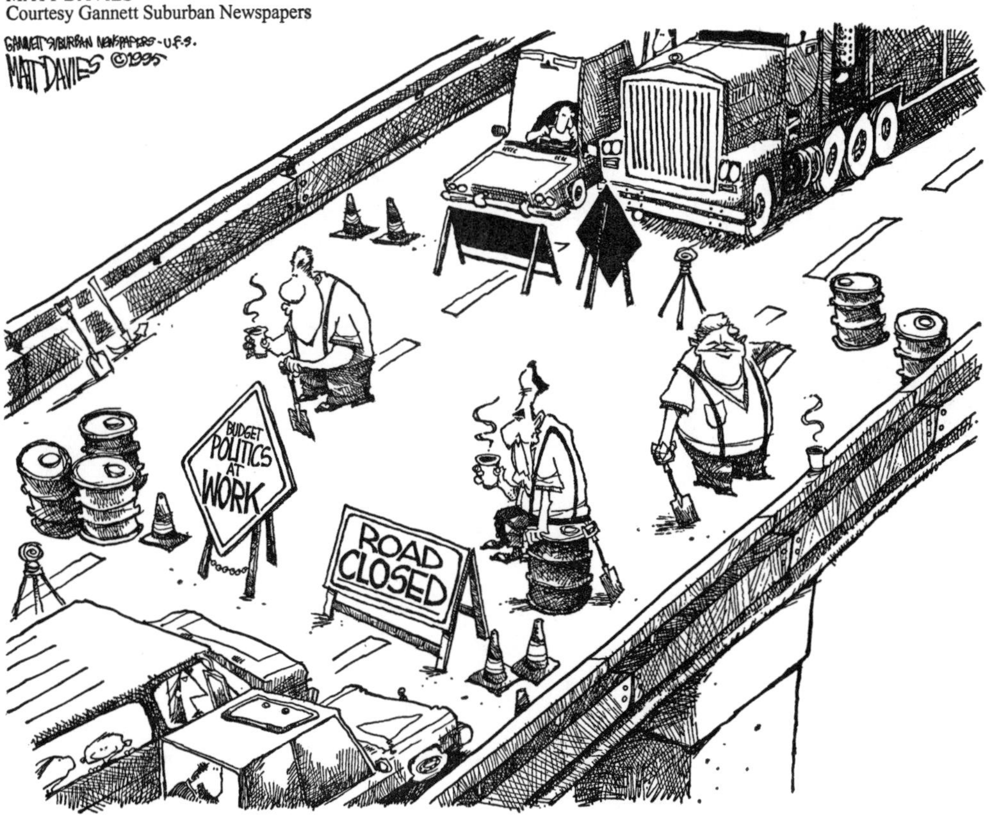
MATT DAVIES ©1995
BUDGET POLITICS AT WORK
ROAD CLOSED

ETTA HULME
Courtesy Ft. Worth Star-Telegram

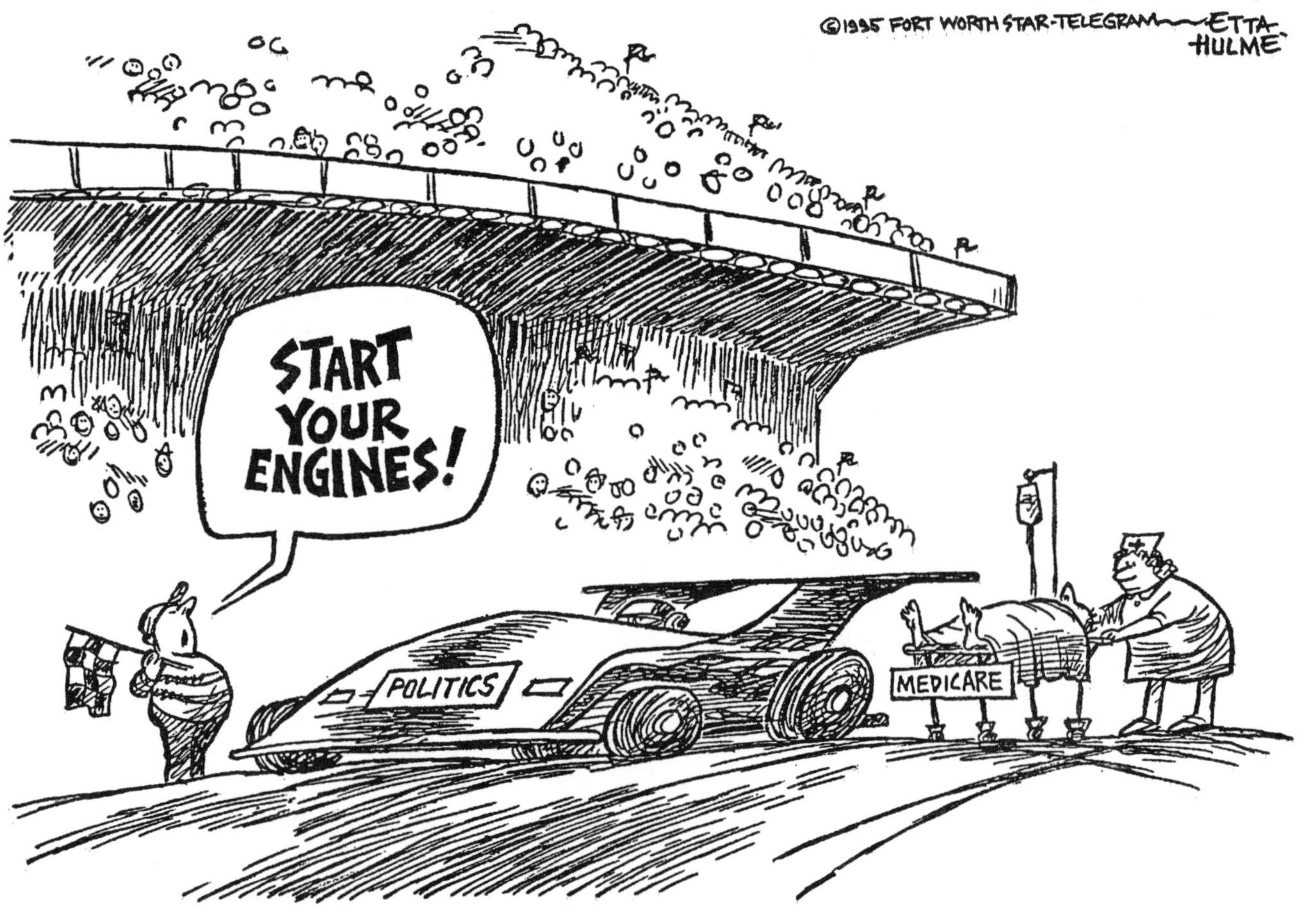
©1995 FORT WORTH STAR-TELEGRAM ETTA HULME
START YOUR ENGINES!
POLITICS
MEDICARE

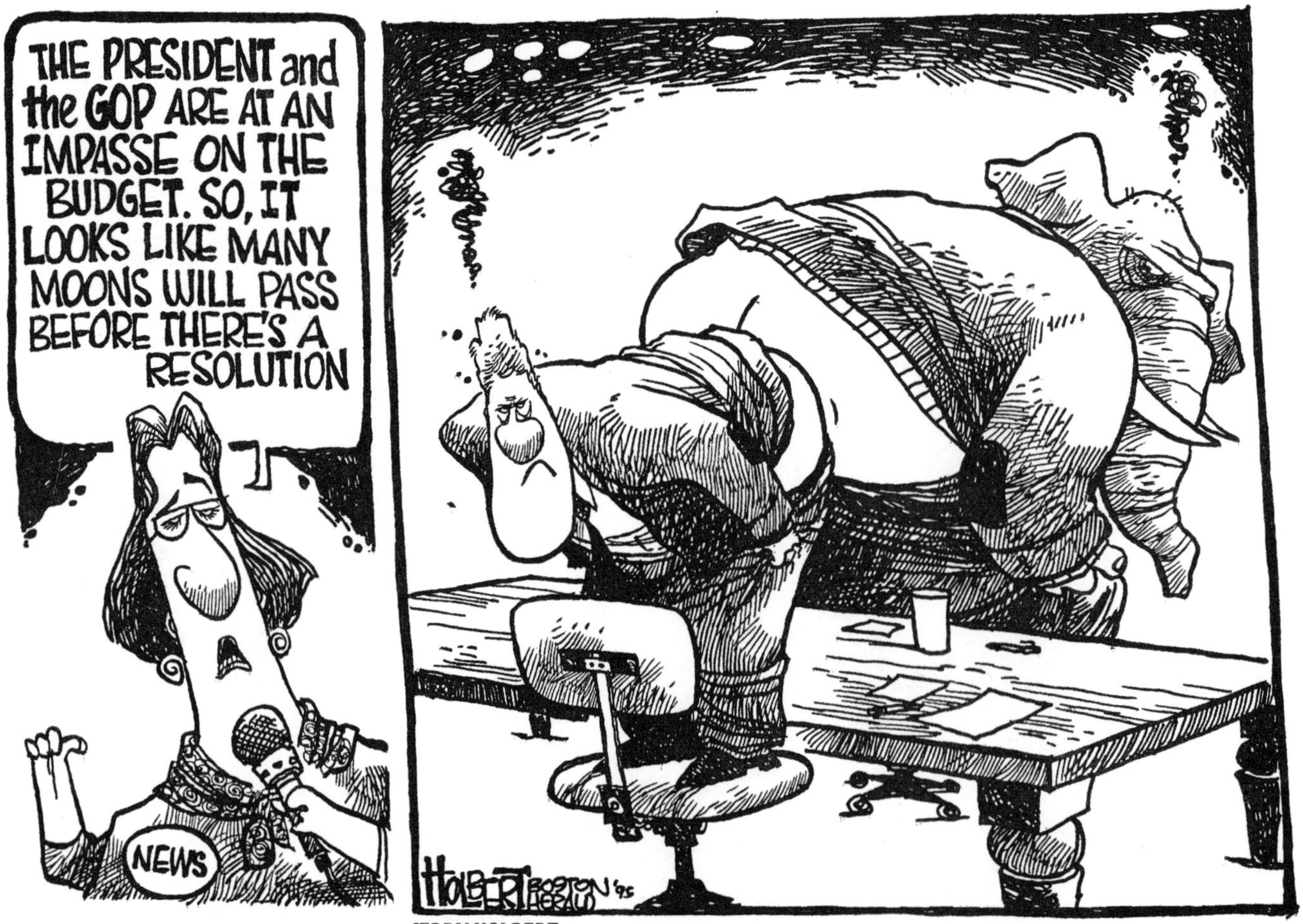
THE PRESIDENT and the GOP ARE AT AN IMPASSE ON THE BUDGET. SO, IT LOOKS LIKE MANY MOONS WILL PASS BEFORE THERE'S A RESOLUTION
NEWS
HOLBERT BOSTON HERALD '95

JERRY HOLBERT
Courtesy Boston Herald

ERIC SMITH
Courtesy Capital Gazette Newspapers

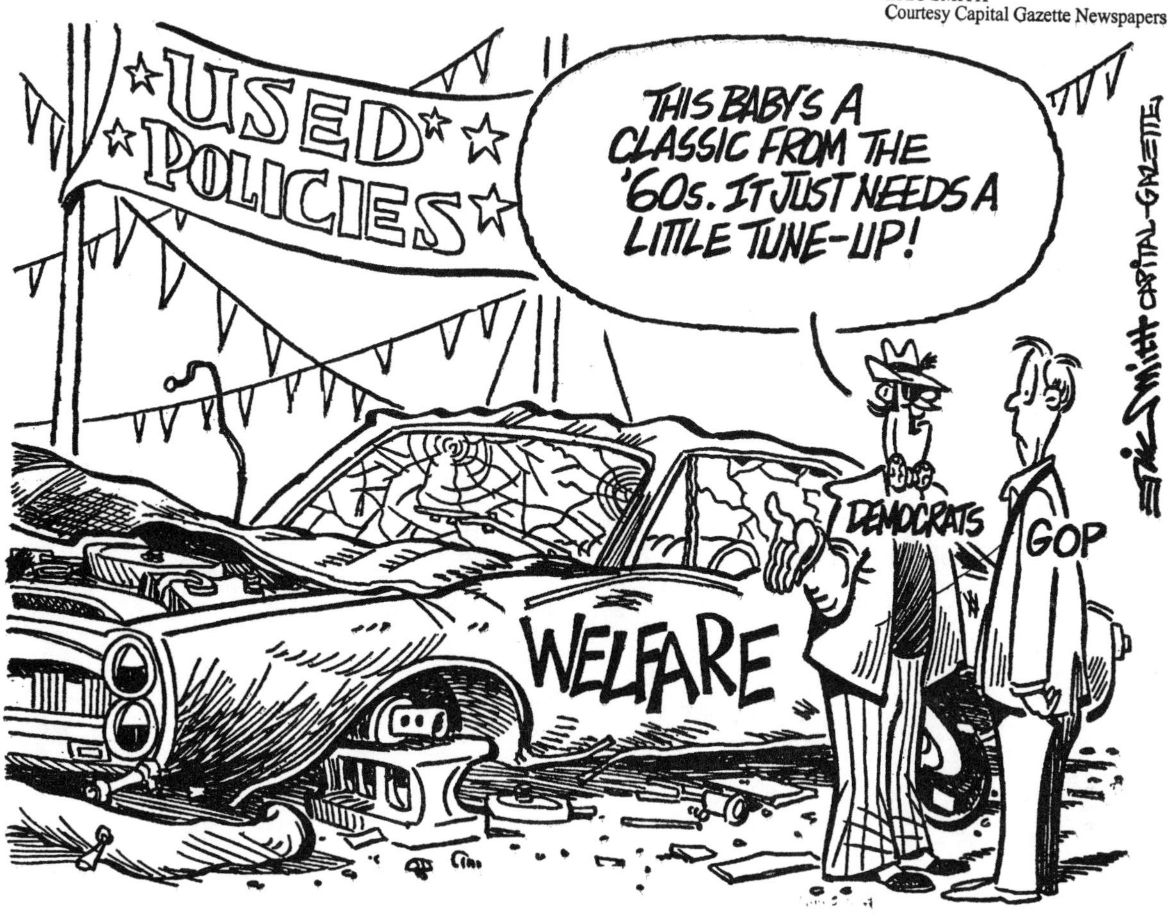
USED POLICIES
THIS BABY'S A CLASSIC FROM THE '60s. IT JUST NEEDS A LITTLE TUNE-UP!
WELFARE
DEMOCRATS
GOP
Eric Smith CAPITAL-GAZETTE

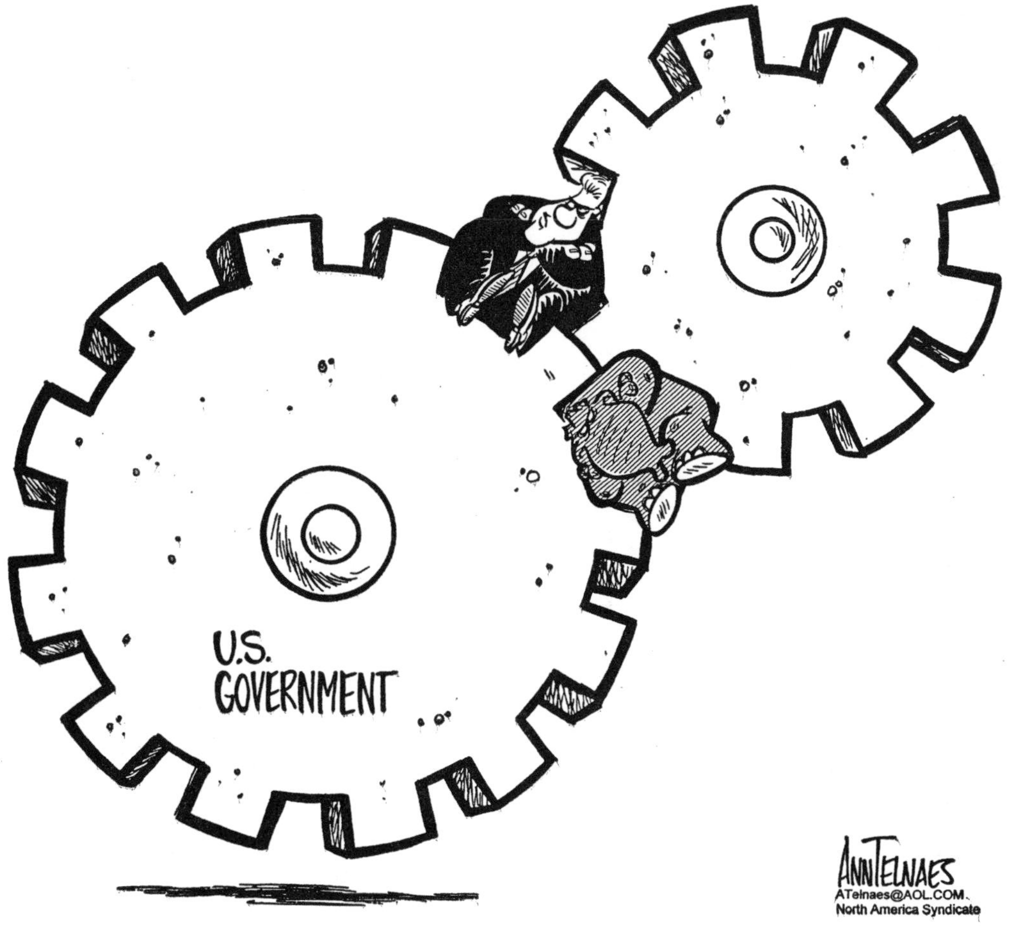
U.S. GOVERNMENT
ANN TELNAES
ATelnaes@AOL.COM
North America Syndicate

ANN TELNAES
Courtesy North America Syndicate

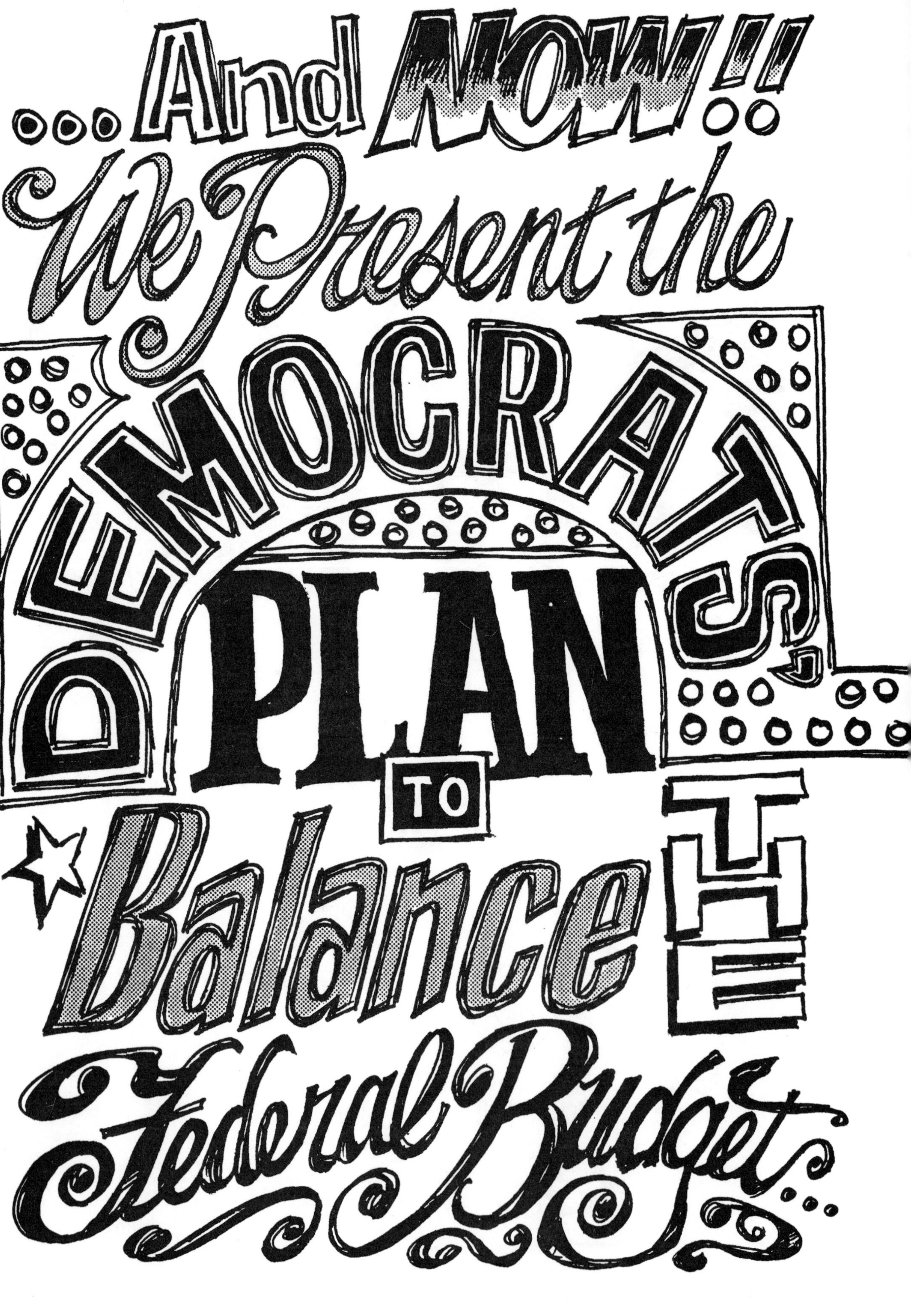
...And NOW!!
We Present the
DEMOCRATS'
PLAN
TO
Balance THE
Federal Budget...

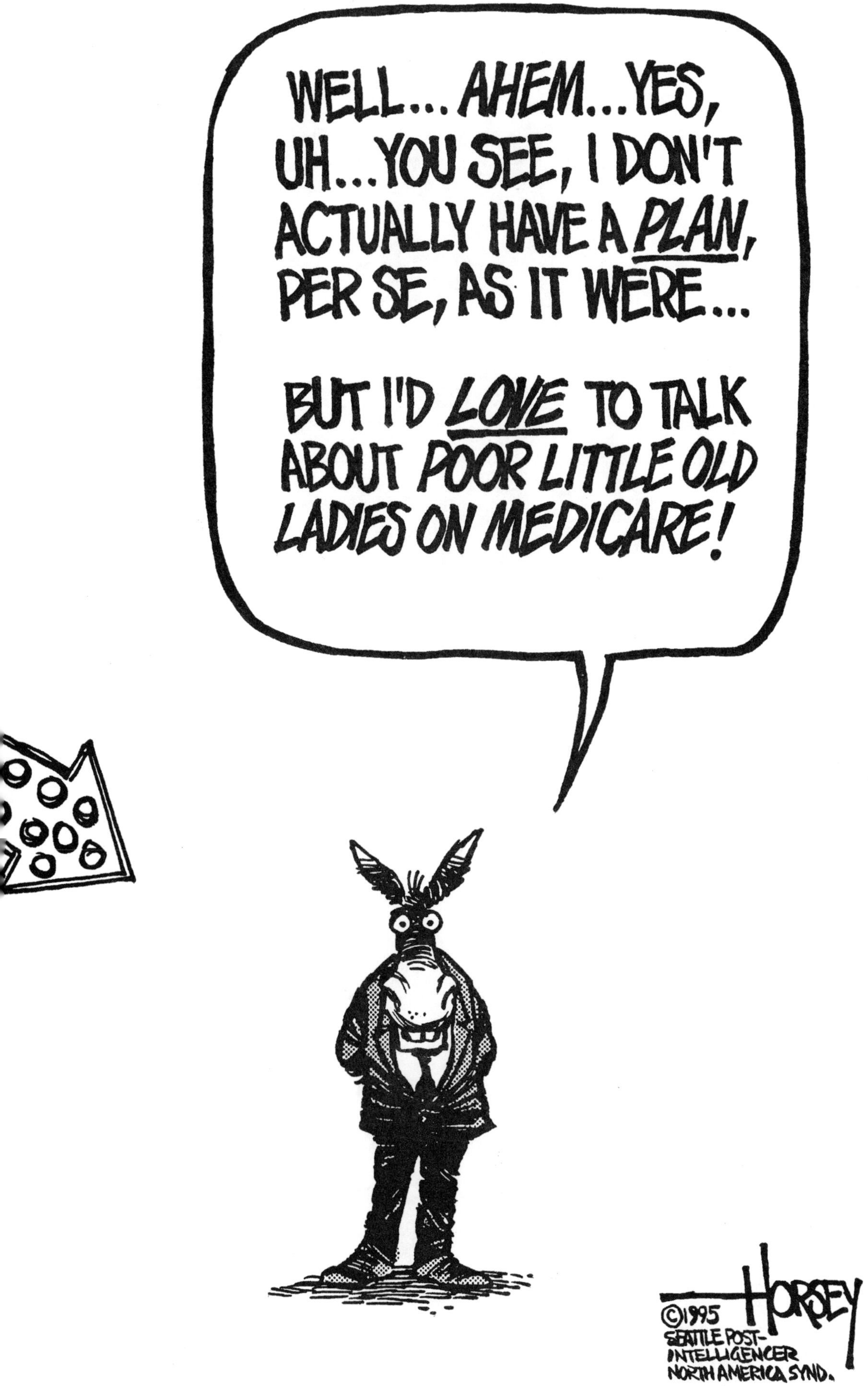
WELL... AHEM... YES, UH... YOU SEE, I DON'T ACTUALLY HAVE A PLAN, PER SE, AS IT WERE...
BUT I'D LOVE TO TALK ABOUT POOR LITTLE OLD LADIES ON MEDICARE!
HORSEY
©1995 SEATTLE POST-INTELLIGENCER NORTH AMERICA SYND.

DAVID HORSEY
Courtesy Seattle Post-Intelligencer

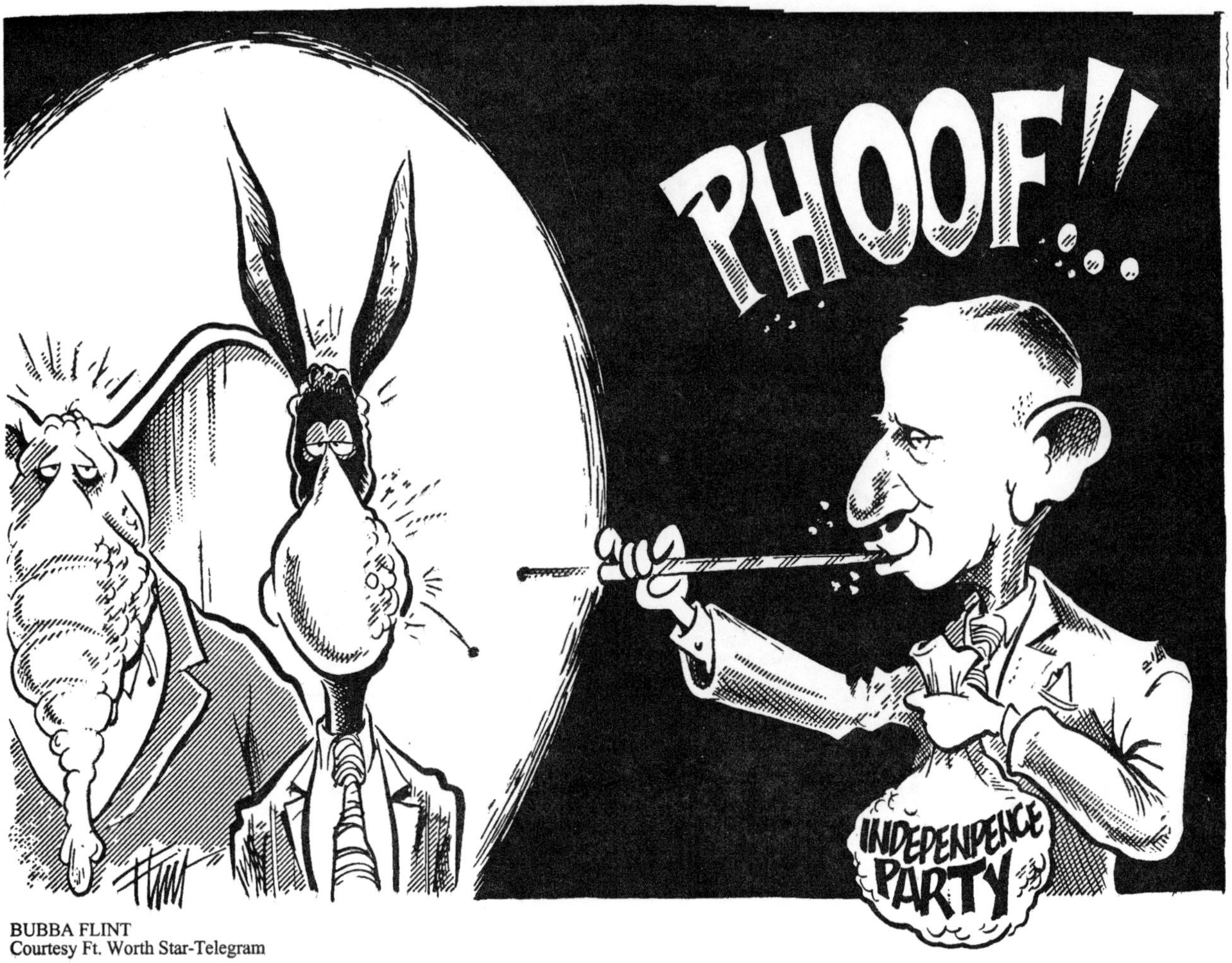
PHOOF!!
INDEPENDENCE PARTY

BUBBA FLINT
Courtesy Ft. Worth Star-Telegram

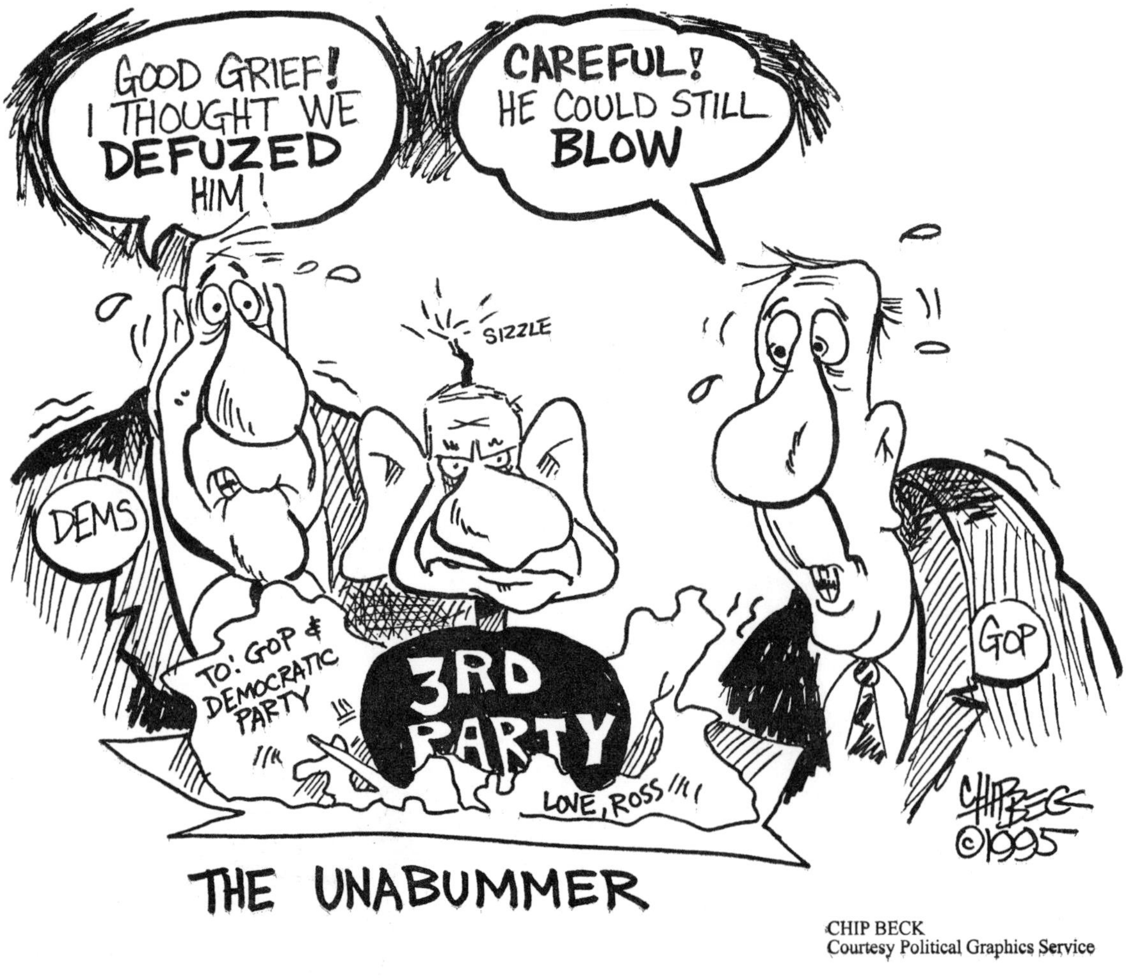
GOOD GRIEF! I THOUGHT WE DEFUZED HIM!
CAREFUL! HE COULD STILL BLOW
SIZZLE
DEMS
GOP
TO: GOP & DEMOCRATIC PARTY
3RD PARTY
LOVE, ROSS
CHIP BECK ©1995
THE UNABUMMER

CHIP BECK
Courtesy Political Graphics Service

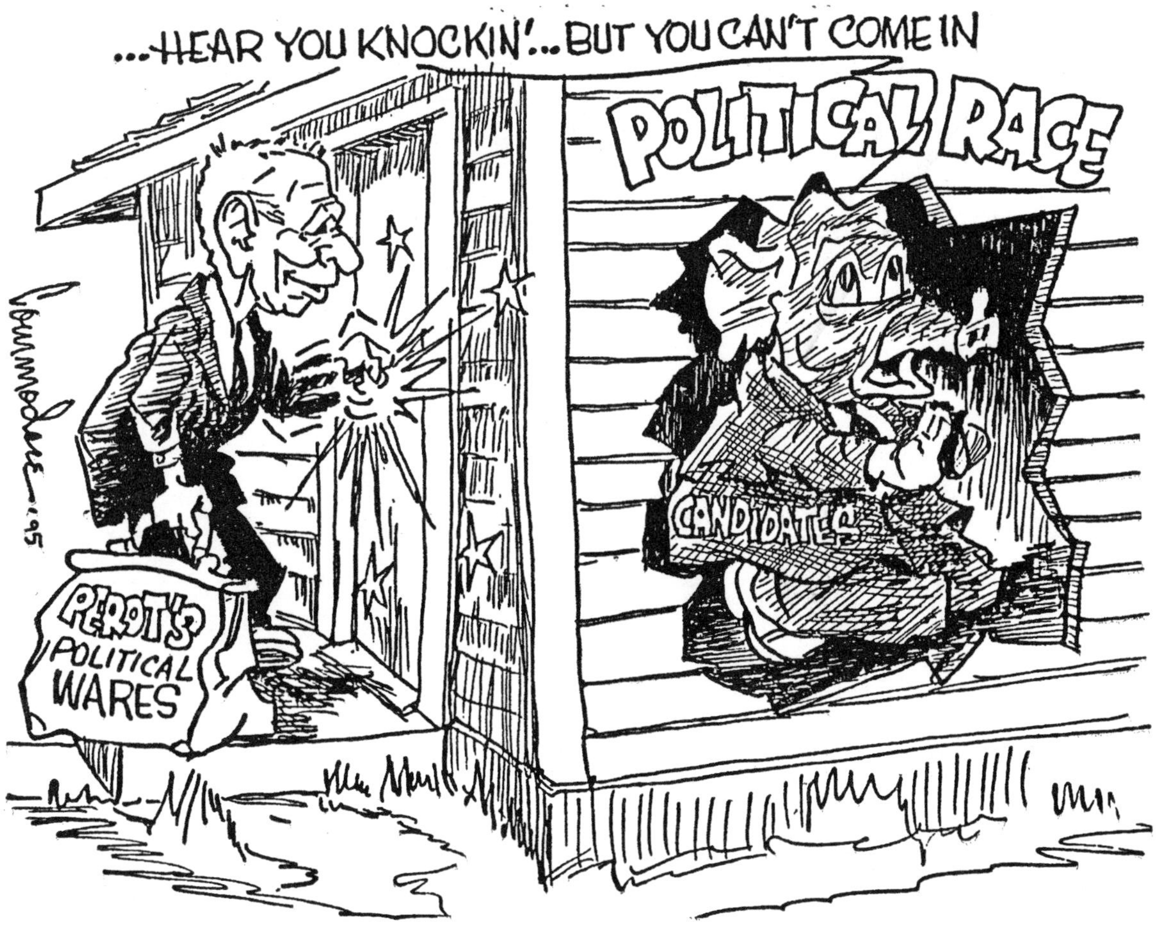
...HEAR YOU KNOCKIN'...BUT YOU CAN'T COME IN
POLITICAL RACE
CANDIDATES
PEROT'S POLITICAL WARES
Commodore '95

CHESTER COMMODORE, SR.
Courtesy Chicago Daily Defender

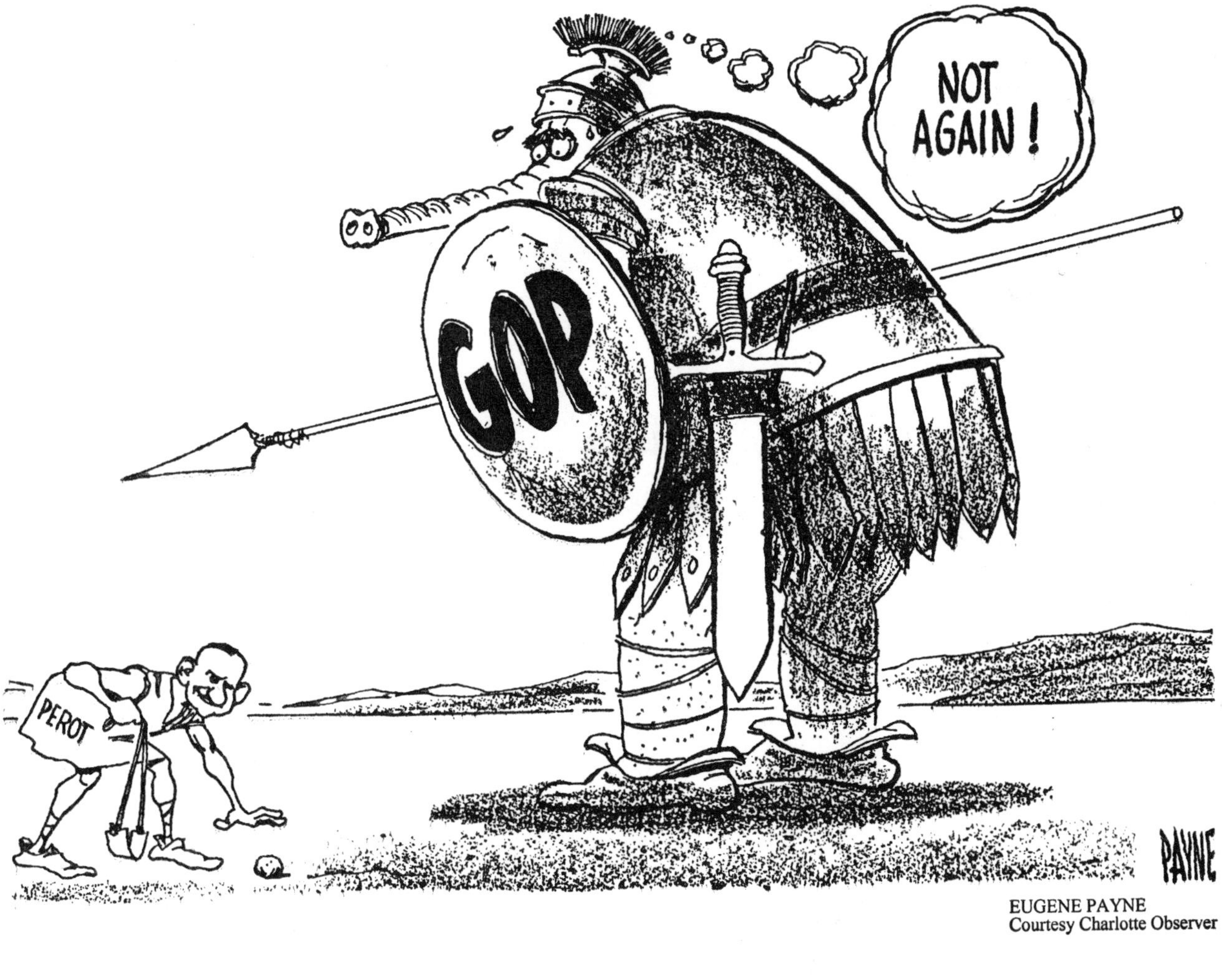
NOT AGAIN!
GOP
PEROT
PAYNE

EUGENE PAYNE
Courtesy Charlotte Observer

MARK CULLUM
Courtesy Birmingham News

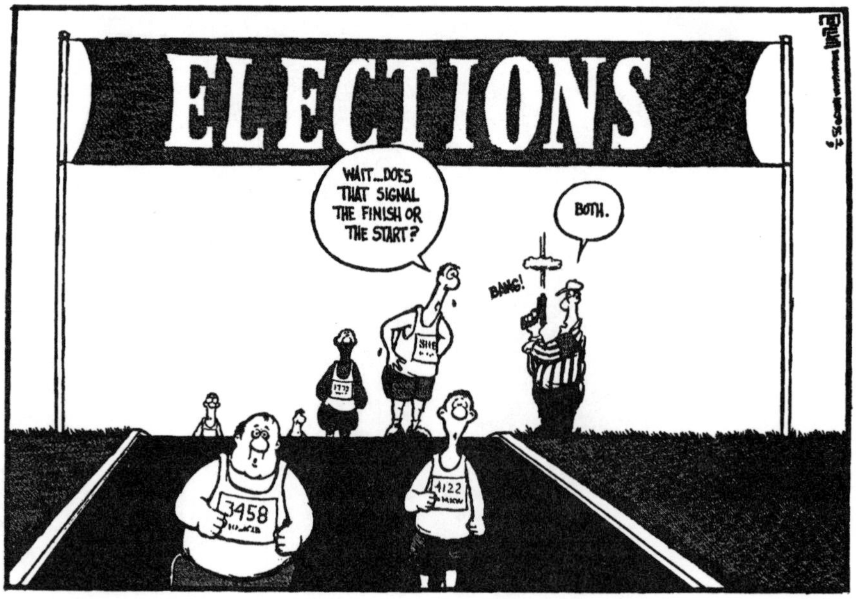
ELECTIONS
WAIT...DOES THAT SIGNAL THE FINISH OR THE START?
BOTH.
BANG!
3458
4122

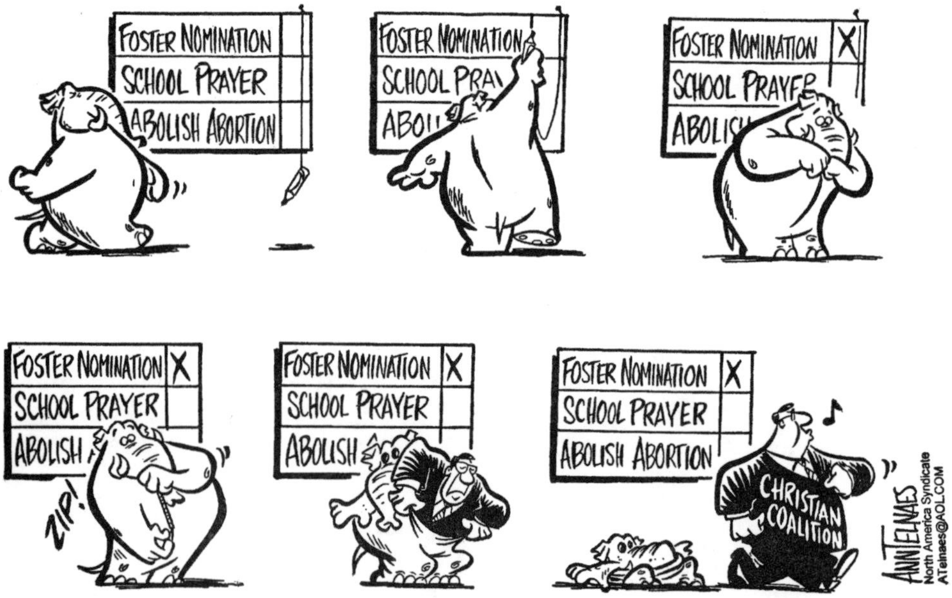
FOSTER NOMINATION
SCHOOL PRAYER
ABOLISH ABORTION
X
ZIP!
CHRISTIAN COALITION
ANN TELNAES
North America Syndicate
ATelnaes@AOL.COM

ANN TELNAES
Courtesy North America Syndicate

STUART CARLSON
Courtesy Milwaukee Journal Sentinel

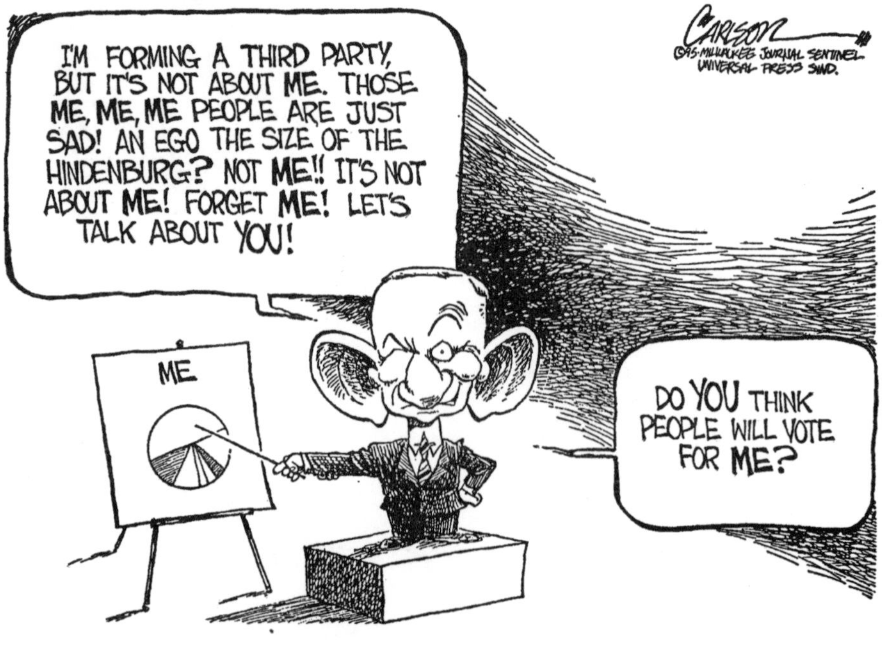
CARLSON
©95 MILWAUKEE JOURNAL SENTINEL UNIVERSAL PRESS SYND.
I'M FORMING A THIRD PARTY, BUT IT'S NOT ABOUT ME. THOSE ME, ME, ME PEOPLE ARE JUST SAD! AN EGO THE SIZE OF THE HINDENBURG? NOT ME!! IT'S NOT ABOUT ME! FORGET ME! LET'S TALK ABOUT YOU!
ME
DO YOU THINK PEOPLE WILL VOTE FOR ME?

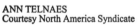

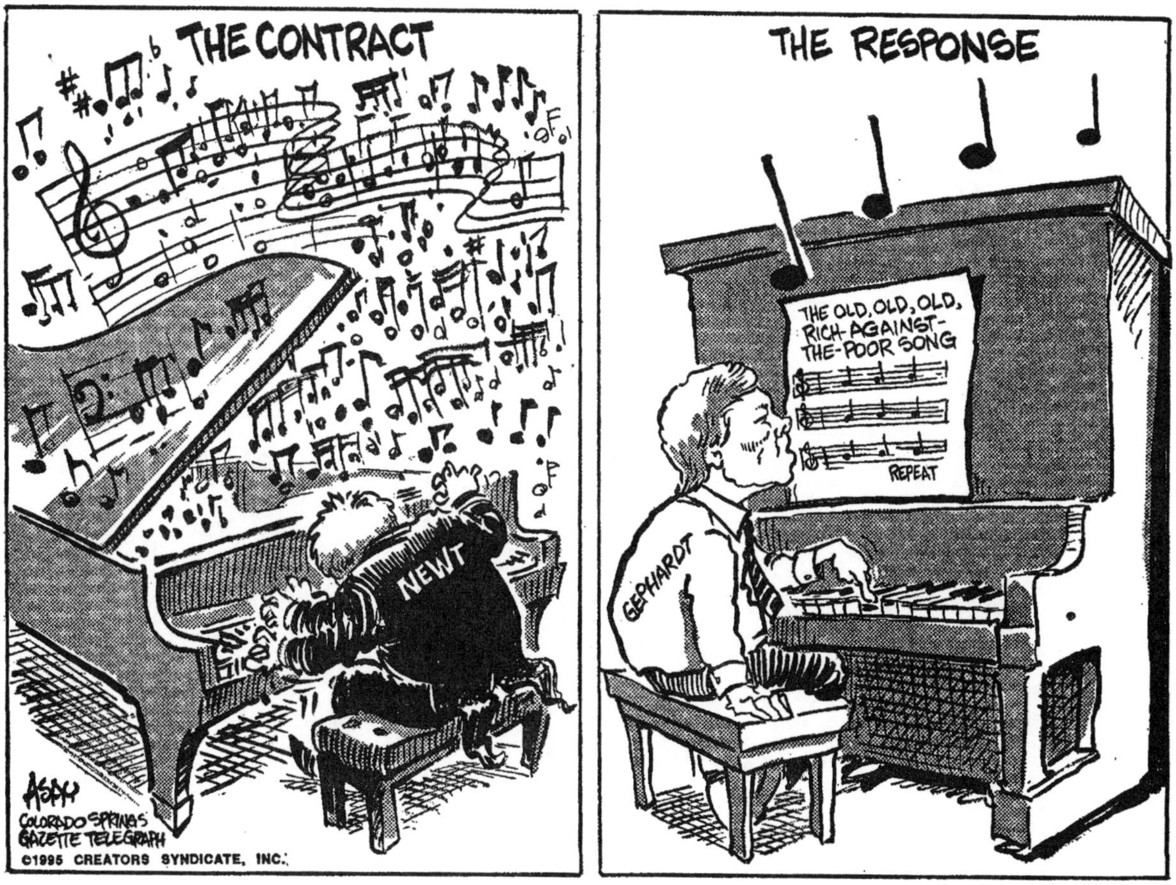
THE CONTRACT
NEWT
THE RESPONSE
THE OLD, OLD, OLD, RICH-AGAINST-THE-POOR SONG
REPEAT
GEPHARDT
ASAY
COLORADO SPRINGS GAZETTE TELEGRAPH
©1995 CREATORS SYNDICATE, INC.

CHUCK ASAY
Courtesy Colorado Springs Gazette Telegraph

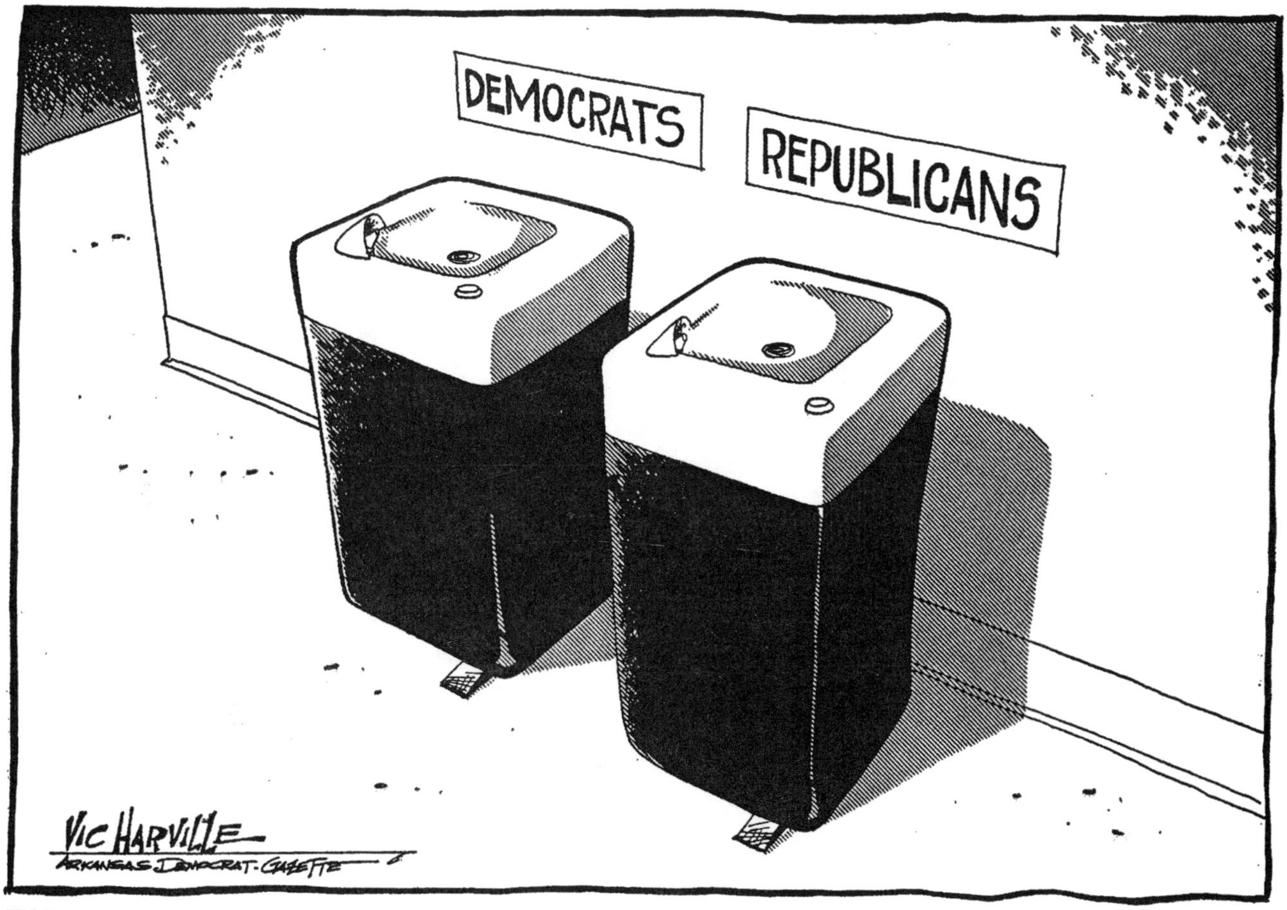
DEMOCRATS
REPUBLICANS
VIC HARVILLE
ARKANSAS DEMOCRAT-GAZETTE

VIC HARVILLE
Courtesy Arkansas Democrat-Gazette

S. C. RAWLS
Courtesy Rockdale Citizen

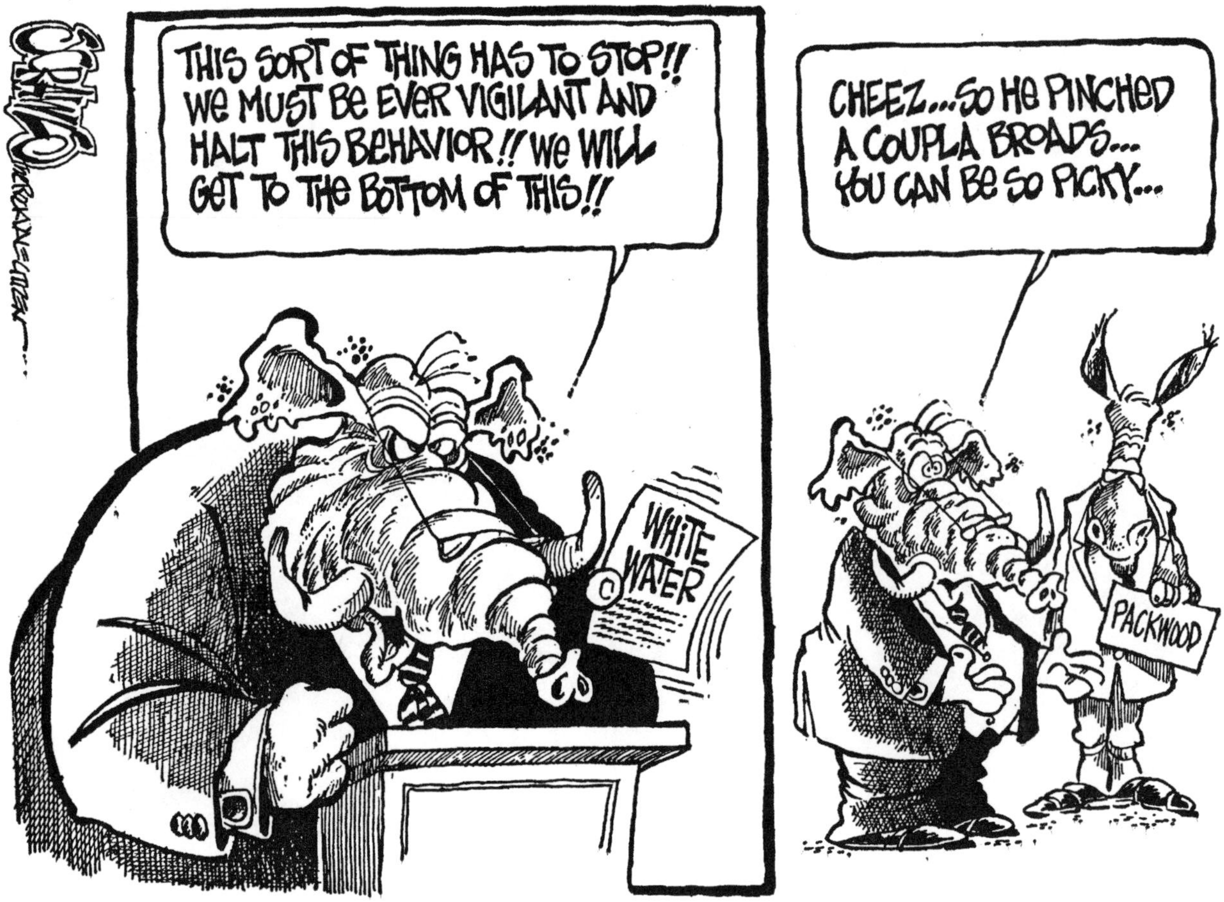
THIS SORT OF THING HAS TO STOP!! WE MUST BE EVER VIGILANT AND HALT THIS BEHAVIOR!! WE WILL GET TO THE BOTTOM OF THIS!!
WHITE WATER
CHEEZ...SO HE PINCHED A COUPLA BROADS... YOU CAN BE SO PICKY...
PACKWOOD

GARY BROOKINS
Courtesy Richmond Times-Dispatch

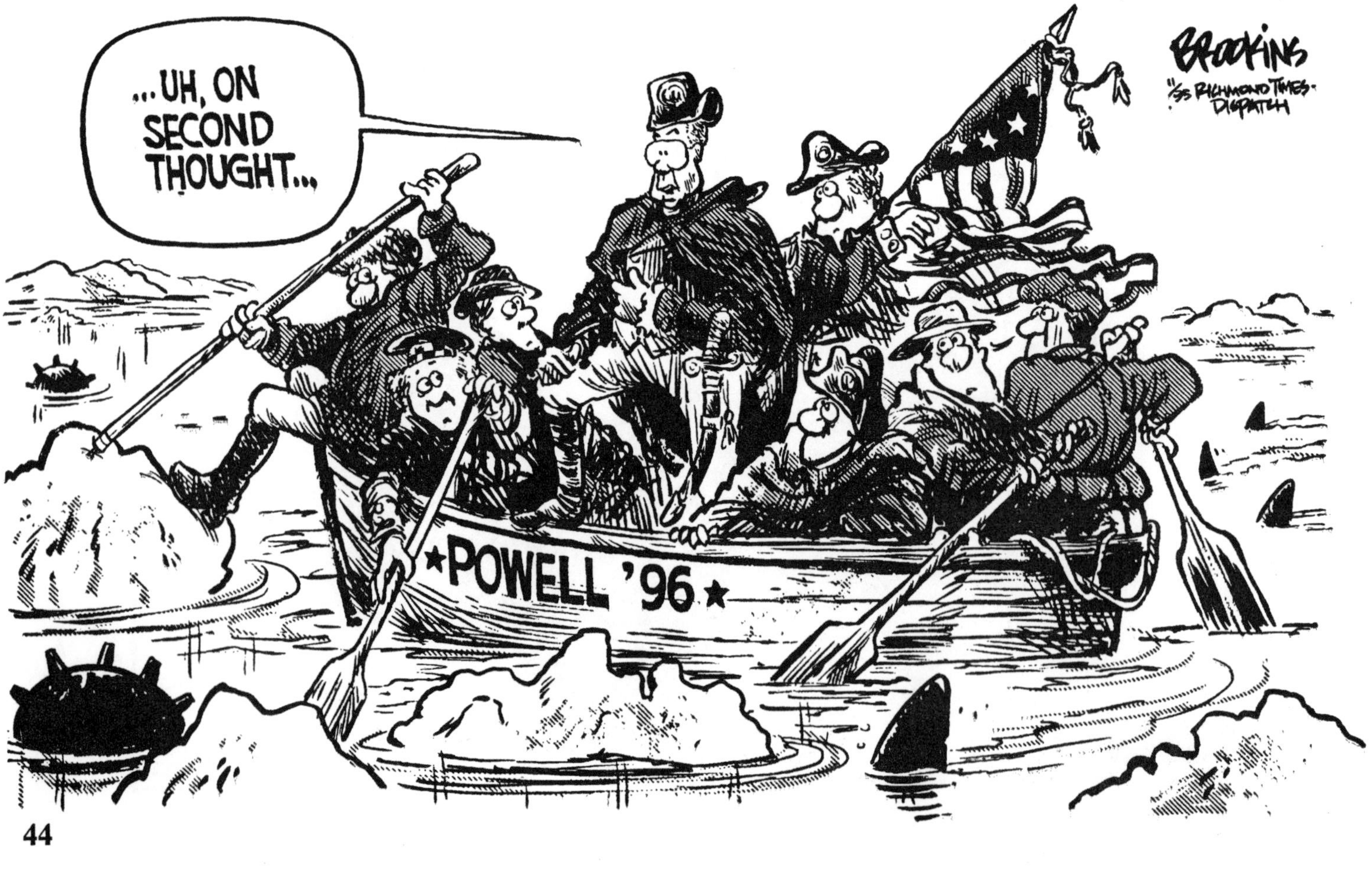
...UH, ON SECOND THOUGHT...
★POWELL '96★

REX BABIN
Courtesy Albany Times Union

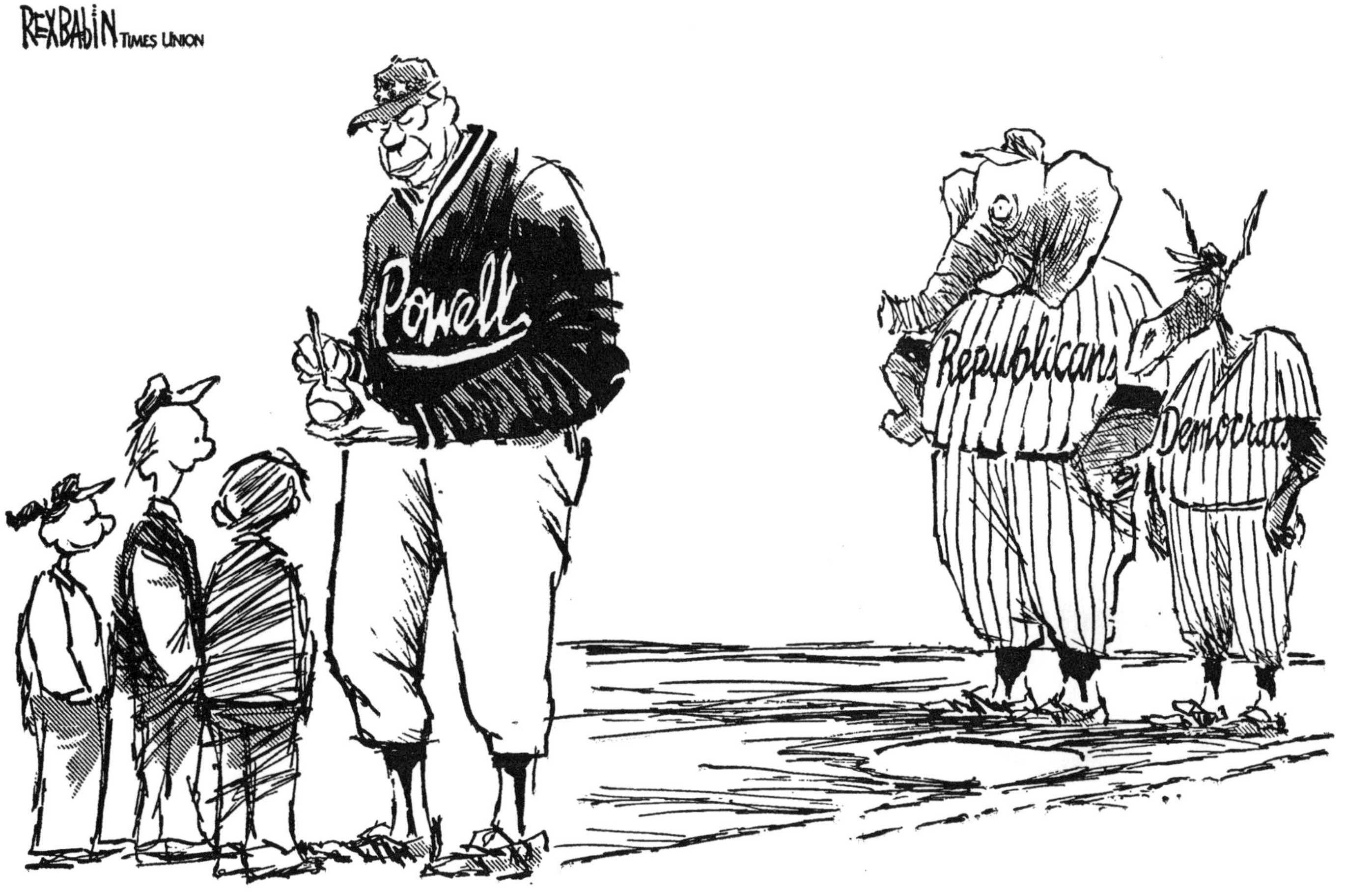
REXBABIN TIMES UNION
Powell
Republicans
Democrats

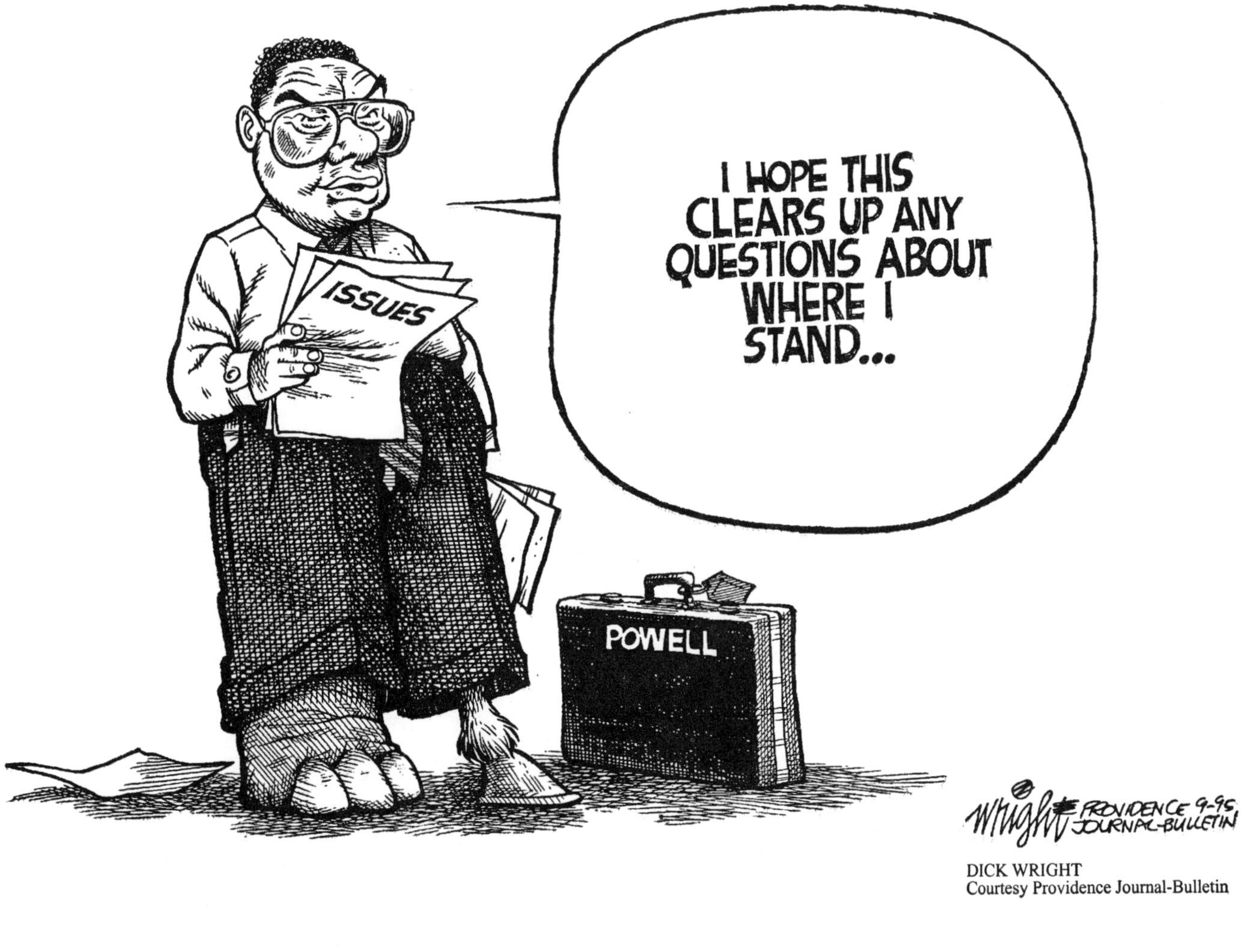
I HOPE THIS CLEARS UP ANY QUESTIONS ABOUT WHERE I STAND...
ISSUES
POWELL
WRIGHT PROVIDENCE 9-95 JOURNAL-BULLETIN

DICK WRIGHT
Courtesy Providence Journal-Bulletin

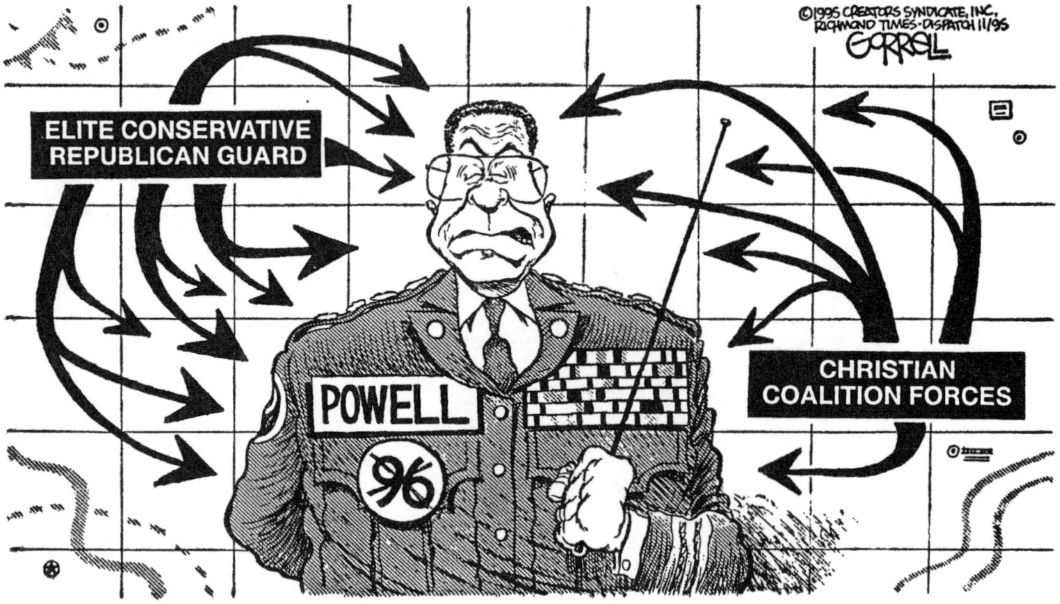
©1995 CREATORS SYNDICATE, INC.
RICHMOND TIMES-DISPATCH 11/95
GORRELL
ELITE CONSERVATIVE
REPUBLICAN GUARD
CHRISTIAN
COALITION FORCES
POWELL
96

BOB GORRELL
Courtesy Richmond Times-Dispatch/
Copley News Service

CLAY JONES
Courtesy Gulfport Daily Leader

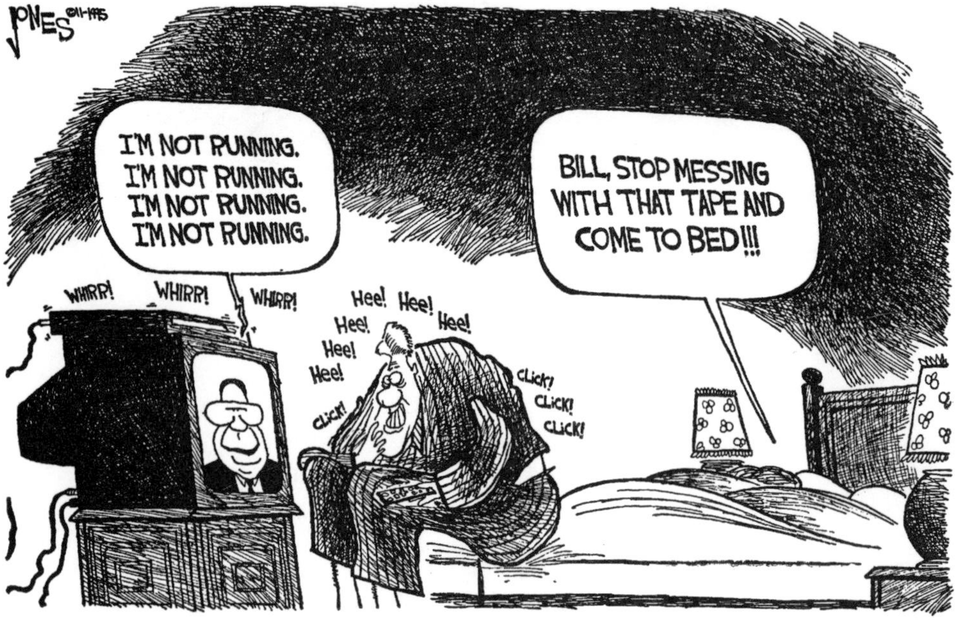
JONES
I'M NOT RUNNING.
I'M NOT RUNNING.
I'M NOT RUNNING.
I'M NOT RUNNING.
BILL, STOP MESSING WITH THAT TAPE AND COME TO BED!!!
WHIRR! WHIRR! WHIRR!
Hee! Hee! Hee! Hee! Hee! Hee!
CLICK! CLICK! CLICK! CLICK!

JOHN SPENCER
Courtesy Philadelphia Business Journal

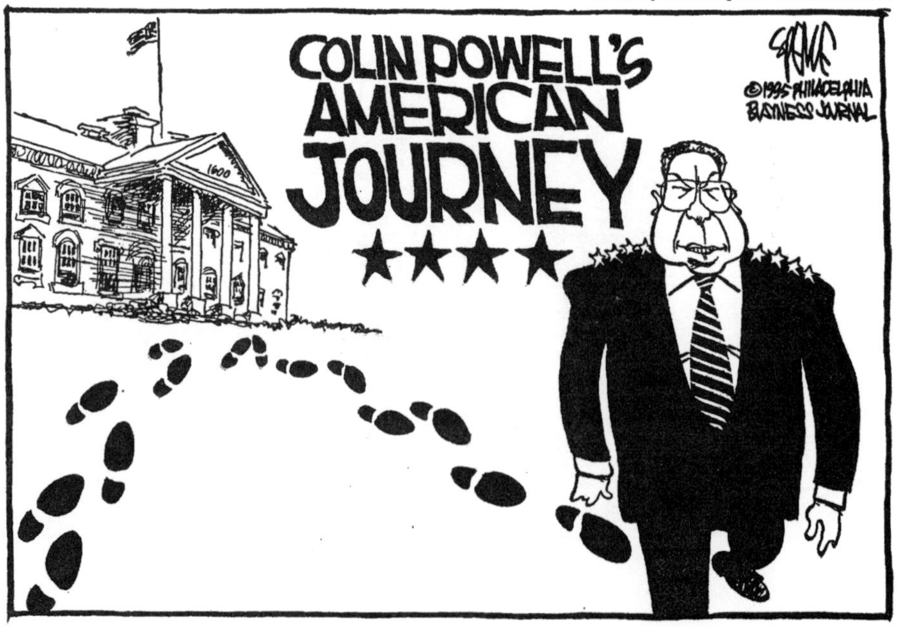
COLIN POWELL'S
AMERICAN
JOURNEY
★★★★
SPENCE
©1995 PHILADELPHIA BUSINESS JOURNAL
1600

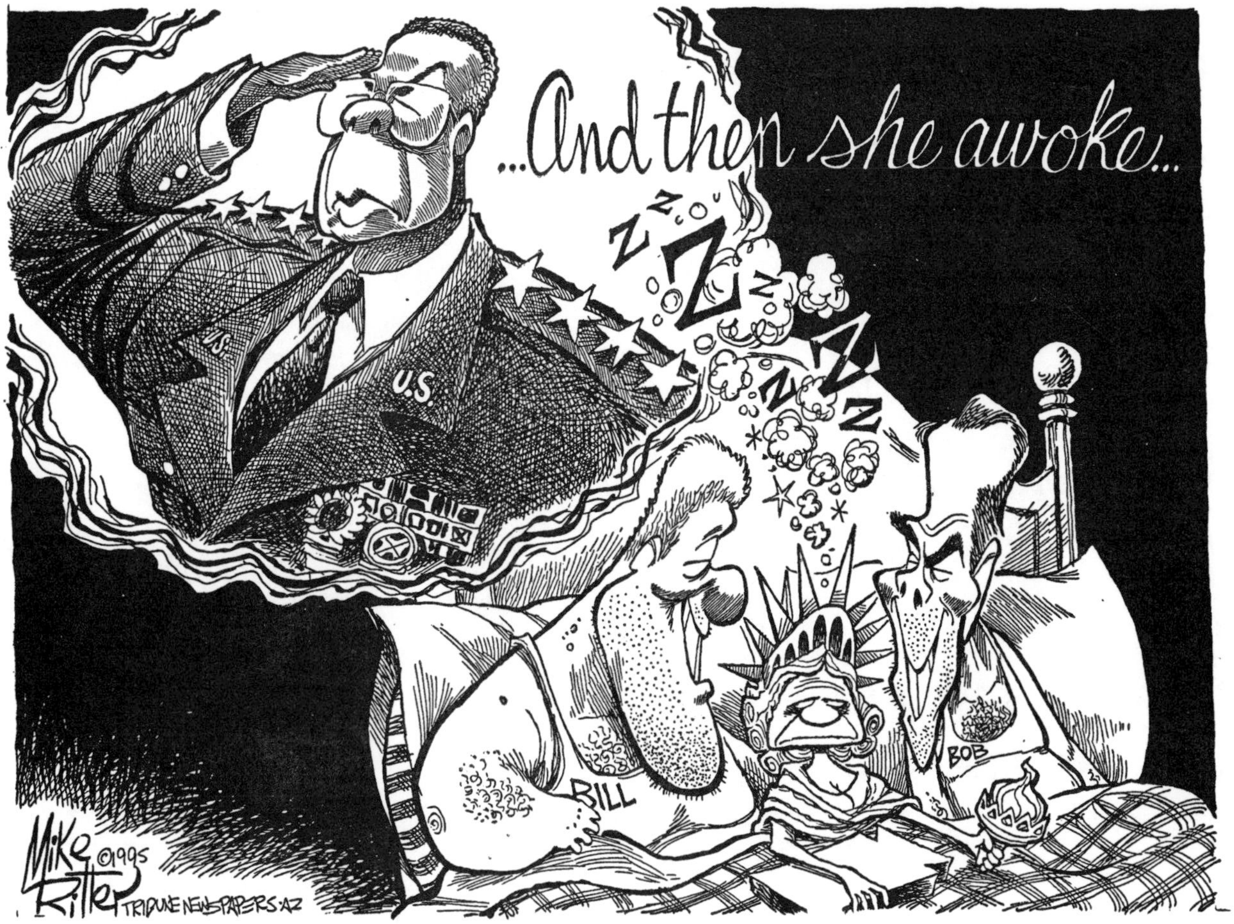
...And then she awoke...
U.S.
BILL
BOB
Mike Ritter ©1995 Tribune Newspapers·AZ

MIKE RITTER
Courtesy Tribune Newspapers

TOM GIBB
Courtesy Rothco

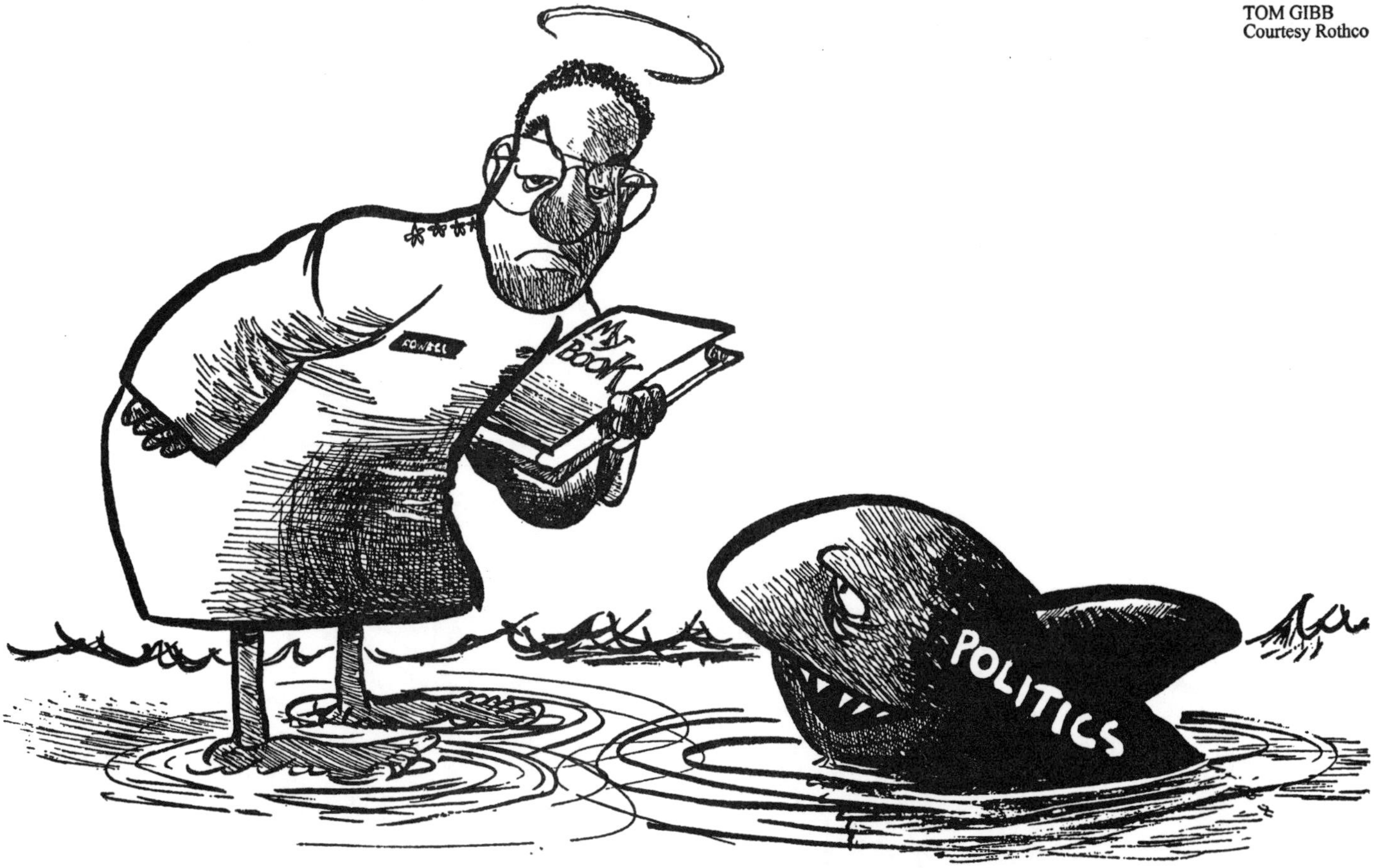
MY BOOK
POLITICS
"WHAT'LL IT BE, GEN. POWELL? YOU GONNA KEEP WALKING ON WATER OR DIVE IN?"

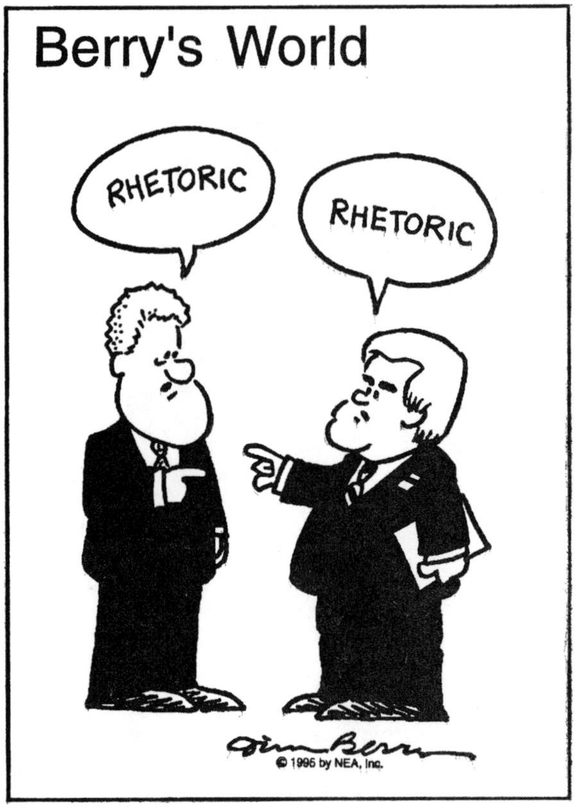
Berry's World
RHETORIC
RHETORIC
Jim Berry
© 1996 by NEA, Inc.

JIM BERRY
Courtesy NEA

ETTA HULME
Courtesy Ft. Worth Star-Telegram

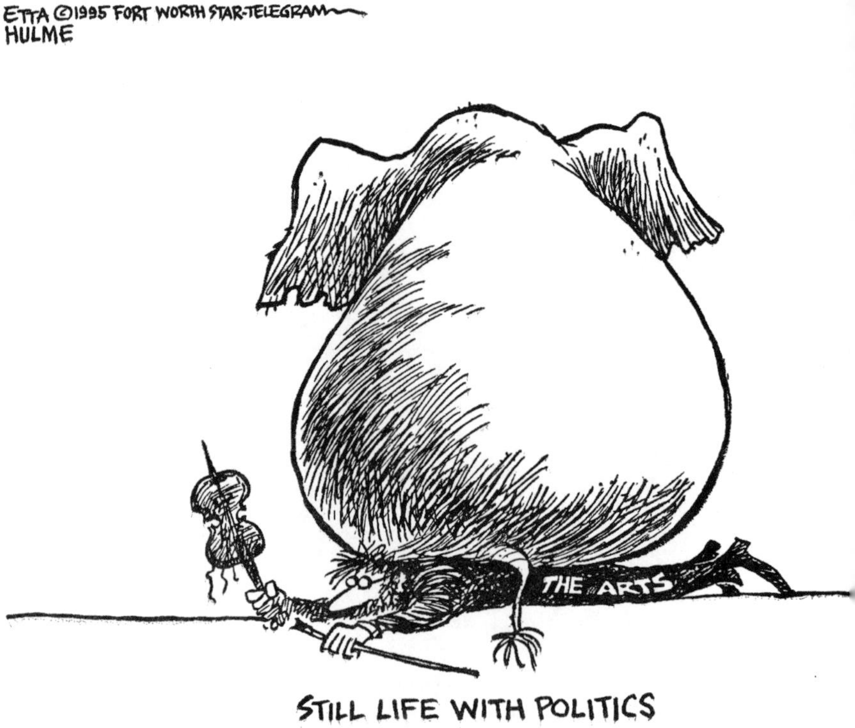
ETTA ©1995 FORT WORTH STAR-TELEGRAM
HULME
THE ARTS
STILL LIFE WITH POLITICS

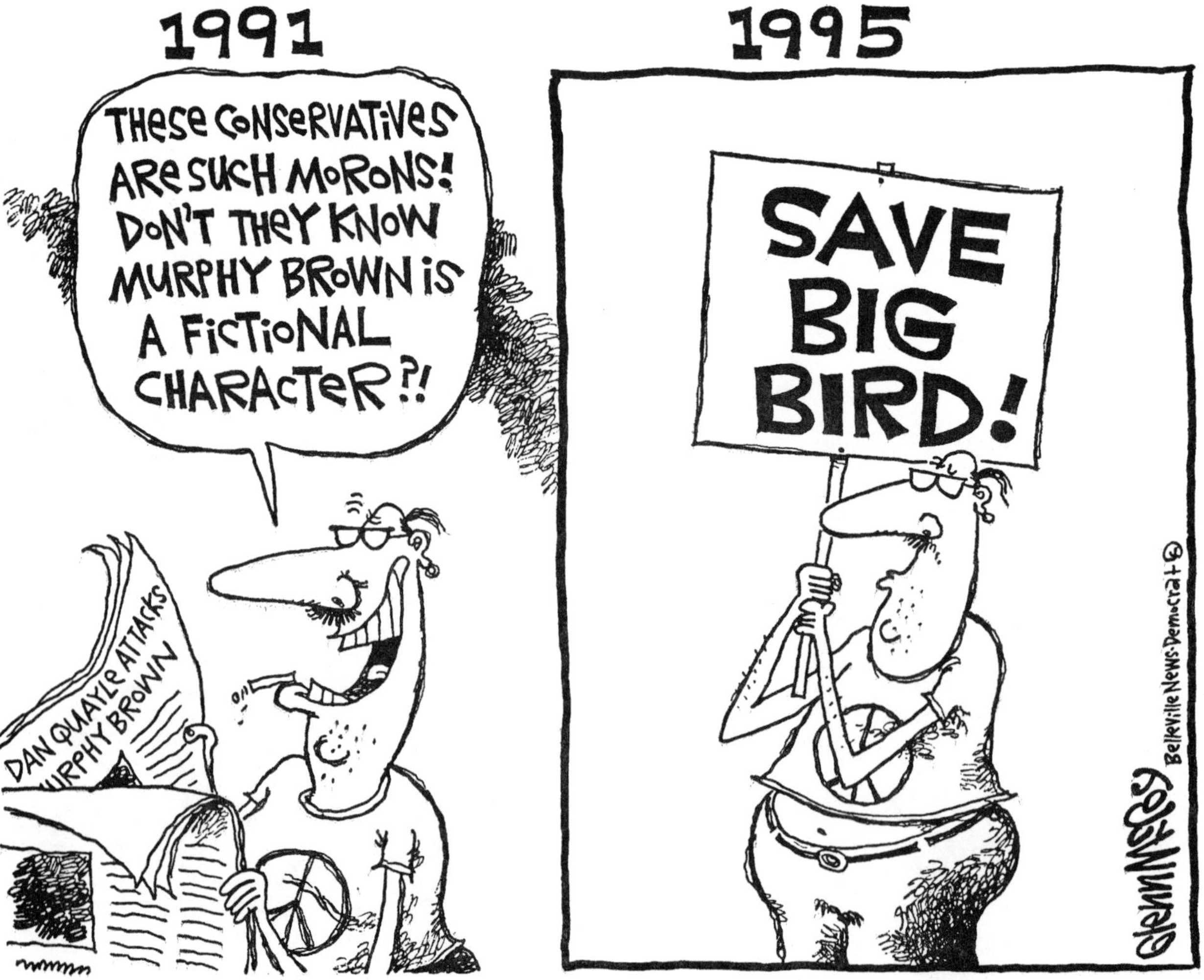
1991
THESE CONSERVATIVES ARE SUCH MORONS! DON'T THEY KNOW MURPHY BROWN IS A FICTIONAL CHARACTER?!
DAN QUAYLE ATTACKS MURPHY BROWN
1995
SAVE BIG BIRD!
GLENN McCOY
Belleville News-Democrat ©

GLENN MCCOY
Courtesy Belleville News-Democrat (Ill.)

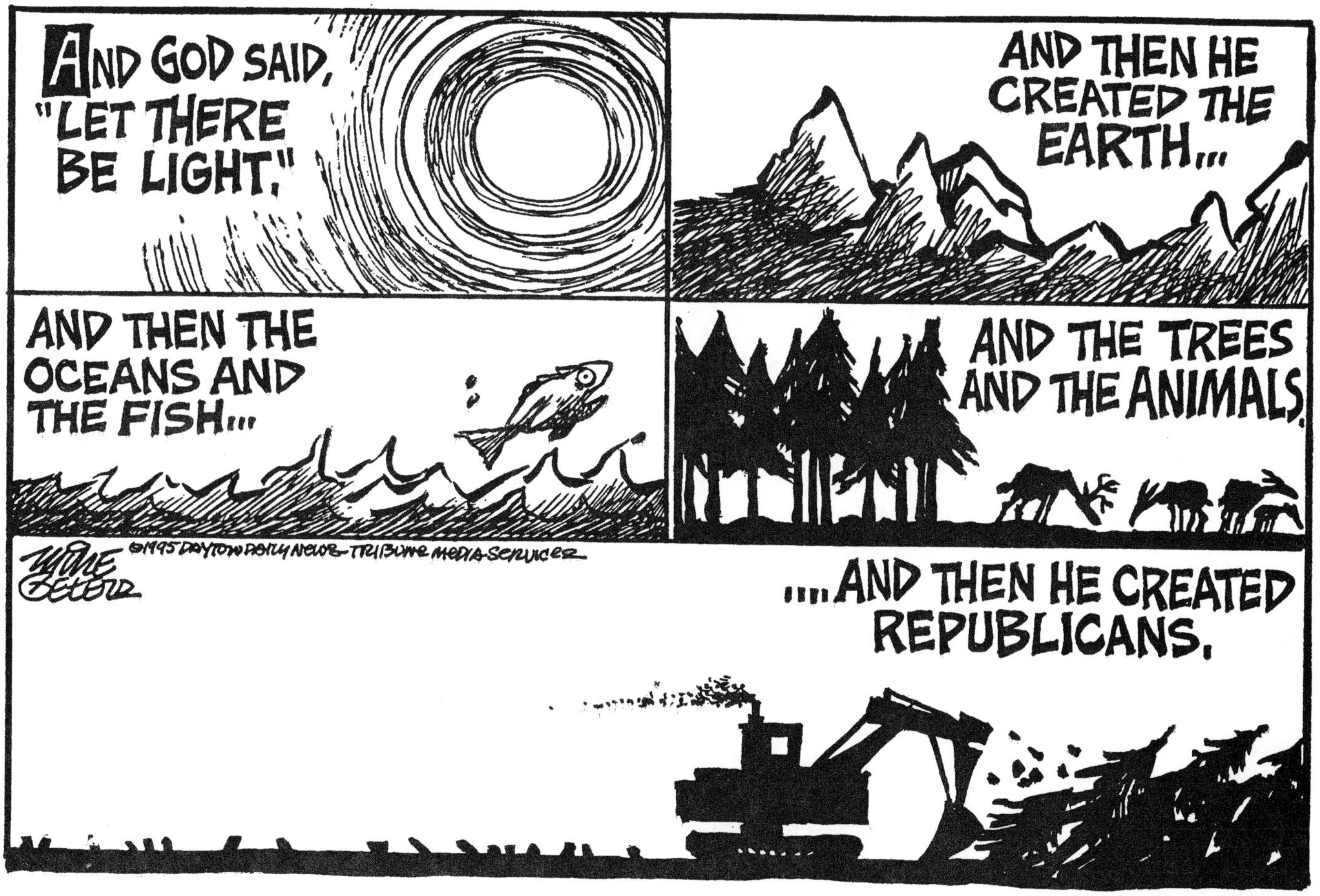
AND GOD SAID, "LET THERE BE LIGHT."
AND THEN HE CREATED THE EARTH...
AND THEN THE OCEANS AND THE FISH...
AND THE TREES AND THE ANIMALS.
....AND THEN HE CREATED REPUBLICANS.

MIKE PETERS
Courtesy Dayton Daily News

ED GAMBLE
Courtesy Florida Times-Union

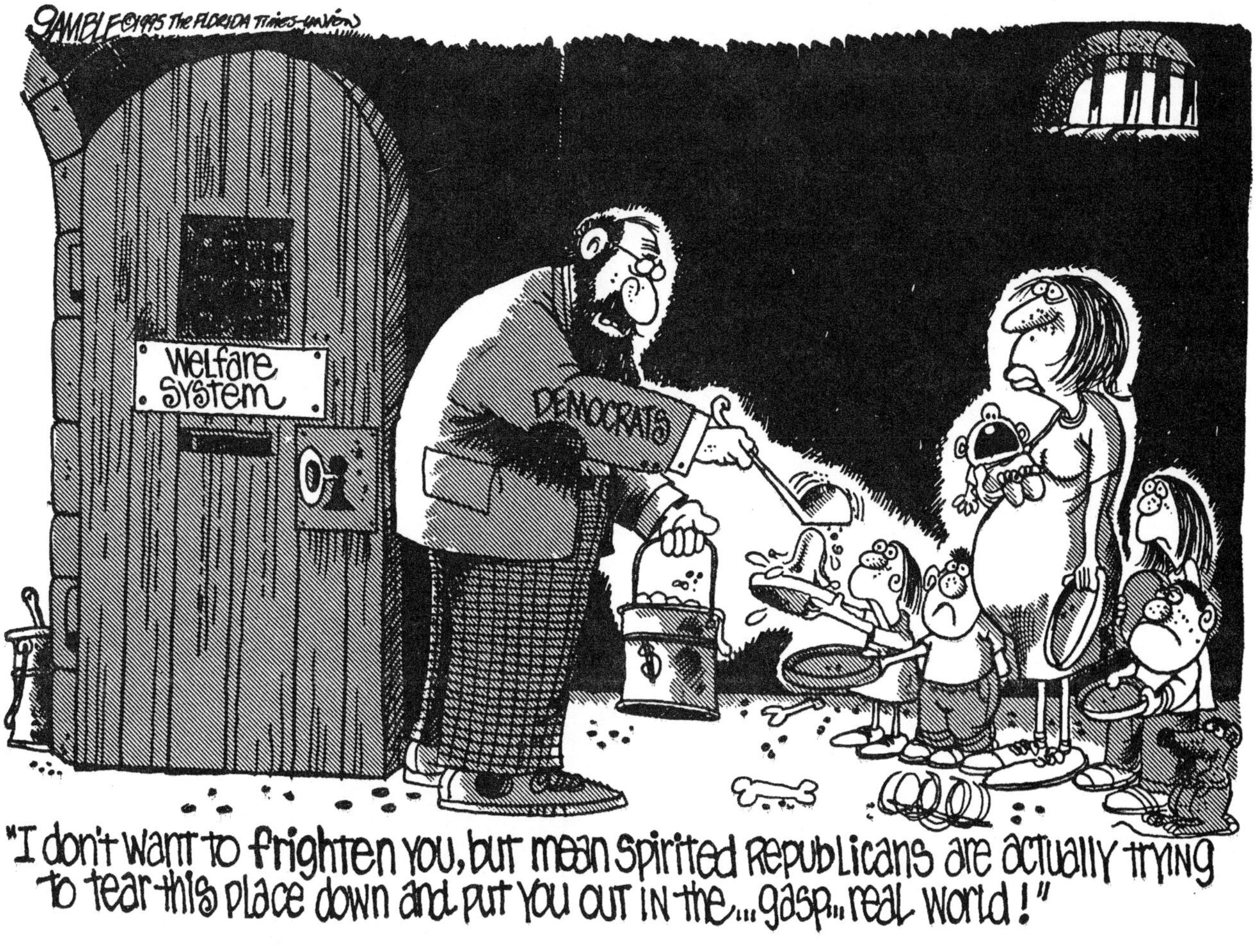
Welfare System
DEMOCRATS
"I don't want to frighten you, but mean spirited Republicans are actually trying to tear this place down and put you out in the... gasp... real world!"

ETTA HULME
Courtesy Ft. Worth Star-Telegram

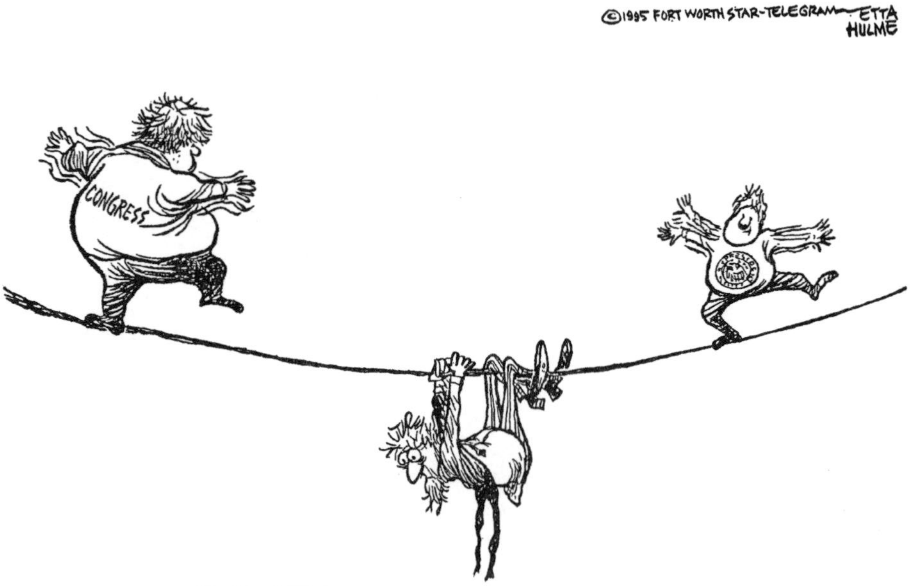
©1995 FORT WORTH STAR-TELEGRAM ETTA HULME
CONGRESS

KIRK ANDERSON
Courtesy Madison (Wis.) Capital Times

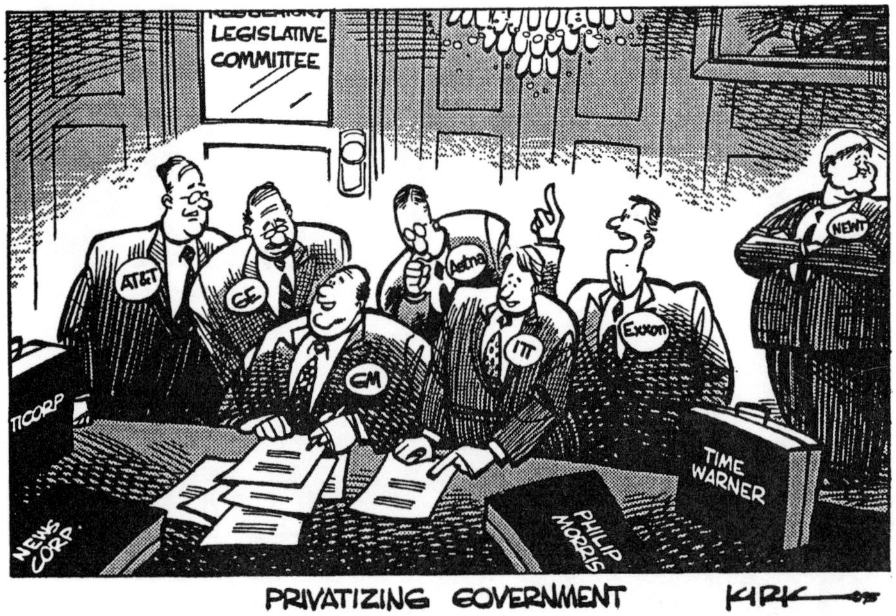
LEGISLATIVE COMMITTEE
AT&T
GE
GM
Aetna
ITT
Exxon
NEWT
TICORP
NEWS CORP.
PHILIP MORRIS
TIME WARNER
PRIVATIZING GOVERNMENT
KIRK

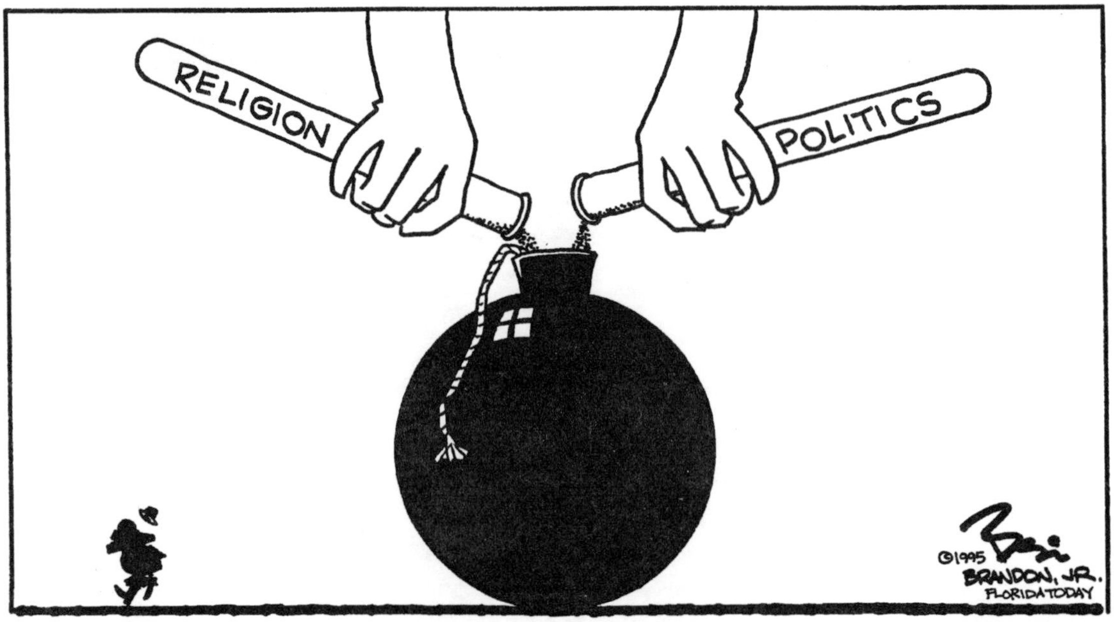
RELIGION
POLITICS
©1995 BRANDON, JR.
FLORIDA TODAY

BRUMSIC BRANDON
Courtesy Florida Today

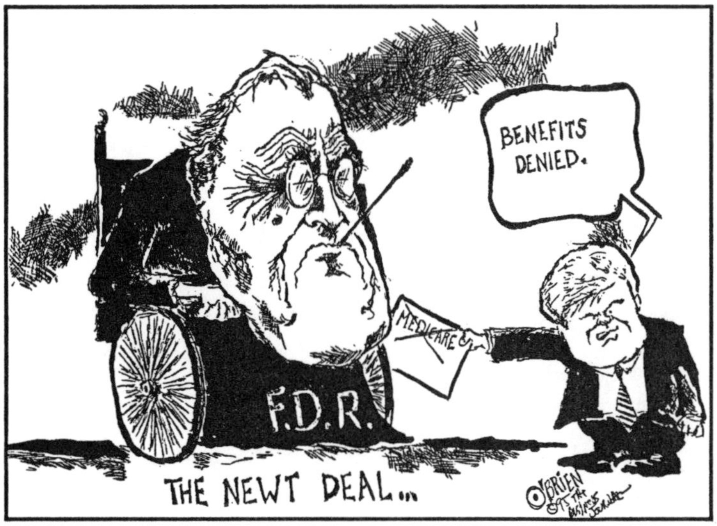
BENEFITS DENIED.
MEDICARE
F.D.R.
THE NEWT DEAL...

DAN O'BRIEN
Courtesy Youngstown Daily Business Journal

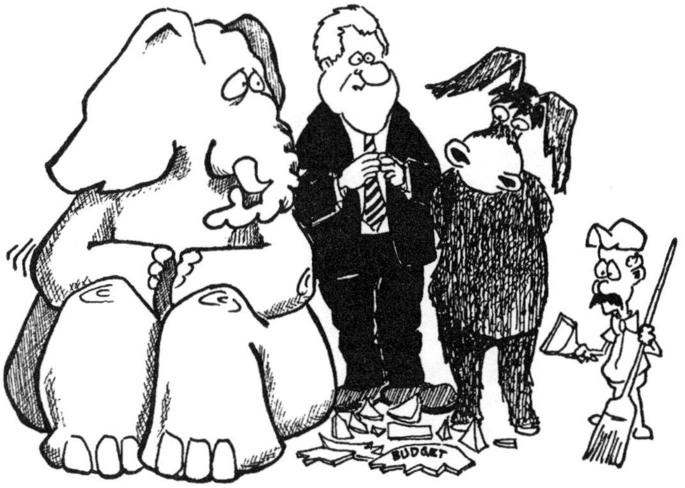
BUDGET

JERRY HUGHES
Courtesy Enterprise-Ledger (Ala.)

BOB DORNFRIED
Courtesy Greenwich News

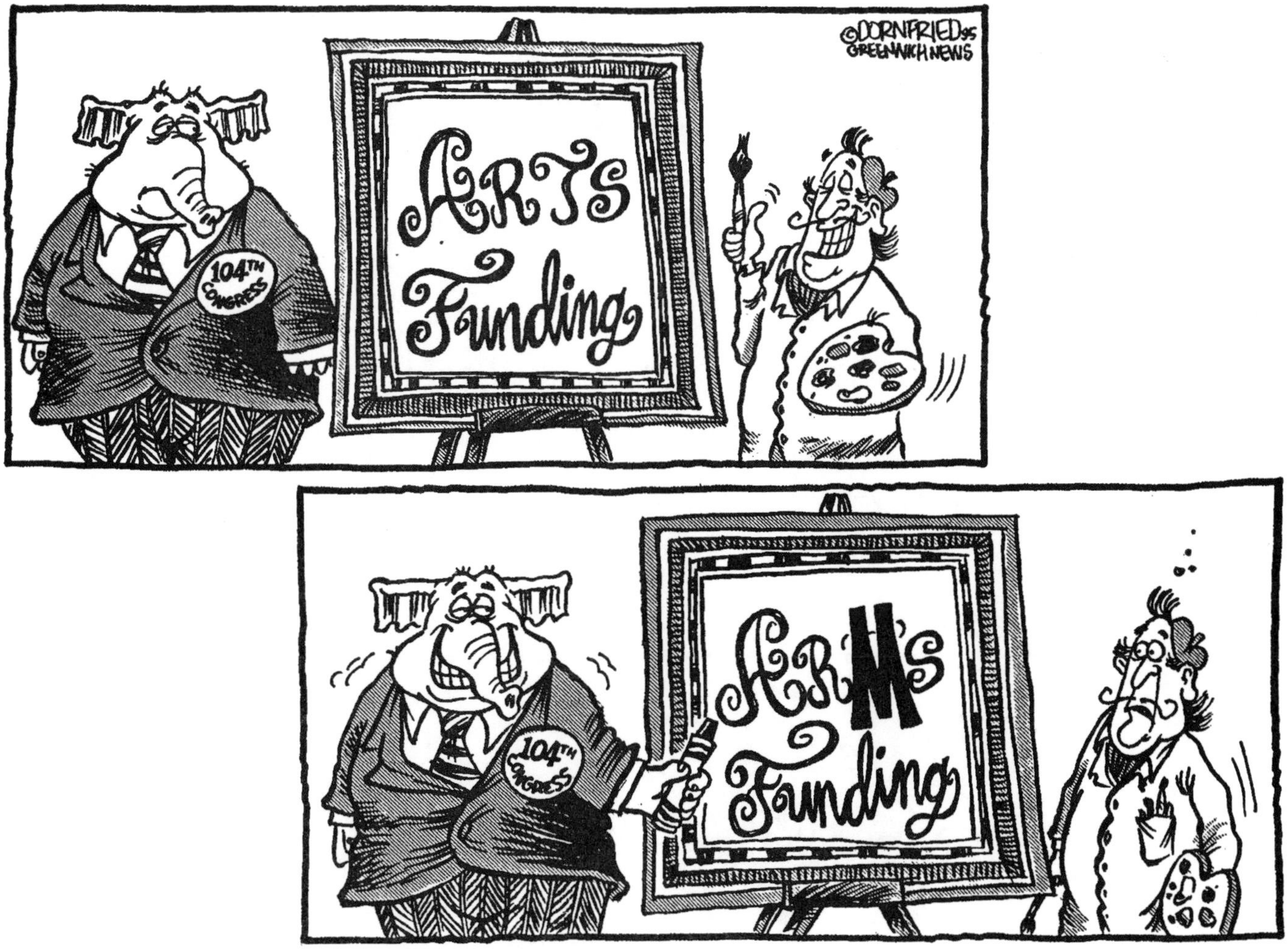
©DORNFRIED95
GREENWICH NEWS
ARTS
Funding
104TH CONGRESS
ARMS
Funding
104TH CONGRESS

MIKE PETERS
Courtesy Dayton Daily News

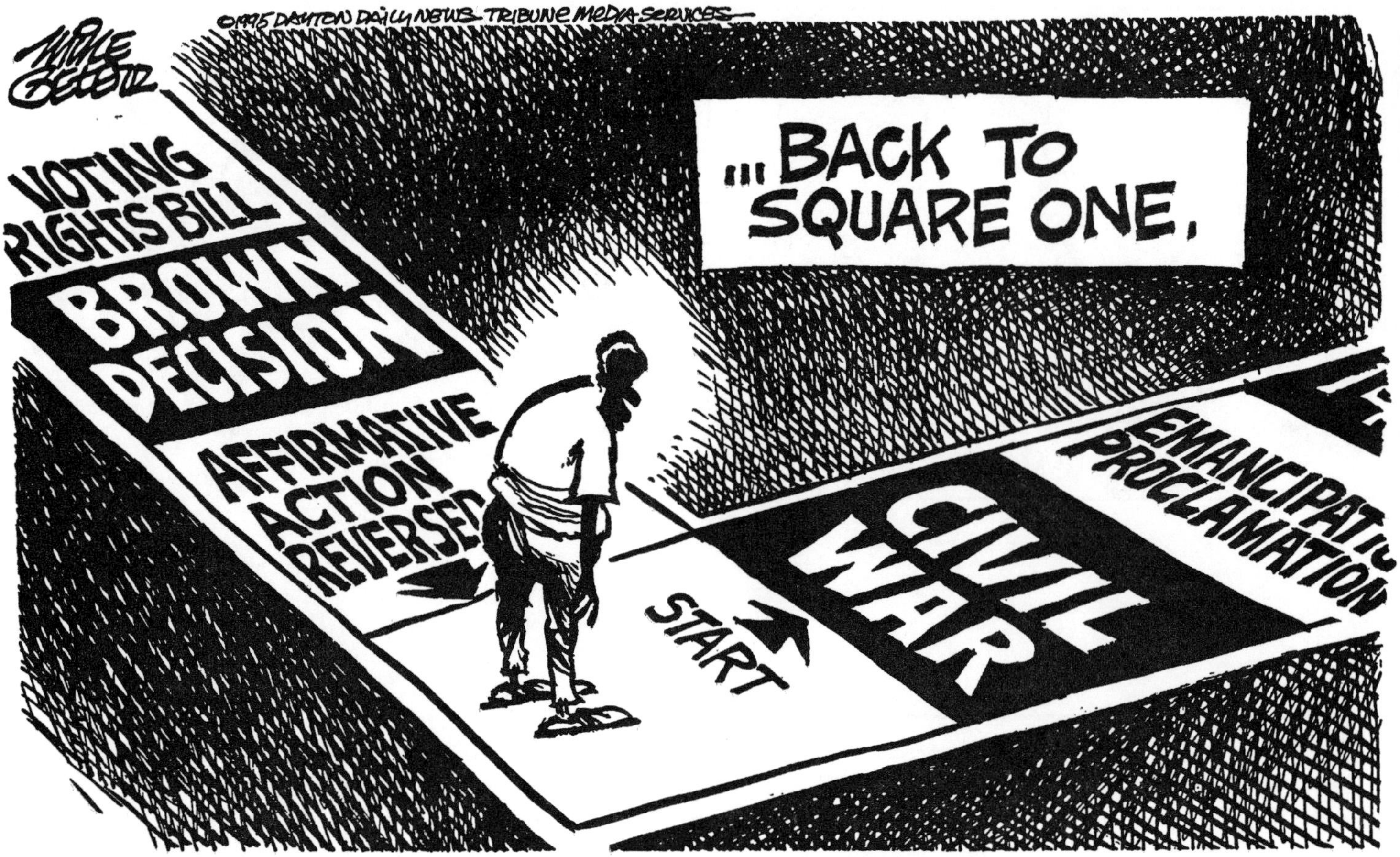
©1995 DAYTON DAILY NEWS-TRIBUNE MEDIA SERVICES
...BACK TO SQUARE ONE.
VOTING RIGHTS BILL
BROWN DECISION
AFFIRMATIVE ACTION REVERSED
START
CIVIL WAR
EMANCIPATIO
PROCLAMATION

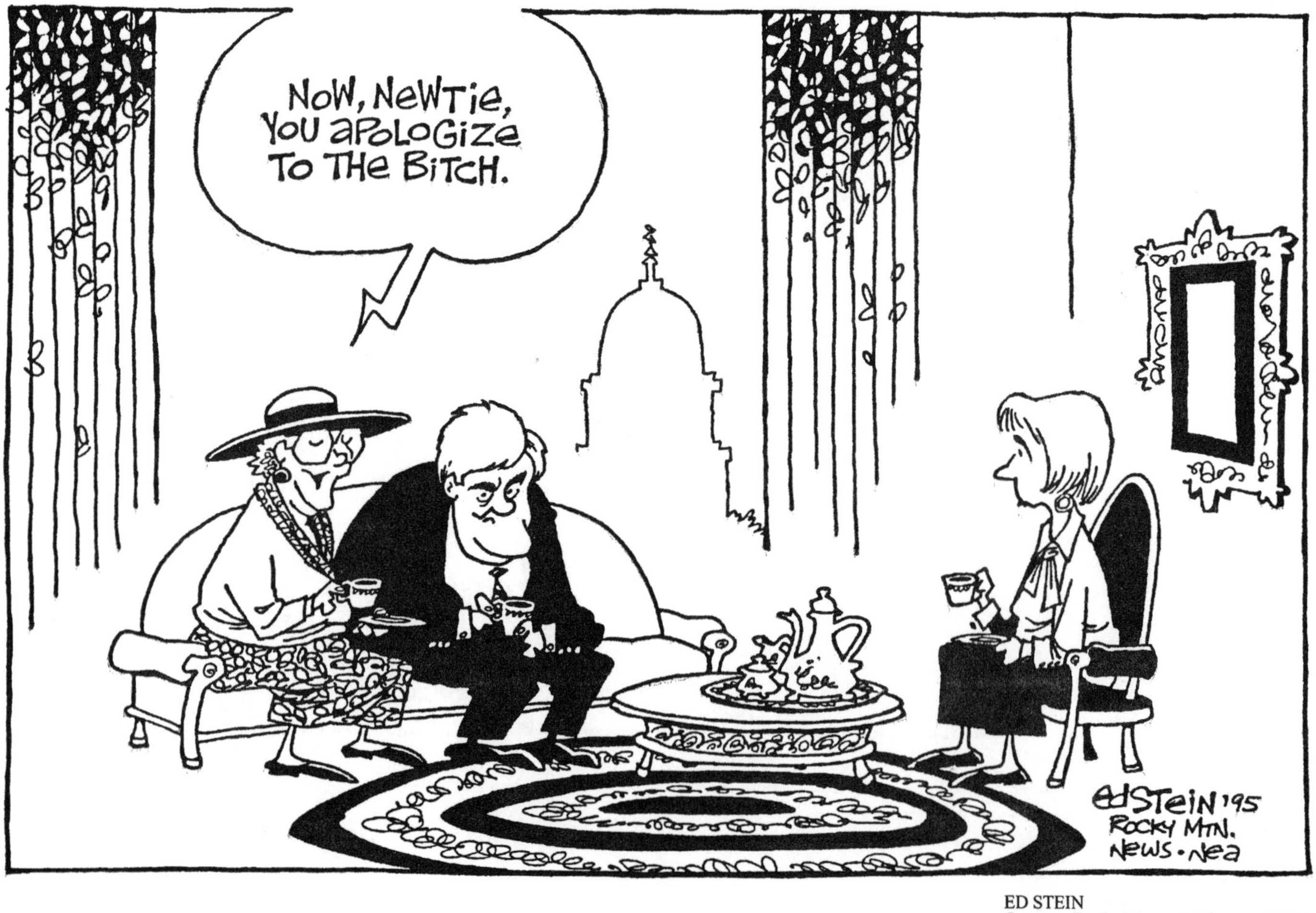
NOW, NEWTIE, YOU APOLOGIZE TO THE BITCH.
EDSTEIN '95 ROCKY MTN. NEWS • NEA

ED STEIN
Courtesy Rocky Mountain News and NEA

The Republicans

The federal budget deficit ranks as the most critical economic issue facing the U.S. Interest charges on the deficit cost taxpayers more than $250 billion a year, a figure that rises annually. There is widespread agreement that America has been living beyond its means for decades. Congress, for example, has "borrowed" $500 billion over the years from Social Security trust funds for various spending projects. As a result, there are few reserves, a lot of IOUs, and a fund that will be bankrupt by 2031 if drastic measures are not taken.

On this, politicians of both parties agree. The disagreement centers on how to fix the problem. Because of huge gains in the last congressional elections, Republicans finally decided to take on the task the Democrats had long neglected. President Clinton has accused the Republicans of proposing massive cuts in social programs to achieve their goal. In reality, many proposals are not cuts at all, but would simply slow the rate of increase, a policy Clinton advocated two years ago. The GOP plan would raise the monthly Medicare premium $42.80 over seven years while the Democrats would increase it $30.90, a difference of $11.90 over a seven-year span.

Clinton insists that the Republican proposal would be too harsh. The GOP must make sure its effort to balance the budget is fair.

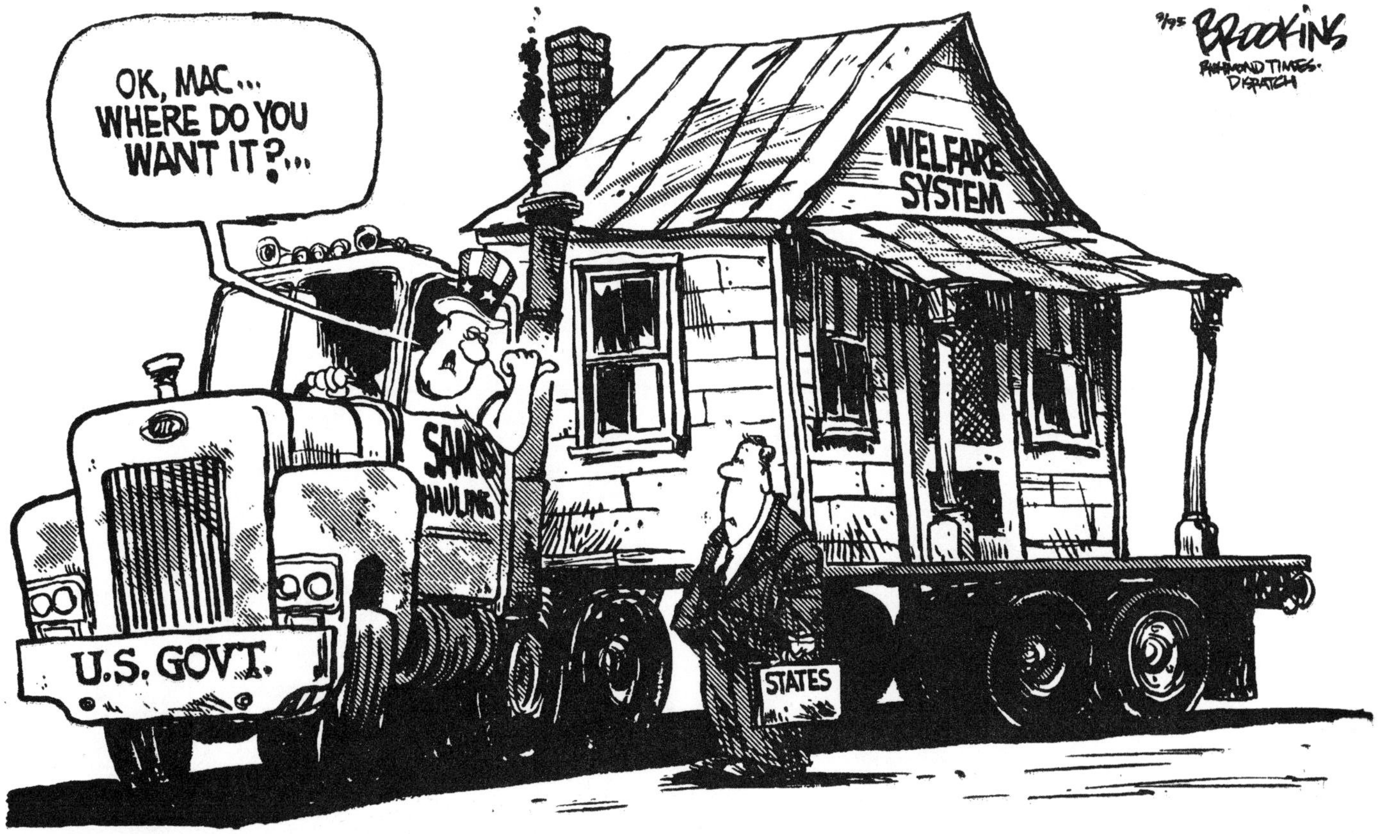
OK, MAC... WHERE DO YOU WANT IT?...
WELFARE SYSTEM
SAM'S HAULING
U.S. GOVT.
STATES
BROOKINS
RICHMOND TIMES-DISPATCH

GARY BROOKINS
Courtesy Richmond Times-Dispatch

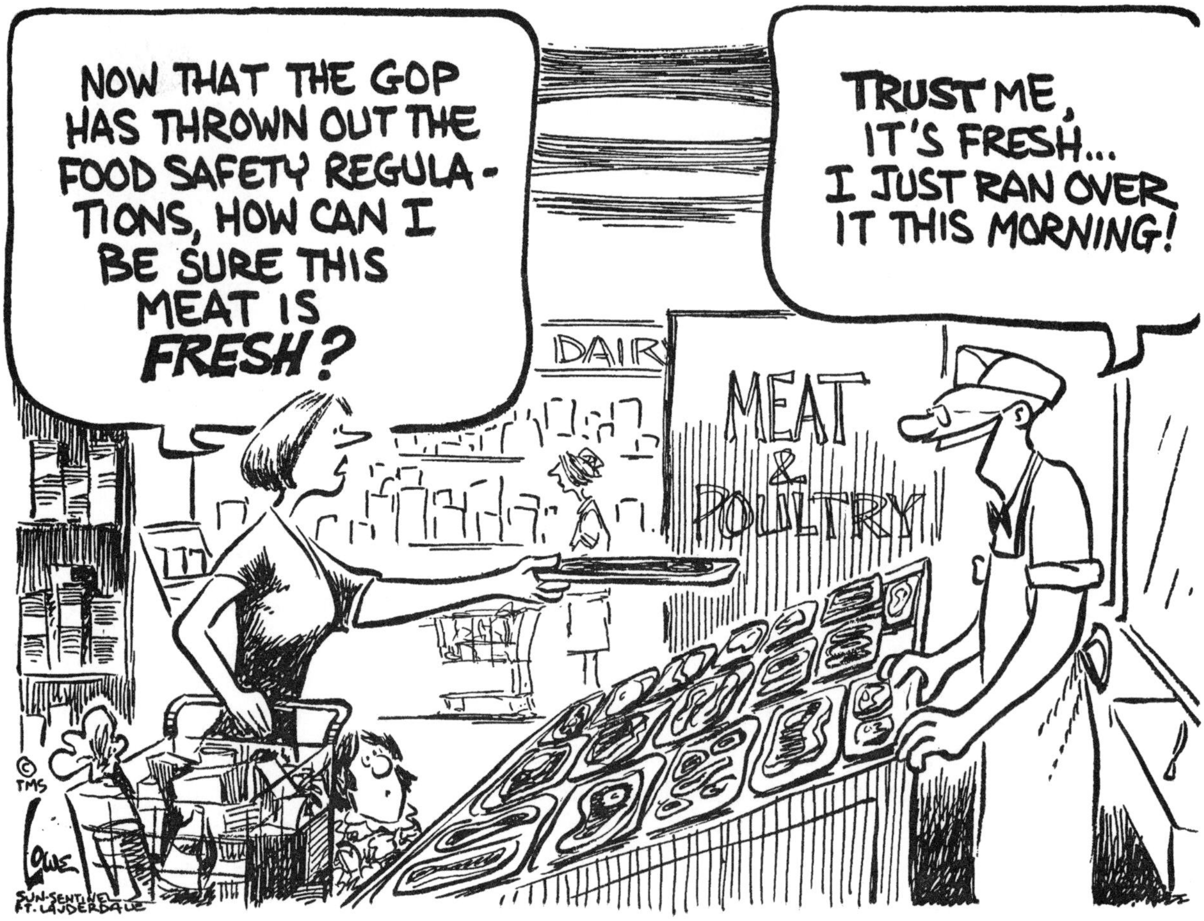
NOW THAT THE GOP HAS THROWN OUT THE FOOD SAFETY REGULATIONS, HOW CAN I BE SURE THIS MEAT IS *FRESH*?
TRUST ME, IT'S FRESH... I JUST RAN OVER IT THIS MORNING!
MEAT & POULTRY
©TMS
LOWE
SUN-SENTINEL FT. LAUDERDALE

CHAN LOWE
Courtesy The News/Sun-Sentinel (Fla.)

JEFF MACNELLY
Courtesy Chicago Tribune and
Tribune Media Services

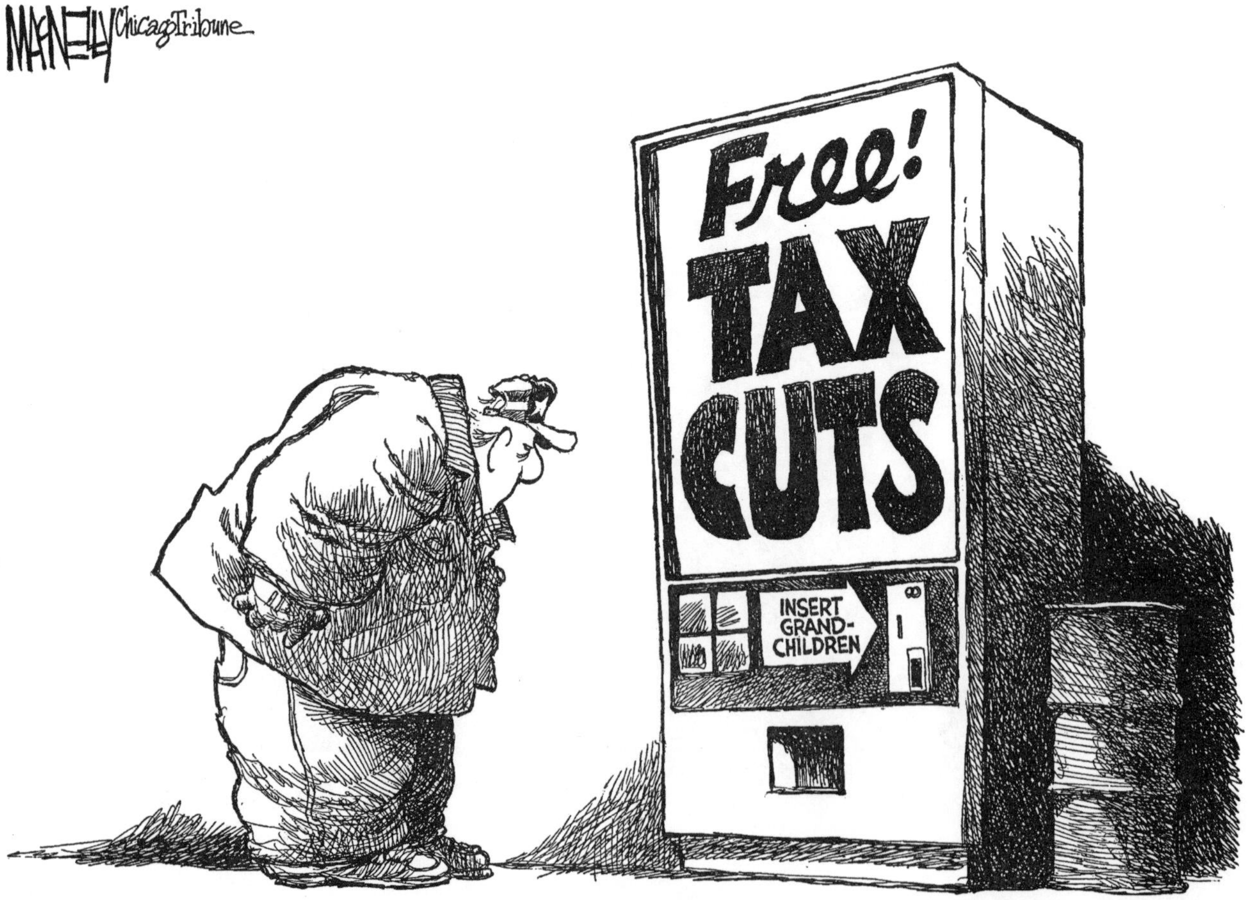
MACNELLY ChicagoTribune
Free!
TAX CUTS
INSERT GRANDCHILDREN

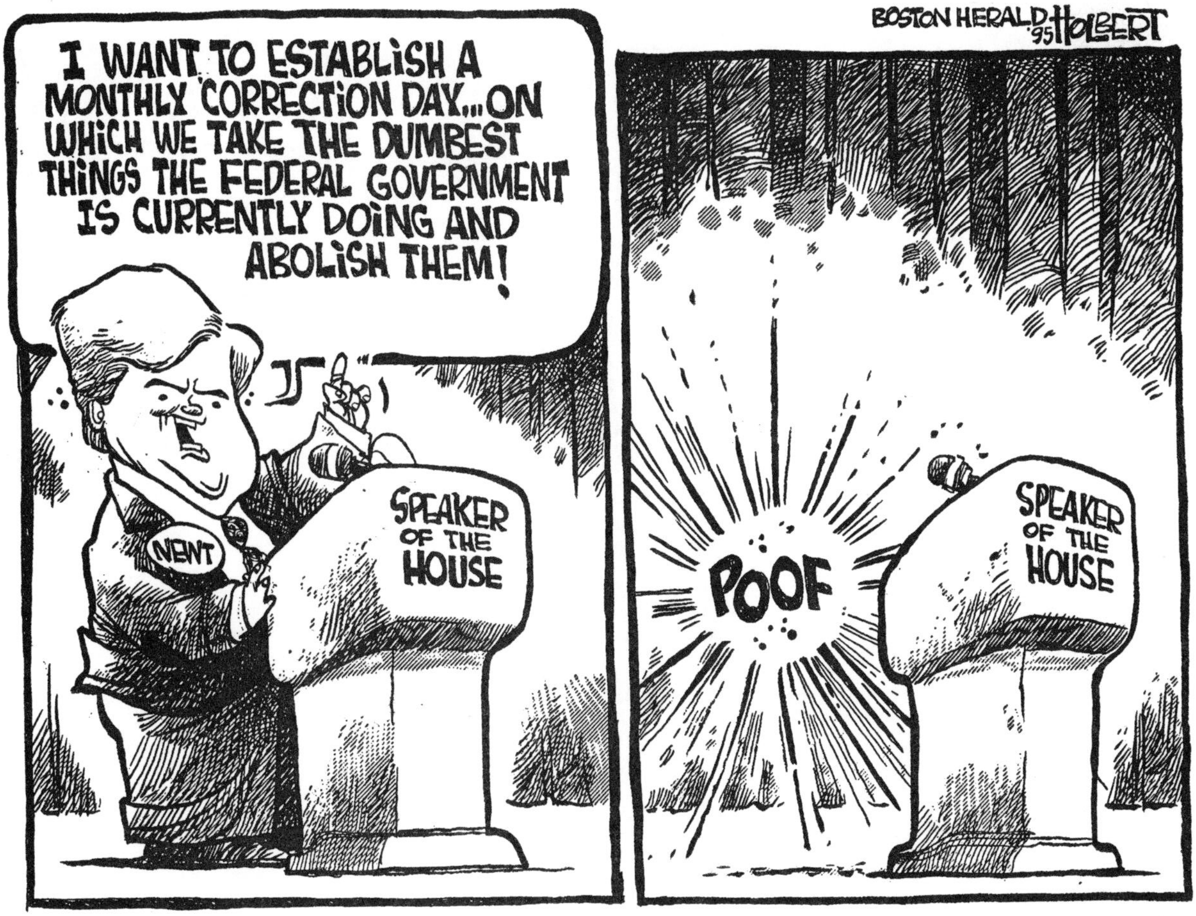
I WANT TO ESTABLISH A MONTHLY CORRECTION DAY...ON WHICH WE TAKE THE DUMBEST THINGS THE FEDERAL GOVERNMENT IS CURRENTLY DOING AND ABOLISH THEM!
NEWT
SPEAKER OF THE HOUSE
POOF
SPEAKER OF THE HOUSE
BOSTON HERALD '95 HOLBERT

JERRY HOLBERT
Courtesy Boston Herald

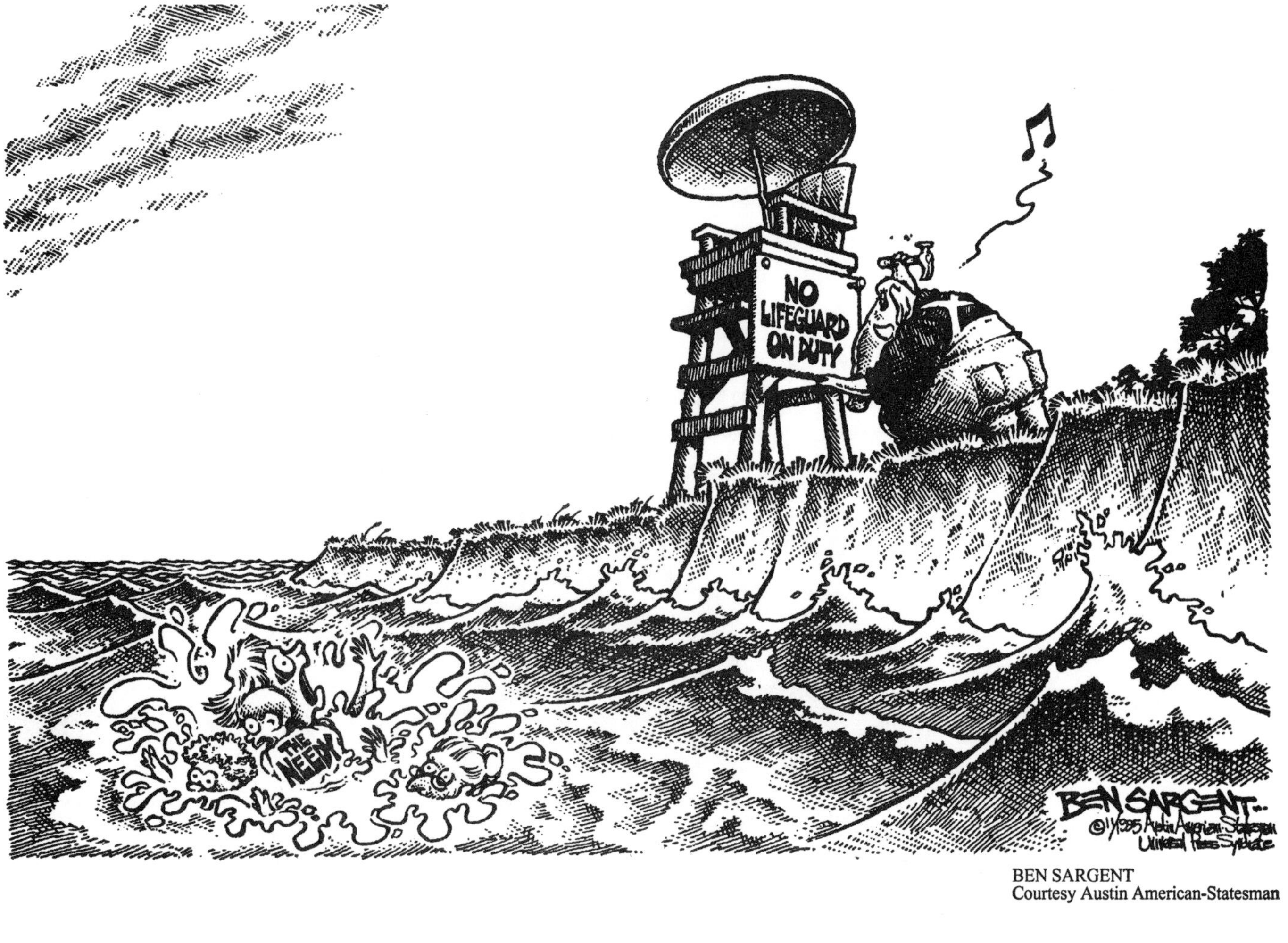
NO LIFEGUARD ON DUTY
THE NEEDY
BEN SARGENT

BEN SARGENT
Courtesy Austin American-Statesman

STEVE GREENBERG
Courtesy Seattle Post-Intelligencer

G.O.P. BUDGET
THE RICH
THE POOR

MIKE LUCKOVICH
Courtesy Atlanta Constitution

MIKE LUCKOVICH ATLANTA CONSTITUTION '95
I baptize you a Republican....
Christian Coalition

WHY THE SPHINX HAS NO NOSE...
I DON'T GIVE A FLYING HOOT HOW CLOSE YOU ARE— NO MORE PUBLIC FINANCING!
NEWT
Mike Keefe THE DENVER POST '95

MIKE KEEFE
Courtesy Denver Post

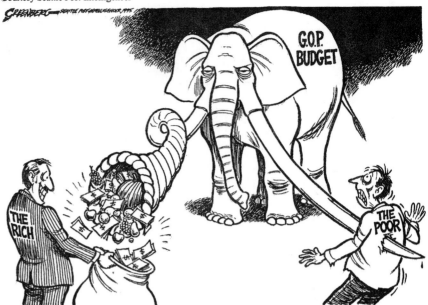

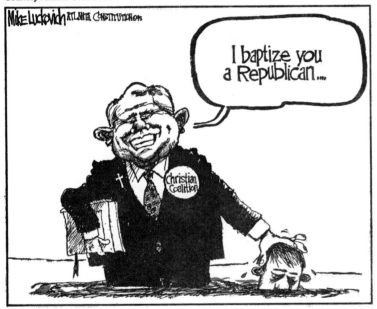

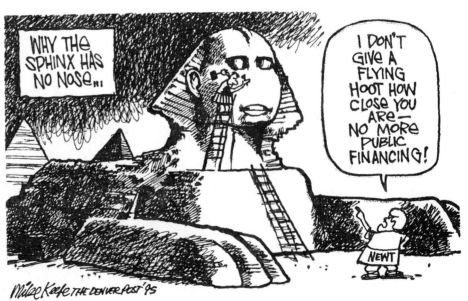

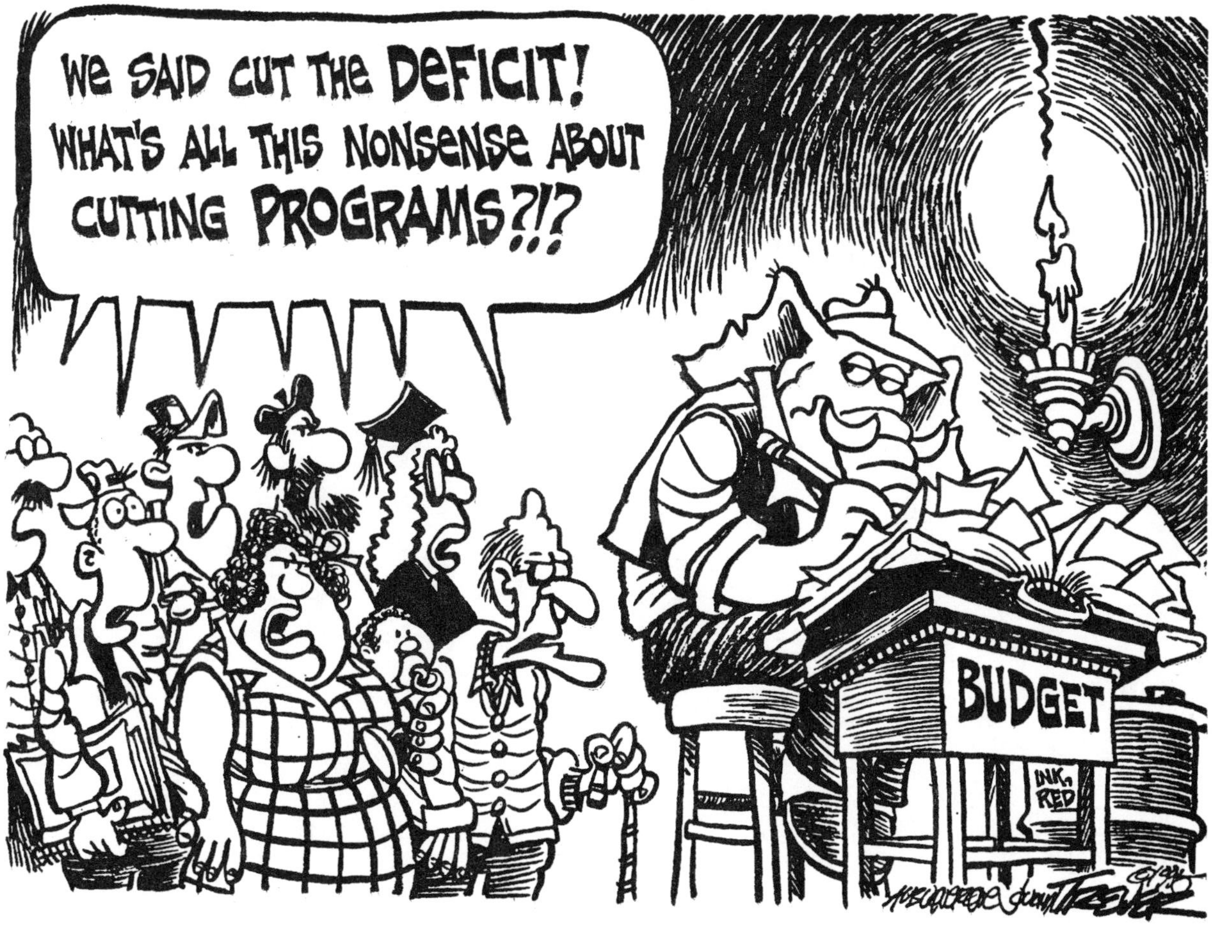
WE SAID CUT THE DEFICIT! WHAT'S ALL THIS NONSENSE ABOUT CUTTING PROGRAMS?!?
BUDGET
INK, RED

JOHN TREVER
Courtesy Albuquerque Journal

ROBERT ARIAIL
Courtesy The State (S.C

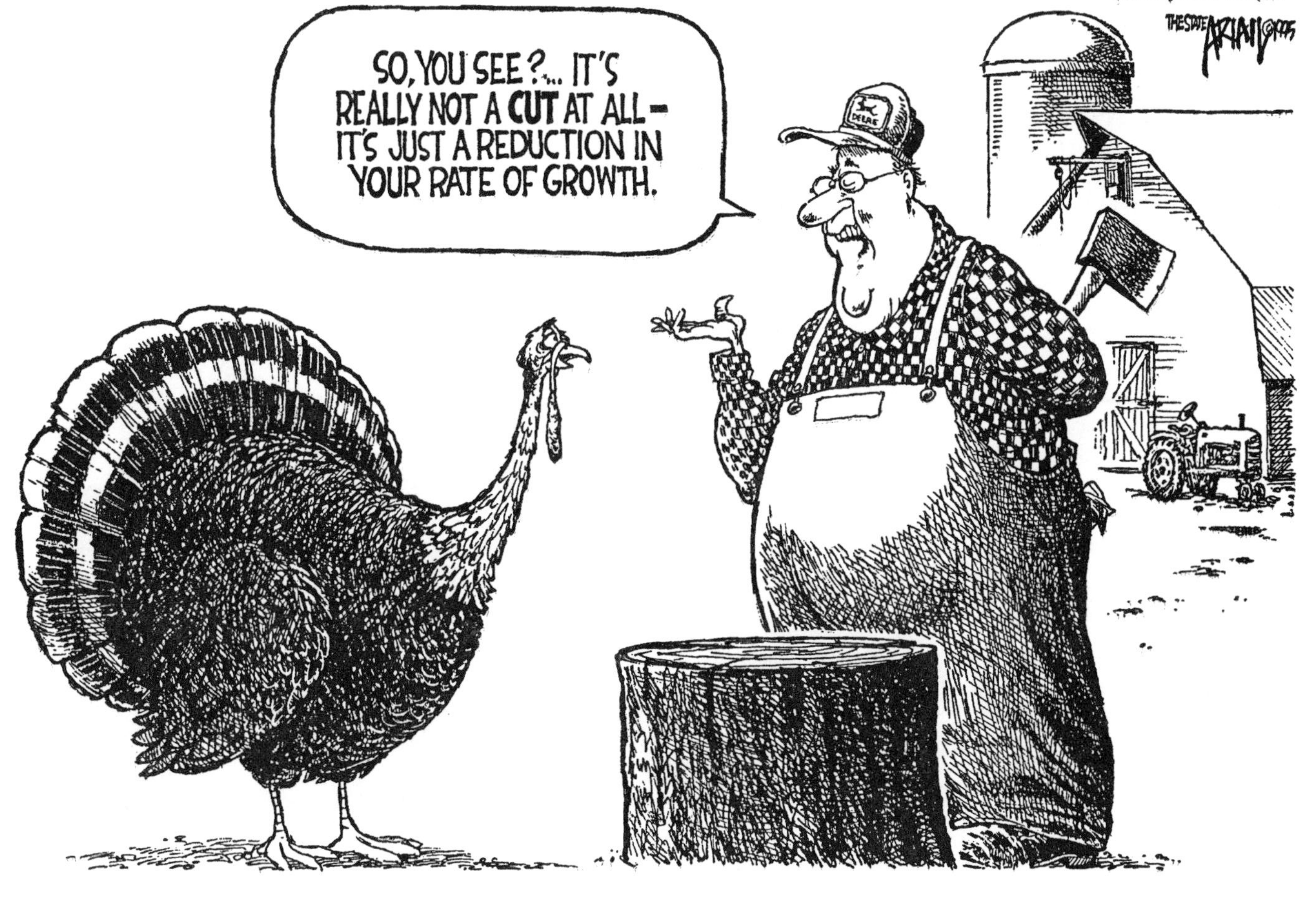
SO, YOU SEE?... IT'S REALLY NOT A CUT AT ALL - IT'S JUST A REDUCTION IN YOUR RATE OF GROWTH.

FRANK CAMMUSO
Courtesy Syracuse Herald-American

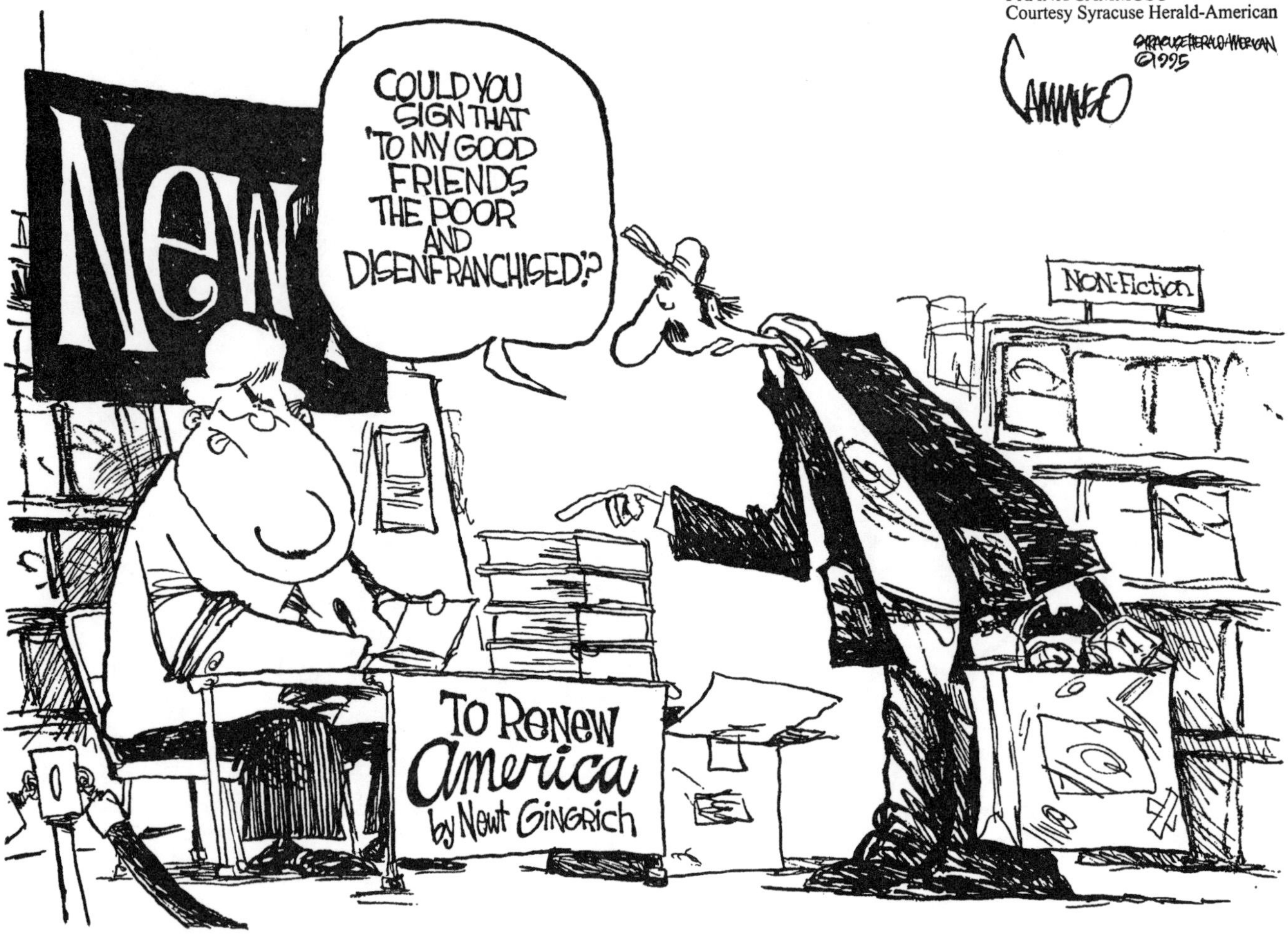
CAMMUSO
SYRACUSE HERALD-AMERICAN ©1995
New
COULD YOU SIGN THAT 'TO MY GOOD FRIENDS THE POOR AND DISENFRANCHISED'?
NON-Fiction
TV
To Renew America by Newt Gingrich

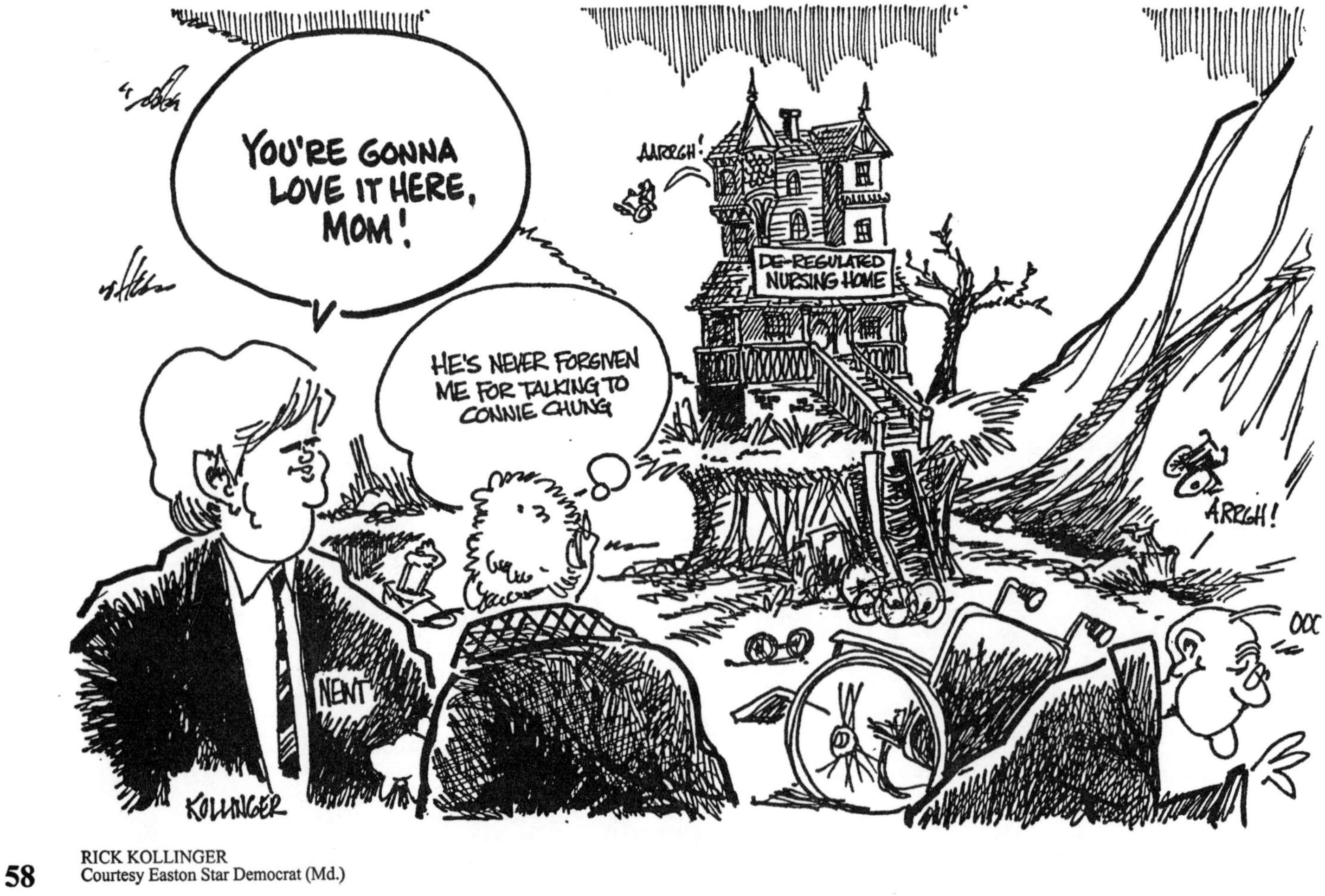
YOU'RE GONNA LOVE IT HERE, MOM!
HE'S NEVER FORGIVEN ME FOR TALKING TO CONNIE CHUNG
AARRGH!
DE-REGULATED NURSING HOME
ARRGH!
OOC
NEWT
KOLLINGER

RICK KOLLINGER
Courtesy Easton Star Democrat (Md.)

PAUL CONRAD
Courtesy Los Angeles Times

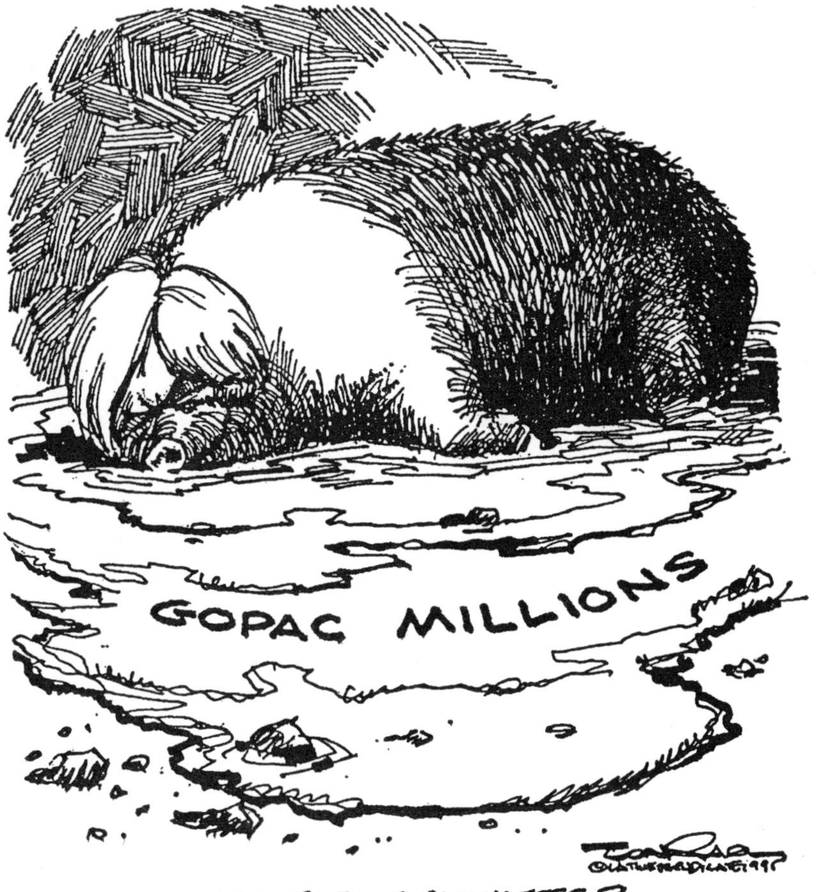

GOPAC MILLIONS

WHAT ETHICS COMMITTEE?

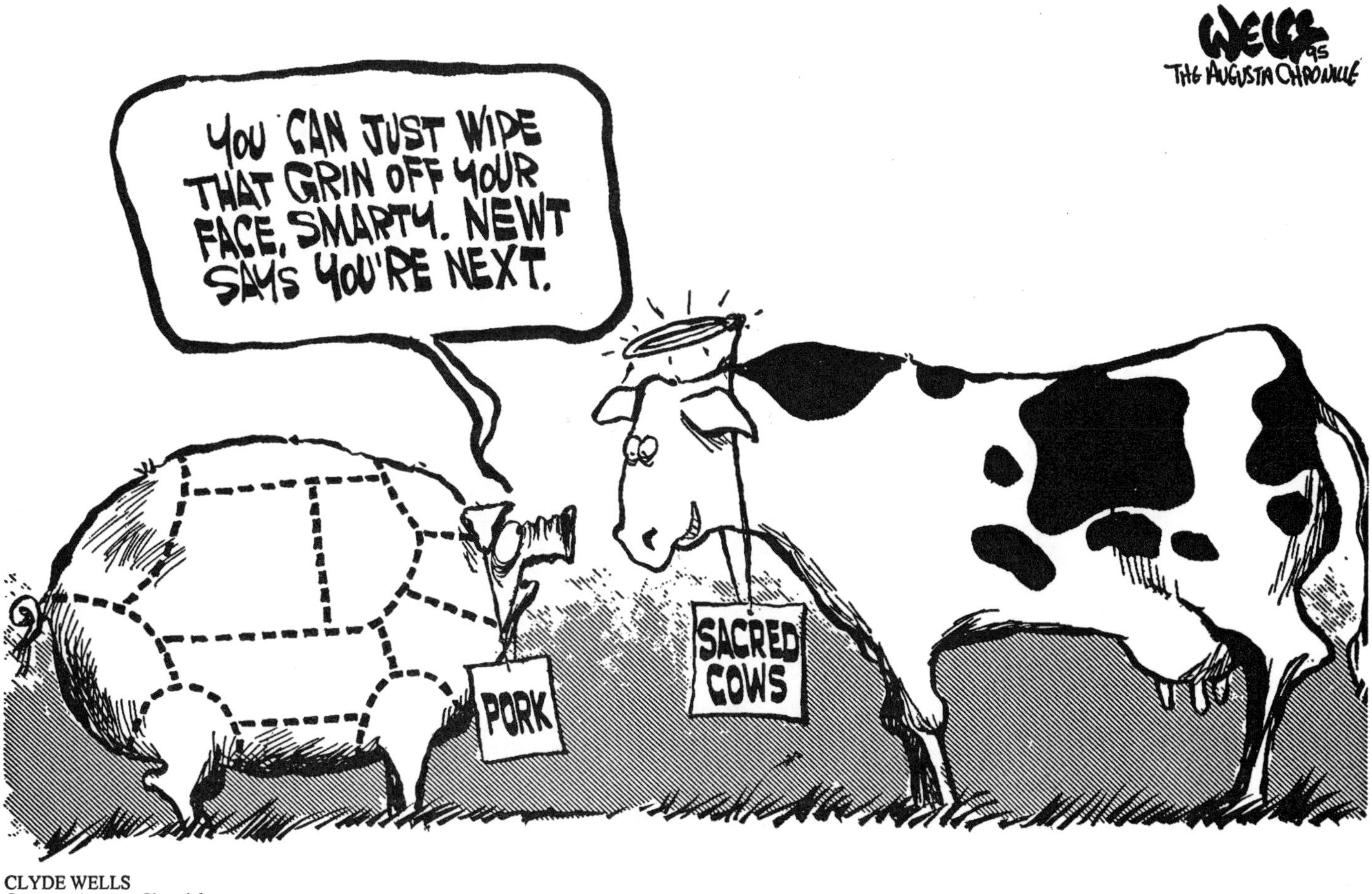

WELLS 95
THE AUGUSTA CHRONICLE
YOU CAN JUST WIPE THAT GRIN OFF YOUR FACE, SMARTY. NEWT SAYS YOU'RE NEXT.
PORK
SACRED COWS

CLYDE WELLS
Courtesy Augusta Chronicle

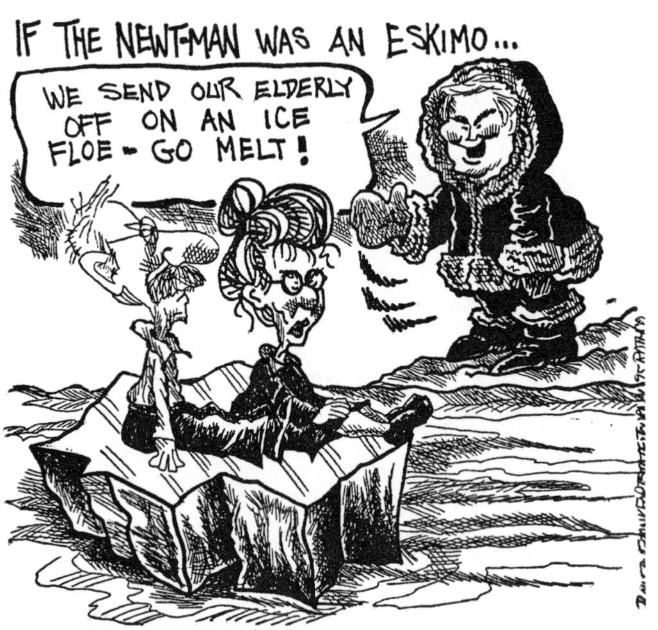
IF THE NEWT-MAN WAS AN ESKIMO...
WE SEND OUR ELDERLY OFF ON AN ICE FLOE – GO MELT!

LINDA BOILEAU
Courtesy Frankfort State Journal

DICK WALLMEYER
Courtesy Long Beach Press-Telegram

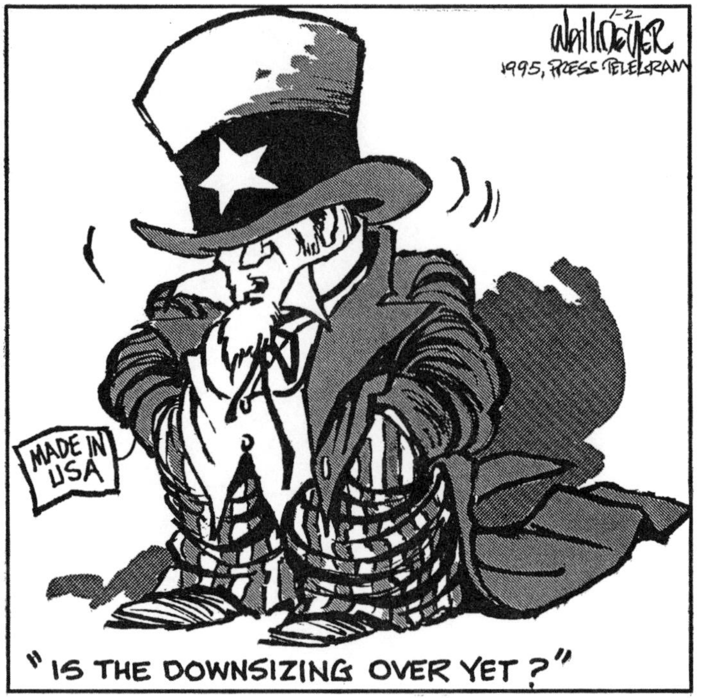
Wallmeyer 1-2
1995, PRESS TELEGRAM
MADE IN USA
"IS THE DOWNSIZING OVER YET?"

JIM BORGMAN
Courtesy Cincinnati Enquirer

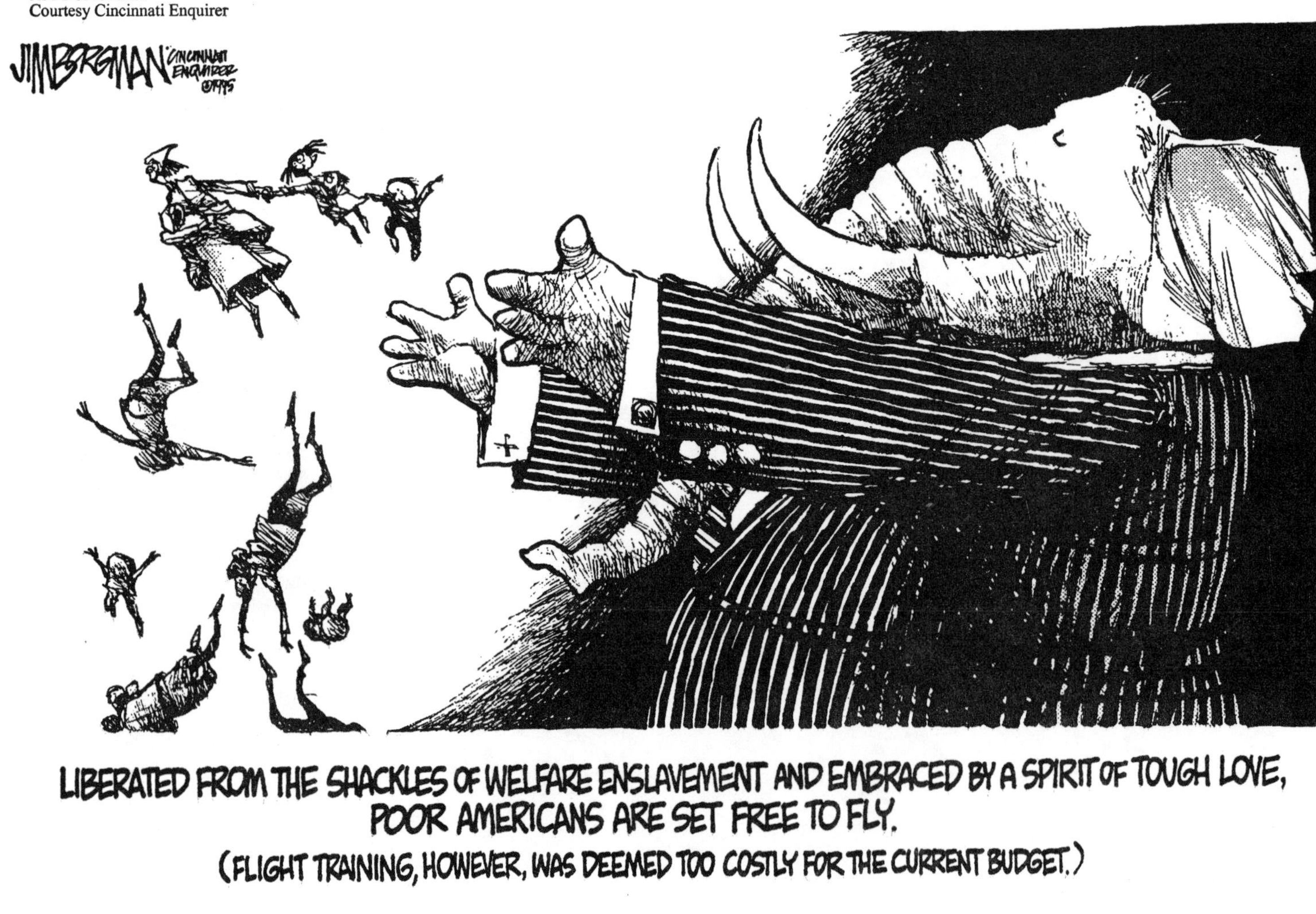
JIM BORGMAN CINCINNATI ENQUIRER ©1995
LIBERATED FROM THE SHACKLES OF WELFARE ENSLAVEMENT AND EMBRACED BY A SPIRIT OF TOUGH LOVE, POOR AMERICANS ARE SET FREE TO FLY.
(FLIGHT TRAINING, HOWEVER, WAS DEEMED TOO COSTLY FOR THE CURRENT BUDGET.)

DOUG MACGREGOR
Courtesy Ft. Meyers News-Press

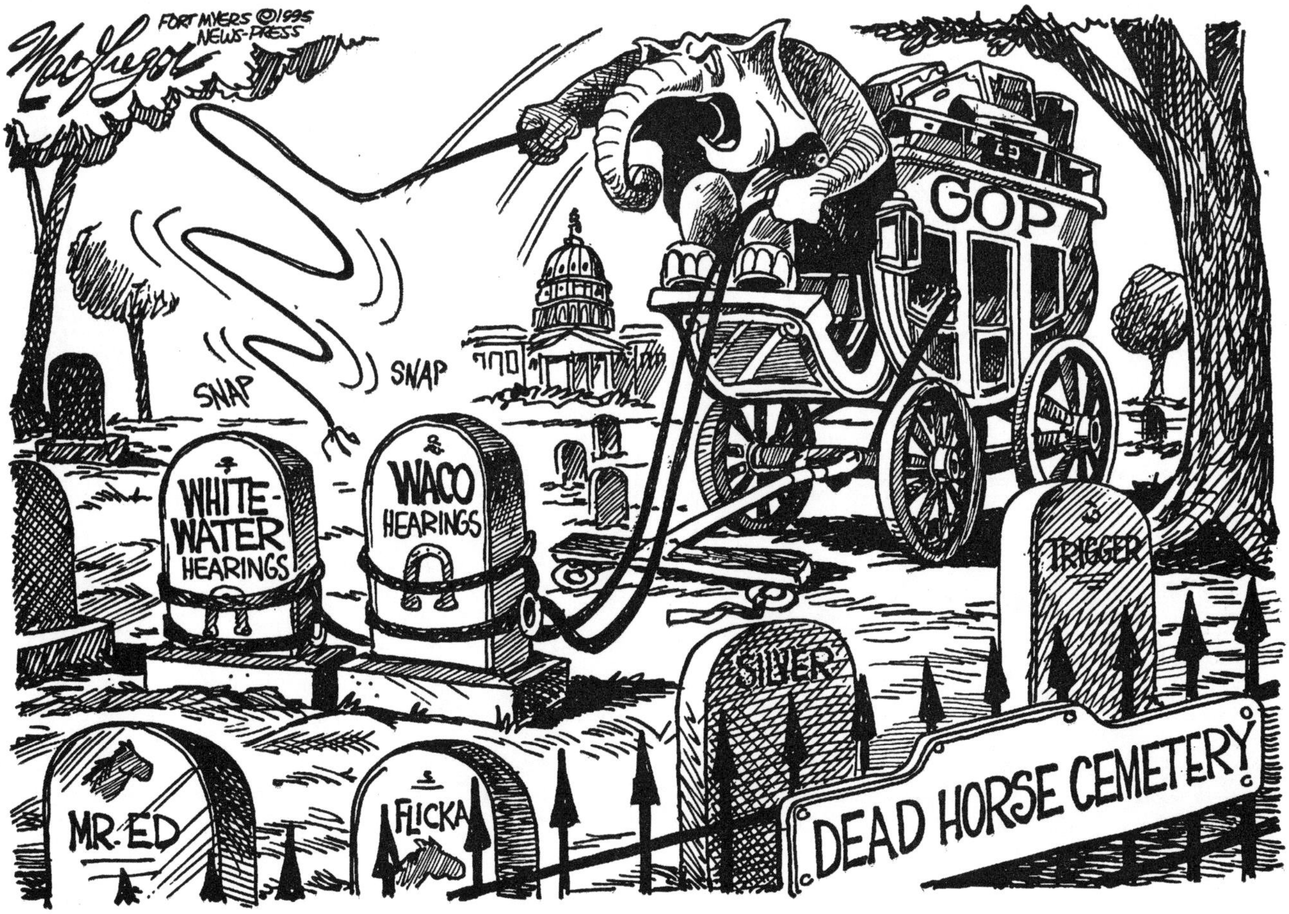
MacGregor
FORT MYERS ©1995 NEWS-PRESS
GOP
SNAP
SNAP
WHITE-WATER HEARINGS
WACO HEARINGS
TRIGGER
SILVER
DEAD HORSE CEMETERY
MR. ED
FLICKA

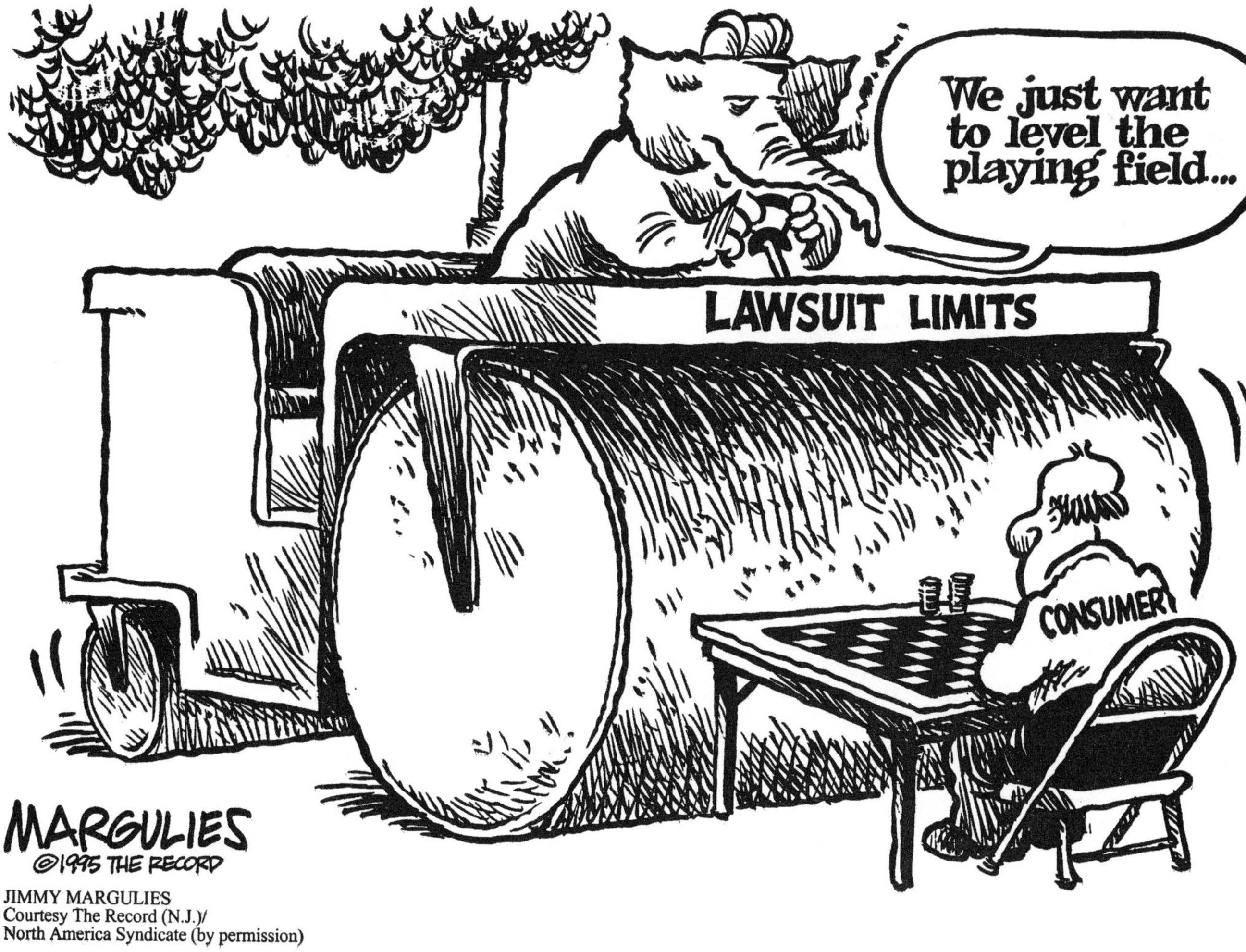
We just want to level the playing field...
LAWSUIT LIMITS
CONSUMER
MARGULIES
©1995 THE RECORD

JIMMY MARGULIES
Courtesy The Record (N.J.)/
North America Syndicate (by permission)

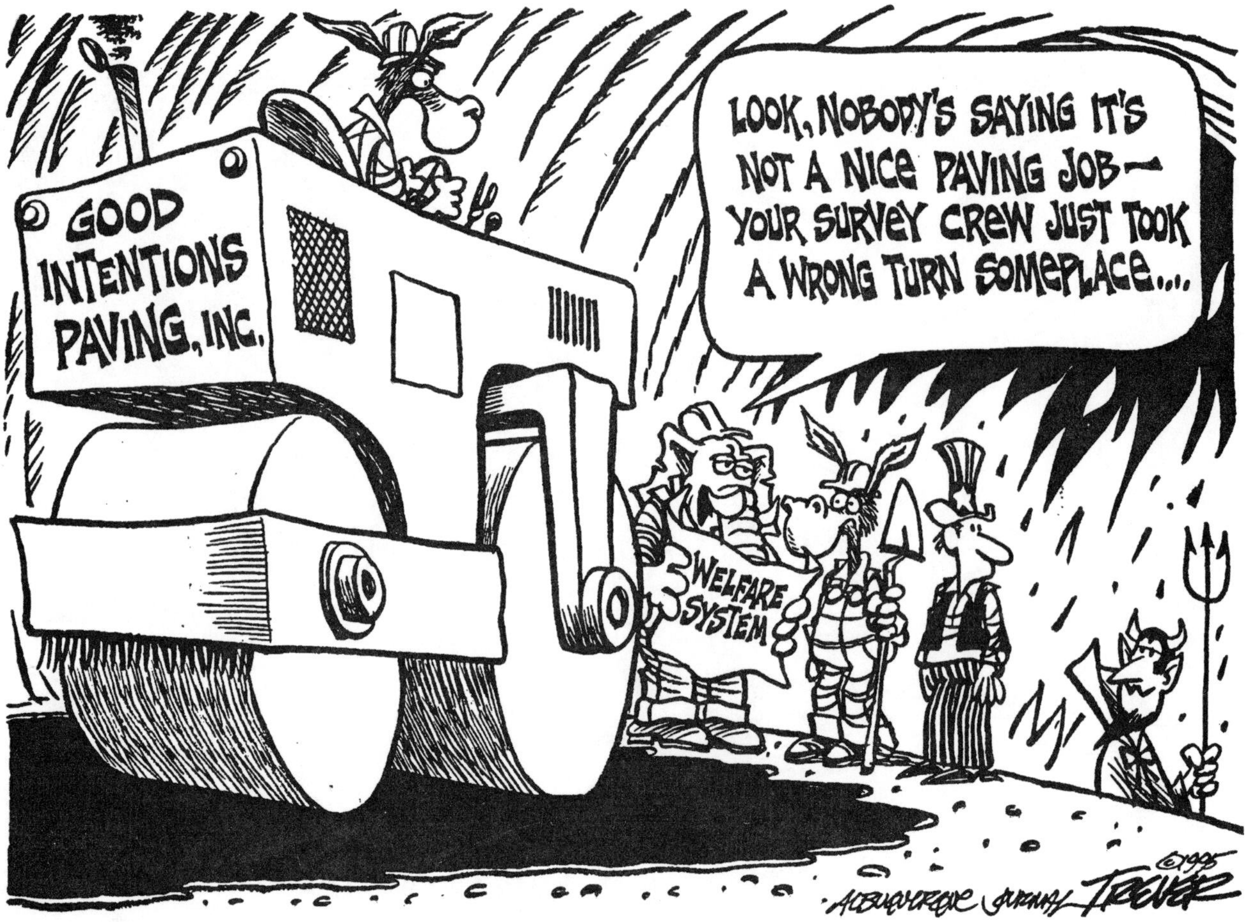
GOOD INTENTIONS PAVING, INC.
LOOK, NOBODY'S SAYING IT'S NOT A NICE PAVING JOB— YOUR SURVEY CREW JUST TOOK A WRONG TURN SOMEPLACE....
WELFARE SYSTEM
©1995 ALBUQUERQUE JOURNAL TREVER

JOHN TREVER
Courtesy Albuquerque Journal

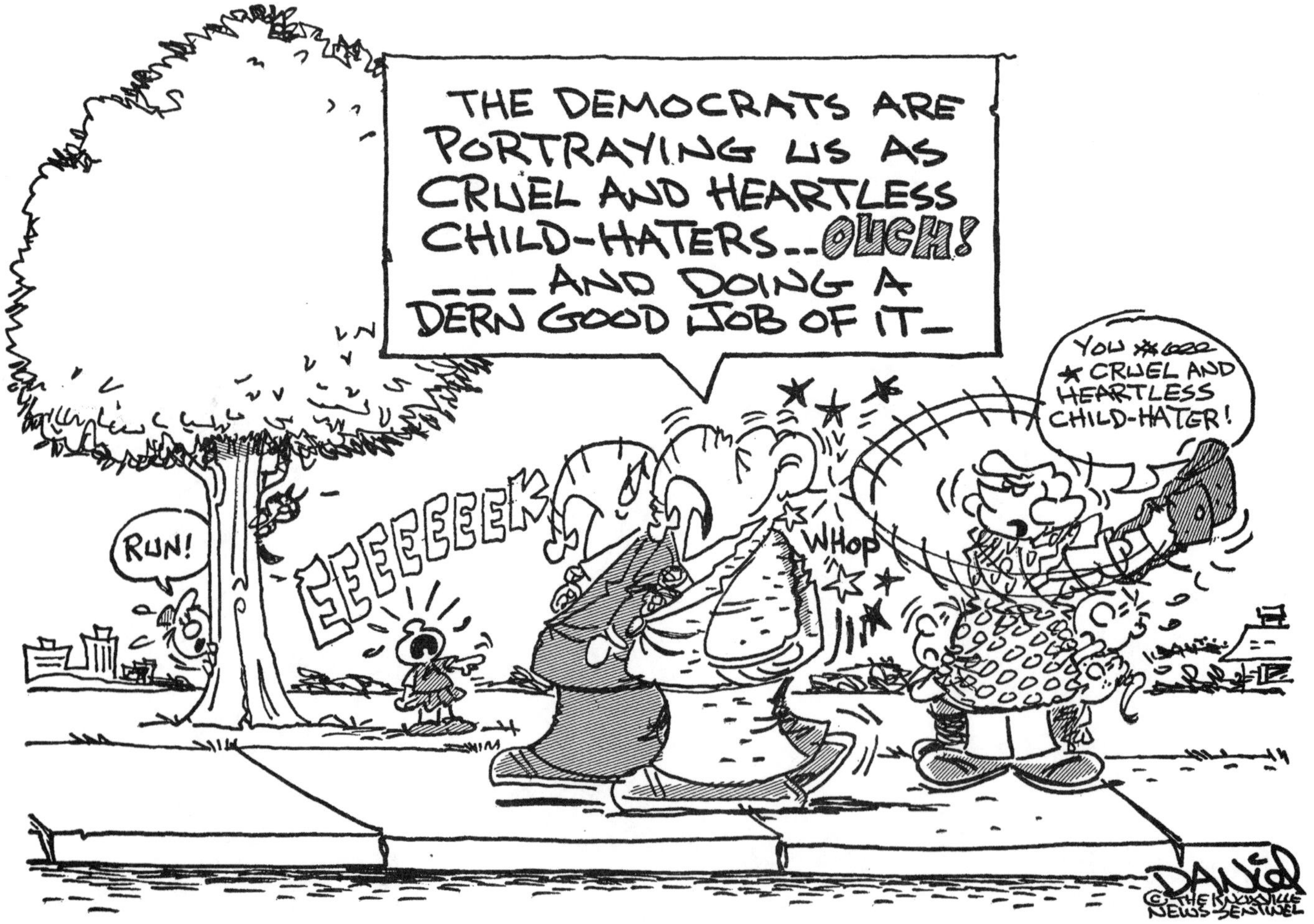
THE DEMOCRATS ARE PORTRAYING US AS CRUEL AND HEARTLESS CHILD-HATERS...OUCH! ...AND DOING A DERN GOOD JOB OF IT_
YOU CRUEL AND HEARTLESS CHILD-HATER!
RUN!
WHop
DANIEL © THE KNOXVILLE NEWS-SENTINEL

CHARLES DANIEL
Courtesy Knoxville News-Sentinel

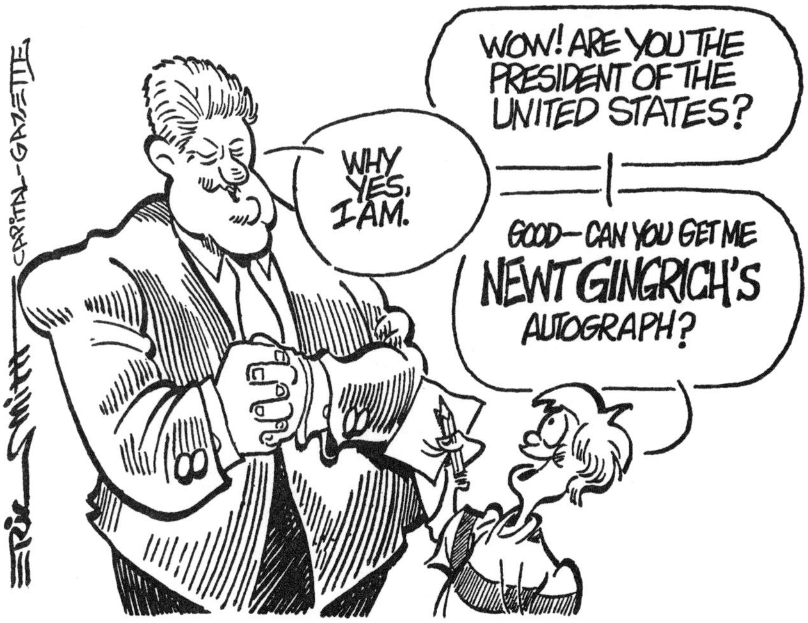
WOW! ARE YOU THE PRESIDENT OF THE UNITED STATES?
WHY YES, I AM.
GOOD—CAN YOU GET ME NEWT GINGRICH'S AUTOGRAPH?
CAPITAL-GAZETTE

ERIC SMITH
Courtesy Capital Gazette Newspapers

TOM ENGELHARDT
Courtesy St. Louis Post-Dispatch

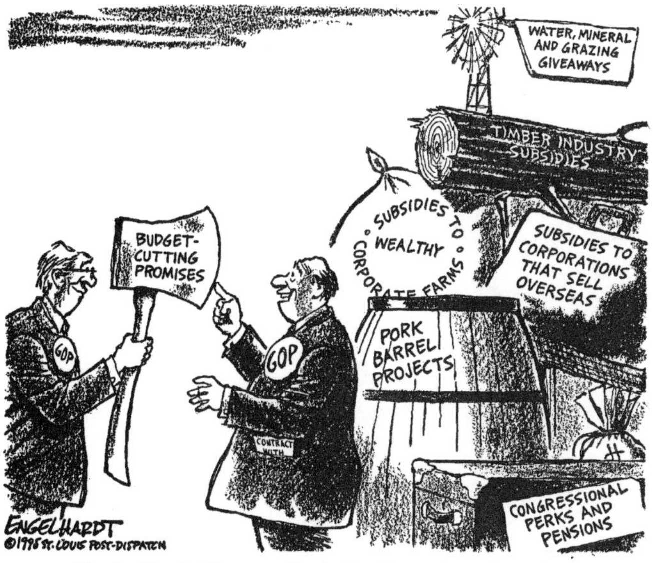
WATER, MINERAL AND GRAZING GIVEAWAYS
TIMBER INDUSTRY SUBSIDIES
SUBSIDIES TO WEALTHY CORPORATE FARMS
SUBSIDIES TO CORPORATIONS THAT SELL OVERSEAS
BUDGET-CUTTING PROMISES
GOP
GOP
PORK BARREL PROJECTS
CONGRESSIONAL PERKS AND PENSIONS
ENGELHARDT
©1995 ST. LOUIS POST-DISPATCH

'Oooh, That's Sharp — Let's Try It On Some Poor Kids, Old Folks And Elitist Cultural Snobs First'

MARK STREETER
Courtesy Savannah Morning News

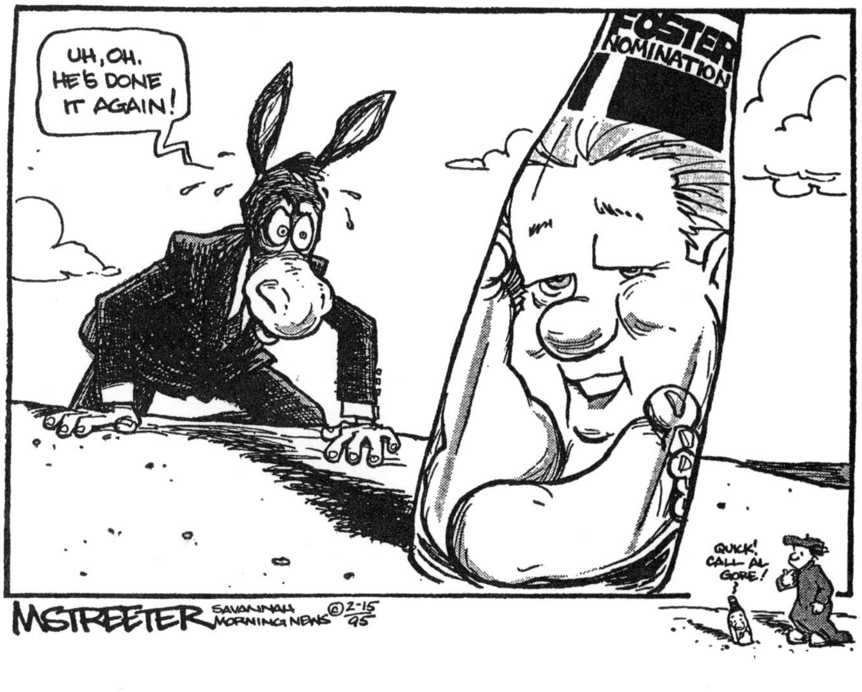
UH, OH. HE'S DONE IT AGAIN!
FOSTER NOMINATION
QUICK! CALL AL GORE!
MSTREETER SAVANNAH MORNING NEWS ©2-15 95

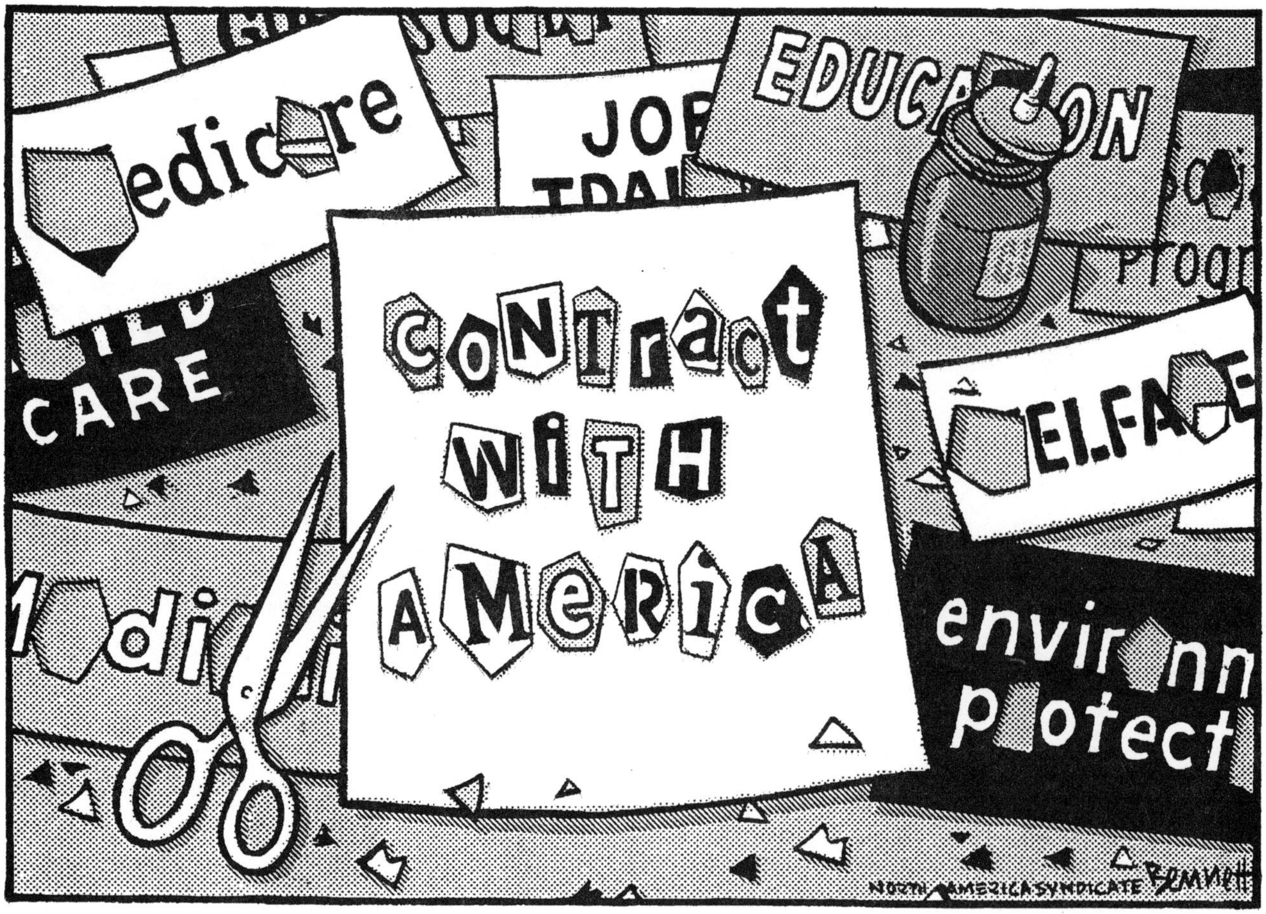
CONTRACT WITH AMERICA
CARE
NORTH AMERICA SYNDICATE BENNETT

CLAY BENNETT
Courtesy North America Syndicate

LAZARO FRESQUET
Courtesy El Nuevo Herald (Miami)

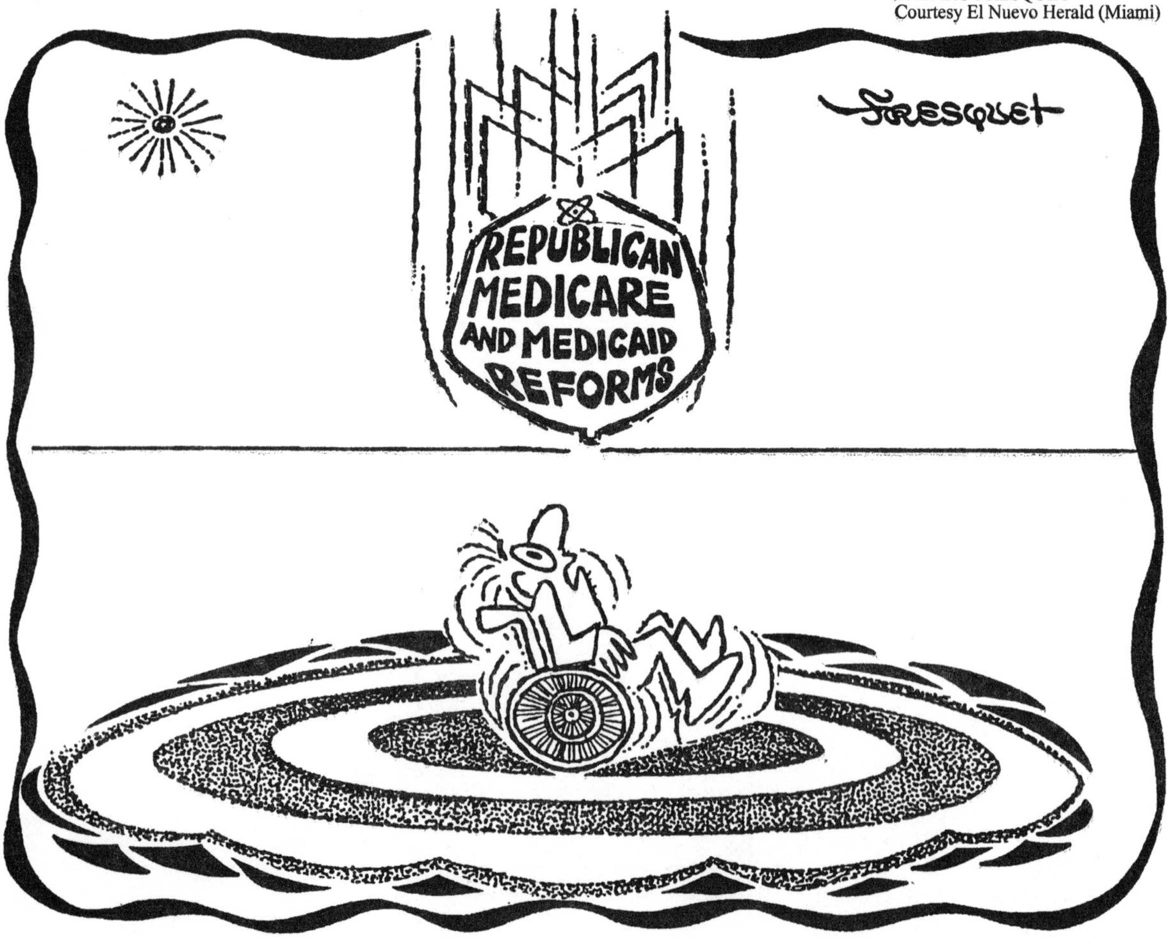
FRESQUET
REPUBLICAN MEDICARE AND MEDICAID REFORMS

SCOTT WILLIS
Courtesy San Jose Mercury

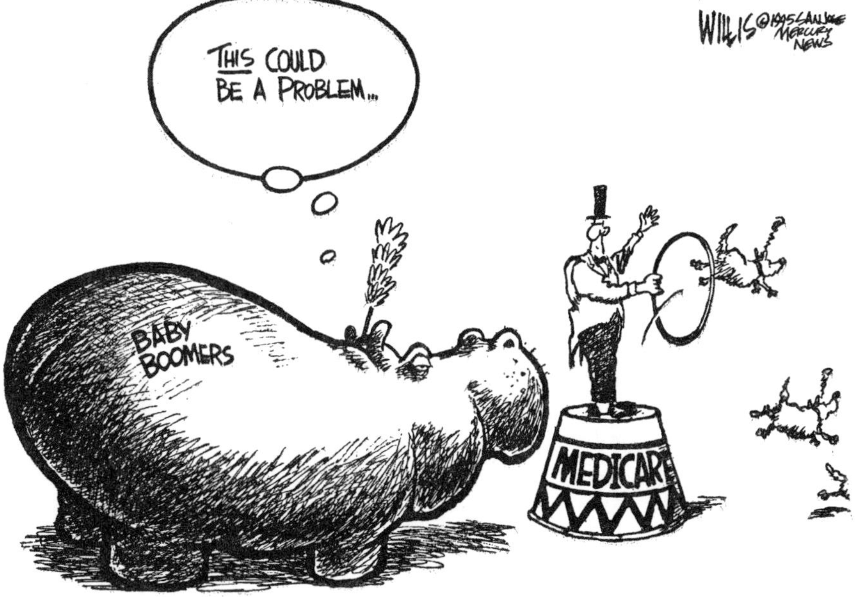
THIS COULD BE A PROBLEM...
BABY BOOMERS
MEDICARE

SVEN VAN ASSCHE
Courtesy Darien Times

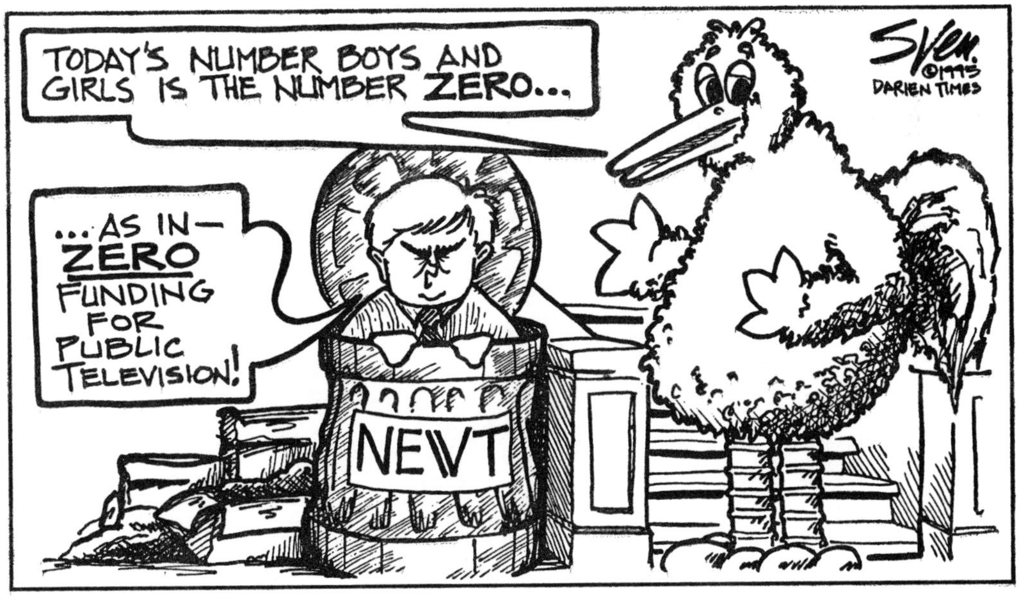
TODAY'S NUMBER BOYS AND GIRLS IS THE NUMBER ZERO...
...AS IN— ZERO FUNDING FOR PUBLIC TELEVISION!
NEWT

JOE MAJESKI
Courtesy The Times-Leader (Pa.)

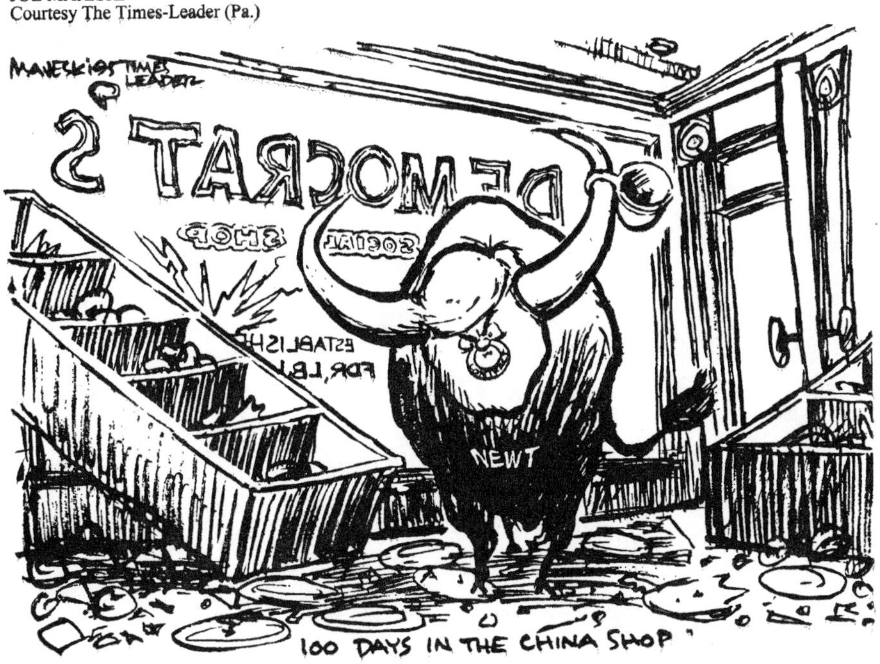
NEWT
100 DAYS IN THE CHINA SHOP

FRED CURATOLO
Courtesy Edmonton Sun

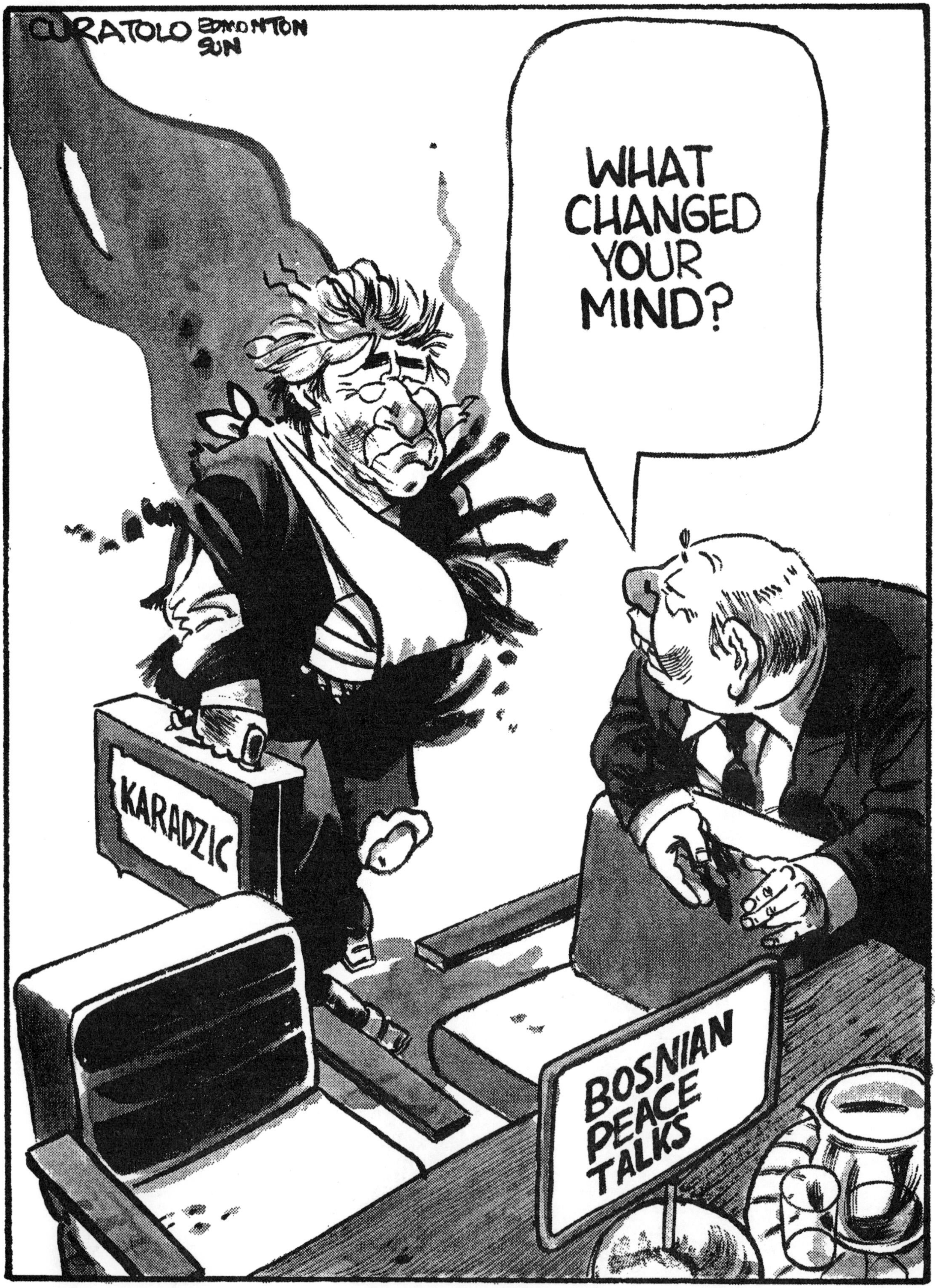

CURATOLO EDMONTON SUN
WHAT CHANGED YOUR MIND?
KARADZIC
BOSNIAN PEACE TALKS

Bosnia

As the bloody war in Bosnia dragged on, the Clinton administration spent much of the year struggling to develop a clear policy. Complicating matters was the capture of more than three hundred United Nations peace-keepers by the Bosnian Serbs. But in November, Balkan leaders Milosevic Izetbegovic and Franjo Tudjman, refereed by U.S. Secretary of State Warren Christopher, signed a peace accord in Dayton, Ohio. Tortuous negotiations had been conducted in Spartan quarters on a U.S. air base. Bosnian Serbs quickly declared opposition to the agreement, and many members of Congress expressed doubt that it would work.

The agreement gave numerous "ethnically cleansed" towns and regions to the federation composed of Bosnia's Croats and the Muslim-dominated government. It ratifies, for now, the de facto dismemberment of Bosnia.

In early December, President Clinton made the decision to send 20,000 U.S. troops to Bosnia to begin peace-keeping duties. Polls showed that a majority of Americans opposed the action, and there was considerable opposition in Congress as well. As the year ended, a fragile, controlled semipeace settled across the war-weary land. Troubling questions, however, remained. Is Bosnia America's fight? Should U.S. troops even be there? And what will happen if U.S. troops leave after a year, as President Clinton promised?

DICK LOCHER
Courtesy Chicago Tribune

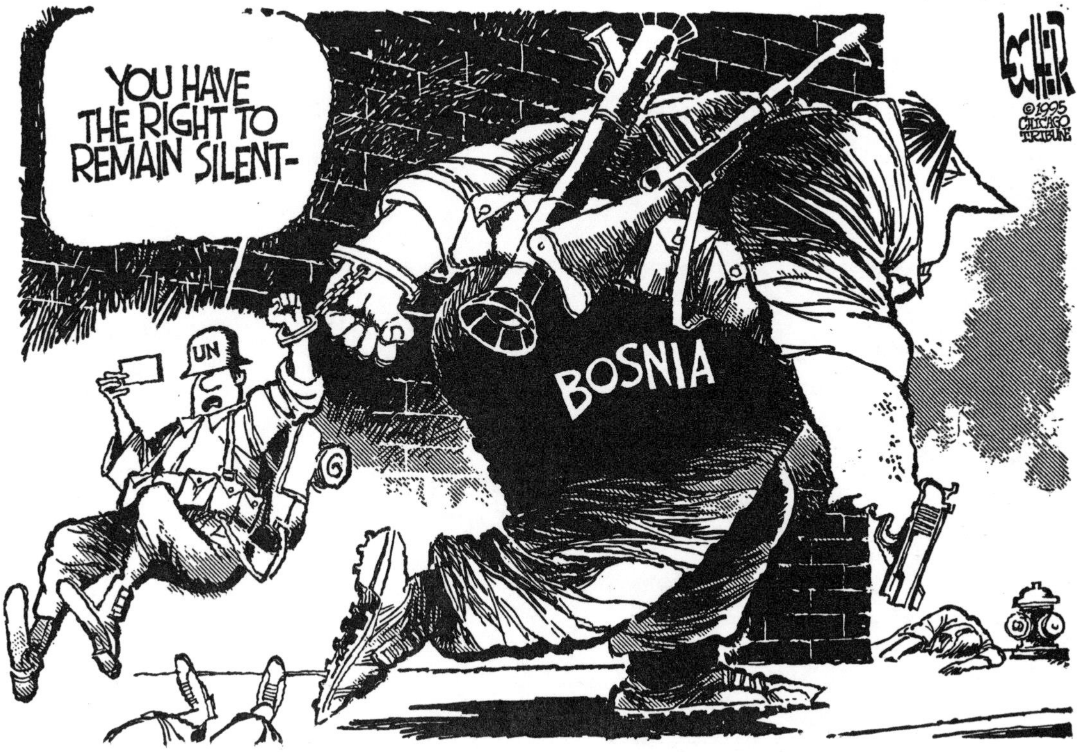
YOU HAVE THE RIGHT TO REMAIN SILENT-
UN
BOSNIA
LOCHER
©1995 CHICAGO TRIBUNE

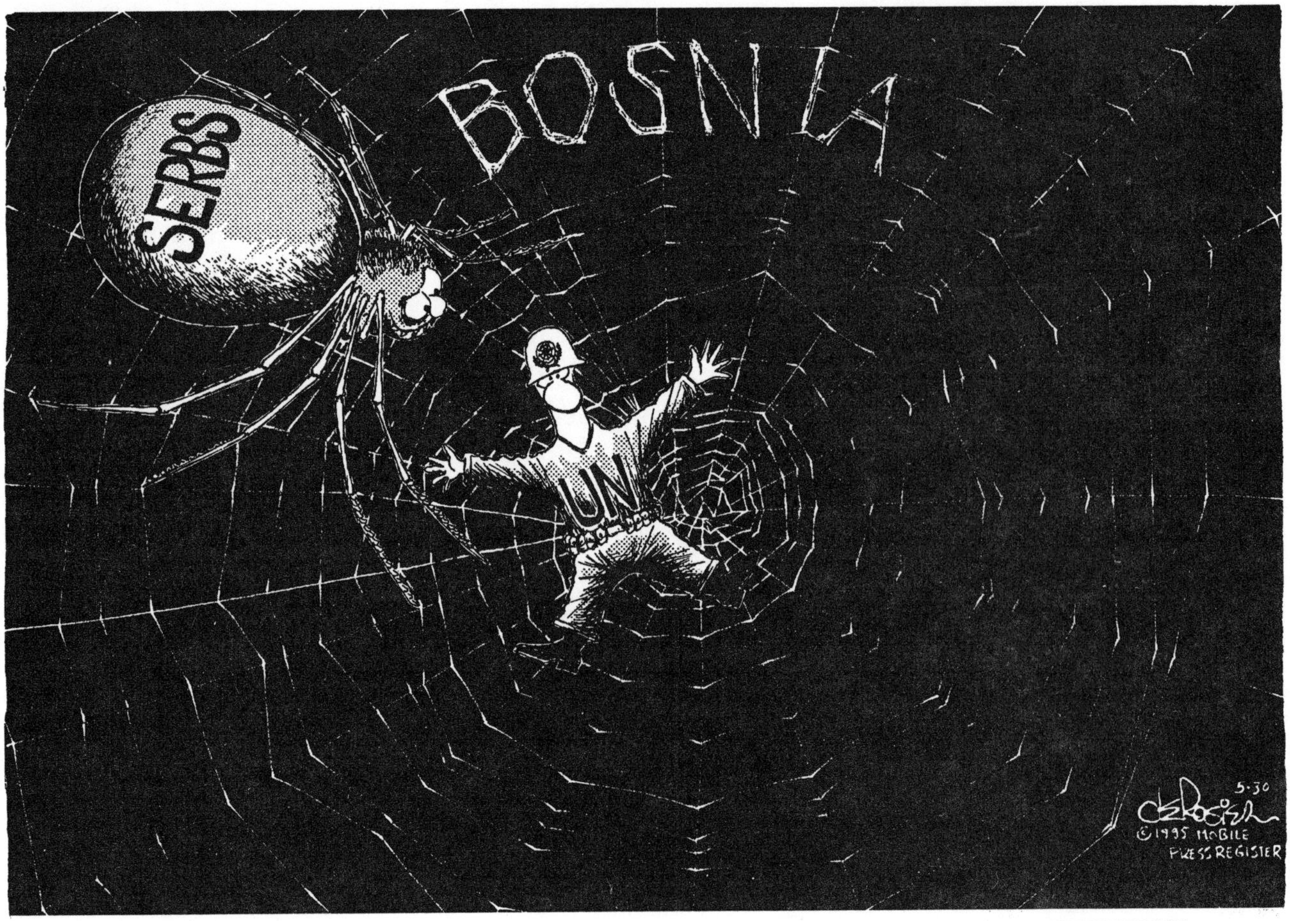
BOSNIA
SERBS
UN
5-30
©1995 MOBILE PRESS REGISTER

JOHN DEROSIER
Courtesy Mobile Press Register

MICHAEL RAMIREZ
Courtesy Memphis Commercial Appeal

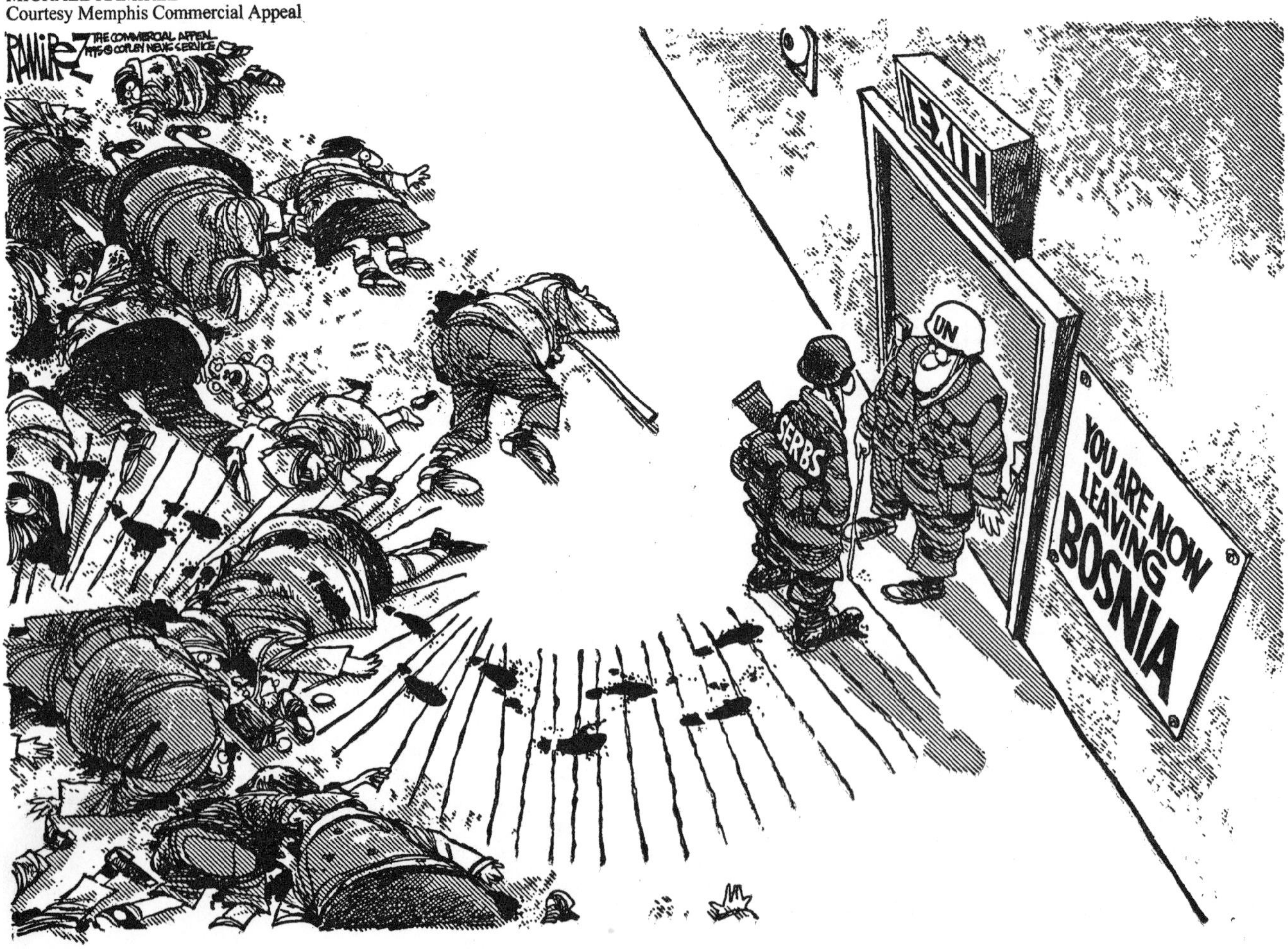
RAMIREZ
THE COMMERCIAL APPEAL 1995 © COPLEY NEWS SERVICE
EXIT
UN
SERBS
YOU ARE NOW LEAVING BOSNIA

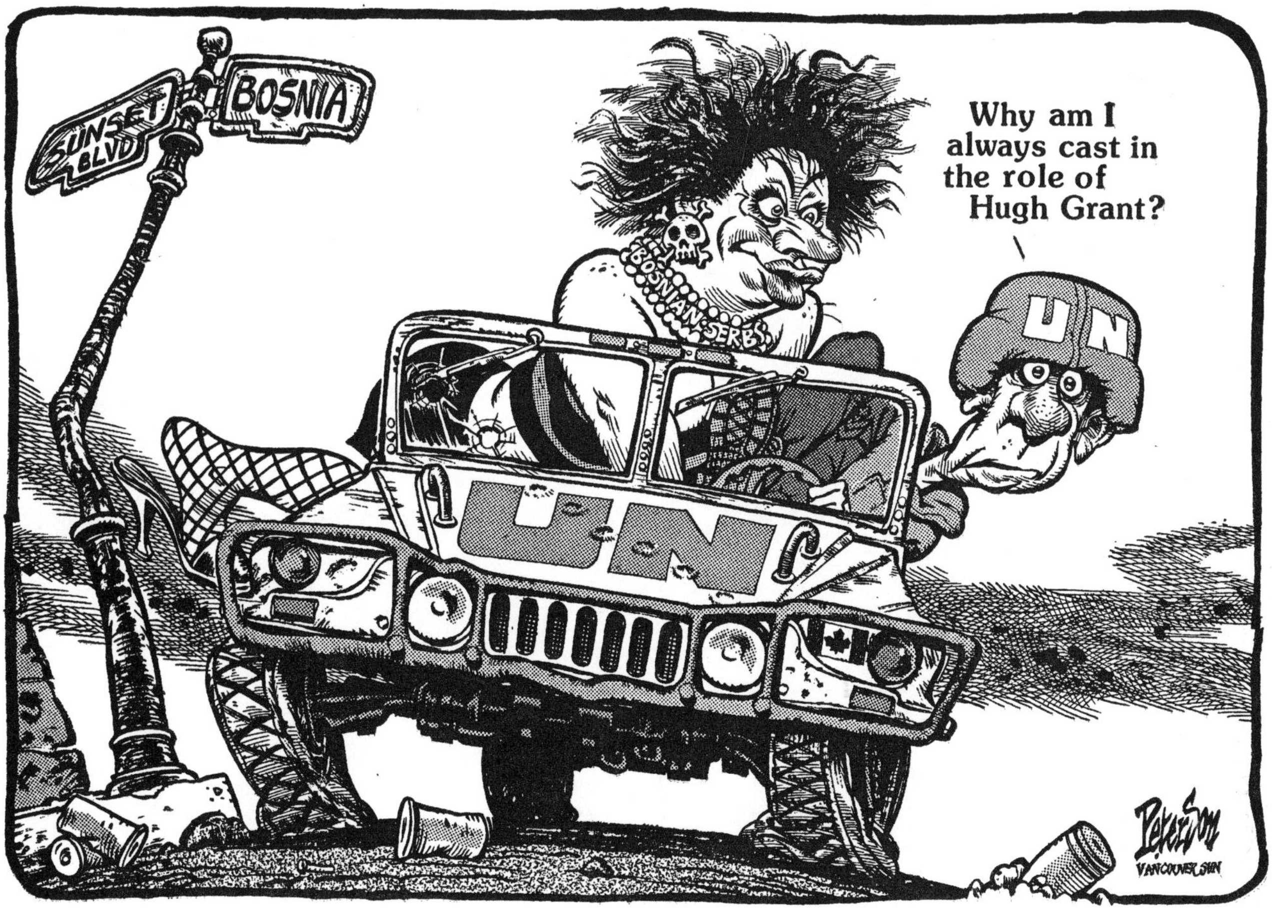
SUNSET BLVD
BOSNIA
Why am I always cast in the role of Hugh Grant?
BOSNIAN SERBS
UN
U N
PETERSON
VANCOUVER SUN

ROY PETERSON
Courtesy Vancouver Sun

DOUG MACGREGOR
Courtesy Ft. Meyers News-Press

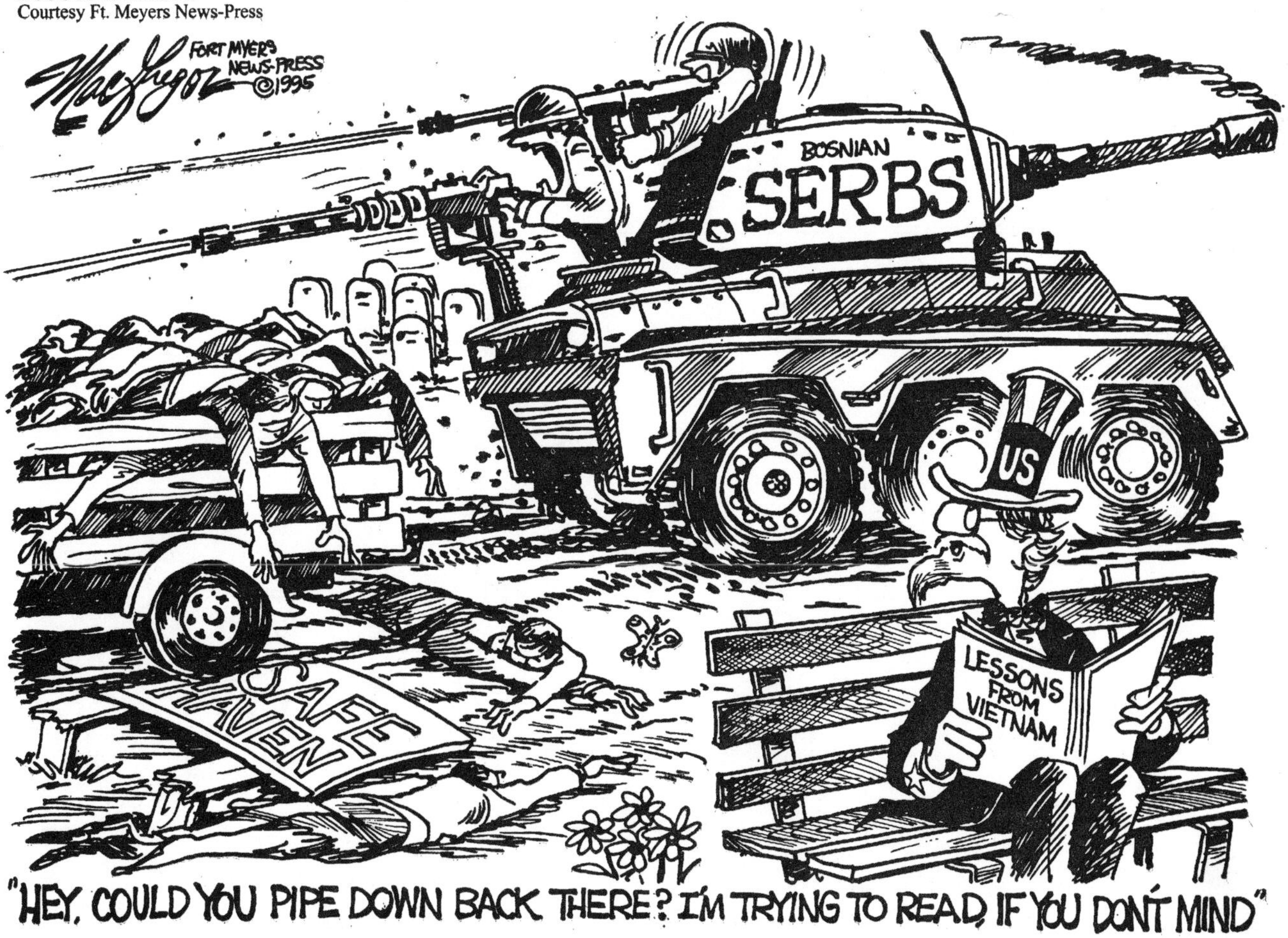
MacGregor
FORT MYERS NEWS-PRESS ©1995
BOSNIAN
SERBS
US
SAFE HAVEN
LESSONS FROM VIETNAM
"HEY, COULD YOU PIPE DOWN BACK THERE? I'M TRYING TO READ, IF YOU DON'T MIND"

MIKE KEEFE
Courtesy Denver Post

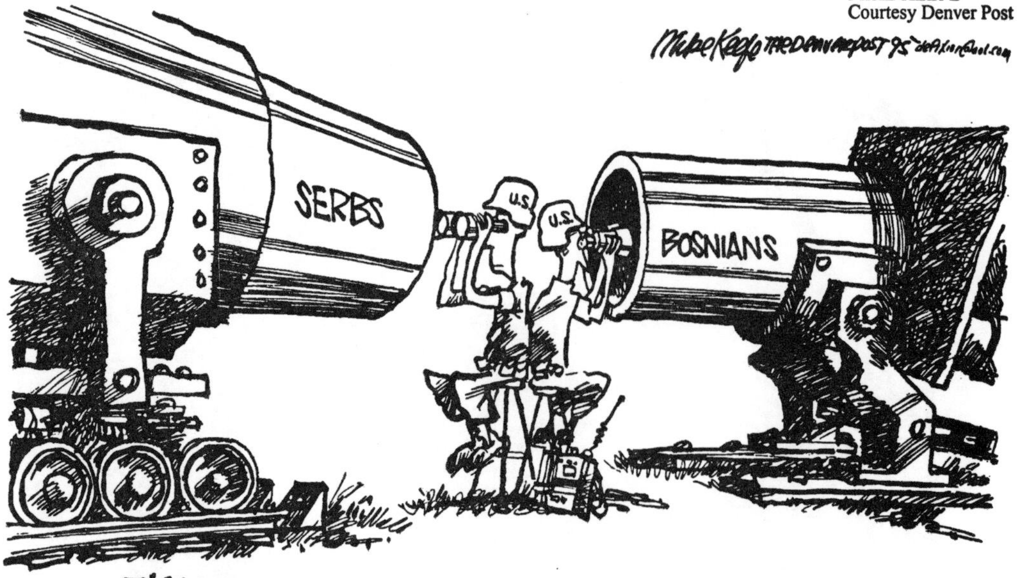
SERBS
U.S.
U.S.
BOSNIANS

THE MISSION: RADIO IN IF YOU SEE ANYTHING FUNNY.

LAMBERT DER
Courtesy Houston Post

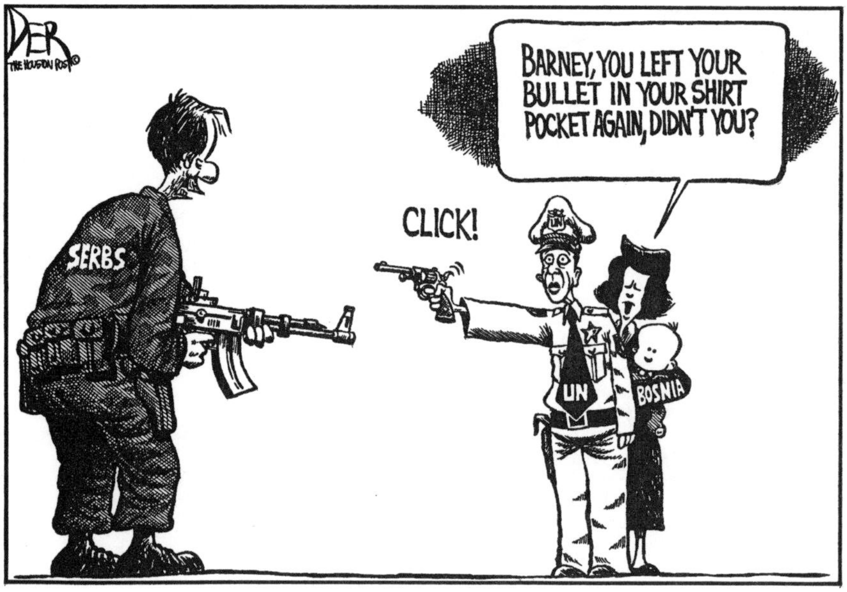
DER
BARNEY, YOU LEFT YOUR BULLET IN YOUR SHIRT POCKET AGAIN, DIDN'T YOU?
CLICK!
SERBS
UN
UN
BOSNIA

CARLOS GARY
Courtesy Ft. Wayne News-Sentinel

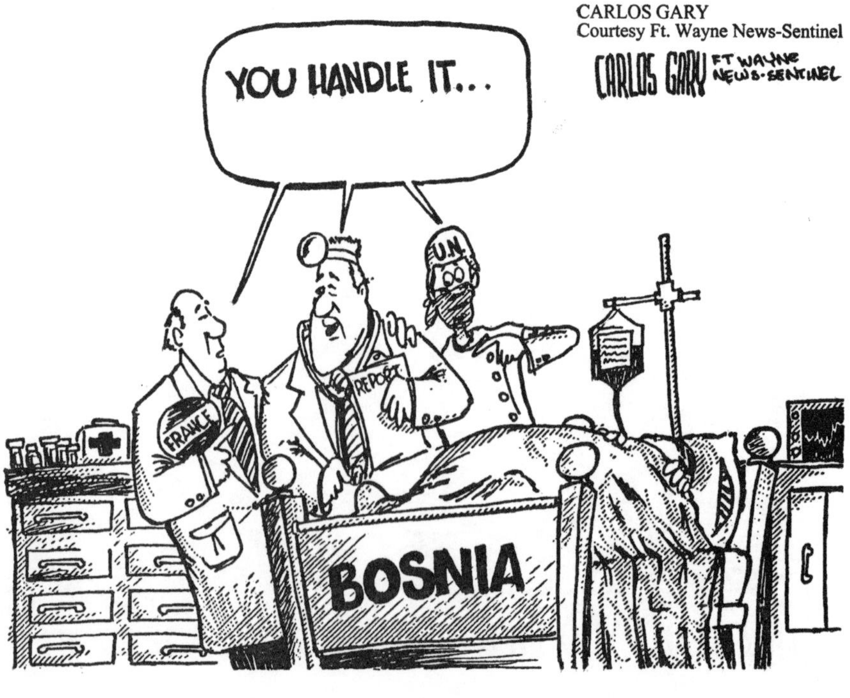
CARLOS GARY FT WAYNE NEWS-SENTINEL
YOU HANDLE IT...
U.N.
FRANCE
REPORT
BOSNIA

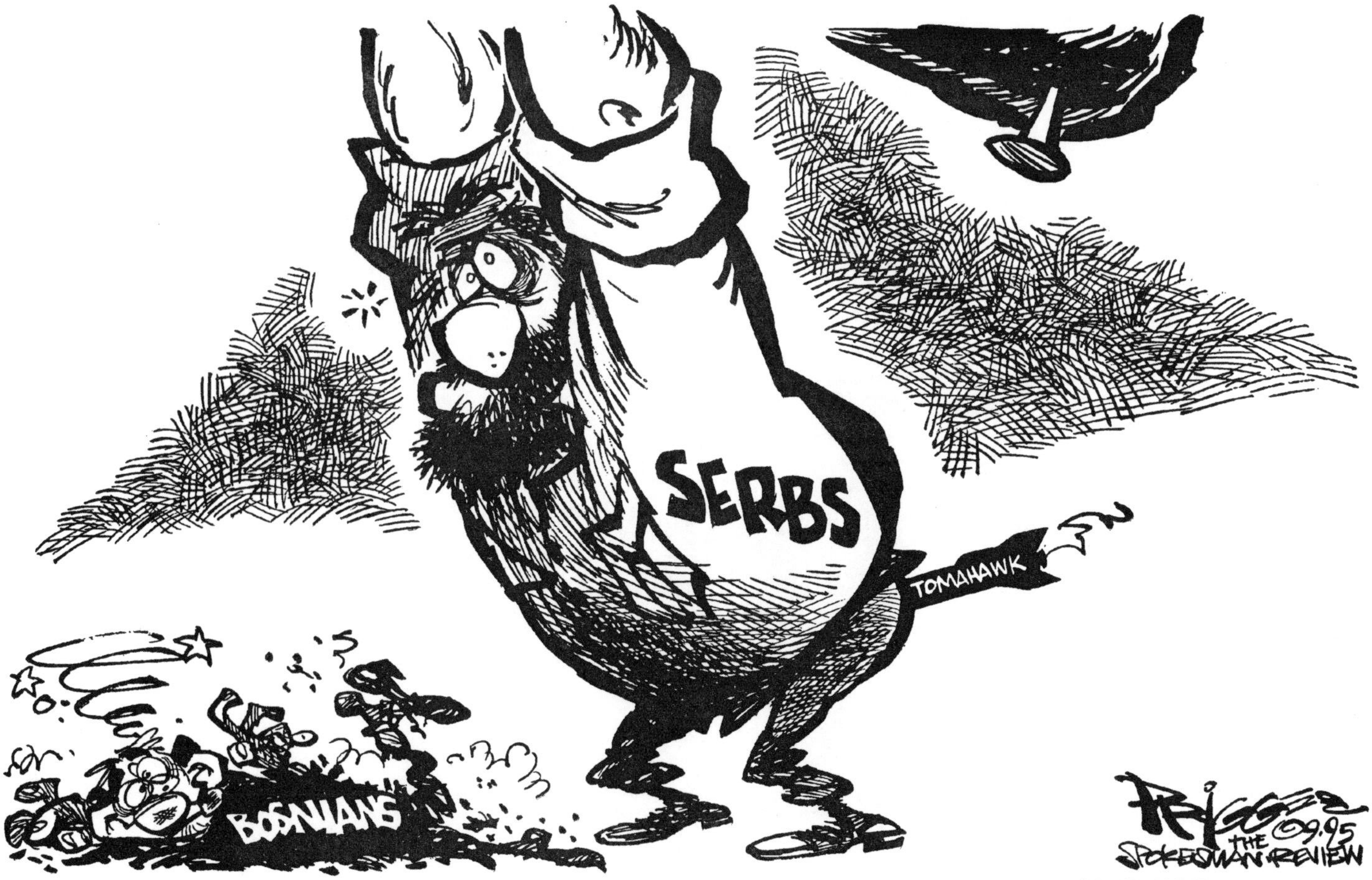
SERBS
TOMAHAWK
BOSNIANS

MILT PRIGGEE
Courtesy Spokane Spokesman-Review

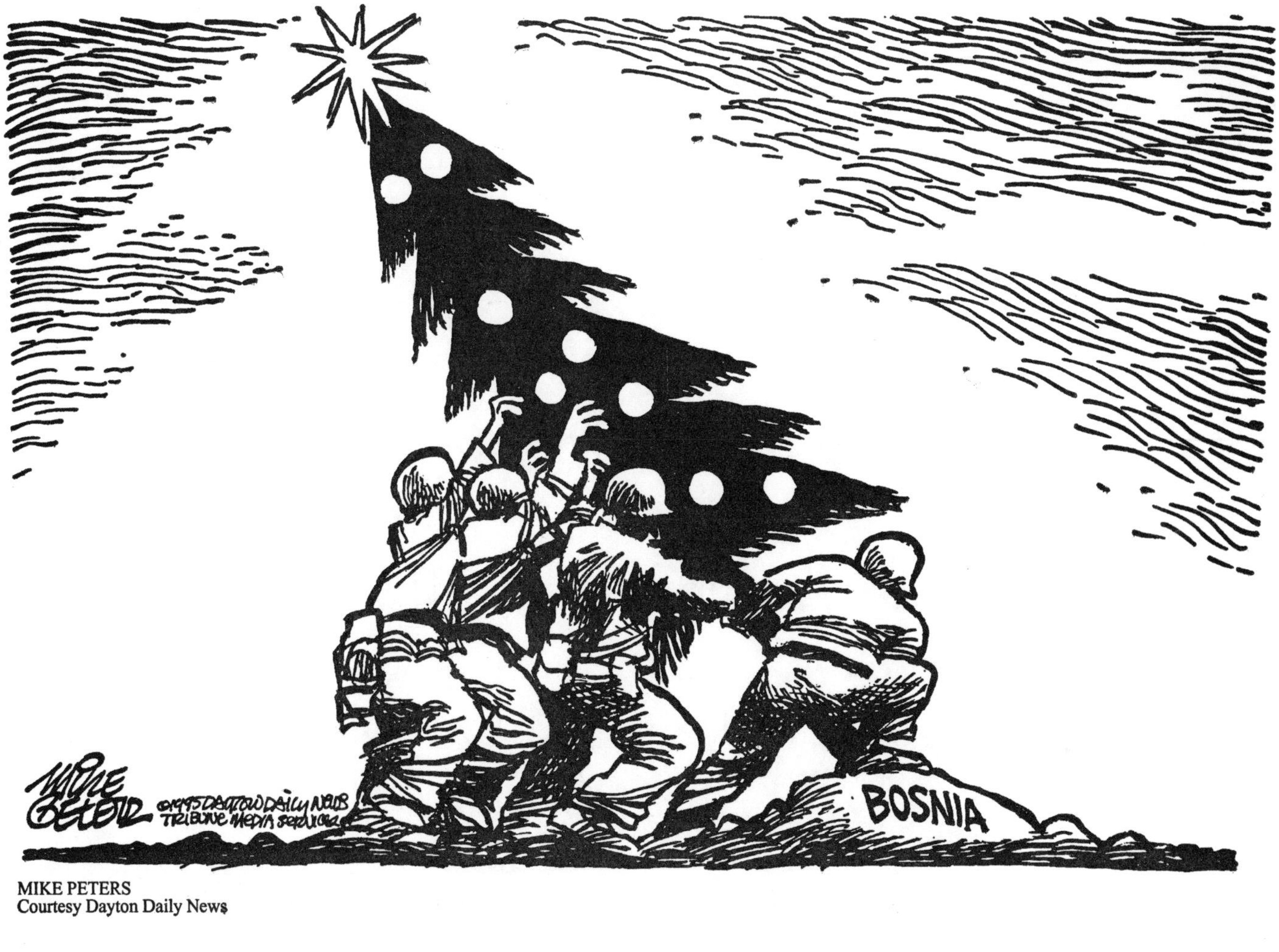
BOSNIA

MIKE PETERS
Courtesy Dayton Daily News

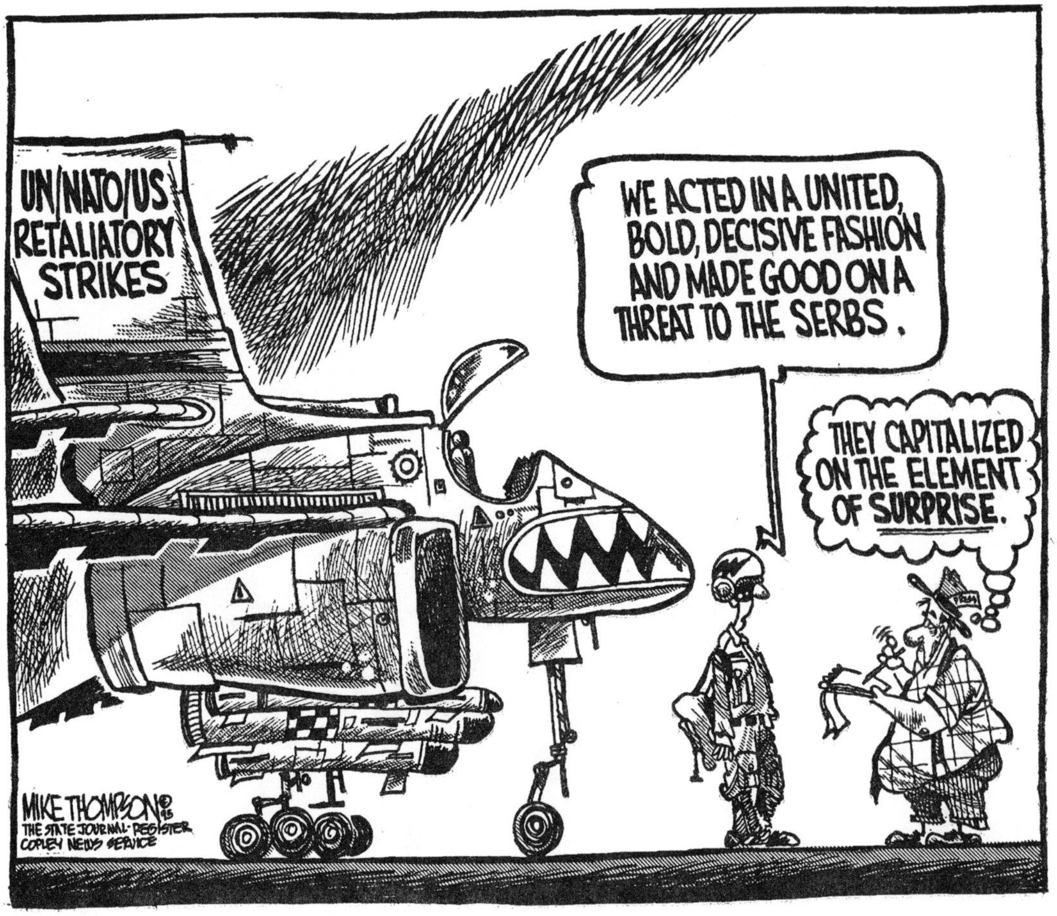
UN/NATO/US
RETALIATORY
STRIKES
WE ACTED IN A UNITED, BOLD, DECISIVE FASHION AND MADE GOOD ON A THREAT TO THE SERBS.
THEY CAPITALIZED ON THE ELEMENT OF SURPRISE.
MIKE THOMPSON ©95
THE STATE JOURNAL-REGISTER
COPLEY NEWS SERVICE

MIKE THOMPSON
Courtesy State Journal-Register (Ill.)

DENNY PRITCHARD
Courtesy Ottawa Citizen

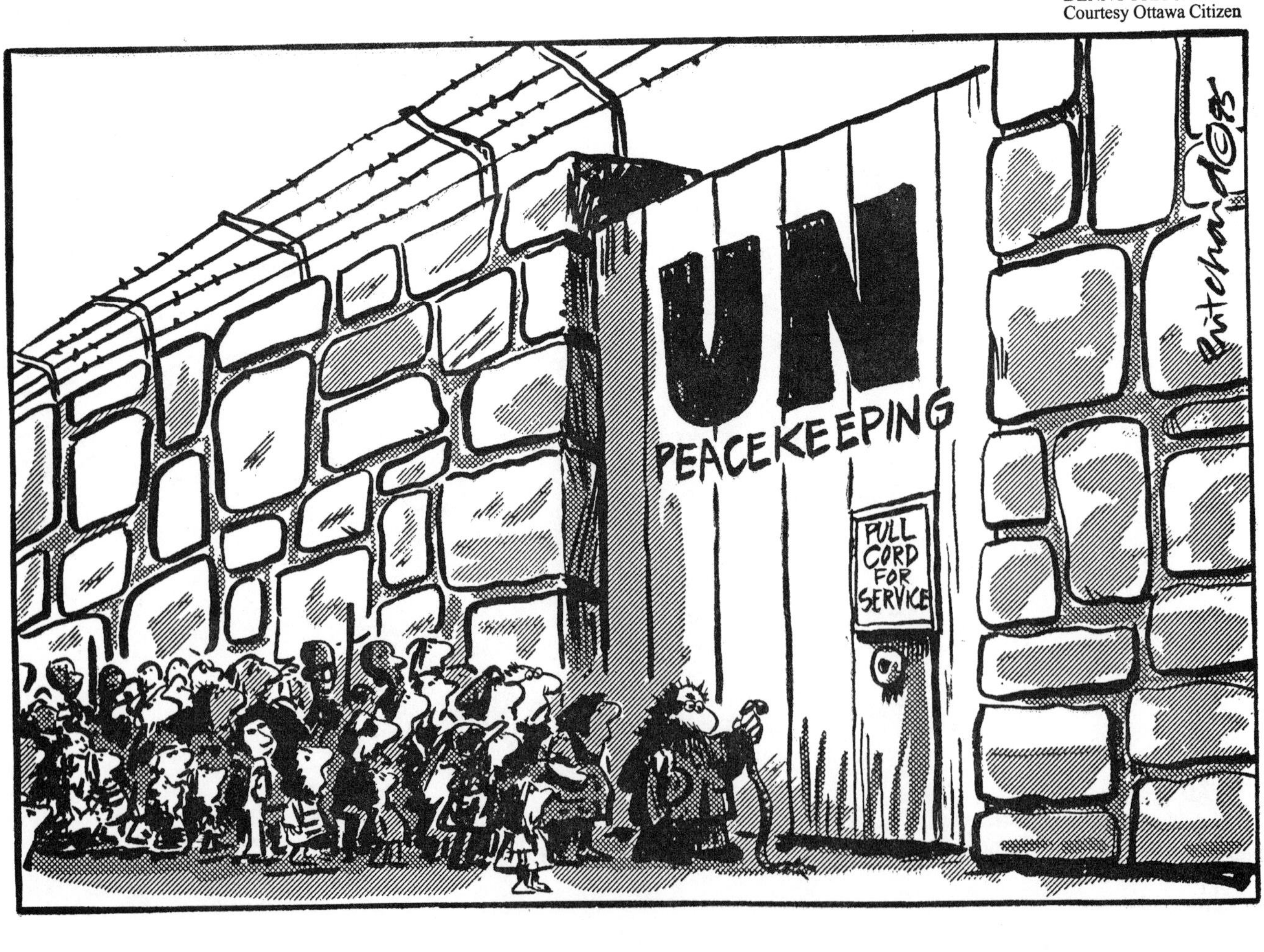
UN
PEACEKEEPING
PULL CORD FOR SERVICE

FRED CURATOLO
Courtesy Edmonton Sun

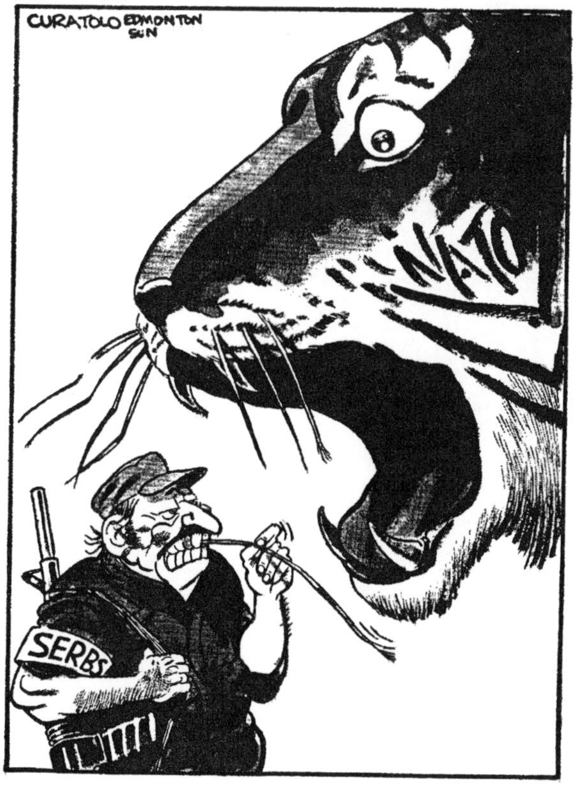
CURATOLO EDMONTON SUN
NATO
SERBS

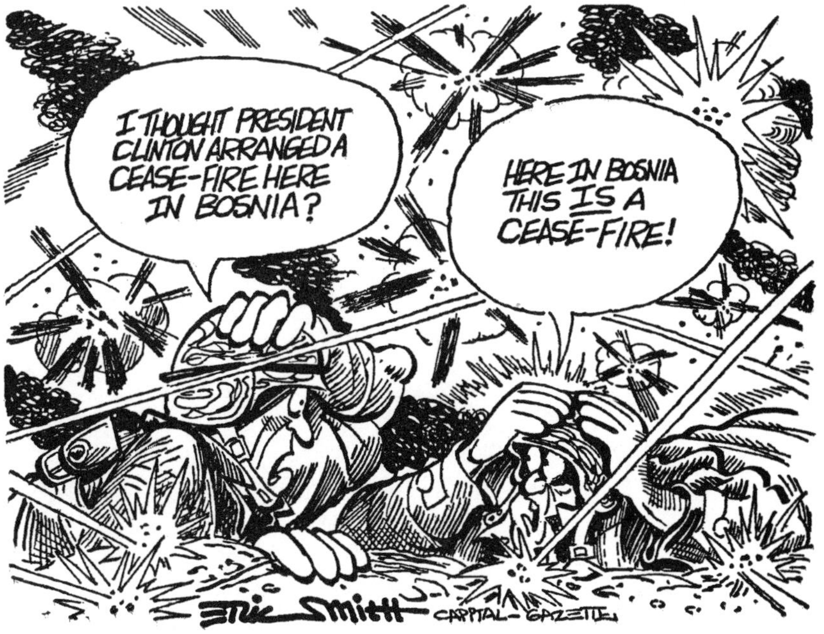
I THOUGHT PRESIDENT CLINTON ARRANGED A CEASE-FIRE HERE IN BOSNIA?
HERE IN BOSNIA THIS IS A CEASE-FIRE!
ERIC SMITH CAPITAL-GAZETTE

ERIC SMITH
Courtesy Capital Gazette Newspapers

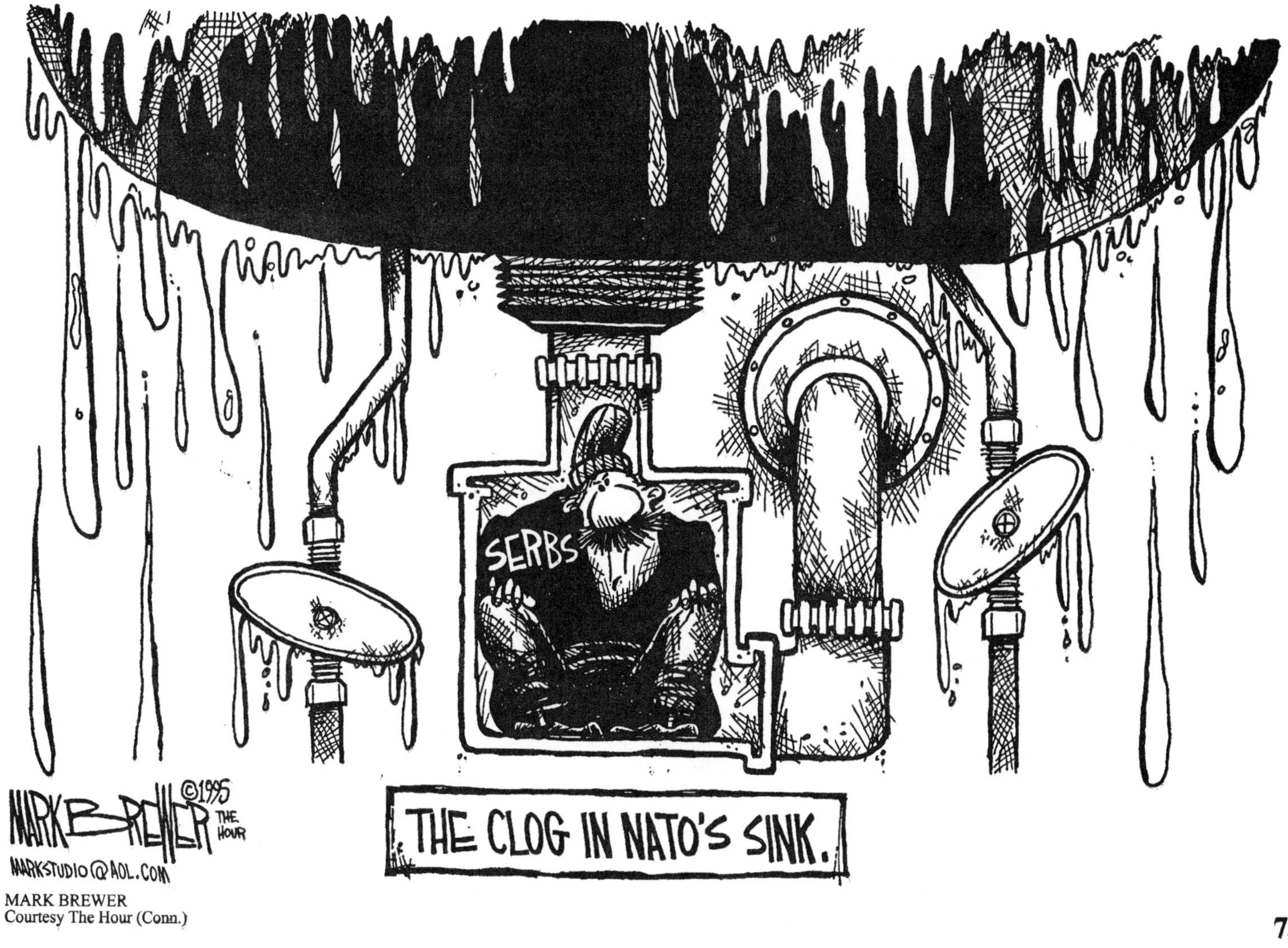
SERBS
MARK BREWER ©1995 THE HOUR
MARKSTUDIO@AOL.COM
THE CLOG IN NATO'S SINK.

MARK BREWER
Courtesy The Hour (Conn.)

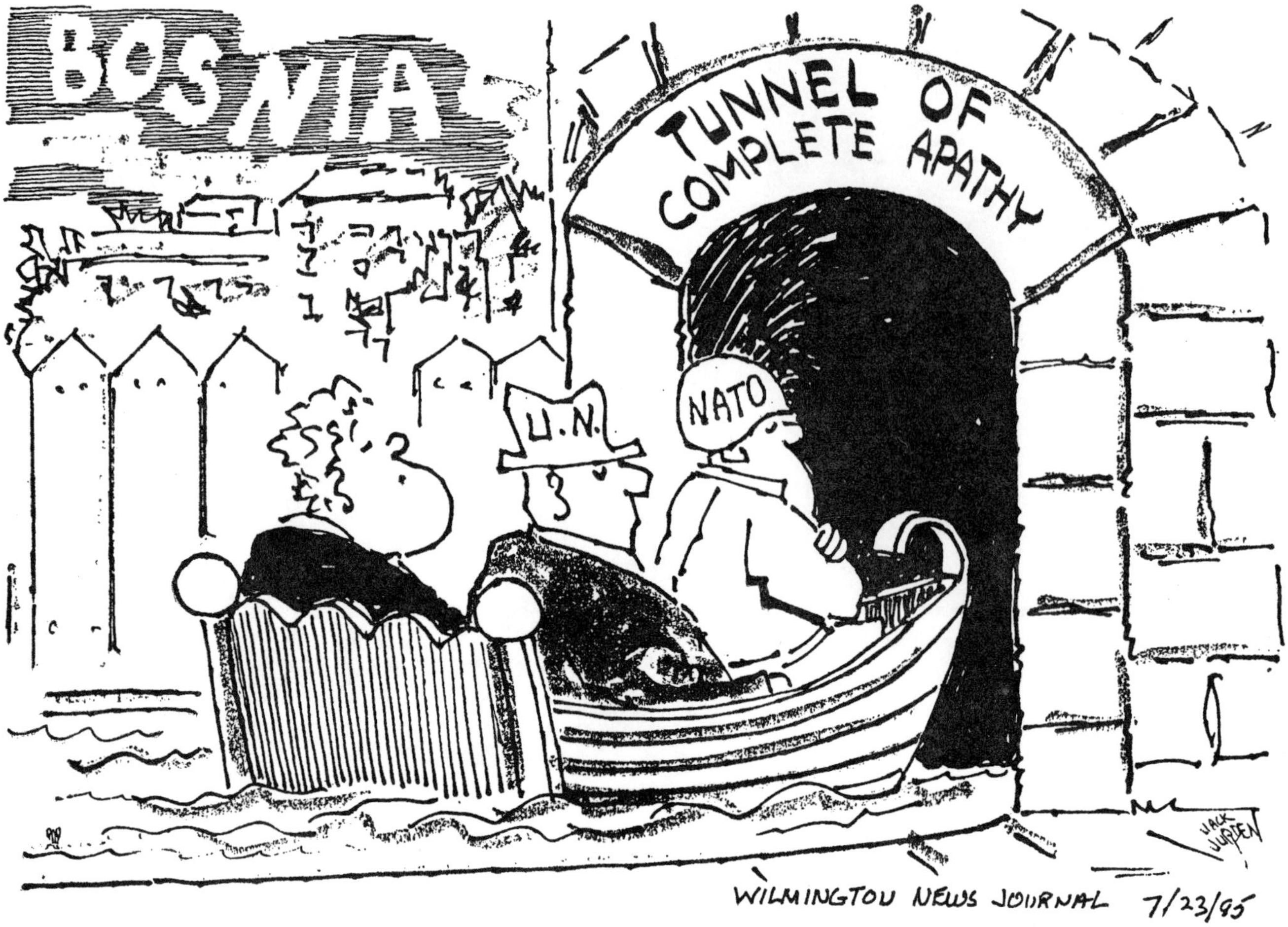
BOSNIA
TUNNEL OF COMPLETE APATHY
U.N.
NATO
JACK JURDEN
WILMINGTON NEWS JOURNAL 7/23/95

JACK JURDEN
Courtesy Wilmington News Journal

BILL GARNER
Courtesy Washington Times

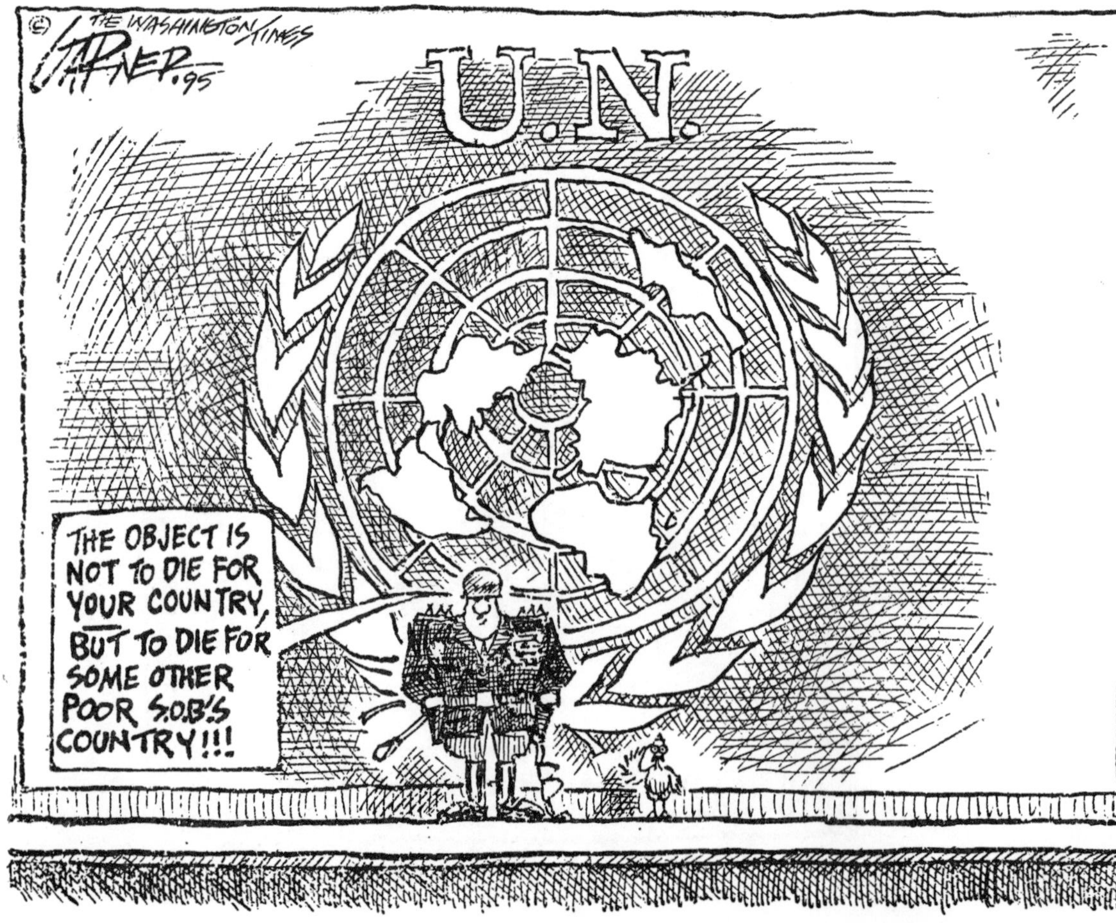
© THE WASHINGTON TIMES
GARNER '95
U.N.
THE OBJECT IS NOT TO DIE FOR YOUR COUNTRY, BUT TO DIE FOR SOME OTHER POOR S.O.B'S COUNTRY!!!

LINDA BOILEAU
Courtesy Frankfort State Journal

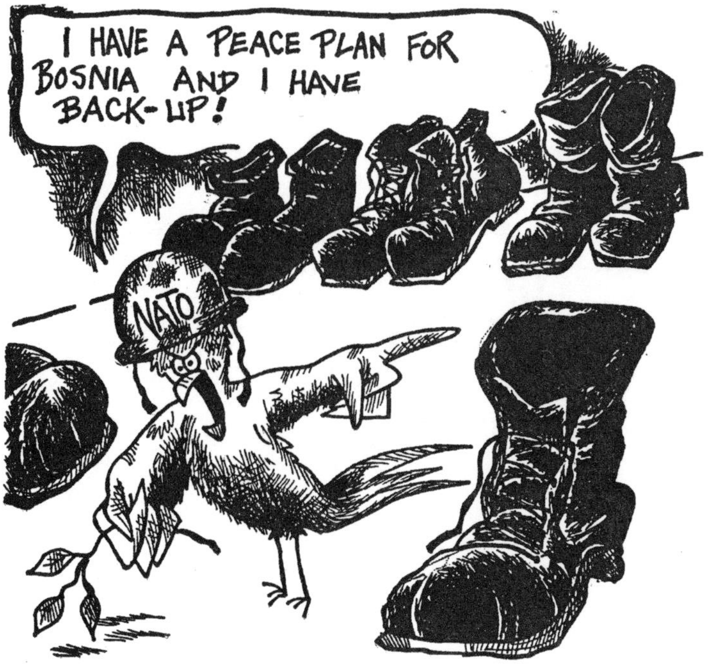
I HAVE A PEACE PLAN FOR BOSNIA AND I HAVE BACK-UP!
NATO

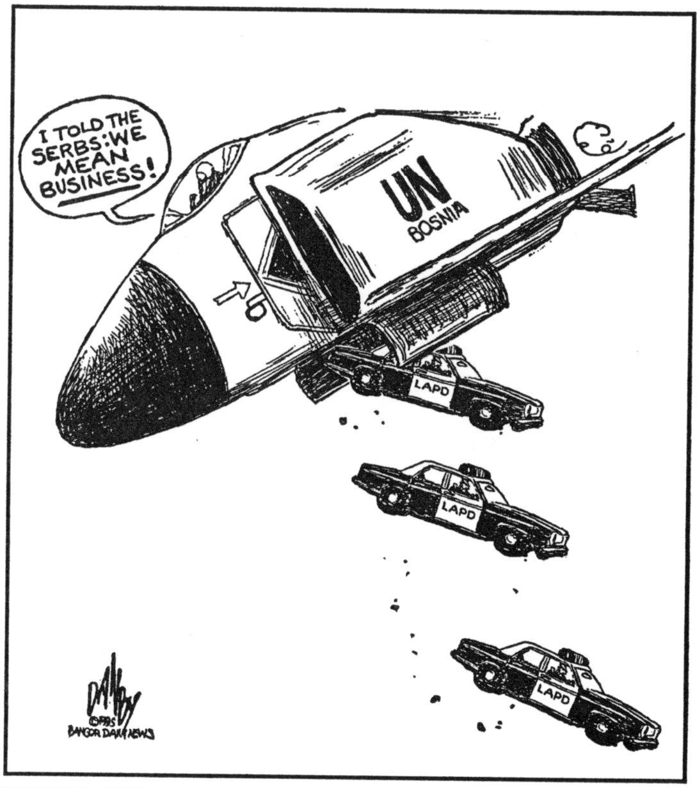
I TOLD THE SERBS: WE MEAN BUSINESS!
UN
BOSNIA
LAPD
LAPD
LAPD

GEORGE DANBY
Courtesy Bangor Daily News

PAUL SZEP
Courtesy Boston Globe

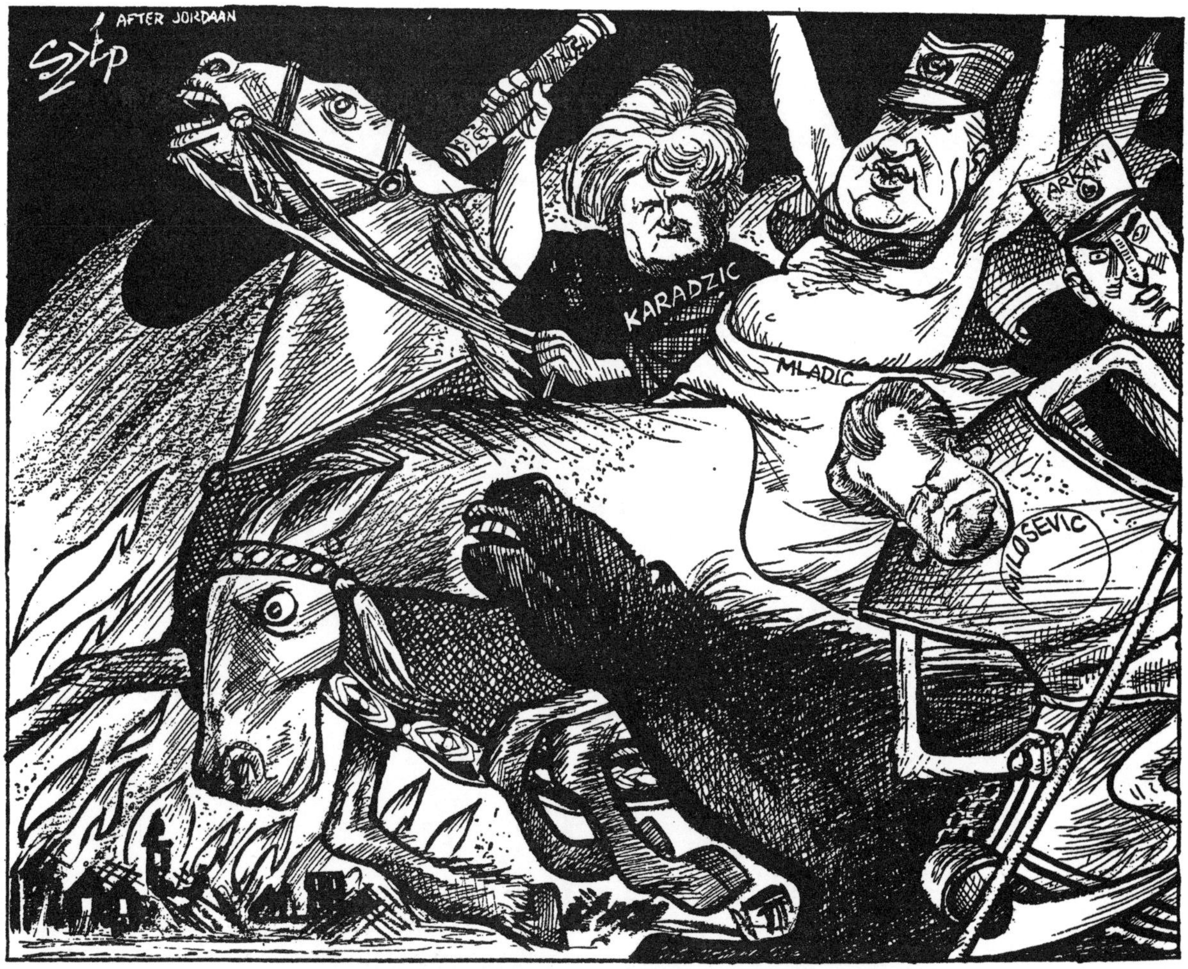
AFTER JORDAAN
KARADZIC
MLADIC
ARKAN
LOSEVIC

THE FOUR SERBMEN OF THE ATROCITIES

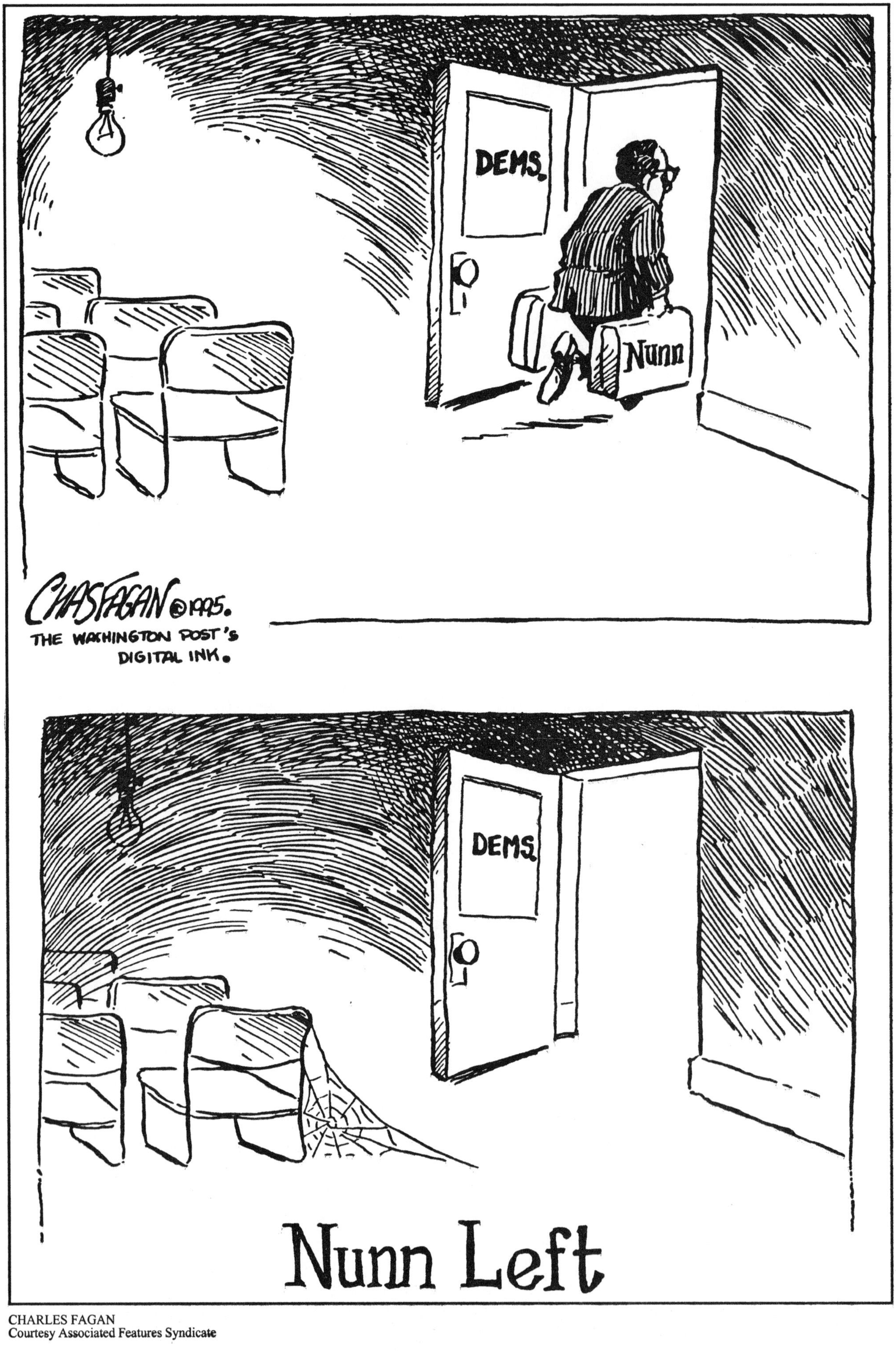
DEMS
Nunn
CHAS FAGAN ©1995.
THE WASHINGTON POST'S
DIGITAL INK.
DEMS
Nunn Left

CHARLES FAGAN
Courtesy Associated Features Syndicate

Congress

The newly elected Republican majority took control of Congress. Using their Contract With America as a blueprint, they set about changing the political landscape. The first order of business was to make Congress subject to its own laws. Under Democratic control, Congress had exempted itself from most of the laws it passed. As the first 100 days came to a close, the Republicans celebrated the fact that they had kept their Contract With America, having brought up everything on their agenda for a vote and having passed many of the items. The two parties were still battling at year's end over a balanced budget.

Out of power for the first time in forty years, the Democrats continued to lose strength as nine party stalwarts announced they would not seek reelection. Others were switching to the Republican party, particularly in the South. Sen. Bob Packwood, an Oregon Republican, resigned after allegations of longtime sexual misconduct.

One popular item, term limits for members of Congress, failed to win the two-thirds majority necessary to place a constitutional amendment on the ballot. The Supreme Court ruled that states did not have the power to limit the terms of their own federal representatives. Much was said about lobby reform by new GOP members, but little has changed. An army of lobbyists still plies the halls of the Capitol.

DICK WRIGHT
Courtesy Providence Journal-Bulletin

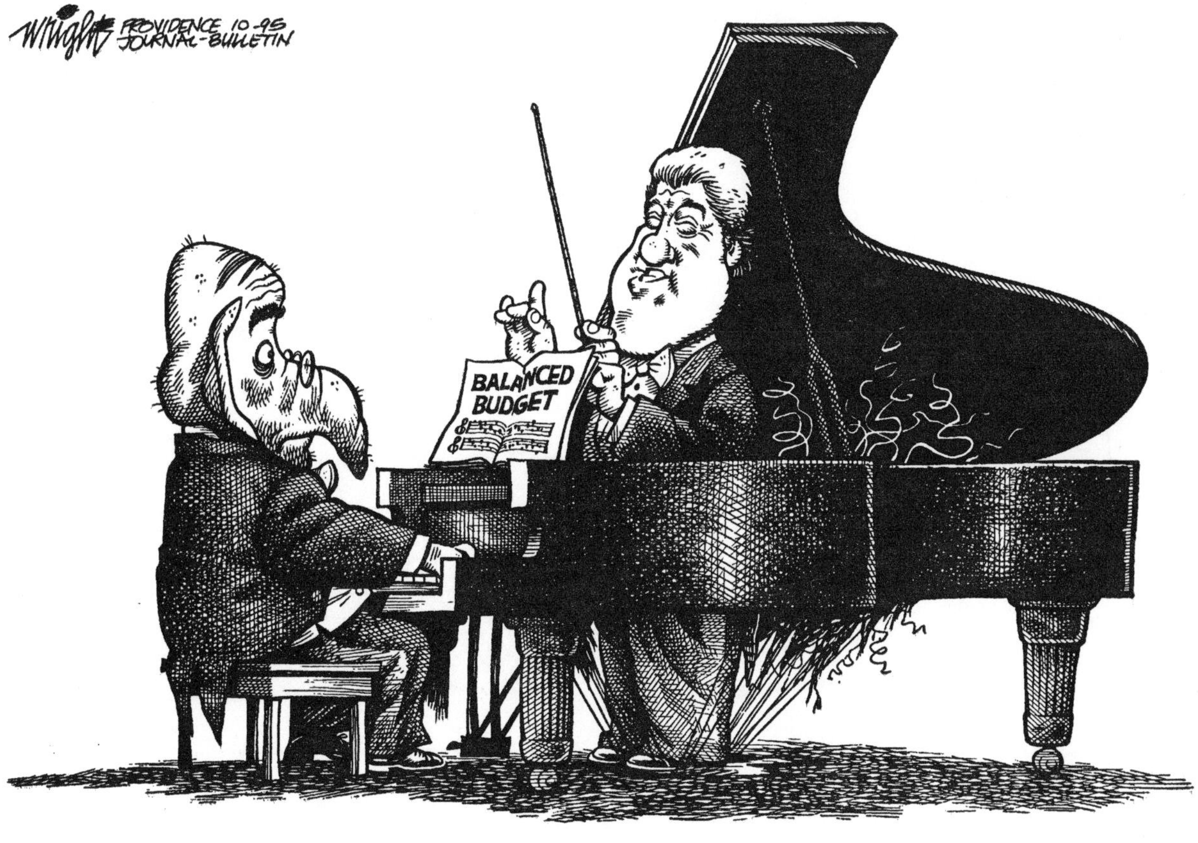
WRIGHT PROVIDENCE 10-95 JOURNAL-BULLETIN
BALANCED BUDGET

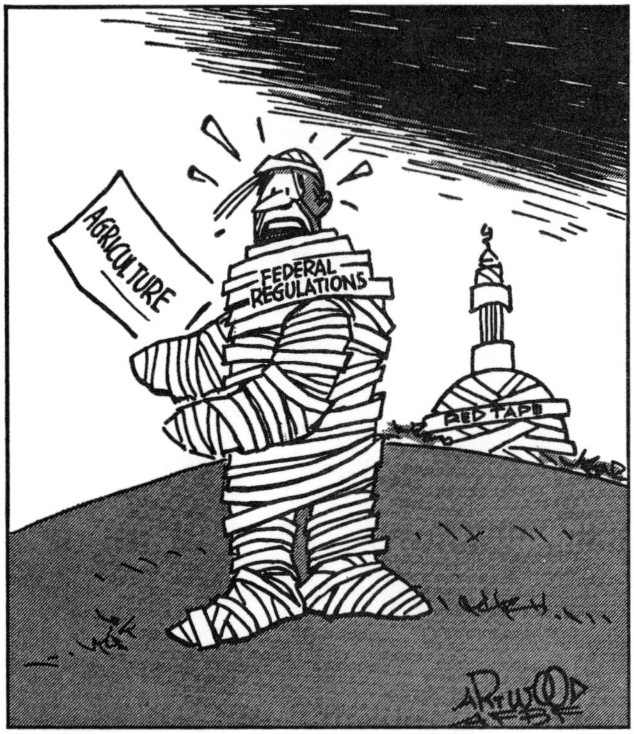
AGRICULTURE
FEDERAL REGULATIONS
RED TAPE

ART WOOD
Courtesy Farm Bureau News

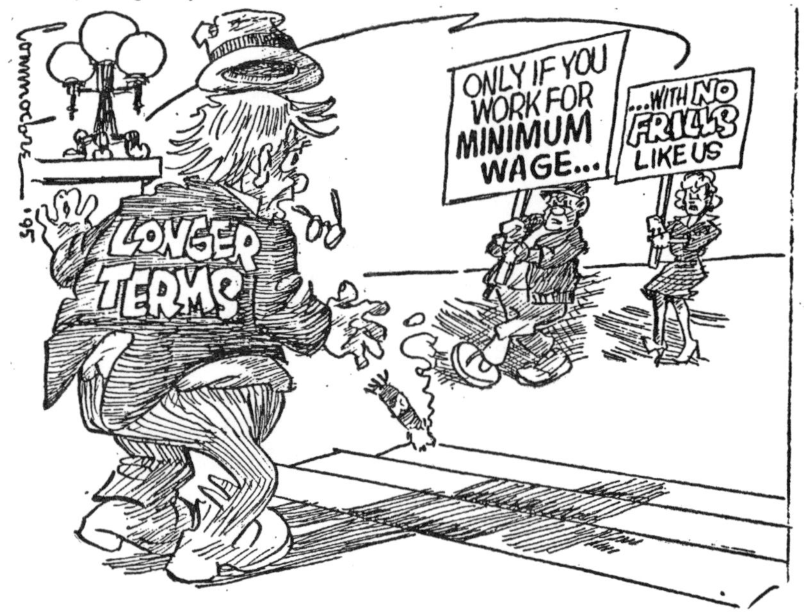
LONGER TERMS
ONLY IF YOU WORK FOR MINIMUM WAGE...
...WITH NO FRILLS LIKE US

CHESTER COMMODORE, SR.
Courtesy Chicago Daily Defender

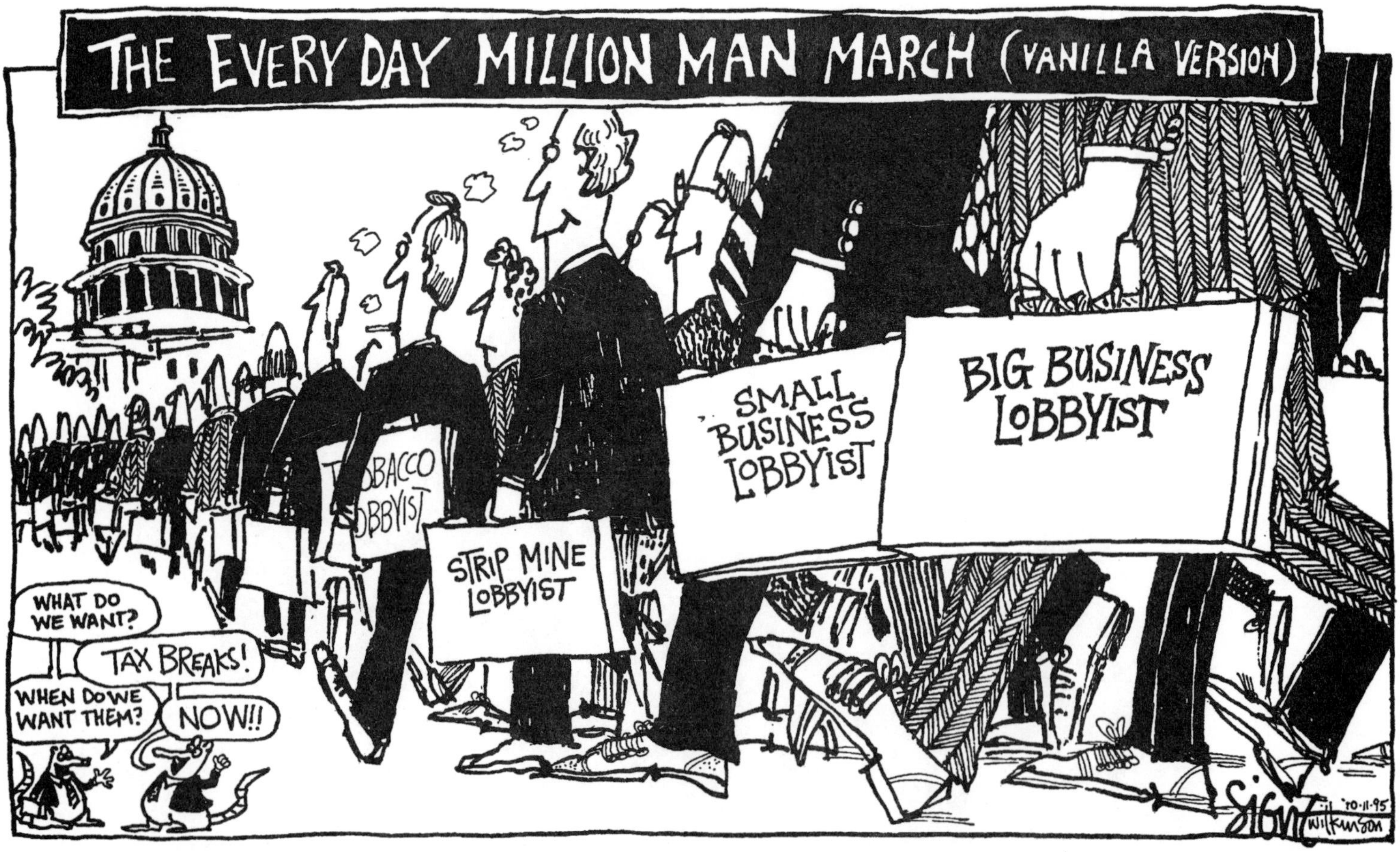
THE EVERY DAY MILLION MAN MARCH (VANILLA VERSION)
SMALL BUSINESS LOBBYIST
BIG BUSINESS LOBBYIST
STRIP MINE LOBBYIST
WHAT DO WE WANT?
TAX BREAKS!
WHEN DO WE WANT THEM?
NOW!!

SIGNE WILKINSON
Courtesy Philadelphia Daily News

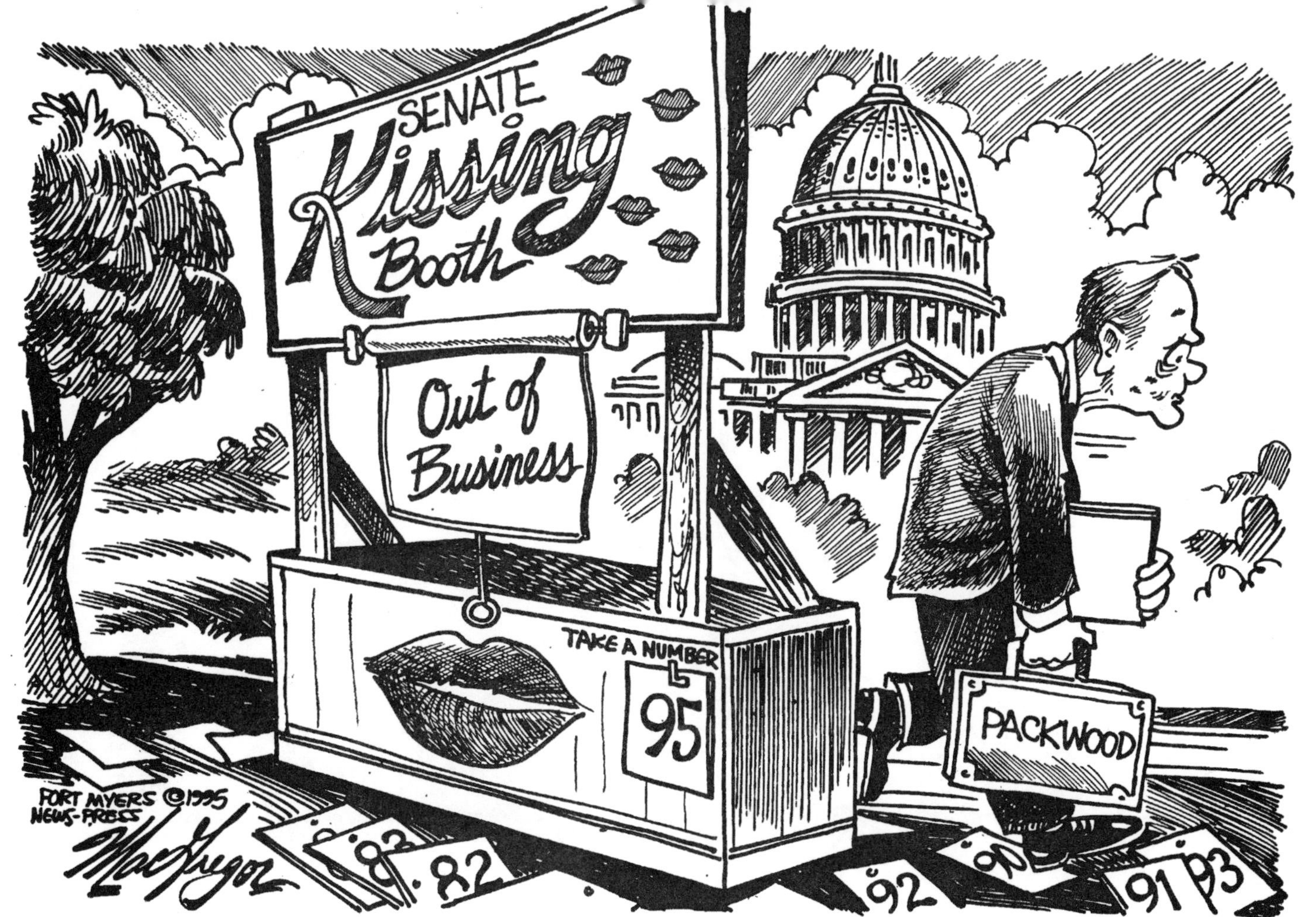
SENATE
Kissing
Booth
Out of
Business
TAKE A NUMBER
95
PACKWOOD
FORT MYERS ©1995
NEWS-PRESS
MacGregor
82
92
91
93

DOUG MACGREGOR
Courtesy Ft. Meyers News-Press

GARY BROOKINS
Courtesy Richmond Times-Dispatch

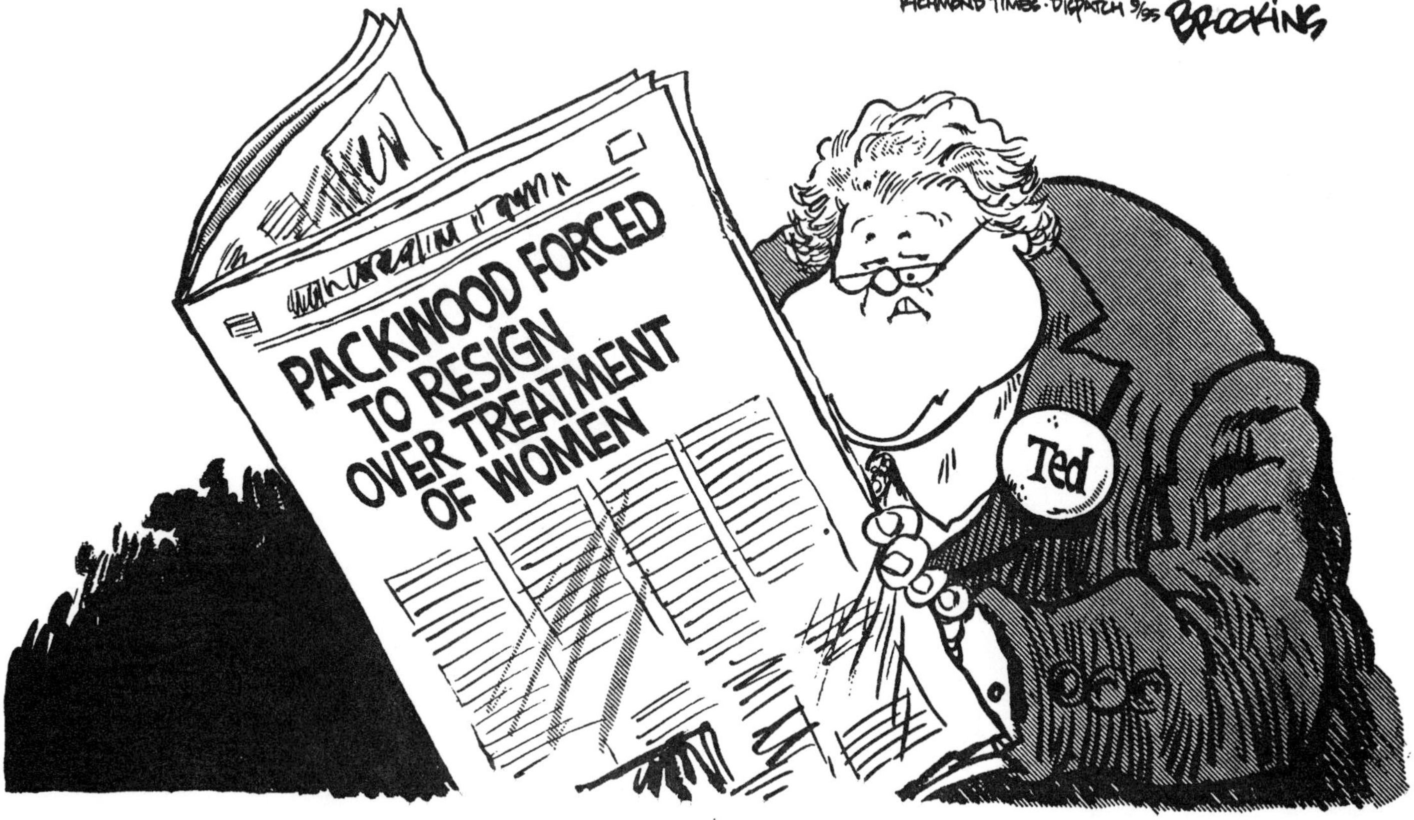
RICHMOND TIMES-DISPATCH 9/95 BROOKINS
PACKWOOD FORCED
TO RESIGN
OVER TREATMENT
OF WOMEN
Ted

BOB GORRELL
Courtesy Richmond Times-Dispatch/
Copley News Service

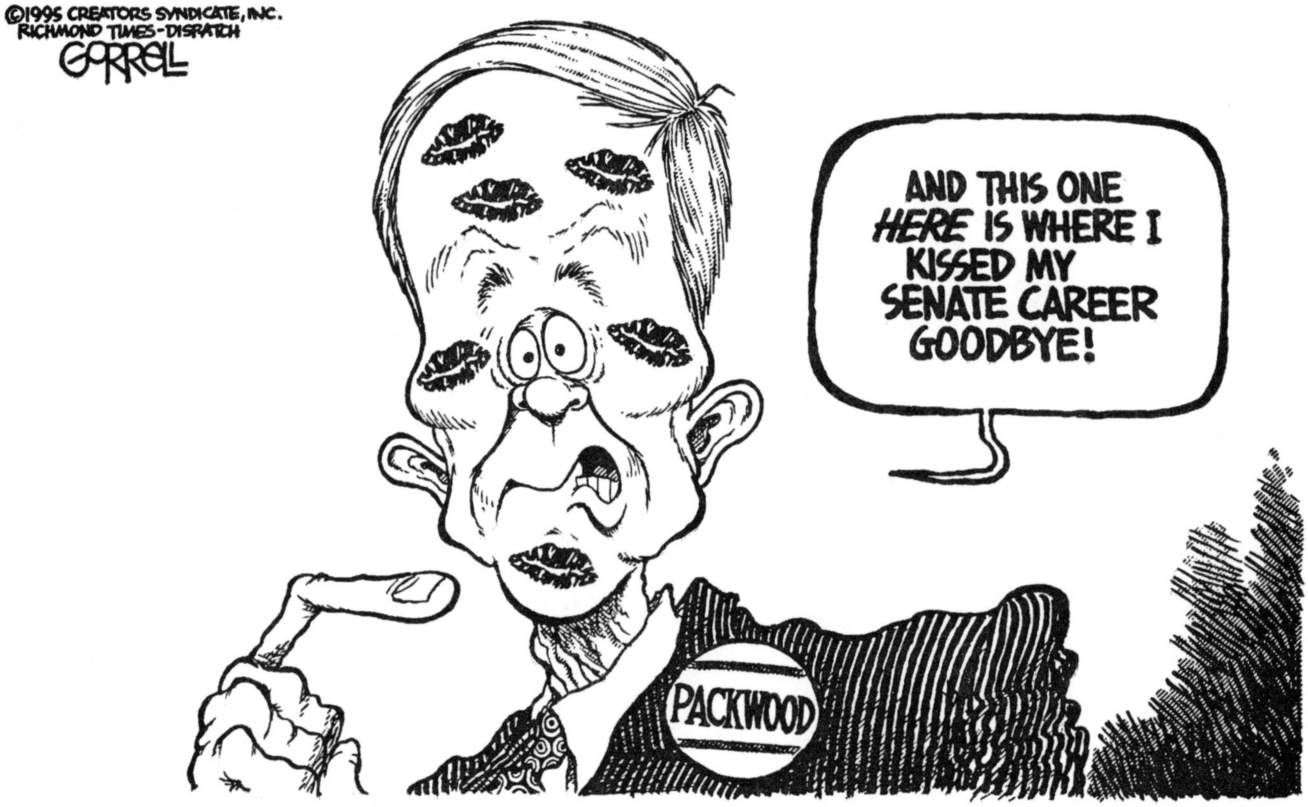
©1995 CREATORS SYNDICATE, INC.
RICHMOND TIMES-DISPATCH
GORRELL
AND THIS ONE *HERE* IS WHERE I KISSED MY SENATE CAREER GOODBYE!
PACKWOOD

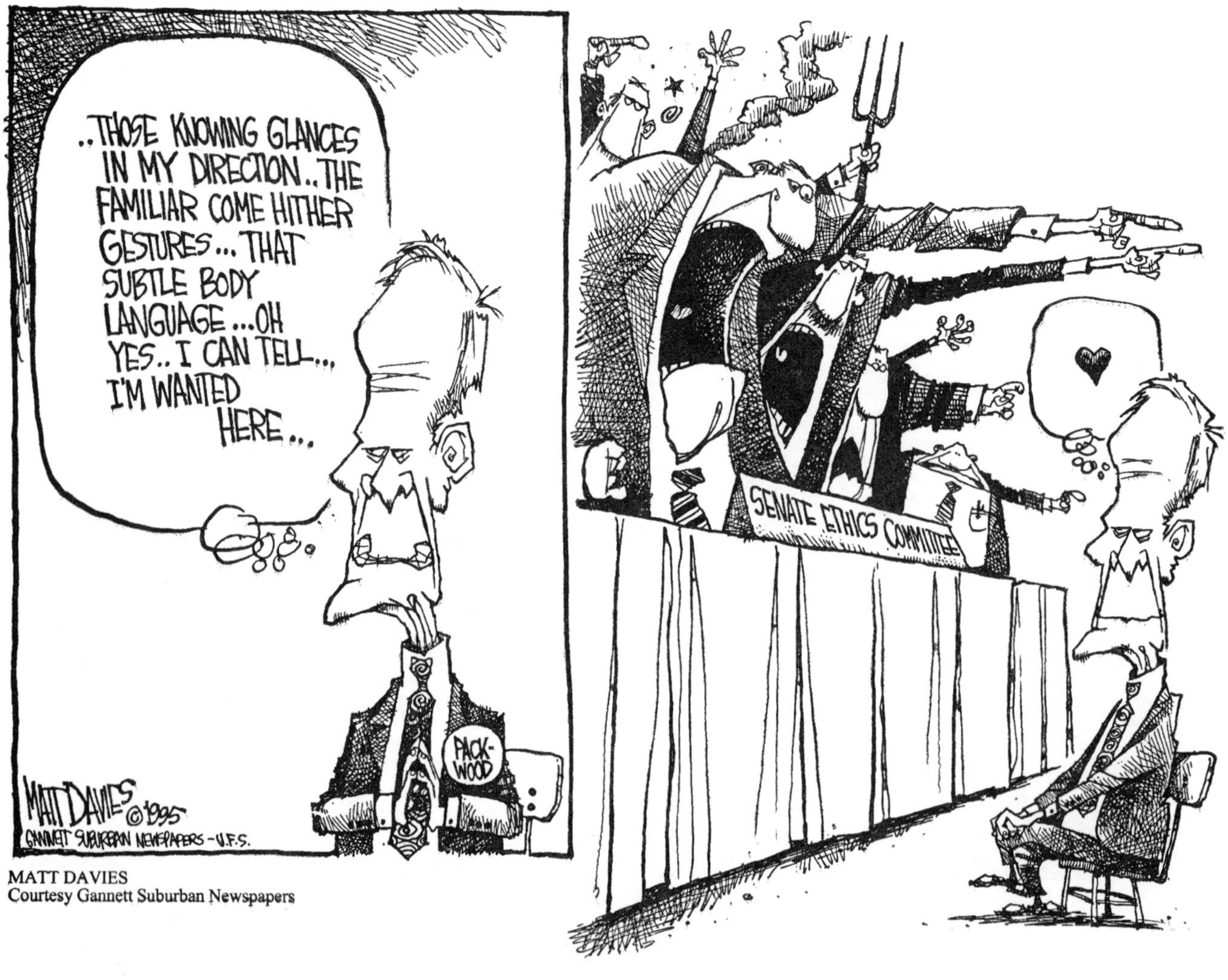
..THOSE KNOWING GLANCES IN MY DIRECTION..THE FAMILIAR COME HITHER GESTURES... THAT SUBTLE BODY LANGUAGE ...OH YES.. I CAN TELL... I'M WANTED HERE...
PACK-WOOD
MATT DAVIES ©1995
GANNETT SUBURBAN NEWSPAPERS - U.F.S.
SENATE ETHICS COMMITTEE

MATT DAVIES
Courtesy Gannett Suburban Newspapers

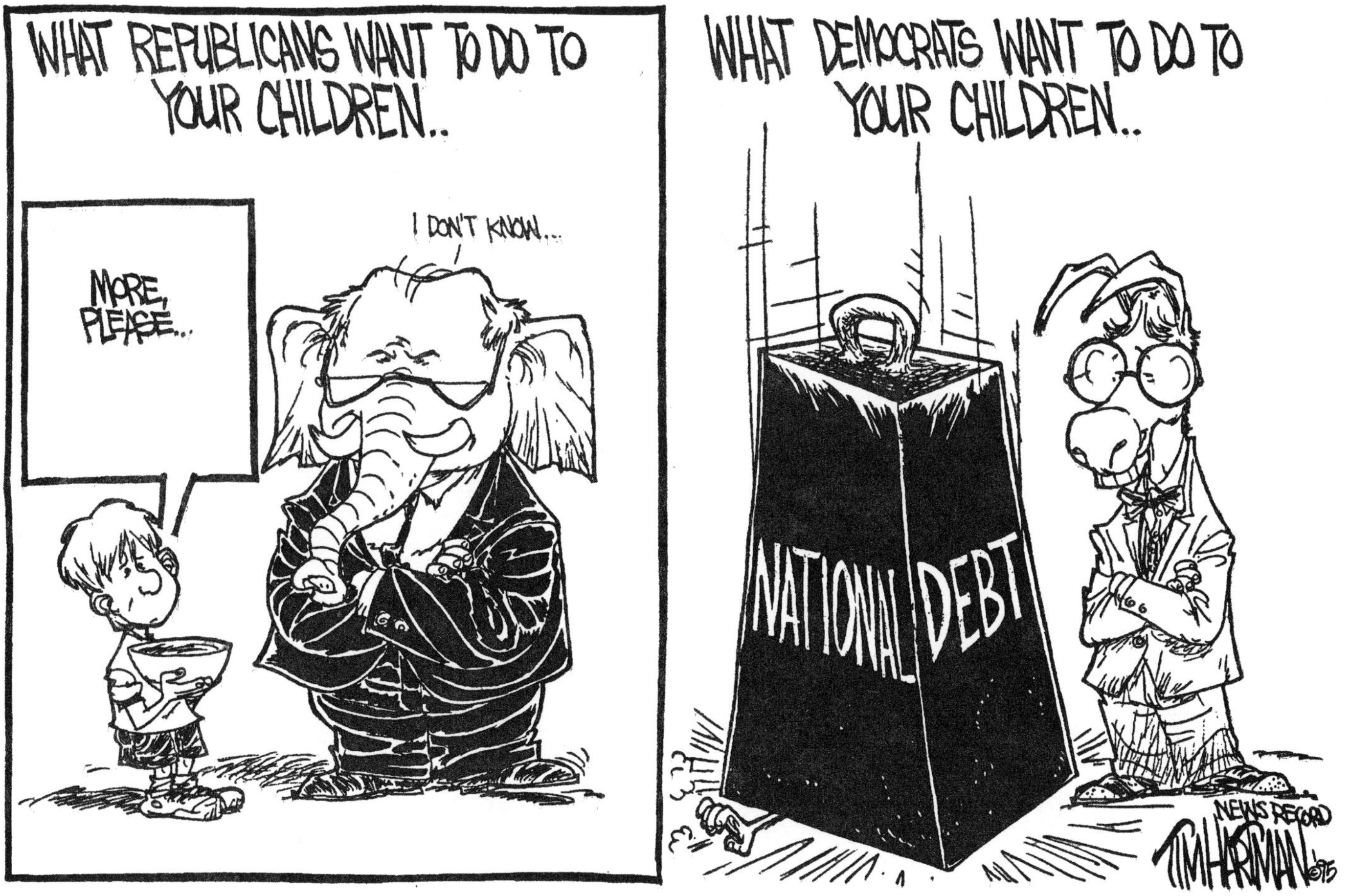
WHAT REPUBLICANS WANT TO DO TO YOUR CHILDREN..
MORE, PLEASE...
I DON'T KNOW...
WHAT DEMOCRATS WANT TO DO TO YOUR CHILDREN..
NATIONAL DEBT
NEWS RECORD
TIM HARTMAN ©95

TIM HARTMAN
Courtesy North Hills News Record (Pa.)

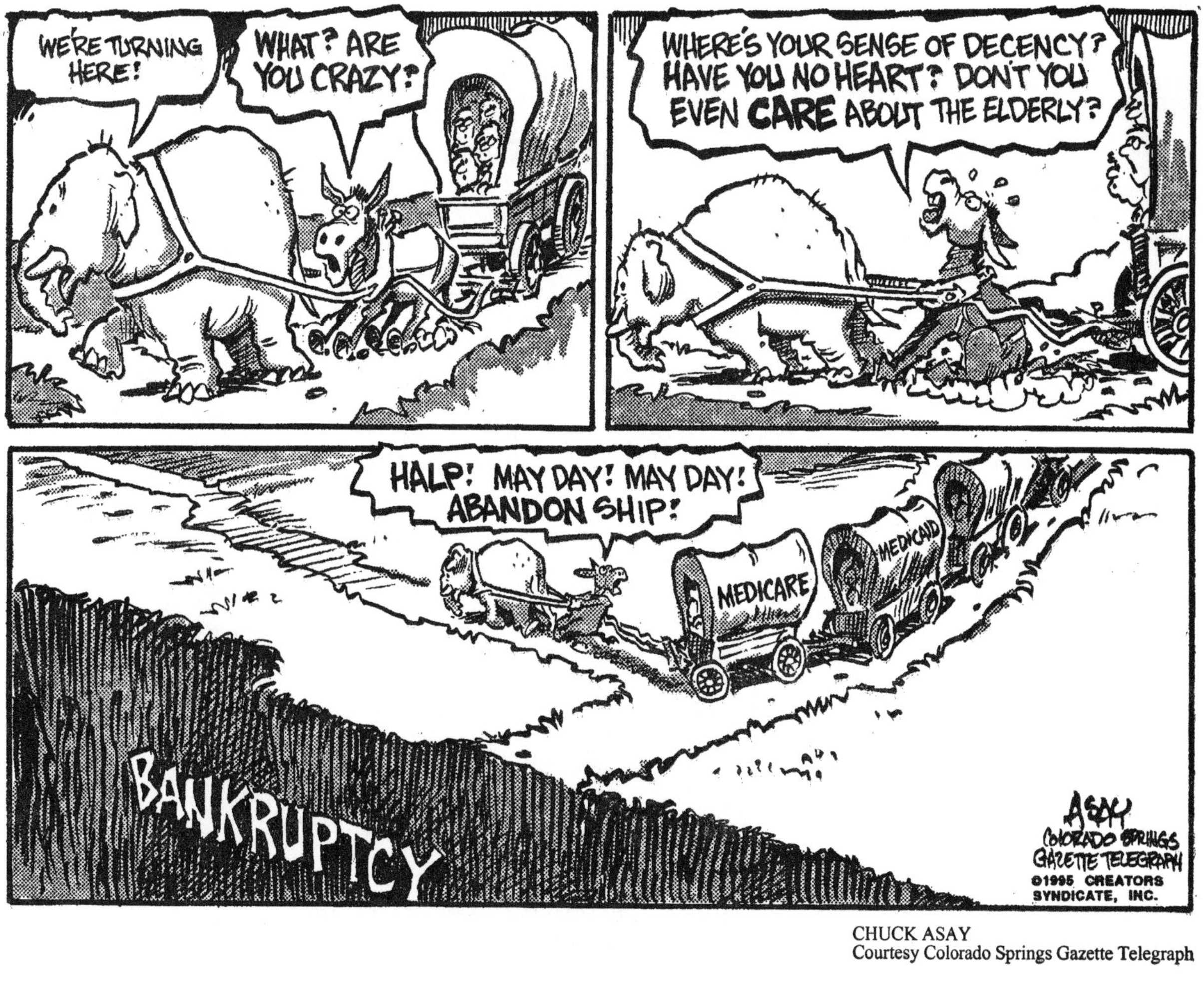
WE'RE TURNING HERE!
WHAT? ARE YOU CRAZY?
WHERE'S YOUR SENSE OF DECENCY? HAVE YOU NO HEART? DON'T YOU EVEN CARE ABOUT THE ELDERLY?
HALP! MAY DAY! MAY DAY! ABANDON SHIP!
MEDICARE
MEDICAID
BANKRUPTCY
ASAY
COLORADO SPRINGS GAZETTE TELEGRAPH
©1995 CREATORS SYNDICATE, INC.

CHUCK ASAY
Courtesy Colorado Springs Gazette Telegraph

JERRY BUCKLEY
Courtesy Express Newspapers

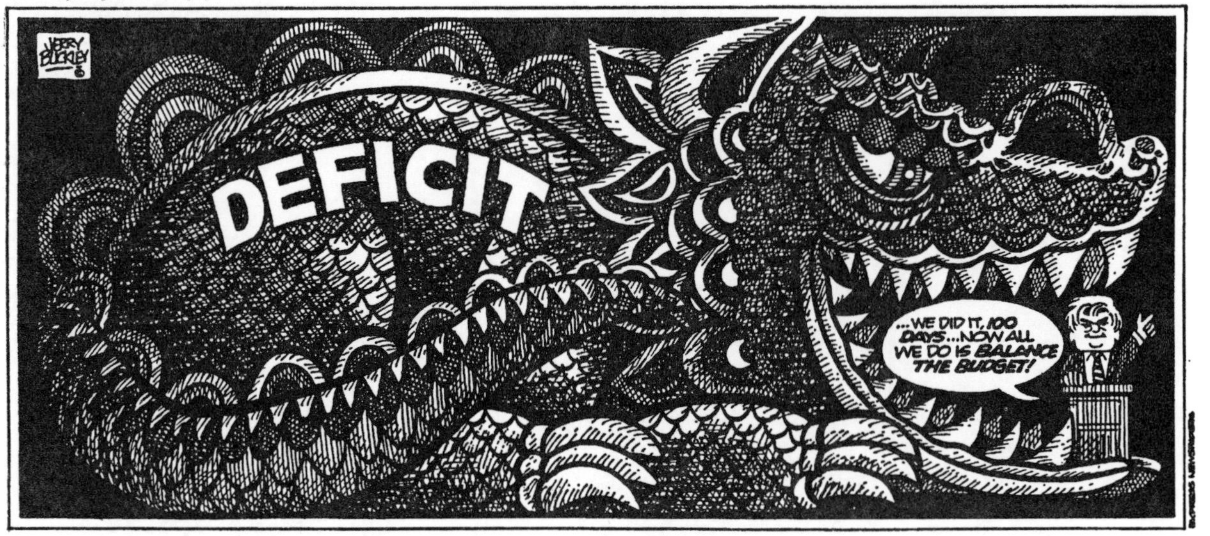
DEFICIT
...WE DID IT, 100 DAYS...NOW ALL WE DO IS BALANCE THE BUDGET!

JIM BORGMAN
Courtesy Cincinnati Enquirer

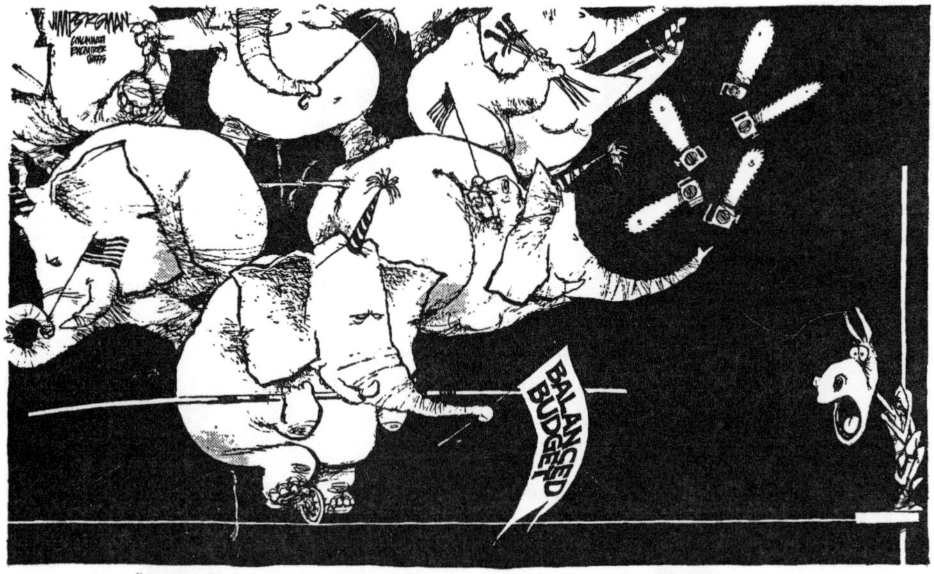
BALANCED BUDGET

"HAVE YOU EVER ONCE CONSIDERED WHAT THIS IS DOING TO MY SELF-ESTEEM?"

PAUL DUGINSKI
Courtesy Fresno Bee

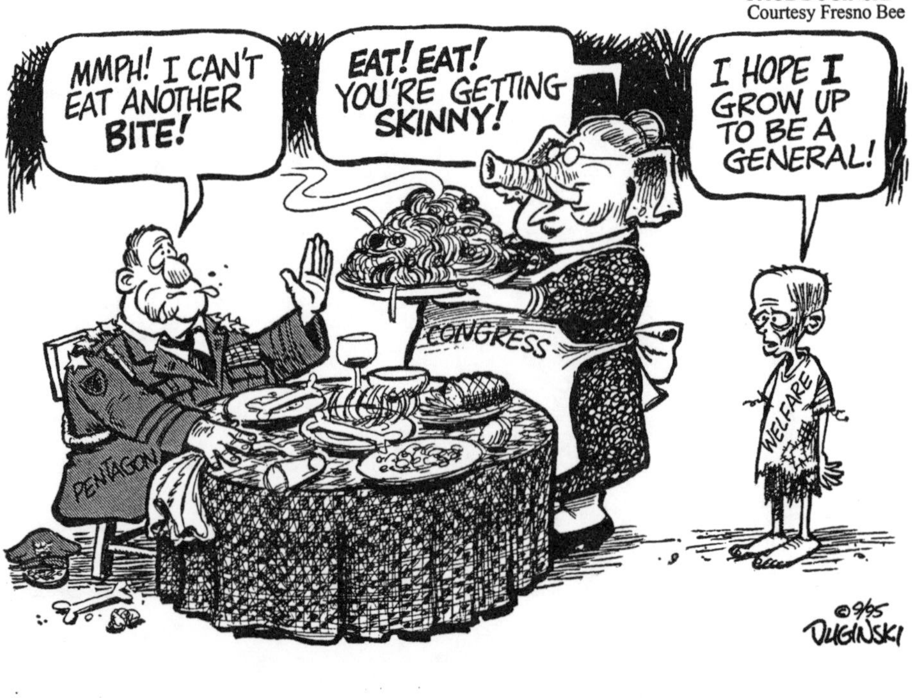
MMPH! I CAN'T EAT ANOTHER BITE!
EAT! EAT! YOU'RE GETTING SKINNY!
I HOPE I GROW UP TO BE A GENERAL!
CONGRESS
PENTAGON
WELFARE

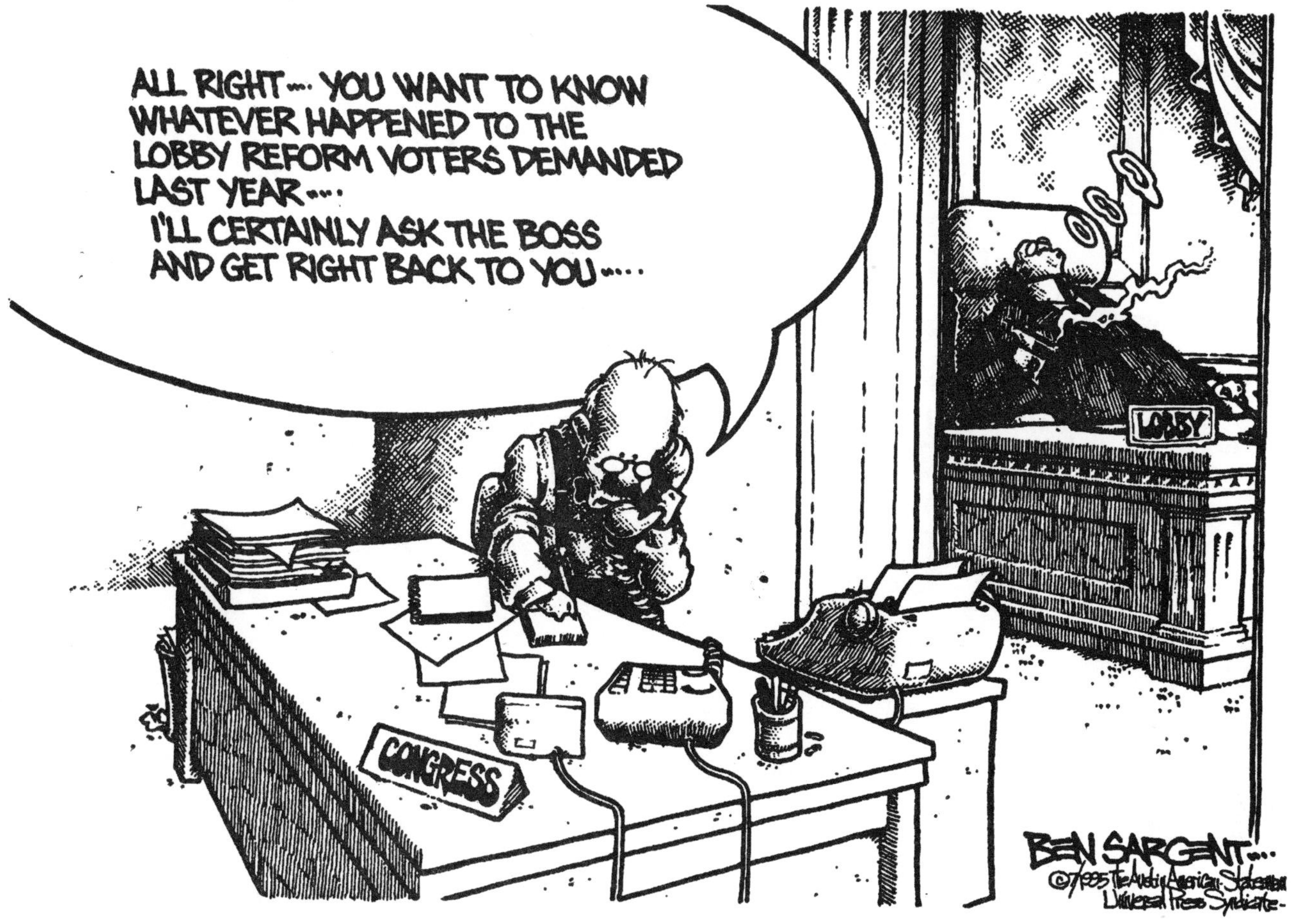
ALL RIGHT.... YOU WANT TO KNOW WHATEVER HAPPENED TO THE LOBBY REFORM VOTERS DEMANDED LAST YEAR.... I'LL CERTAINLY ASK THE BOSS AND GET RIGHT BACK TO YOU.....
LOBBY
CONGRESS
BEN SARGENT...

BEN SARGENT
Courtesy Austin American-Statesman

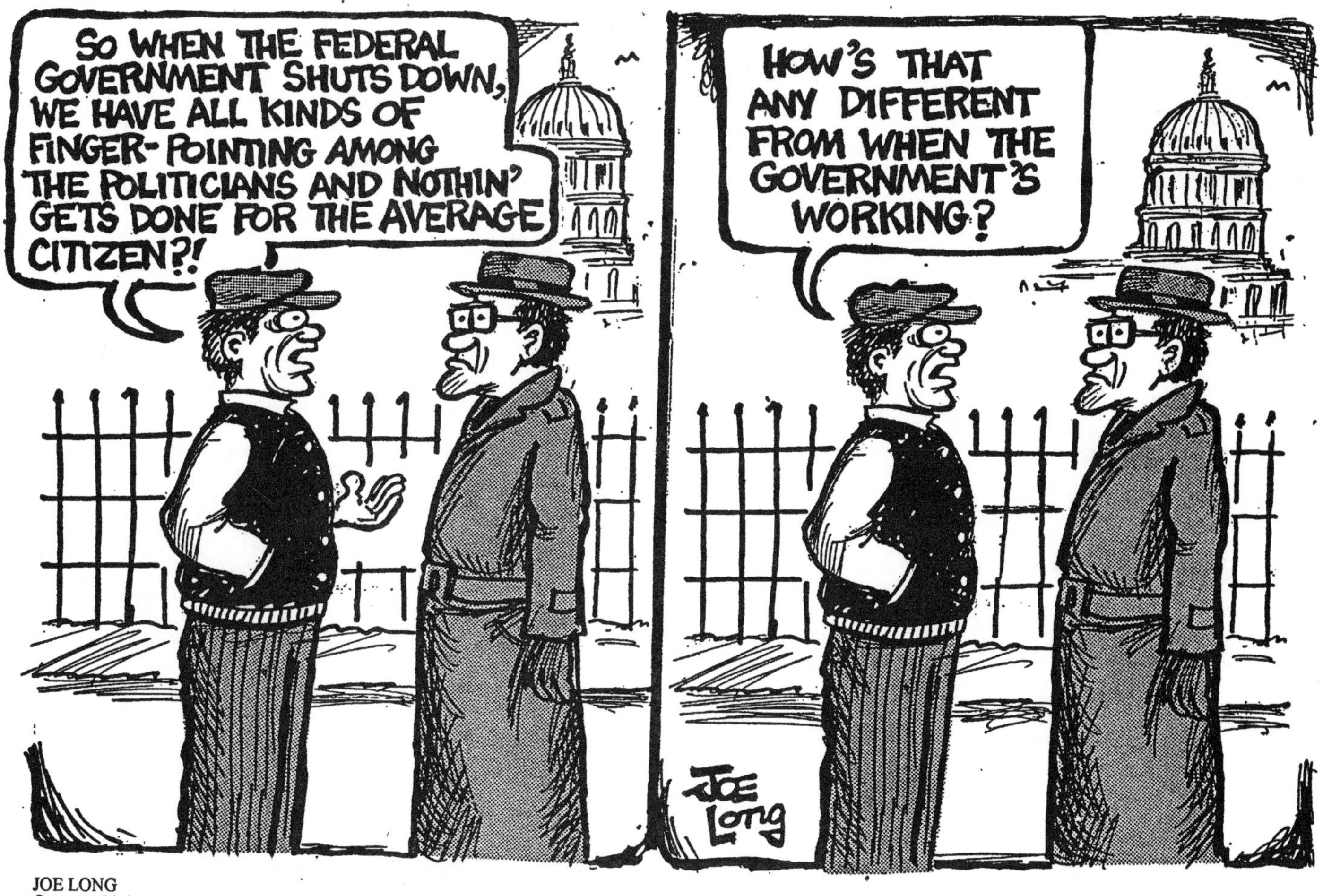
SO WHEN THE FEDERAL GOVERNMENT SHUTS DOWN, WE HAVE ALL KINDS OF FINGER-POINTING AMONG THE POLITICIANS AND NOTHIN' GETS DONE FOR THE AVERAGE CITIZEN?!
HOW'S THAT ANY DIFFERENT FROM WHEN THE GOVERNMENT'S WORKING?
JOE Long

JOE LONG
Courtesy Little Falls Evening Times (N.Y.)

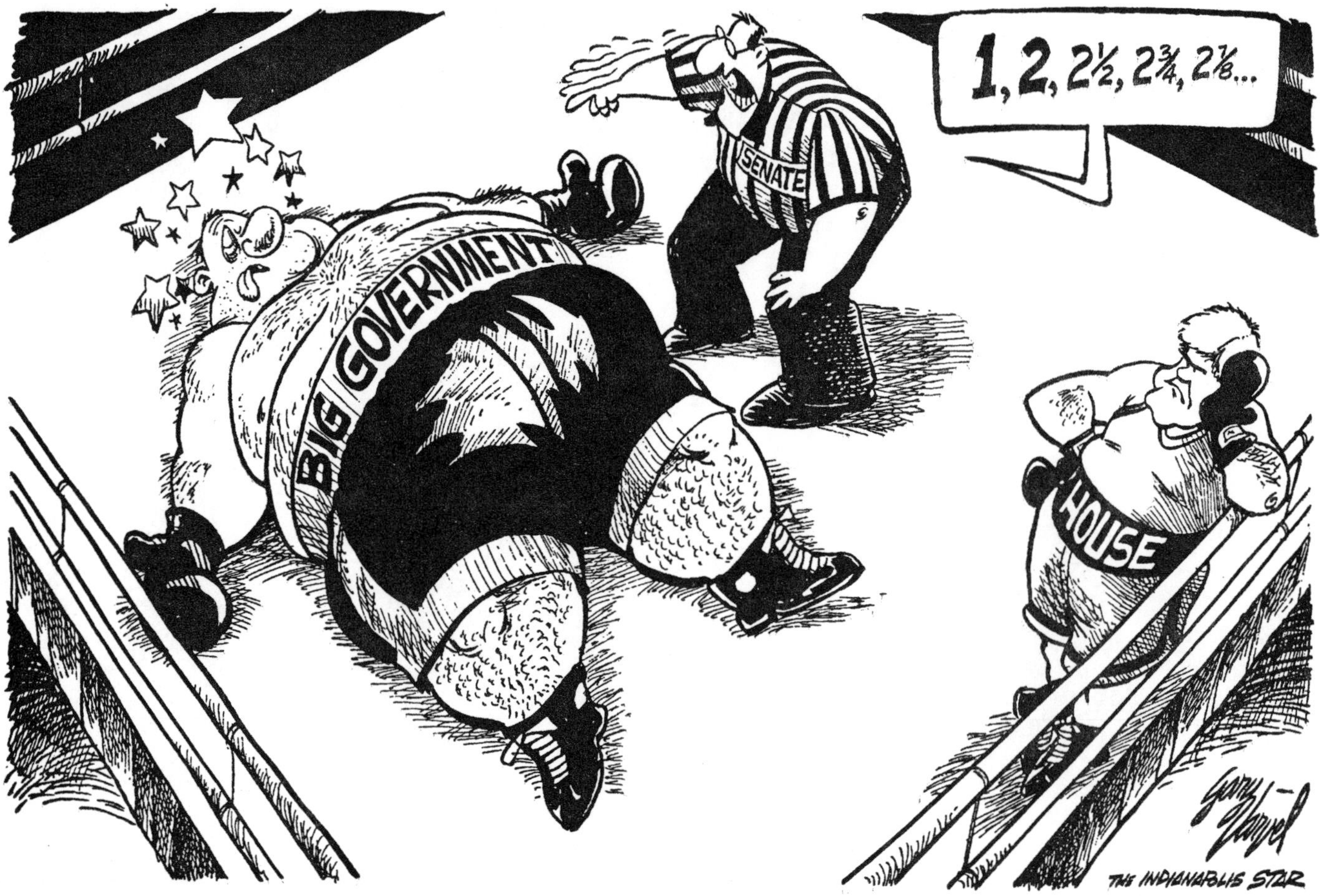
1, 2, 2½, 2¾, 2⅞...
SENATE
BIG GOVERNMENT
HOUSE
Gary Varvel
THE INDIANAPOLIS STAR

GARY VARVEL
Courtesy Indianapolis Star

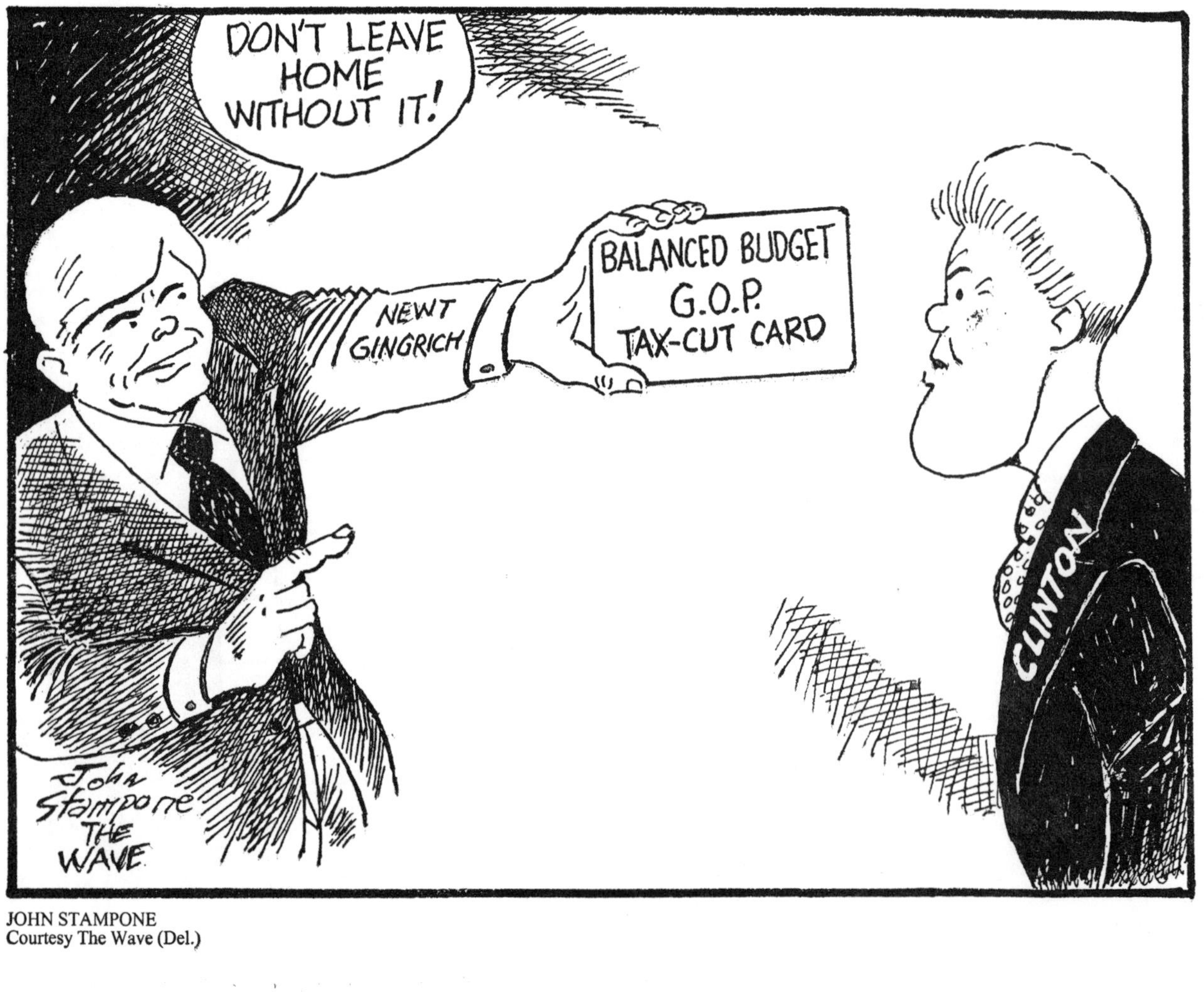
DON'T LEAVE HOME WITHOUT IT!
BALANCED BUDGET
G.O.P.
TAX-CUT CARD
NEWT GINGRICH
CLINTON
John Stampone
THE WAVE

JOHN STAMPONE
Courtesy The Wave (Del.)

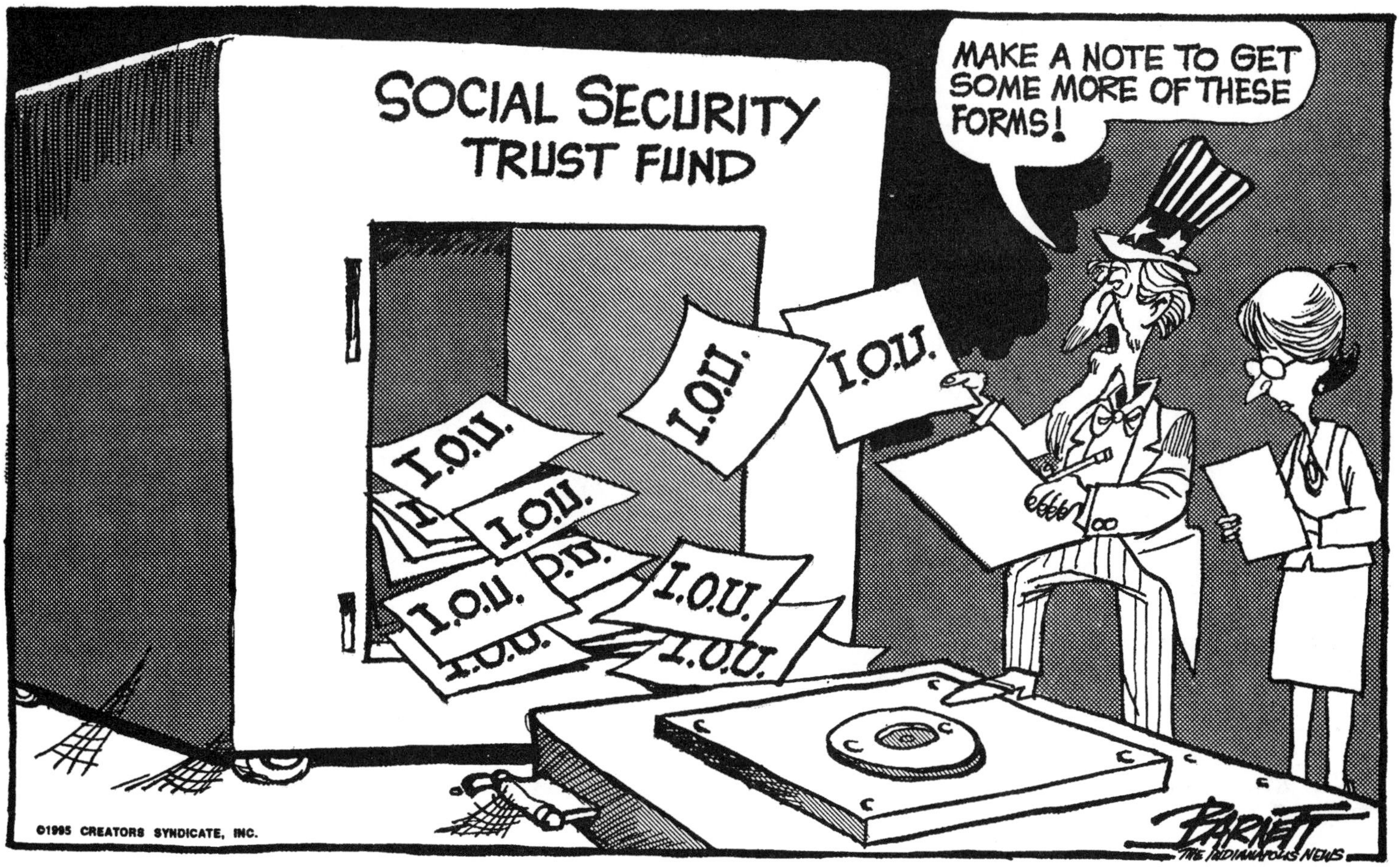
SOCIAL SECURITY
TRUST FUND
MAKE A NOTE TO GET SOME MORE OF THESE FORMS!
I.O.U.
©1995 CREATORS SYNDICATE, INC.
BARNETT
THE INDIANAPOLIS NEWS

JERRY BARNETT
Courtesy Indianapolis News

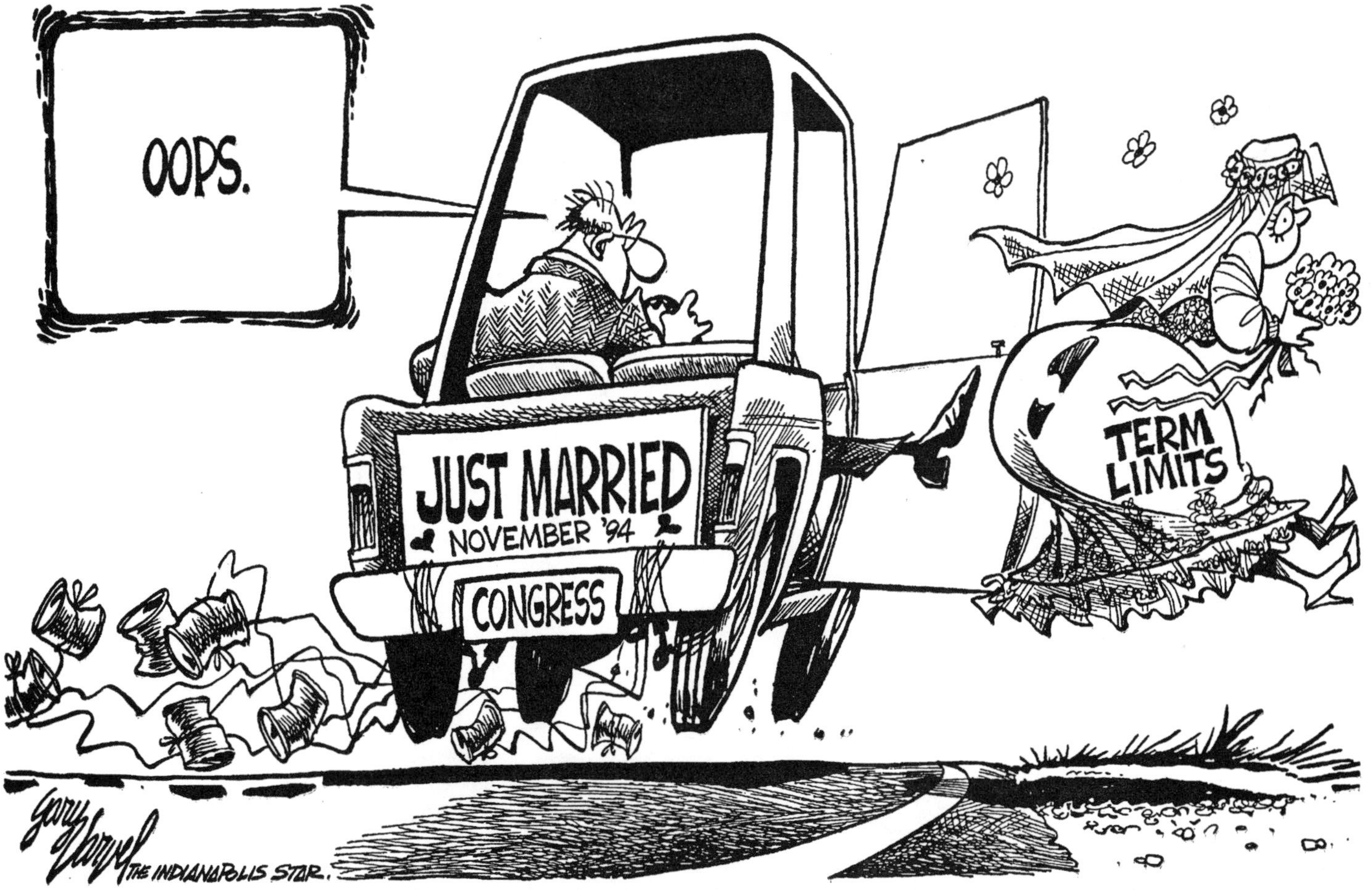
OOPS.
JUST MARRIED
NOVEMBER '94
CONGRESS
TERM LIMITS
Gary Varvel
THE INDIANAPOLIS STAR

GARY VARVEL
Courtesy Indianapolis Star

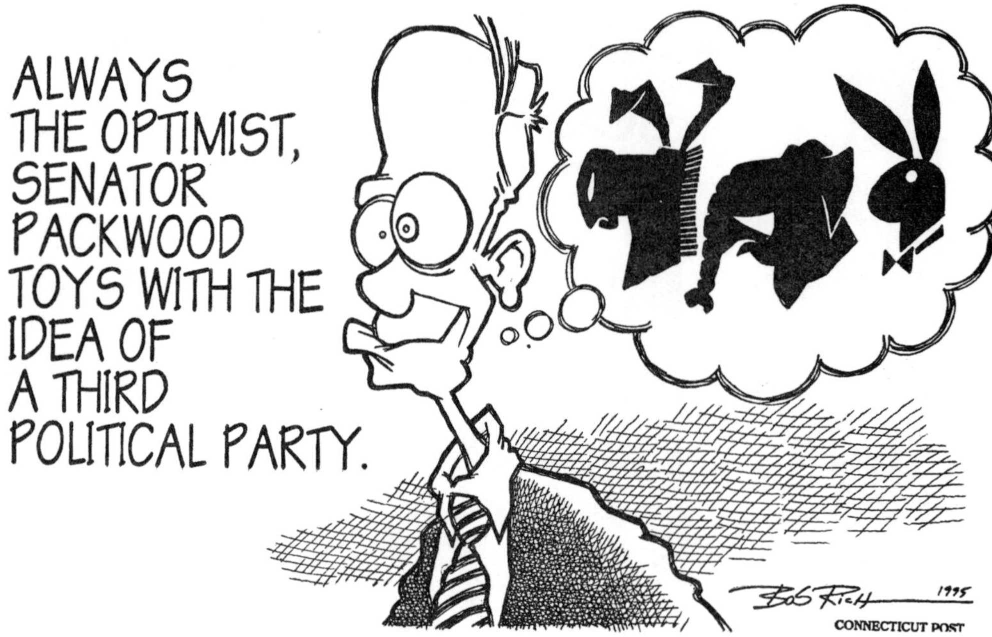
ALWAYS THE OPTIMIST, SENATOR PACKWOOD TOYS WITH THE IDEA OF A THIRD POLITICAL PARTY.
BOB RICH 1995
CONNECTICUT POST

BOB RICH
Courtesy Connecticut Post

ED STEIN
Courtesy Rocky Mountain News and NEA

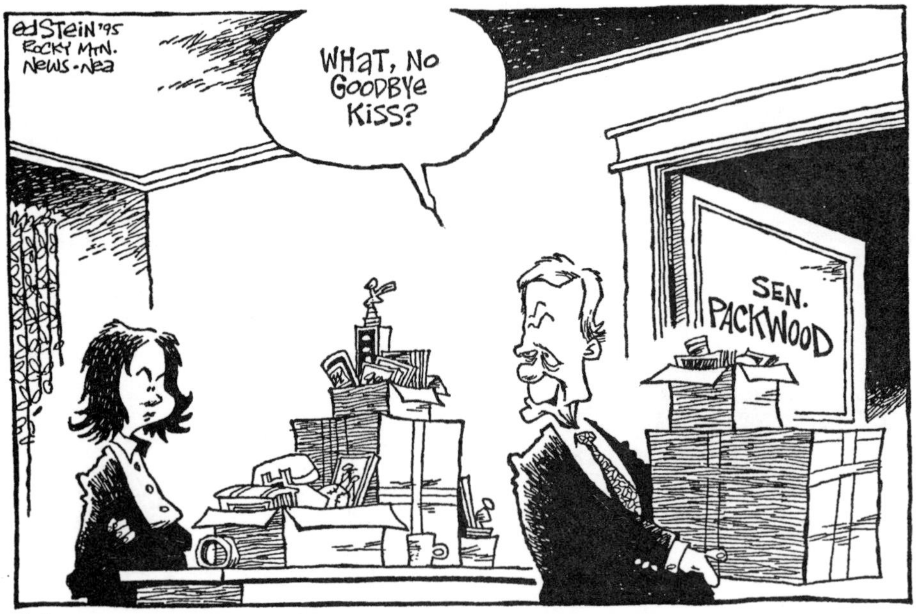
edSTEIN '95 ROCKY MTN. NEWS-NEA
WHAT, NO GOODBYE KISS?
SEN. PACKWOOD

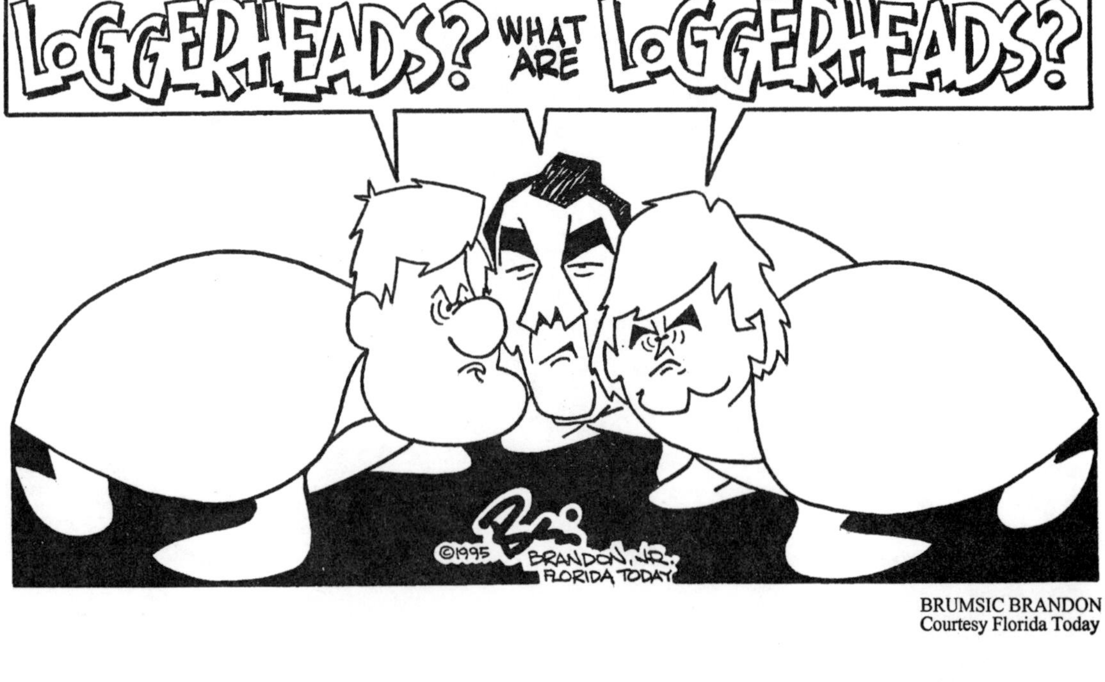
LOGGERHEADS? WHAT ARE LOGGERHEADS?
©1995 BRANDON, JR. FLORIDA TODAY

BRUMSIC BRANDON
Courtesy Florida Today

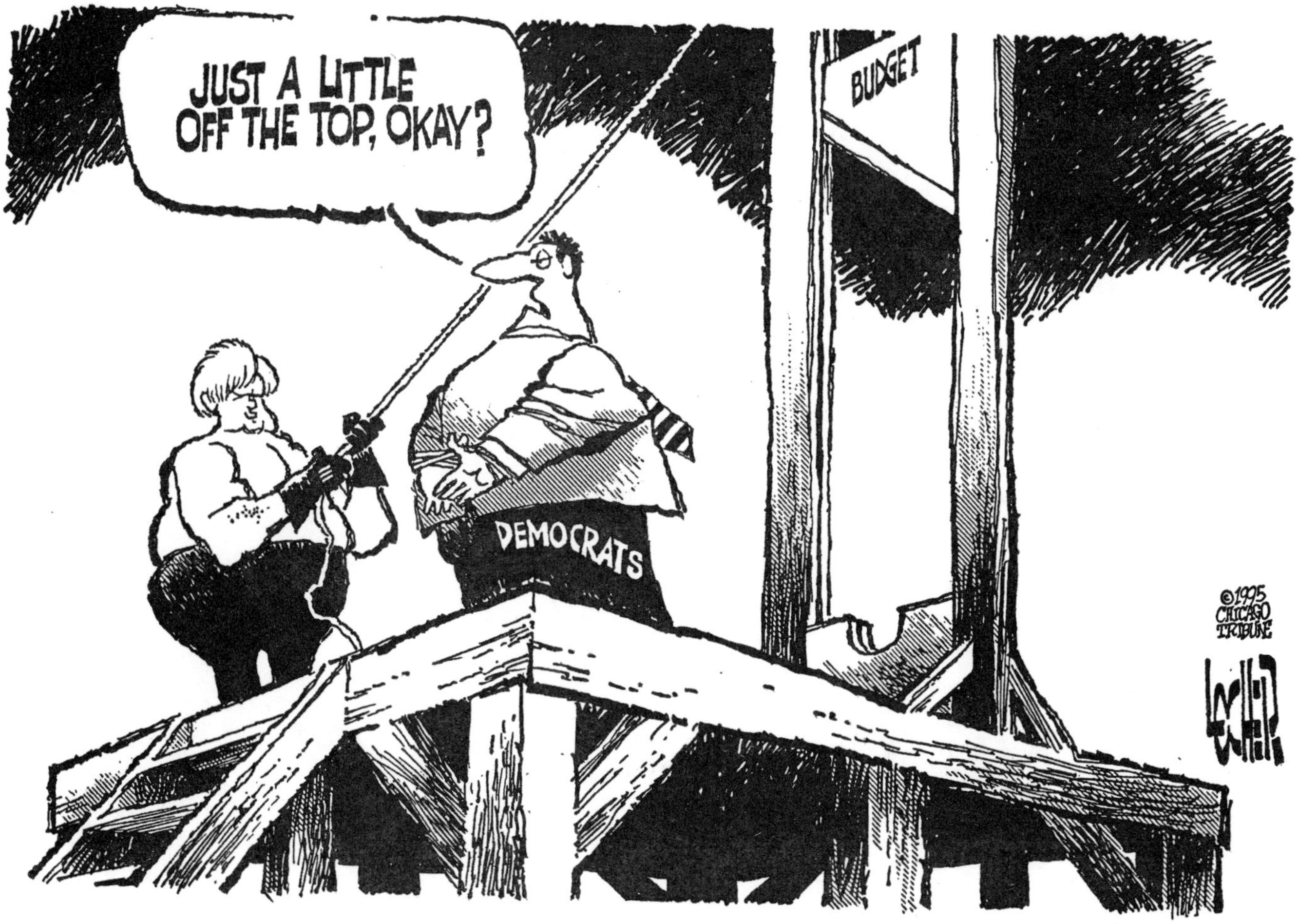
JUST A LITTLE OFF THE TOP, OKAY?
BUDGET
DEMOCRATS
©1995 CHICAGO TRIBUNE
LOCHER

DICK LOCHER
Courtesy Chicago Tribune

MIKE PETERS
Courtesy Dayton Daily News

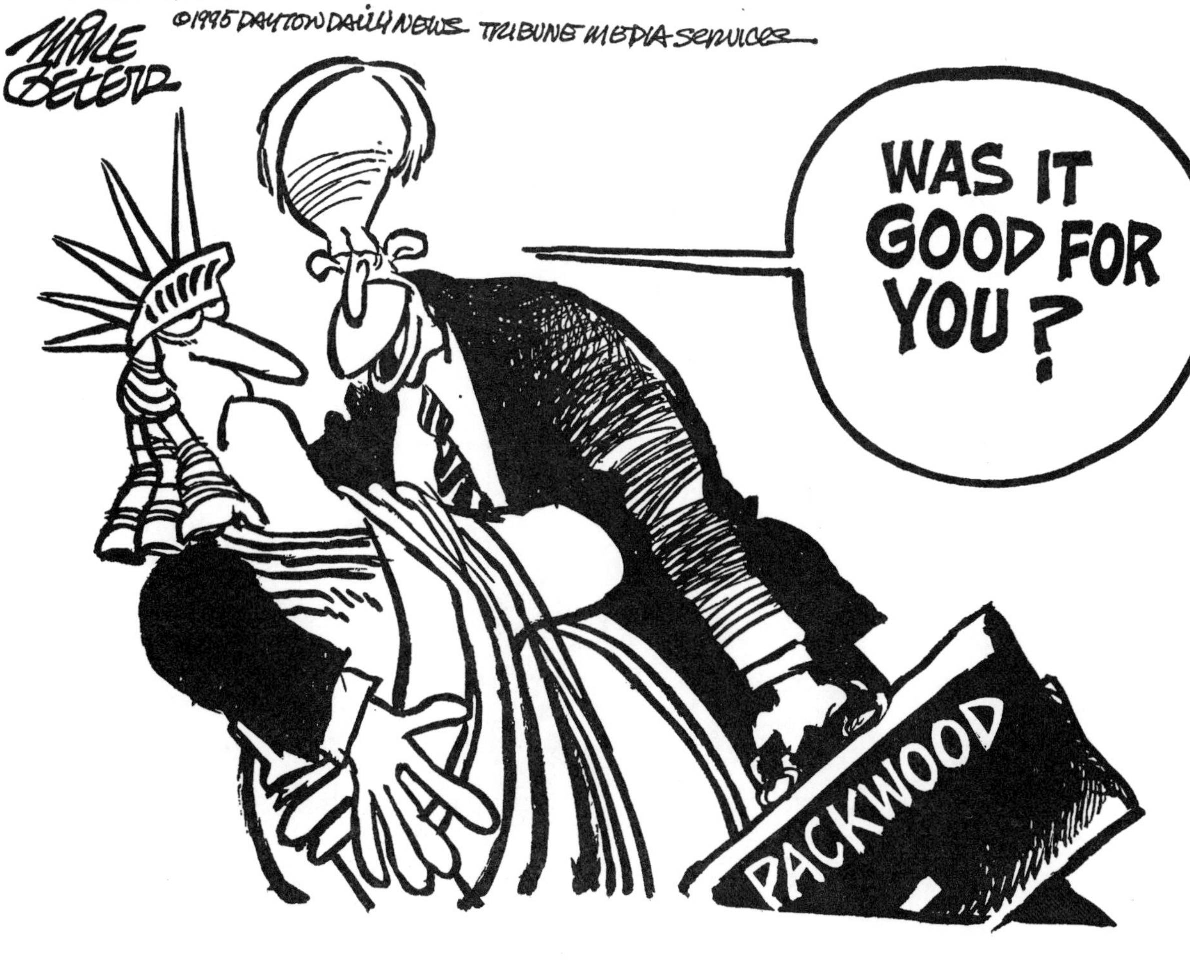
©1995 DAYTON DAILY NEWS TRIBUNE MEDIA SERVICES
MIKE PETERS
WAS IT GOOD FOR YOU?
PACKWOOD

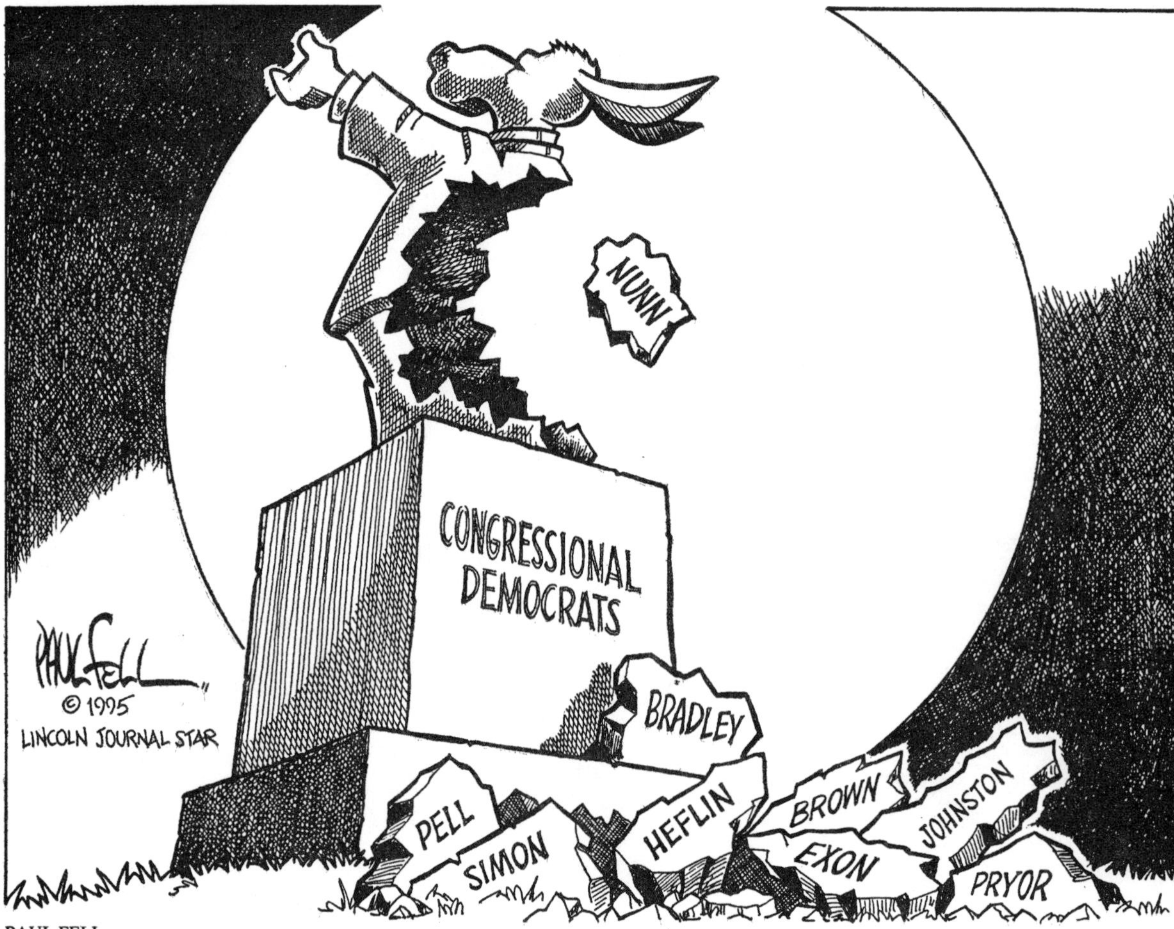
NUNN
CONGRESSIONAL DEMOCRATS
PAUL FELL
© 1995
LINCOLN JOURNAL STAR
BRADLEY
PELL
SIMON
HEFLIN
BROWN
EXON
JOHNSTON
PRYOR

PAUL FELL
Courtesy Lincoln Journal

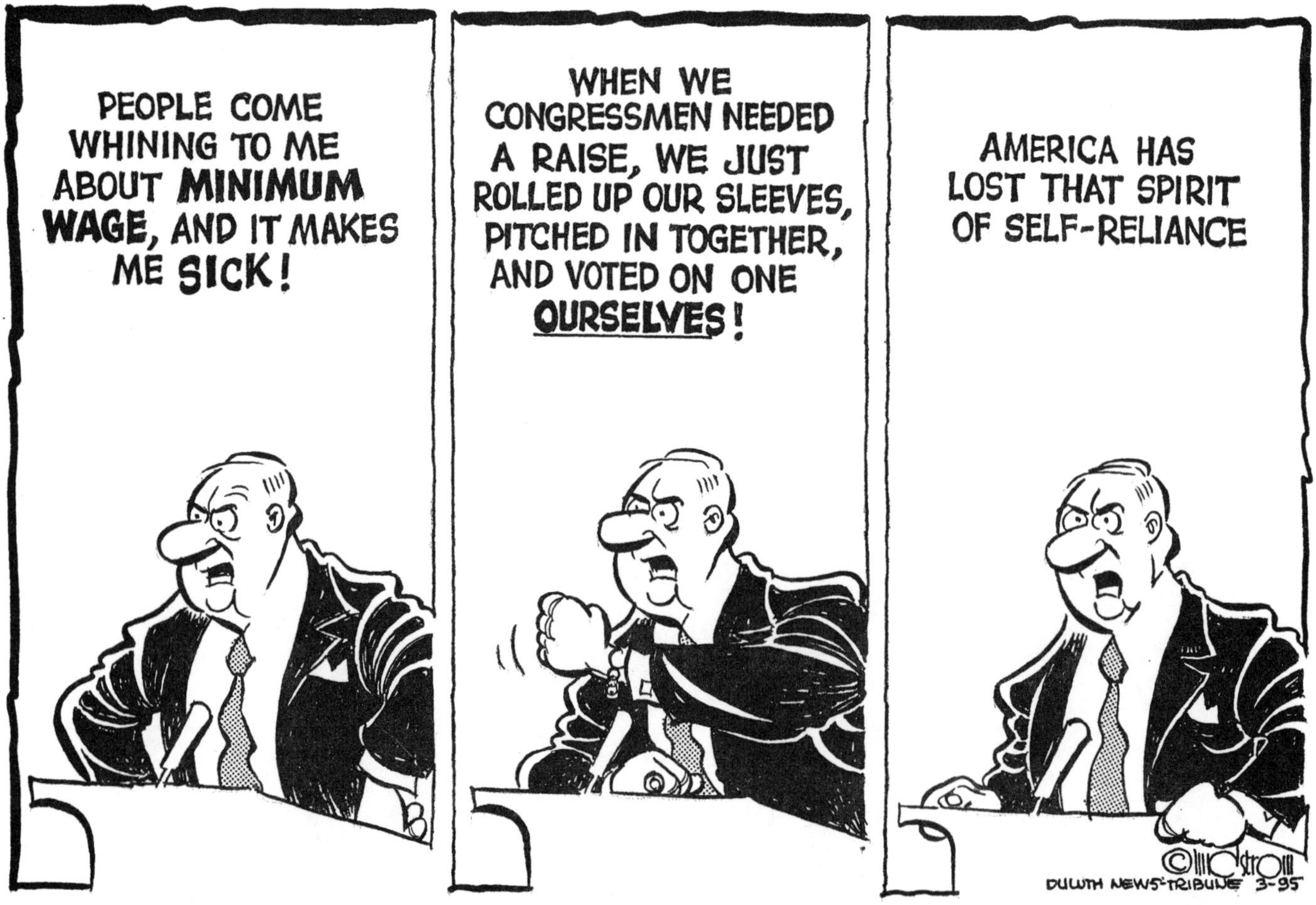
PEOPLE COME WHINING TO ME ABOUT MINIMUM WAGE, AND IT MAKES ME SICK!
WHEN WE CONGRESSMEN NEEDED A RAISE, WE JUST ROLLED UP OUR SLEEVES, PITCHED IN TOGETHER, AND VOTED ON ONE OURSELVES!
AMERICA HAS LOST THAT SPIRIT OF SELF-RELIANCE
DULUTH NEWS-TRIBUNE 3-95

STEVE LINDSTROM
Courtesy Duluth News-Tribune

LAZARO FRESQUET
Courtesy El Nuevo Herald (Miami)

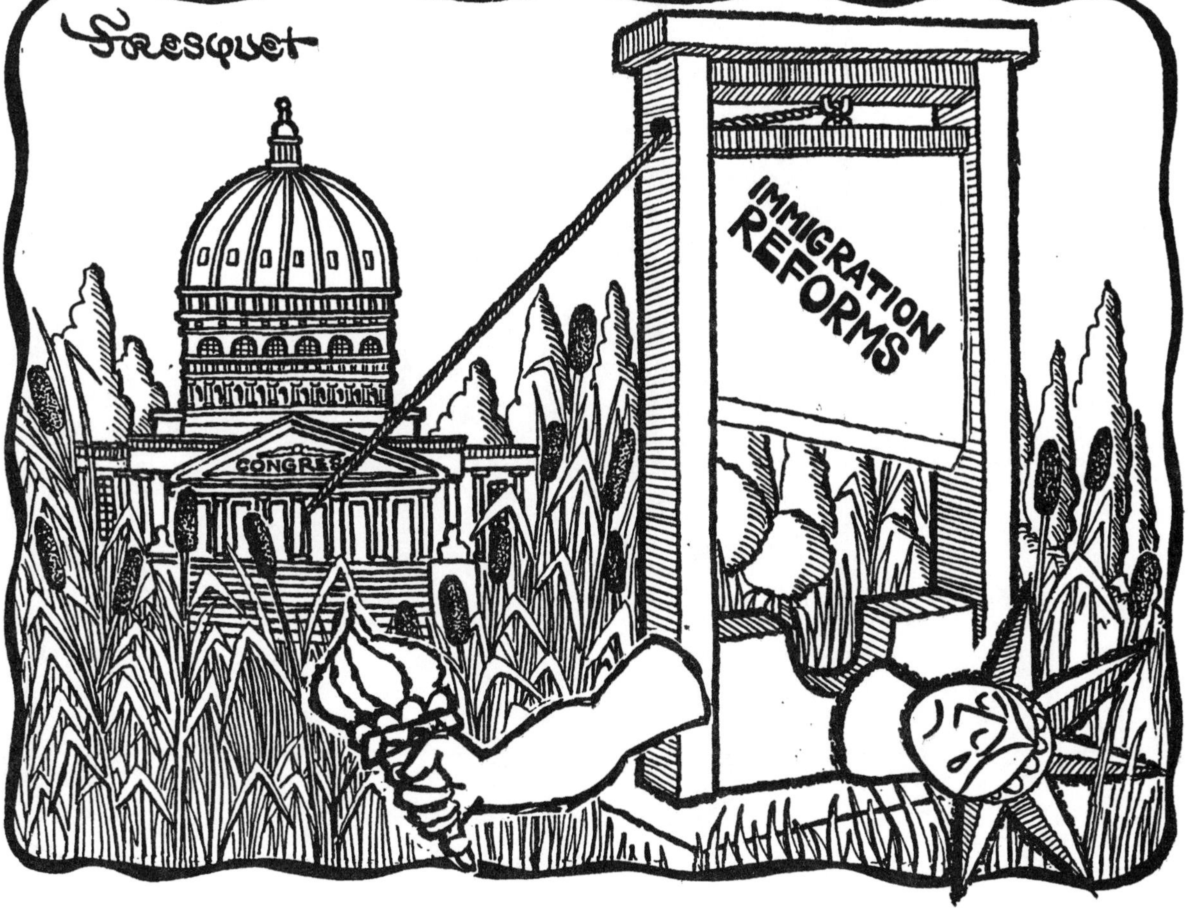
FRESQUET
CONGRESS
IMMIGRATION REFORMS

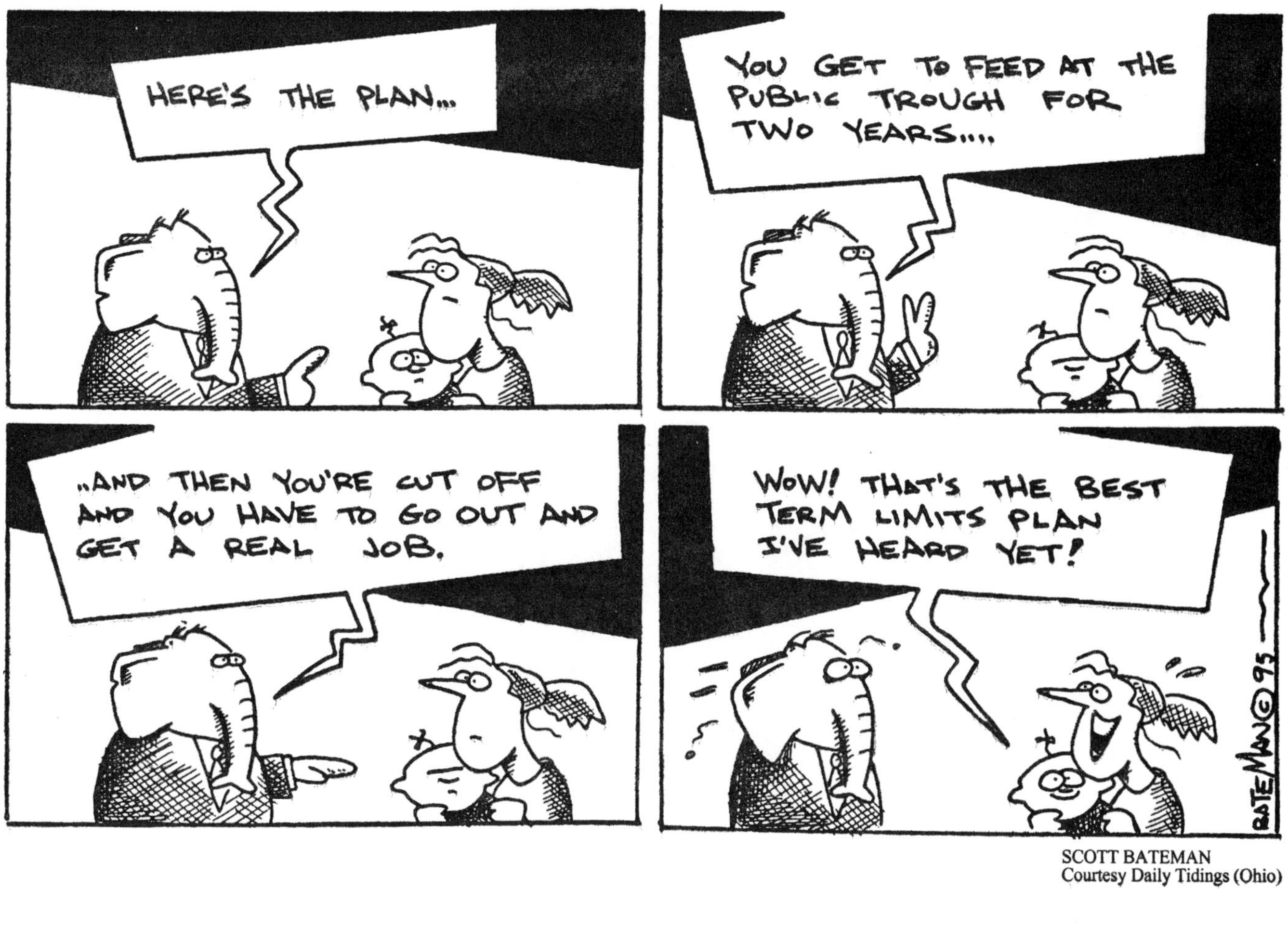
HERE'S THE PLAN...
YOU GET TO FEED AT THE PUBLIC TROUGH FOR TWO YEARS....
..AND THEN YOU'RE CUT OFF AND YOU HAVE TO GO OUT AND GET A REAL JOB.
WOW! THAT'S THE BEST TERM LIMITS PLAN I'VE HEARD YET!
BATEMAN © 95

SCOTT BATEMAN
Courtesy Daily Tidings (Ohio)

PAUL SZEP
Courtesy Boston Globe

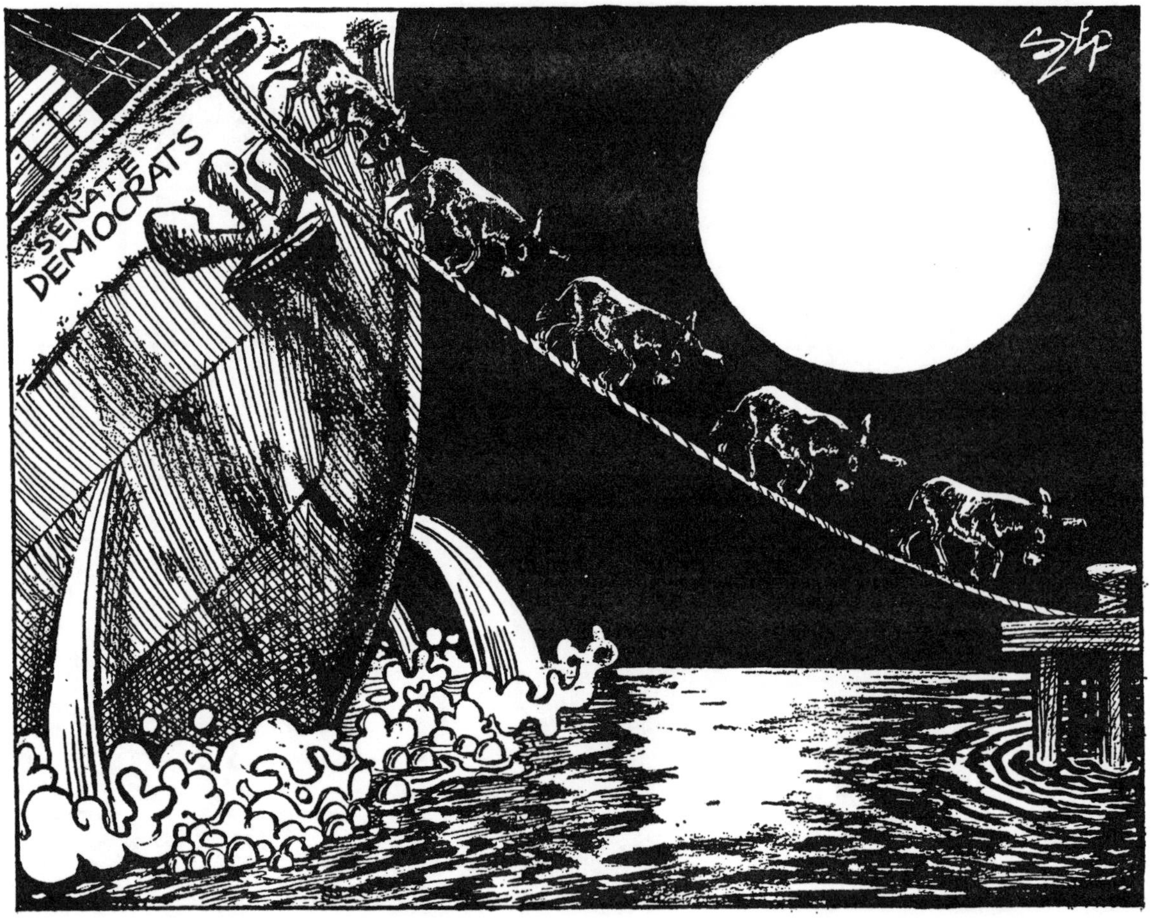
SZEP
SENATE DEMOCRATS

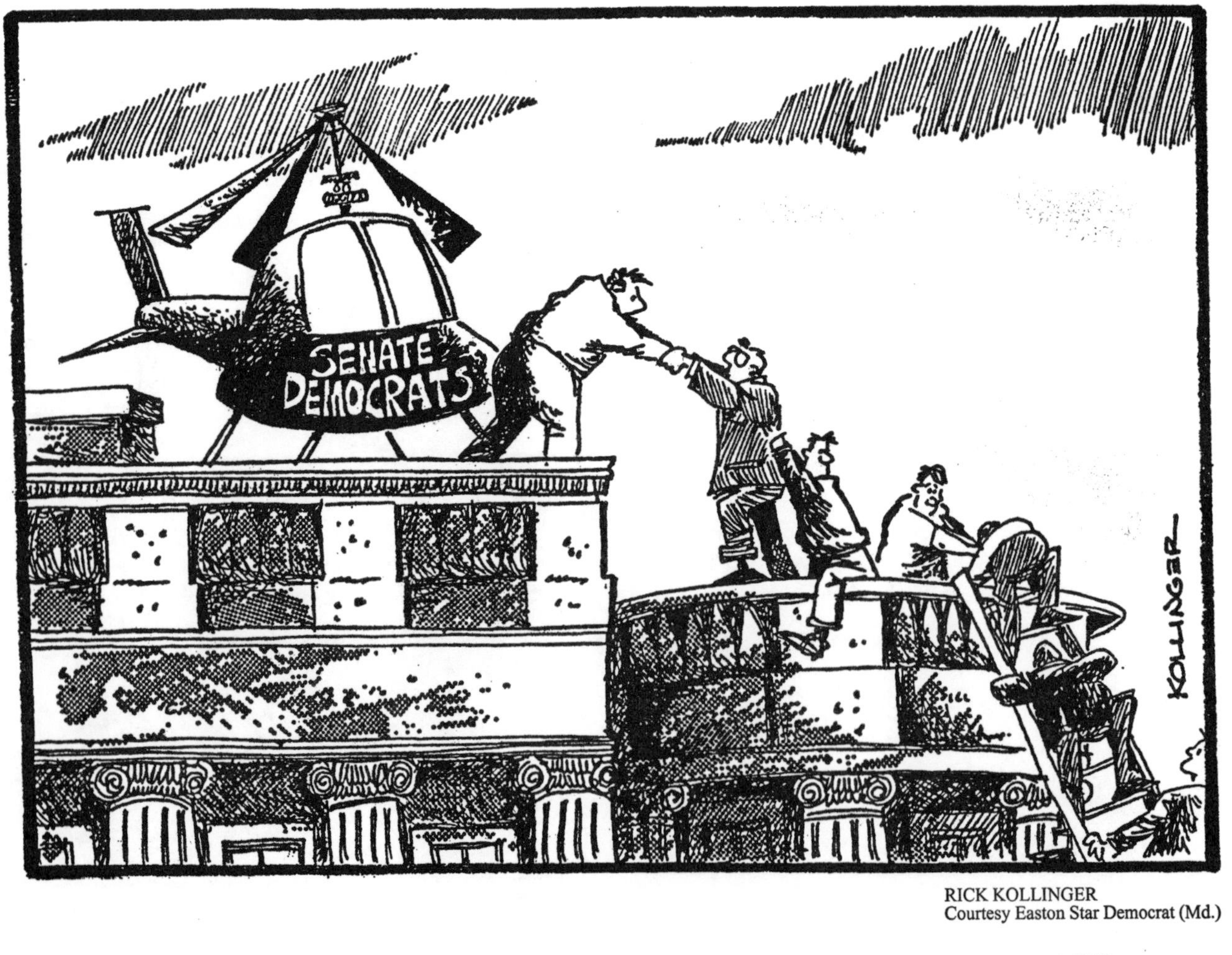
SENATE DEMOCRATS
KOLLINGER

RICK KOLLINGER
Courtesy Easton Star Democrat (Md.)

Foreign Affairs

President Clinton announced early in the year that the U.S. would guarantee $40 billion of Mexico's debt to avert a global financial crisis. The move did stave off financial disaster, but the Mexican economy continues to be plagued by bad loans and political uncertainty.

In British elections, the ruling Conservative party was handed its worst thrashing of this century, winning only 8 of 323 contested councils. The royal family found itself in the news again. Prince Charles confessed to adultery with Camilla Parker Bowles while both were married. And his wife, Princess Di, admitted in a television interview to an adulterous affair of her own. Queen Elizabeth urged that they get a divorce.

Activist Harry Wu, an American citizen, was arrested while videotaping human rights abuses in China's prison system. He was sentenced to fifteen years in jail and then expelled from the country. Chinese officialdom expressed outrage when the Clinton administration approved an official visit from the president of Taiwan.

Clinton also opened normal relations with Vietnam, Pres. Jacques Chirac of France decided to resume nuclear testing in the South Pacific, and thousands of women from throughout the world convened in China to discuss women's rights and human rights in general.

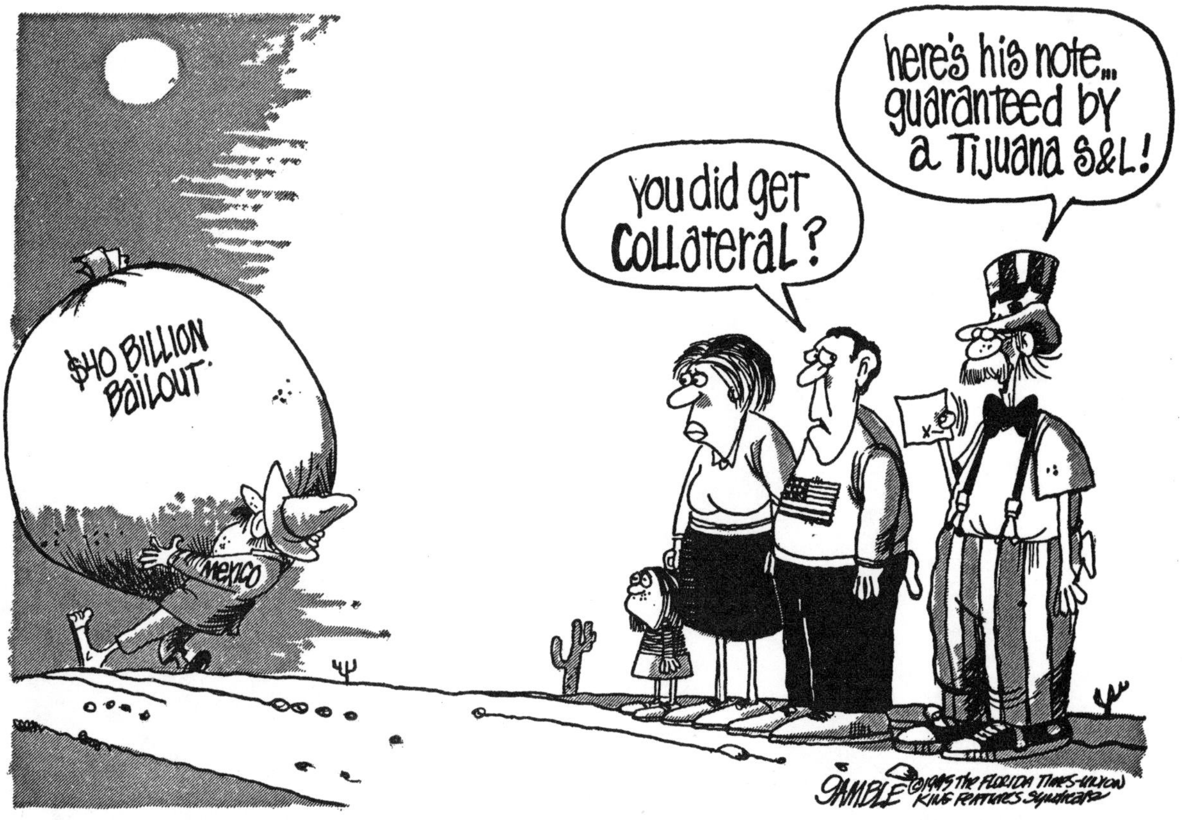

$40 BILLION BAILOUT
MEXICO
You did get collateral?
here's his note... guaranteed by a Tijuana S&L!
GAMBLE ©1995 The Florida Times-Union King Features Syndicate

ED GAMBLE
Courtesy Florida Times-Union

DON LEE
Courtesy Sandusky Register

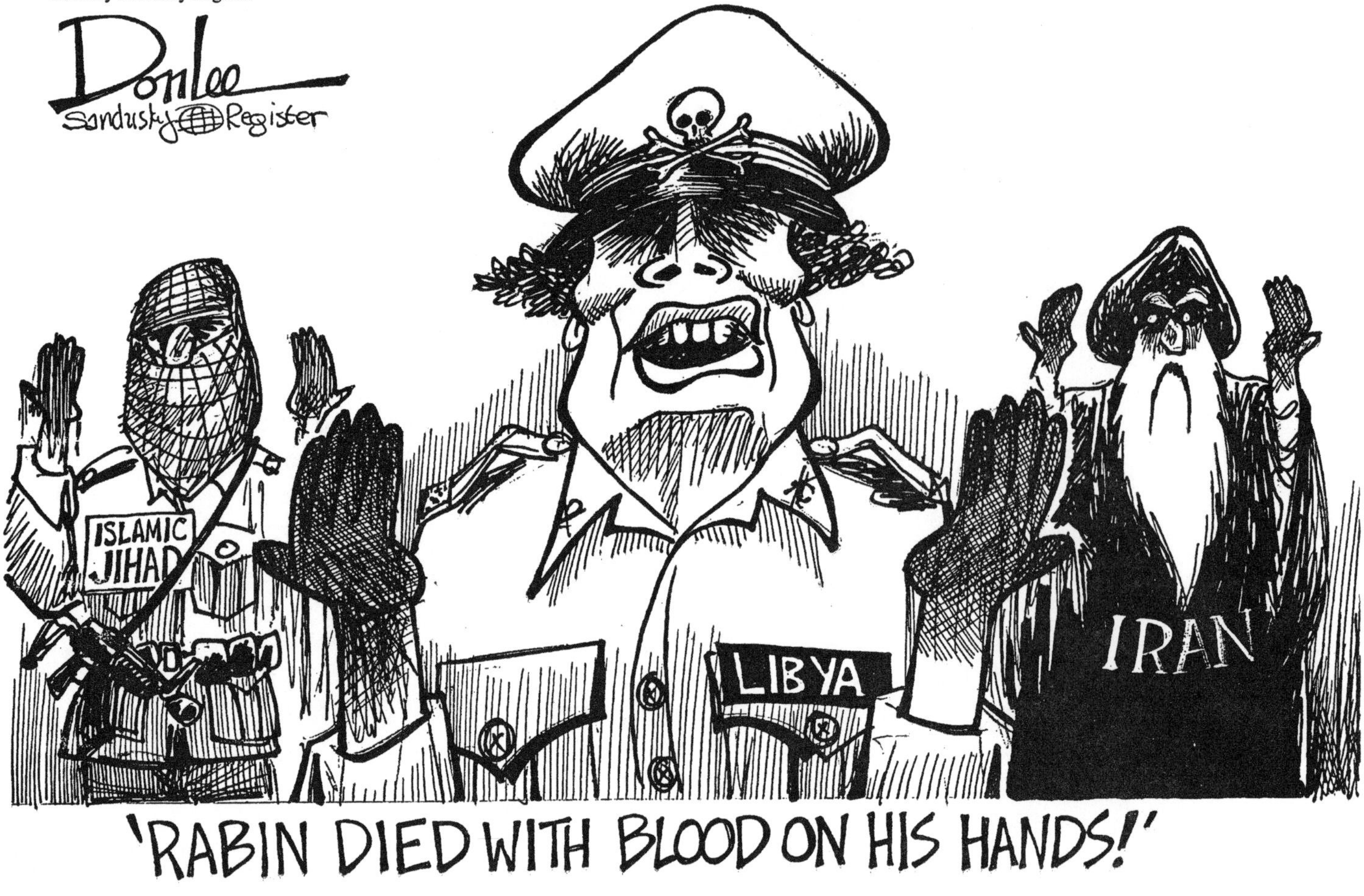
Donlee
Sandusky Register
ISLAMIC JIHAD
LIBYA
IRAN
'RABIN DIED WITH BLOOD ON HIS HANDS!'

JEFF MACNELLY
Courtesy Chicago Tribune and
Tribune Media Services

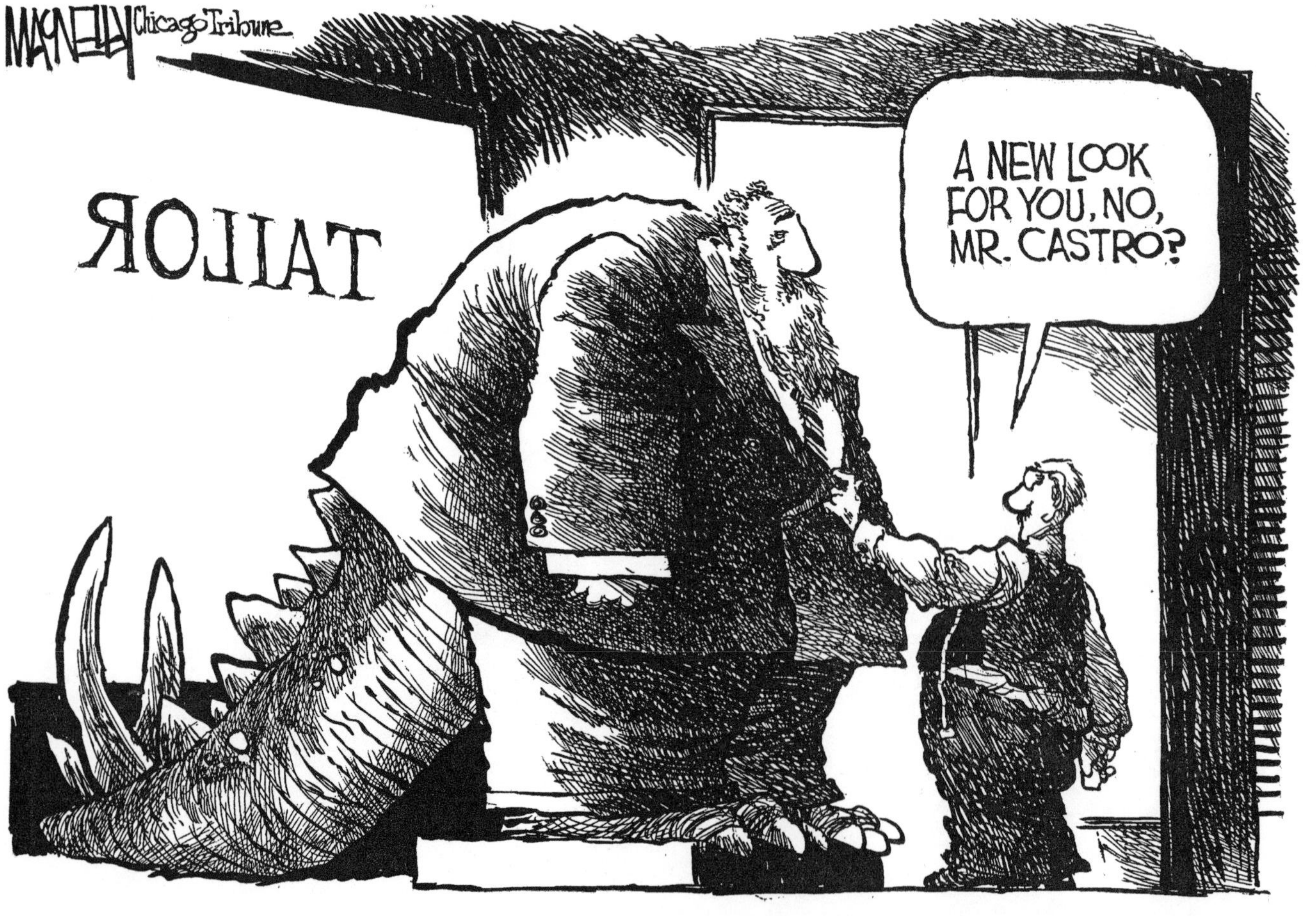
MACNELLY Chicago Tribune
TAILOR
A NEW LOOK FOR YOU, NO, MR. CASTRO?

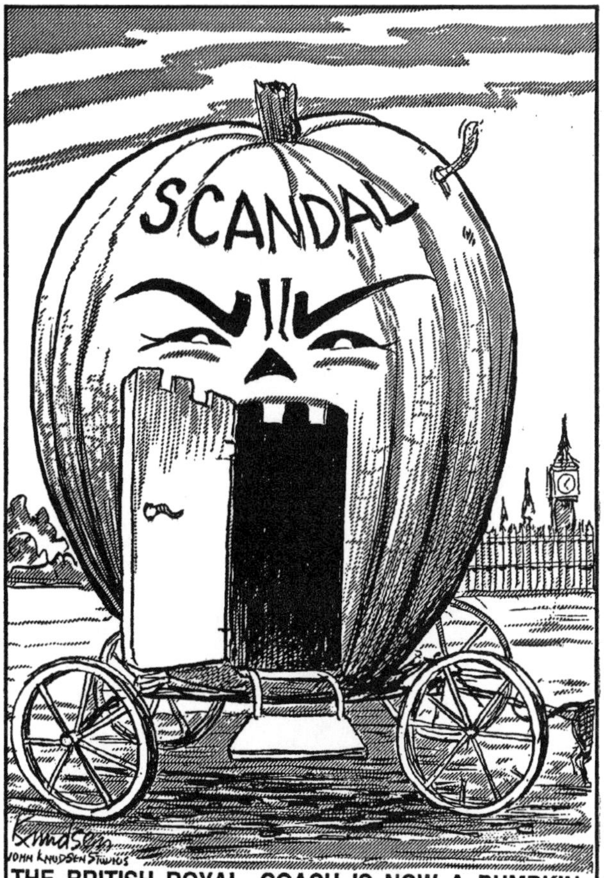
SCANDAL
Knudsen
JOHN KNUDSEN STUDIOS

THE BRITISH ROYAL COACH IS NOW A PUMPKIN

JOHN KNUDSEN
Courtesy The Tidings (Calif.)

FRED CURATOLO
Courtesy Edmonton Sun

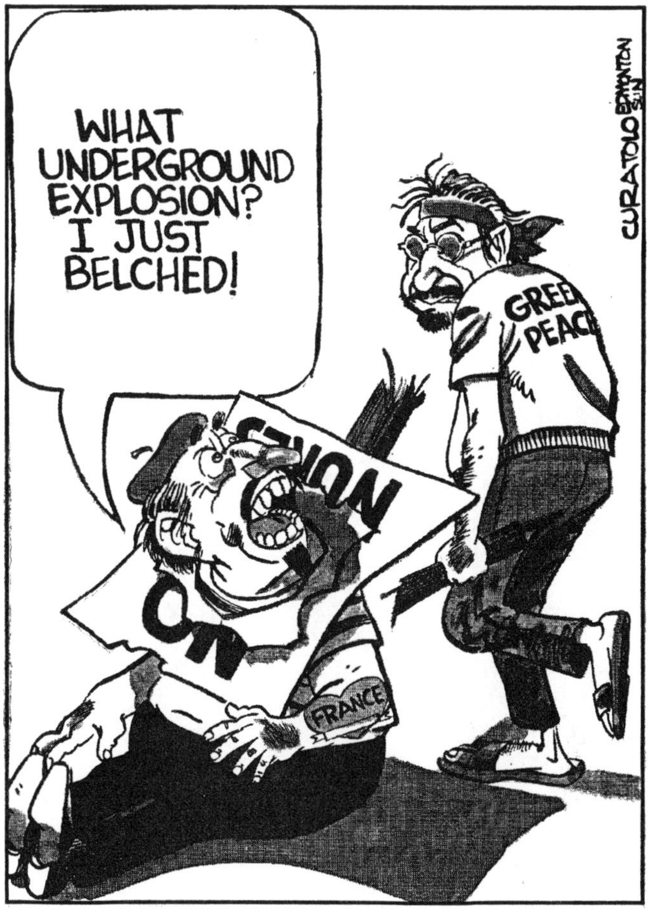
WHAT UNDERGROUND EXPLOSION? I JUST BELCHED!
GREEN PEACE
FRANCE
CURATOLO EDMONTON SUN

MALCOLM MAYES
Courtesy Edmonton Journal

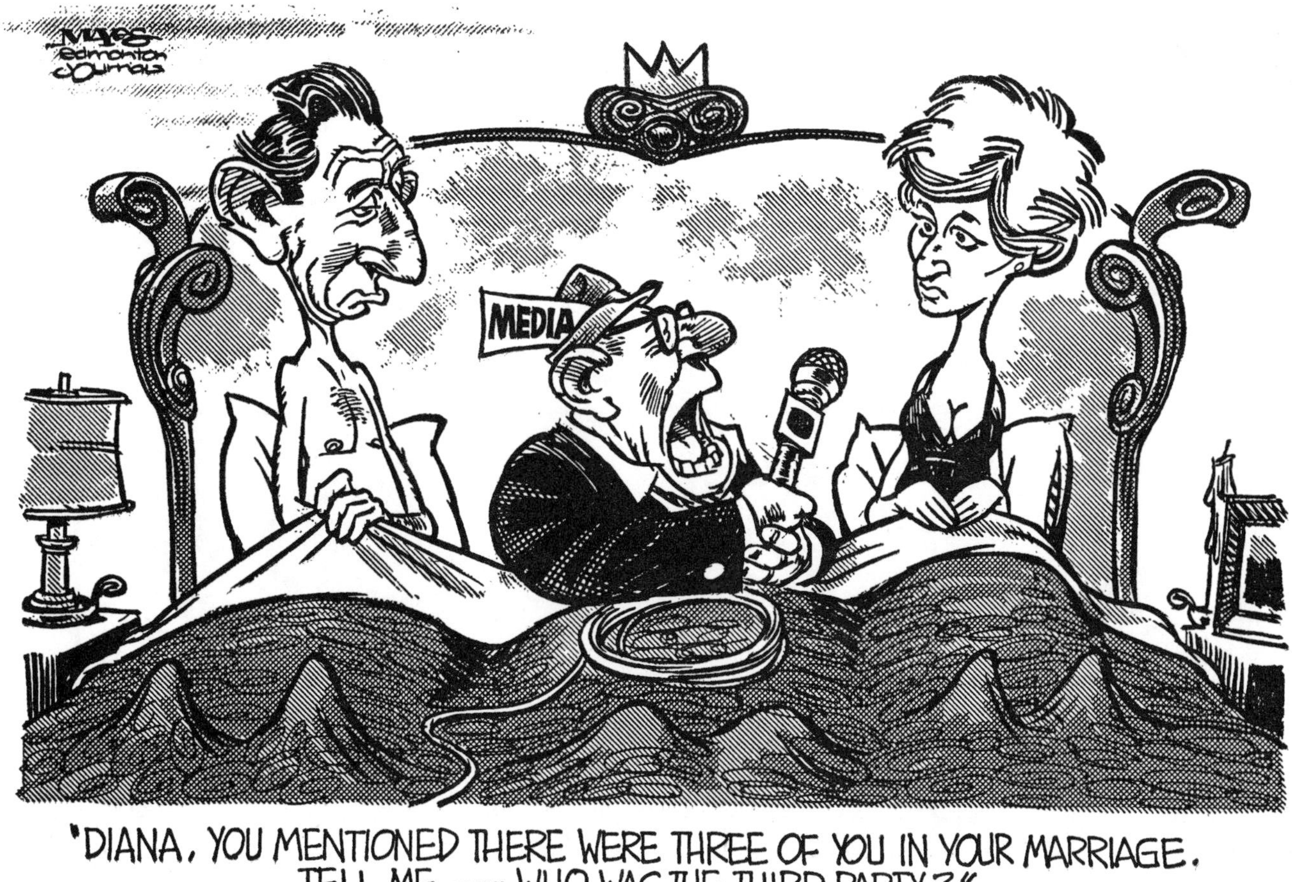
MAYES Edmonton Journal
MEDIA

"DIANA, YOU MENTIONED THERE WERE THREE OF YOU IN YOUR MARRIAGE.
TELL ME — WHO WAS THE THIRD PARTY?"

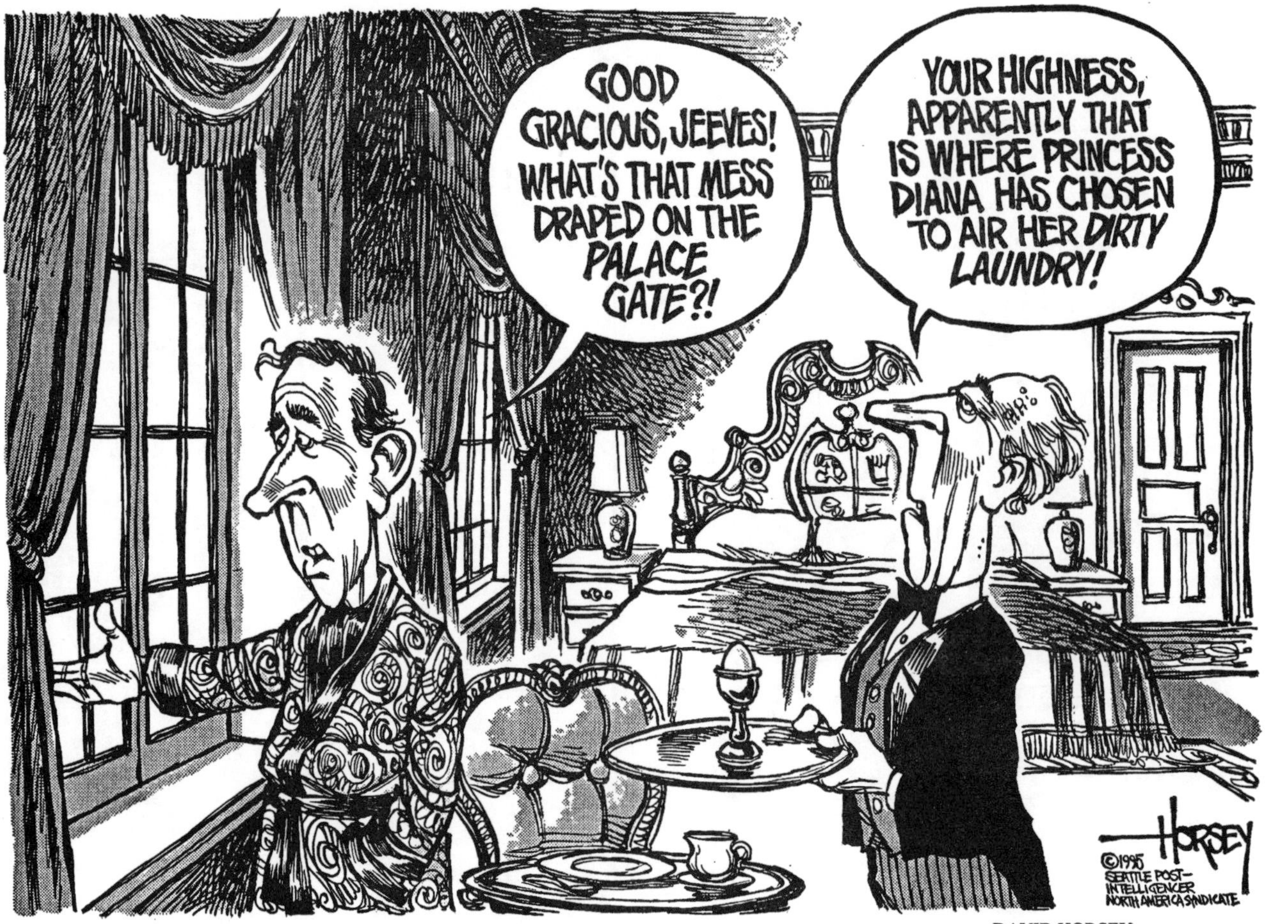
GOOD GRACIOUS, JEEVES! WHAT'S THAT MESS DRAPED ON THE PALACE GATE?!
YOUR HIGHNESS, APPARENTLY THAT IS WHERE PRINCESS DIANA HAS CHOSEN TO AIR HER DIRTY LAUNDRY!
HORSEY
©1995 SEATTLE POST-INTELLIGENCER NORTH AMERICA SYNDICATE

DAVID HORSEY
Courtesy Seattle Post-Intelligencer

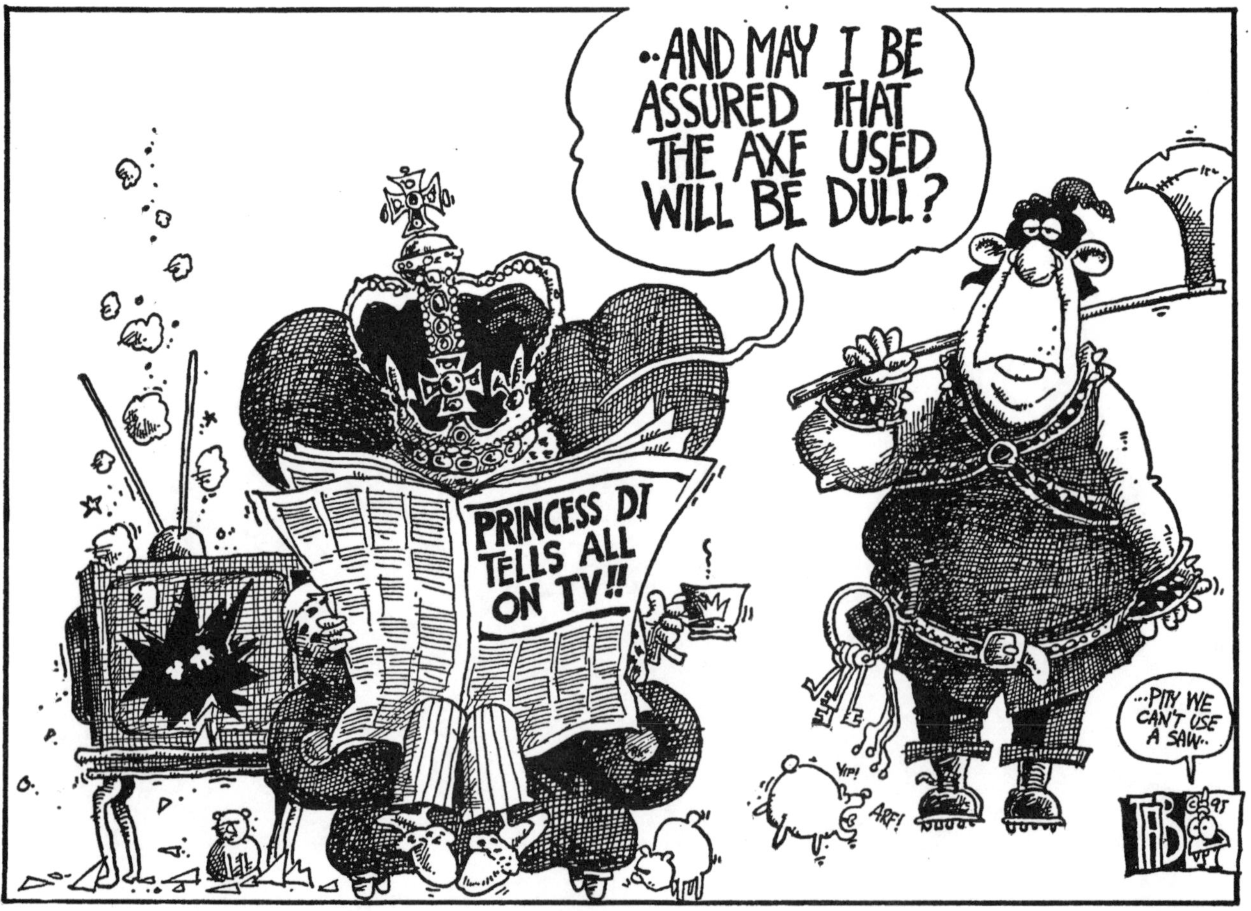
..AND MAY I BE ASSURED THAT THE AXE USED WILL BE DULL?
PRINCESS DI TELLS ALL ON TV!!
..PITY WE CAN'T USE A SAW..
YIP!
ARF!
TAB

THOMAS BOLDT
Courtesy Calgary Herald

RANAN LURIE
Courtesy Cartoonews International

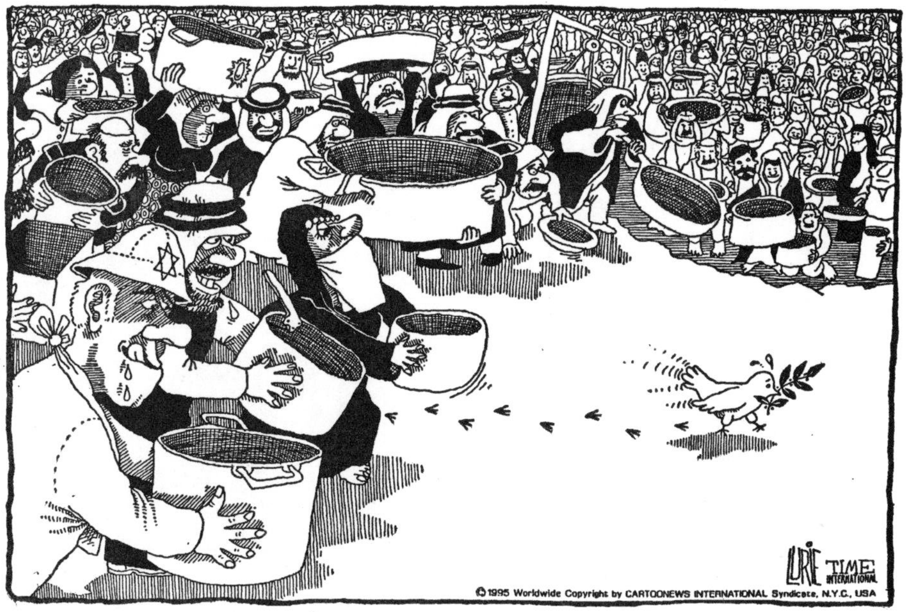
LURIE
TIME INTERNATIONAL
©1995 Worldwide Copyright by CARTOONEWS INTERNATIONAL Syndicate, N.Y.C., USA

The Middle East looking forward to the economic eggs

DAVID DONAR
Courtesy Macomb Daily (Miss.)

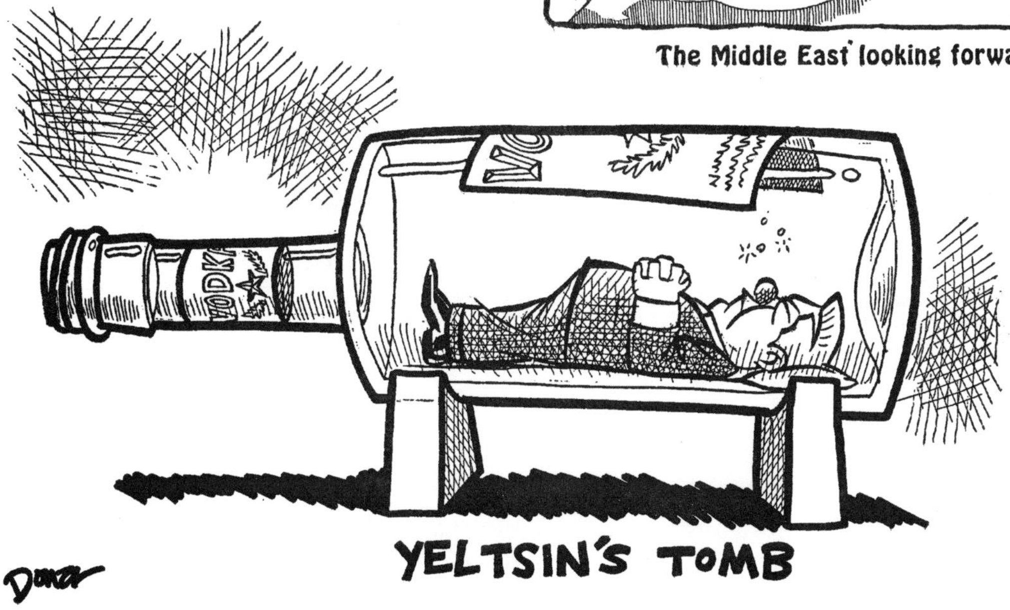
VODKA
DONAR

YELTSIN'S TOMB

Russian Wheat Harvest Worst in 30 Years

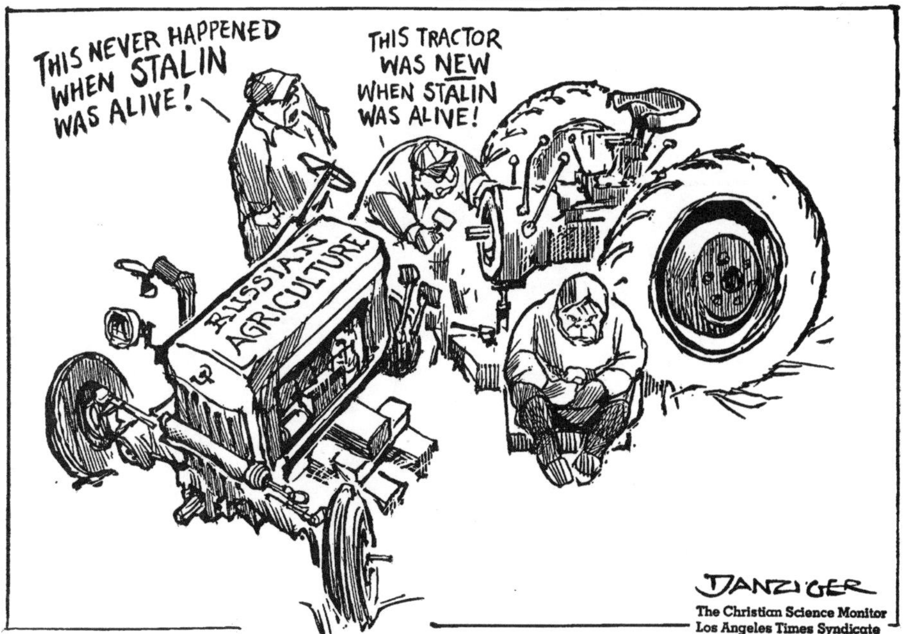
THIS NEVER HAPPENED WHEN STALIN WAS ALIVE!
THIS TRACTOR WAS NEW WHEN STALIN WAS ALIVE!
RUSSIAN AGRICULTURE
DANZIGER
The Christian Science Monitor
Los Angeles Times Syndicate

JEFF DANZIGER
Courtesy Christian Science Monitor

TRACY ROSIENE
Courtesy Norwich Bulletin

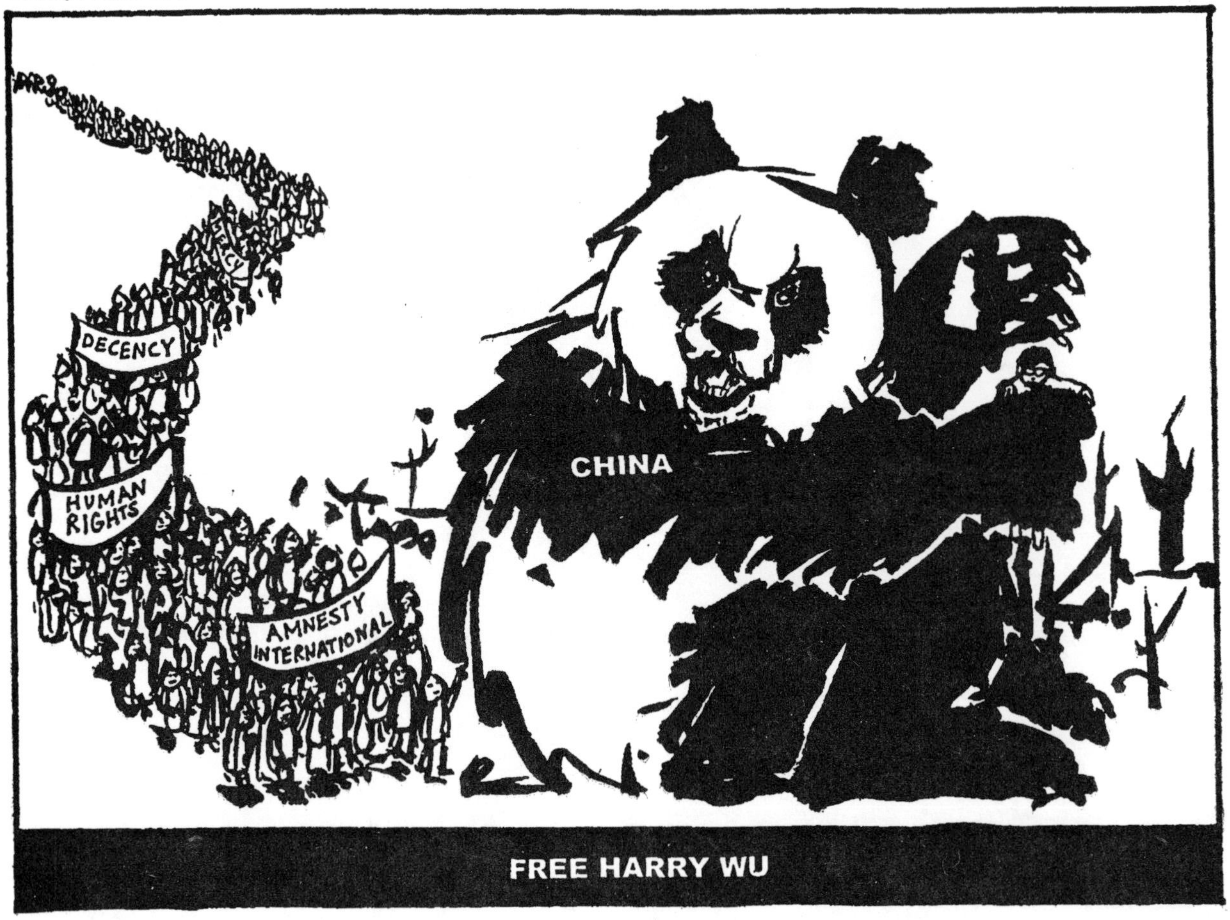
DECENCY
HUMAN RIGHTS
AMNESTY INTERNATIONAL
CHINA
FREE HARRY WU

JEFF MACNELLY
Courtesy Chicago Tribune and
Tribune Media Services

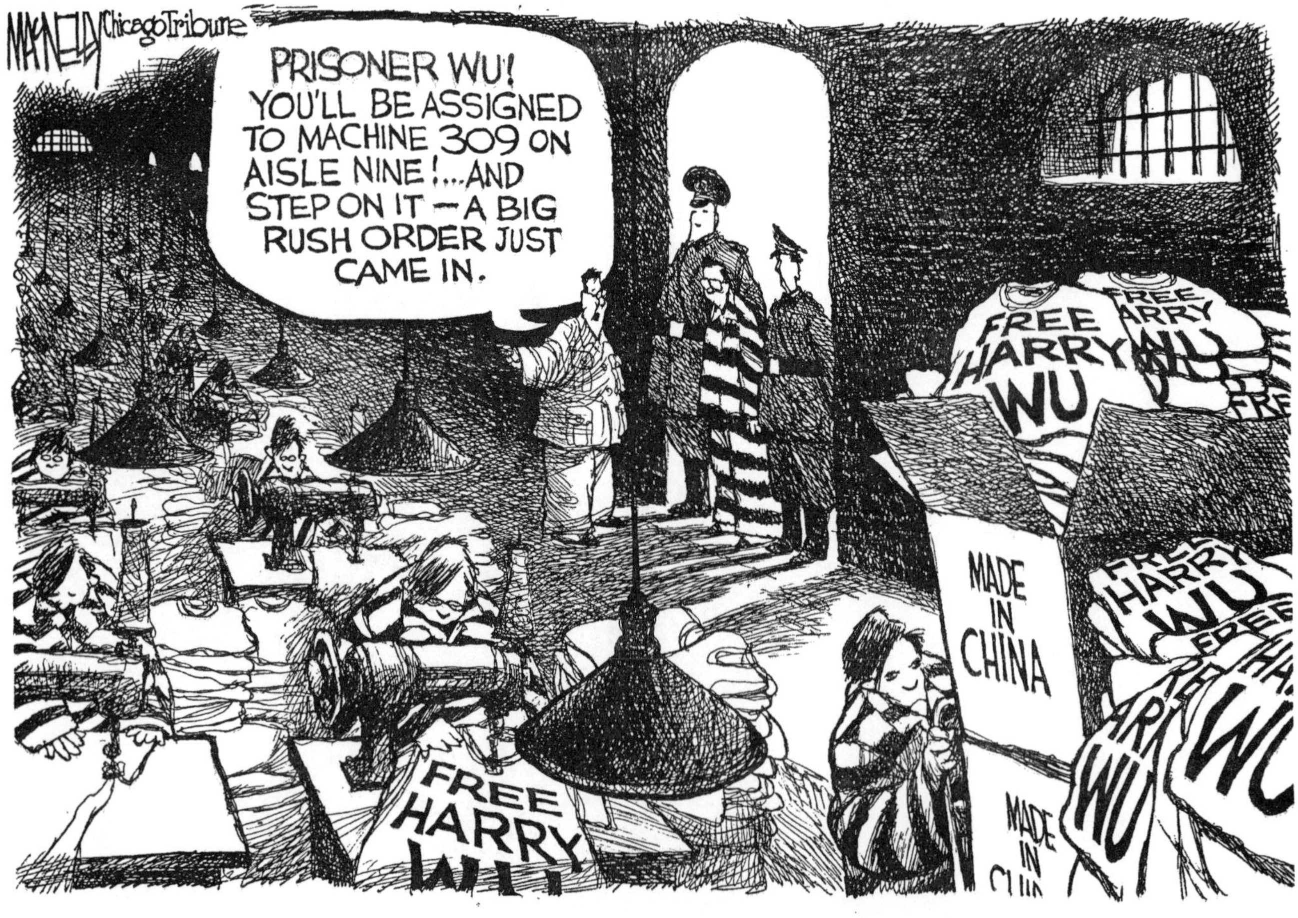
MACNELLY Chicago Tribune
PRISONER WU! YOU'LL BE ASSIGNED TO MACHINE 309 ON AISLE NINE!...AND STEP ON IT—A BIG RUSH ORDER JUST CAME IN.
FREE HARRY WU
MADE IN CHINA
FREE HARRY

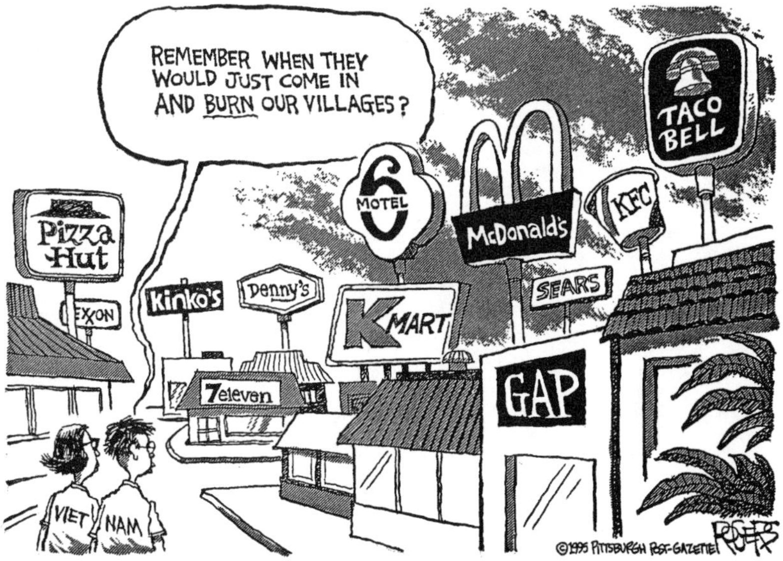
REMEMBER WHEN THEY WOULD JUST COME IN AND BURN OUR VILLAGES?
TACO BELL
MOTEL 6
McDonald's
KFC
Pizza Hut
EXXON
kinko's
Denny's
K MART
SEARS
GAP
7eleven
VIET
NAM
©1995 PITTSBURGH POST-GAZETTE
ROGERS

ROB ROGERS
Courtesy Pittsburgh Post-Gazette

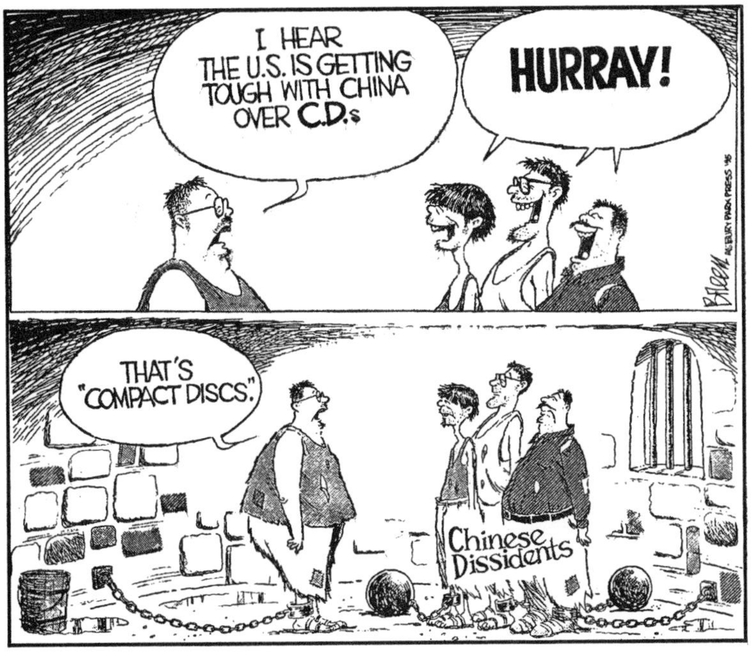
I HEAR THE U.S. IS GETTING TOUGH WITH CHINA OVER C.D.s
HURRAY!
BREEN
THAT'S "COMPACT DISCS."
Chinese Dissidents

STEVE BREEN
Courtesy Asbury Park Press (N.J.)

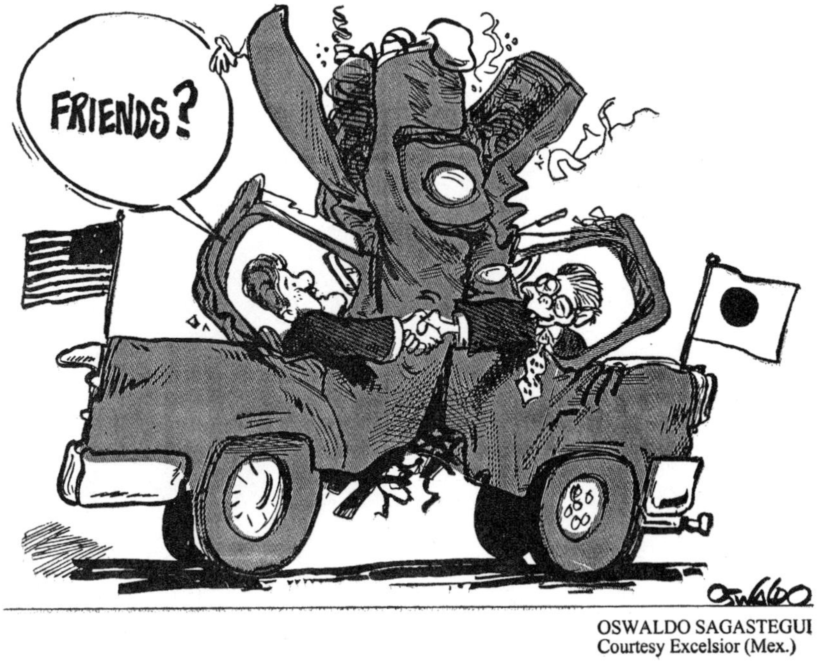
FRIENDS?
OSWALDO

OSWALDO SAGASTEGUI
Courtesy Excelsior (Mex.)

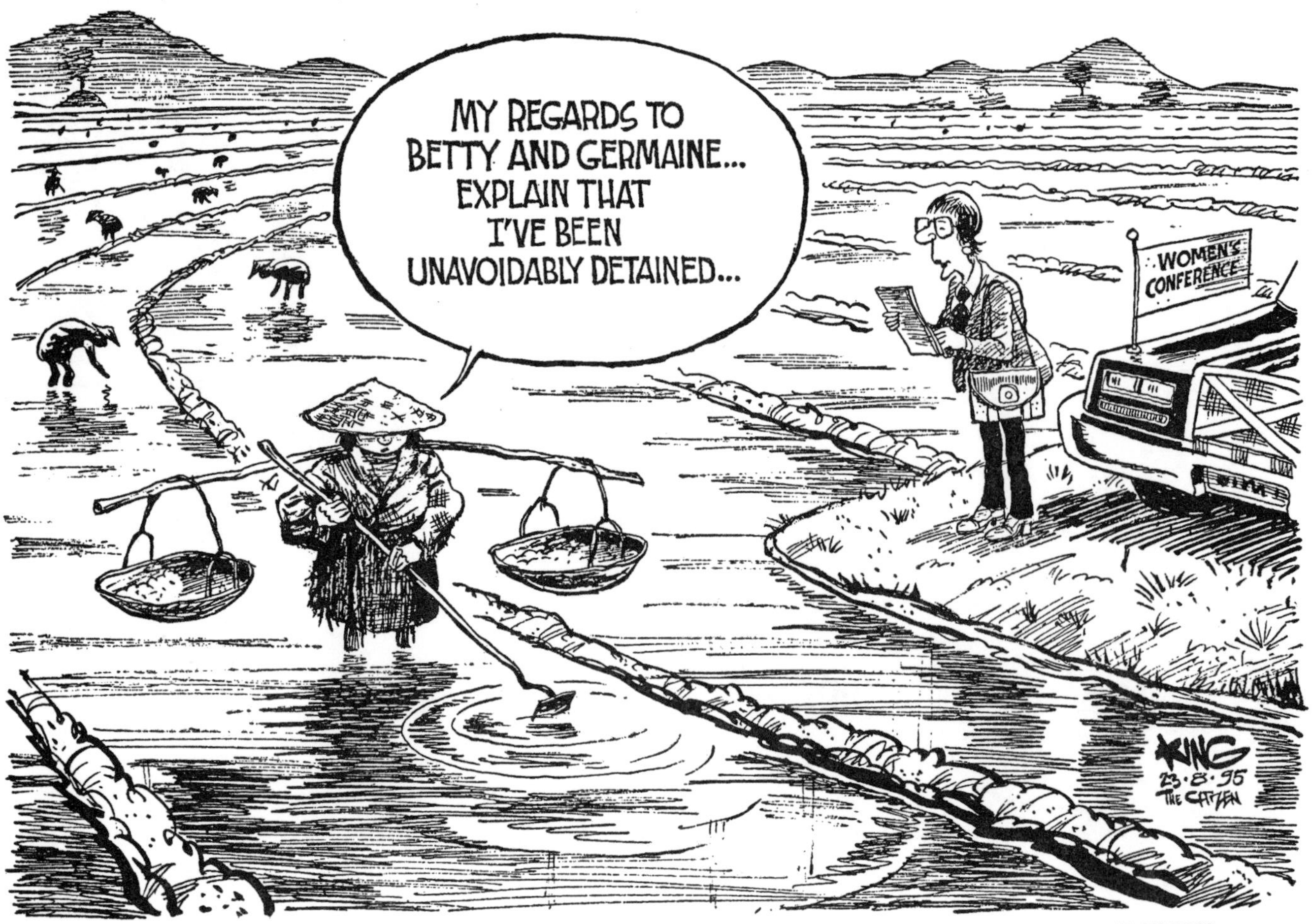
MY REGARDS TO BETTY AND GERMAINE... EXPLAIN THAT I'VE BEEN UNAVOIDABLY DETAINED...
WOMEN'S CONFERENCE
KING 23·8·95 THE CITIZEN

ALAN KING
Courtesy Ottawa Citizen

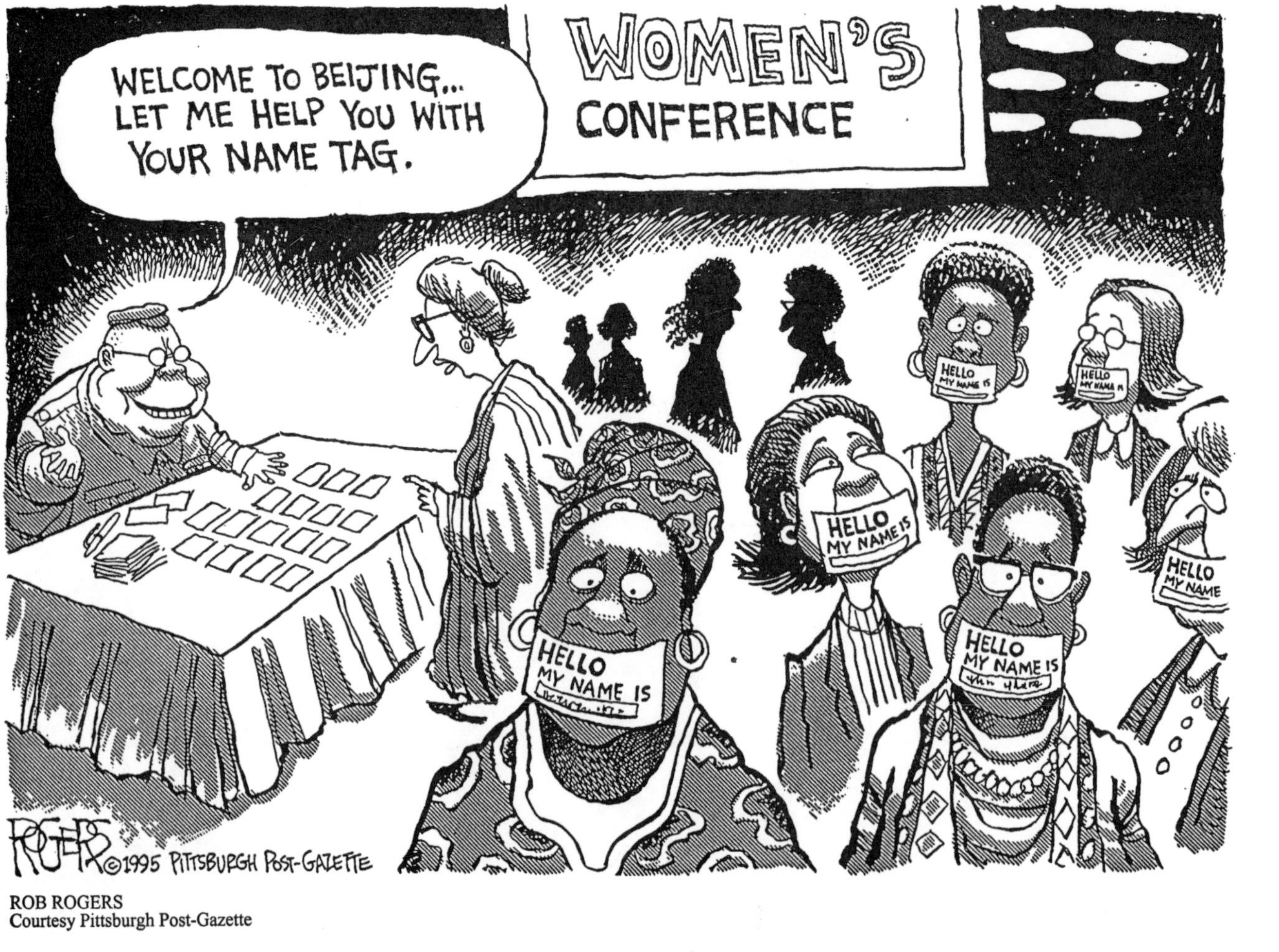
WELCOME TO BEIJING... LET ME HELP YOU WITH YOUR NAME TAG.
WOMEN'S CONFERENCE
HELLO MY NAME IS
HELLO MY NAME IS
HELLO MY NAME IS
HELLO MY NAME IS
HELLO MY NAME IS
HELLO MY NAME
ROGERS ©1995 PITTSBURGH POST-GAZETTE

ROB ROGERS
Courtesy Pittsburgh Post-Gazette

ETTA HULME
Courtesy Ft. Worth Star-Telegram

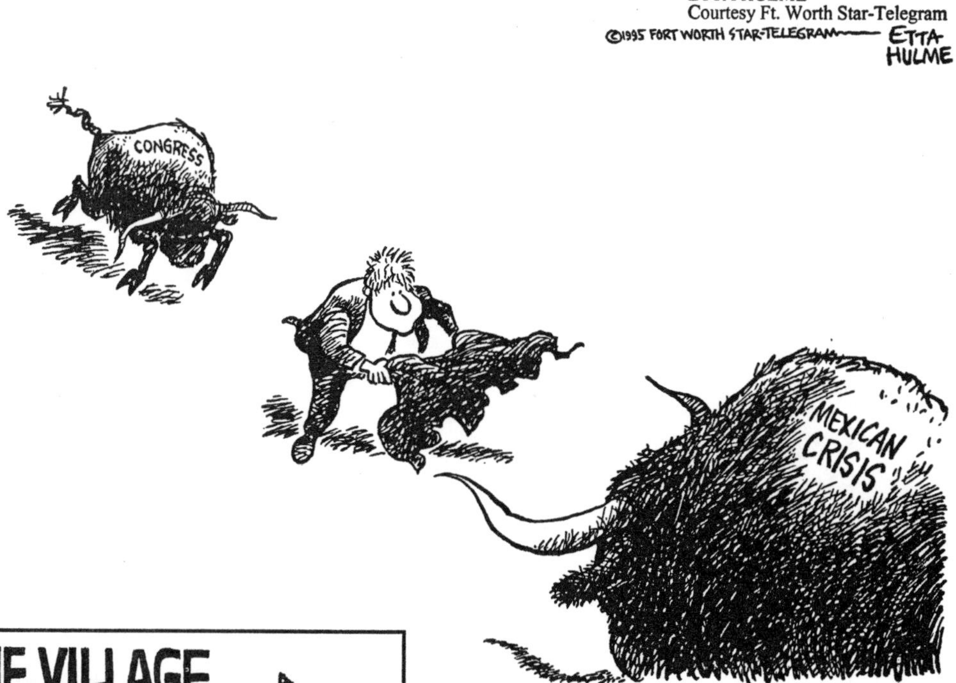
©1995 FORT WORTH STAR-TELEGRAM ETTA HULME
CONGRESS
MEXICAN CRISIS

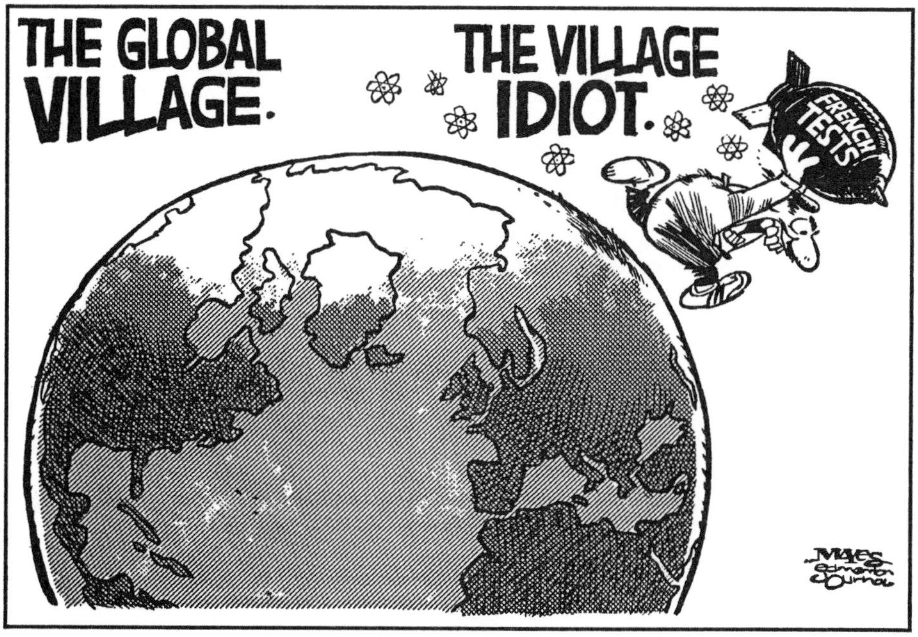
THE GLOBAL VILLAGE.
THE VILLAGE IDIOT.
FRENCH TESTS
MAYES Edmonton Journal

MALCOLM MAYES
Courtesy Edmonton Journal

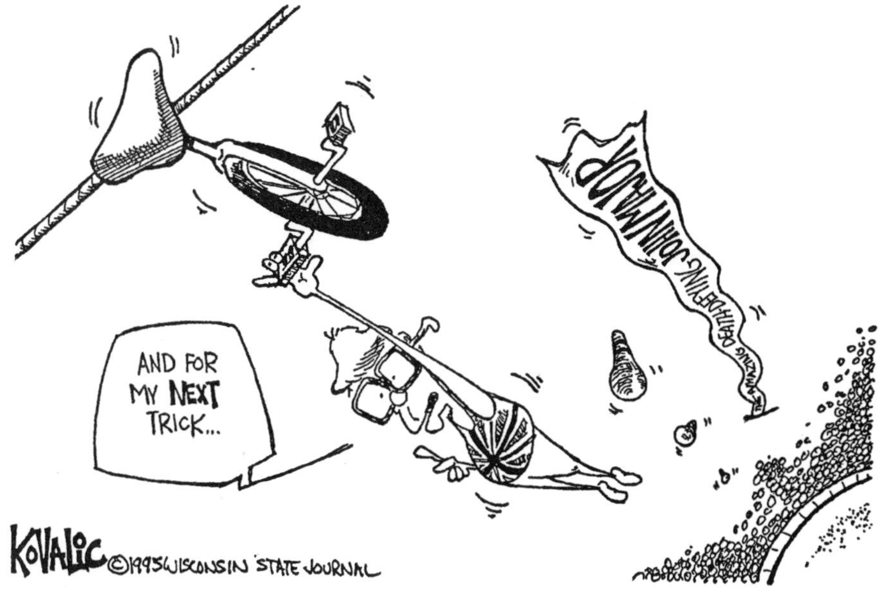
AND FOR MY NEXT TRICK...
KOVALIC ©1995 WISCONSIN STATE JOURNAL

JOHN KOVALIC
Courtesy Wisconsin State Journal

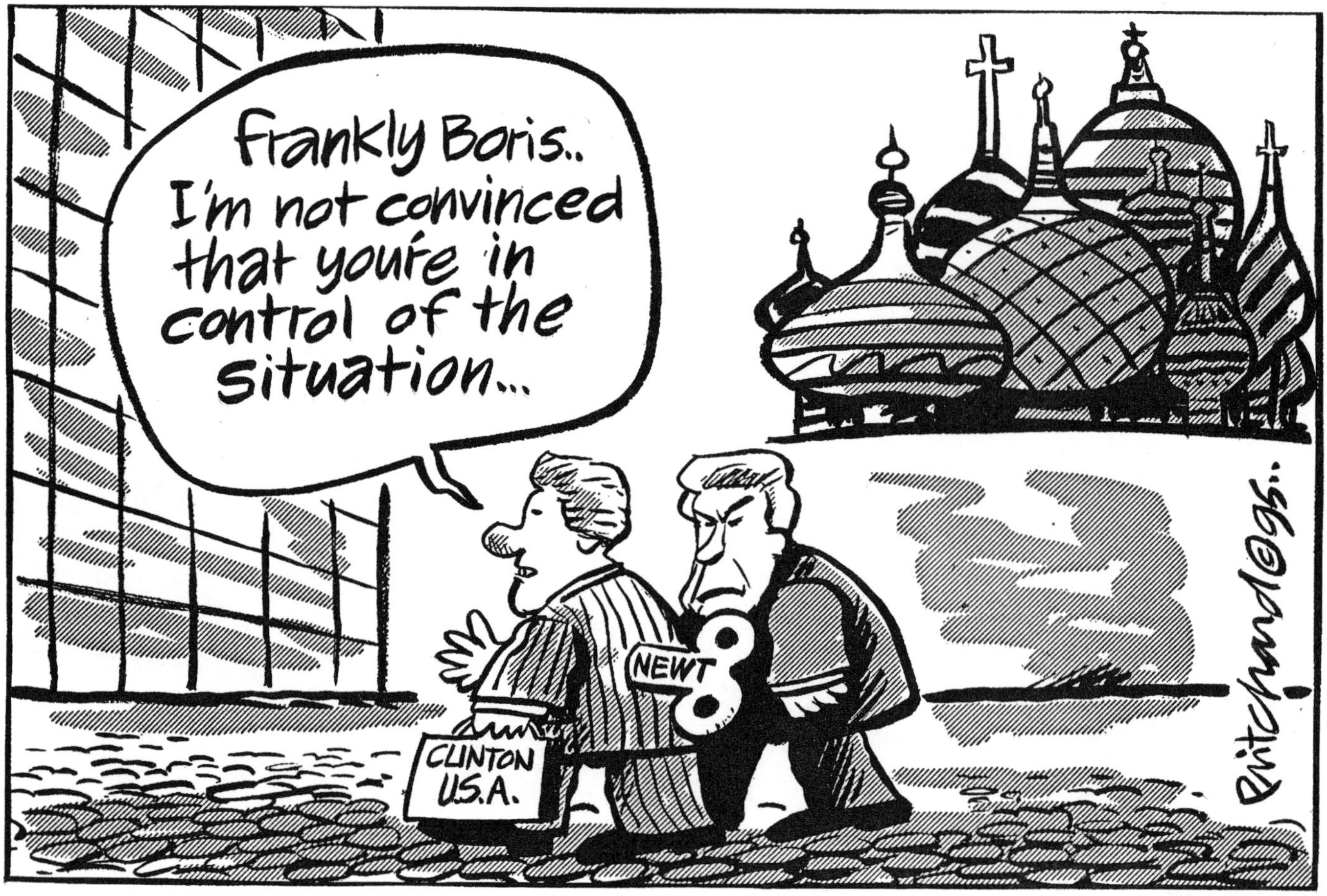
Frankly Boris.. I'm not convinced that you're in control of the situation...
NEWT
CLINTON U.S.A.
Pritchard©95..

DENNY PRITCHARD
Courtesy Ottawa Citizen

WALT HANDELSMAN
Courtesy Times-Picayune (N.O.)

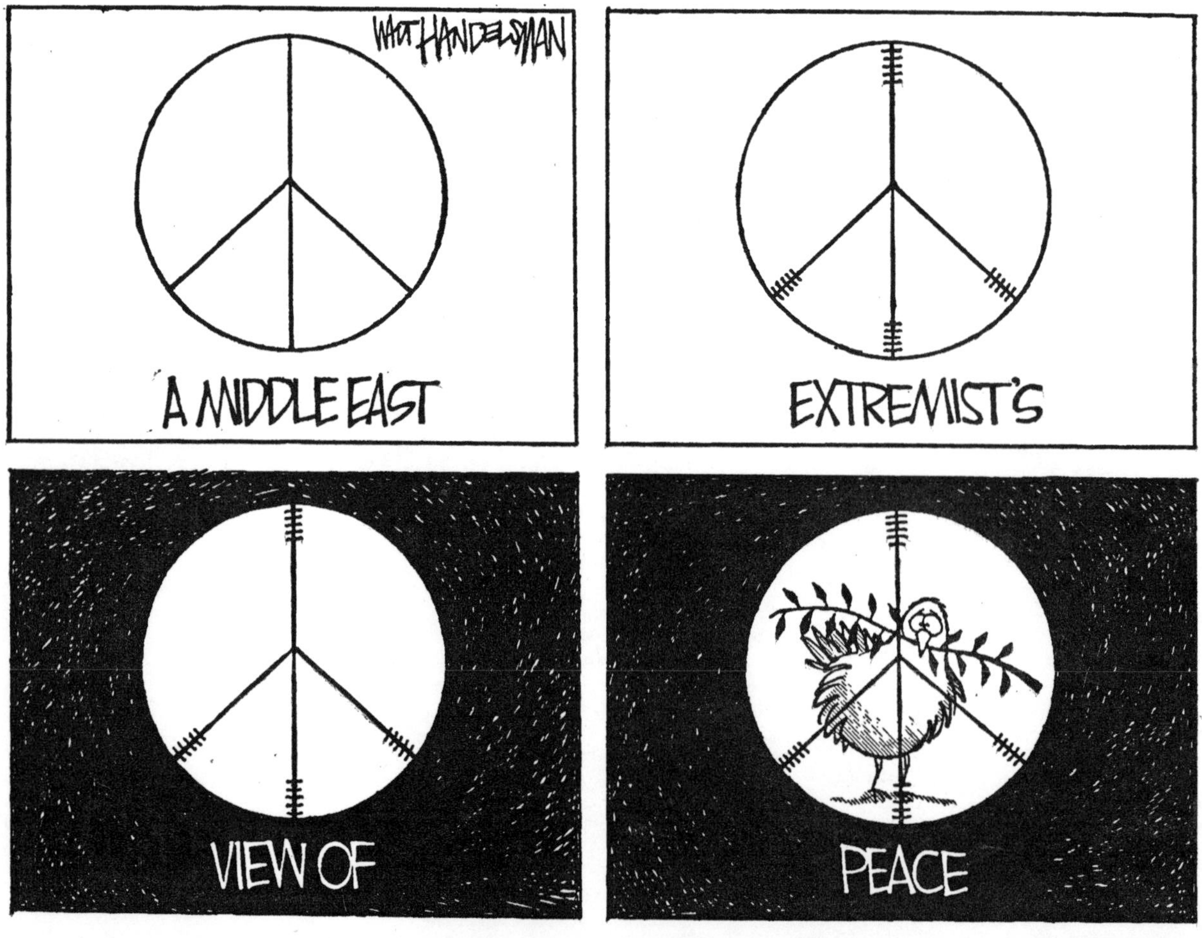
WALT HANDELSMAN
A MIDDLE EAST
EXTREMIST'S
VIEW OF
PEACE

JOHN SHERFFIUS
Courtesy Ventura Star-Free Press

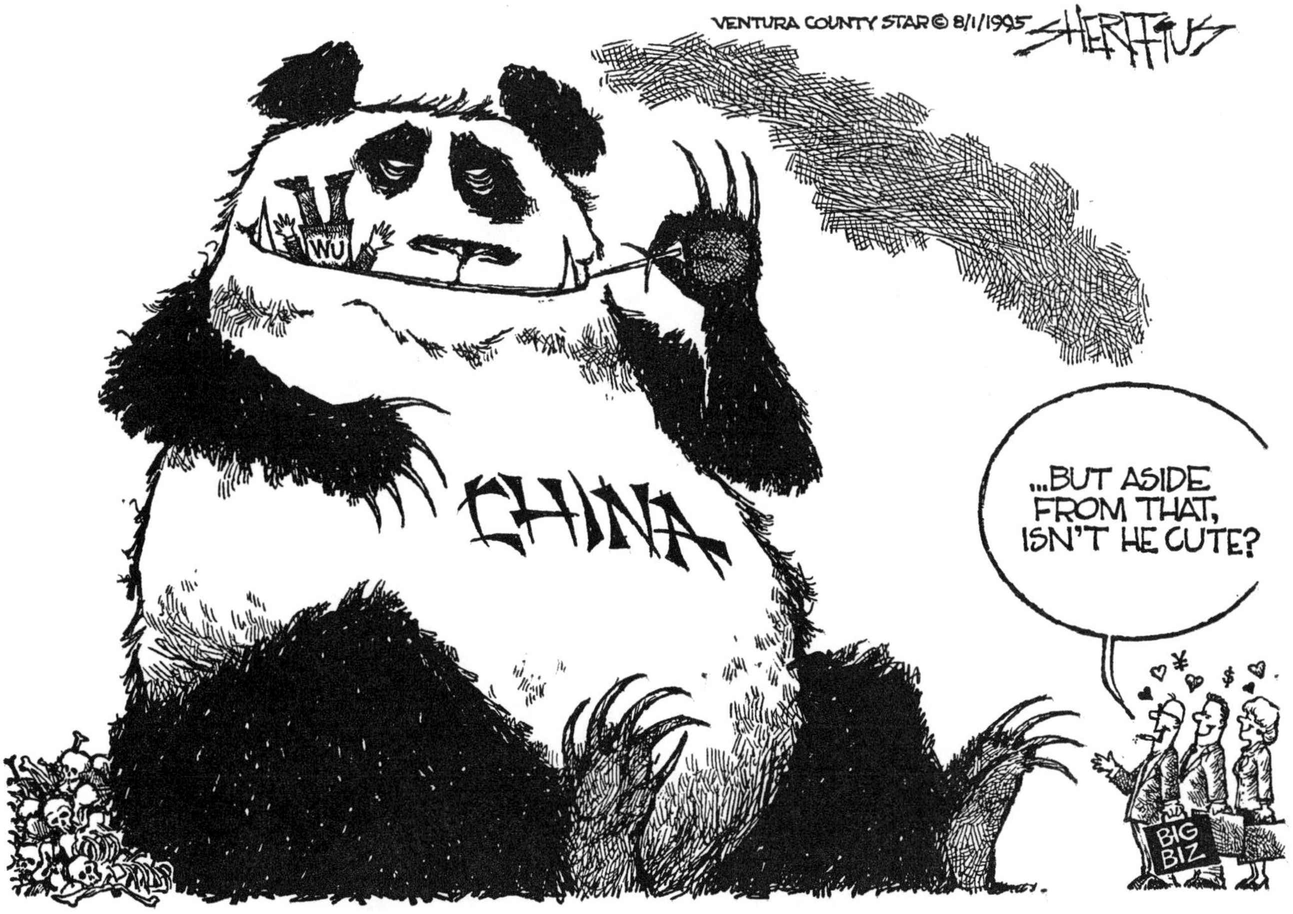
VENTURA COUNTY STAR © 8/1/1995 SHERFFIUS
WU
CHINA
...BUT ASIDE FROM THAT, ISN'T HE CUTE?
BIG BIZ

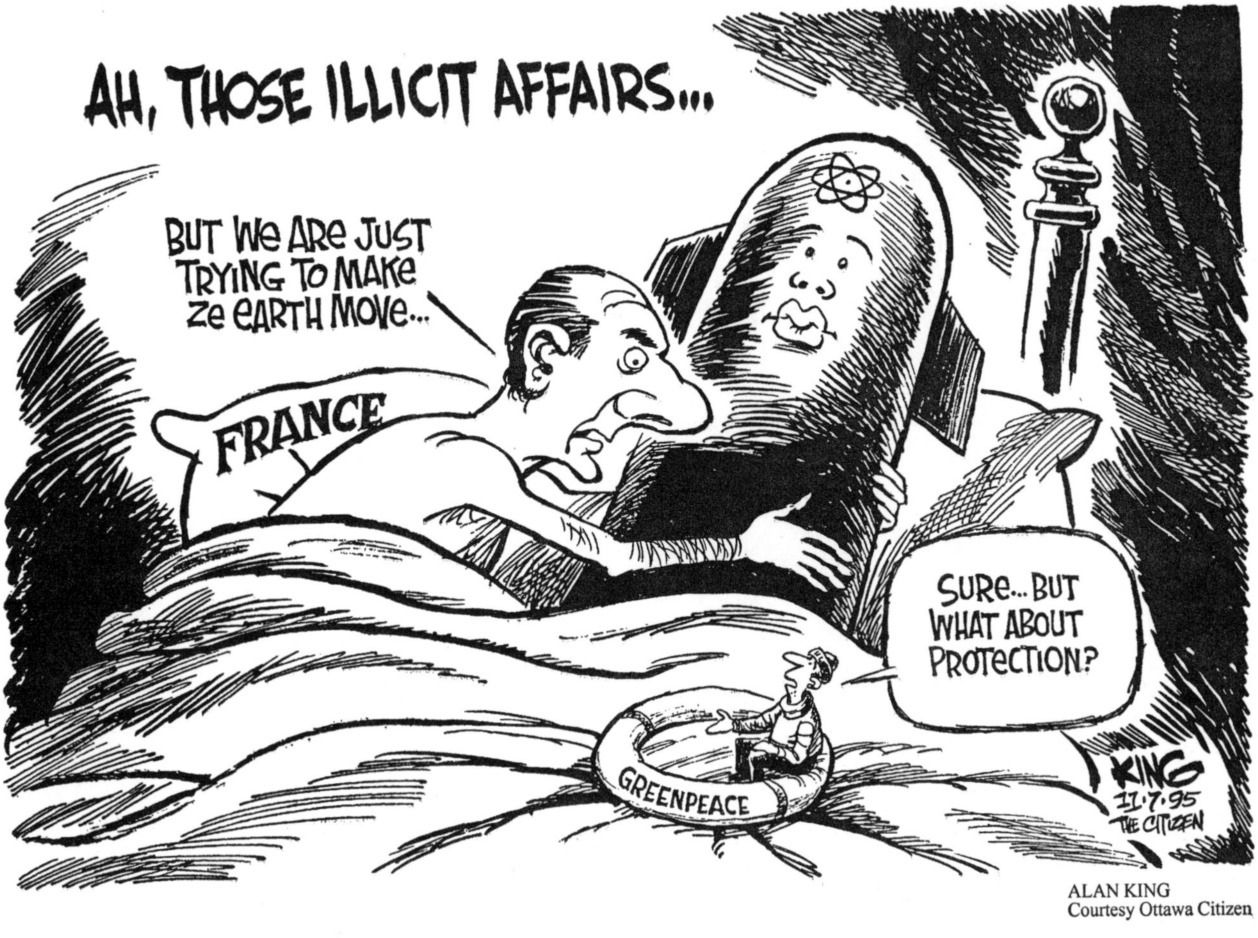
AH, THOSE ILLICIT AFFAIRS...
BUT WE ARE JUST TRYING TO MAKE ZE EARTH MOVE...
FRANCE
SURE... BUT WHAT ABOUT PROTECTION?
GREENPEACE
KING 11·7·95 THE CITIZEN

ALAN KING
Courtesy Ottawa Citizen

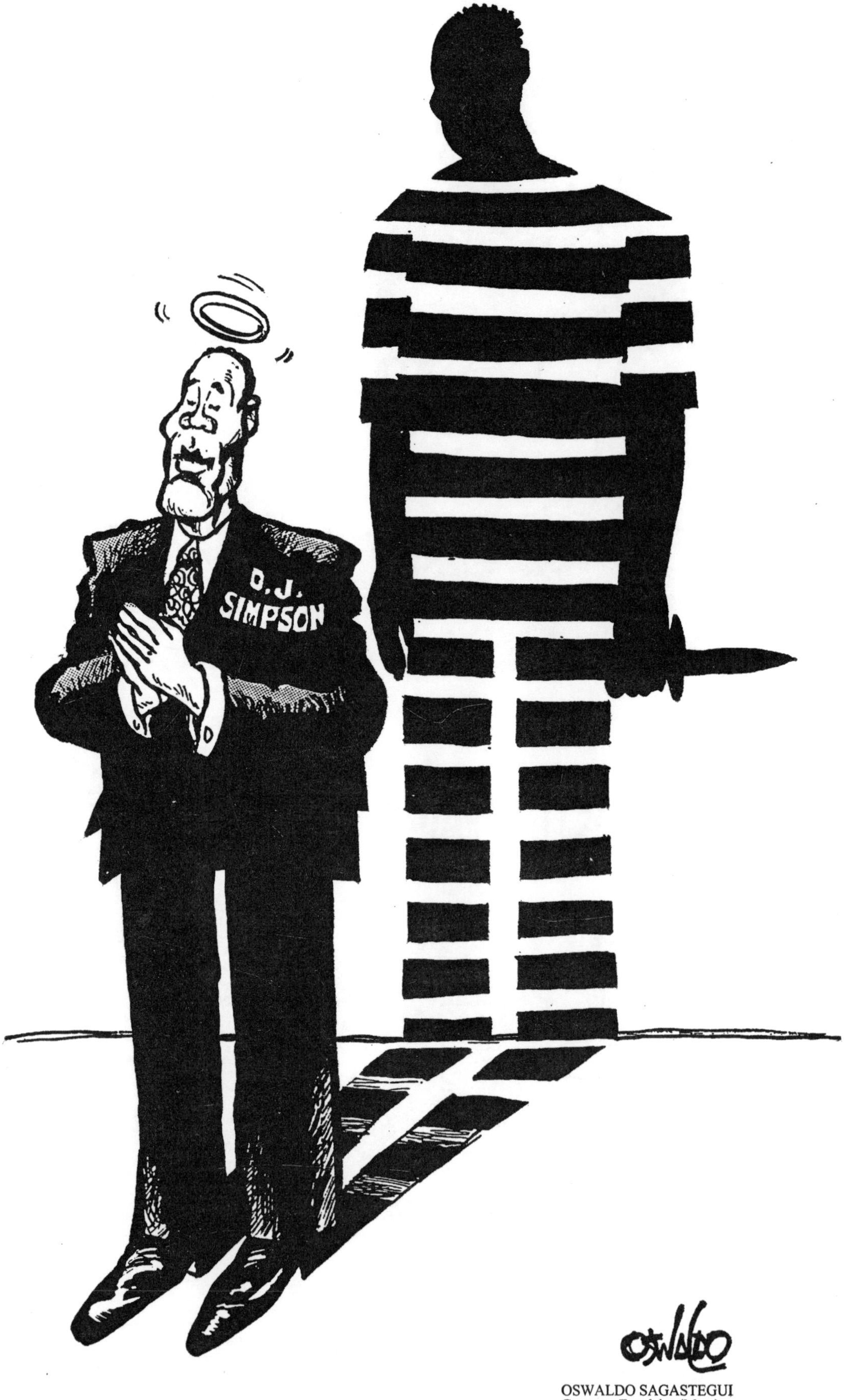
O.J.
SIMPSON
OSWALDO

OSWALDO SAGASTEGUI
Courtesy Excelsior (Mex.)

O. J. Simpson

The seemingly interminable murder trial of former football star O. J. Simpson ended in October with a "Not Guilty" verdict. Simpson had been charged with murdering his ex-wife, Nicole Brown Simpson, and Ronald Goldman. The sequestered jury had spent a record nine months listening to 126 witnesses. Simpson's defense was handled by a bevy of high-powered lawyers, dubbed "the Dream Team."

Some blacks applauded and cheered the verdict while many whites were dumbfounded. Polls had showed that a majority of blacks felt that Simpson was innocent, while an overwhelming percentage of whites thought he was guilty. The verdict, pundits concluded, underscored once again the deep chasm between the races. At the time it reached its verdict, the jury was composed of nine blacks, two whites, and one Hispanic.

Many Americans felt that the verdict demonstrated that there is a different brand of justice available to those who have money. Many observers began to question the American system of justice. Millions wondered whether any trial should be allowed to run as long as Simpson's did. Many also felt that the trial proved conclusively that television cameras have no place in the courtroom.

JEFF MACNELLY
Courtesy Chicago Tribune and
Tribune Media Services

MACNELLY Chicago Tribune
SO. ARE YOU GOING TO BELIEVE US OR THOSE LYING EYES OF YOURS?
O.J.
DREAM TEAM

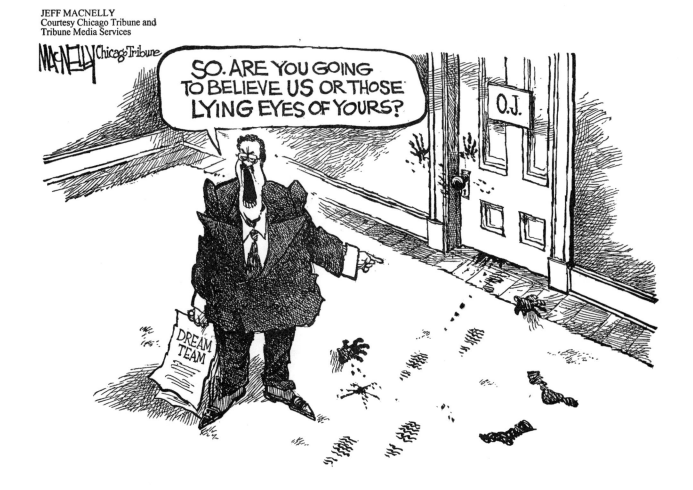

FRED SEBASTIAN
Courtesy Law Times

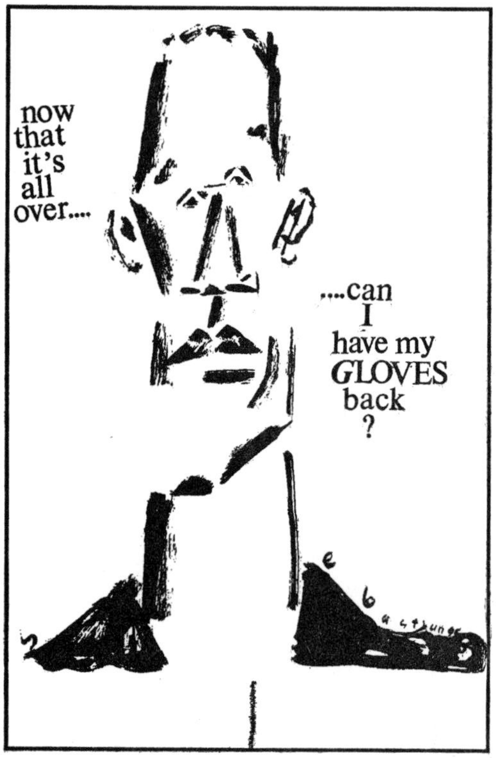
now that it's all over....
....can I have my GLOVES back ?

BOB ENGLEHART
Courtesy Hartford Courant

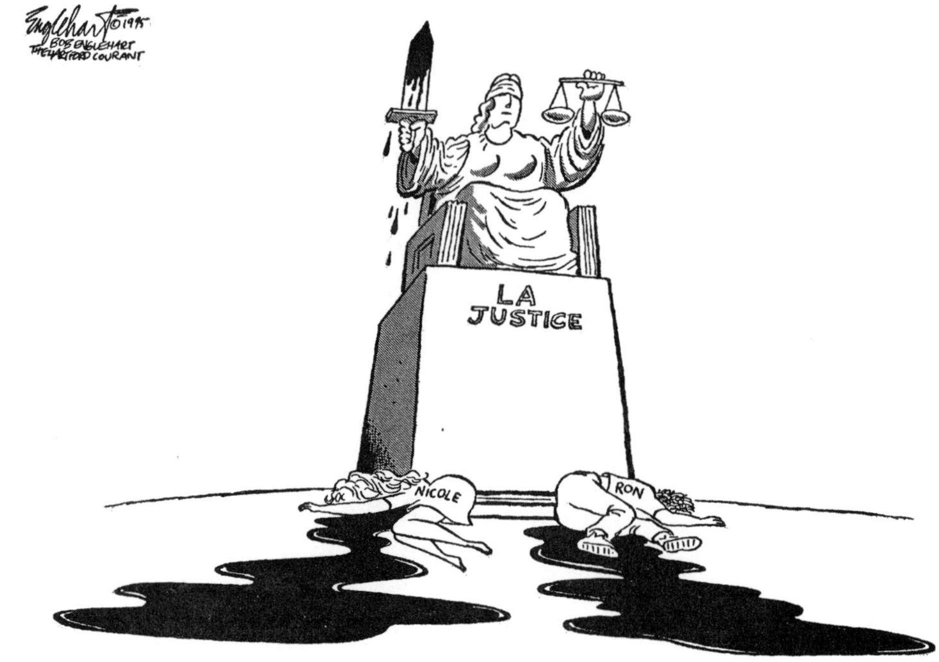
LA JUSTICE
NICOLE
RON

SCOTT NICKEL
Courtesy Antelope Valley Press (Calif.)

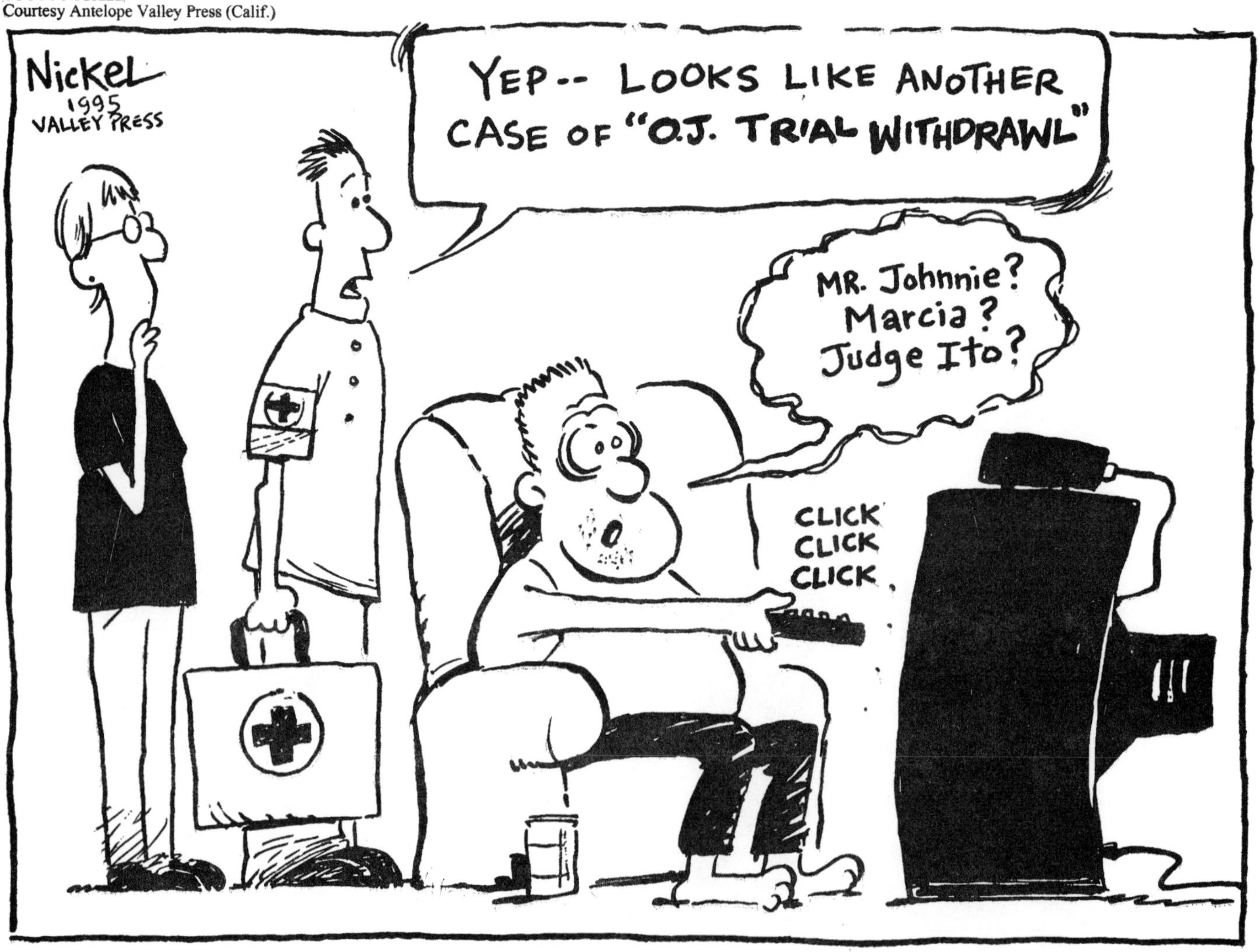
NICKEL 1995 VALLEY PRESS
YEP -- LOOKS LIKE ANOTHER CASE OF "O.J. TRIAL WITHDRAWL"
MR. Johnnie? Marcia? Judge Ito?
CLICK CLICK CLICK

JIM BORGMAN
Courtesy Cincinnati Enquirer

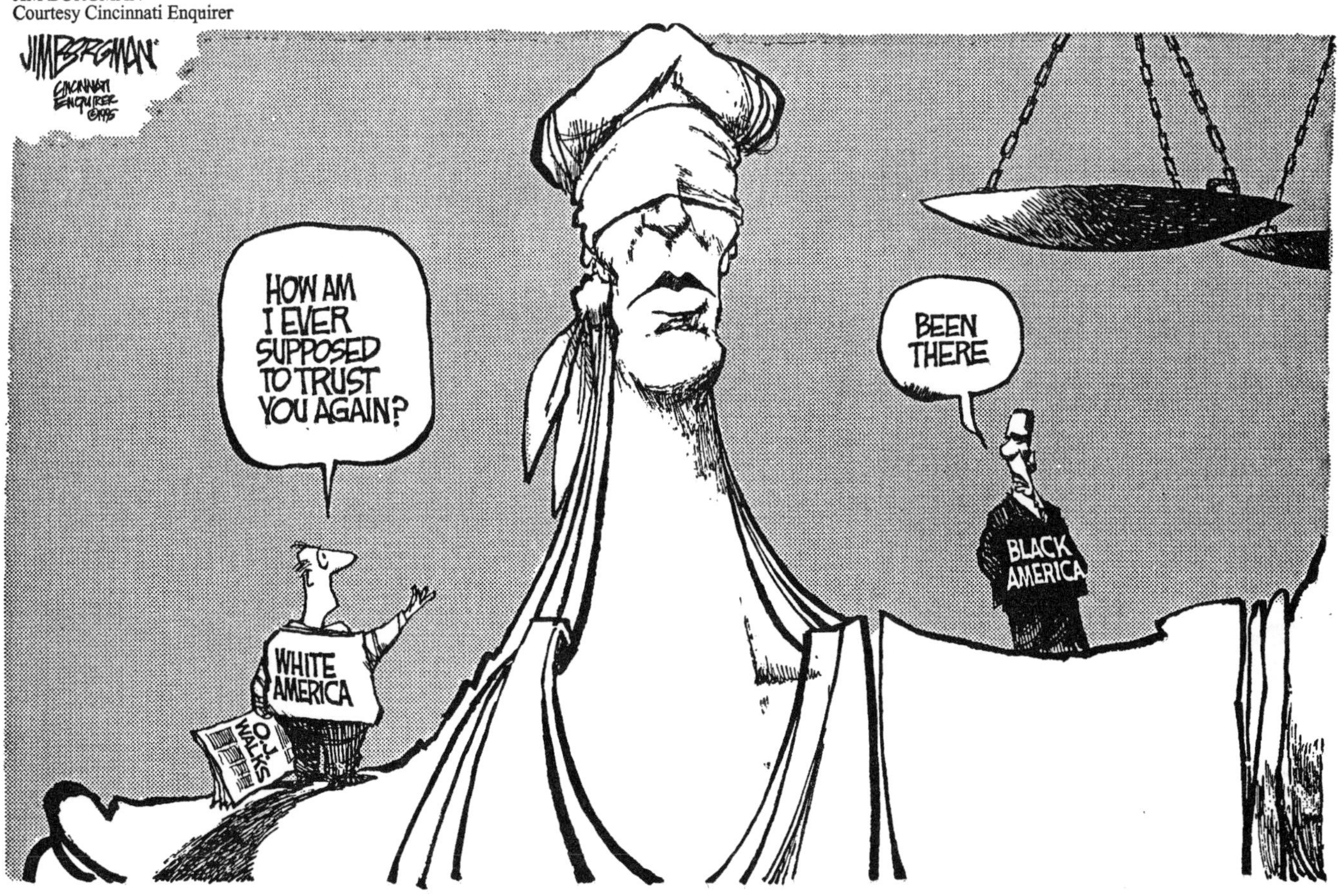

JIMBORGMAN
CINCINNATI ENQUIRER ©1995
HOW AM I EVER SUPPOSED TO TRUST YOU AGAIN?
BEEN THERE
WHITE AMERICA
BLACK AMERICA
O.J. WALKS

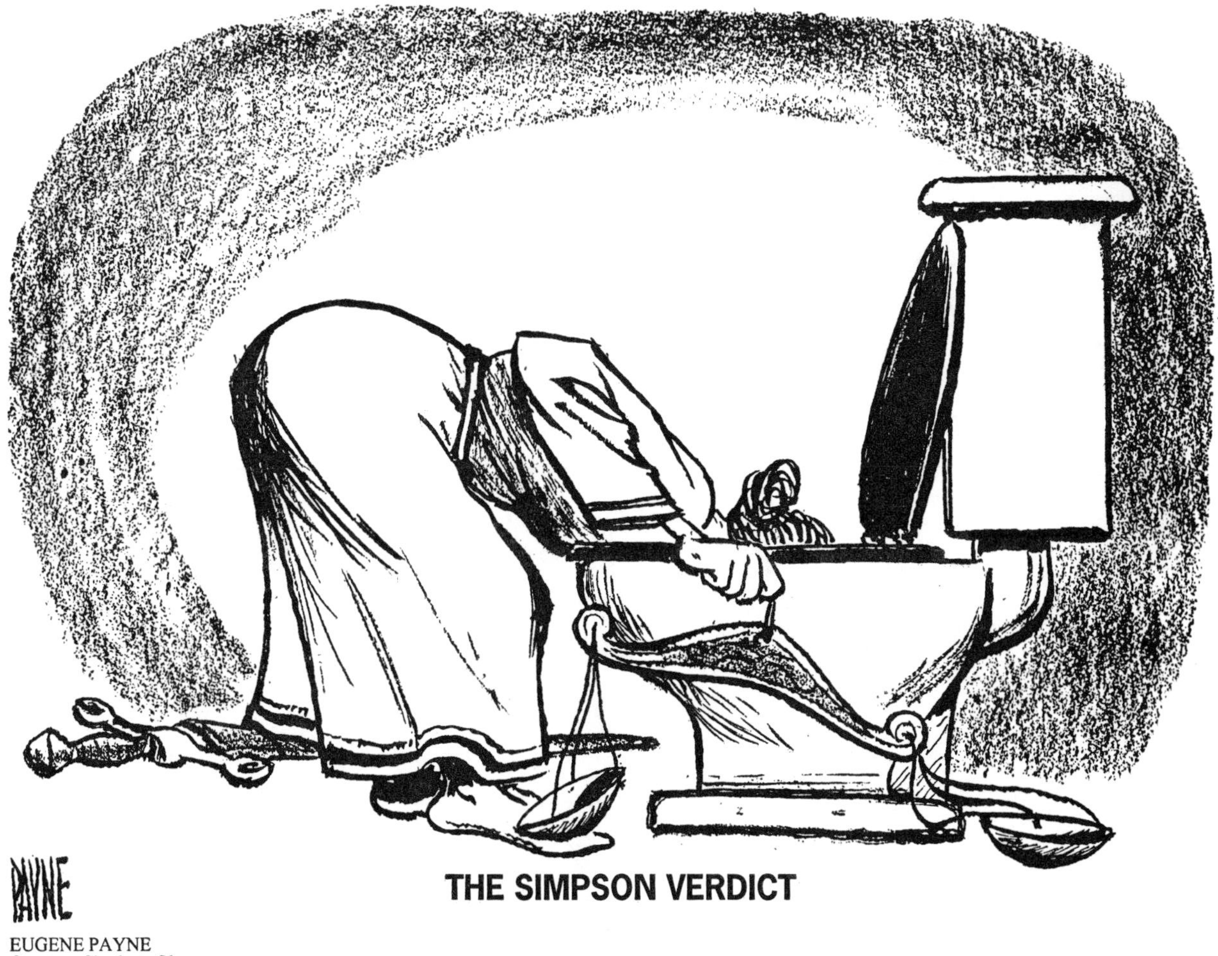

PAYNE

THE SIMPSON VERDICT

EUGENE PAYNE
Courtesy Charlotte Observer

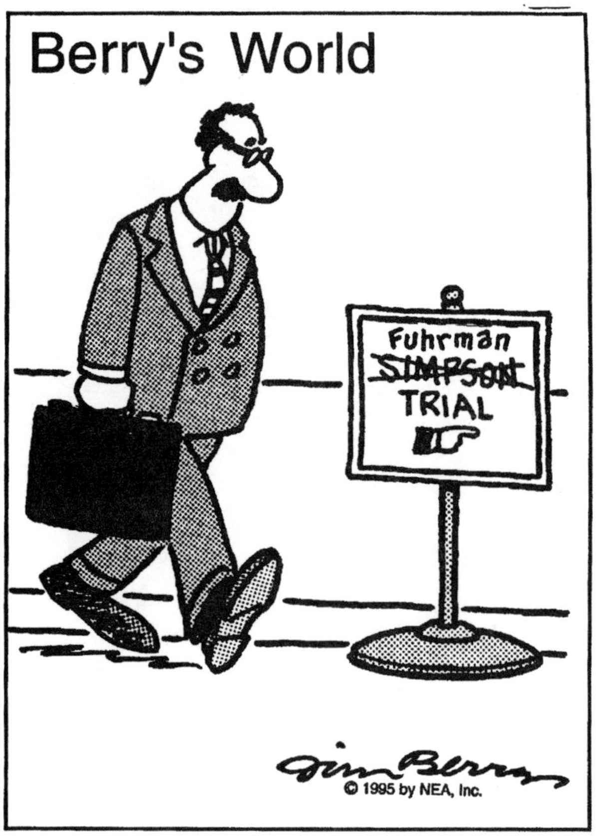
Berry's World
Fuhrman
SIMPSON
TRIAL
© 1995 by NEA, Inc.

JIM BERRY
Courtesy NEA

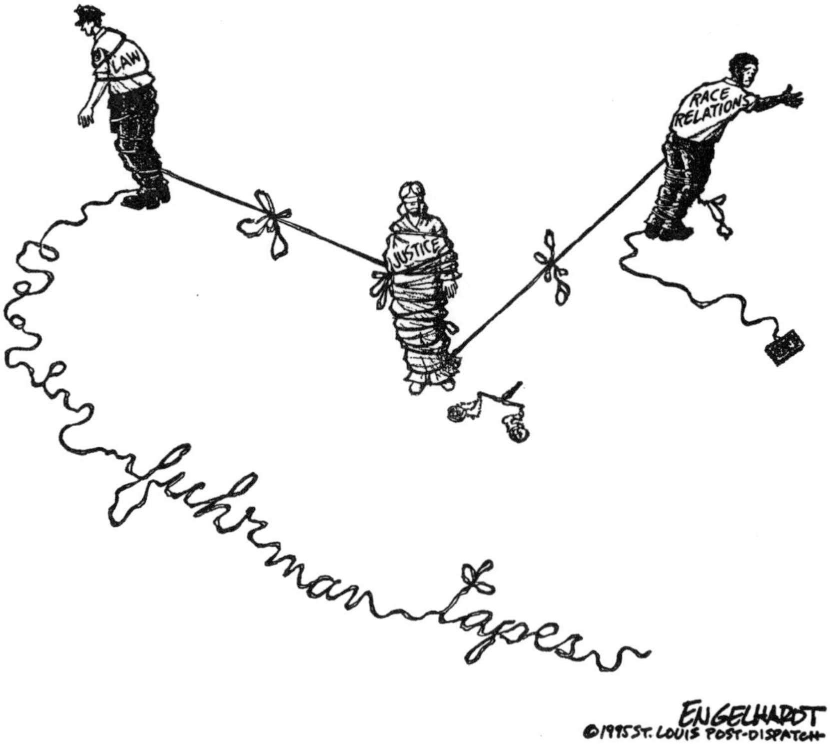
LAW
JUSTICE
RACE RELATIONS
fuhrman tapes
ENGELHARDT
©1995 ST. LOUIS POST-DISPATCH

TOM ENGELHARDT
Courtesy St. Louis Post-Dispatch

WALT HANDELSMAN
Courtesy Times-Picayune (N.O.)

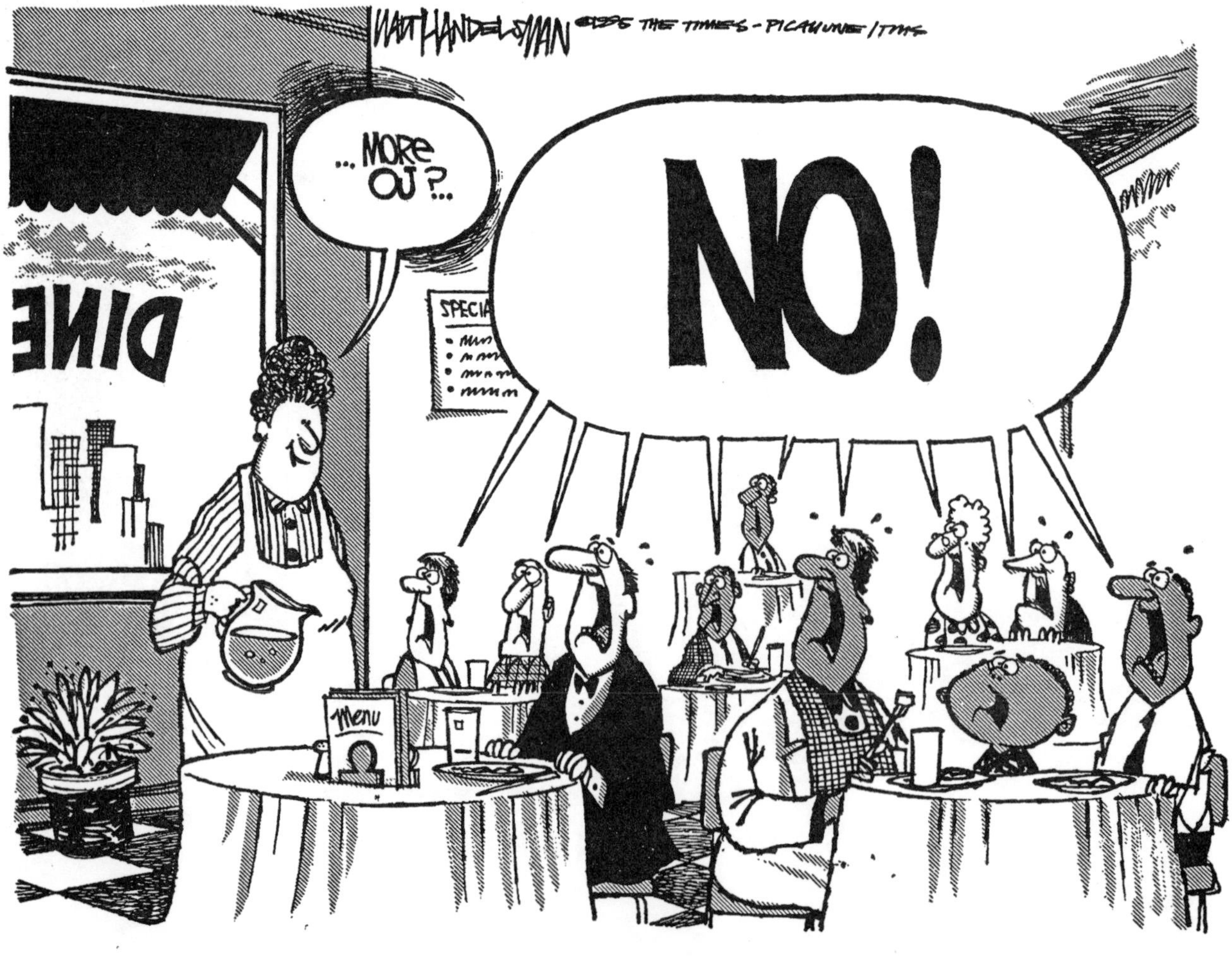
WALT HANDELSMAN ©1995 THE TIMES-PICAYUNE / TMS
...MORE OJ?...
NO!
DINE
SPECIA
Menu

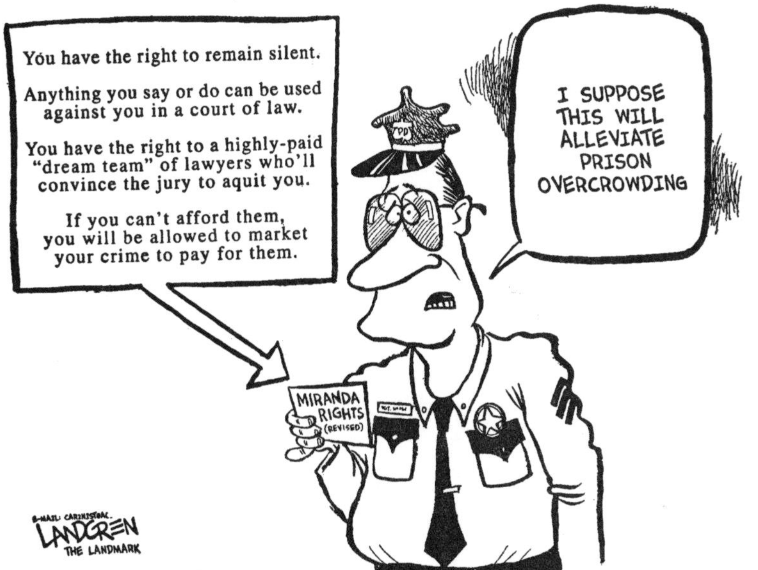
You have the right to remain silent.
Anything you say or do can be used against you in a court of law.
You have the right to a highly-paid "dream team" of lawyers who'll convince the jury to aquit you.
If you can't afford them, you will be allowed to market your crime to pay for them.
I SUPPOSE THIS WILL ALLEVIATE PRISON OVERCROWDING
MIRANDA RIGHTS (REVISED)
LANDGREN
THE LANDMARK

DON LANDGREN, JR.
Courtesy Clinton Daily Item (Mass.)

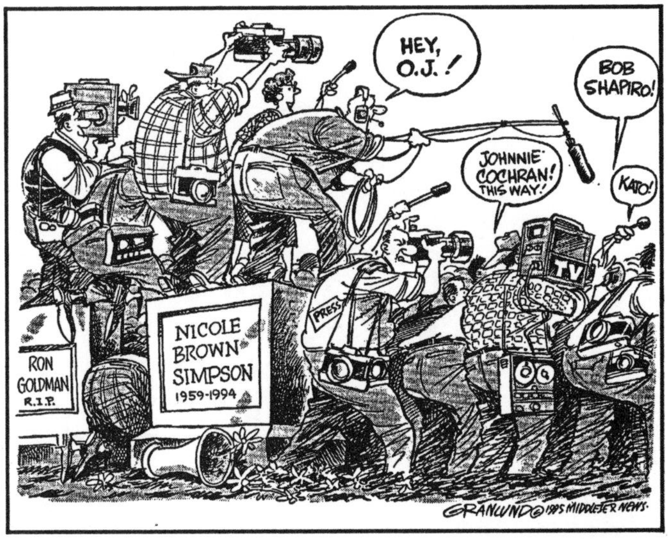
HEY, O.J.!
BOB SHAPIRO!
JOHNNIE COCHRAN! THIS WAY!
KATO!
TV
PRESS
NICOLE BROWN SIMPSON 1959-1994
RON GOLDMAN R.I.P.
GRANLUND ©1995 MIDDLESEX NEWS

DAVID GRANLUND
Courtesy Middlesex News

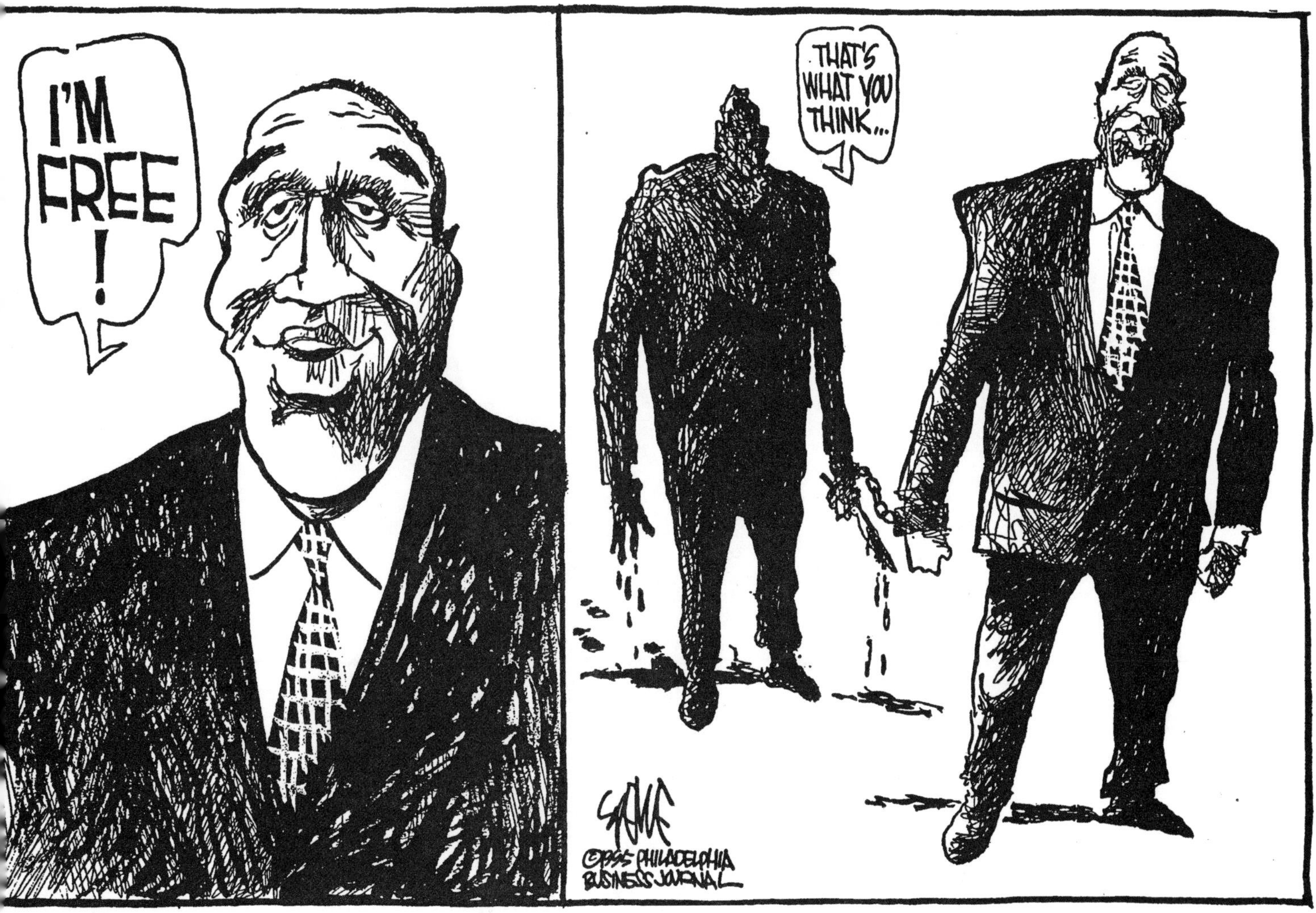
I'M FREE!
THAT'S WHAT YOU THINK...
©1995 PHILADELPHIA BUSINESS JOURNAL

OHN SPENCER
ourtesy Philadelphia Business Journal

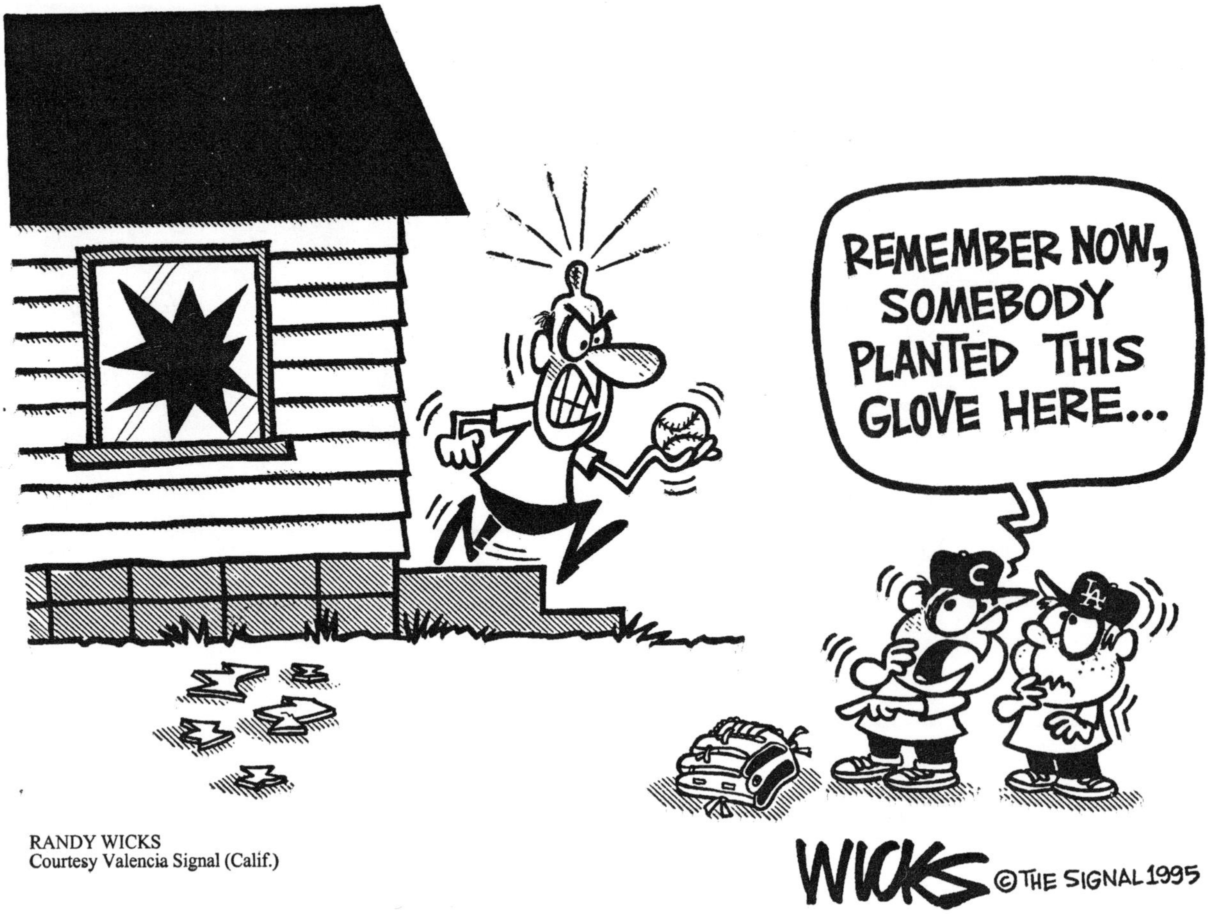
REMEMBER NOW, SOMEBODY PLANTED THIS GLOVE HERE...
WICKS ©THE SIGNAL 1995

RANDY WICKS
Courtesy Valencia Signal (Calif.)

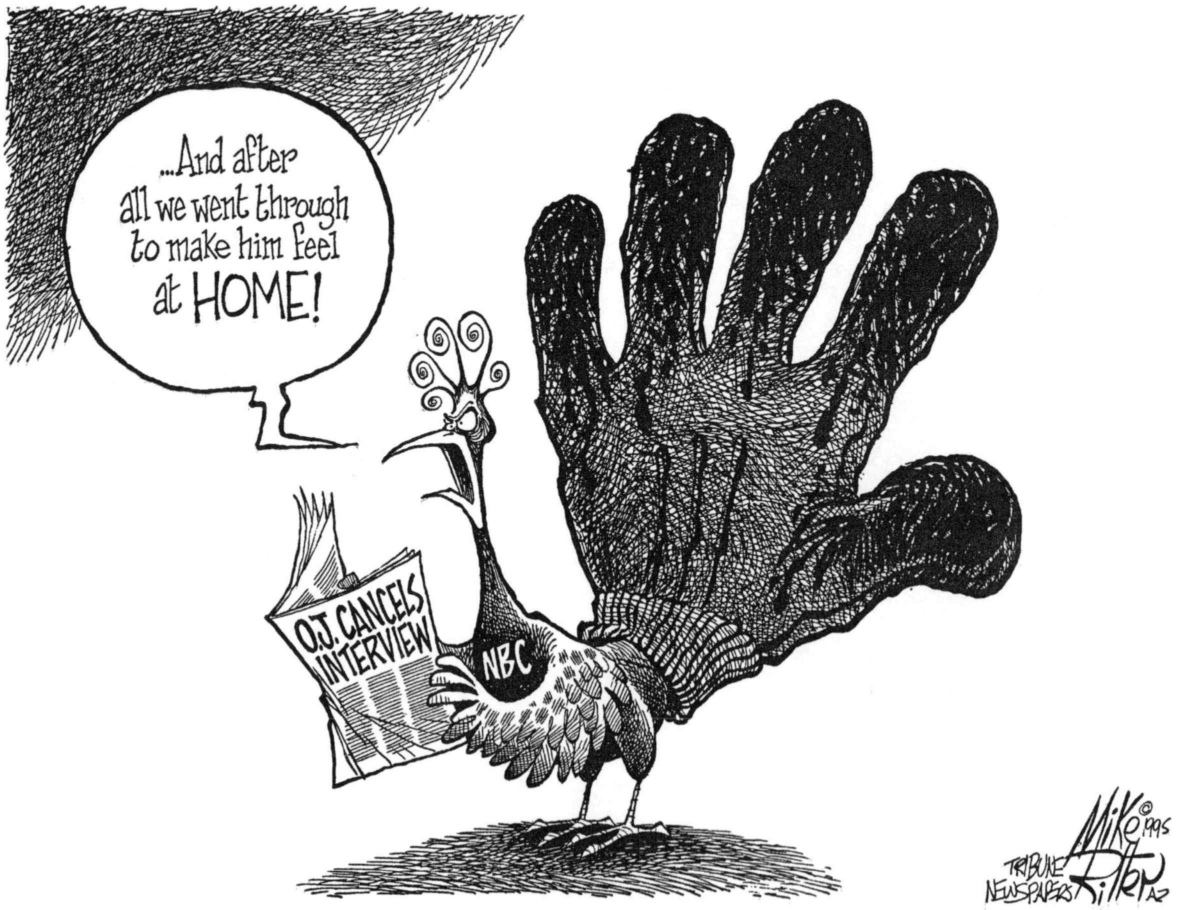
...And after all we went through to make him feel at HOME!
O.J. CANCELS INTERVIEW
NBC

MIKE RITTER
Courtesy Tribune Newspapers

BEN SARGENT
Courtesy Austin American-Statesman

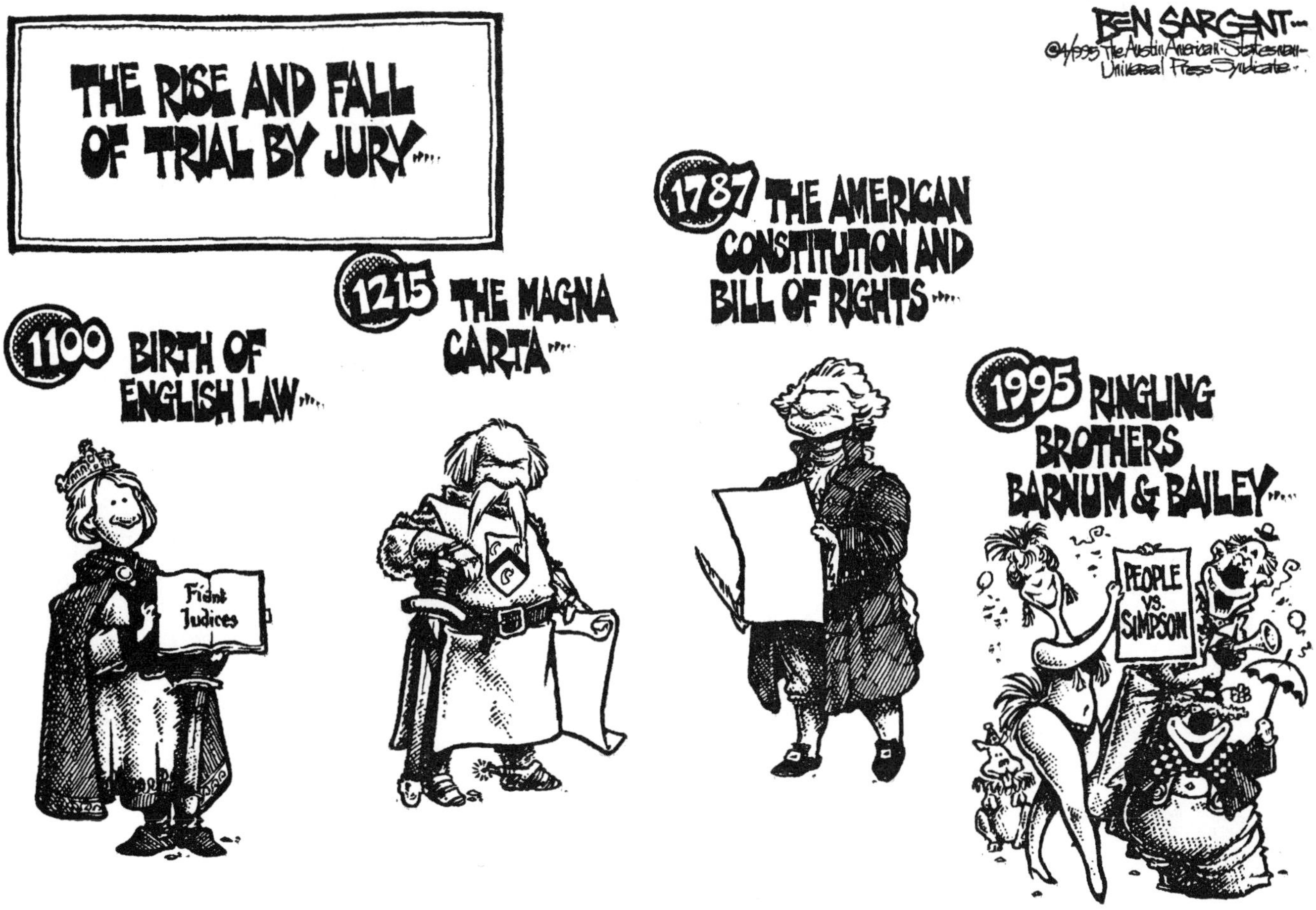
BEN SARGENT
THE RISE AND FALL OF TRIAL BY JURY......
1100 BIRTH OF ENGLISH LAW......
Fiant Judices
1215 THE MAGNA CARTA......
1787 THE AMERICAN CONSTITUTION AND BILL OF RIGHTS......
1995 RINGLING BROTHERS BARNUM & BAILEY......
PEOPLE vs. SIMPSON

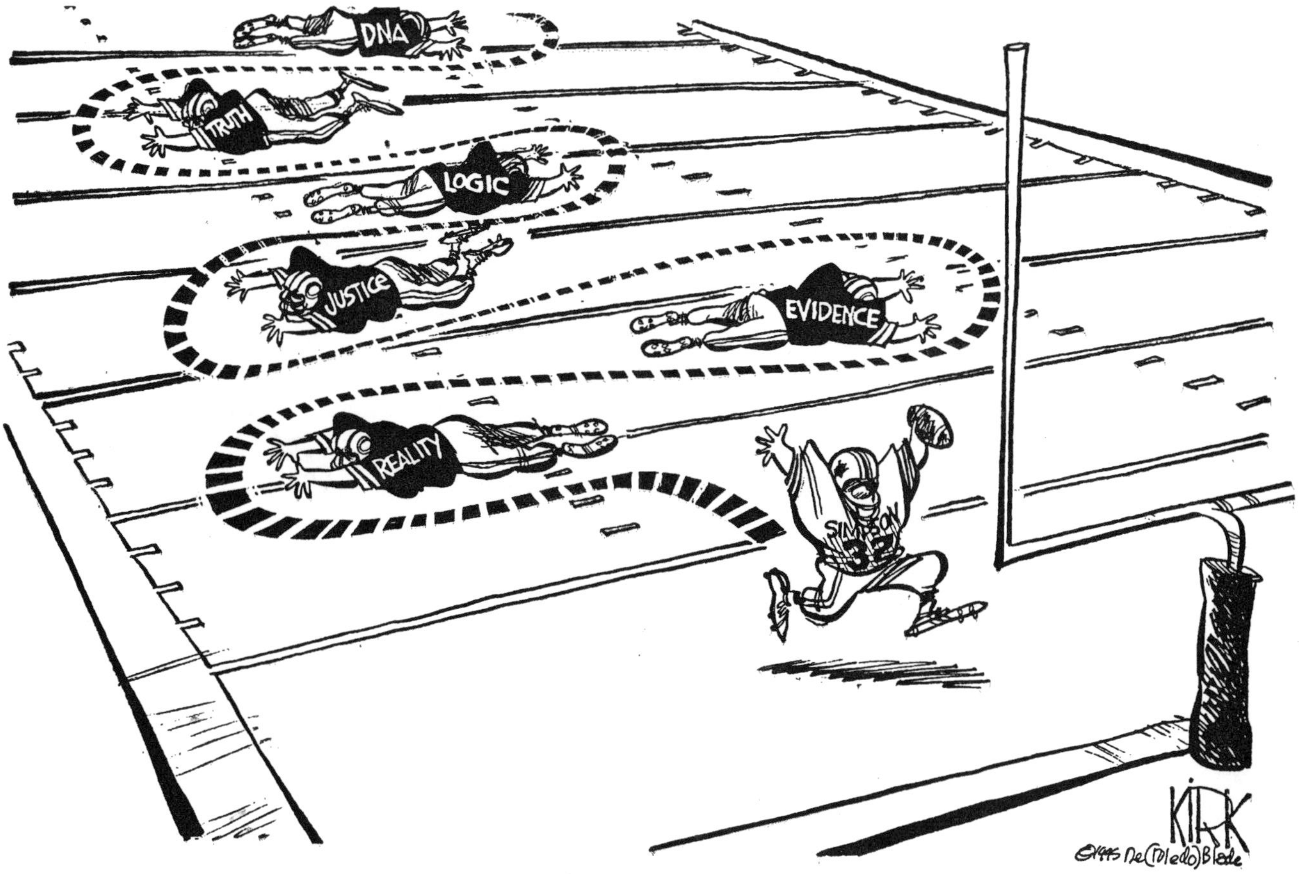
DNA
TRUTH
LOGIC
JUSTICE
EVIDENCE
REALITY
KIRK

KIRK WALTERS
Courtesy Toledo Blade

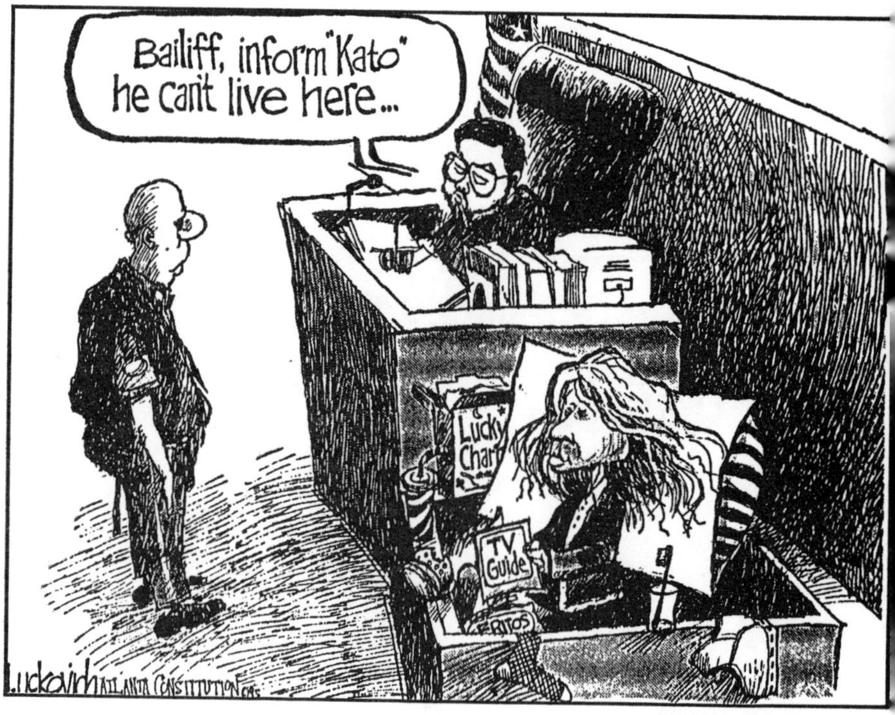
Bailiff, inform "Kato" he can't live here...
TV Guide

MIKE LUCKOVICH
Courtesy Atlanta Constitution

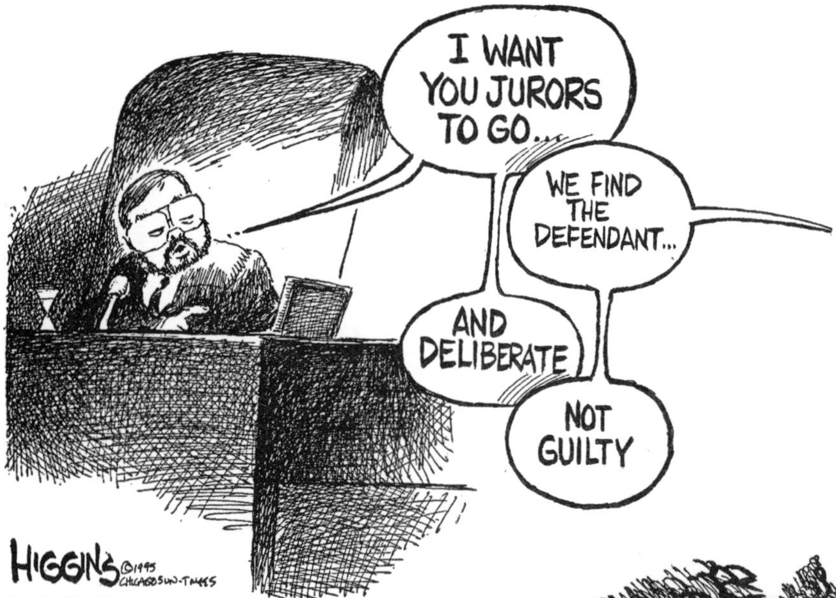
I WANT YOU JURORS TO GO...
AND DELIBERATE
WE FIND THE DEFENDANT...
NOT GUILTY

JACK HIGGINS
Courtesy Chicago Sun-Times

STEVEN LAIT
Courtesy Oakland Tribune

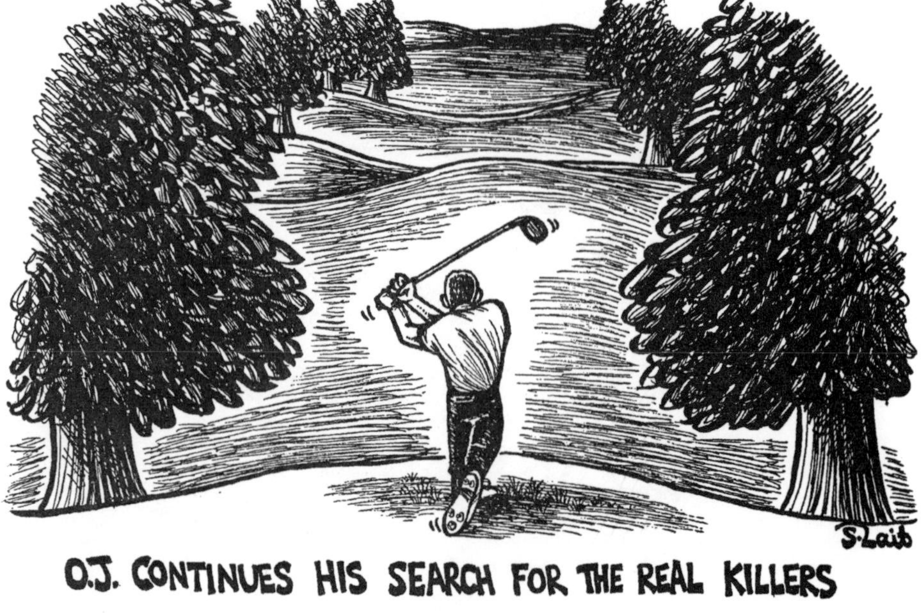

O.J. CONTINUES HIS SEARCH FOR THE REAL KILLERS

Society and the Family

When Vice-Pres. Dan Quayle declared in 1992 that the breakup of families was undermining America and that society needed caring fathers in the home, he was derided as an idiot. Things have changed. Many of Quayle's critics have become champions of the family as polls repeatedly show that children living in homes without fathers are more likely to become ensnared by drugs and crime and doomed to poverty.

In October, a heralded Million Man March of black men called by Louis Farrakhan took place in Washington. The purpose of the march was to acknowledge that two-parent families are the bedrock of a stable culture and to call upon absent fathers to come home.

"Trash" television talk shows, such as those hosted by Sally Jessy Raphael, Ricki Lake, Maury Povich, and Montel Williams, attracted their share of criticism. As the sleaze on the airwaves increased, Sen. Sam Nunn and William Bennett urged viewers to boycott products advertised on such shows.

Child pornographers have moved from dark alleys to on-line computer networks to ply their trade, and Congress began seeking ways to control what children can see in cyberspace. Calvin Klein ads featuring teenagers in suggestive poses raised a storm of protest. Critics demanded the ads be withdrawn, and they were.

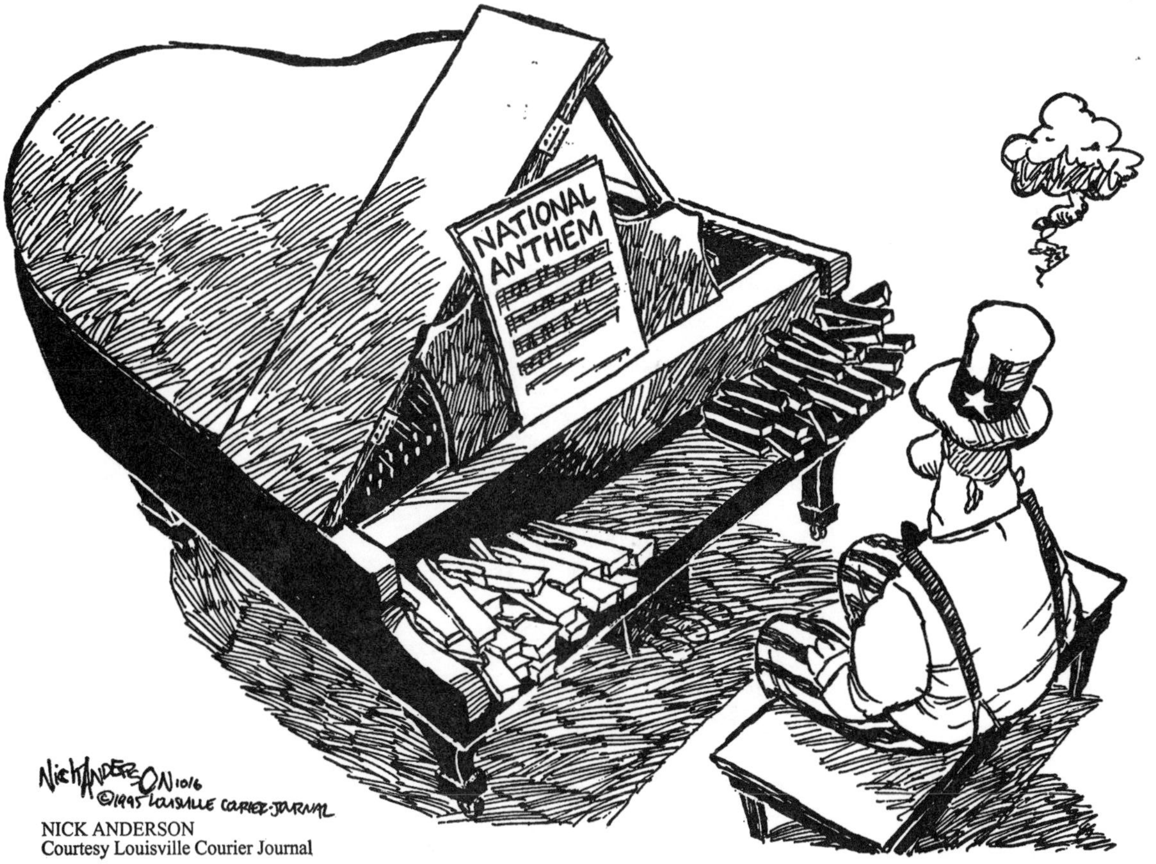
NATIONAL ANTHEM

NICK ANDERSON
Courtesy Louisville Courier Journal

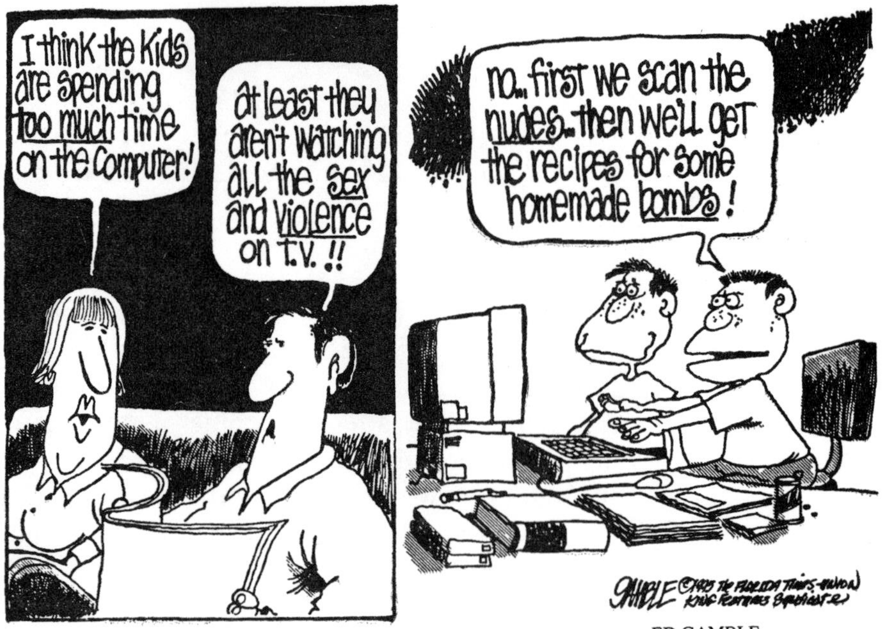
I think the Kids are spending too much time on the Computer!
at least they aren't watching all the sex and violence on t.v. !!
no... first we scan the nudes... then we'll get the recipes for some homemade bombs!

ED GAMBLE
Courtesy Florida Times-Union

JOE HELLER
Courtesy Green Bay Press-Gazette

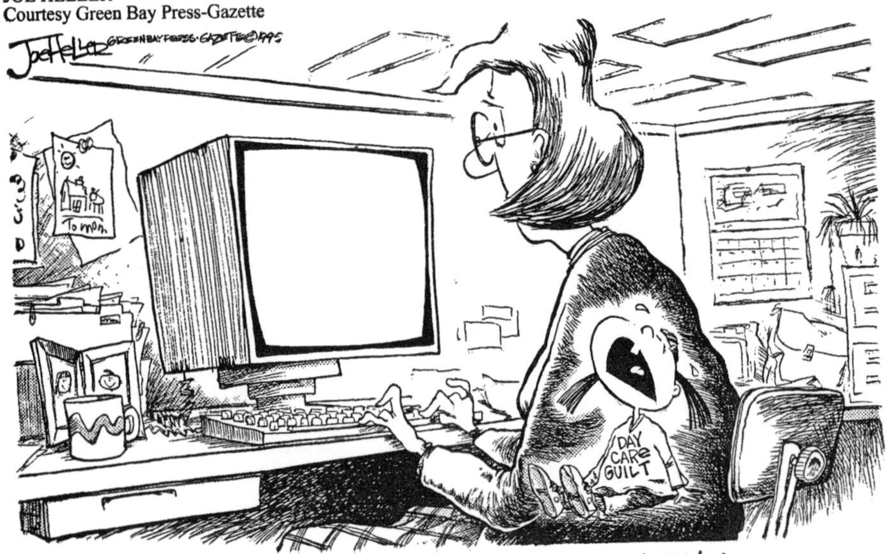
JoeHeller Green Bay Press-Gazette ©1995
To mom
DAY CARE GUILT

THE INNER CHILD THAT GOES TO WORK WITH YOU

JOHN BRANCH
Courtesy San Antonio Express-News

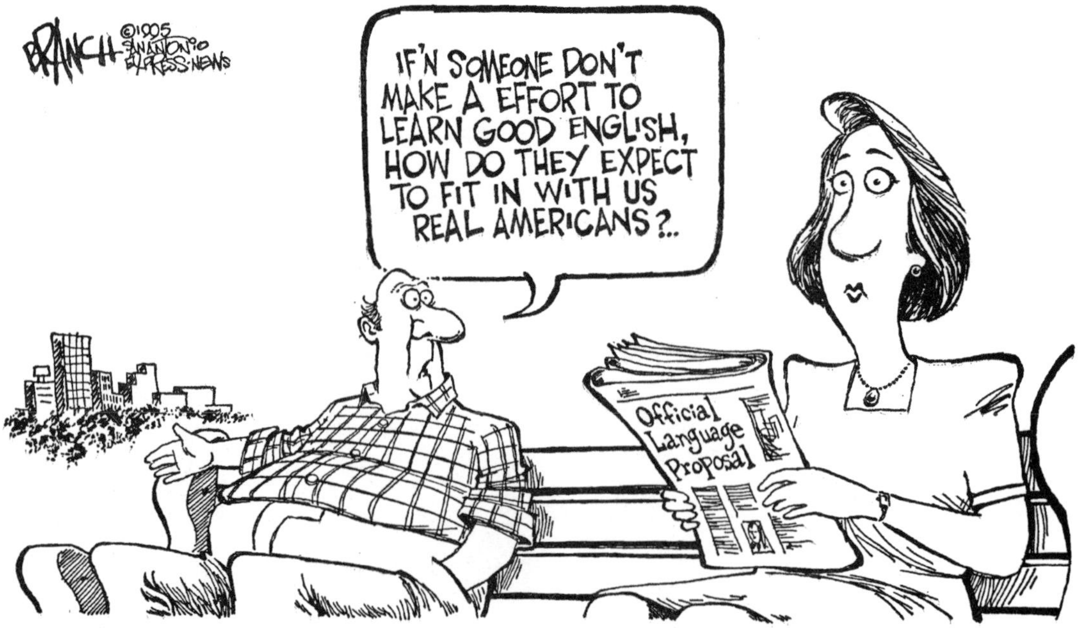
BRANCH ©1995 San Antonio Express-News
IF'N SOMEONE DON'T MAKE A EFFORT TO LEARN GOOD ENGLISH, HOW DO THEY EXPECT TO FIT IN WITH US REAL AMERICANS?..
Official Language Proposal

DAVID HORSEY
Courtesy Seattle Post-Intelligencer

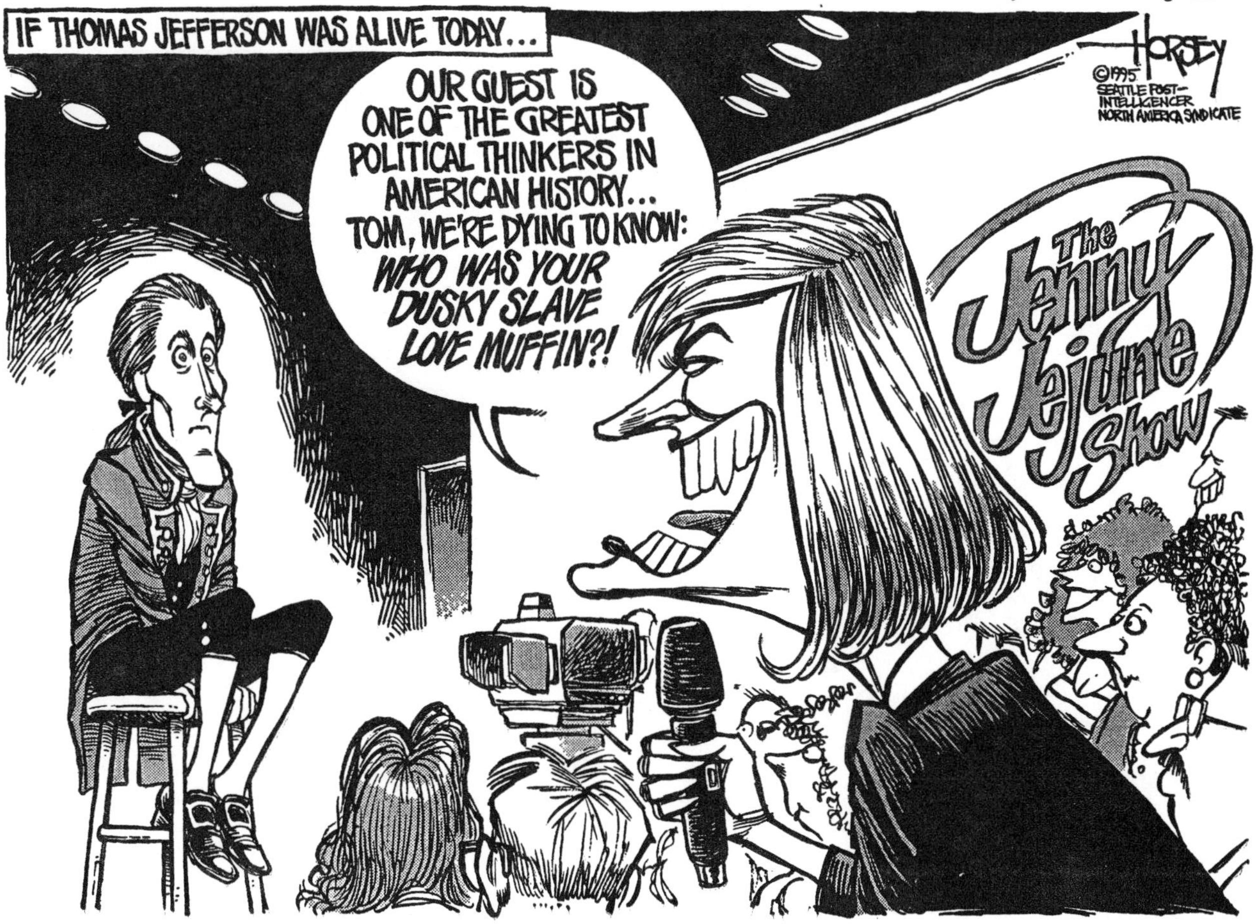
IF THOMAS JEFFERSON WAS ALIVE TODAY...
OUR GUEST IS ONE OF THE GREATEST POLITICAL THINKERS IN AMERICAN HISTORY... TOM, WE'RE DYING TO KNOW: WHO WAS YOUR DUSKY SLAVE LOVE MUFFIN?!
The Jenny Jejune Show
HORSEY
©1995 SEATTLE POST-INTELLIGENCER NORTH AMERICA SYNDICATE

MICHAEL RAMIREZ
Courtesy Memphis Commercial Appeal

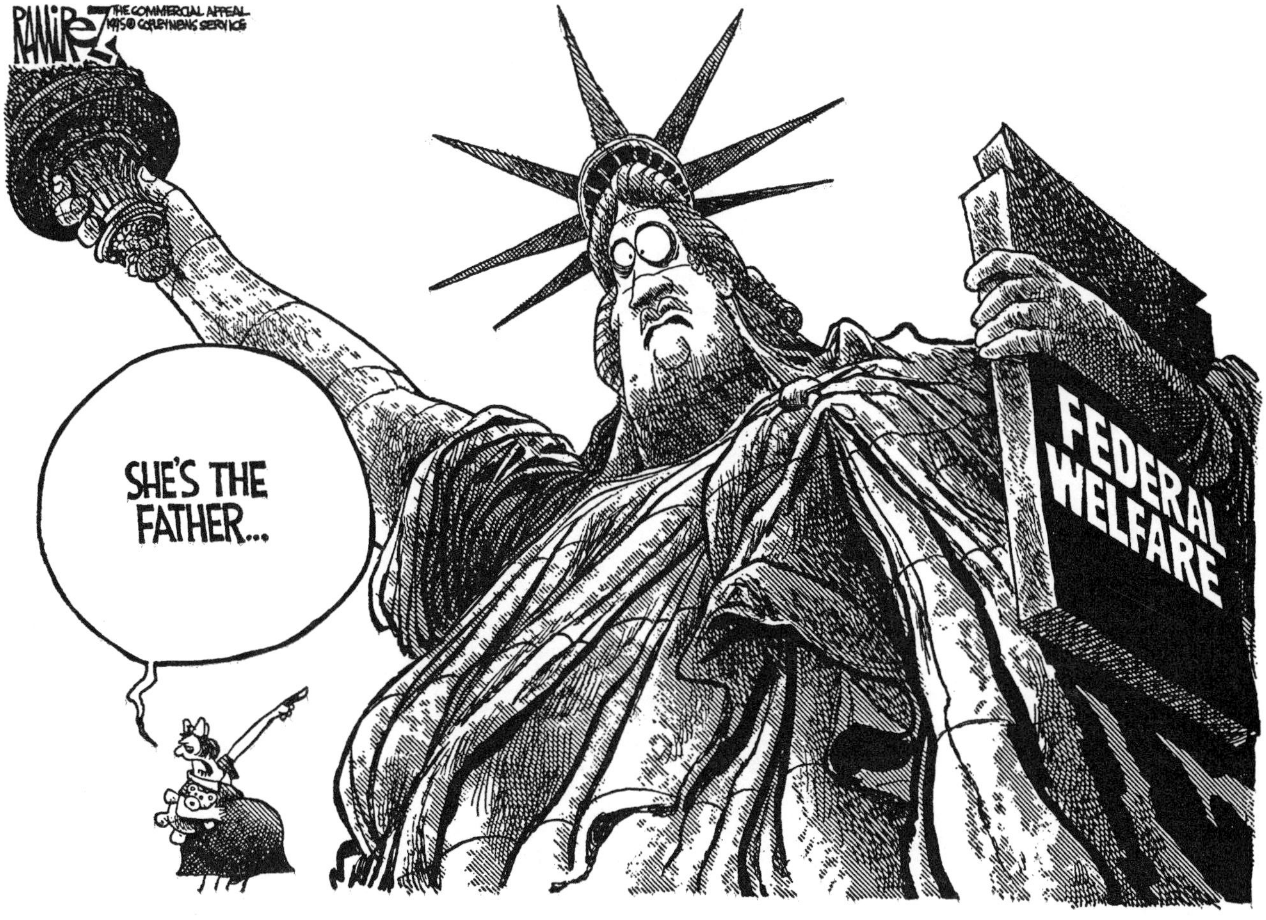
RAMIREZ
THE COMMERCIAL APPEAL 1995© COPLEY NEWS SERVICE
SHE'S THE FATHER...
FEDERAL WELFARE

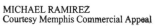

JEFF STAHLER
Courtesy Cincinnati Post

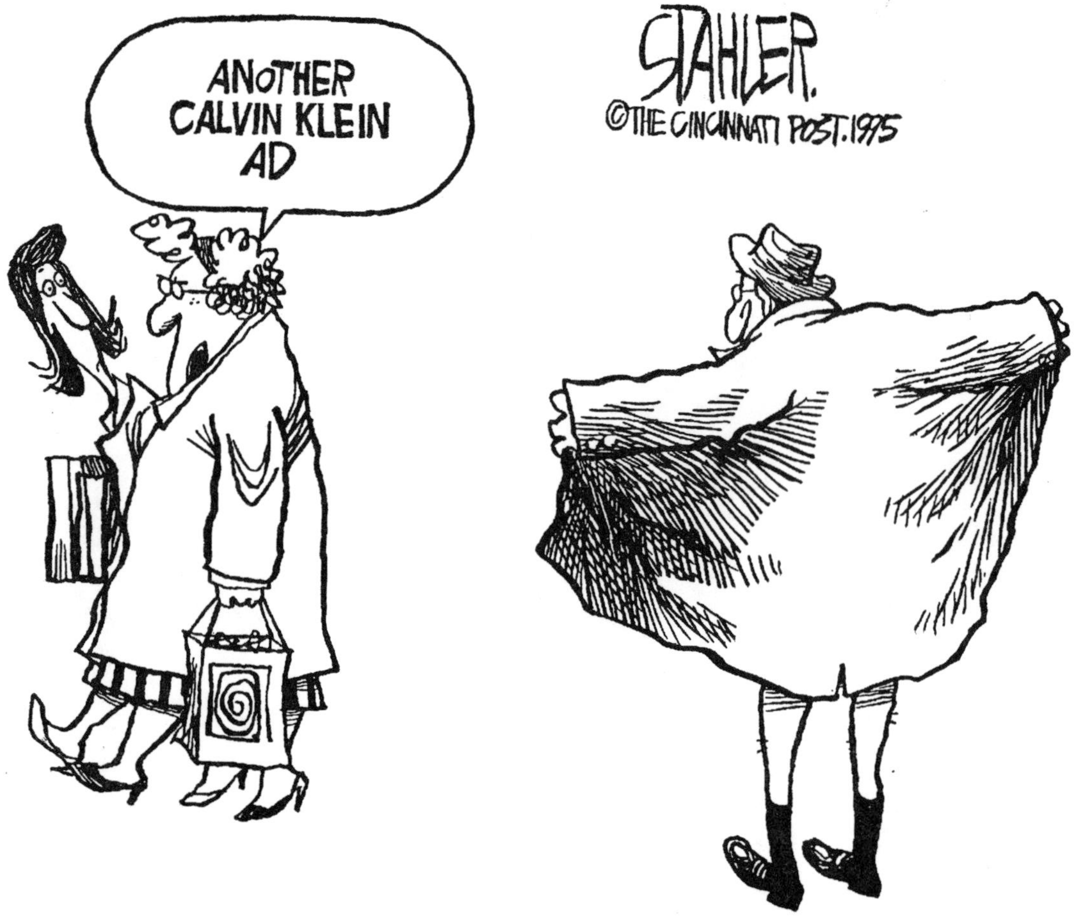
STAHLER.
©THE CINCINNATI POST.1995
ANOTHER CALVIN KLEIN AD

GARY VARVEL
Courtesy Indianapolis Star

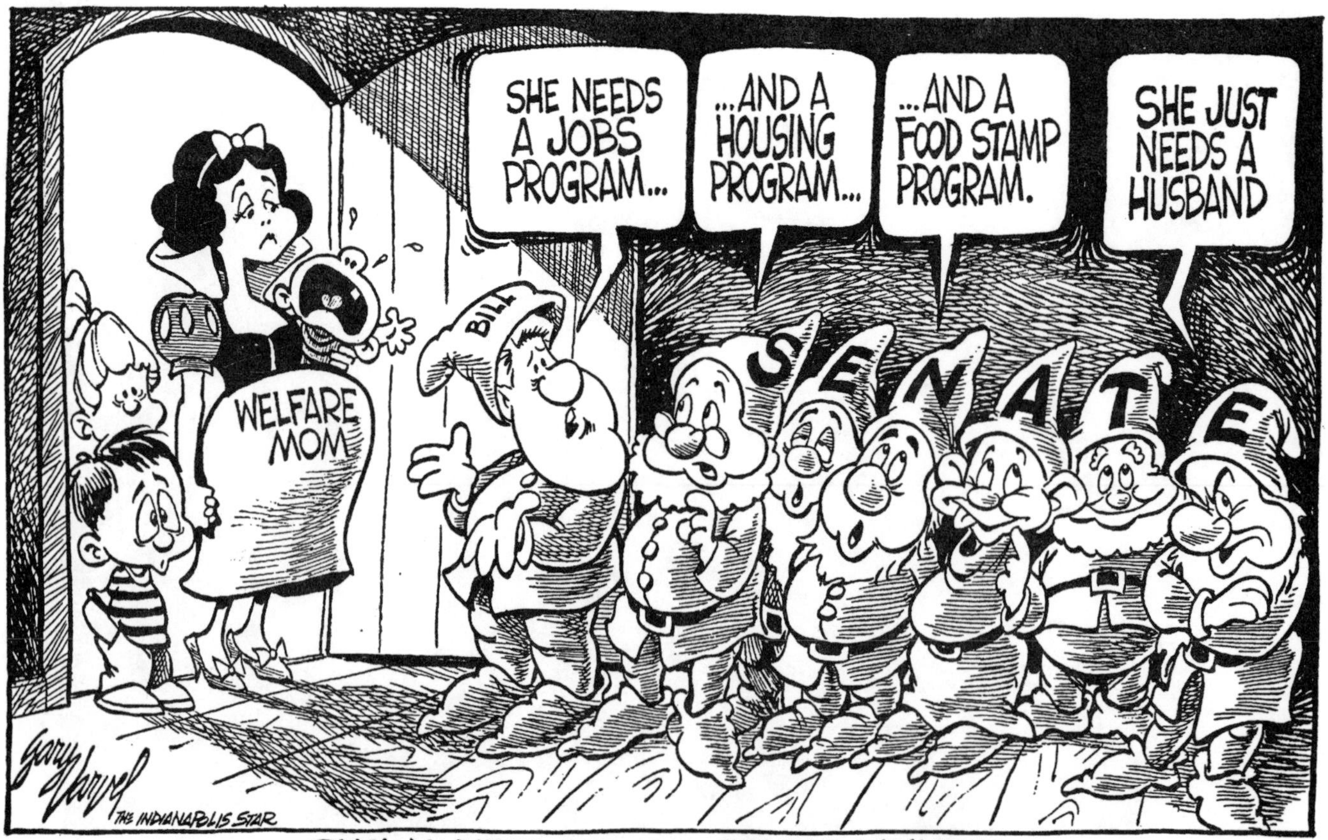
SHE NEEDS A JOBS PROGRAM...
...AND A HOUSING PROGRAM...
...AND A FOOD STAMP PROGRAM.
SHE JUST NEEDS A HUSBAND
WELFARE MOM
BILL
SENATE
Gary Varvel
THE INDIANAPOLIS STAR

SNOW WHINE AND THE SEVEN DWARFS

MATT DAVIES
Courtesy Gannett Suburban Newspapers

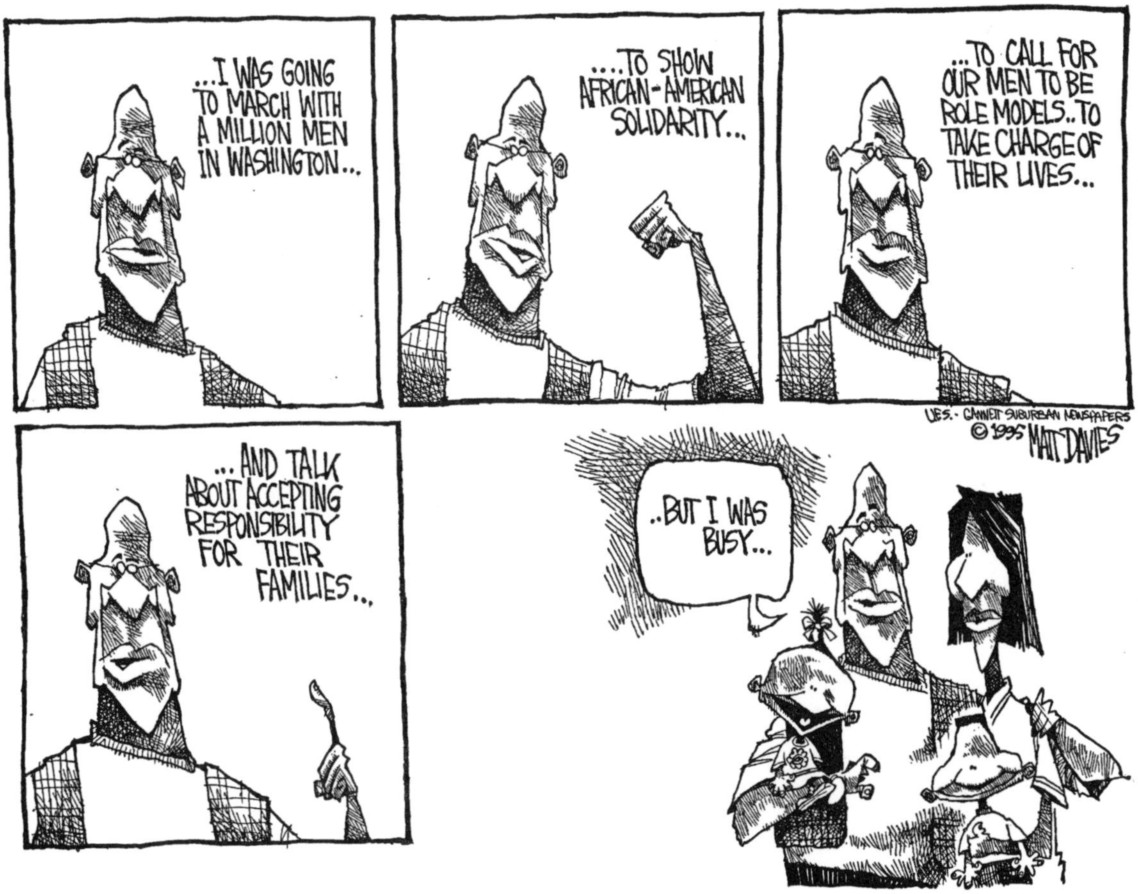
...I WAS GOING TO MARCH WITH A MILLION MEN IN WASHINGTON...
....TO SHOW AFRICAN-AMERICAN SOLIDARITY...
...TO CALL FOR OUR MEN TO BE ROLE MODELS..TO TAKE CHARGE OF THEIR LIVES...
...AND TALK ABOUT ACCEPTING RESPONSIBILITY FOR THEIR FAMILIES...
..BUT I WAS BUSY...
©1995 MATT DAVIES

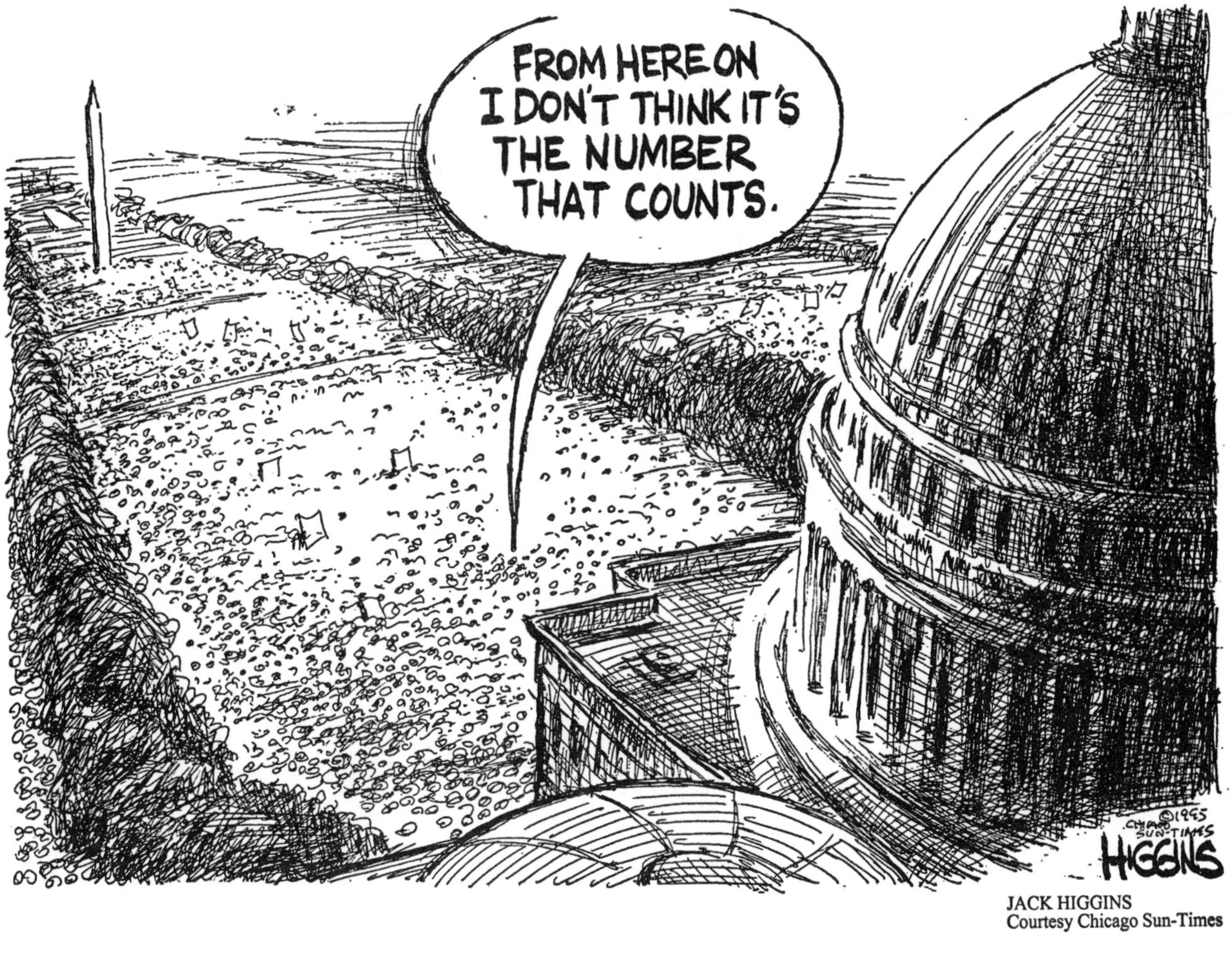
FROM HERE ON I DON'T THINK IT'S THE NUMBER THAT COUNTS.
©1995 HIGGINS

JACK HIGGINS
Courtesy Chicago Sun-Times

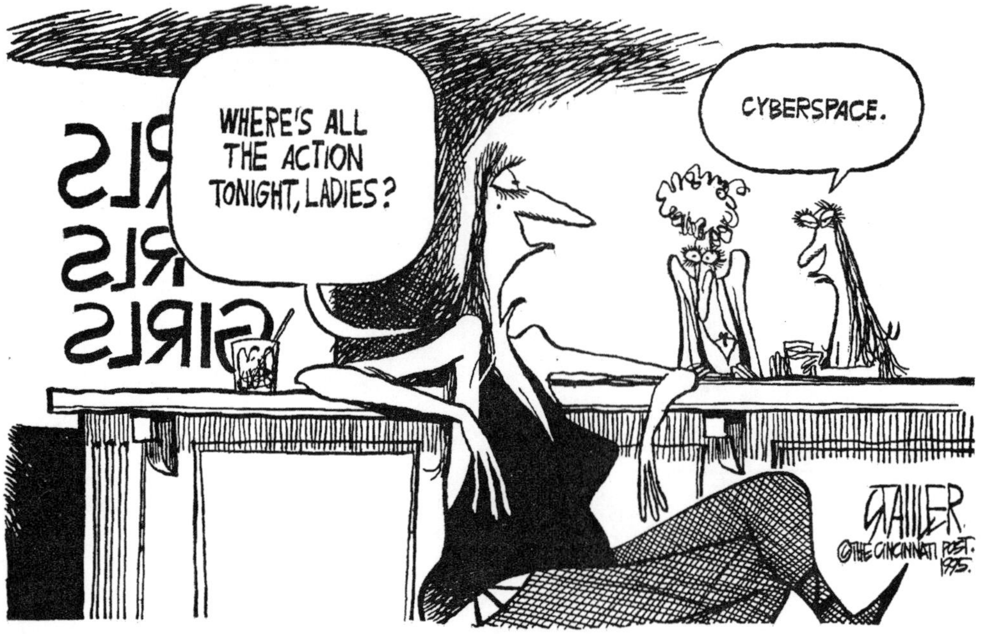

WHERE'S ALL THE ACTION TONIGHT, LADIES?
CYBERSPACE.
STAHLER
©THE CINCINNATI POST. 1995.

JEFF STAHLER
Courtesy Cincinnati Post

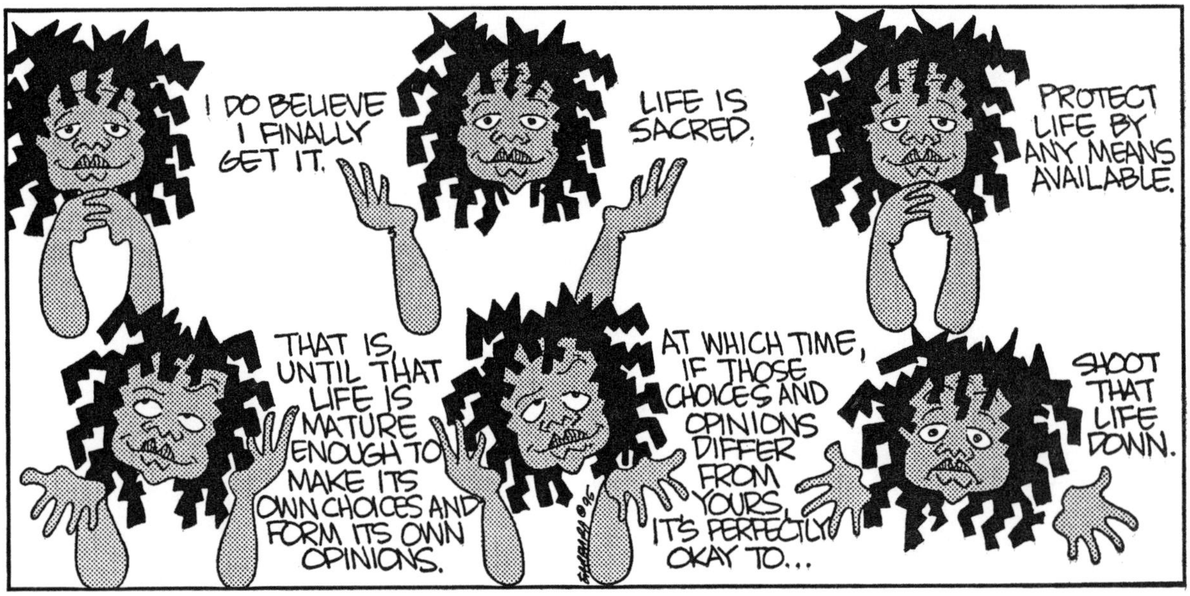

I DO BELIEVE I FINALLY GET IT.
LIFE IS SACRED.
PROTECT LIFE BY ANY MEANS AVAILABLE.
THAT IS, UNTIL THAT LIFE IS MATURE ENOUGH TO MAKE ITS OWN CHOICES AND FORM ITS OWN OPINIONS.
AT WHICH TIME, IF THOSE CHOICES AND OPINIONS DIFFER FROM YOURS, IT'S PERFECTLY OKAY TO...
SHOOT THAT LIFE DOWN.

BARBARA BRANDON
Courtesy Universal Press Syndicate

STEVE SACK
Courtesy Minneapolis Star-Tribune

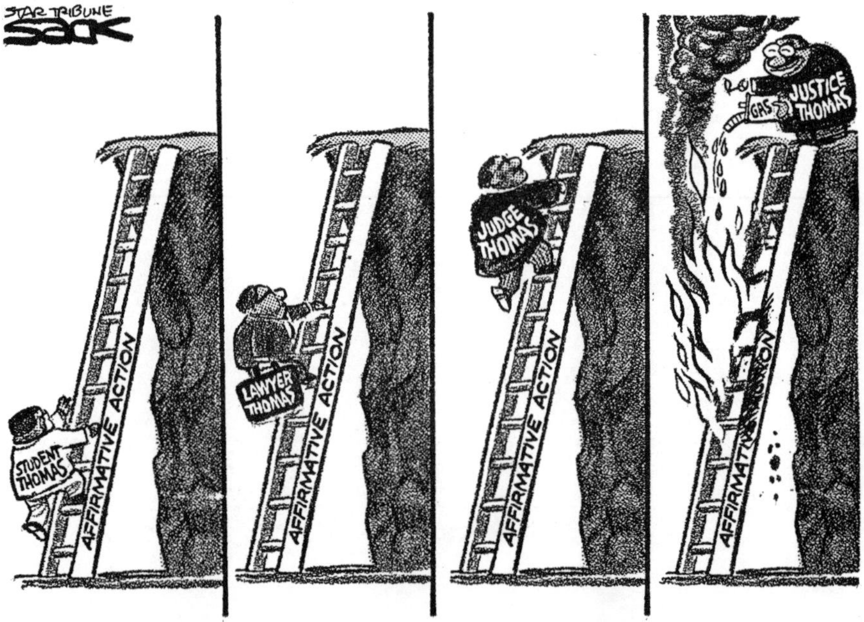

STAR TRIBUNE
SACK
STUDENT THOMAS
AFFIRMATIVE ACTION
LAWYER THOMAS
AFFIRMATIVE ACTION
JUDGE THOMAS
AFFIRMATIVE ACTION
JUSTICE THOMAS
GAS

DICK WALLMEYER
Courtesy Long Beach Press-Telegram

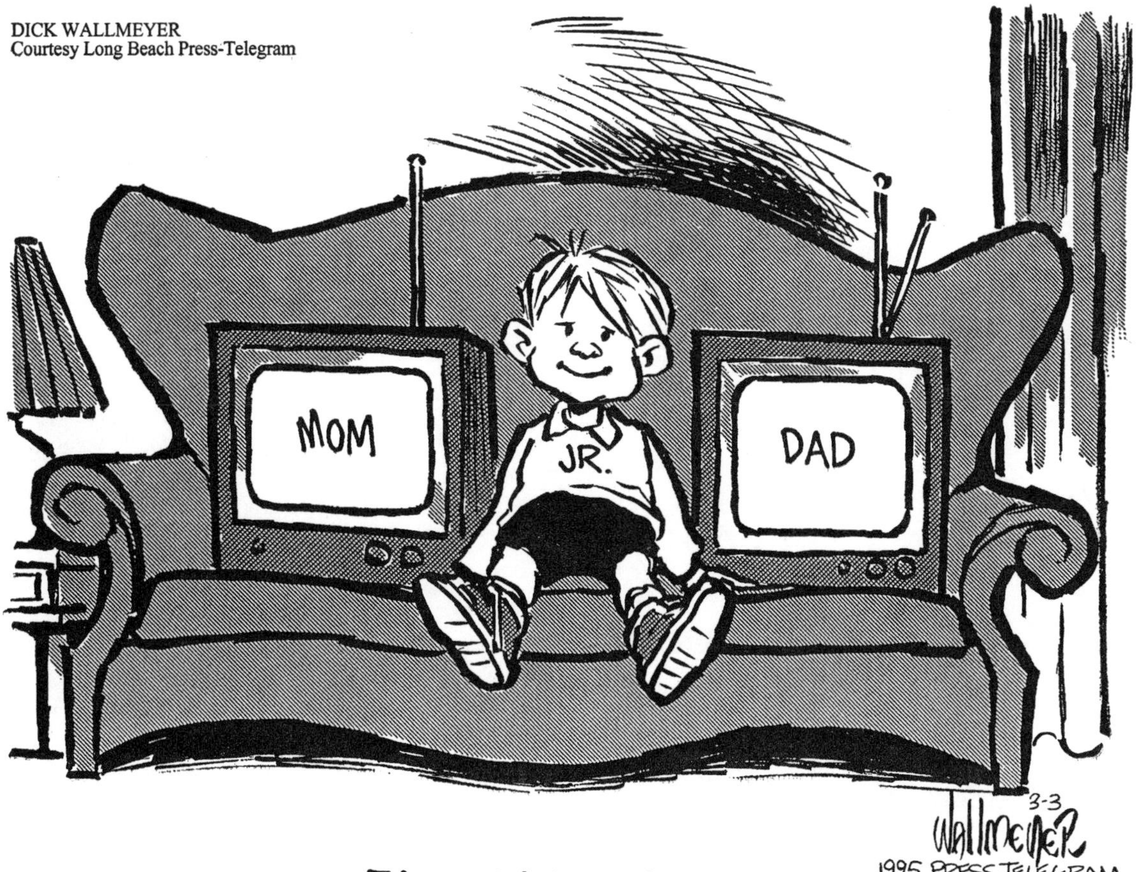

MOM
JR.
DAD
3-3
Wallmeyer
1995, PRESS-TELEGRAM

FAMILY PORTRAIT

STEVE KELLEY
Courtesy San Diego Union

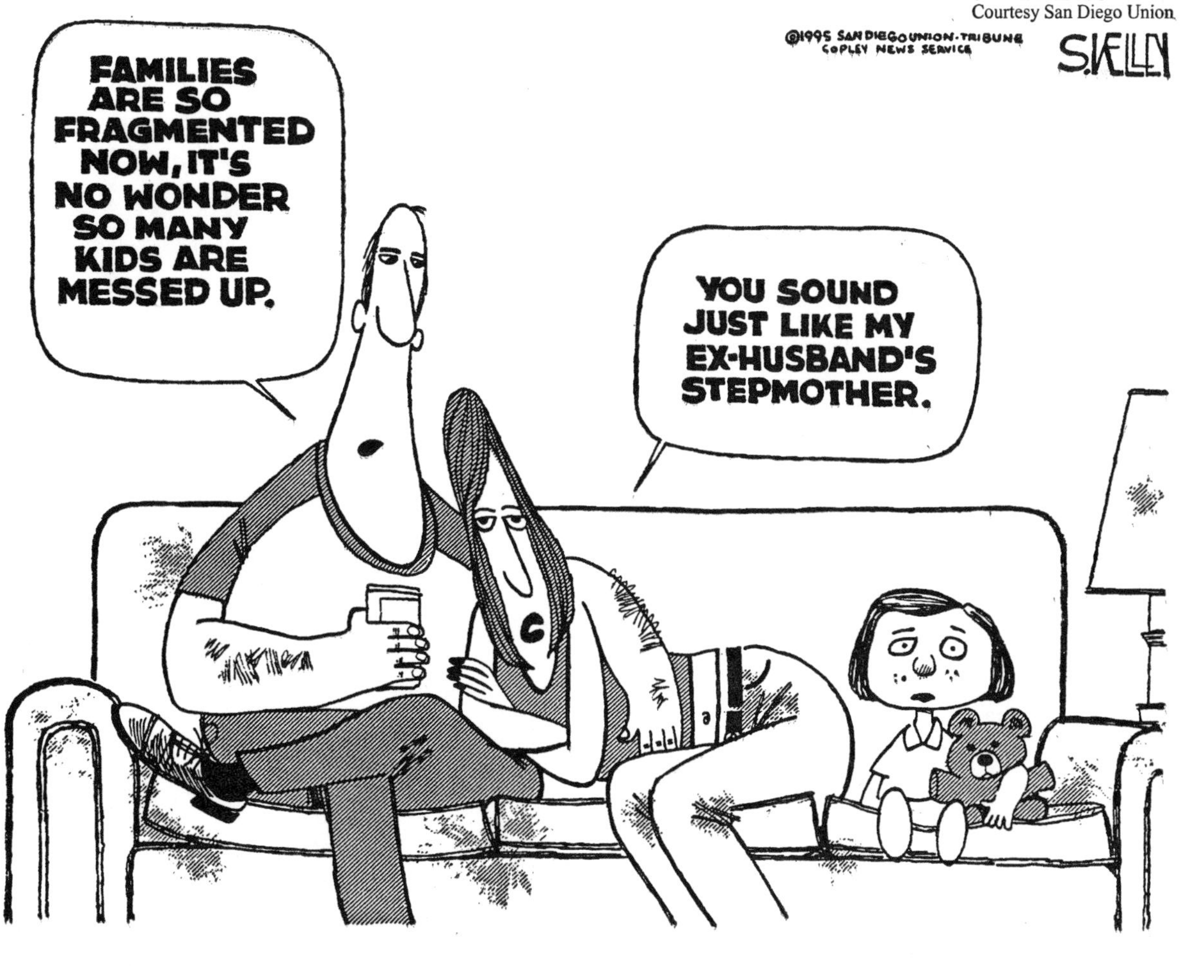

©1995 SAN DIEGO UNION-TRIBUNE COPLEY NEWS SERVICE
S.KELLEY
FAMILIES ARE SO FRAGMENTED NOW, IT'S NO WONDER SO MANY KIDS ARE MESSED UP.
YOU SOUND JUST LIKE MY EX-HUSBAND'S STEPMOTHER.

WALT HANDELSMAN
Courtesy Times-Picayune (N.O.)

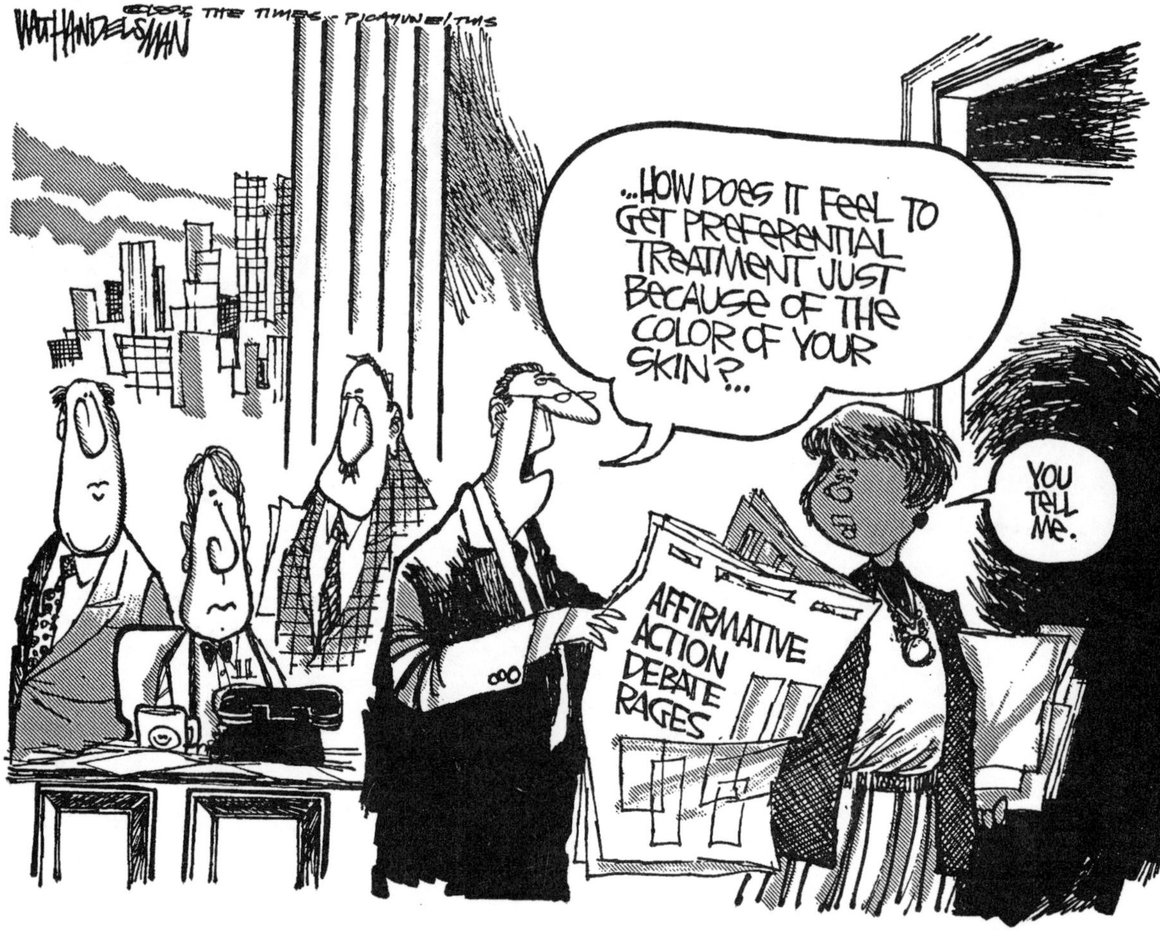
...HOW DOES IT FEEL TO GET PREFERENTIAL TREATMENT JUST BECAUSE OF THE COLOR OF YOUR SKIN?...
YOU TELL ME.
AFFIRMATIVE ACTION DEBATE RAGES

STEVE KELLEY
Courtesy San Diego Union

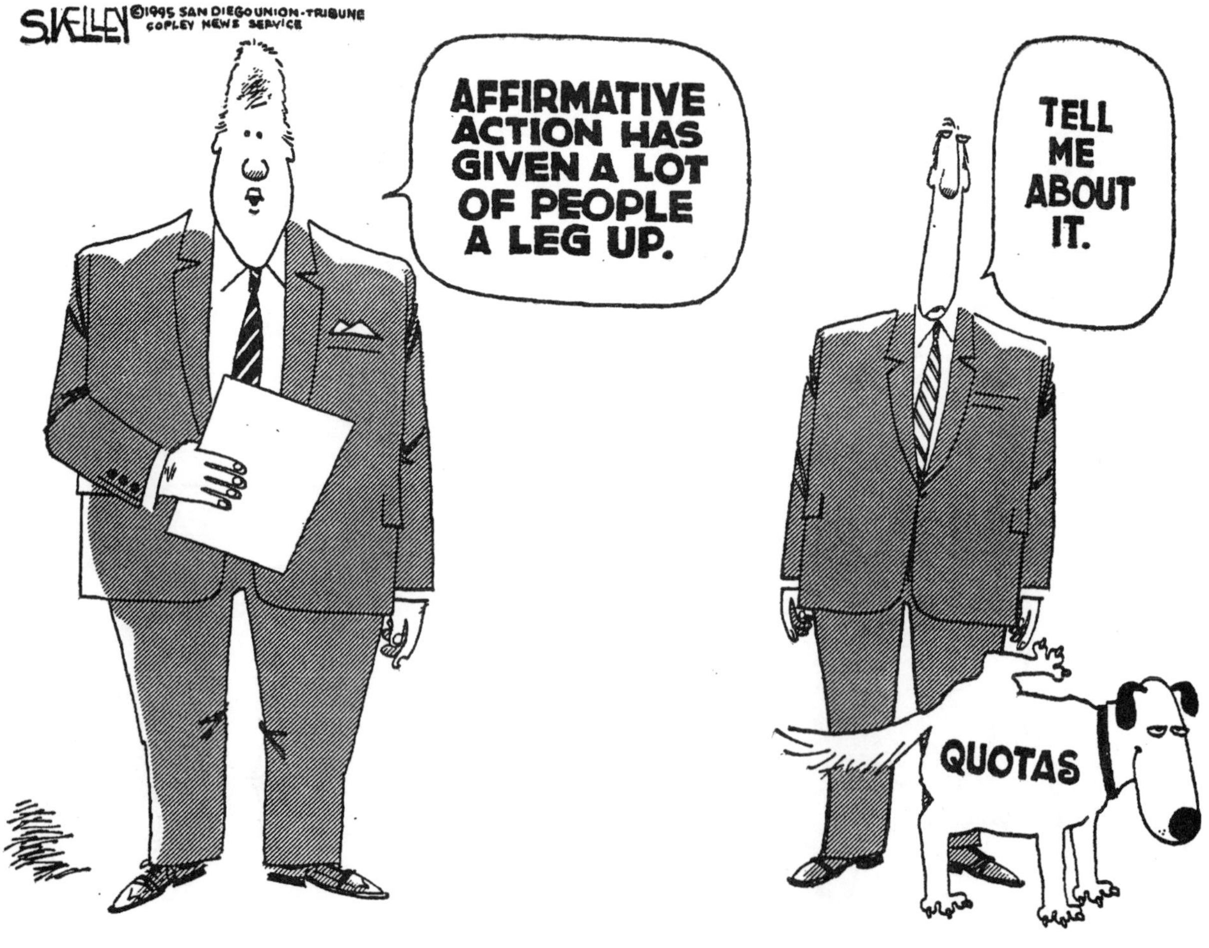
S.KELLEY ©1995 SAN DIEGO UNION-TRIBUNE COPLEY NEWS SERVICE
AFFIRMATIVE ACTION HAS GIVEN A LOT OF PEOPLE A LEG UP.
TELL ME ABOUT IT.
QUOTAS

JOHN TREVER
Courtesy Albuquerque Journal

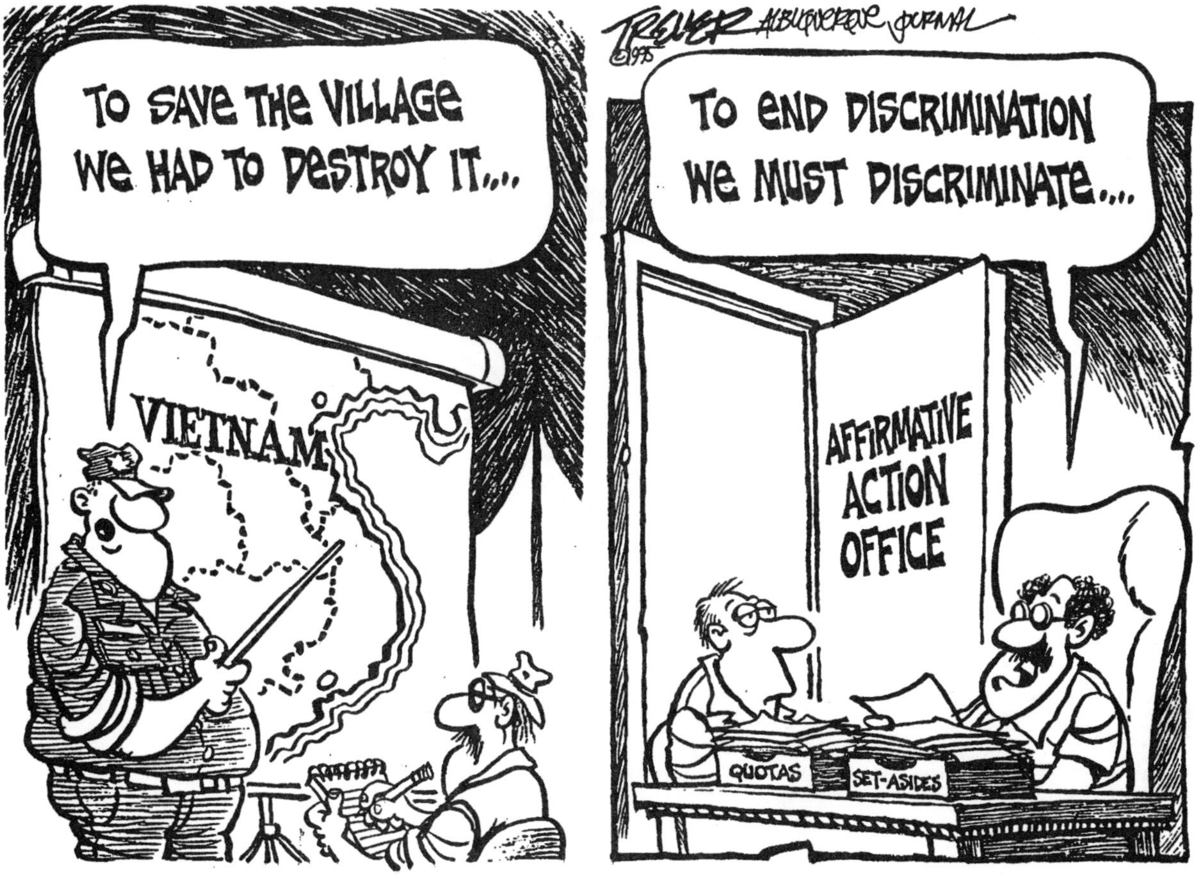

TO SAVE THE VILLAGE WE HAD TO DESTROY IT....
VIETNAM
TO END DISCRIMINATION WE MUST DISCRIMINATE....
AFFIRMATIVE ACTION OFFICE
QUOTAS
SET-ASIDES

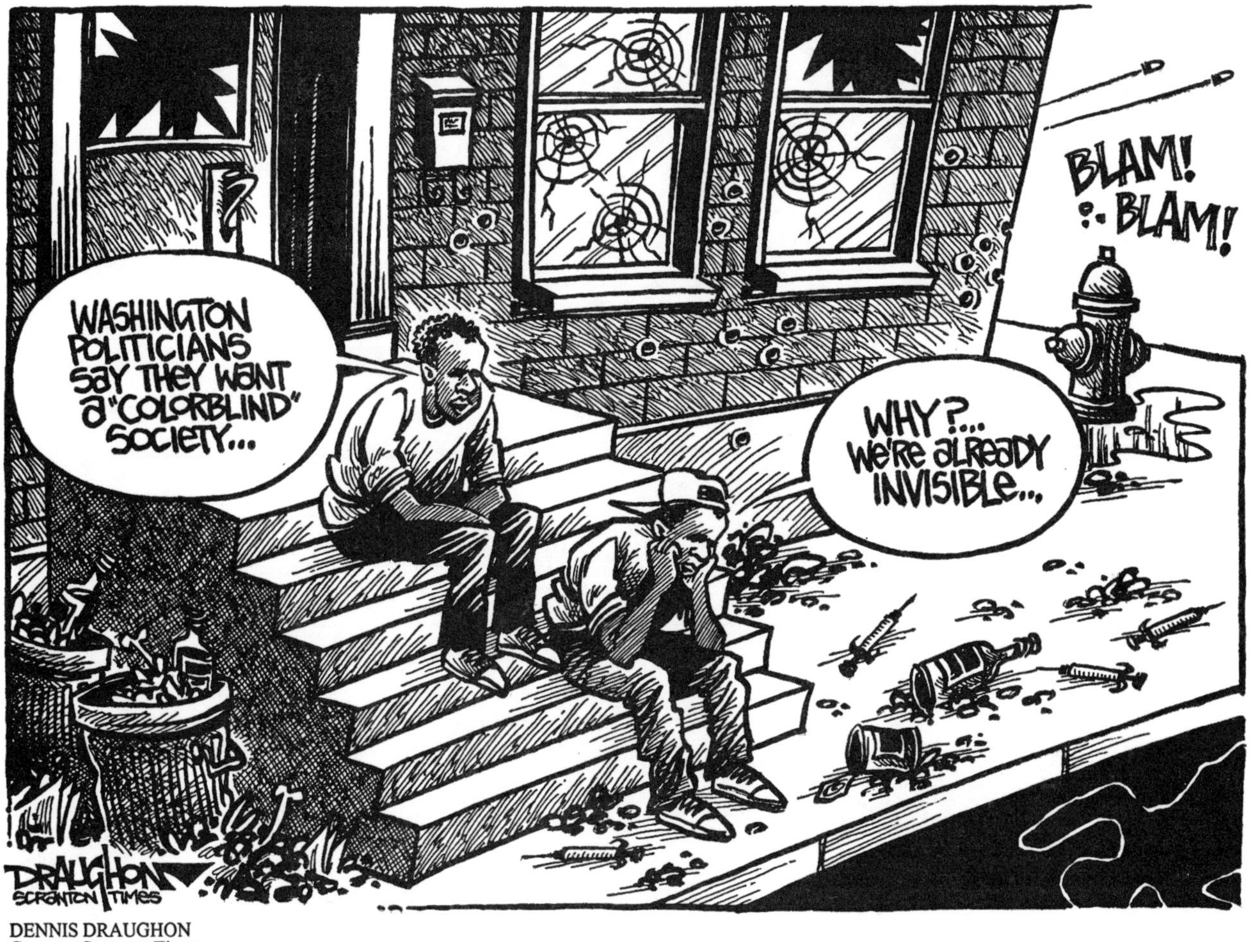

BLAM! BLAM!
WASHINGTON POLITICIANS SAY THEY WANT A "COLORBLIND" SOCIETY...
WHY?... WE'RE ALREADY INVISIBLE...
DRAUGHON SCRANTON TIMES

DENNIS DRAUGHON
Courtesy Scranton Times

ALAN VITELLO
Courtesy Daily Reporter-Herald (Colo.)

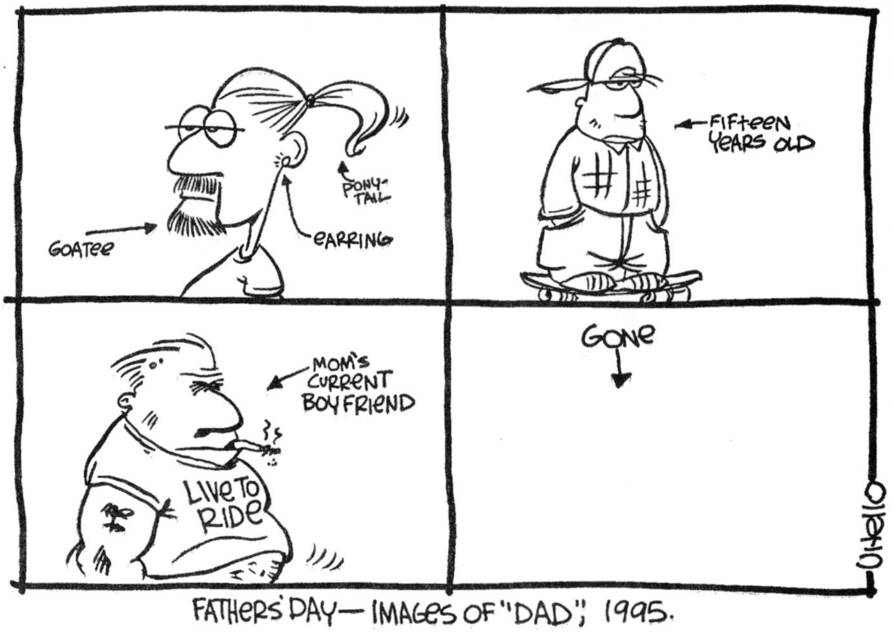
GOATEE
EARRING
PONY-TAIL
FIFTEEN YEARS OLD
MOM'S CURRENT BOYFRIEND
LIVE TO RIDE
GONE
VITELLO
FATHERS' DAY— IMAGES OF "DAD," 1995.

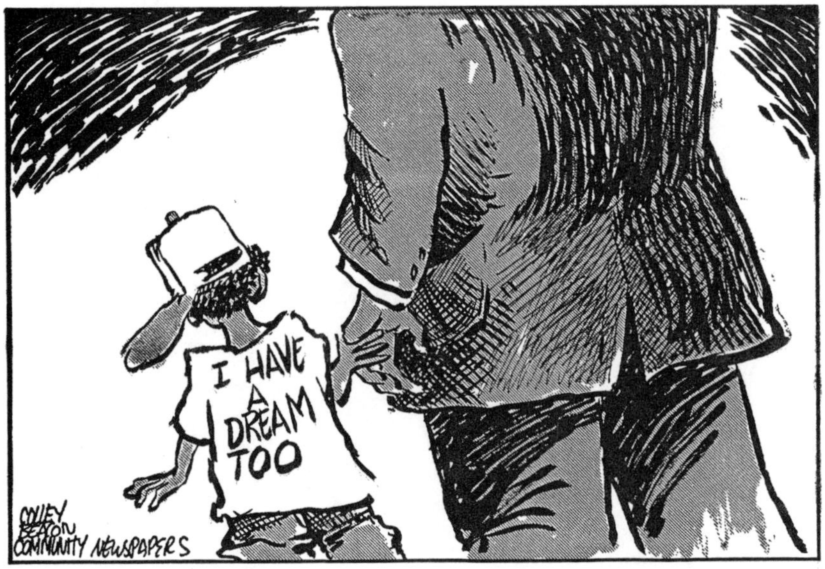
I HAVE A DREAM TOO
COLLEY BEACON COMMUNITY NEWSPAPERS

ED COLLEY
Courtesy Memorial Press Group

JEFF STAHLER
Courtesy Cincinnati Post

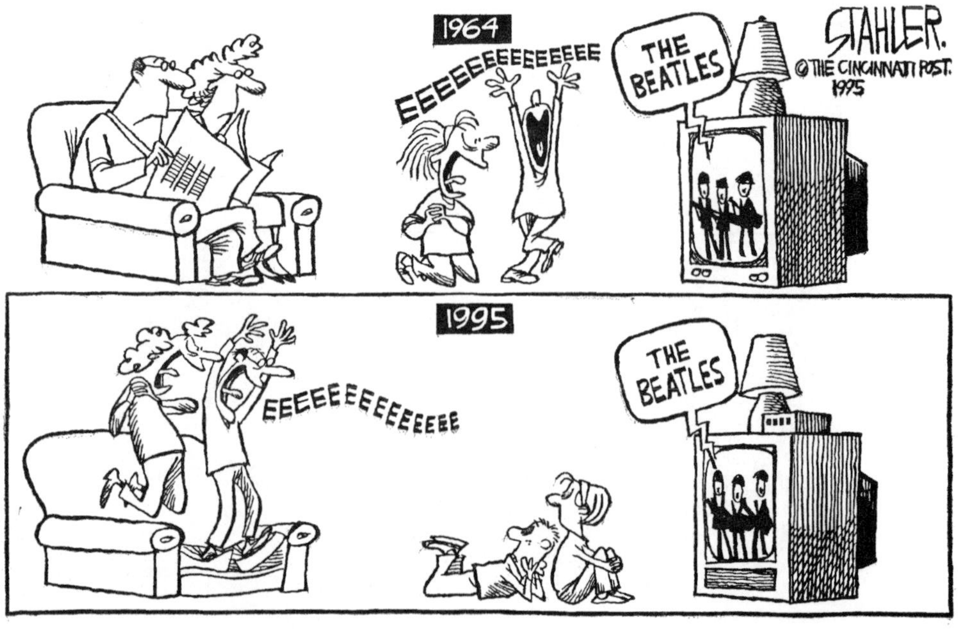
1964
EEEEEEEEEEEEEEE
THE BEATLES
STAHLER. © THE CINCINNATI POST. 1995
1995
EEEEEEEEEEEEEEE
THE BEATLES

CLAY BENNETT
Courtesy North America Syndicate

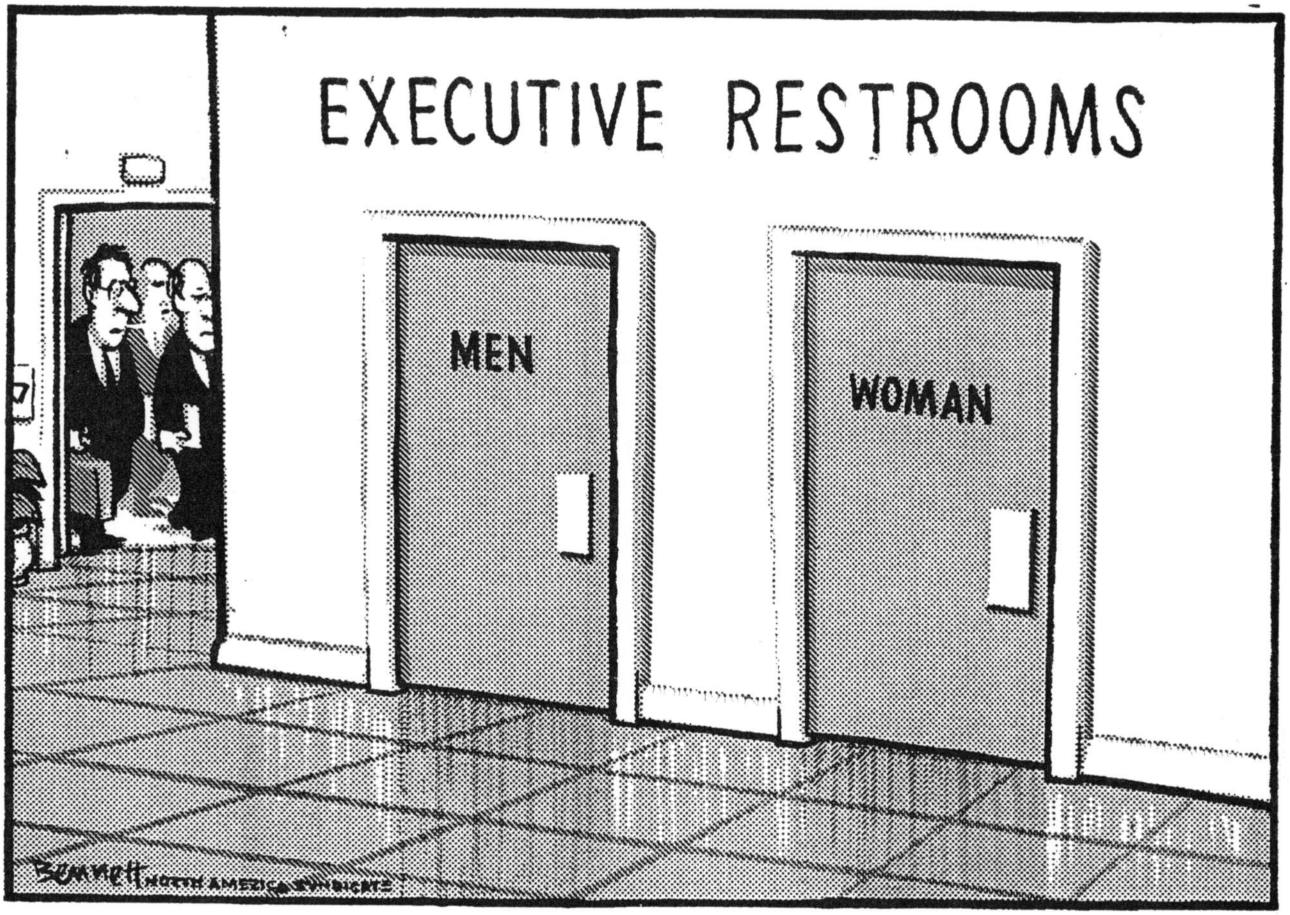
EXECUTIVE RESTROOMS
MEN
WOMAN
BENNETT NORTH AMERICA SYNDICATE

MIKE PETERS
Courtesy Dayton Daily News

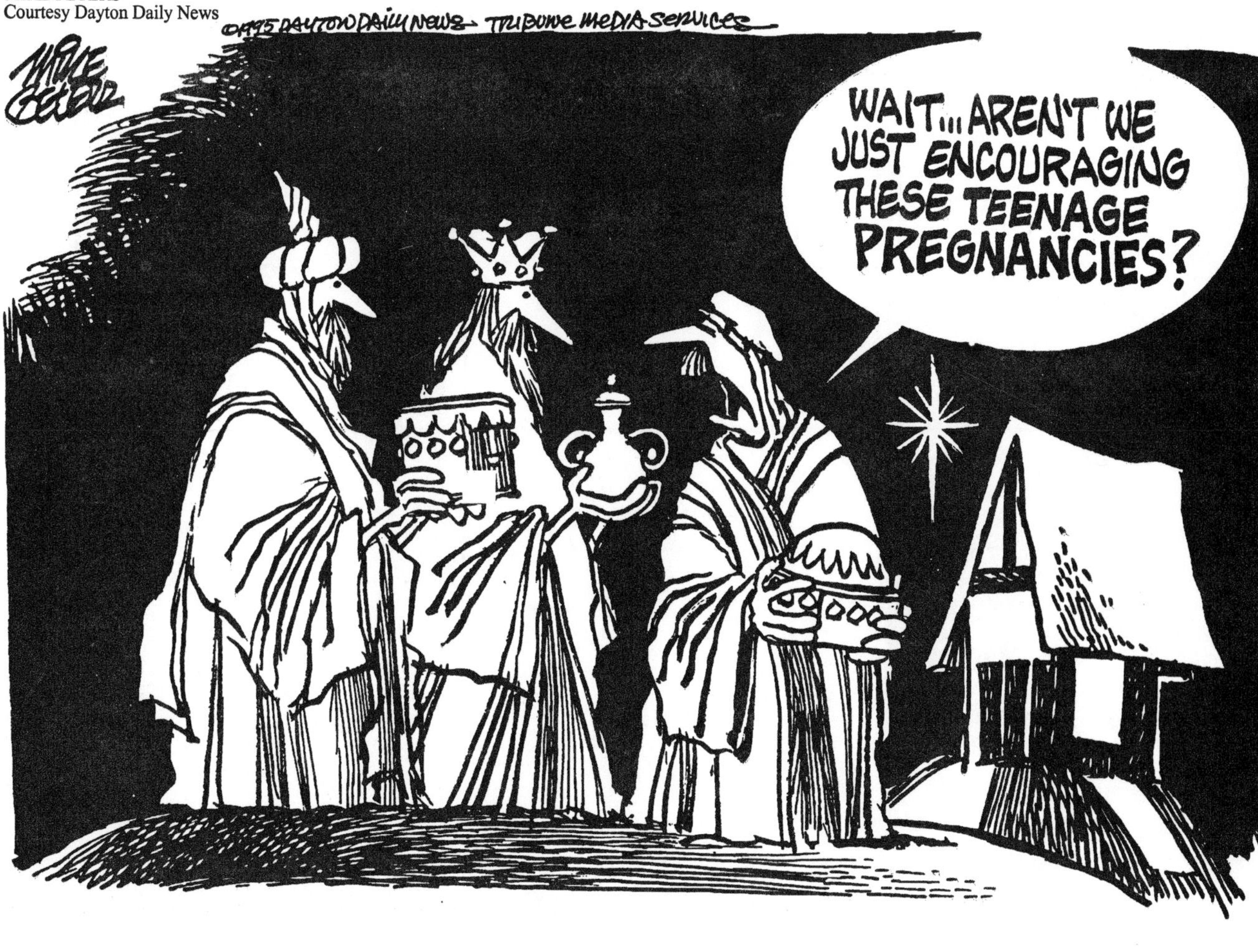
©1995 DAYTON DAILY NEWS TRIBUNE MEDIA SERVICES
MIKE PETERS
WAIT... AREN'T WE JUST ENCOURAGING THESE TEENAGE PREGNANCIES?

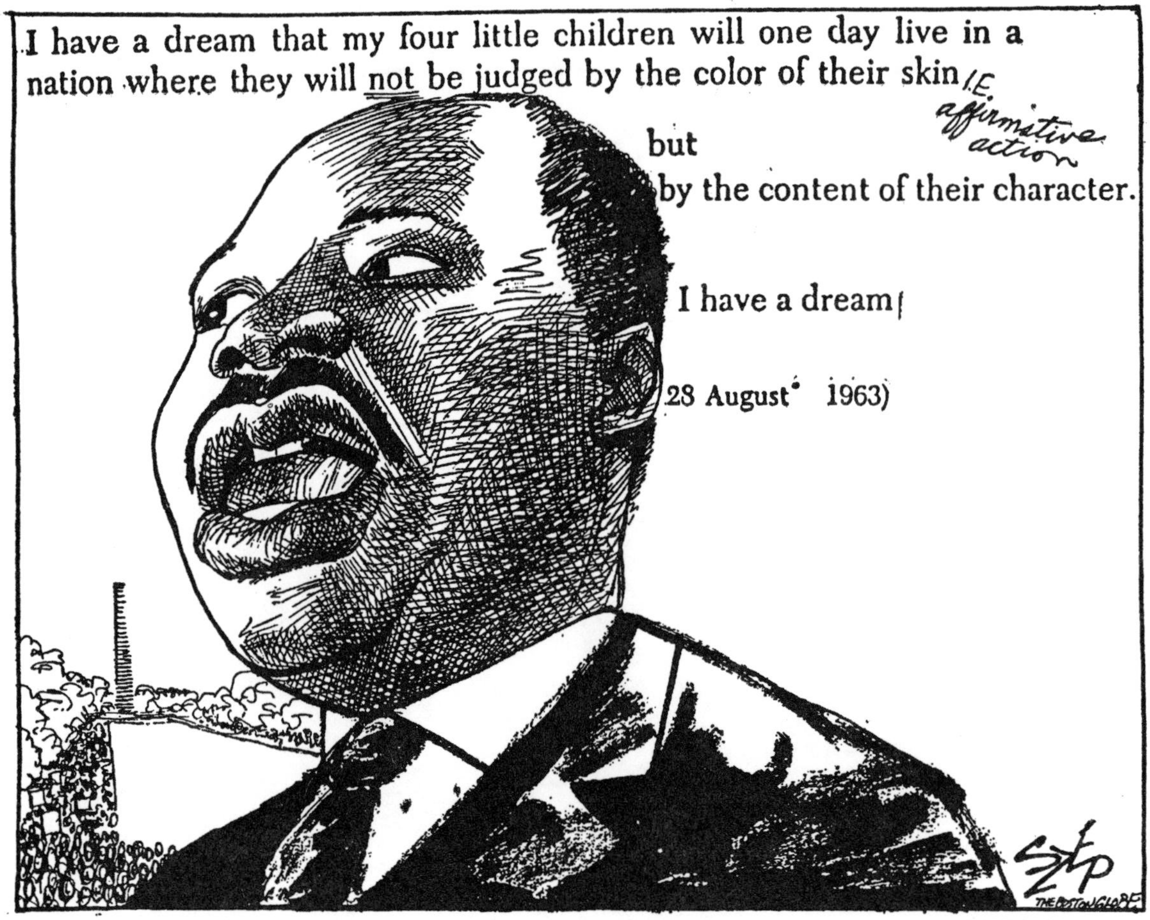
I have a dream that my four little children will one day live in a nation where they will not be judged by the color of their skin
I.E. affirmative action
but
by the content of their character.
I have a dream
28 August 1963
SZEP
THE BOSTON GLOBE

PAUL SZEP
Courtesy Boston Globe

FRANK CAMMUSO
Courtesy Syracuse Herald-Journal

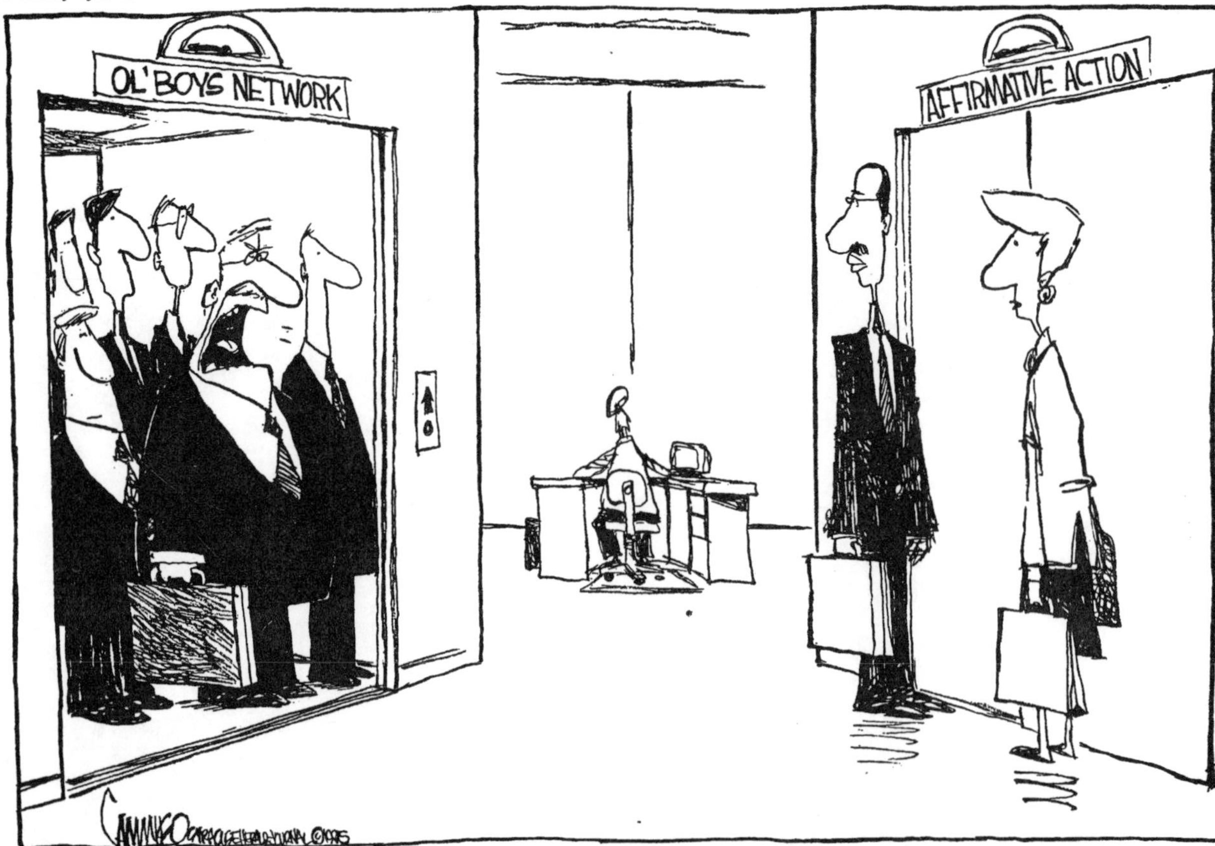
OL' BOYS NETWORK
AFFIRMATIVE ACTION

"FREE LOADERS!"

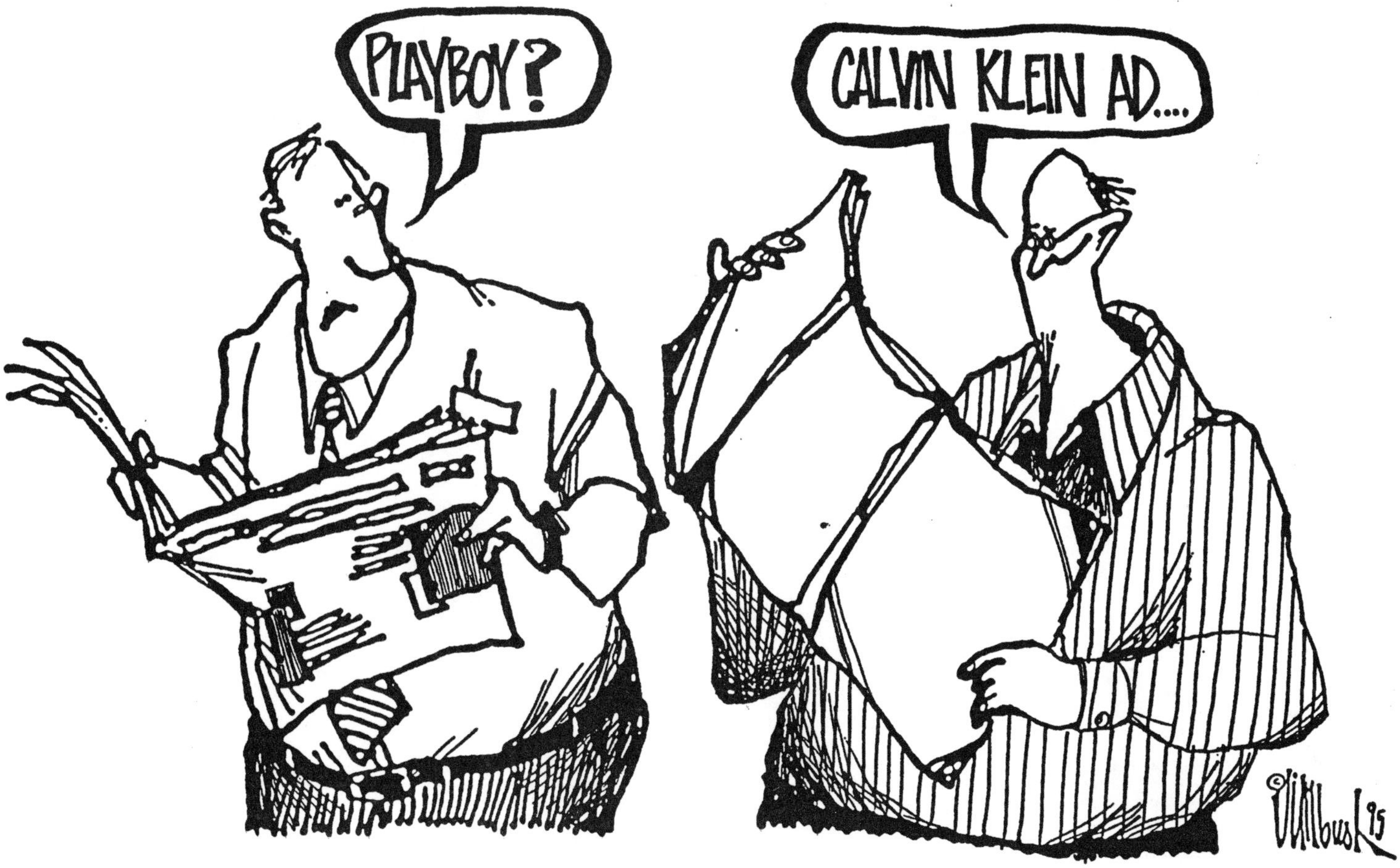
PLAYBOY?
CALVIN KLEIN AD....
©JIMBUSH '95

JIM BUSH
Courtesy Providence Journal Bulletin

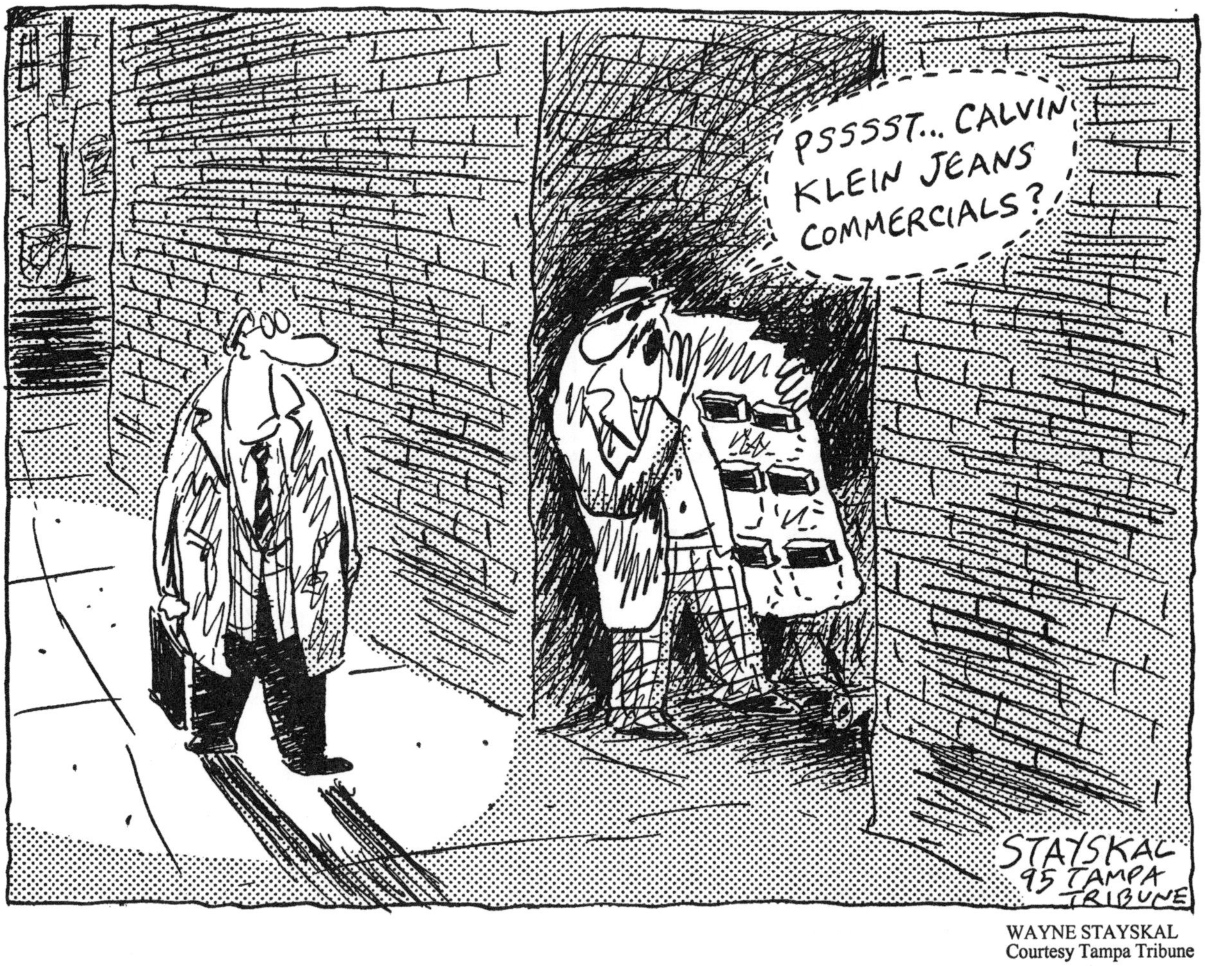
PSSSST... CALVIN KLEIN JEANS COMMERCIALS?
STAYSKAL '95 TAMPA TRIBUNE

WAYNE STAYSKAL
Courtesy Tampa Tribune

JOHN KNUDSEN
Courtesy The Tidings (Calif.)

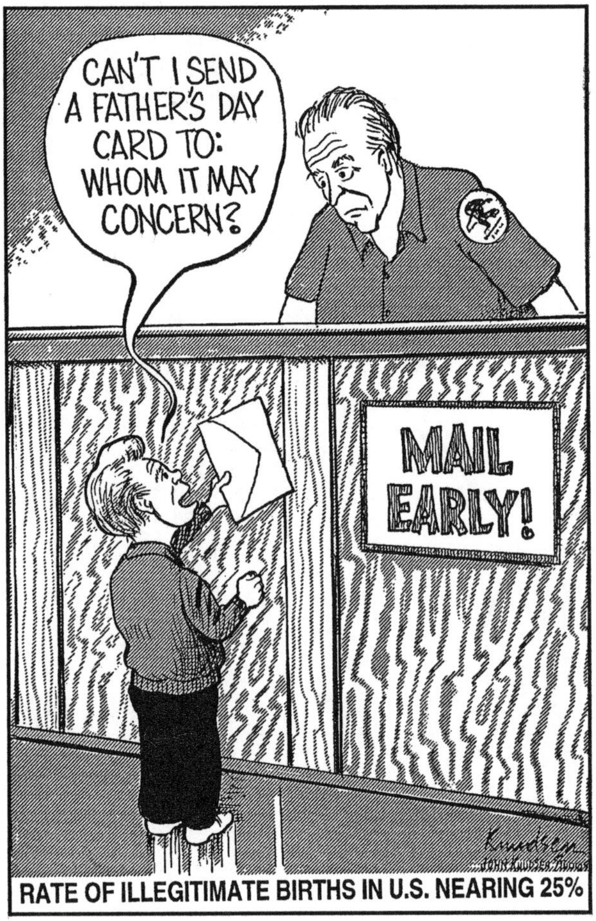
CAN'T I SEND A FATHER'S DAY CARD TO: WHOM IT MAY CONCERN?
MAIL EARLY!
RATE OF ILLEGITIMATE BIRTHS IN U.S. NEARING 25%

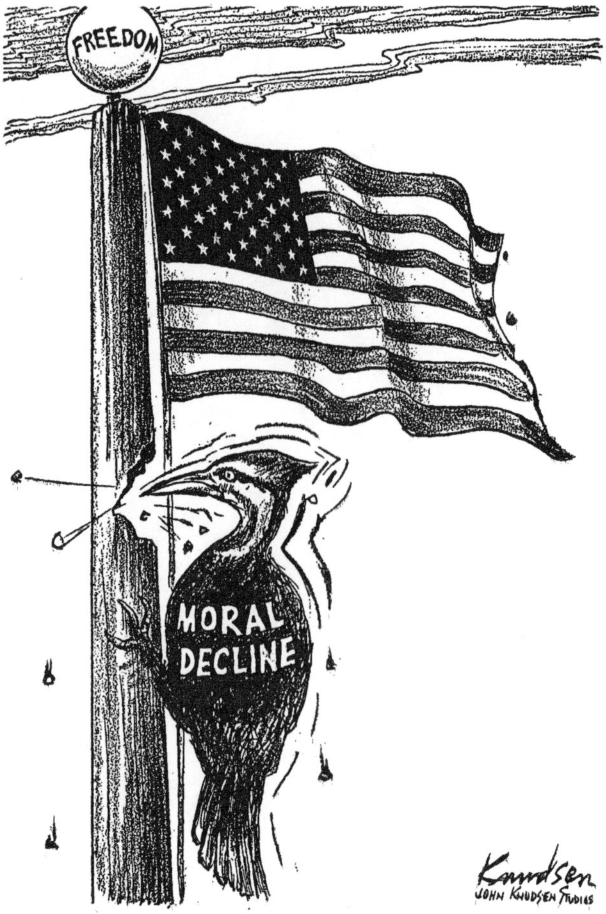
FREEDOM
MORAL DECLINE
Knudsen
JOHN KNUDSEN STUDIOS

JOHN KNUDSEN
Courtesy The Tidings (Calif.)

JOEL PETT
Courtesy Lexington Herald-Leader

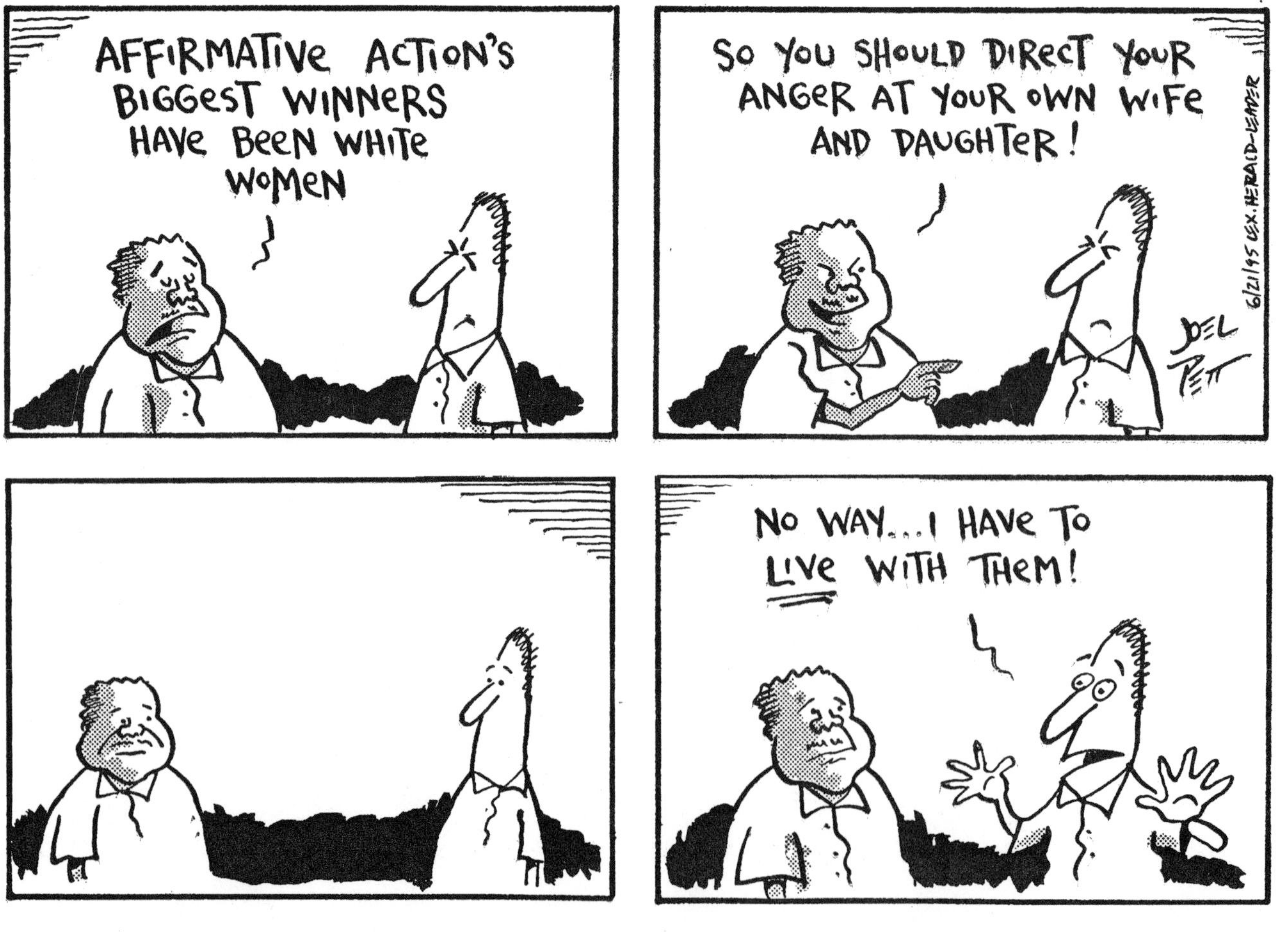
AFFIRMATIVE ACTION'S BIGGEST WINNERS HAVE BEEN WHITE WOMEN
SO YOU SHOULD DIRECT YOUR ANGER AT YOUR OWN WIFE AND DAUGHTER!
6/21/95 LEX. HERALD-LEADER
JOEL PETT
NO WAY... I HAVE TO LIVE WITH THEM!

TED RALL
Courtesy Chronicle Features

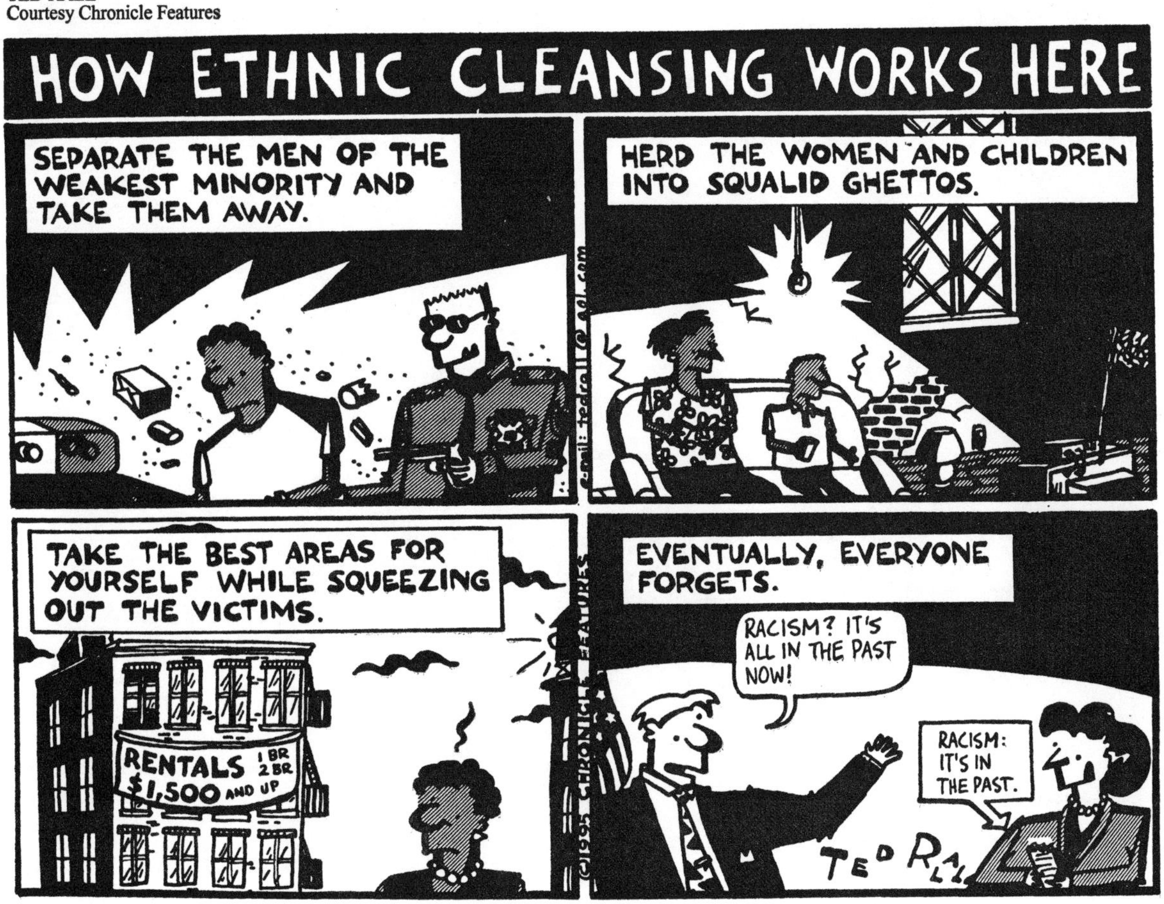
HOW ETHNIC CLEANSING WORKS HERE
SEPARATE THE MEN OF THE WEAKEST MINORITY AND TAKE THEM AWAY.
HERD THE WOMEN AND CHILDREN INTO SQUALID GHETTOS.
TAKE THE BEST AREAS FOR YOURSELF WHILE SQUEEZING OUT THE VICTIMS.
RENTALS 1 BR 2 BR $1,500 AND UP
EVENTUALLY, EVERYONE FORGETS.
RACISM? IT'S ALL IN THE PAST NOW!
RACISM: IT'S IN THE PAST.
TED RALL

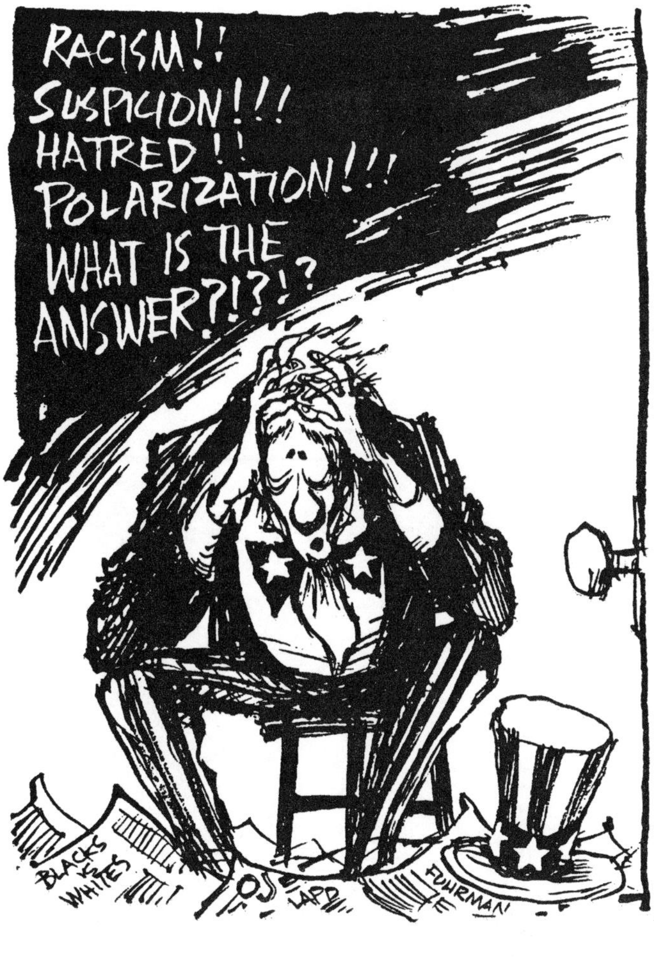
RACISM!!
SUSPICION!!!
HATRED!!
POLARIZATION!!!
WHAT IS THE ANSWER?!?!?
BLACKS WHITES
OJ
LAPD
FUHRMAN

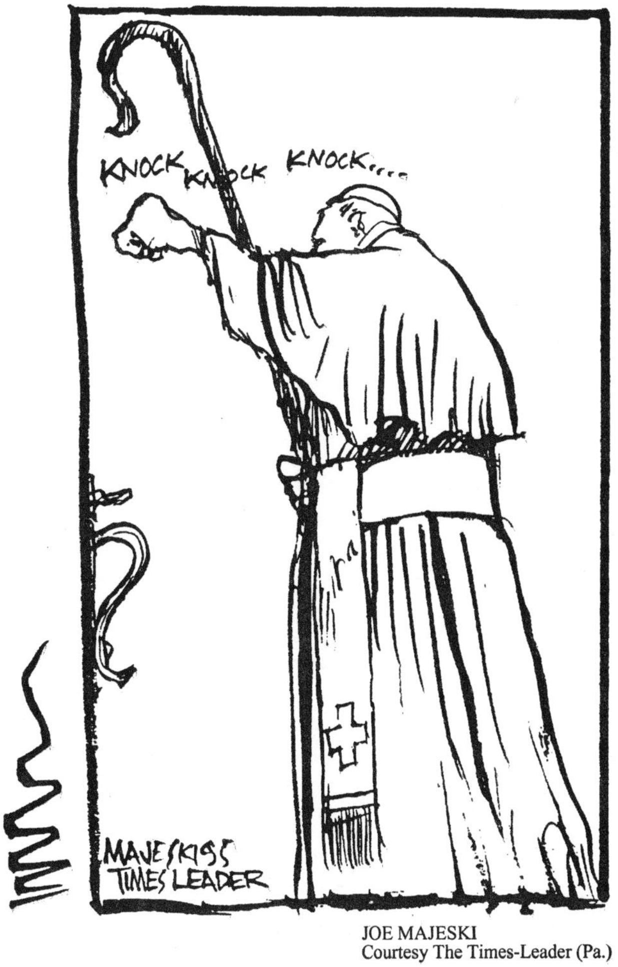
KNOCK KNOCK KNOCK....
MAJESKI©95
TIMES LEADER

JOE MAJESKI
Courtesy The Times-Leader (Pa.)

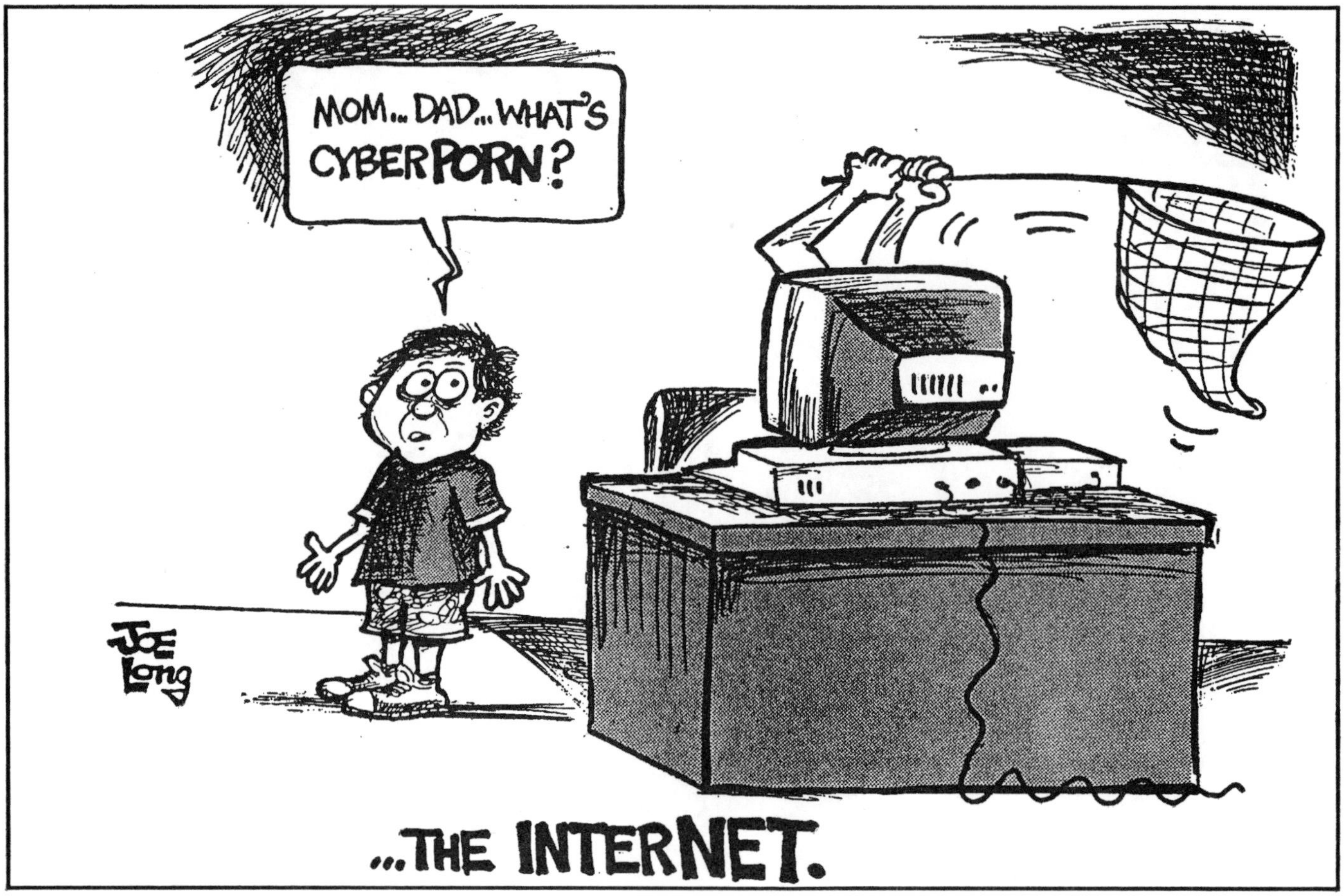
MOM... DAD... WHAT'S CYBERPORN?
JOE LONG
...THE INTERNET.

JOE LONG
Courtesy Little Falls Evening Times (N.Y.)

WALT HANDELSMAN
Courtesy Times-Picayune (N.O.)

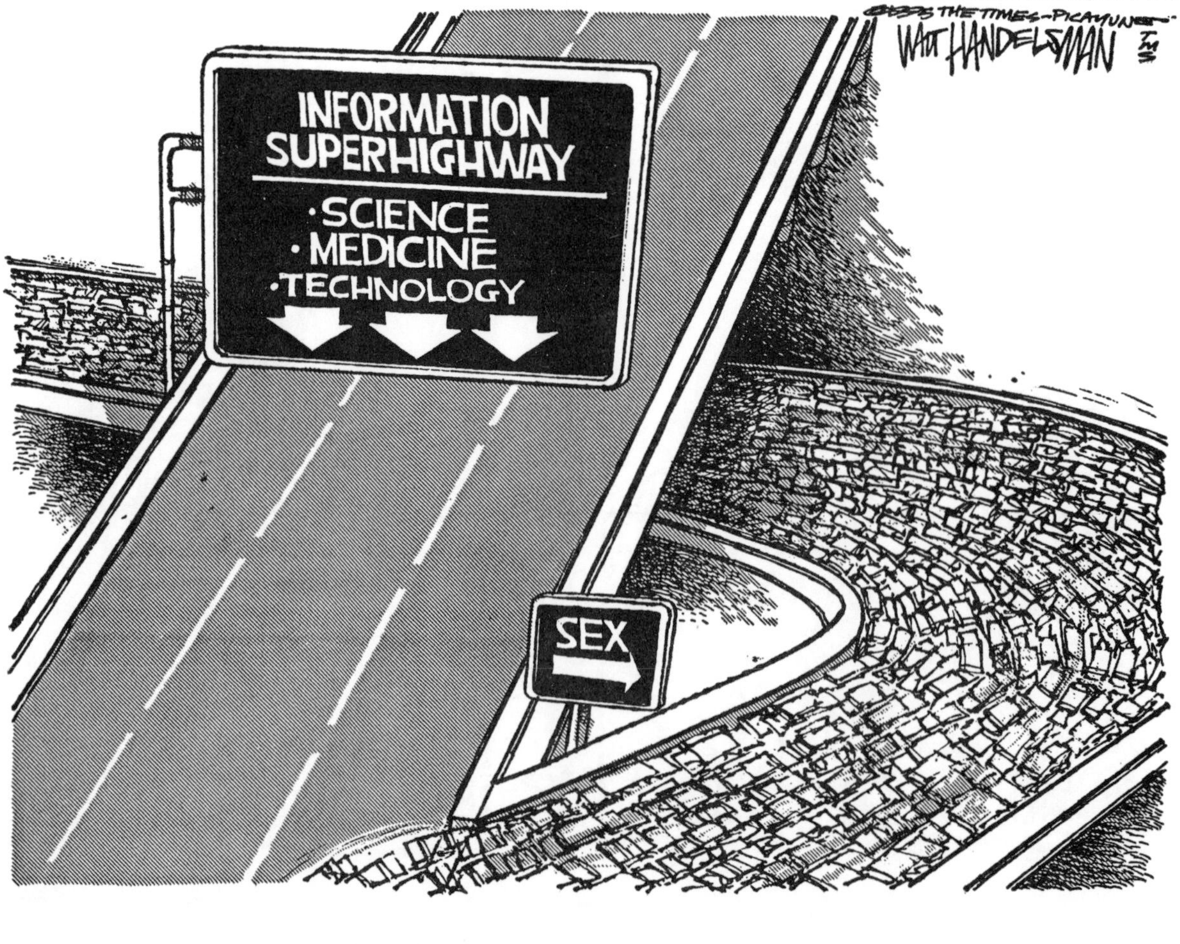
WALT HANDELSMAN
INFORMATION SUPERHIGHWAY
·SCIENCE
·MEDICINE
·TECHNOLOGY
SEX

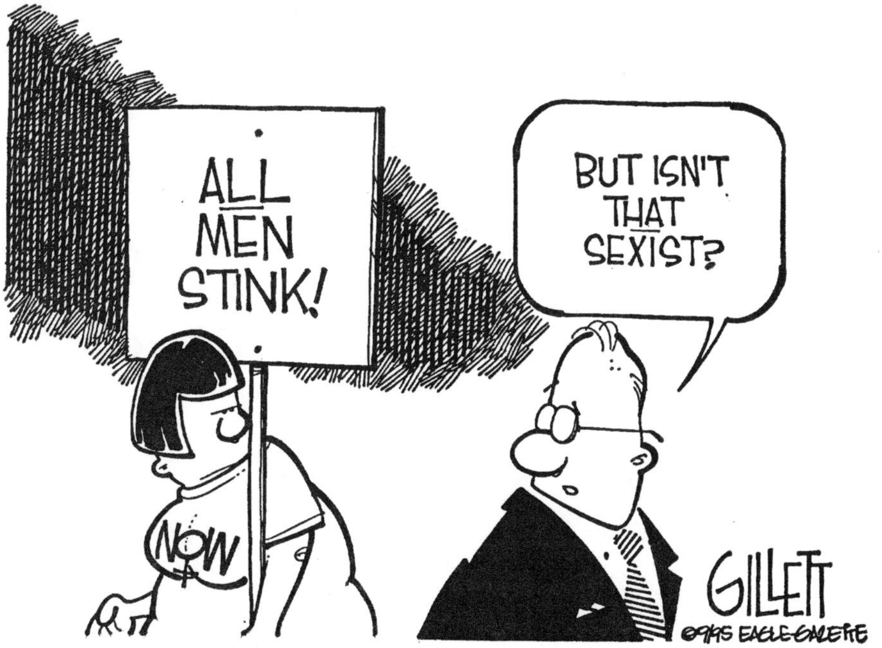
ALL MEN STINK!
BUT ISN'T THAT SEXIST?
NOW
GILLETT
©1995 EAGLE-GAZETTE

MICHAEL GILLETT
Courtesy Lancaster Eagle-Gazette (Ohio)

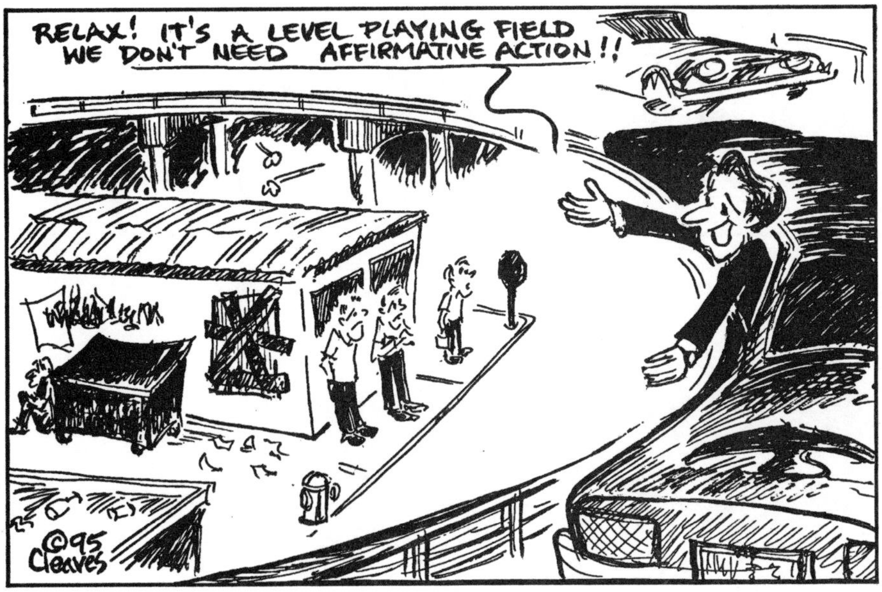
RELAX! IT'S A LEVEL PLAYING FIELD WE DON'T NEED AFFIRMATIVE ACTION!!
©95 Cleaves

ANN CLEAVES
Courtesy La Prensa (San Diego)

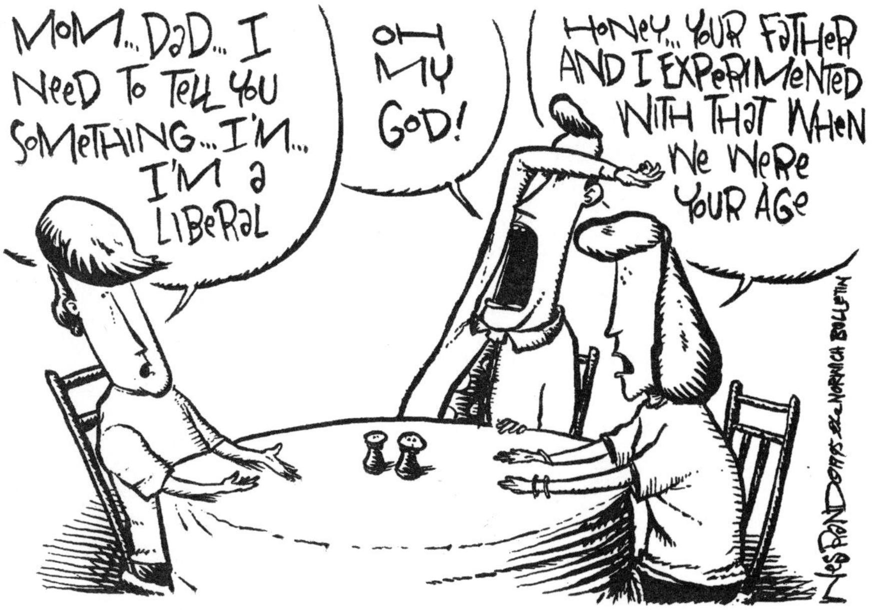
MOM... DAD... I NEED TO TELL YOU SOMETHING... I'M... I'M A LIBERAL
OH MY GOD!
HONEY... YOUR FATHER AND I EXPERIMENTED WITH THAT WHEN WE WERE YOUR AGE
NORWICH BULLETIN

WES RAND
Courtesy Norwich Bulletin

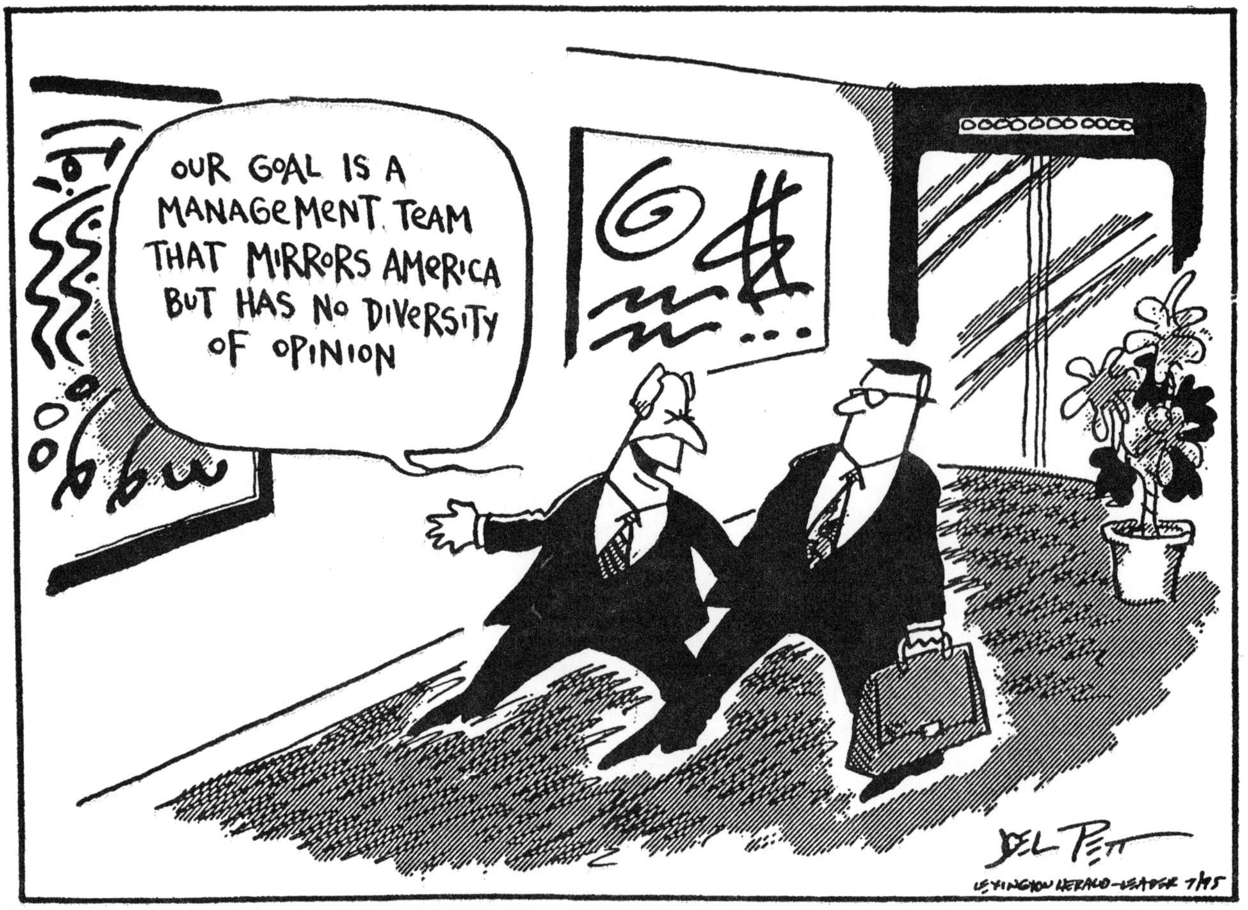
OUR GOAL IS A MANAGEMENT TEAM THAT MIRRORS AMERICA BUT HAS NO DIVERSITY OF OPINION

JOEL PETT
Courtesy Lexington Herald-Leader

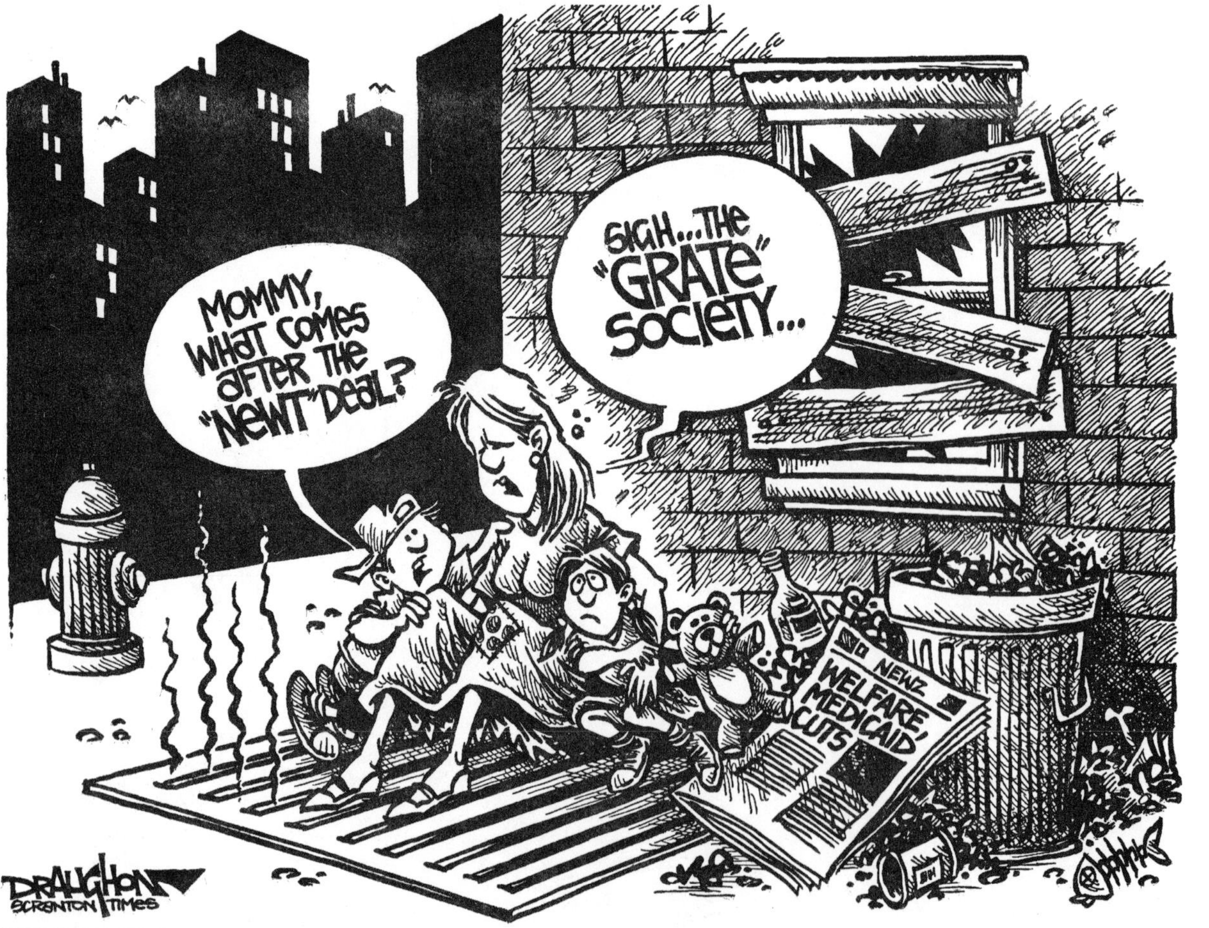
MOMMY, WHAT COMES AFTER THE "NEWT" DEAL?
SIGH...THE "GRATE" SOCIETY...
NEWZ
WELFARE, MEDICAID CUTS
DRAUGHON
SCRANTON TIMES

DENNIS DRAUGHON
Courtesy Scranton Times

JIM MCCLOSKEY
Courtesy Staunton Daily News Leader

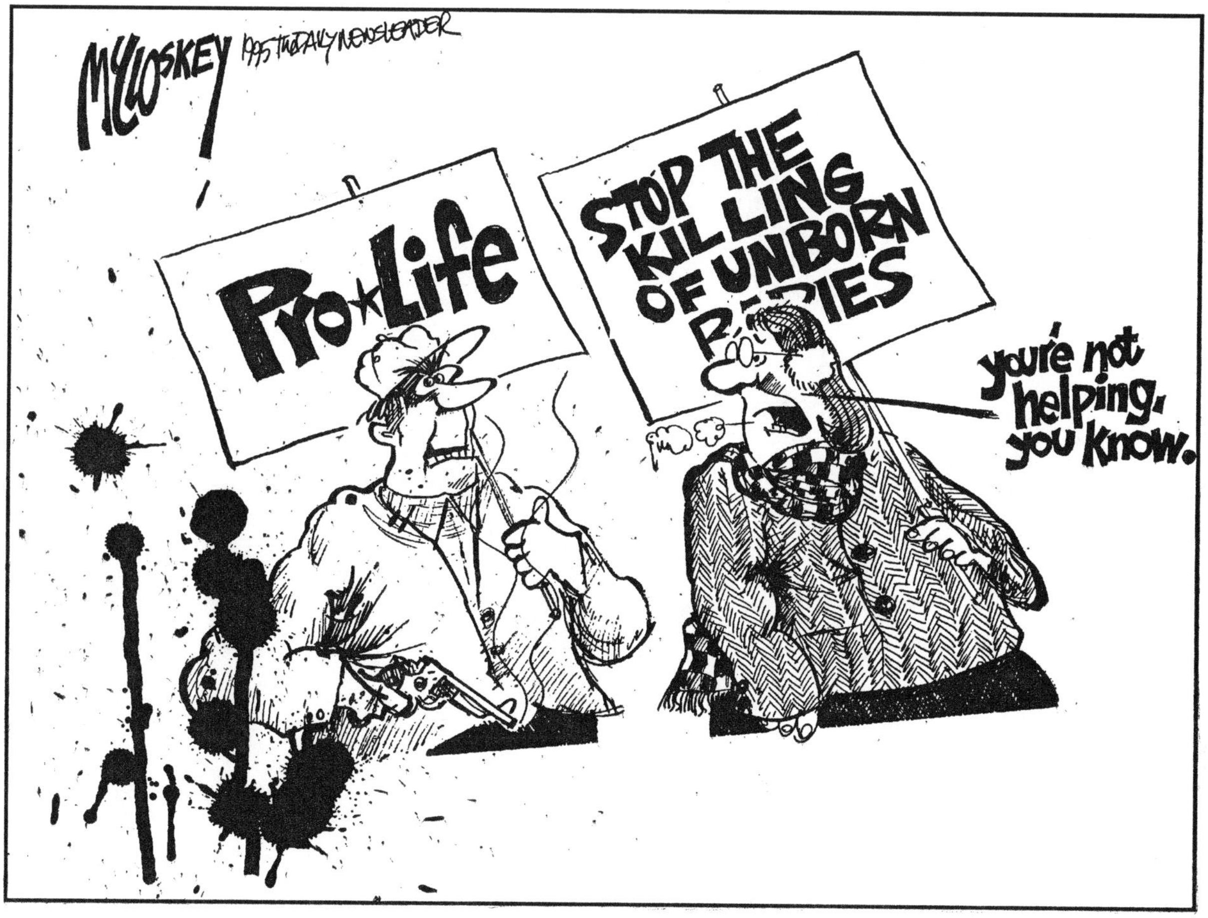
McCLOSKEY 1995 THE DAILY NEWS LEADER
Pro-Life
STOP THE KILLING OF UNBORN BABIES
you're not helping, you know.

ED FISCHER
Courtesy Rochester Post-Bulletin

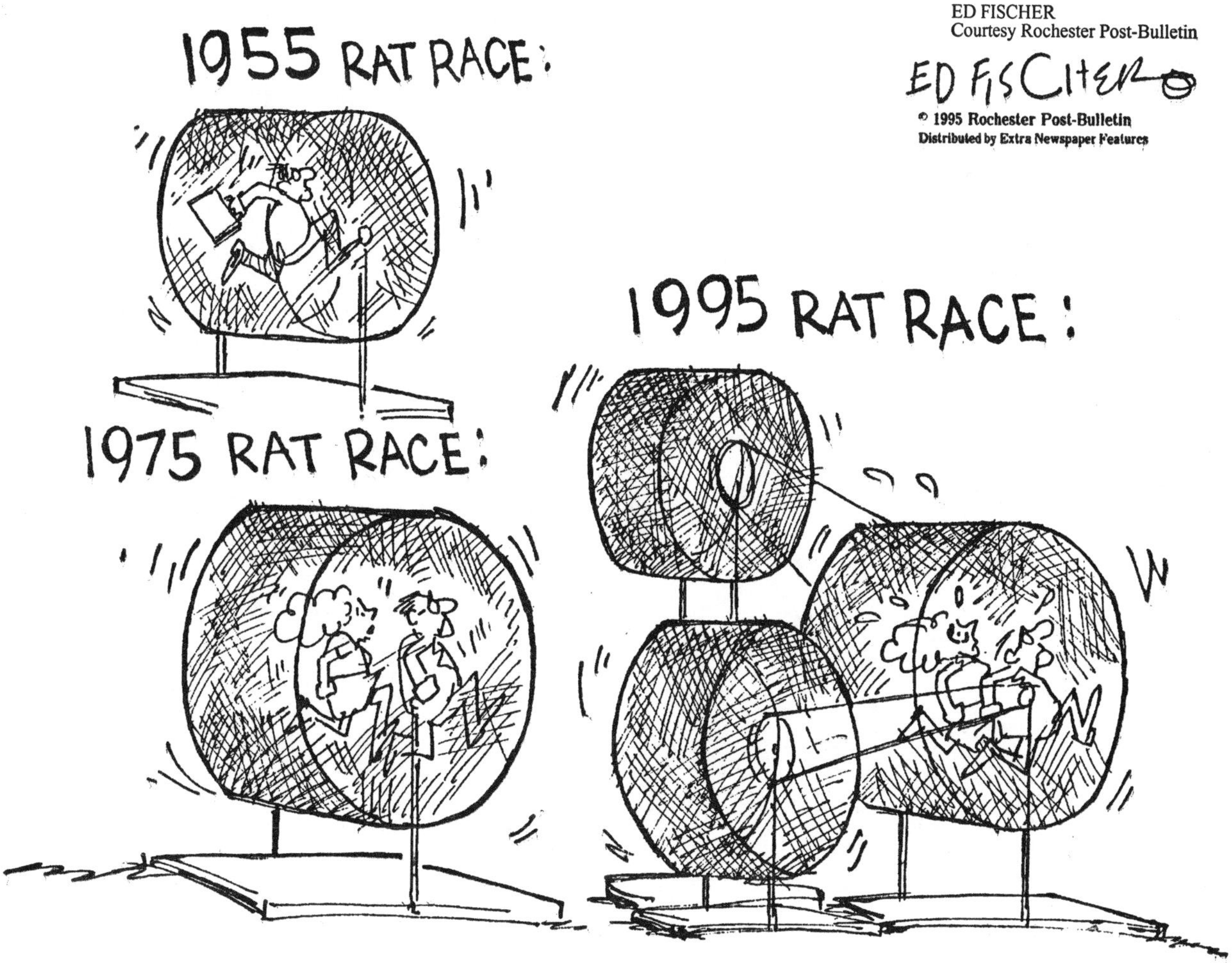
ED FISCHER
© 1995 Rochester Post-Bulletin
Distributed by Extra Newspaper Features
1955 RAT RACE:
1975 RAT RACE:
1995 RAT RACE:

HANK MCCLURE
Courtesy Lawton Constitution

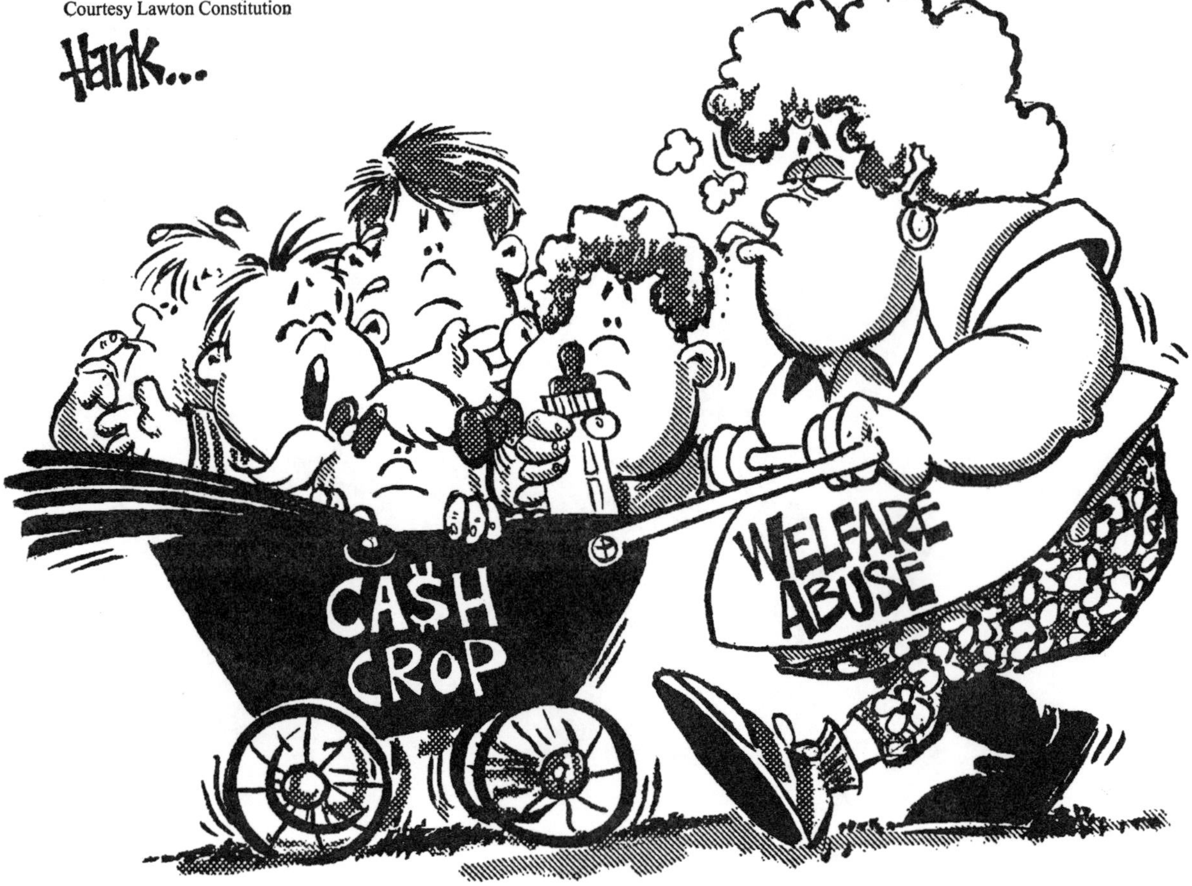
HANK...
CA$H CROP
WELFARE ABUSE

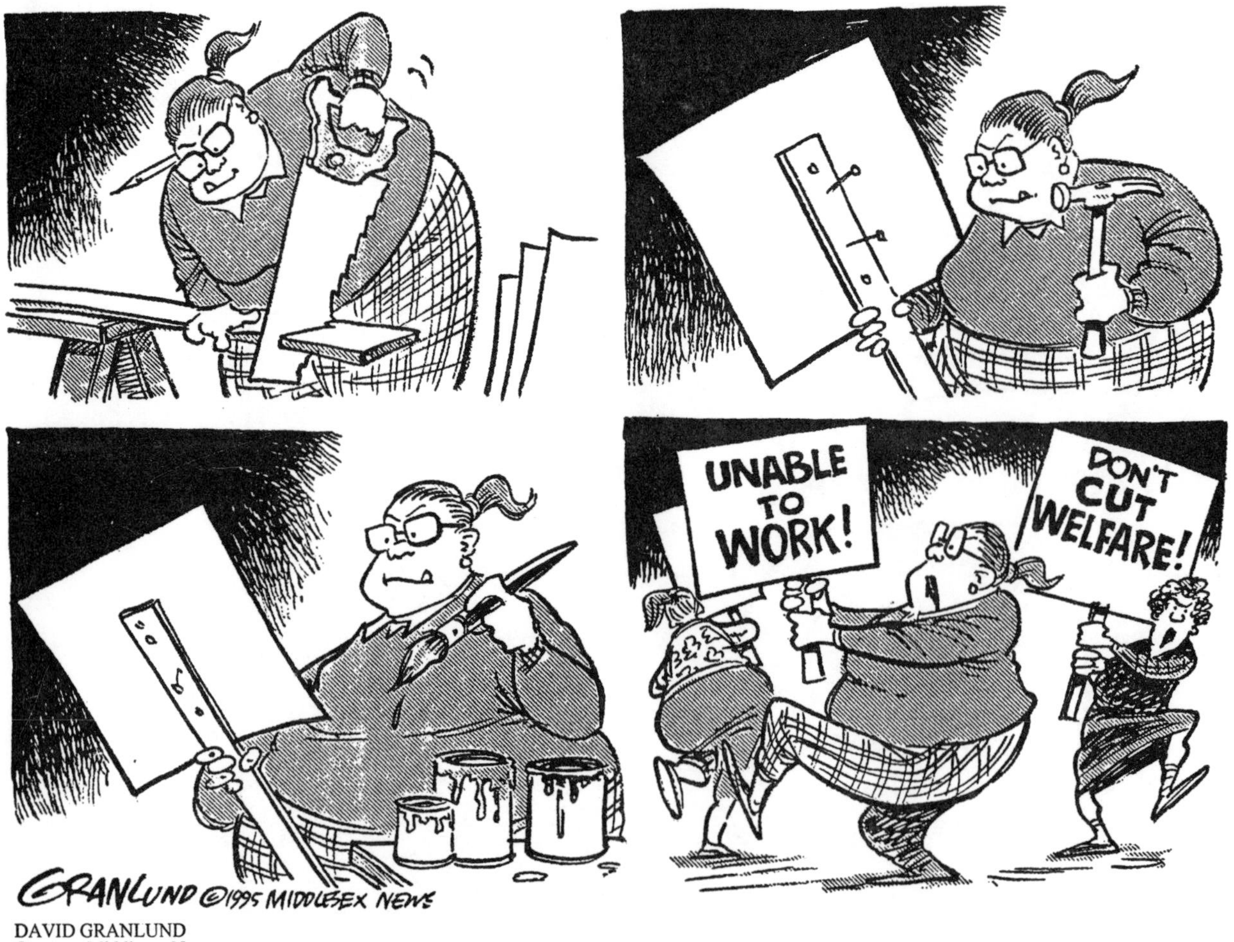
UNABLE TO WORK!
DON'T CUT WELFARE!
GRANLUND ©1995 MIDDLESEX NEWS

DAVID GRANLUND
Courtesy Middlesex News

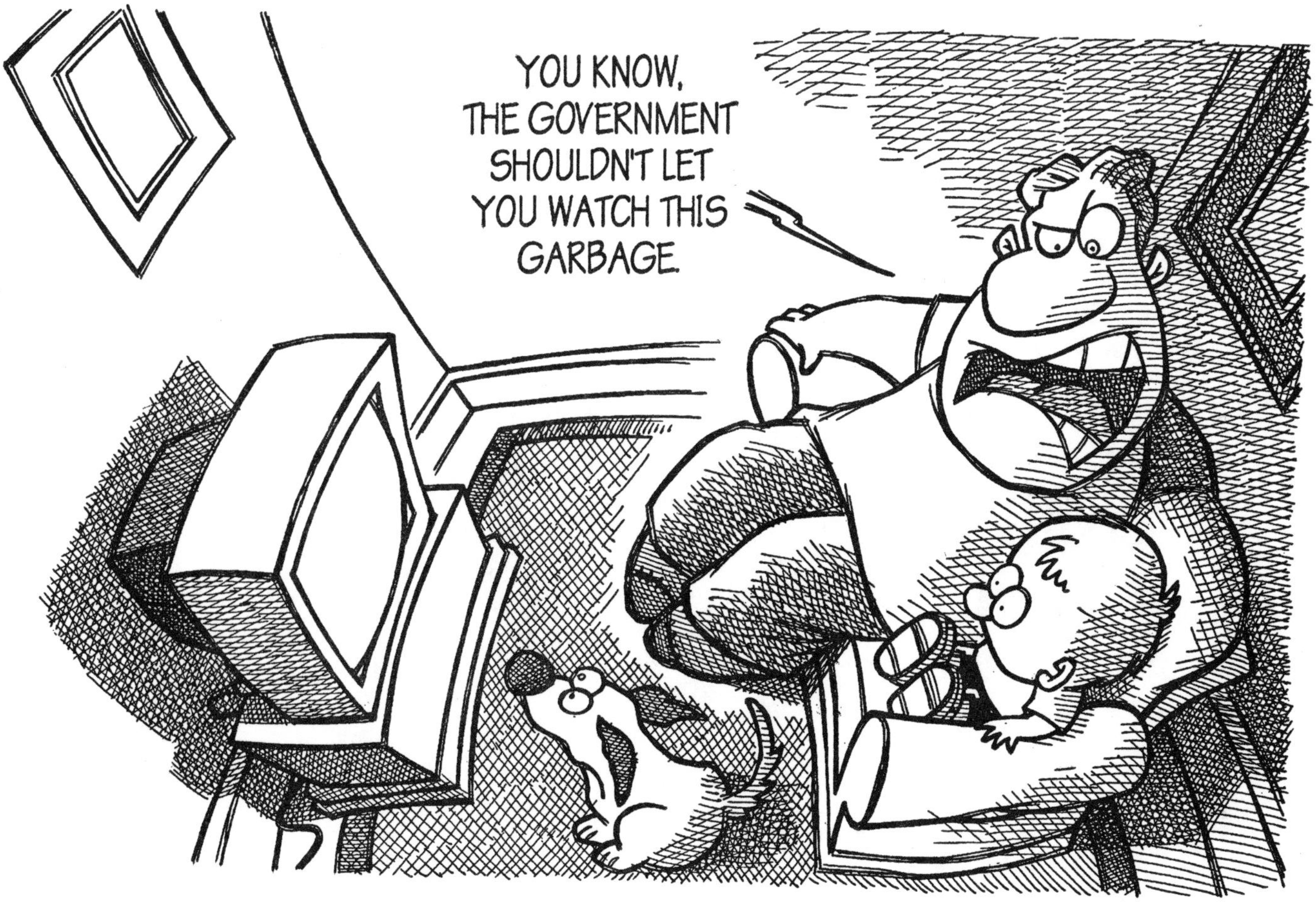
YOU KNOW, THE GOVERNMENT SHOULDN'T LET YOU WATCH THIS GARBAGE.

BOB RICH
Courtesy Connecticut Post

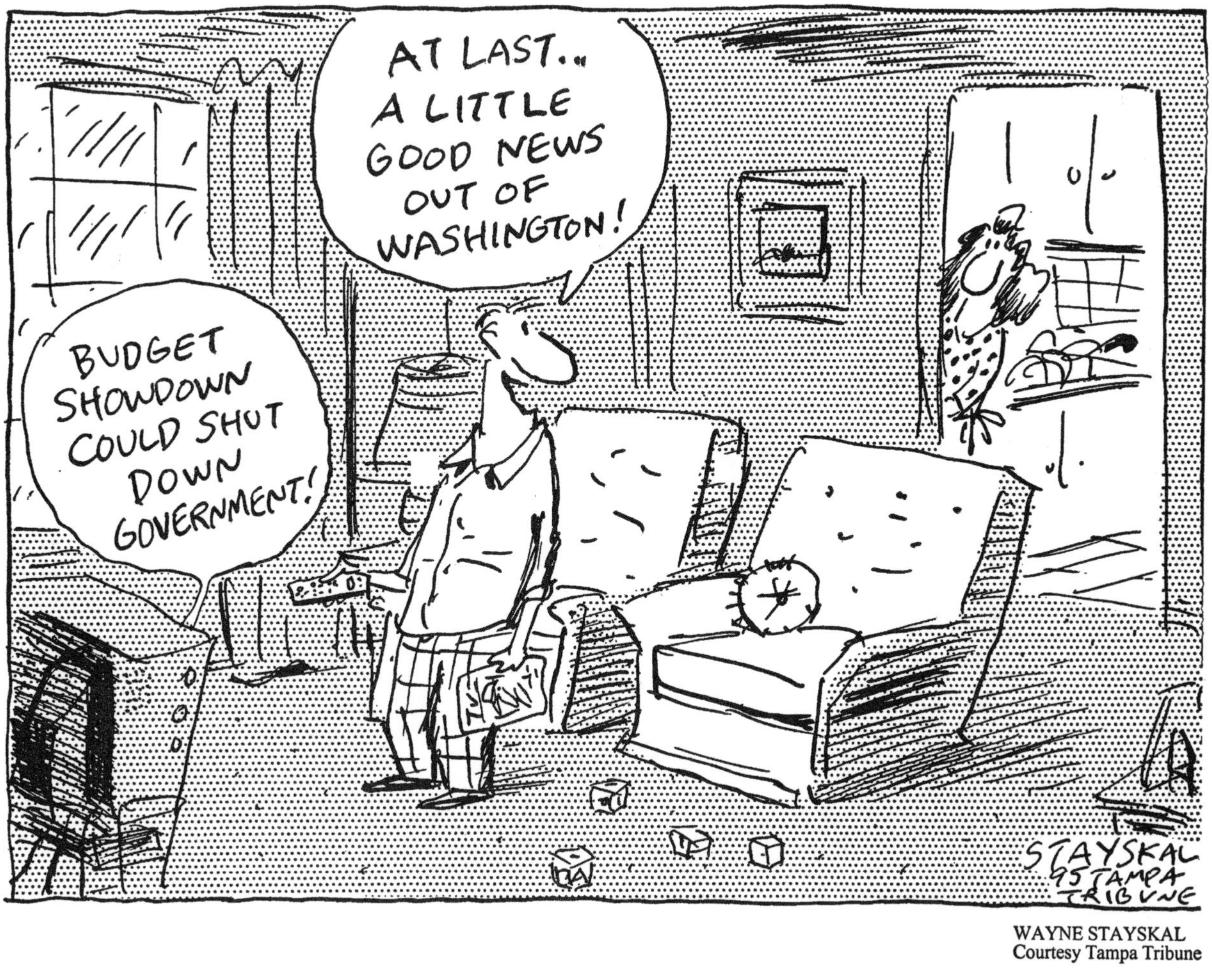
BUDGET SHOWDOWN COULD SHUT DOWN GOVERNMENT!
AT LAST... A LITTLE GOOD NEWS OUT OF WASHINGTON!
STAYSKAL '95 TAMPA TRIBUNE

WAYNE STAYSKAL
Courtesy Tampa Tribune

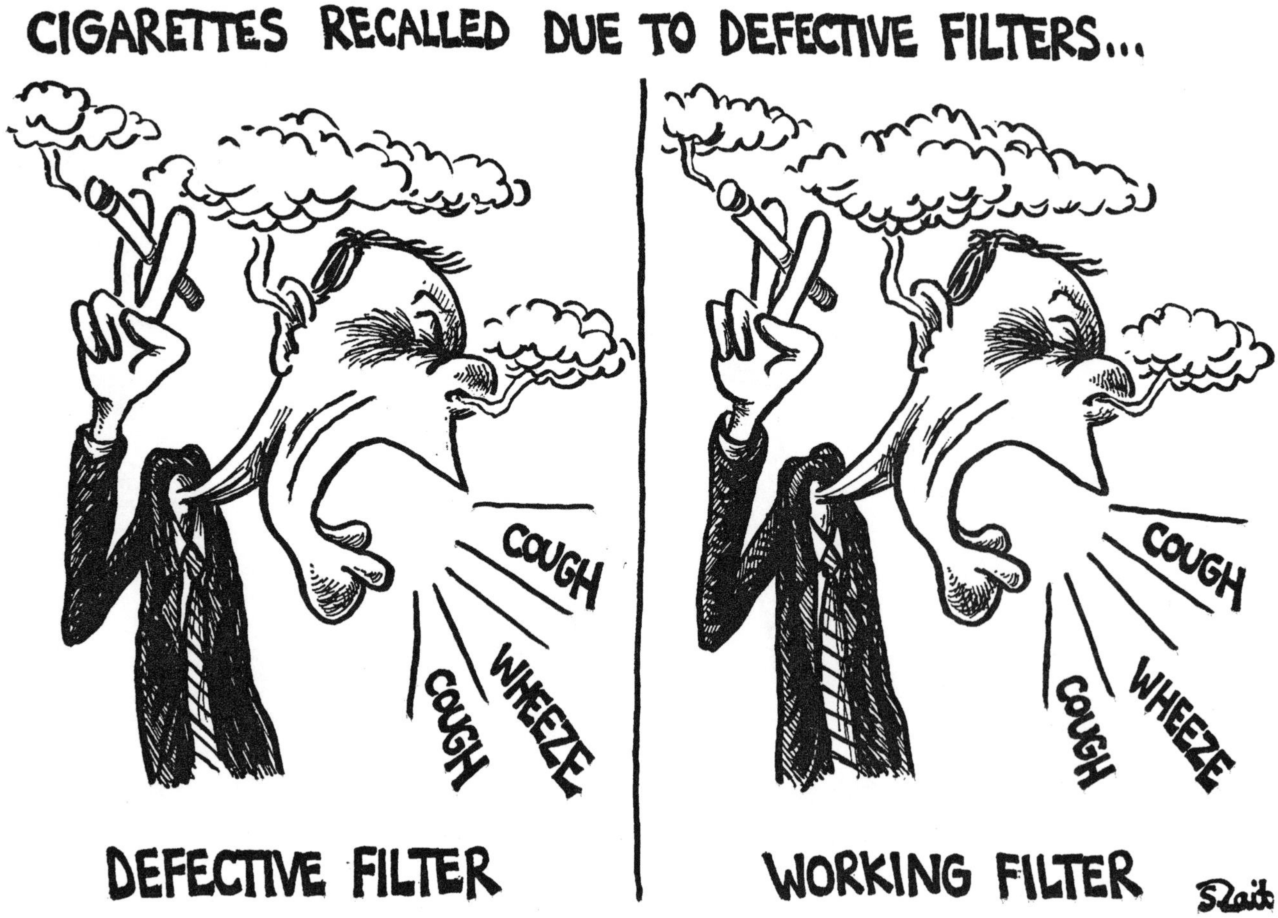
CIGARETTES RECALLED DUE TO DEFECTIVE FILTERS...
COUGH
WHEEZE
COUGH
DEFECTIVE FILTER
COUGH
WHEEZE
COUGH
WORKING FILTER
SLait

STEVEN LAIT
Courtesy Oakland Tribune

PAUL FELL
Courtesy Lincoln Journal

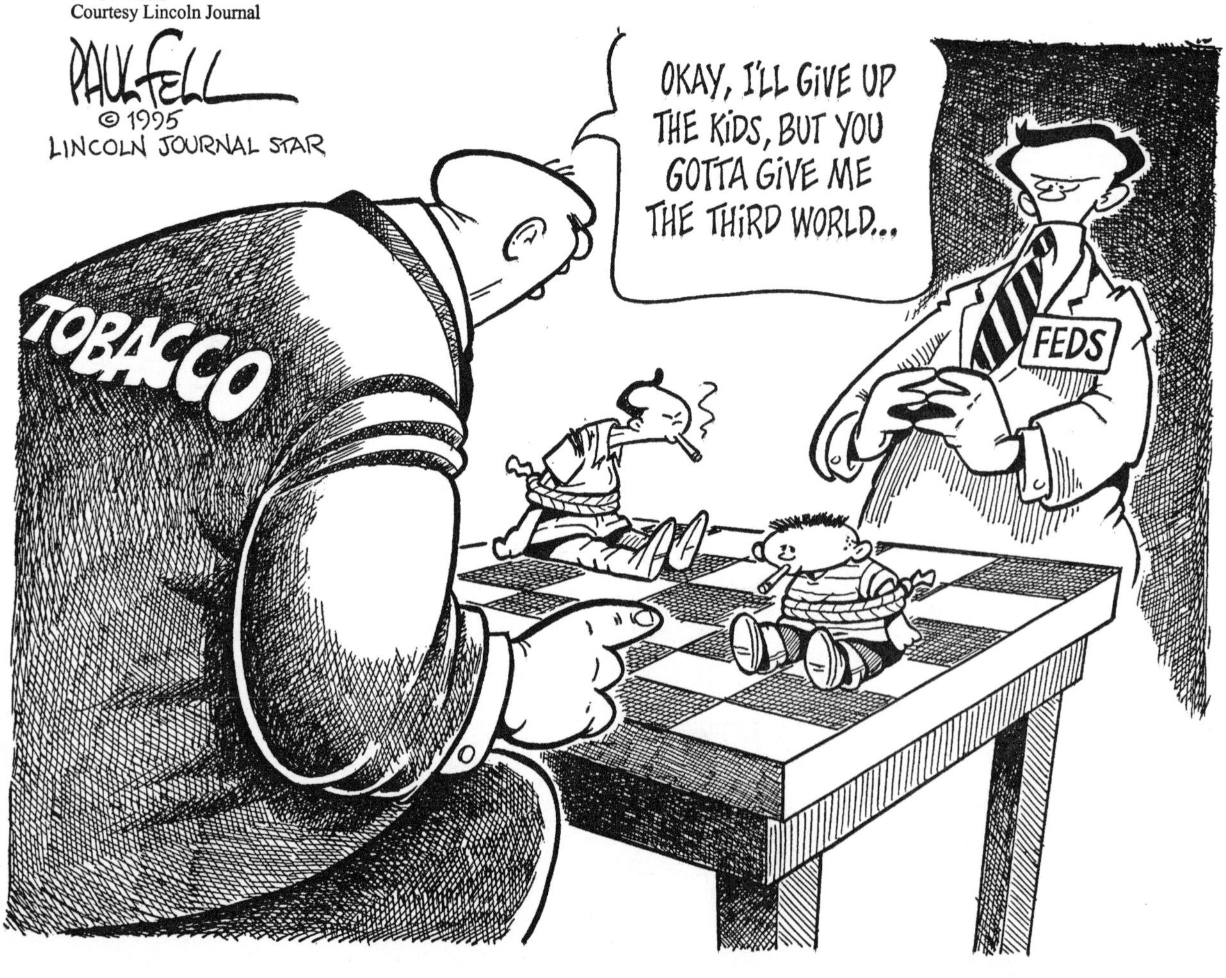
PAUL FELL
© 1995
LINCOLN JOURNAL STAR
OKAY, I'LL GIVE UP THE KIDS, BUT YOU GOTTA GIVE ME THE THIRD WORLD...
TOBACCO
FEDS

Health

Declaring tobacco an addictive drug, President Clinton issued wide-ranging policies aimed at keeping teenagers from becoming smokers. The plan included restrictions on cigarette advertising and the banning of cigarette vending machines in certain locations. Tobacco companies immediately filed suit, calling the president's actions unconstitutional, and critics charged that the real objective was to ban tobacco outright. Sen. Jesse Helms of North Carolina was a special target because of his continuing support of the tabacco industry, one of his state's largest employers.

Dr. Henry Foster was nominated to replace Dr. Joycelyn Elders as U.S. surgeon general, but quickly came under fire when it was disclosed that he had performed numerous abortions. His nomination was rejected by the Senate.

The Republican-controlled Congress is attempting to reduce the growth of Medicare to 6 percent from the recent rate of 10 percent, but faces an uphill battle. Time is running out. The program will go broke by the year 2002, when the baby-boom generation begins to reach retirement age.

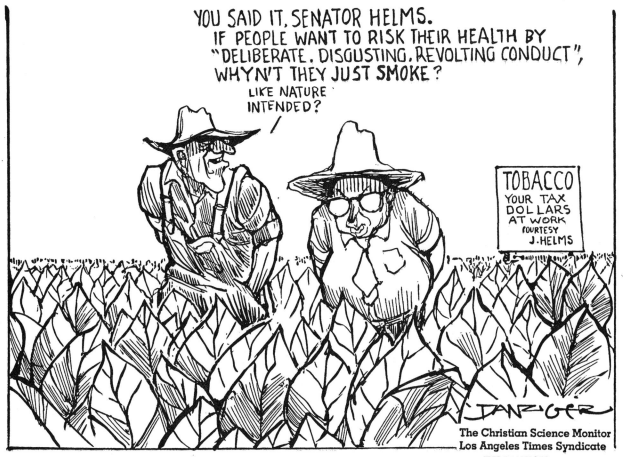

YOU SAID IT, SENATOR HELMS. IF PEOPLE WANT TO RISK THEIR HEALTH BY "DELIBERATE, DISGUSTING, REVOLTING CONDUCT", WHYN'T THEY JUST SMOKE?
LIKE NATURE INTENDED?
TOBACCO YOUR TAX DOLLARS AT WORK COURTESY J. HELMS
DANZIGER
The Christian Science Monitor
Los Angeles Times Syndicate

JEFF DANZIGER
Courtesy Christian Science Monitor

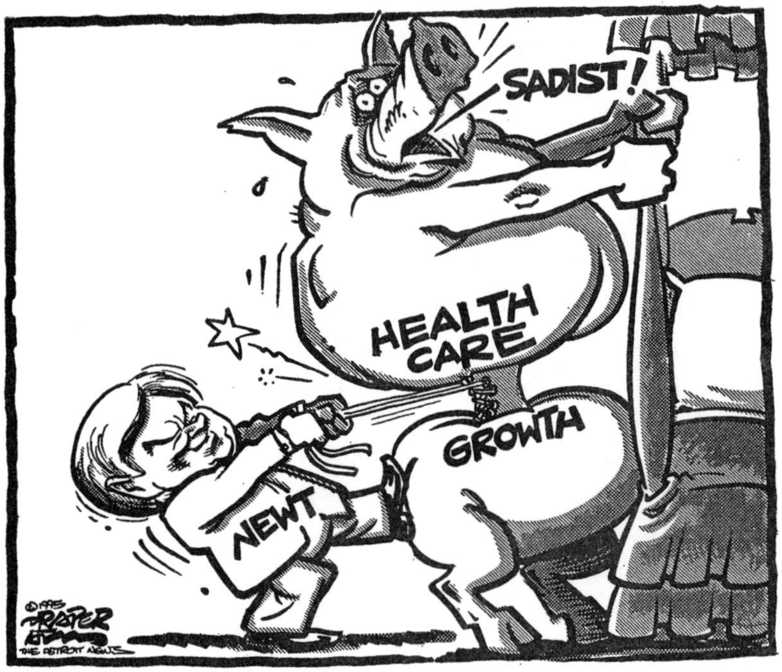
SADIST!
HEALTH CARE
GROWTH
NEWT
©1995 DRAPER HILL
THE DETROIT NEWS

DRAPER HILL
Courtesy Detroit News

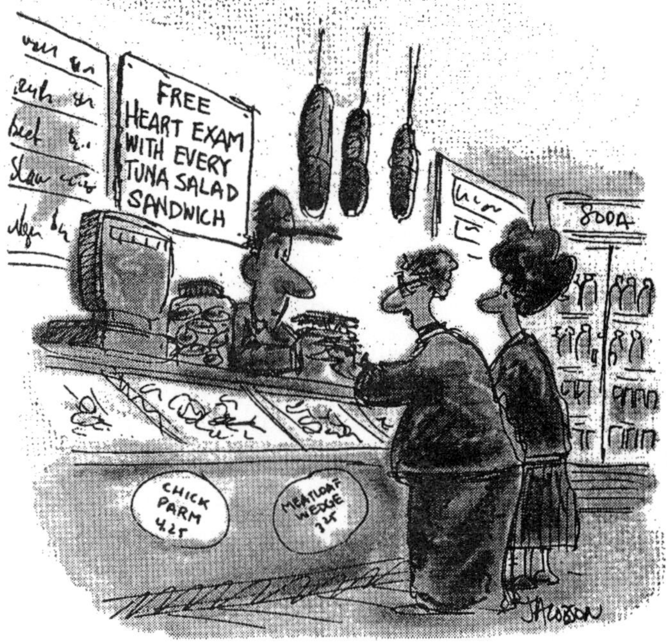
FREE HEART EXAM WITH EVERY TUNA SALAD SANDWICH
CHICK PARM 4.25
MEATLOAF WEDGE
JACOBSON

DAVID JACOBSON
Courtesy Gannett Newspapers

STUART CARLSON
Courtesy Milwaukee Journal Sentinel

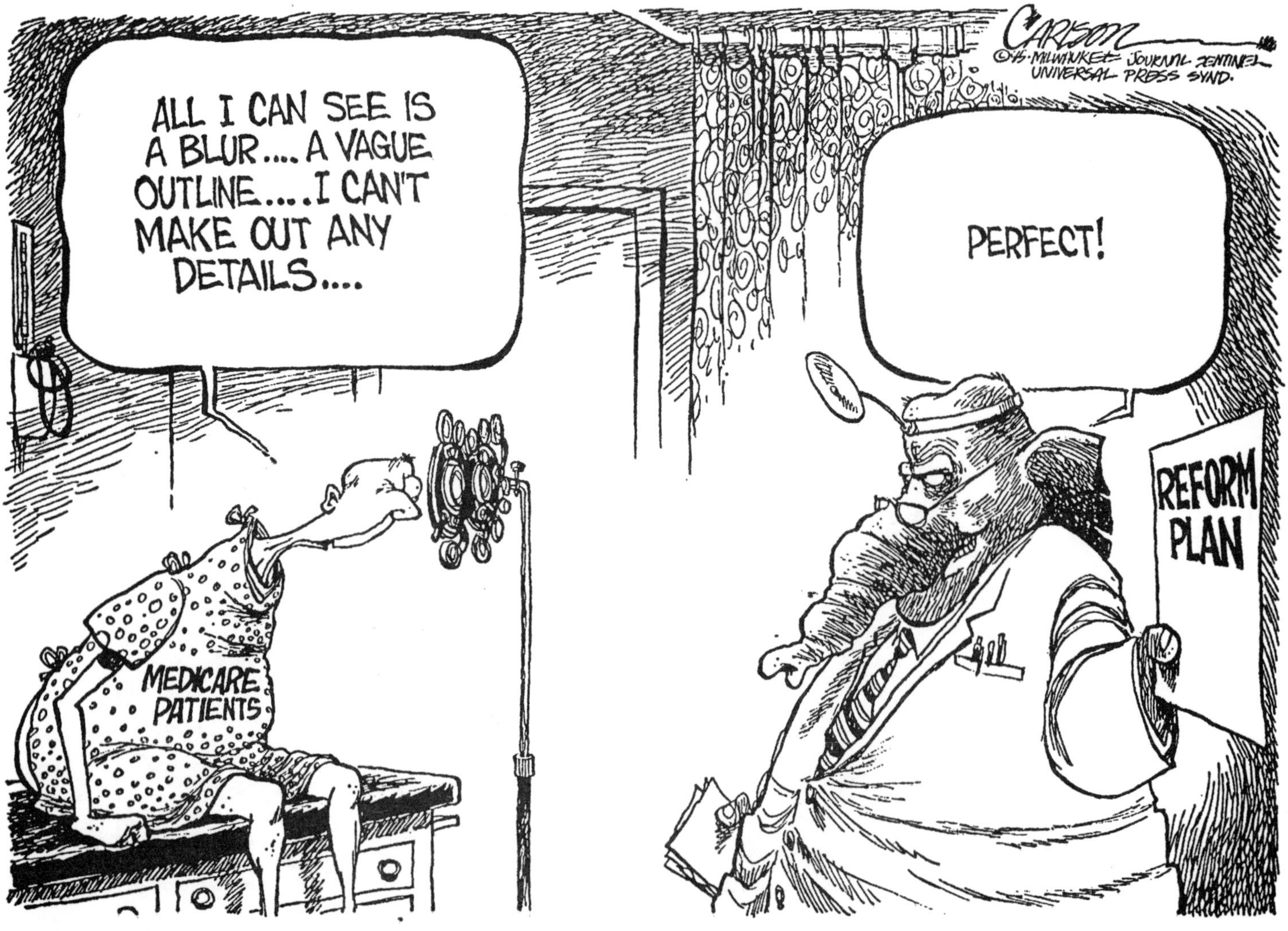
CARLSON
©'95 MILWAUKEE JOURNAL SENTINEL
UNIVERSAL PRESS SYND.
ALL I CAN SEE IS A BLUR.... A VAGUE OUTLINE.....I CAN'T MAKE OUT ANY DETAILS....
PERFECT!
MEDICARE PATIENTS
REFORM PLAN

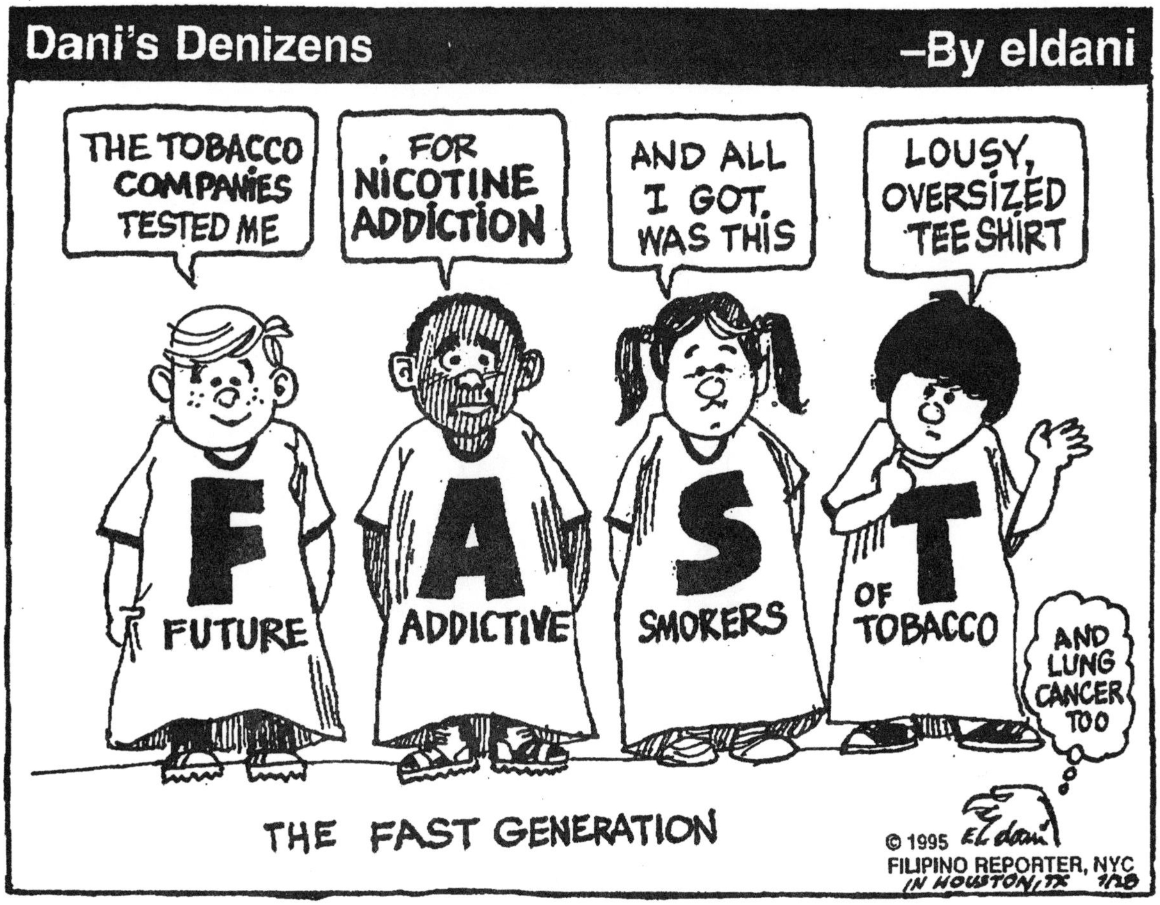
Dani's Denizens
–By eldani
THE TOBACCO COMPANIES TESTED ME
FOR NICOTINE ADDICTION
AND ALL I GOT WAS THIS
LOUSY, OVERSIZED TEE SHIRT
F
FUTURE
A
ADDICTIVE
S
SMOKERS
T
OF TOBACCO
AND LUNG CANCER TOO
THE FAST GENERATION
© 1995
FILIPINO REPORTER, NYC
IN HOUSTON, TX 1/28

DANI AGUILA
Courtesy Filipino Reporter

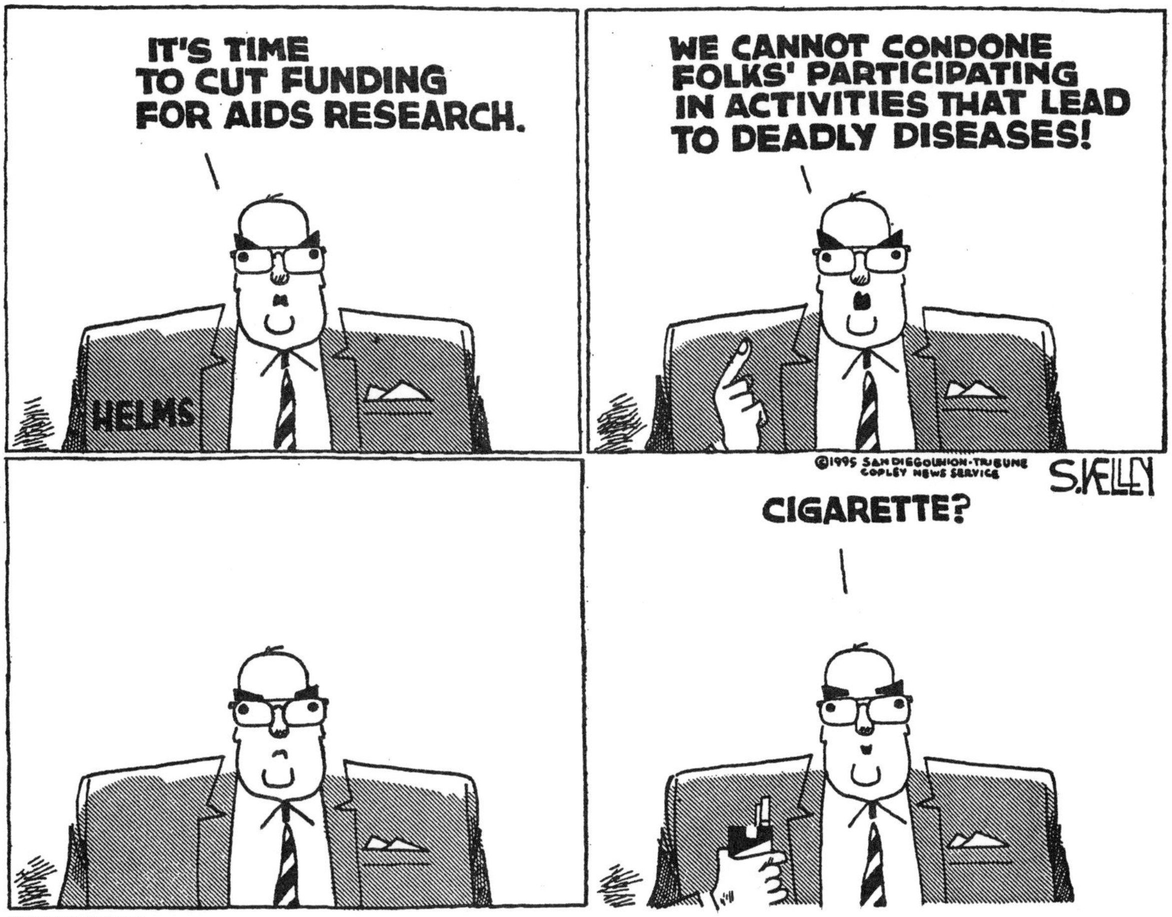
IT'S TIME TO CUT FUNDING FOR AIDS RESEARCH.
HELMS
WE CANNOT CONDONE FOLKS' PARTICIPATING IN ACTIVITIES THAT LEAD TO DEADLY DISEASES!
©1995 SAN DIEGO UNION-TRIBUNE COPLEY NEWS SERVICE
S.KELLEY
CIGARETTE?

STEVE KELLEY
Courtesy San Diego Union

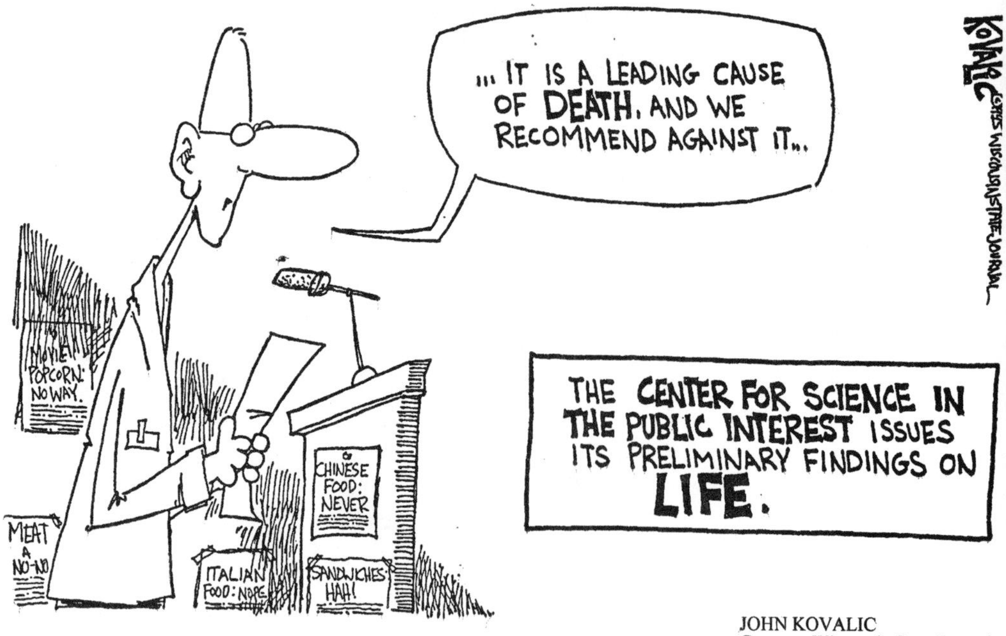

... IT IS A LEADING CAUSE OF DEATH, AND WE RECOMMEND AGAINST IT...
MOVIE POPCORN: NO WAY.
CHINESE FOOD: NEVER
MEAT A NO-NO
ITALIAN FOOD: NOPE
SANDWICHES: HAH!
THE CENTER FOR SCIENCE IN THE PUBLIC INTEREST ISSUES ITS PRELIMINARY FINDINGS ON LIFE.

JOHN KOVALIC
Courtesy Wisconsin State Journal

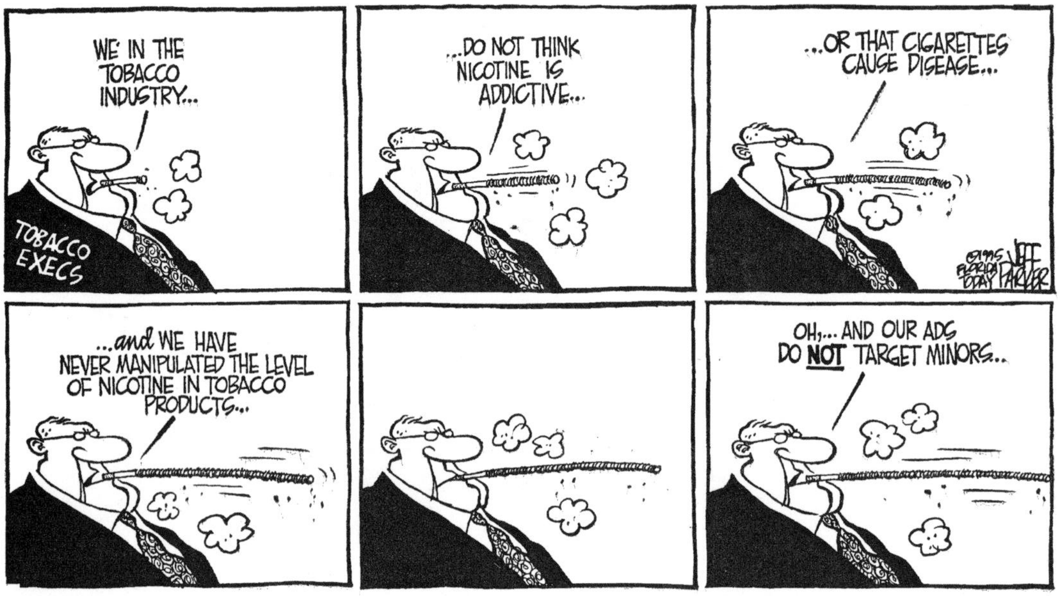

WE IN THE TOBACCO INDUSTRY...
TOBACCO EXECS
...DO NOT THINK NICOTINE IS ADDICTIVE...
...OR THAT CIGARETTES CAUSE DISEASE...
...and WE HAVE NEVER MANIPULATED THE LEVEL OF NICOTINE IN TOBACCO PRODUCTS...
OH,... AND OUR ADS DO NOT TARGET MINORS..

JEFF PARKER
Courtesy Florida Today

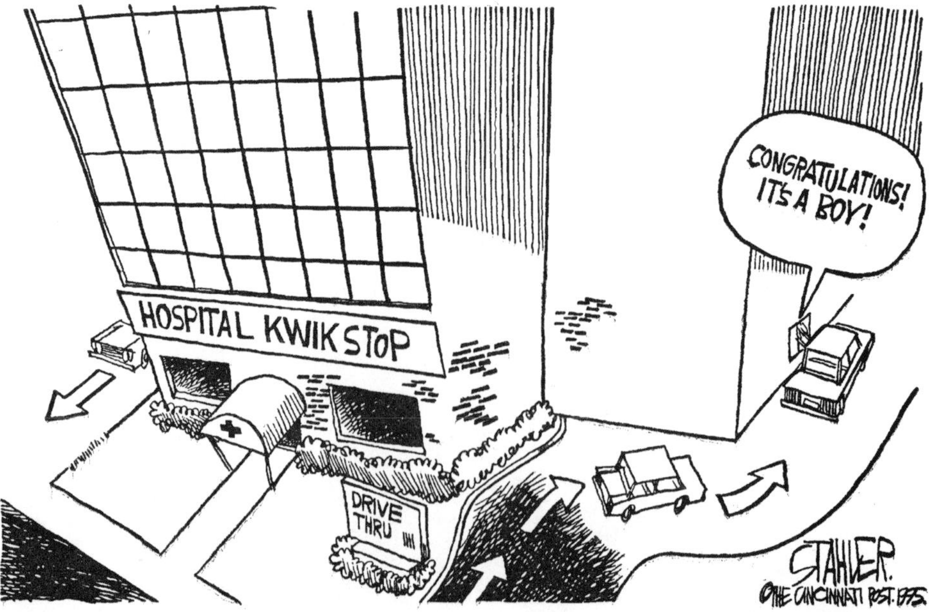

CONGRATULATIONS! IT'S A BOY!
HOSPITAL KWIK STOP
DRIVE THRU

JEFF STAHLER
Courtesy Cincinnati Post

J. R. ROSE
Courtesy Byrd Newspapers

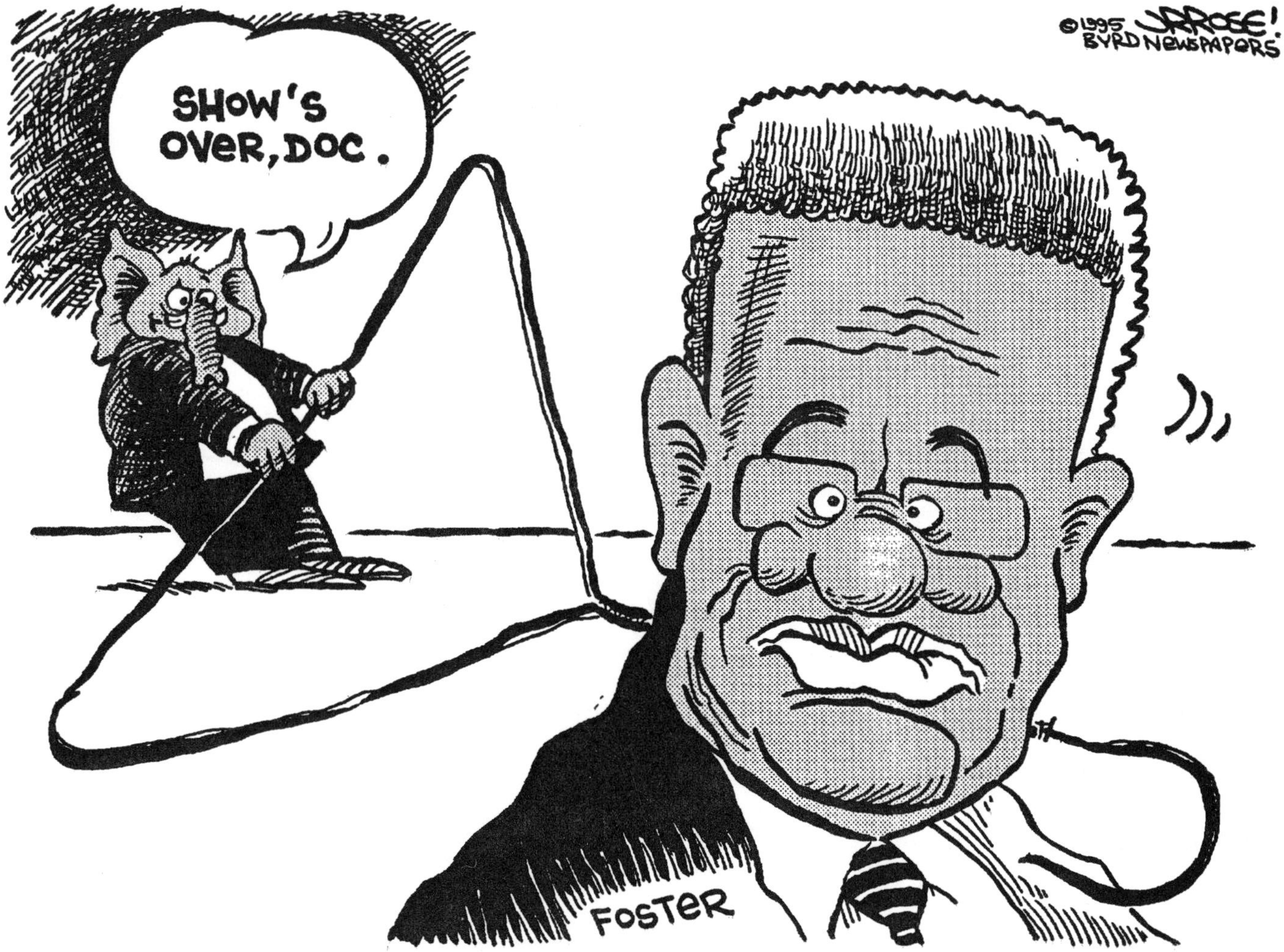
©1995 JRROSE!
BYRD NEWSPAPERS
SHOW'S OVER, DOC.
FOSTER

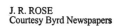

ROGER SCHILLERSTROM
Courtesy Crain Communications

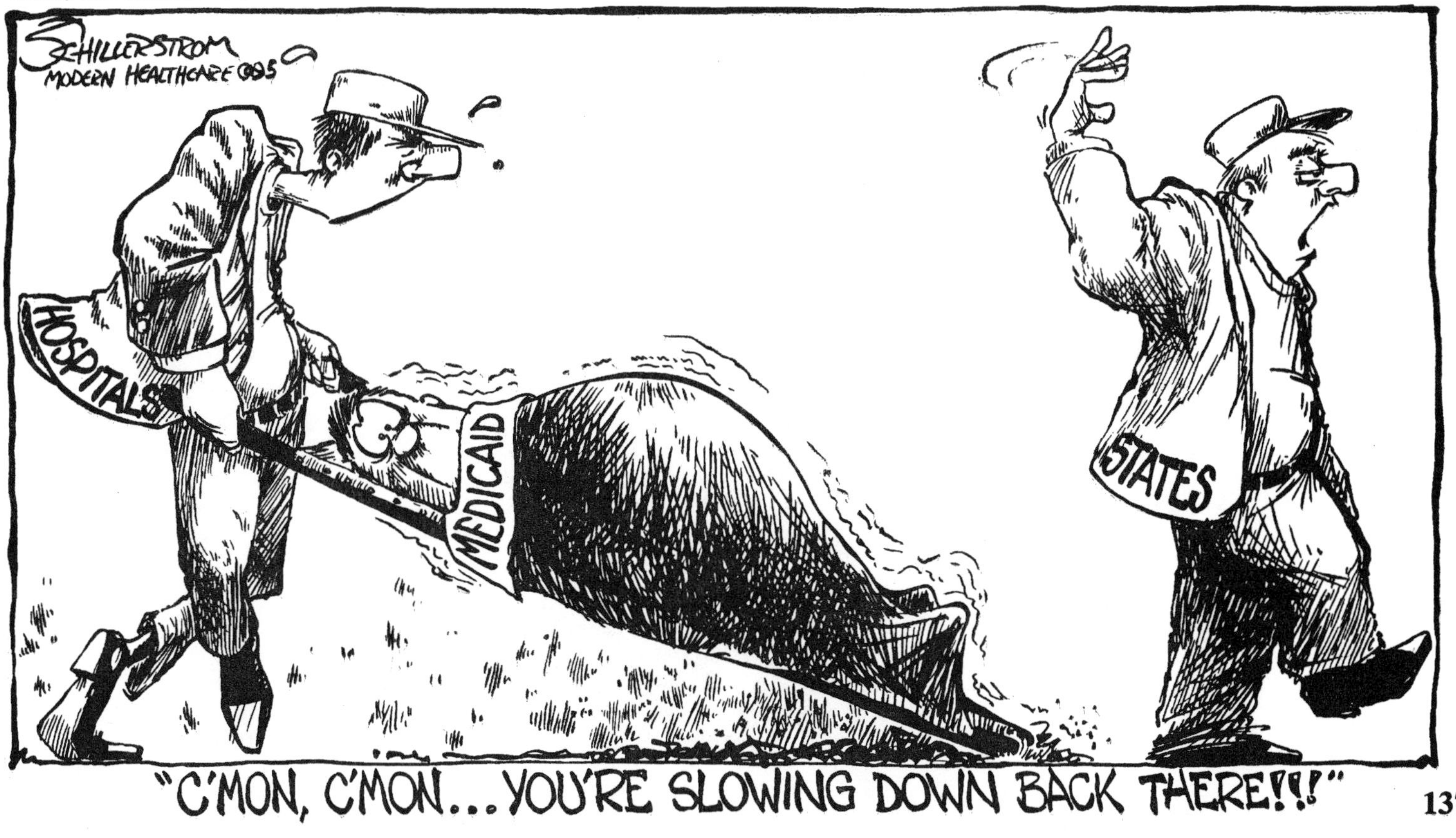
SCHILLERSTROM
MODERN HEALTHCARE ©95
HOSPITALS
MEDICAID
STATES

"C'MON, C'MON... YOU'RE SLOWING DOWN BACK THERE!!!"

SCOTT WILLIS
Courtesy San Jose Mercury

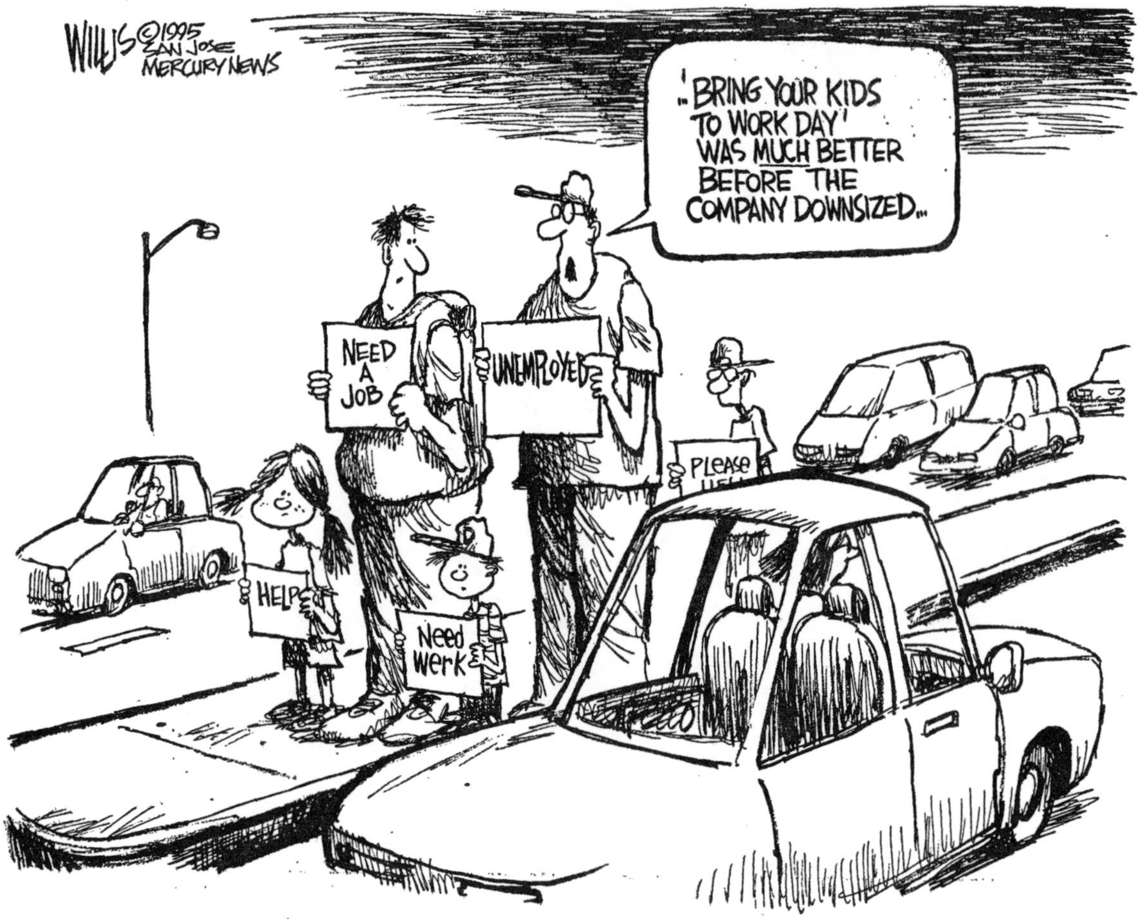
WILLIS ©1995 SAN JOSE MERCURY NEWS
..'BRING YOUR KIDS TO WORK DAY' WAS MUCH BETTER BEFORE THE COMPANY DOWNSIZED...
NEED A JOB
UNEMPLOYED
HELP
Need Werk
PLEASE

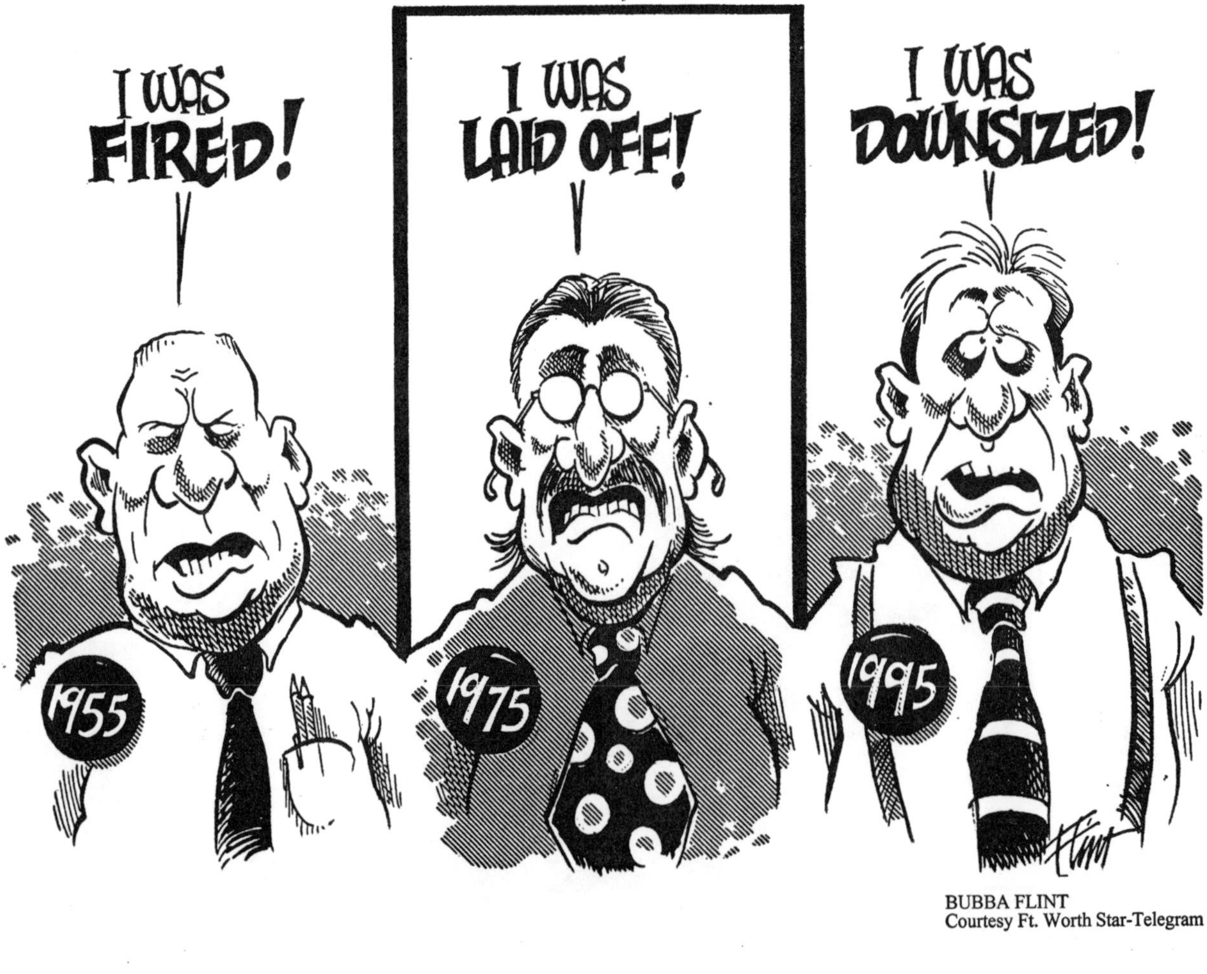
I WAS FIRED!
I WAS LAID OFF!
I WAS DOWNSIZED!
1955
1975
1995
Flint

BUBBA FLINT
Courtesy Ft. Worth Star-Telegram

The Economy

The U.S. economy grew at a tepid rate of 2.5 percent during the year as companies downsized while wages stagnated. Several big chains filed for bankruptcy, and Kmart closed more than two hundred stores.

Just as Ross Perot predicted, the hotly debated NAFTA agreement appeared to be costing the U.S. heavily. Thousands of jobs, particularly in the textile industry, have been lost to Mexico. Many manufacturing plants closed their doors and moved south of the border to find cheaper labor and lower costs. A trade war with Japan was averted when Japanese officials agreed—once again—to open their markets wider to American cars. The U.S. trade deficit with Japan showed little improvement.

The Walt Disney Company took over Capital Cities/ABC in a $19-billion transaction, the second-largest corporate merger in U.S. history. One day later, CBS purchased Westinghouse for $5.4 billion. An agreement between Time-Warner and Turner Broadcasting System effectively created the number-one company in the entertainment business.

Large banks continued to swallow smaller ones, and public television stepped up its search for operating revenue from commercial sources. More than twenty million people now use the Internet, and the number is growing.

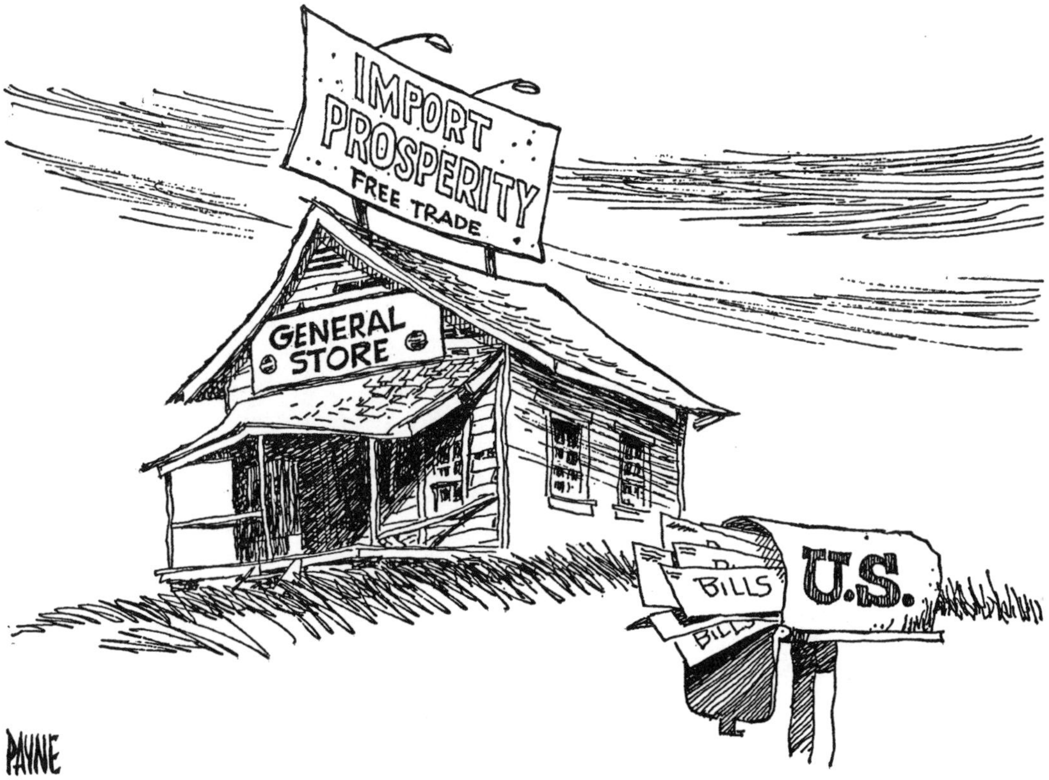
IMPORT PROSPERITY
FREE TRADE
GENERAL STORE
BILLS
U.S.
PAYNE

EUGENE PAYNE
Courtesy Charlotte Observer

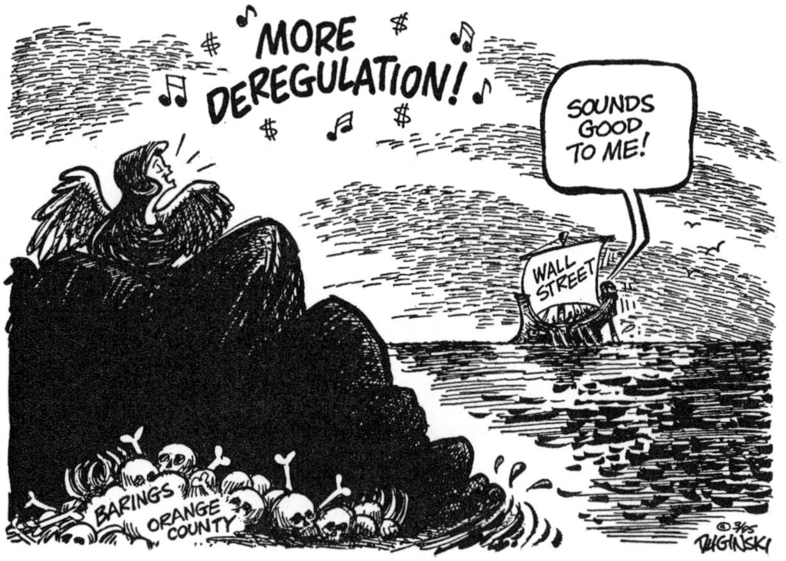
MORE DEREGULATION!
SOUNDS GOOD TO ME!
WALL STREET
BARINGS
ORANGE COUNTY
© 3/95 DUGINSKI

PAUL DUGINSKI
Courtesy Fresno Bee

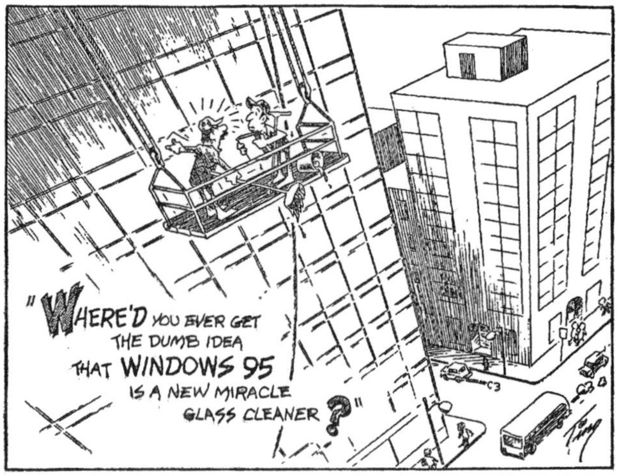
"WHERE'D YOU EVER GET THE DUMB IDEA THAT WINDOWS 95 IS A NEW MIRACLE GLASS CLEANER?"

MERLE R. TINGLEY
Courtesy Montreal Gazette

JEFF PARKER
Courtesy Florida Today

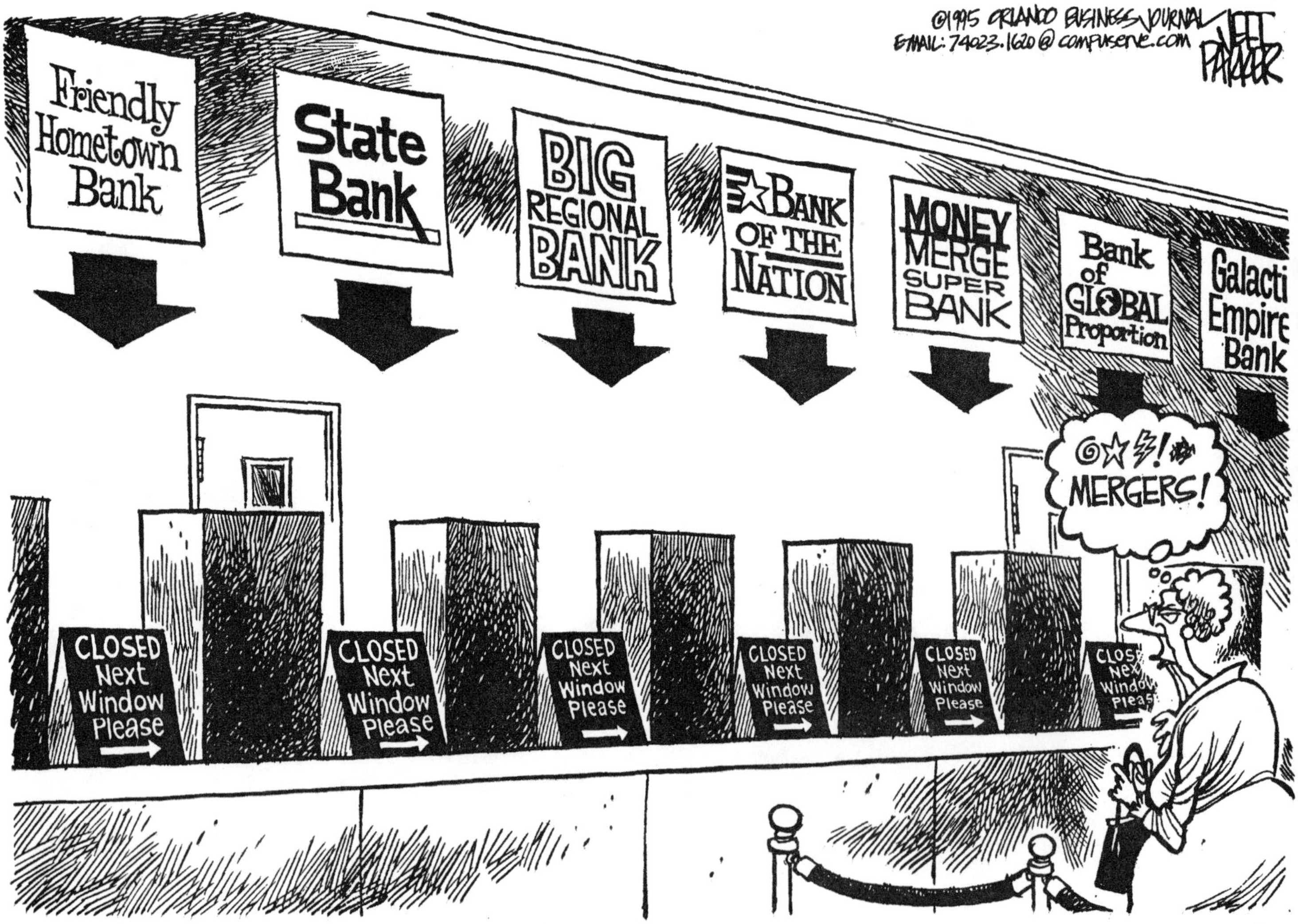
©1995 ORLANDO BUSINESS JOURNAL
E-MAIL: 74023.1620@compuserve.com
JEFF PARKER
Friendly Hometown Bank
State Bank
BIG REGIONAL BANK
BANK OF THE NATION
MONEY MERGE SUPER BANK
Bank of GLOBAL Proportion
Galacti Empire Bank
CLOSED Next Window Please
MERGERS!

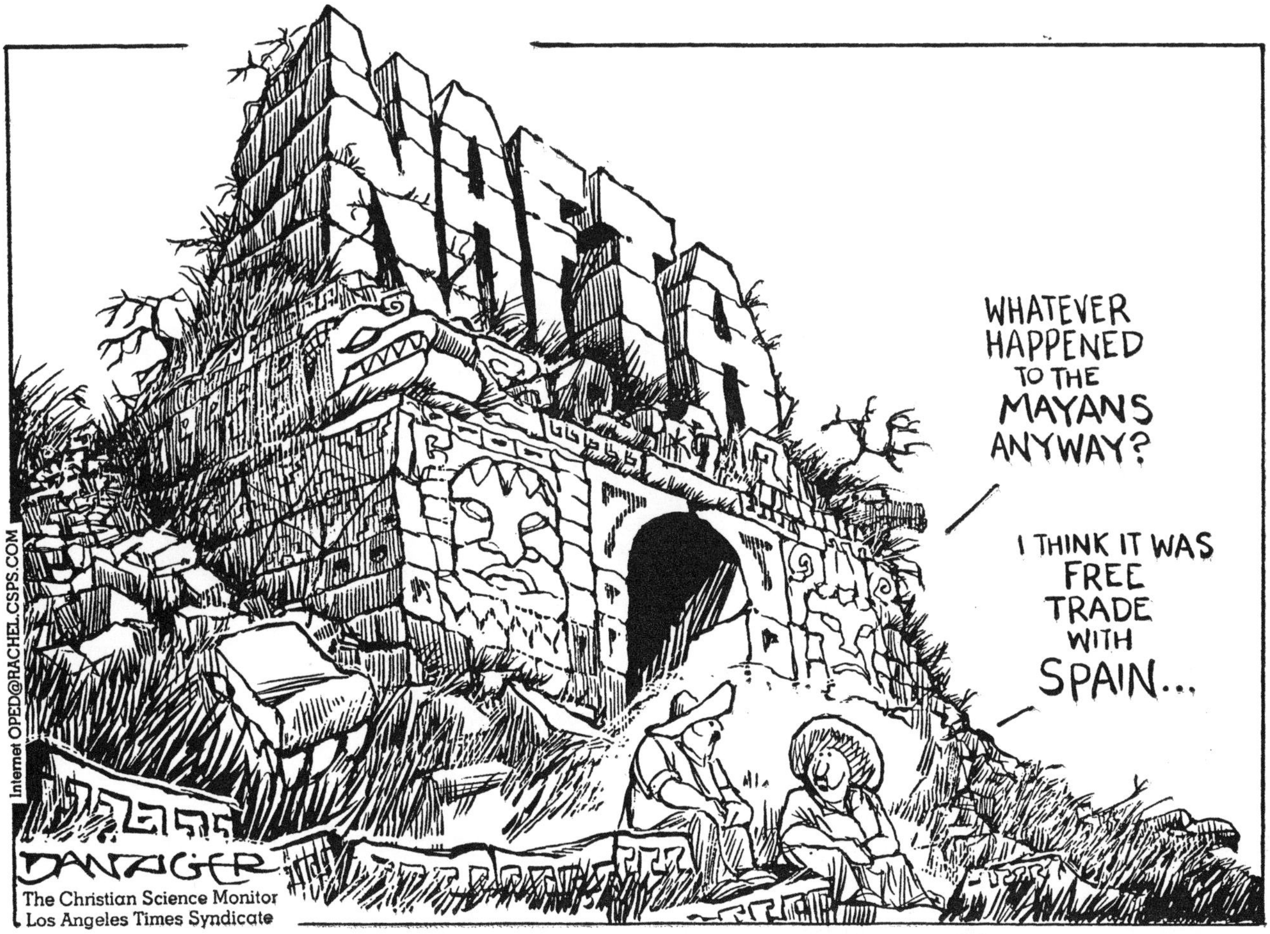
NAFTA
WHATEVER HAPPENED TO THE MAYANS ANYWAY?
I THINK IT WAS FREE TRADE WITH SPAIN...
Internet OPED@RACHEL.CSPS.COM
DANZIGER
The Christian Science Monitor
Los Angeles Times Syndicate

JEFF DANZIGER
Courtesy Christian Science Monitor

DICK LOCHER
Courtesy Chicago Tribune

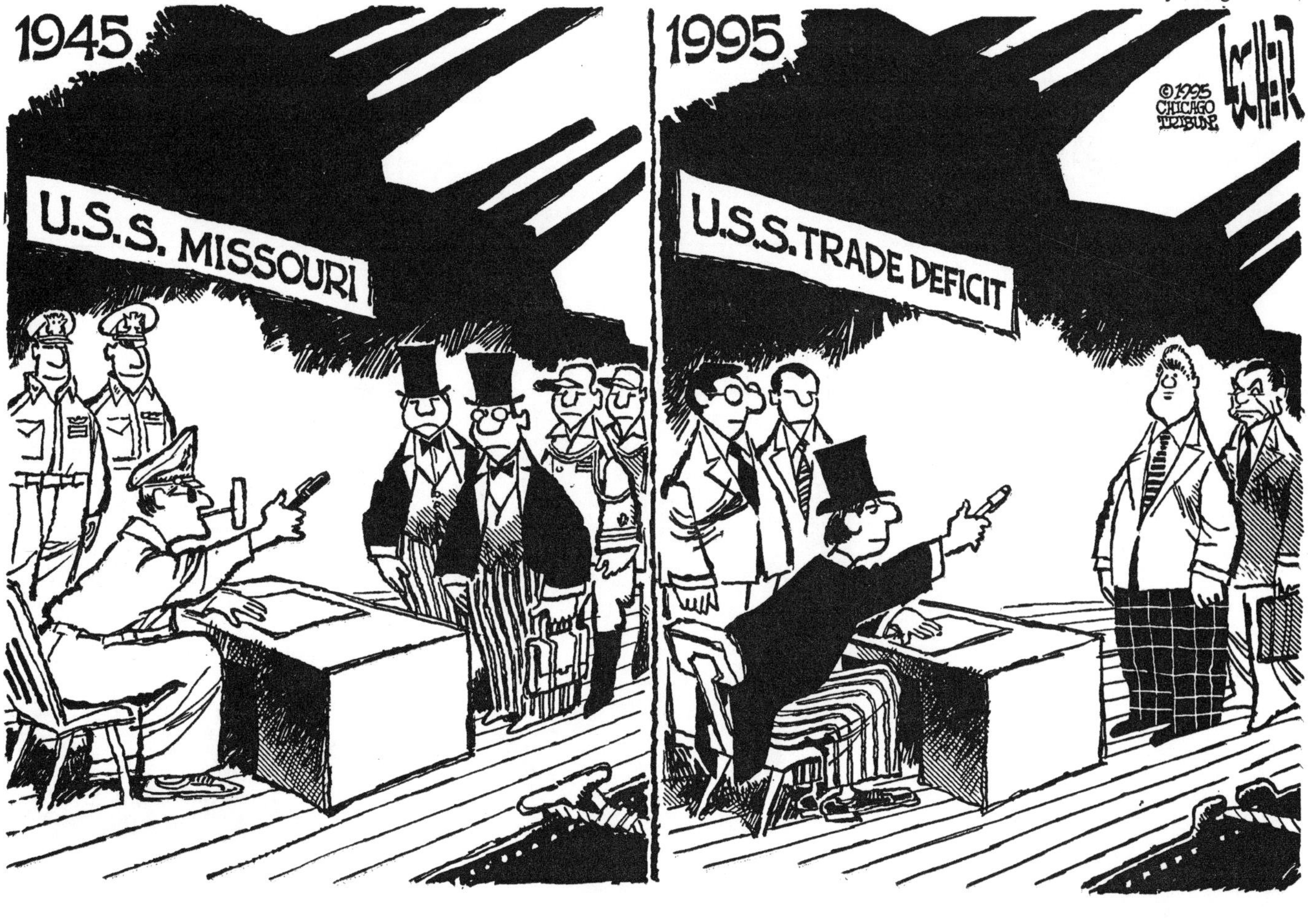
1945
U.S.S. MISSOURI
1995
U.S.S. TRADE DEFICIT
©1995 CHICAGO TRIBUNE
LOCHER

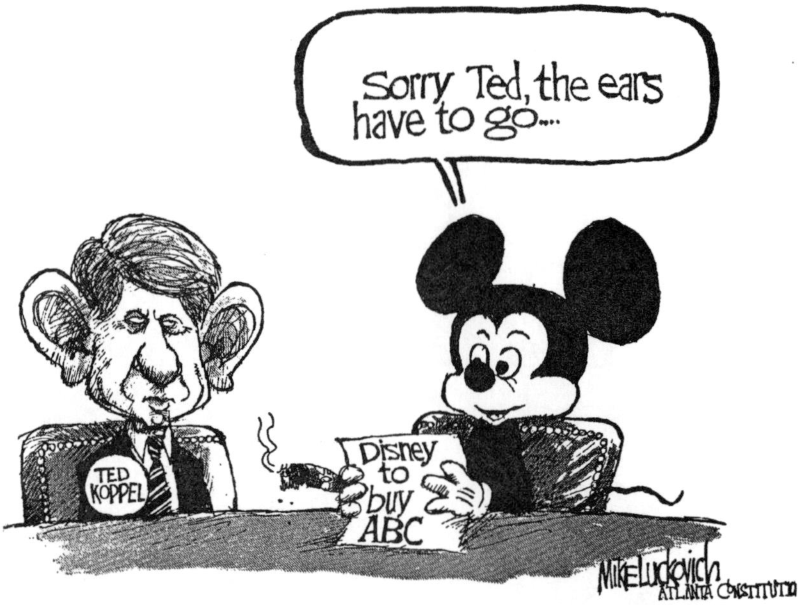
Sorry Ted, the ears have to go....
TED KOPPEL
Disney to buy ABC
MIKE LUCKOVICH ATLANTA CONSTITUTION

MIKE LUCKOVICH
Courtesy Atlanta Constitution

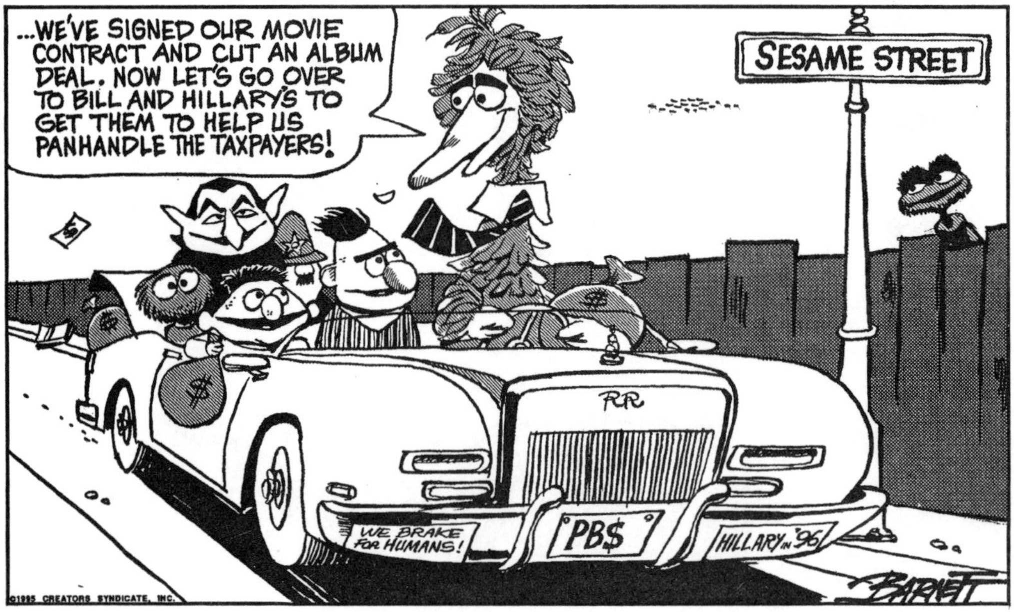
...WE'VE SIGNED OUR MOVIE CONTRACT AND CUT AN ALBUM DEAL. NOW LET'S GO OVER TO BILL AND HILLARY'S TO GET THEM TO HELP US PANHANDLE THE TAXPAYERS!
SESAME STREET
WE BRAKE FOR HUMANS!
PB$
HILLARY IN '96
©1995 CREATORS SYNDICATE, INC.
BARNETT

JERRY BARNETT
Courtesy Indianapolis News

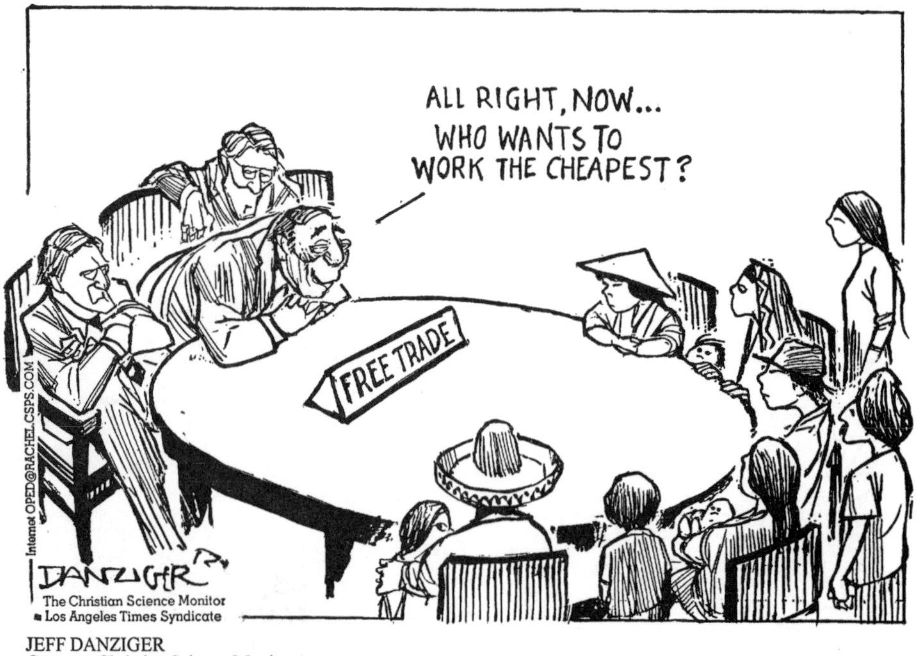
ALL RIGHT, NOW... WHO WANTS TO WORK THE CHEAPEST?
FREE TRADE
Internet OPED@RACHEL.CSPS.COM
DANZIGER
The Christian Science Monitor
Los Angeles Times Syndicate

JEFF DANZIGER
Courtesy Christian Science Monitor

TOM BECK
Courtesy Freeport Journal-Standard (Ill.)

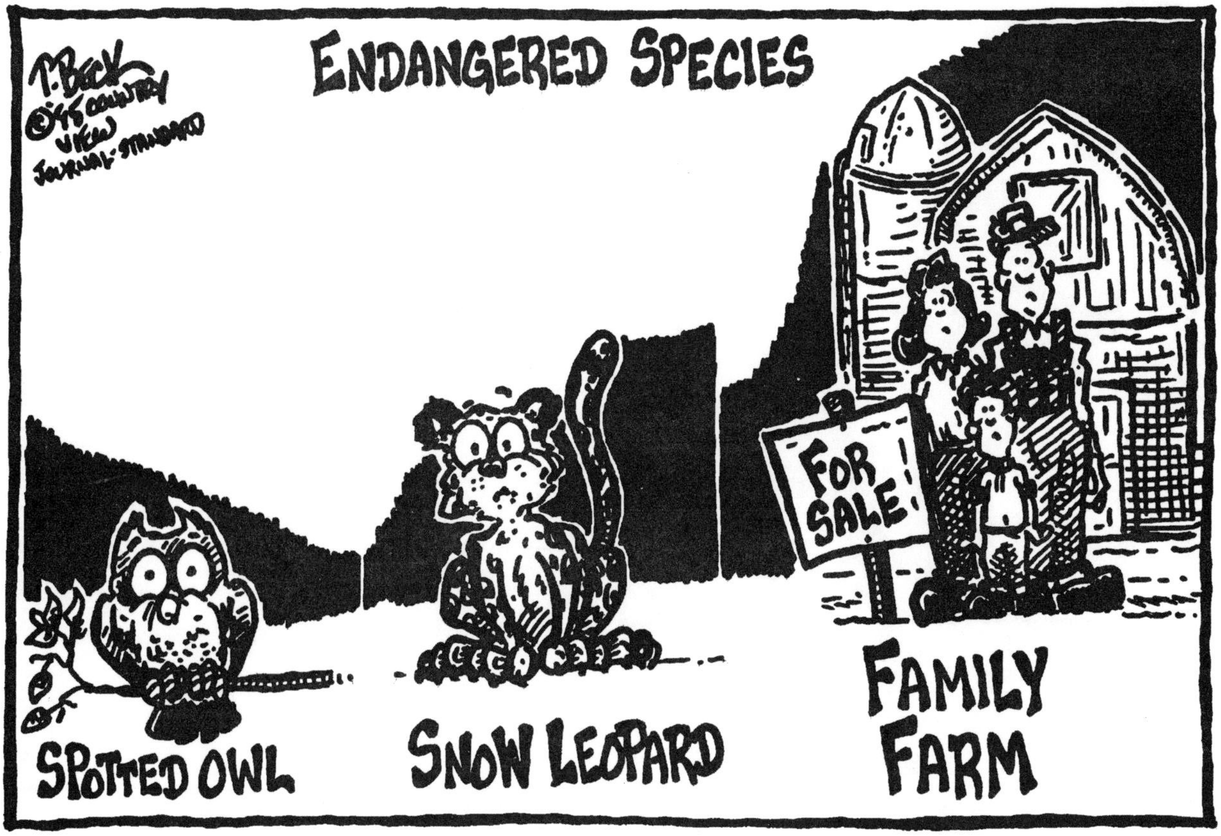
ENDANGERED SPECIES
T. BECK ©95 COUNTRY VIEW JOURNAL-STANDARD
FOR SALE
SPOTTED OWL
SNOW LEOPARD
FAMILY FARM

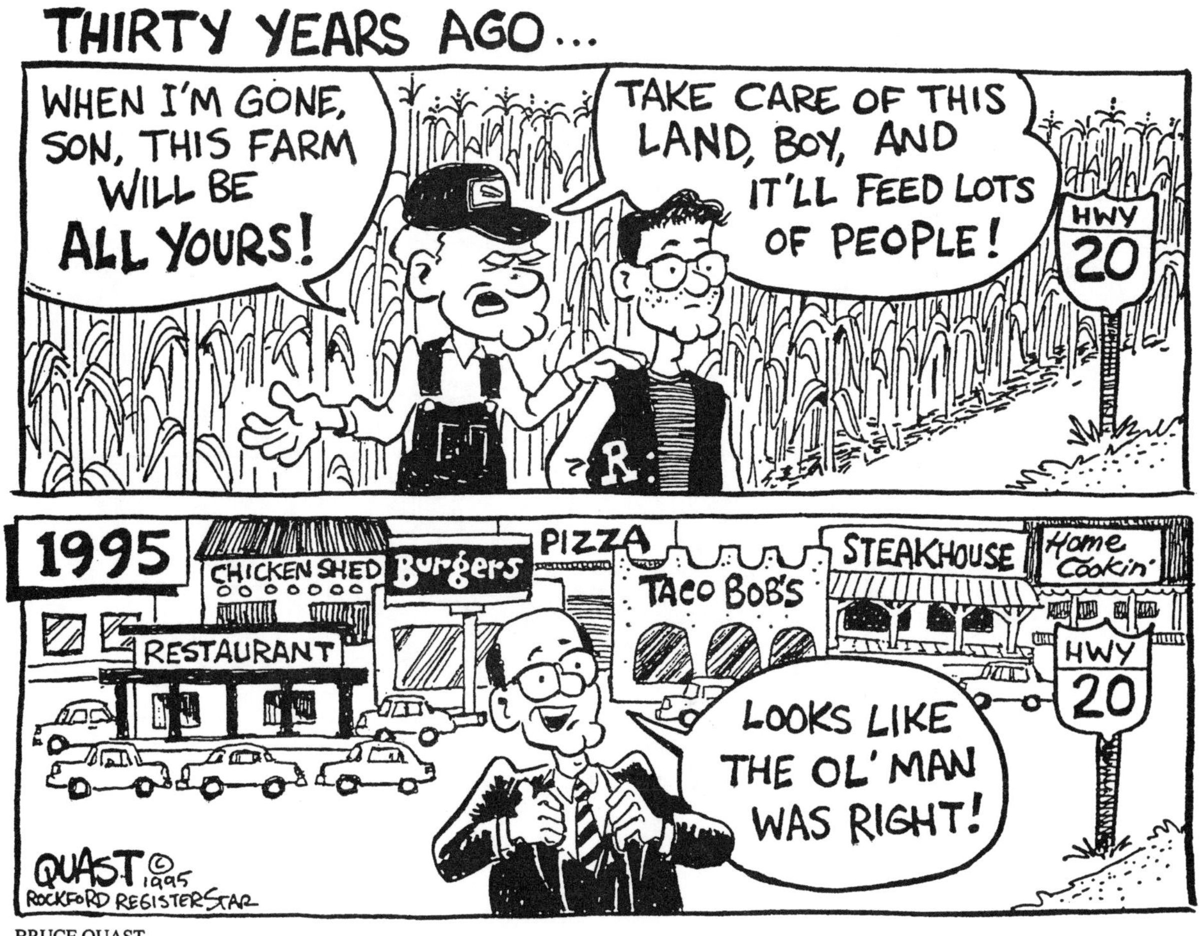
THIRTY YEARS AGO...
WHEN I'M GONE, SON, THIS FARM WILL BE ALL YOURS!
TAKE CARE OF THIS LAND, BOY, AND IT'LL FEED LOTS OF PEOPLE!
HWY 20
1995
CHICKEN SHED
Burgers
PIZZA
TACO BOB'S
STEAKHOUSE
Home Cookin'
RESTAURANT
HWY 20
LOOKS LIKE THE OL' MAN WAS RIGHT!
QUAST © 1995 ROCKFORD REGISTER STAR

BRUCE QUAST
Courtesy Rockford Register-Star

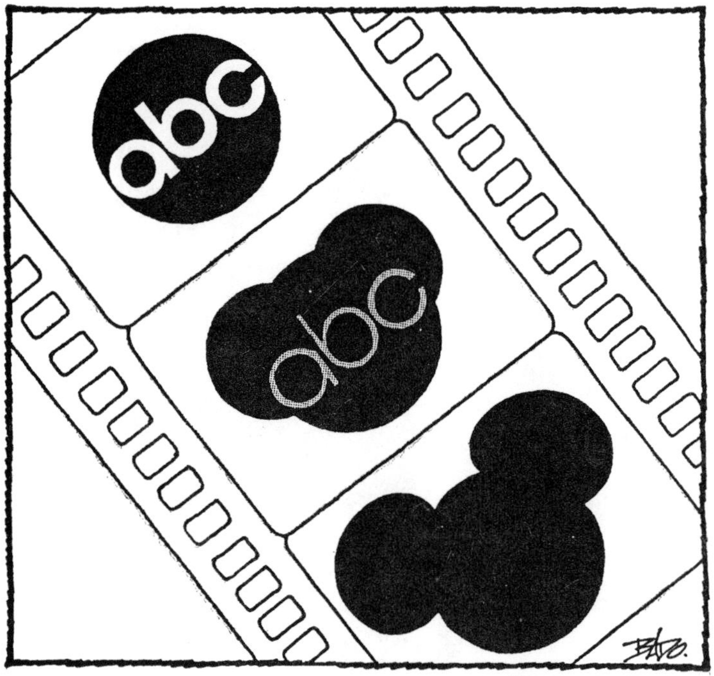
abc
abc

GUY BADEAUX
Courtesy Ottawa Unimedia

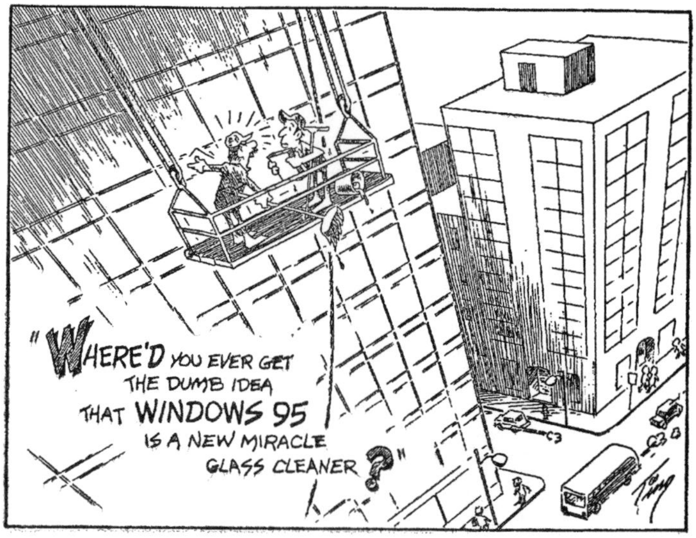
"WHERE'D YOU EVER GET THE DUMB IDEA THAT WINDOWS 95 IS A NEW MIRACLE GLASS CLEANER?"

STEPHEN TEMPLETON
Courtesy Washington Post

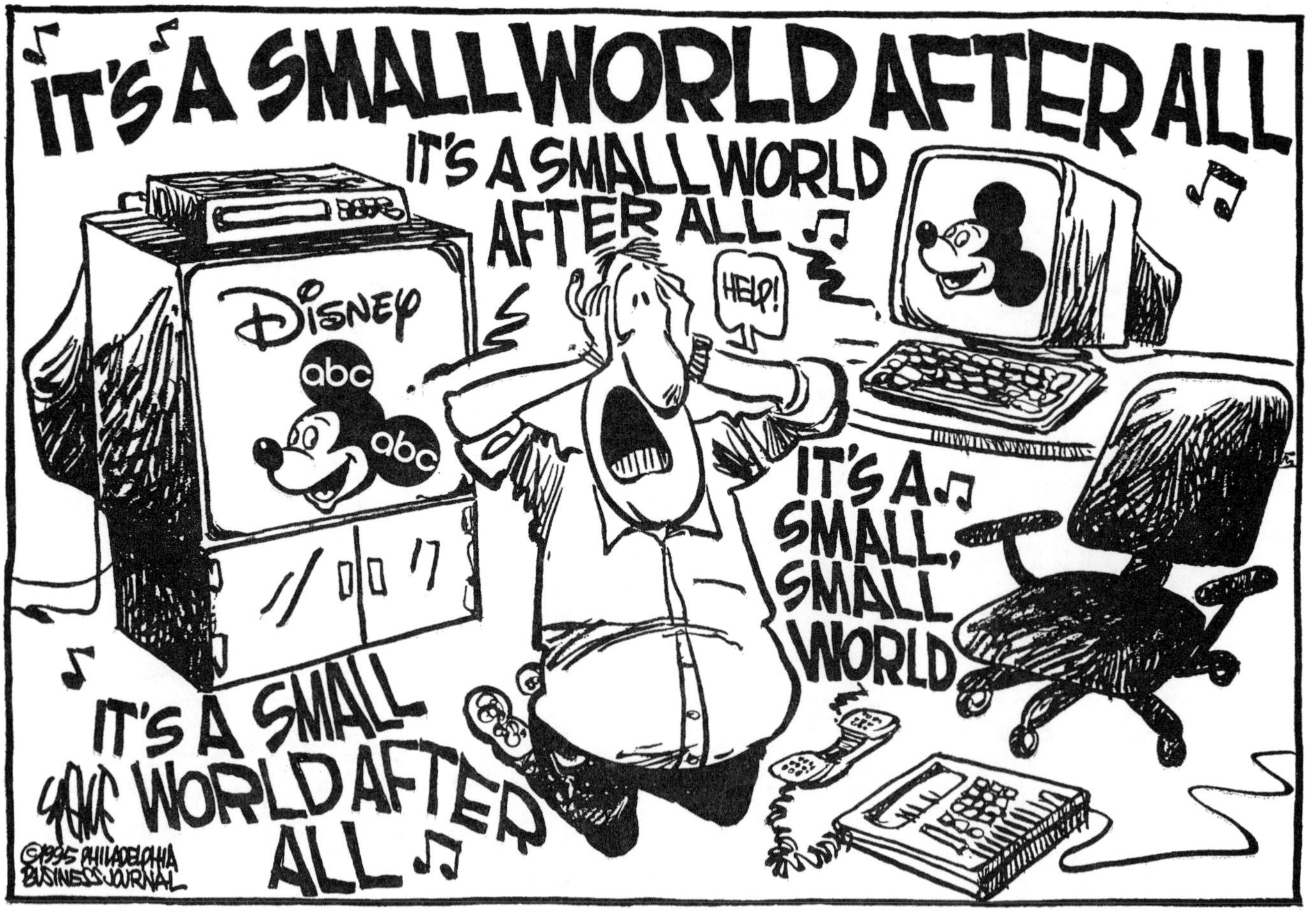
IT'S A SMALL WORLD AFTER ALL
IT'S A SMALL WORLD AFTER ALL
DISNEY
abc
abc
HELP!
IT'S A SMALL, SMALL WORLD
IT'S A SMALL WORLD AFTER ALL
©1995 PHILADELPHIA BUSINESS JOURNAL

JOHN SPENCER
Courtesy Philadelphia Business Journal

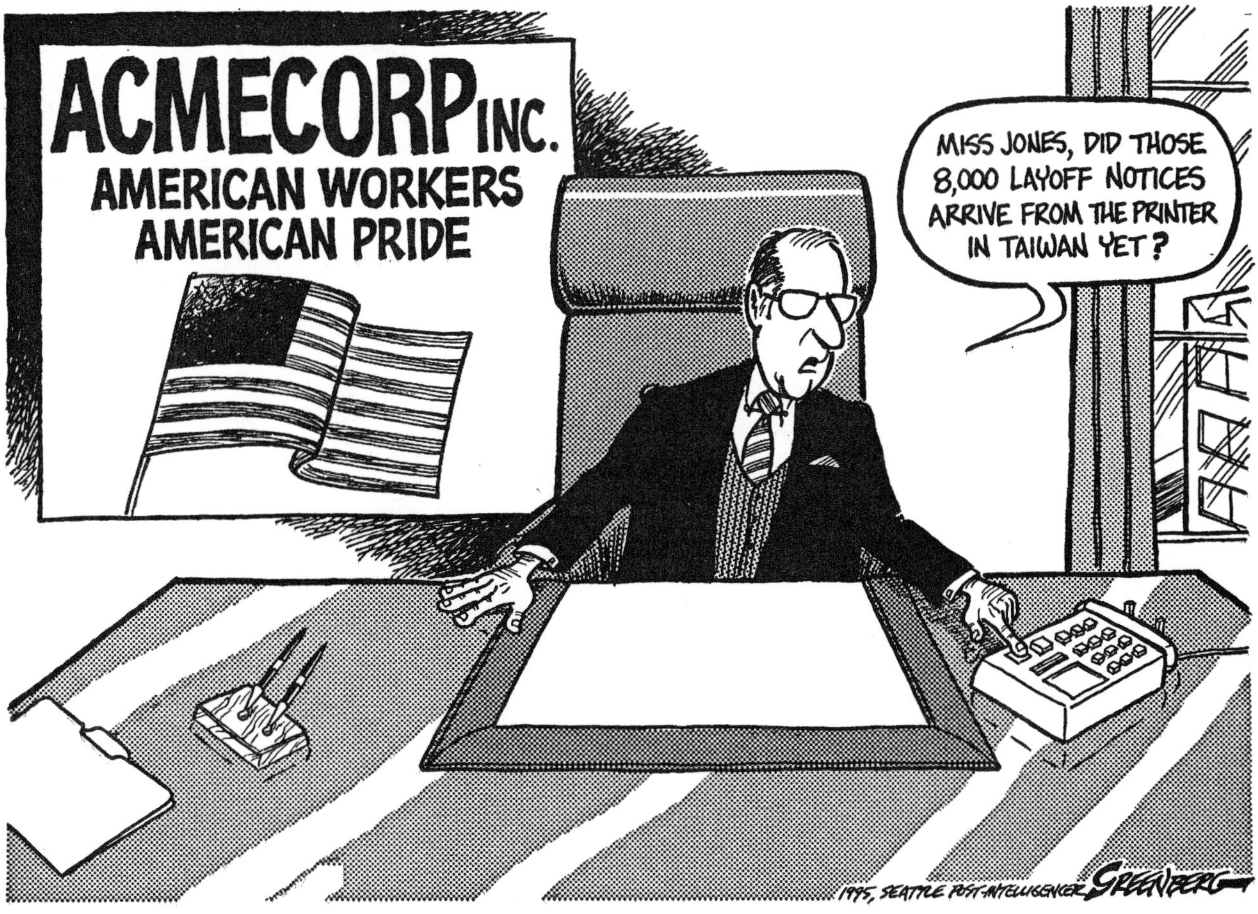
ACMECORP INC.
AMERICAN WORKERS
AMERICAN PRIDE
MISS JONES, DID THOSE 8,000 LAYOFF NOTICES ARRIVE FROM THE PRINTER IN TAIWAN YET?
1995, SEATTLE POST-INTELLIGENCER GREENBERG

STEVE GREENBERG
Courtesy Seattle Post-Intelligencer

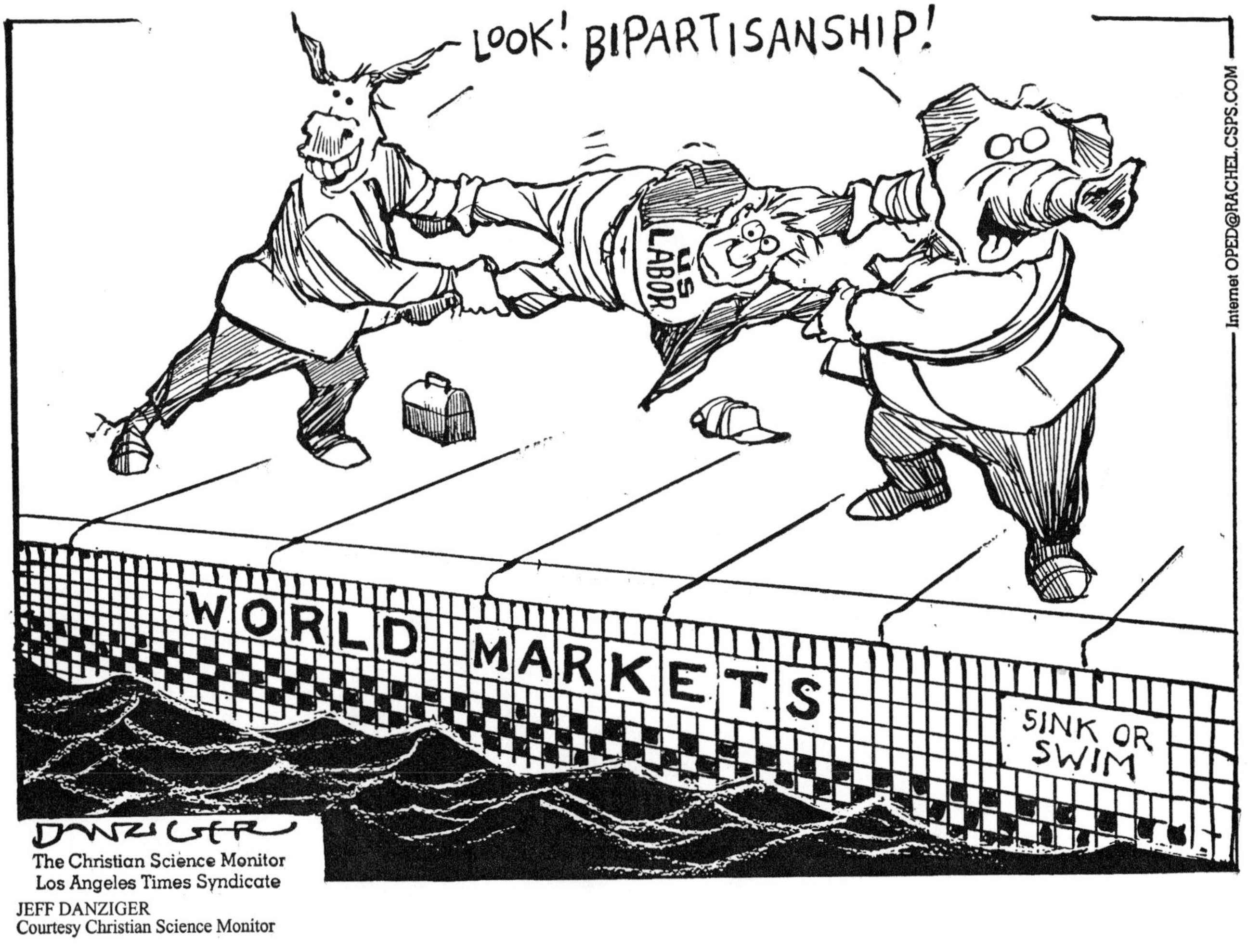
LOOK! BIPARTISANSHIP!
US LABOR
WORLD MARKETS
SINK OR SWIM
Internet OPED@RACHEL.CSPS.COM
DANZIGER
The Christian Science Monitor
Los Angeles Times Syndicate

JEFF DANZIGER
Courtesy Christian Science Monitor

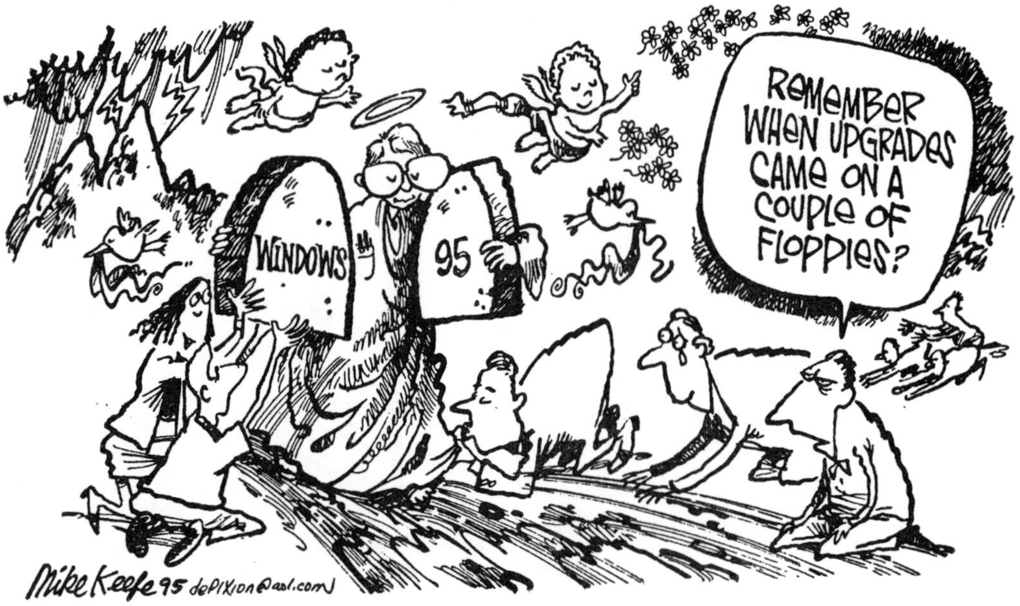
REMEMBER WHEN UPGRADES CAME ON A COUPLE OF FLOPPIES?
WINDOWS
95
MIKE KEEFE 95 dePIXion@aol.com

MIKE KEEFE
Courtesy Denver Post

JERRY LEFLER
Courtesy Ventura County Star-Free Press

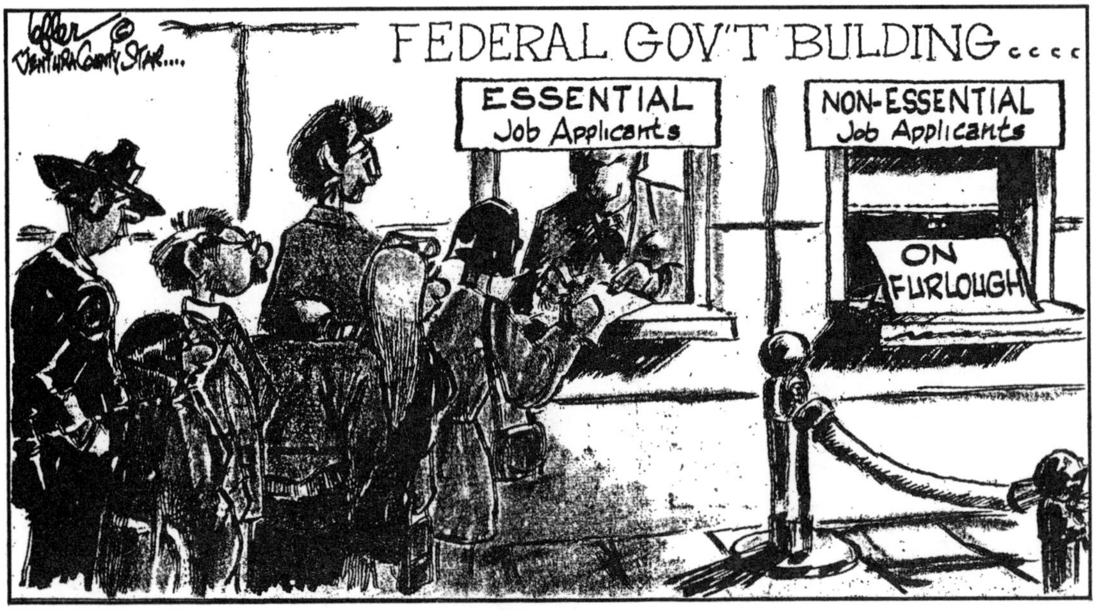
FEDERAL GOV'T BULDING....
ESSENTIAL Job Applicants
NON-ESSENTIAL Job Applicants
ON FURLOUGH

ROGER SCHILLERSTROM
Courtesy Crain Communications

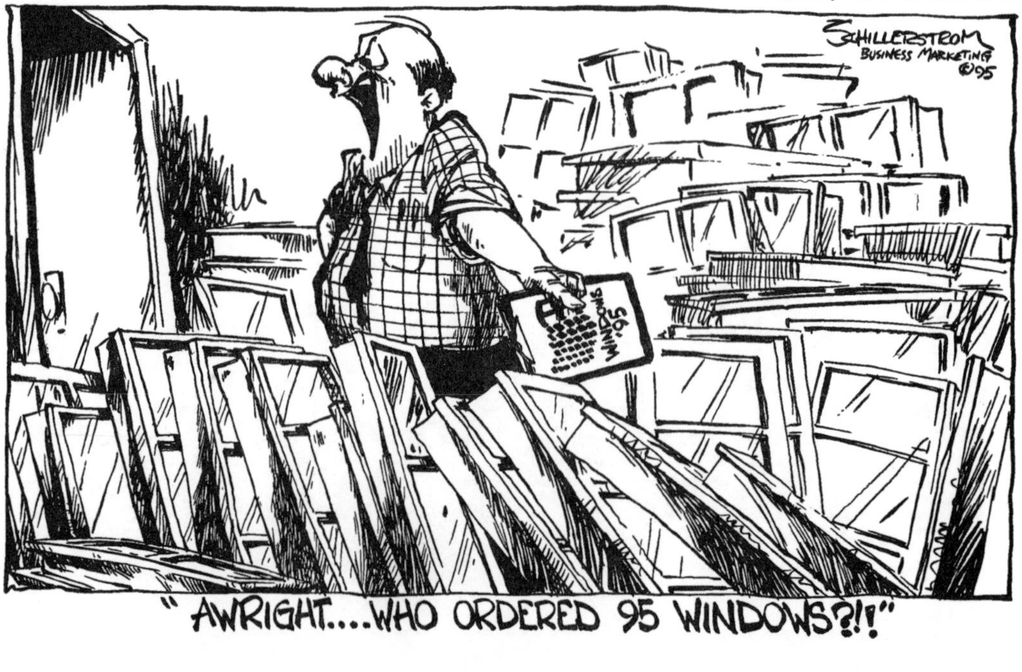
SCHILLERSTROM BUSINESS MARKETING ©95
WINDOWS 95

"AWRIGHT....WHO ORDERED 95 WINDOWS?!!"

ROB ROGERS
Courtesy Pittsburgh Post-Gazette

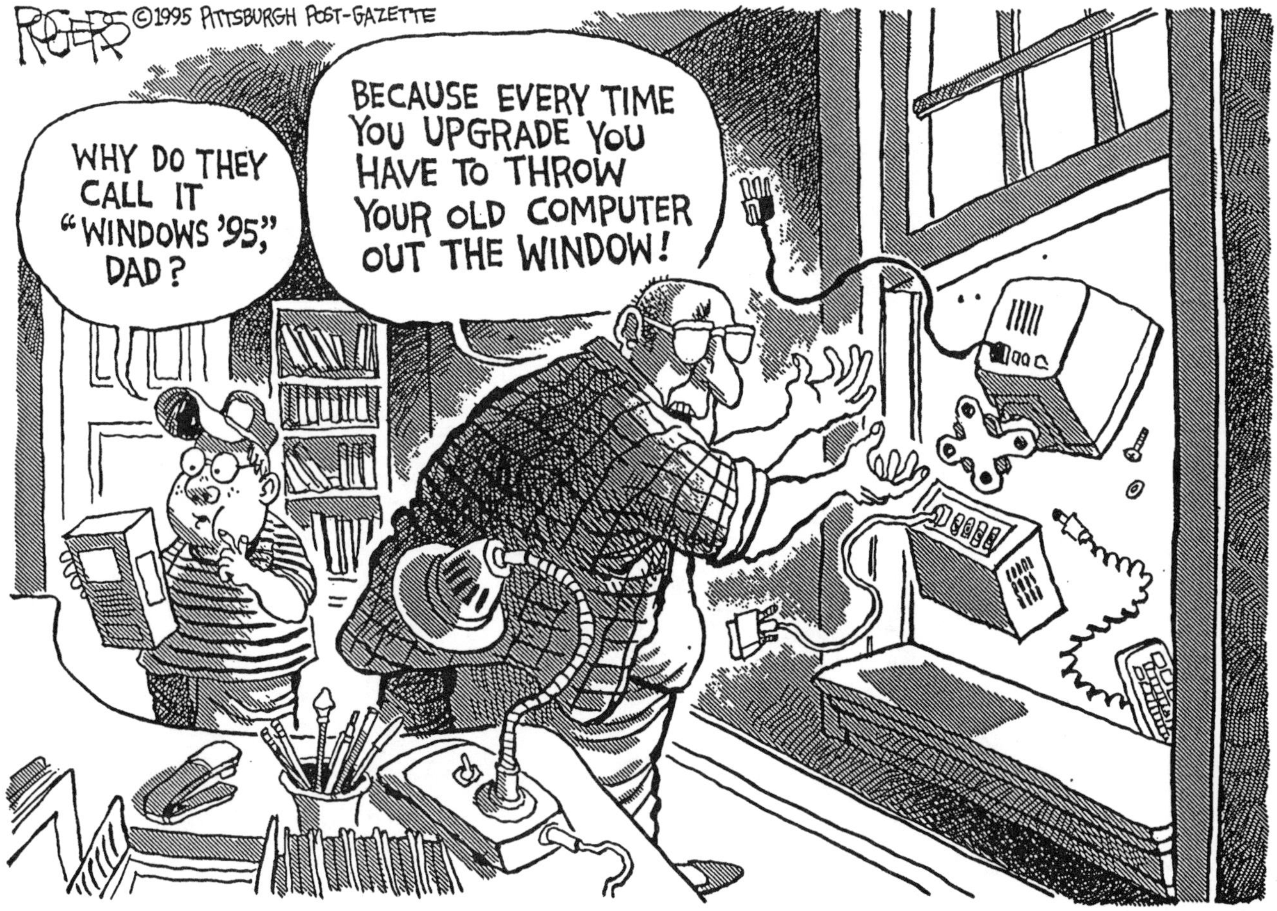
ROGERS ©1995 PITTSBURGH POST-GAZETTE
WHY DO THEY CALL IT "WINDOWS '95," DAD?
BECAUSE EVERY TIME YOU UPGRADE YOU HAVE TO THROW YOUR OLD COMPUTER OUT THE WINDOW!

JOHN SPENCER
Courtesy Philadelphia Business Journal

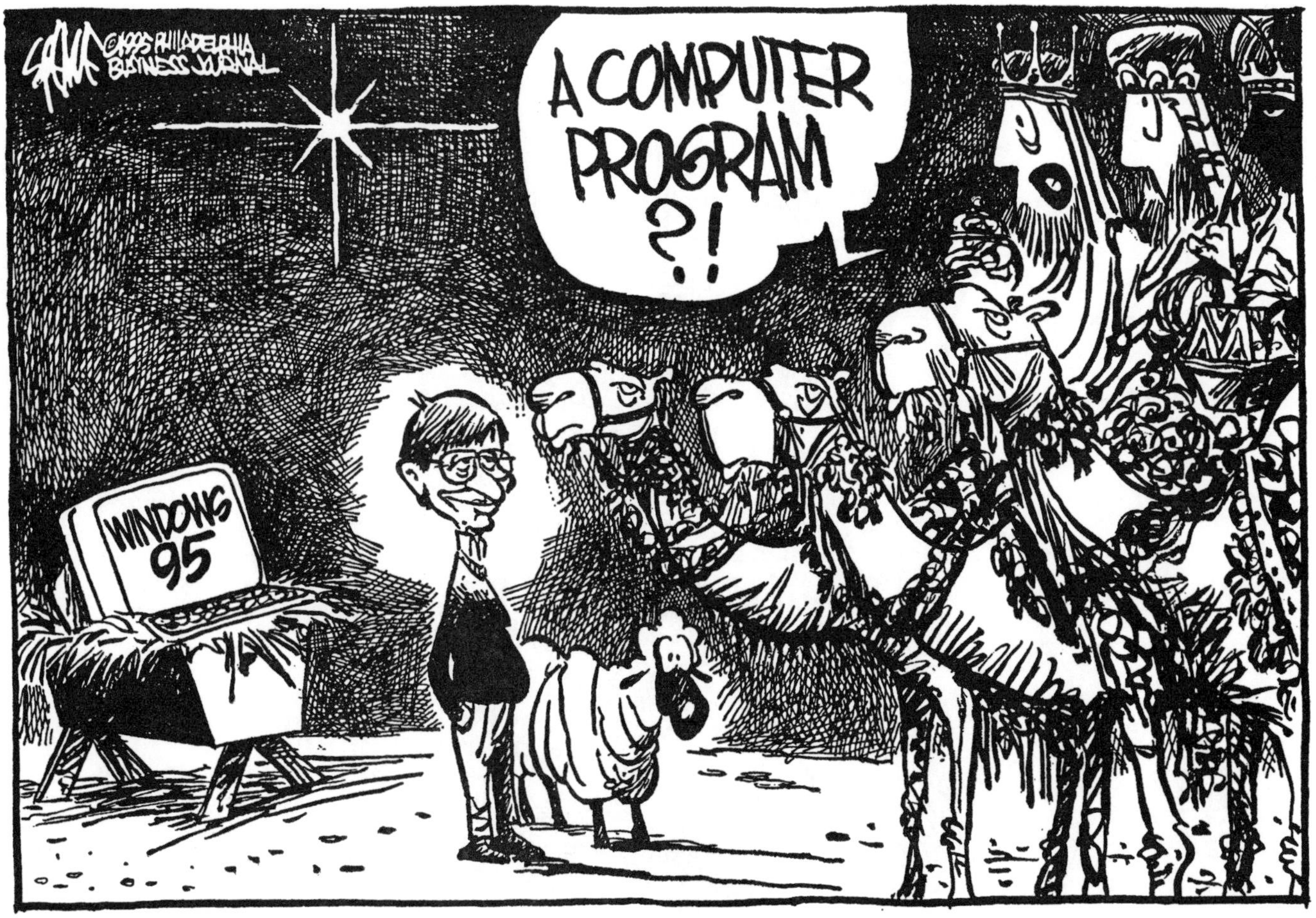
©1995 PHILADELPHIA BUSINESS JOURNAL
A COMPUTER PROGRAM ?!
WINDOWS 95

TOM DARCY
Courtesy Newsday

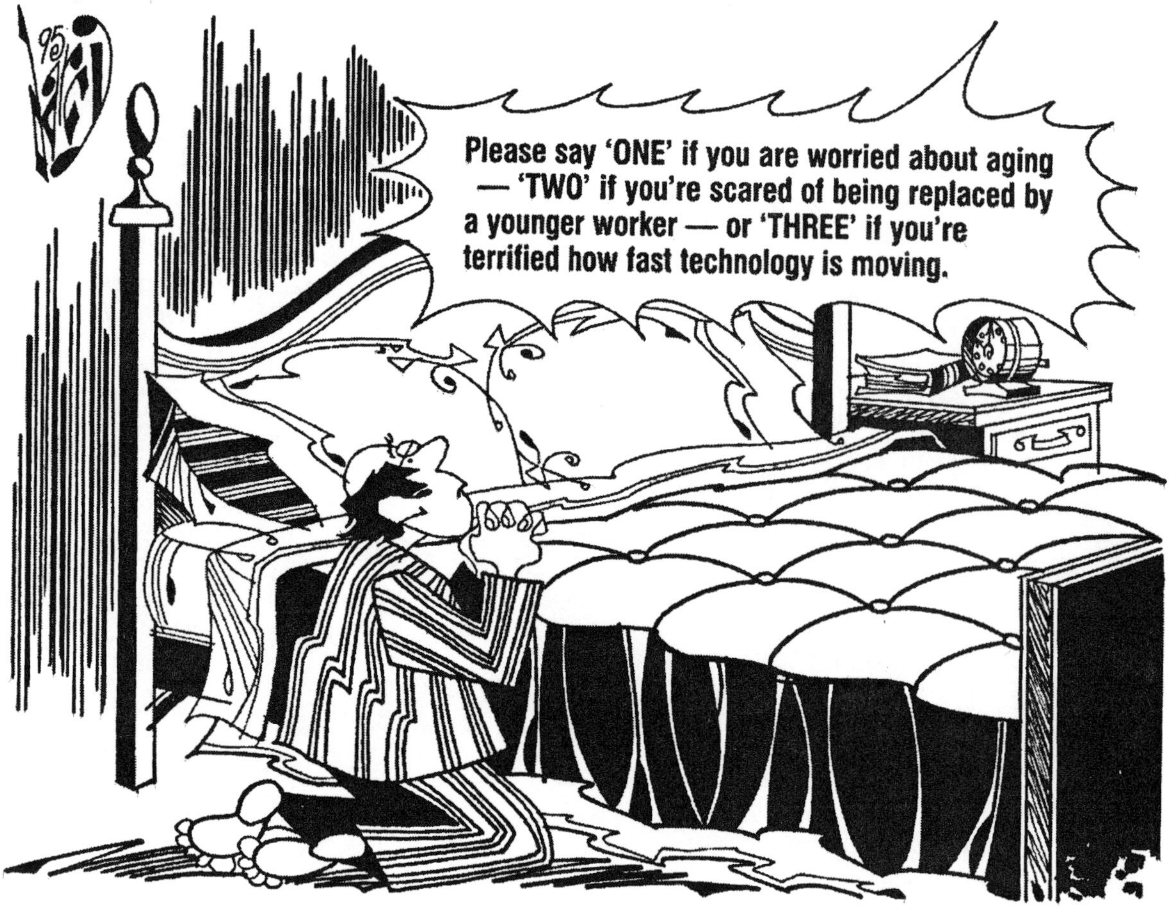
Please say 'ONE' if you are worried about aging — 'TWO' if you're scared of being replaced by a younger worker — or 'THREE' if you're terrified how fast technology is moving.

JOHN SHERFFIUS
Courtesy Ventura Star-Free Press

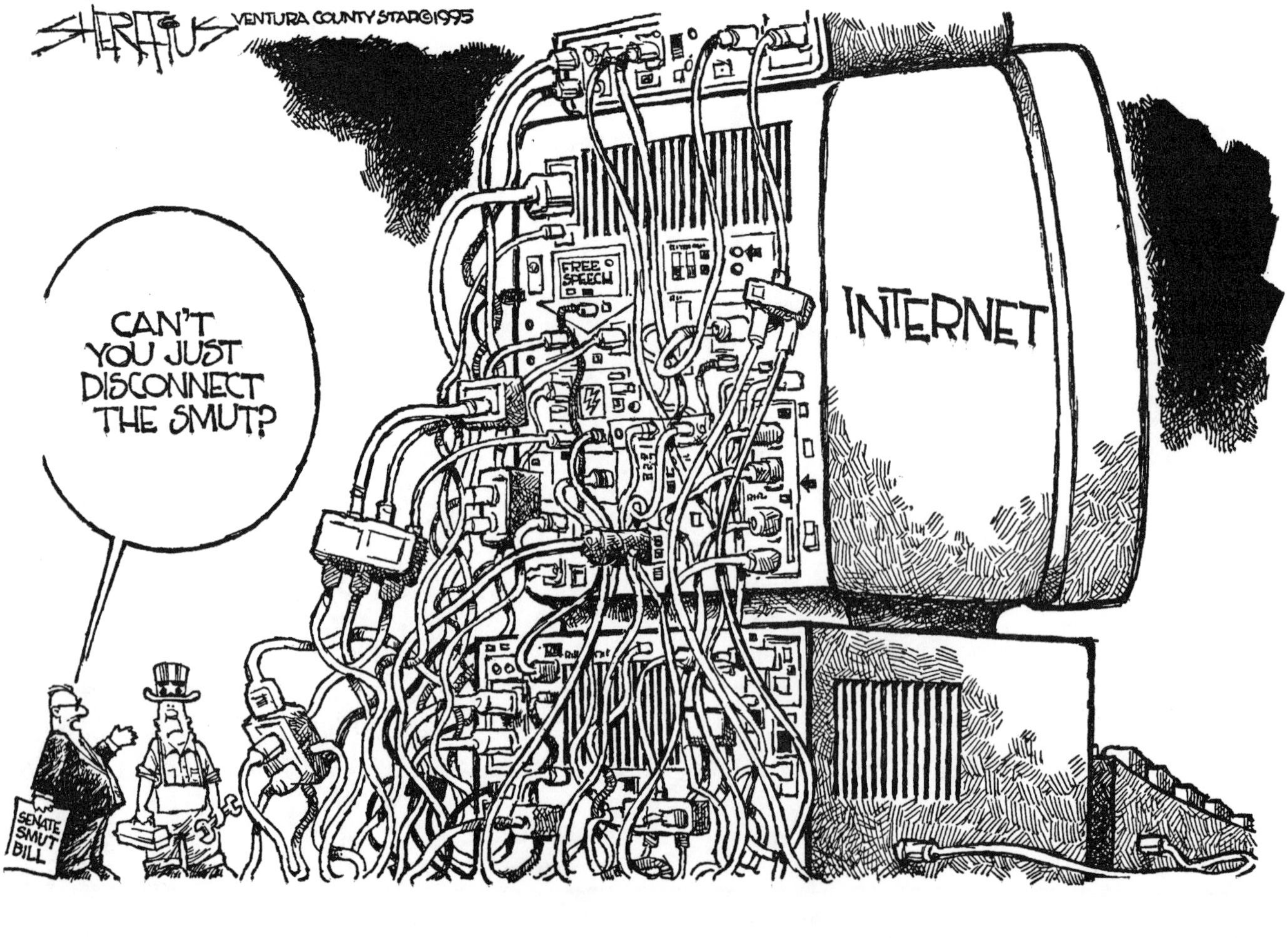
SHERFFIUS VENTURA COUNTY STAR©1995
CAN'T YOU JUST DISCONNECT THE SMUT?
FREE SPEECH
INTERNET
SENATE SMUT BILL

Sports

Baltimore's Cal Ripken, Jr., eclipsed one of baseball's most venerable records in September when he played in his 2,131st consecutive major-league game. The amazing streak that eventually surpassed Iron Man Lou Gehrig's fifty-six-year-old mark stretched from 1982 when Ripken was a twenty-one-year-old rookie.

Ripken's achievement came at a time when baseball needed something—or somebody—heroic. Fans had become disenchanted with the greed of spoiled, wealthy players and owners after the lengthy player strike of 1994, and attendance had declined across the country. The steady, dedicated play of Ripken seemed just what America's National Pastime needed to halt its slide.

Baseball Hall of Famer Mickey Mantle died August 13 as a result of cancer. Mantle ranked eighth on the all-time home-run list with 536.

American Indians renewed their push to persuade sports teams to cease using nicknames and mascots whose origins could be linked to Indian culture. It is degrading and racist practice, some claimed, but few people noticed. And owners of professional sports teams continued to shop around for home cities where they might increase profits on their investments. Fans in Cleveland were furious when the Browns, a National Football League team, announced they were moving to Baltimore.

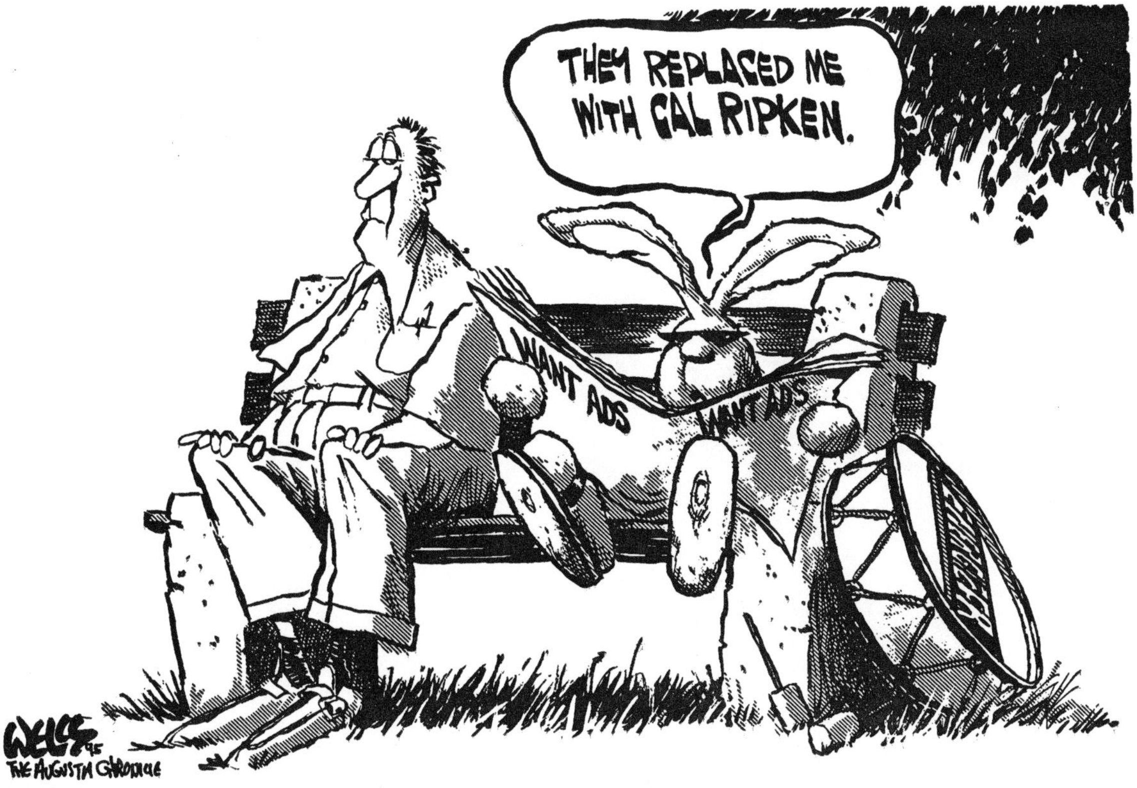
THEY REPLACED ME WITH CAL RIPKEN.
WANT ADS
WANT ADS
WELLS '95
THE AUGUSTA CHRONICLE

CLYDE WELLS
Courtesy Augusta Chronicle

STEVE MCBRIDE
Courtesy Independence Daily Reporter (Kans.)

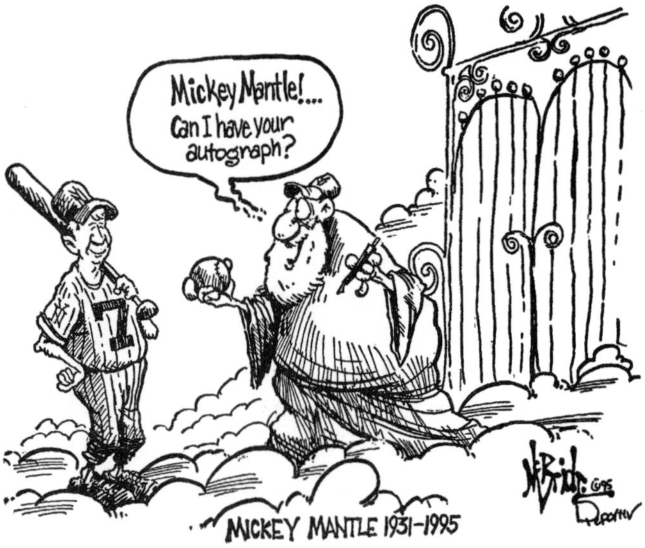
Mickey Mantle!...
Can I have your autograph?
MICKEY MANTLE 1931-1995

One Hundred Years After The Birth Of The Great Bambino

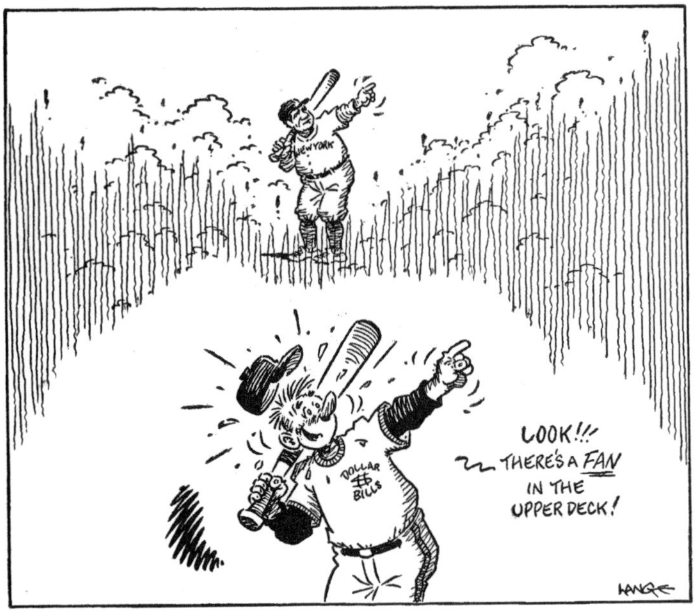
NEW YORK
DOLLAR BILLS
LOOK!!! THERE'S A FAN IN THE UPPER DECK!

JIM LANGE
Courtesy Daily Oklahoman

CHIP BOK
Courtesy Akron Beacon Journal

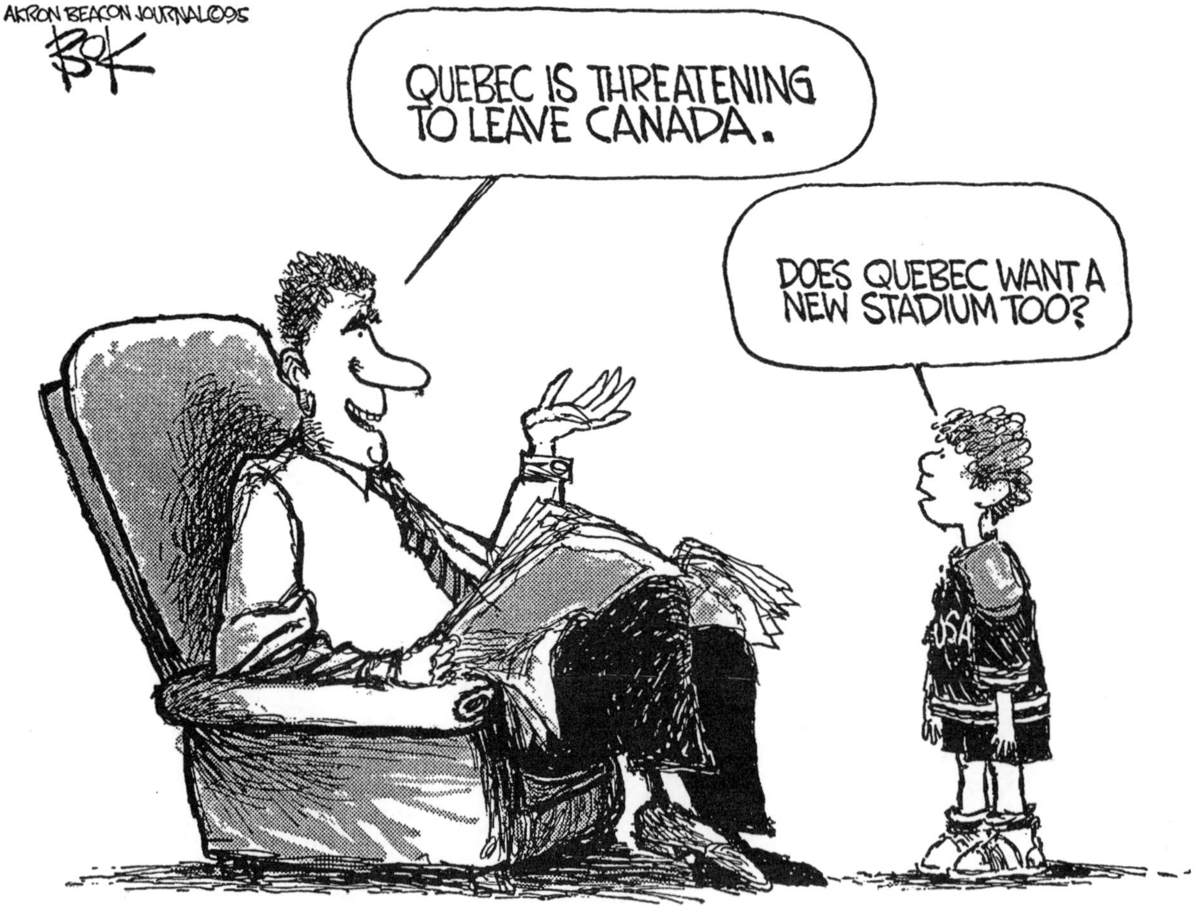
AKRON BEACON JOURNAL©95
QUEBEC IS THREATENING TO LEAVE CANADA.
DOES QUEBEC WANT A NEW STADIUM TOO?
USA

BILL GARNER
Courtesy Washington Times

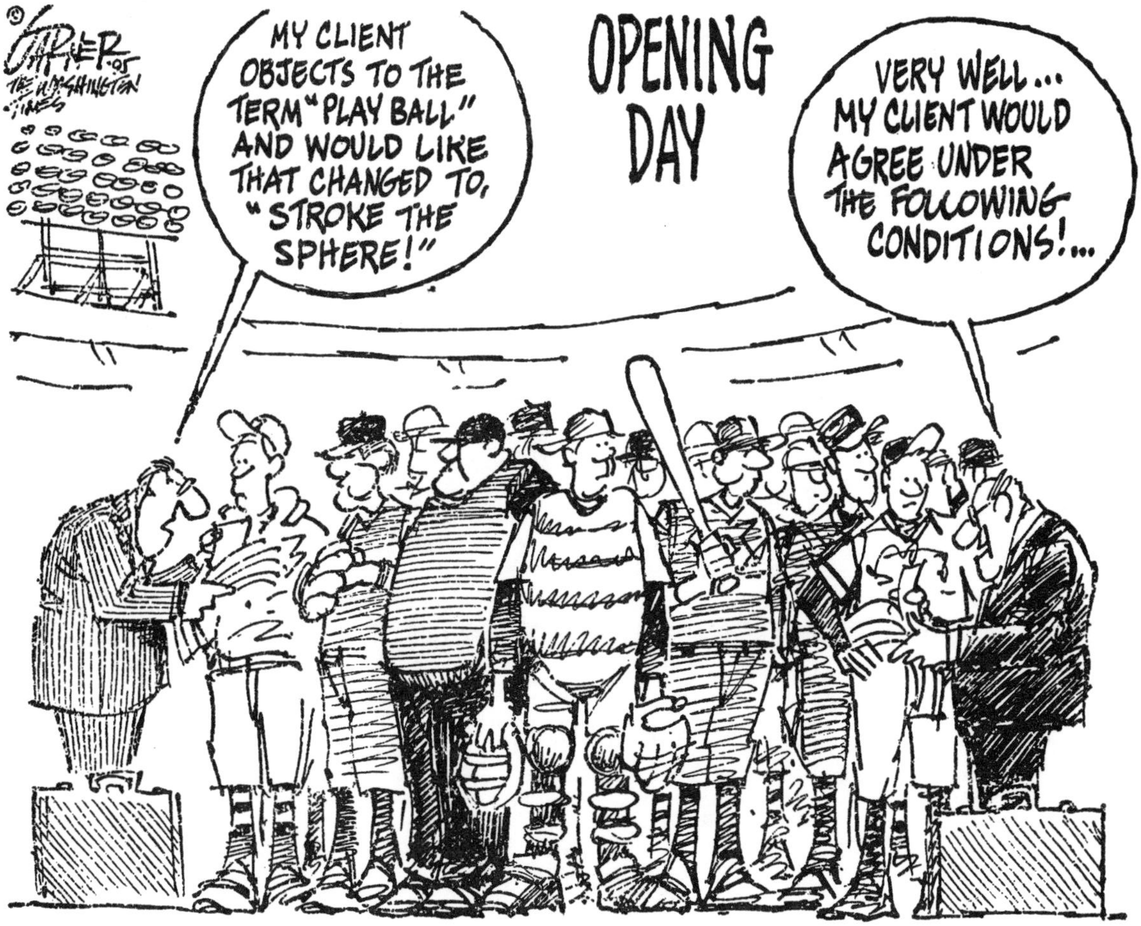
OPENING DAY
MY CLIENT OBJECTS TO THE TERM "PLAY BALL" AND WOULD LIKE THAT CHANGED TO, "STROKE THE SPHERE!"
VERY WELL... MY CLIENT WOULD AGREE UNDER THE FOLLOWING CONDITIONS!...

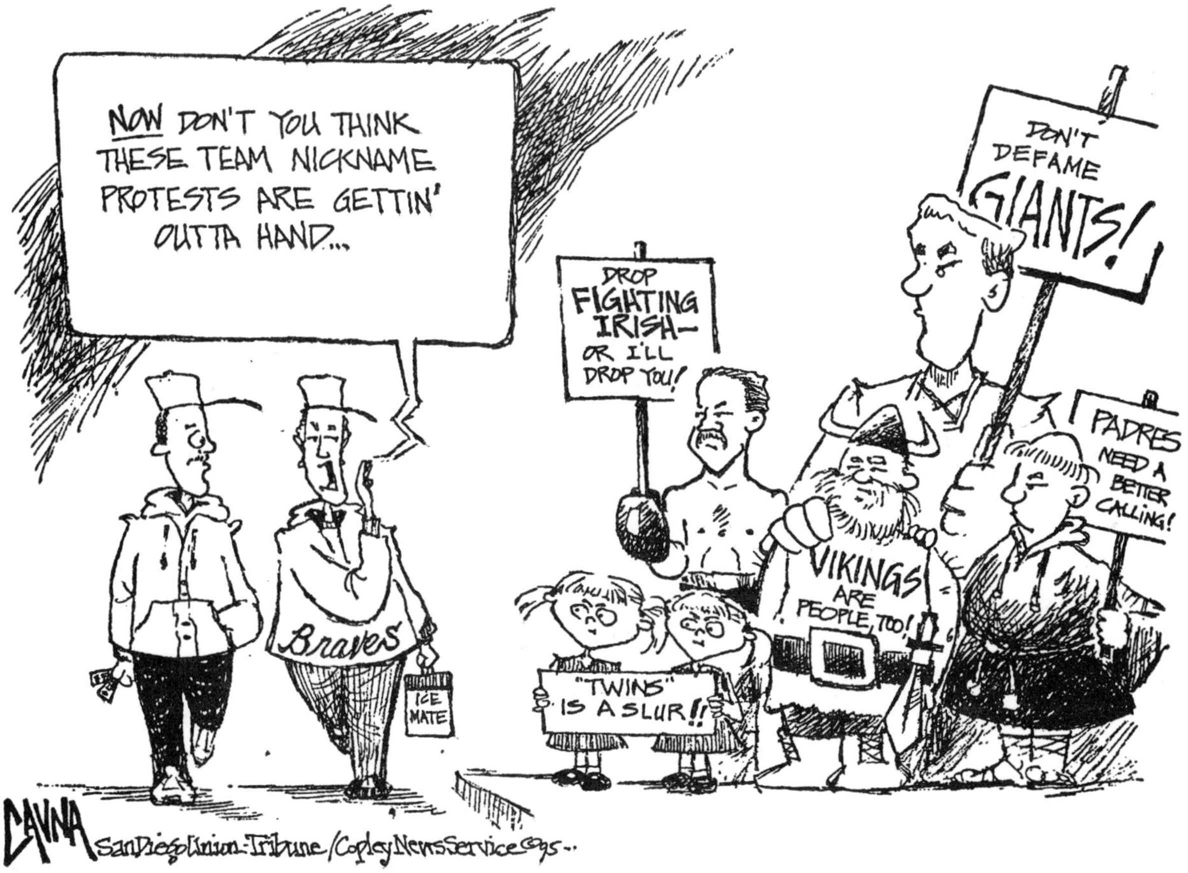
NOW DON'T YOU THINK THESE TEAM NICKNAME PROTESTS ARE GETTIN' OUTTA HAND...
DON'T DEFAME GIANTS!
DROP FIGHTING IRISH— OR I'LL DROP YOU!
PADRES NEED A BETTER CALLING!
VIKINGS ARE PEOPLE, TOO!
"TWINS" IS A SLUR!!
Braves
ICE MATE
CAVNA SanDiegoUnion-Tribune/CopleyNewsService©95

MICHAEL CAVNA
Courtesy San Diego Union-Tribune

PTUI!
FANS
BASEBALL ATTENDANCE DOWN
WELLS
THE AUGUSTA CHRONICLE

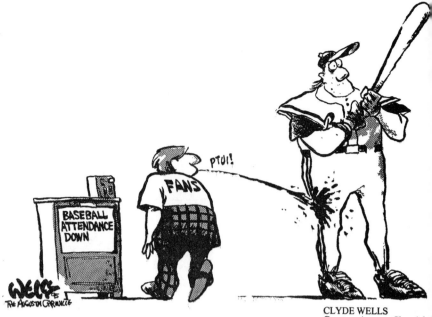

CLYDE WELLS
Courtesy Augusta Chronicle

OLD BASEBALL
NEW BASEBALL
©lindstrom
DULUTH NEWS-TRIBUNE

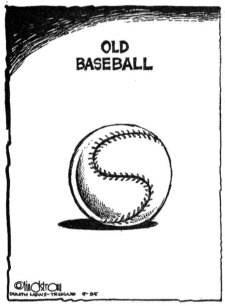

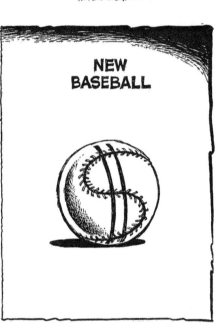

STEVE LINDSTROM
Courtesy Duluth News-Tribune

I'M TELLING YOU SOMEDAY I'LL BREAK CAL RIPKEN'S PLAYING RECORD!
THE WAVE

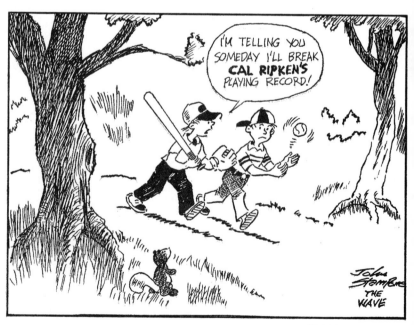

JOHN STAMPONE
Courtesy The Wave (Del.)

DENNY PRITCHARD
Courtesy Ottawa Citizen

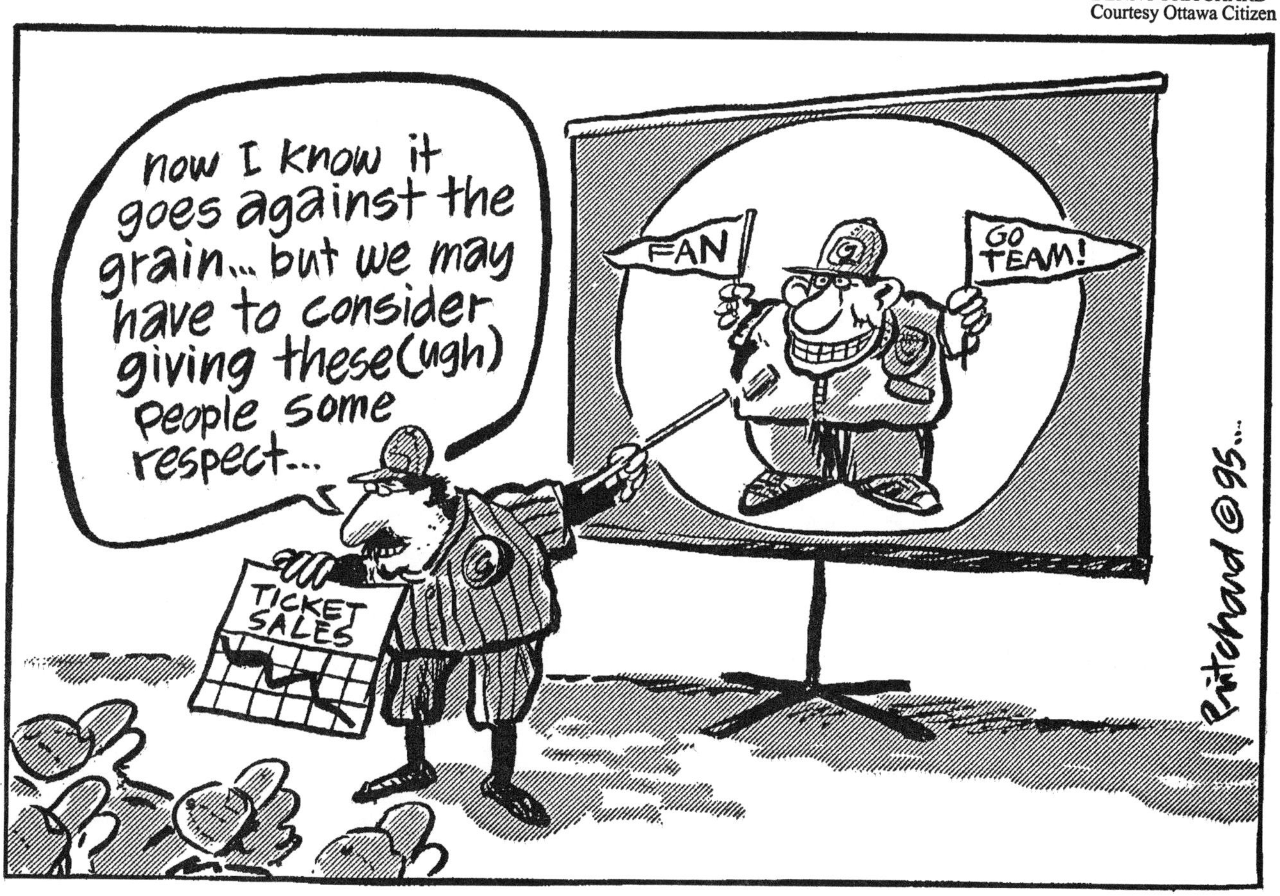
now I know it goes against the grain... but we may have to consider giving these (ugh) people some respect...
FAN
GO TEAM!
TICKET SALES
Pritchard ©95...

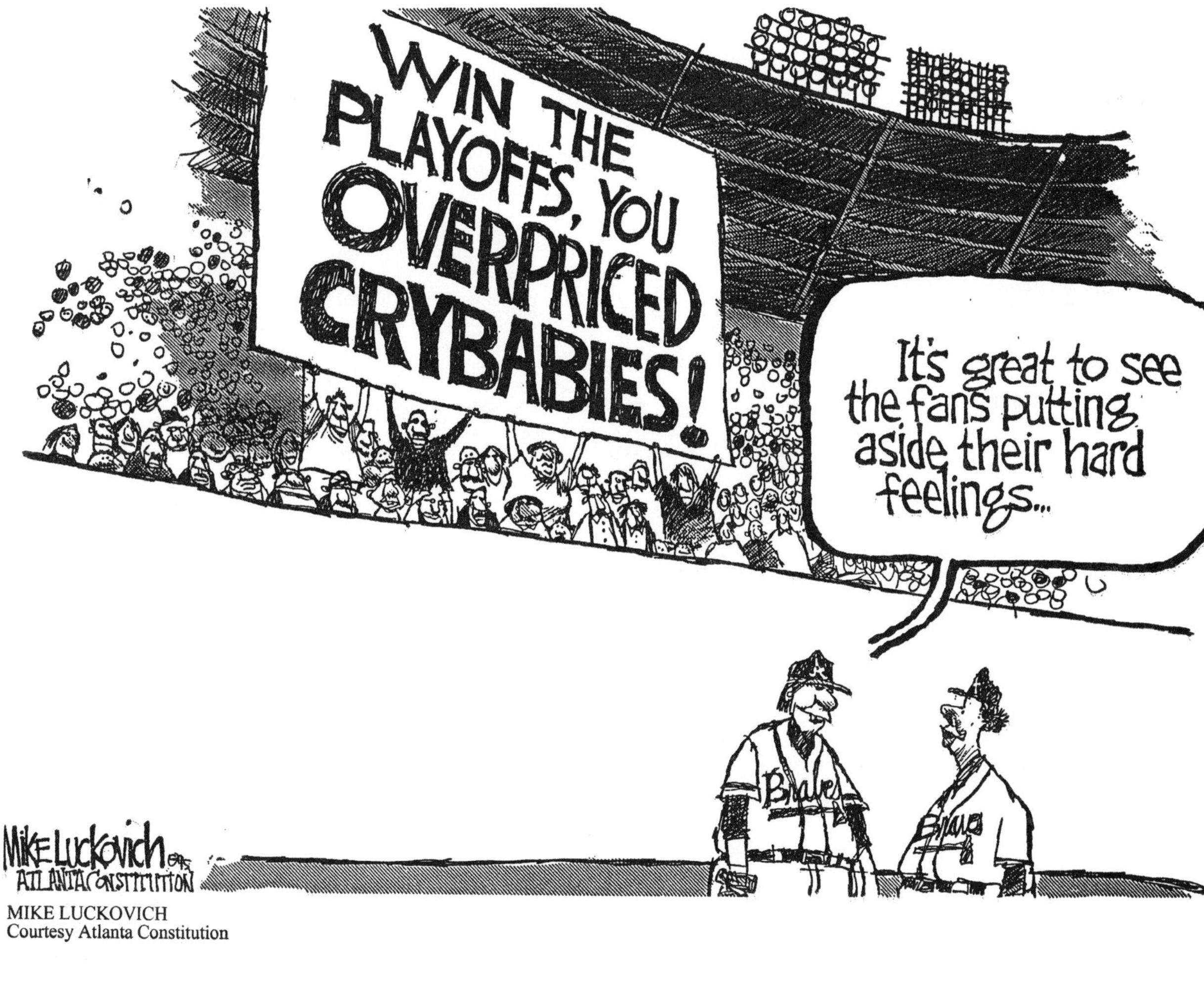
WIN THE PLAYOFFS, YOU OVERPRICED CRYBABIES!
It's great to see the fans putting aside their hard feelings...
MIKE LUCKOVICH ATLANTA CONSTITUTION

MIKE LUCKOVICH
Courtesy Atlanta Constitution

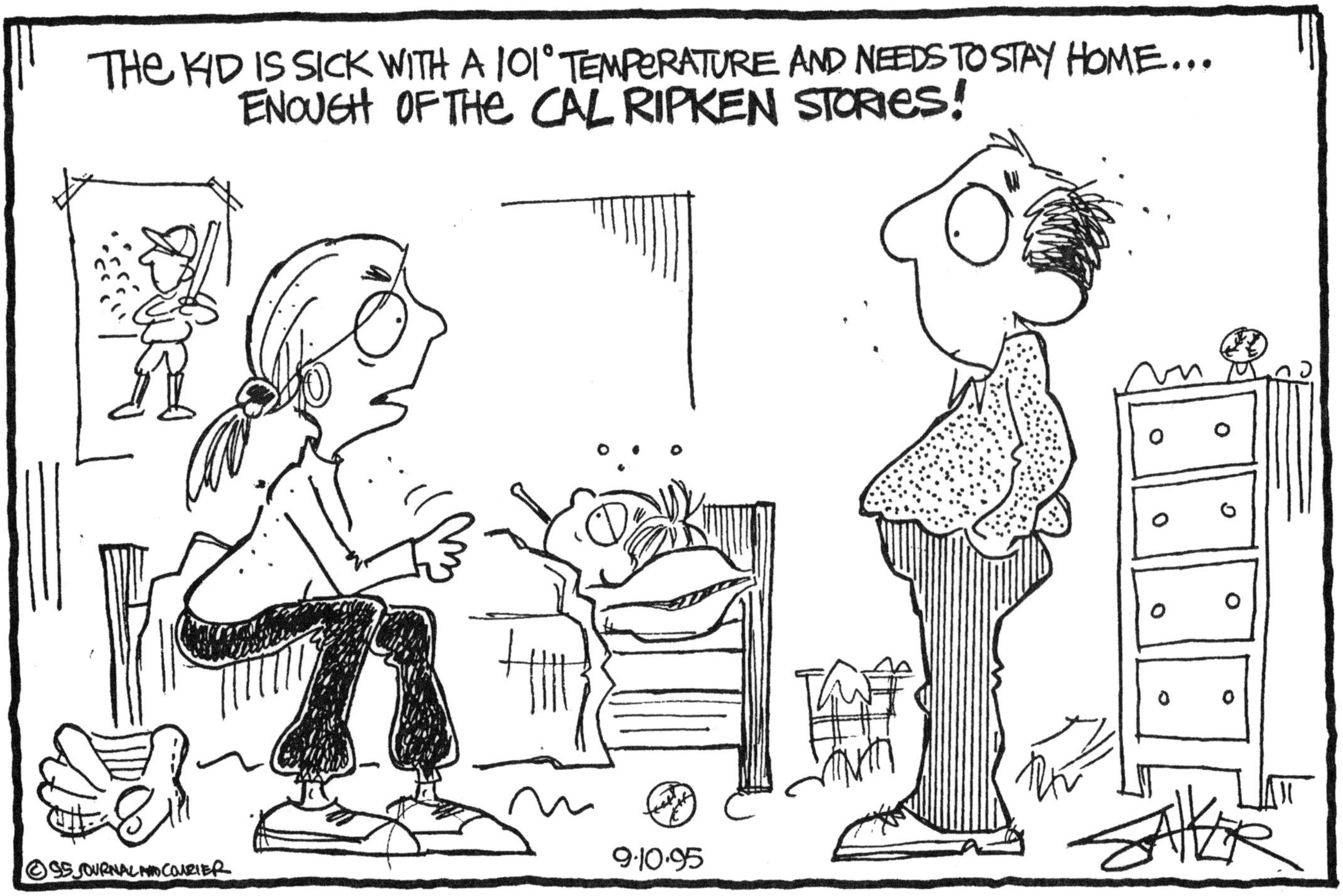
THE KID IS SICK WITH A 101° TEMPERATURE AND NEEDS TO STAY HOME... ENOUGH OF THE CAL RIPKEN STORIES!
©95 JOURNAL AND COURIER
9·10·95

DAVE SATTLER
Courtesy Journal and Courier (Ind.)

JACK HIGGINS
Courtesy Chicago Sun-Times

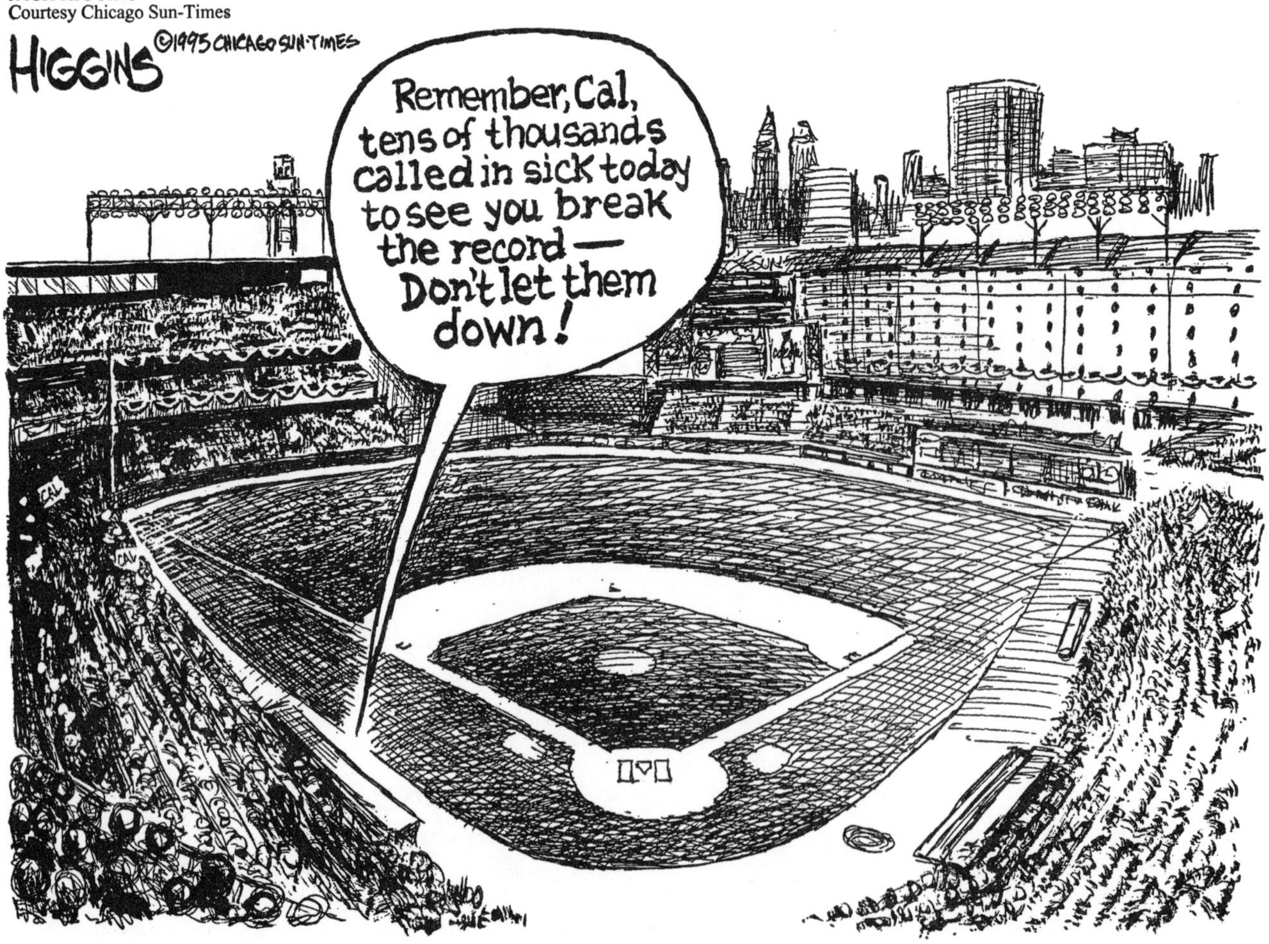
HIGGINS ©1995 CHICAGO SUN-TIMES
Remember, Cal, tens of thousands called in sick today to see you break the record— Don't let them down!

JOE HELLER
Courtesy Green Bay Press-Gazette

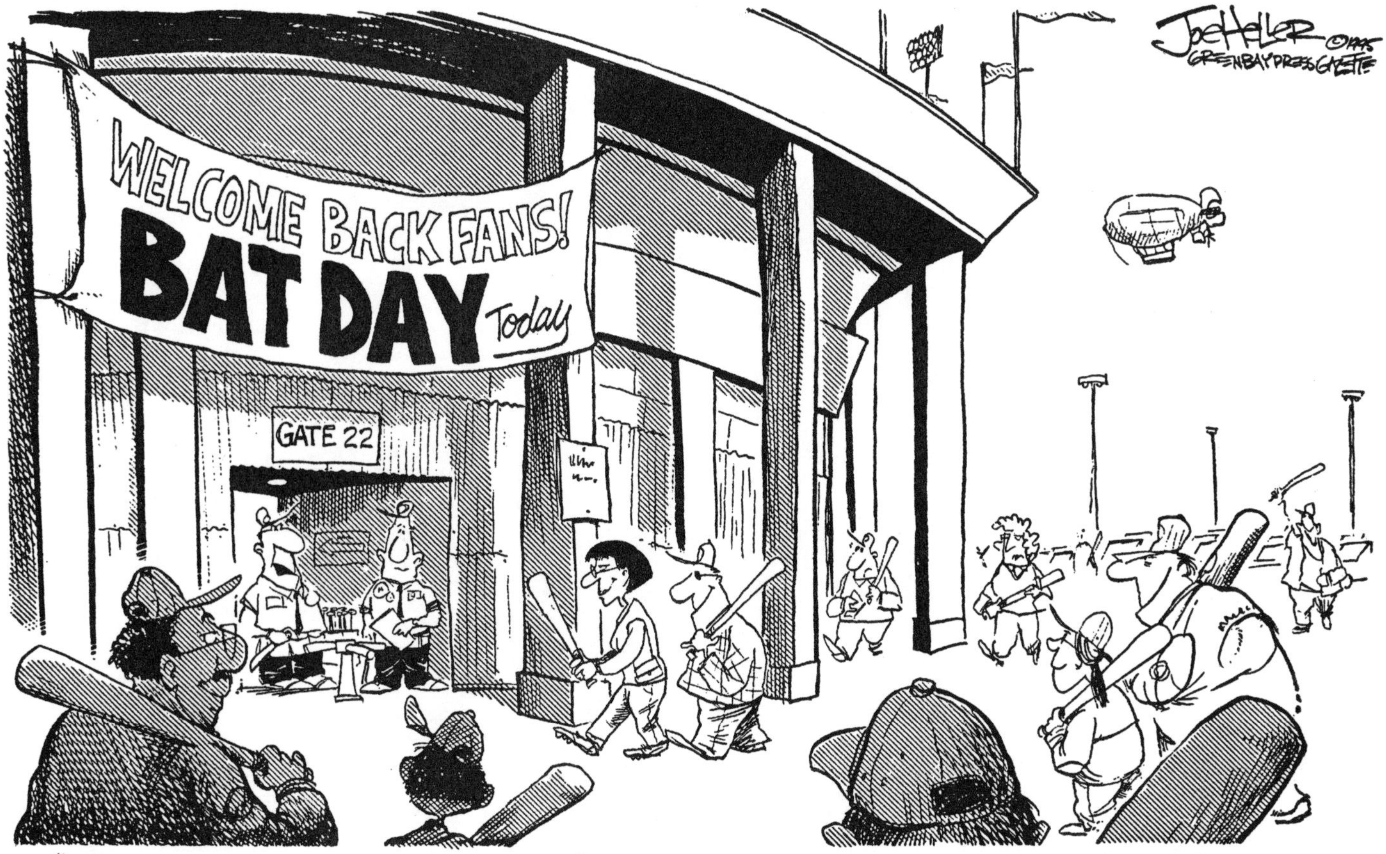
WELCOME BACK FANS!
BAT DAY Today
GATE 22

"THIS DOESN'T LOOK GOOD.... THEY'RE ALL BRINGING THEIR OWN BATS!"

DAVID HITCH
Courtesy Worcester Telegram & Gazette

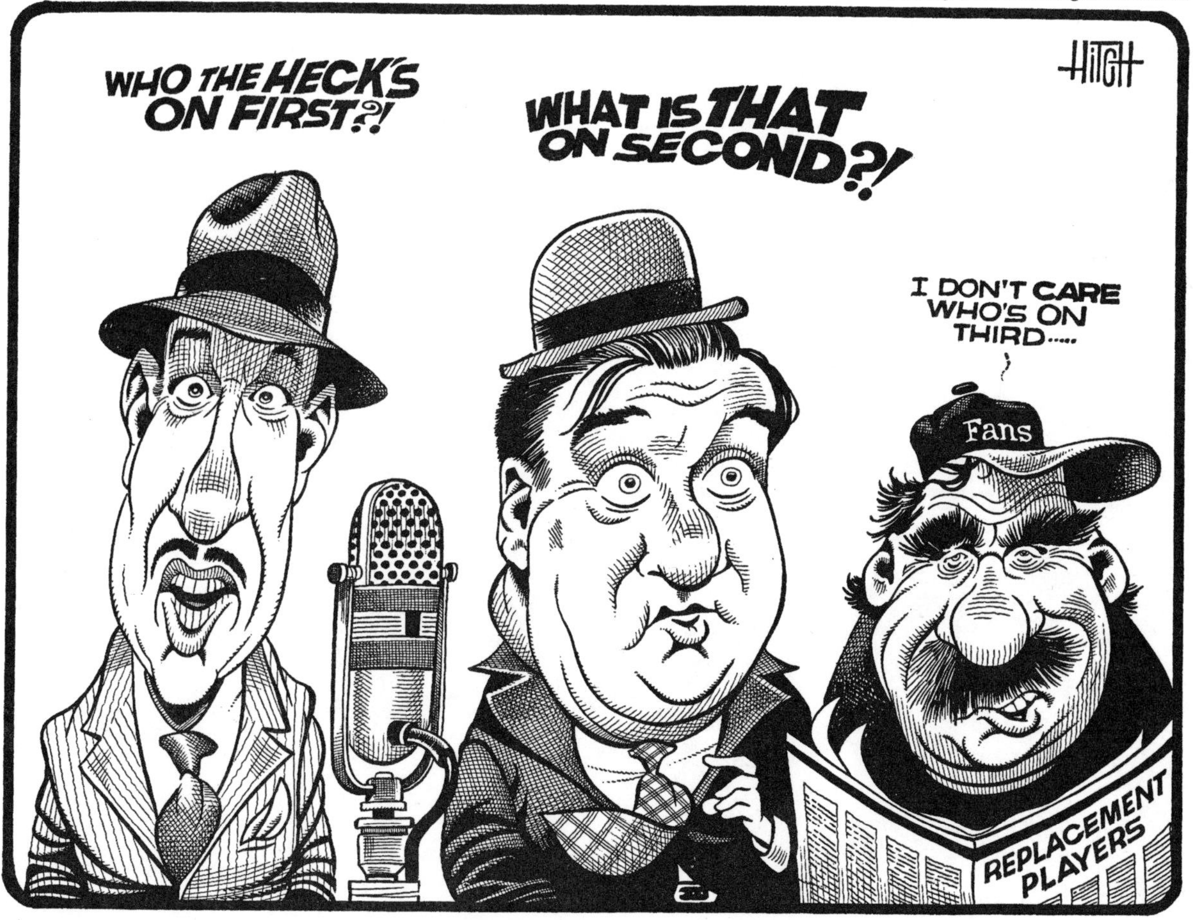
WHO THE HECK'S ON FIRST?!
WHAT IS THAT ON SECOND?!
I DON'T CARE WHO'S ON THIRD.....
Fans
REPLACEMENT PLAYERS

GEORGE DANBY
Courtesy Bangor Daily News

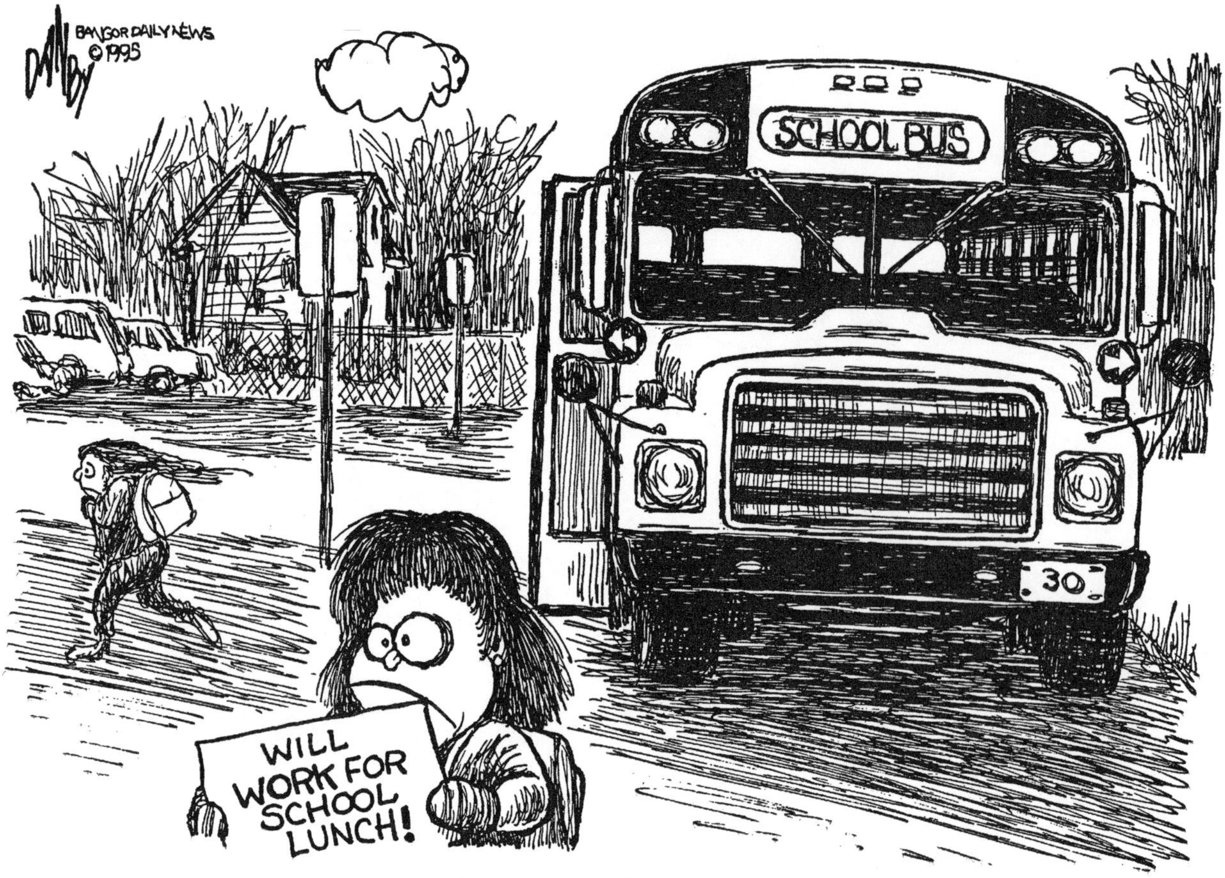
DANBY BANGOR DAILY NEWS ©1995
SCHOOL BUS
30
WILL WORK FOR SCHOOL LUNCH!

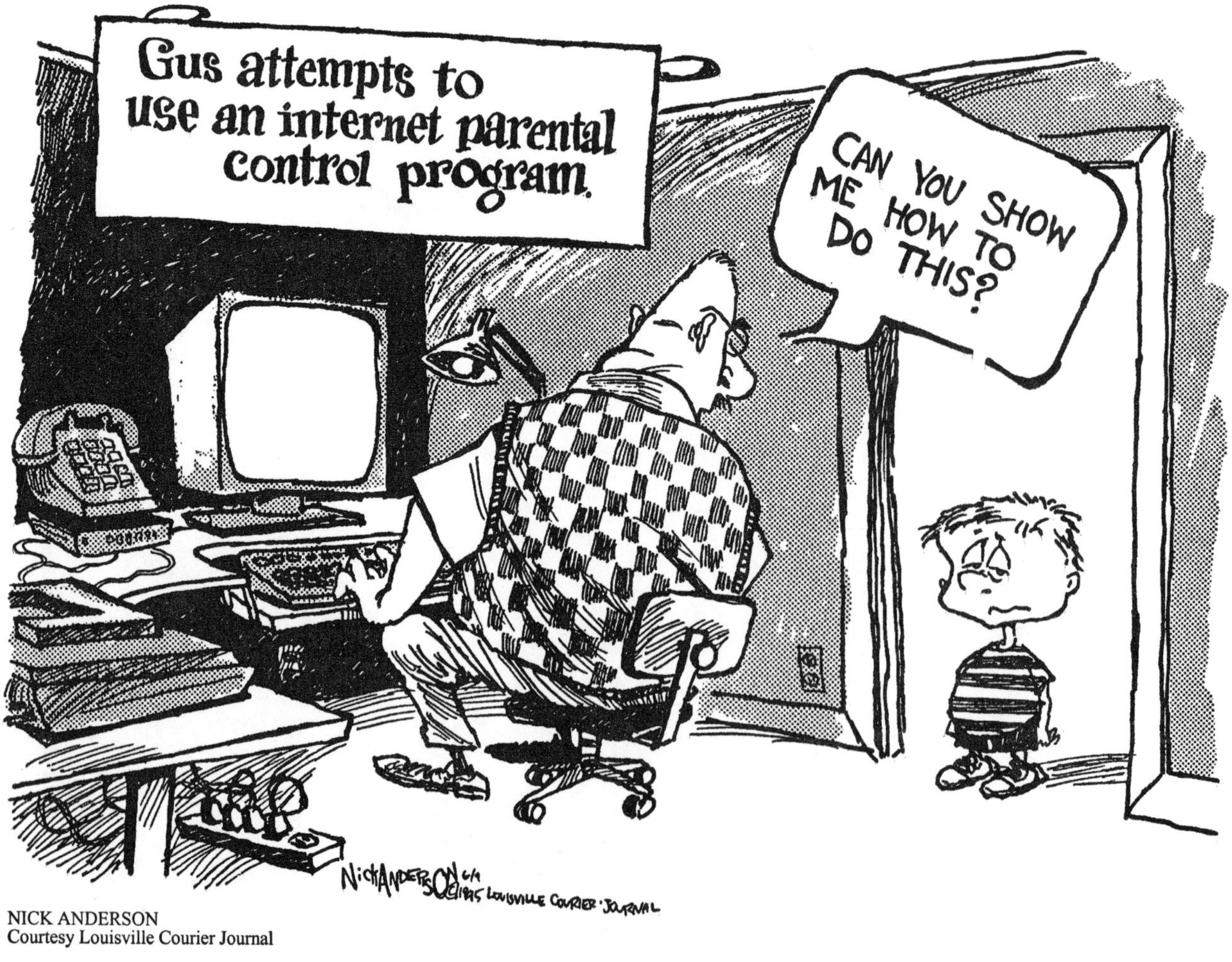
Gus attempts to use an internet parental control program.
CAN YOU SHOW ME HOW TO DO THIS?
NICK ANDERSON ©1995 LOUISVILLE COURIER-JOURNAL

NICK ANDERSON
Courtesy Louisville Courier Journal

Education

The outlook for U.S. public schools showed few signs of improvement during 1995. Irrelevant courses were still being taught, incompetent teachers remained in the classrooms, and drugs and crime continued to confront school administrators. Polls indicate that 12 percent of all students feel unsafe at school, while records show that 19 percent of the girls have been molested in some way. Suicides, school gangs, and cheating were up over the previous year. Marijuana use among high-school students, according to a University of Michigan survey, has almost doubled since 1991.

Although bussing is out of favor with both whites and blacks, the worn-out policy continues in many areas of the country. Many students who cannot read or write well enough to find a place in the modern business world are still receiving diplomas. And they still lag behind students in other industrialized countries in math and science.

Guns, knives, and other potential weapons are still in evidence in many schools. As a result, police have been called upon to assist in maintaining order. Many serious incidents on school grounds have centered around individuals who had no legitimate business there, and school officials and community groups are trying to deal with the problem.

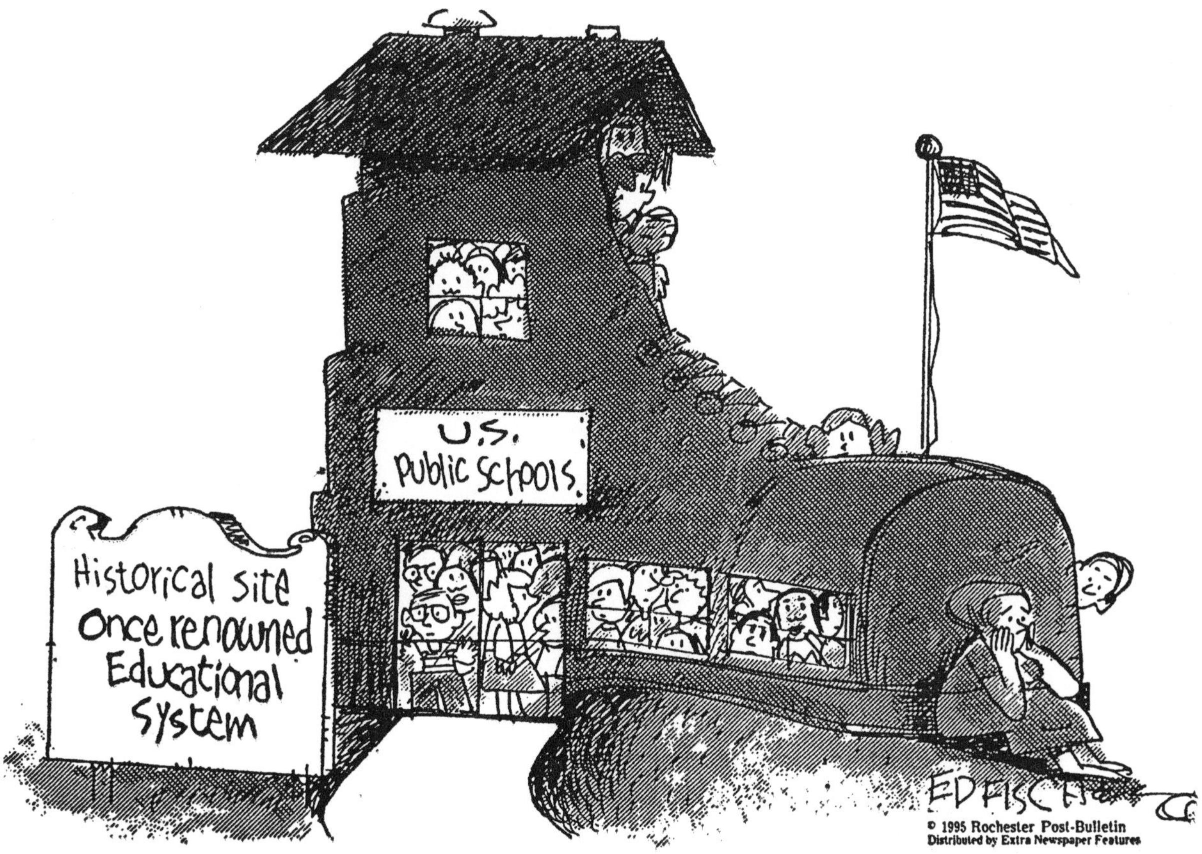
U.S. Public Schools
Historical site Once renowned Educational System
ED FISCHER
© 1995 Rochester Post-Bulletin
Distributed by Extra Newspaper Features

ED FISCHER
Courtesy Rochester Post-Bulletin

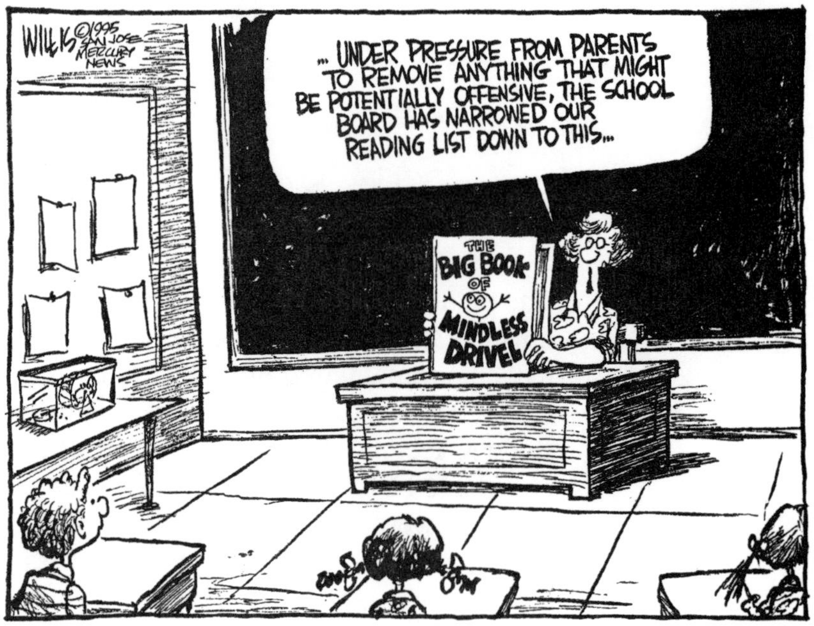
WILLIS ©1995 San Jose Mercury News
... UNDER PRESSURE FROM PARENTS TO REMOVE ANYTHING THAT MIGHT BE POTENTIALLY OFFENSIVE, THE SCHOOL BOARD HAS NARROWED OUR READING LIST DOWN TO THIS...
THE BIG BOOK OF MINDLESS DRIVEL

SCOTT WILLIS
Courtesy San Jose Mercury

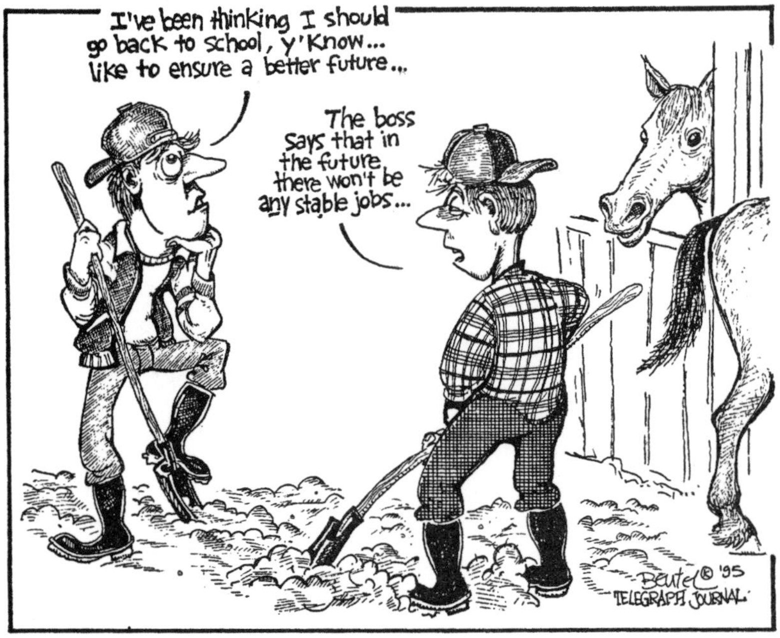
I've been thinking I should go back to school, y'know... like to ensure a better future...
The boss says that in the future there won't be any stable jobs...
BEUTEL® '95 TELEGRAPH JOURNAL

JOSH BEUTEL
Courtesy St. John Telegraph Journal

WAYNE STAYSKAL
Courtesy Tampa Tribune

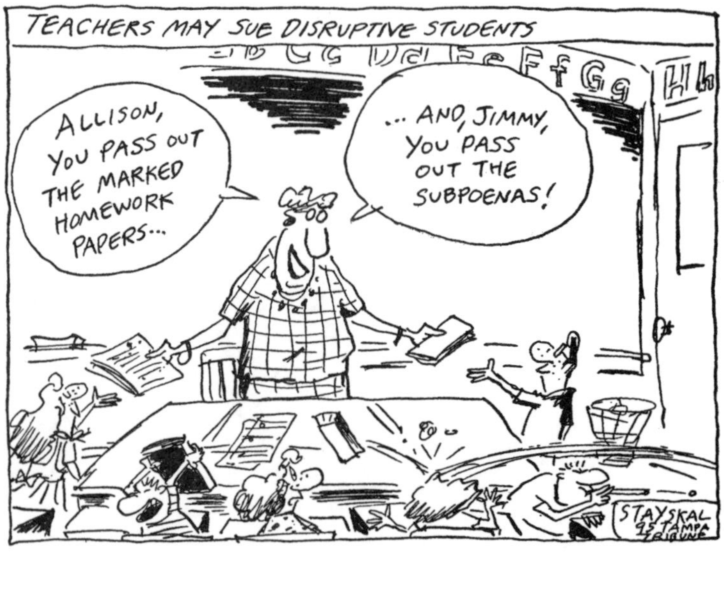
TEACHERS MAY SUE DISRUPTIVE STUDENTS
ALLISON, YOU PASS OUT THE MARKED HOMEWORK PAPERS...
... AND, JIMMY, YOU PASS OUT THE SUBPOENAS!
STAYSKAL '95 TAMPA TRIBUNE

GARY BROOKINS
Courtesy Richmond Times-Dispatch

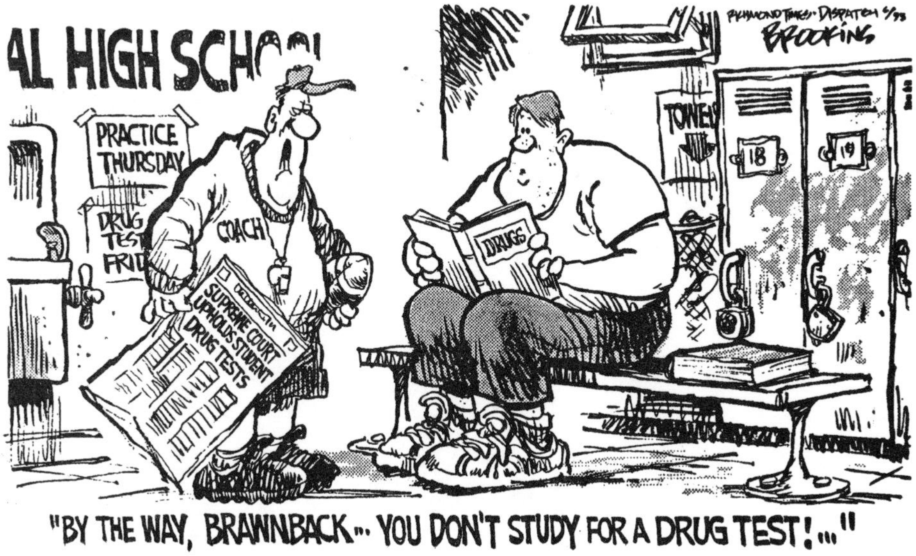

AL HIGH SCHO
PRACTICE THURSDAY
DRUG TES FRI
COACH
SUPREME COURT UPHOLDS STUDENT DRUG TESTS
DRUGS
TOWEL
18
19
"BY THE WAY, BRAWNBACK... YOU DON'T STUDY FOR A DRUG TEST!..."

JEFF MACNELLY
Courtesy Chicago Tribune and
Tribune Media Services

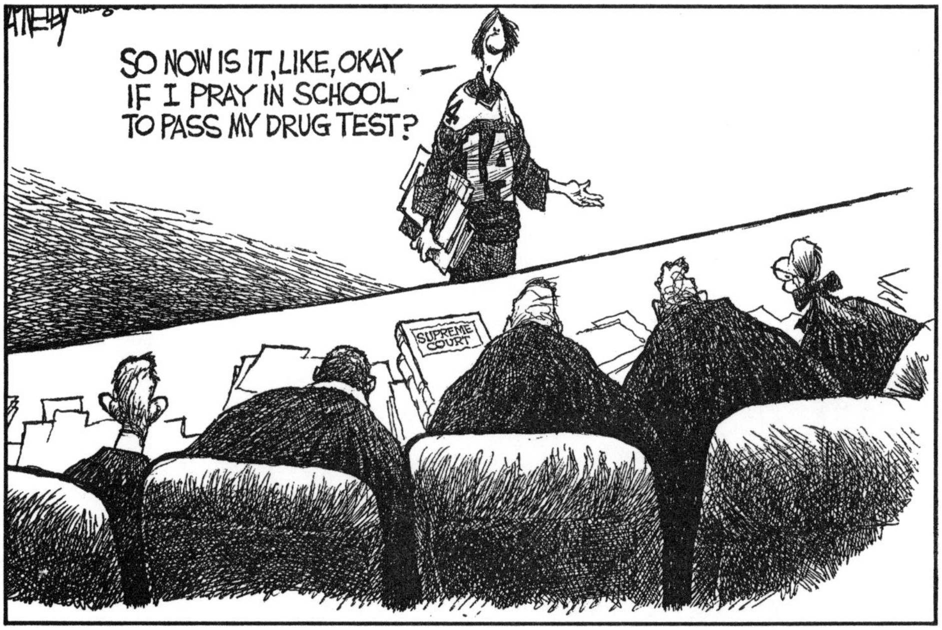

SO NOW IS IT, LIKE, OKAY IF I PRAY IN SCHOOL TO PASS MY DRUG TEST?
14
SUPREME COURT

MIKE SMITH
Courtesy Las Vegas Sun

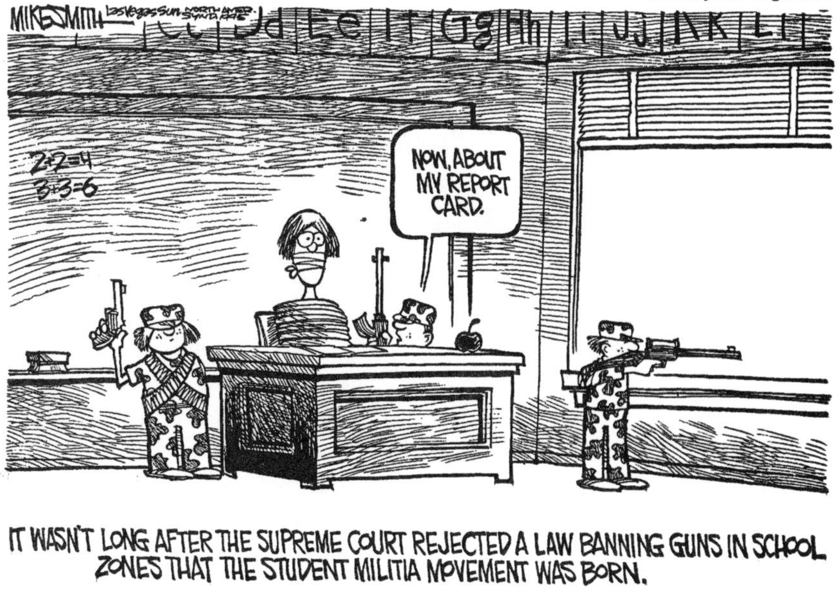

2+2=4
3+3=6
NOW, ABOUT MY REPORT CARD.
IT WASN'T LONG AFTER THE SUPREME COURT REJECTED A LAW BANNING GUNS IN SCHOOL ZONES THAT THE STUDENT MILITIA MOVEMENT WAS BORN.

CHRIS OBRION
Courtesy Free Lance-Star (Va.)

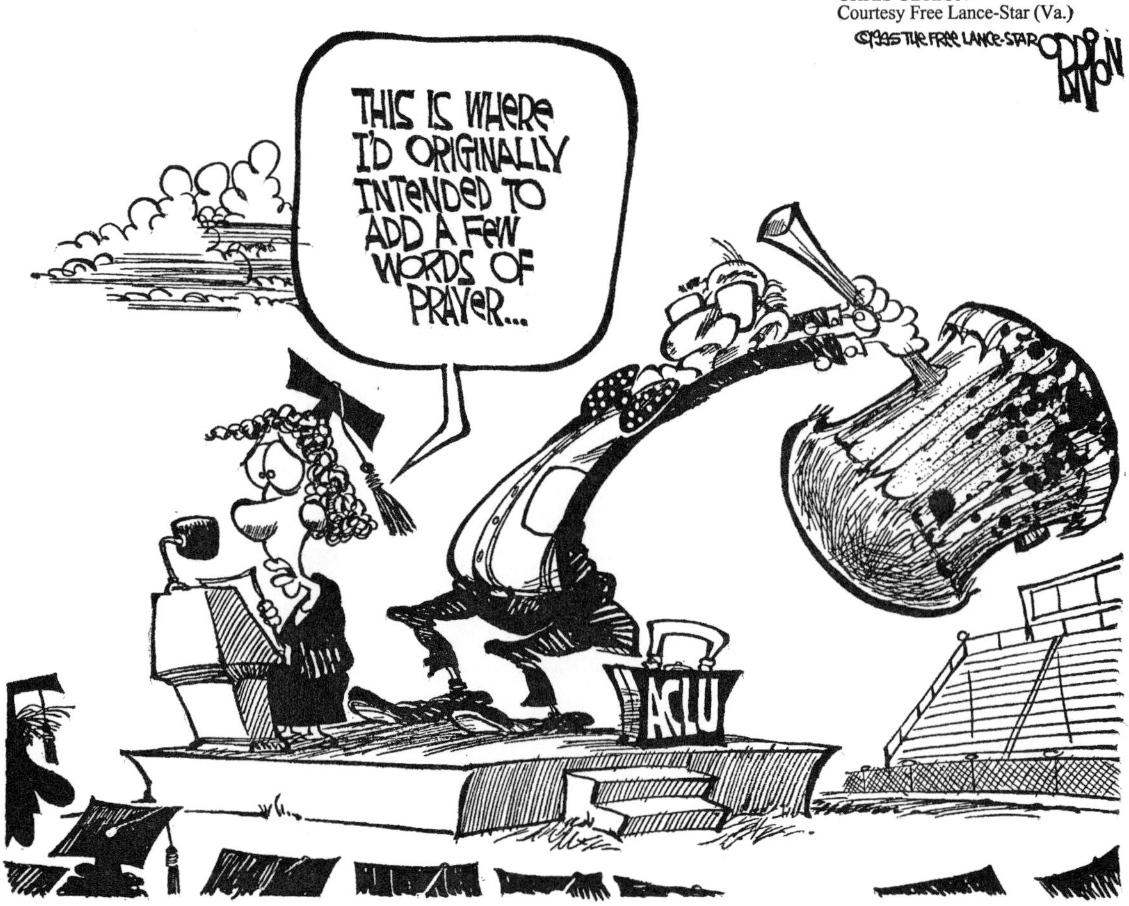
©1995 THE FREE LANCE-STAR OBRION
THIS IS WHERE I'D ORIGINALLY INTENDED TO ADD A FEW WORDS OF PRAYER...
ACLU

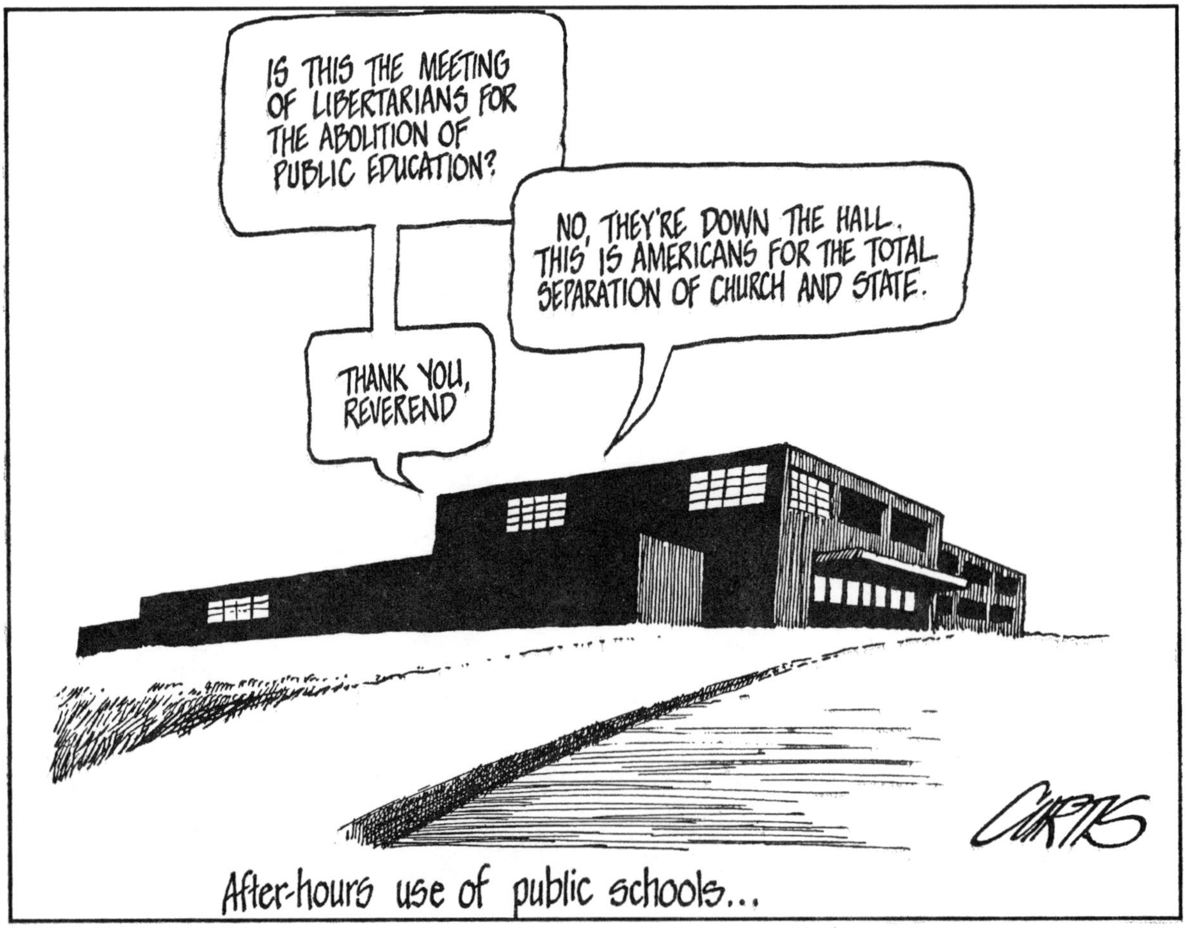
IS THIS THE MEETING OF LIBERTARIANS FOR THE ABOLITION OF PUBLIC EDUCATION?
NO, THEY'RE DOWN THE HALL. THIS IS AMERICANS FOR THE TOTAL SEPARATION OF CHURCH AND STATE.
THANK YOU, REVEREND
CURTIS
After-hours use of public schools...

CHRIS CURTIS
Courtesy Potomac Almanac

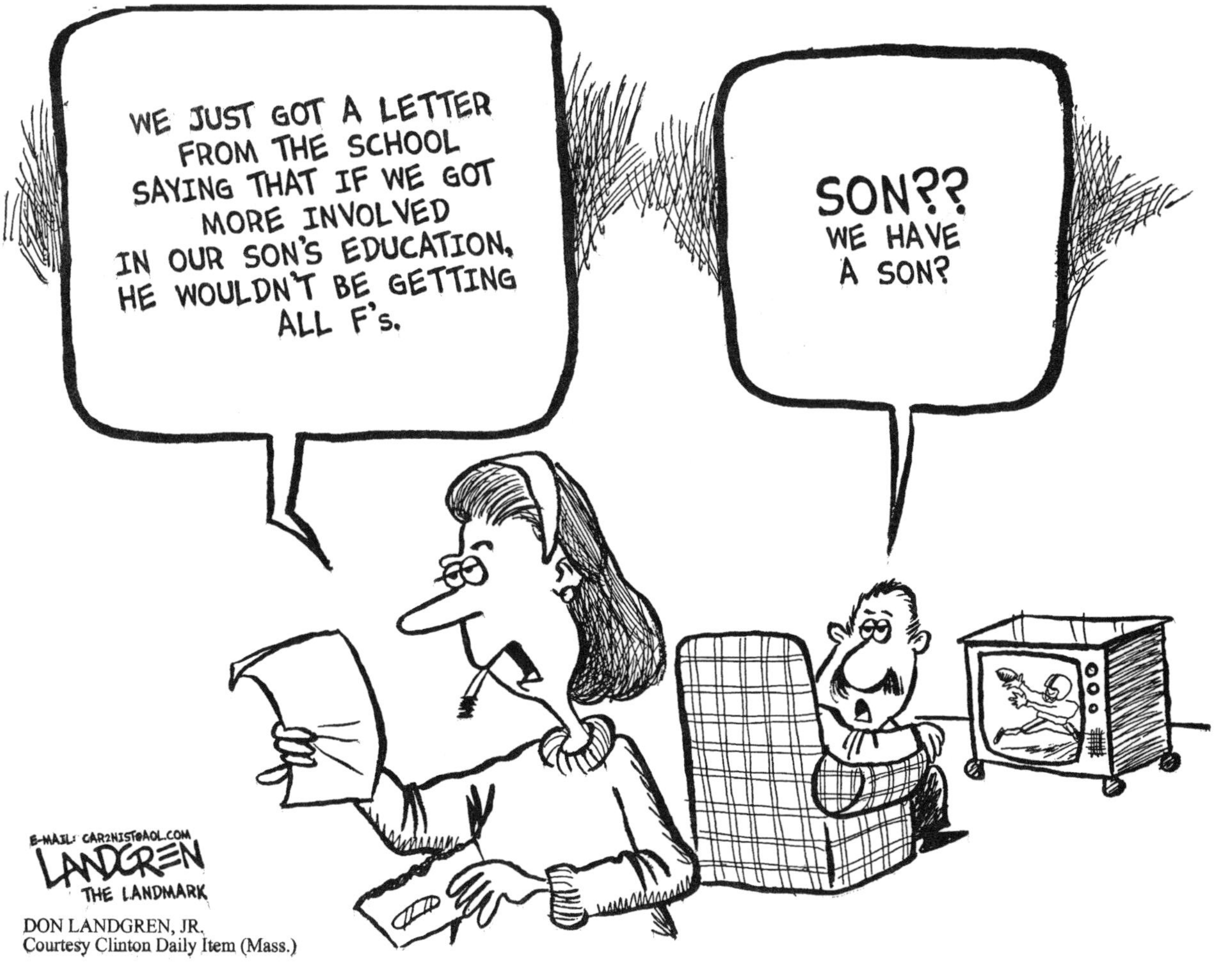
WE JUST GOT A LETTER FROM THE SCHOOL SAYING THAT IF WE GOT MORE INVOLVED IN OUR SON'S EDUCATION, HE WOULDN'T BE GETTING ALL F's.
SON?? WE HAVE A SON?
E-MAIL: CAR2NIST@AOL.COM
LANDGREN
THE LANDMARK

DON LANDGREN, JR.
Courtesy Clinton Daily Item (Mass.)

ED GAMBLE
Courtesy Florida Times-Union

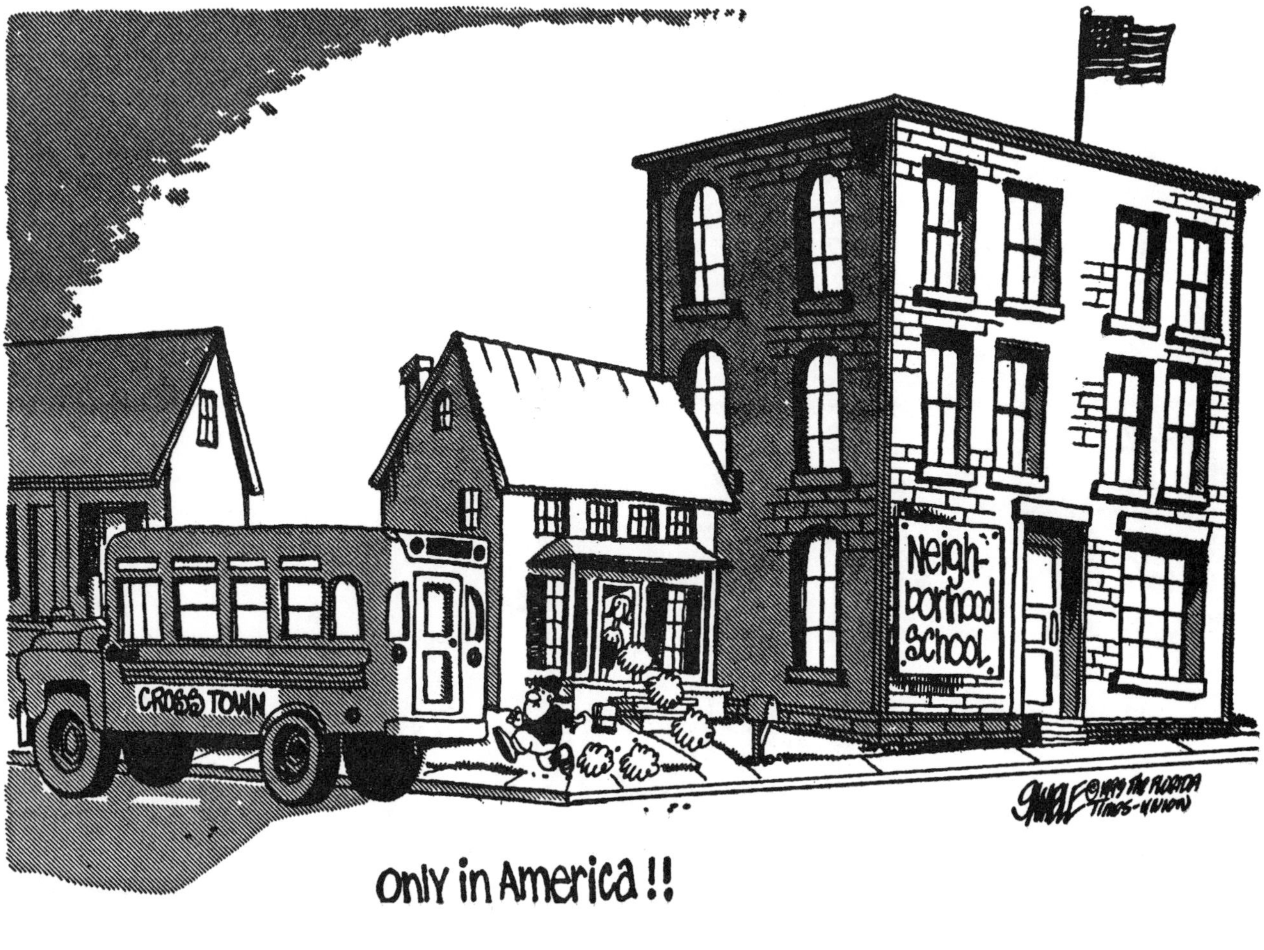
Neighborhood School
CROSS TOWN
GAMBLE ©1999 THE FLORIDA TIMES-UNION

Only in America !!

JAMES CASCIARI
Courtesy Vero Beach Press Journal

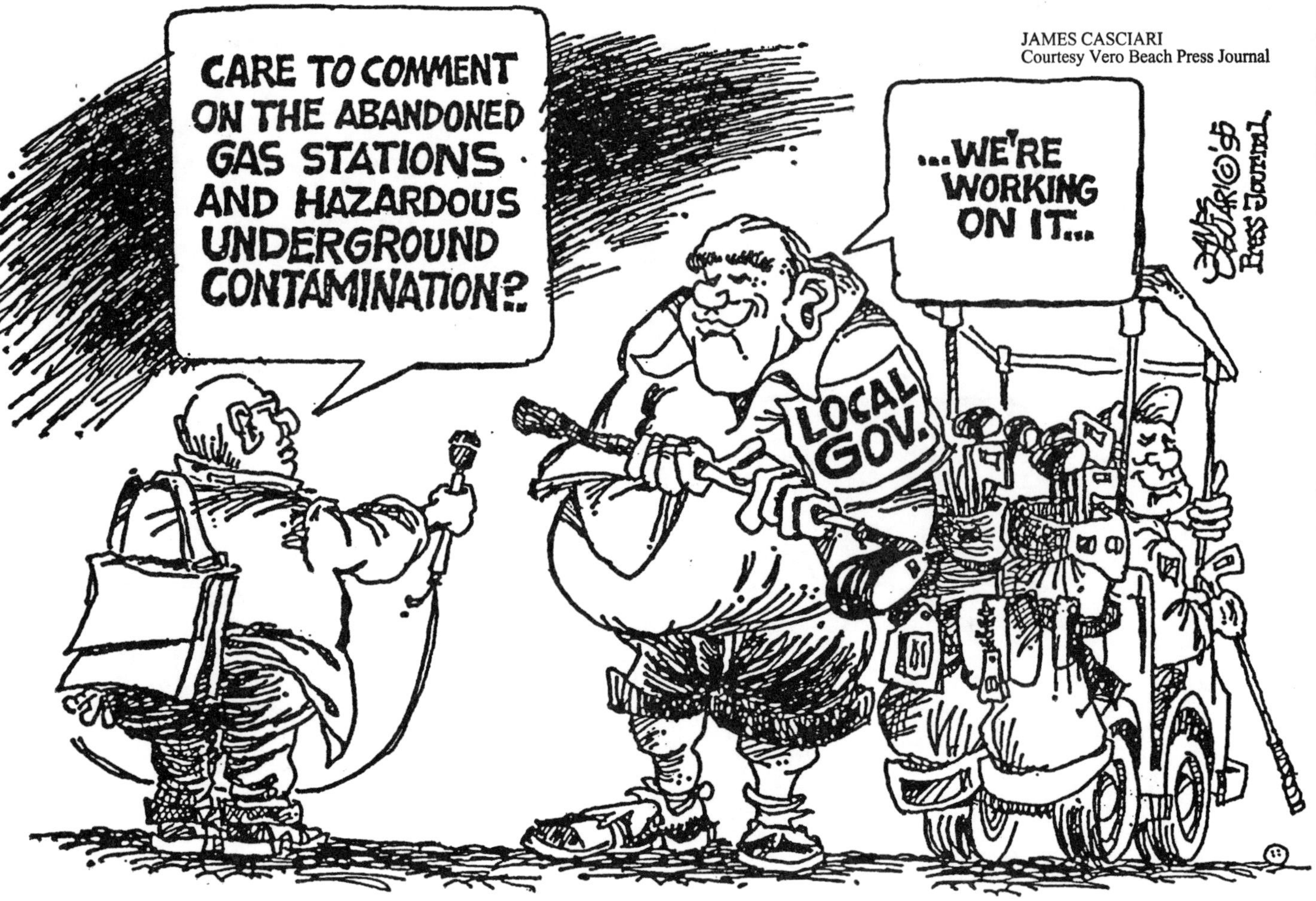

CARE TO COMMENT ON THE ABANDONED GAS STATIONS AND HAZARDOUS UNDERGROUND CONTAMINATION?..
...WE'RE WORKING ON IT...
LOCAL GOV.

JIMMY MARGULIES
Courtesy The Record (N.J.)/
North American Syndicate (by permission)

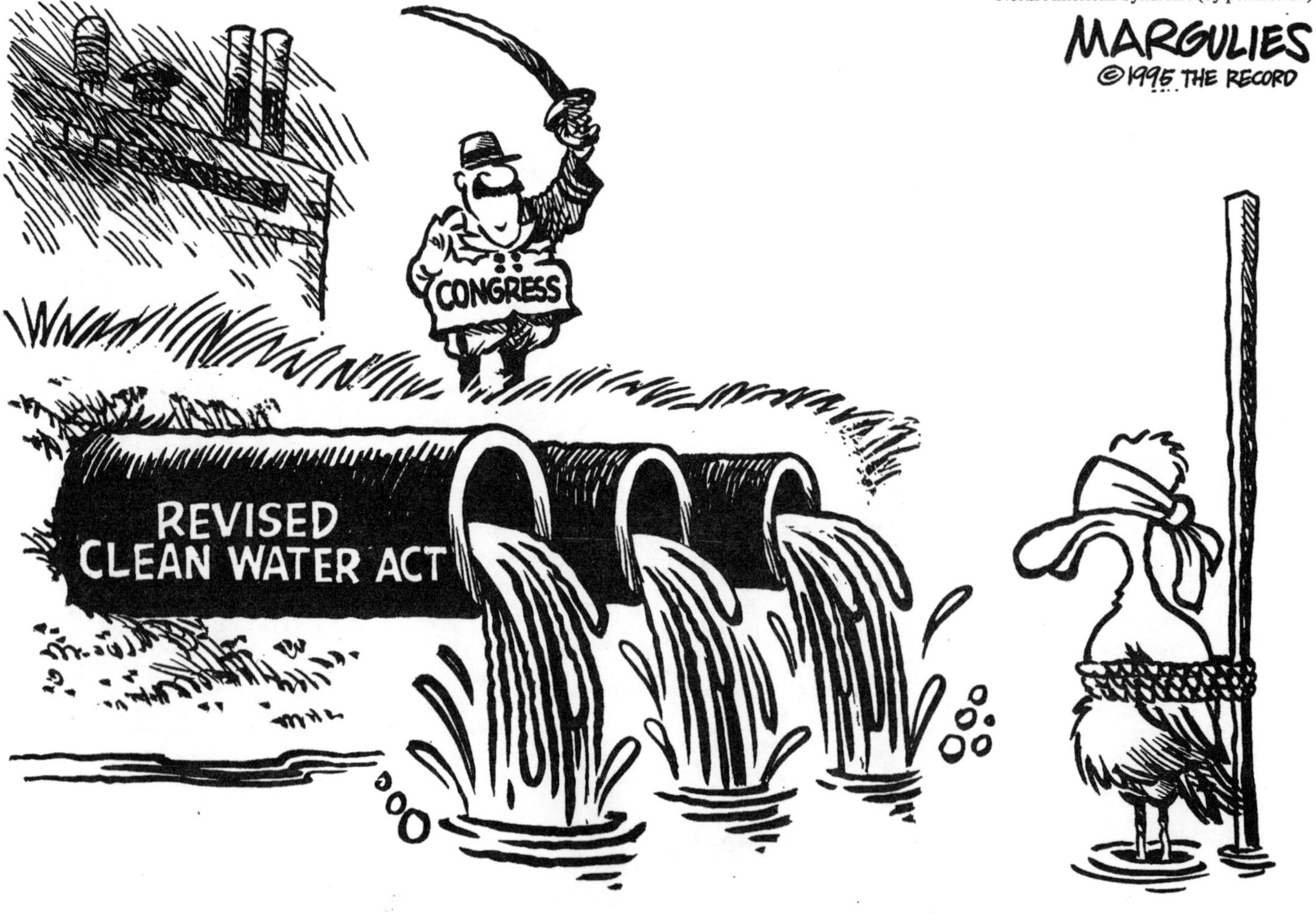

MARGULIES
©1995 THE RECORD
CONGRESS
REVISED CLEAN WATER ACT

The Environment

The Republican party contends that in order to cut spending sufficiently to balance the budget in seven years, sixteen environmental health, safety, and conservation laws must be changed. Sen. Bob Dole and Rep. Newt Gingrich claim that environmentalists have gone too far and that overbearing bureaucracy and inflexible green laws are costing jobs. Even environmentalists now admit that some of their doomsday predictions about threats to the environment were in error. For example, many forecast that the Alaskan ecosystem would not recover for decades—and perhaps never—from the Exxon *Valdez* oil spill in 1989. Today, however, nature has erased virtually all traces of the spill.

The Republican push for environmental law reform has galvanized the weakened green movement, and Democrats are making the environment an issue in upcoming elections. The Environmental Protection Agency claims it will begin to apply common sense to regulation, and the Interior Department expects to take a new approach in the matter of endangered species.

According to the Wilderness Society, a new EPA plan for pollution prevention should improve enforcement, save money, and reduce restraints on new technology. Democrats and environmentalists insist, however, that Republican cuts run too deep.

JIM BORGMAN
Courtesy Cincinnati Enquirer

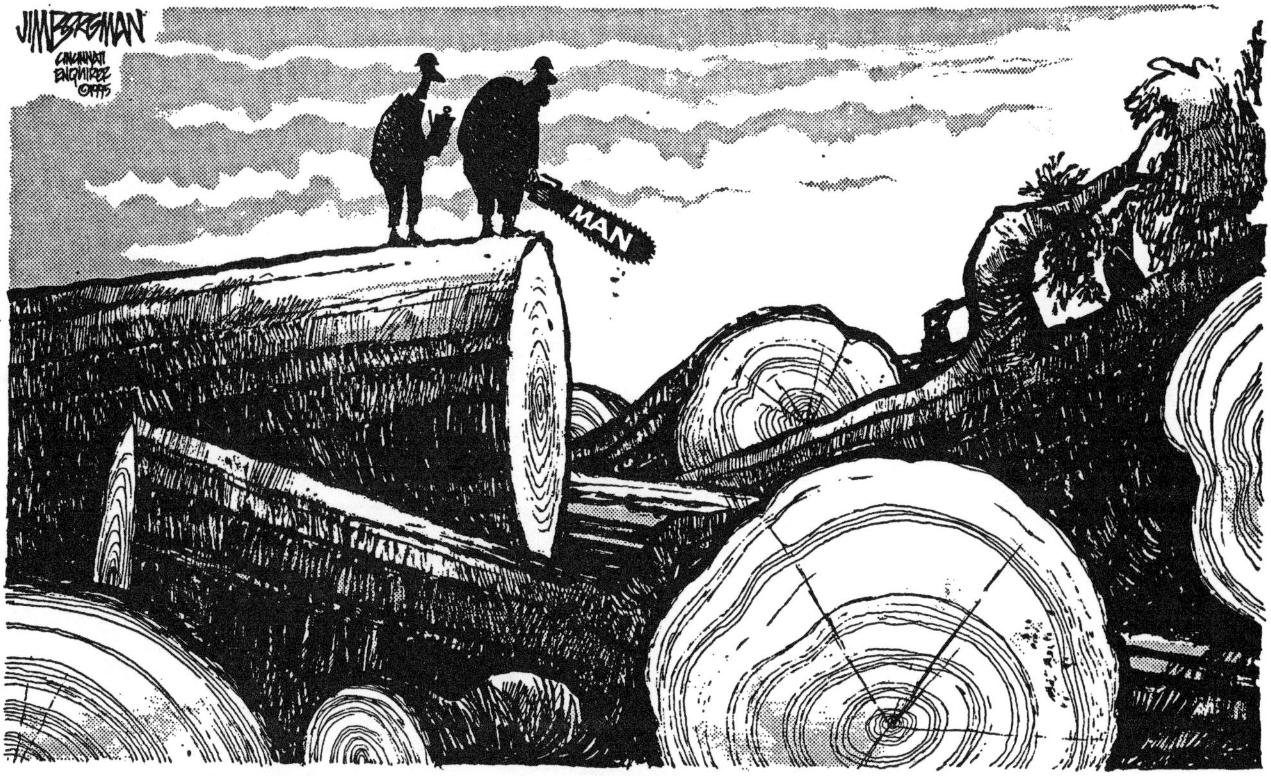
JIMBORGMAN
CINCINNATI ENQUIRER ©1995
MAN

"....ON THE BRIGHT SIDE, THE ENDANGERED SPECIES LIST IS DOWN TO ONE."

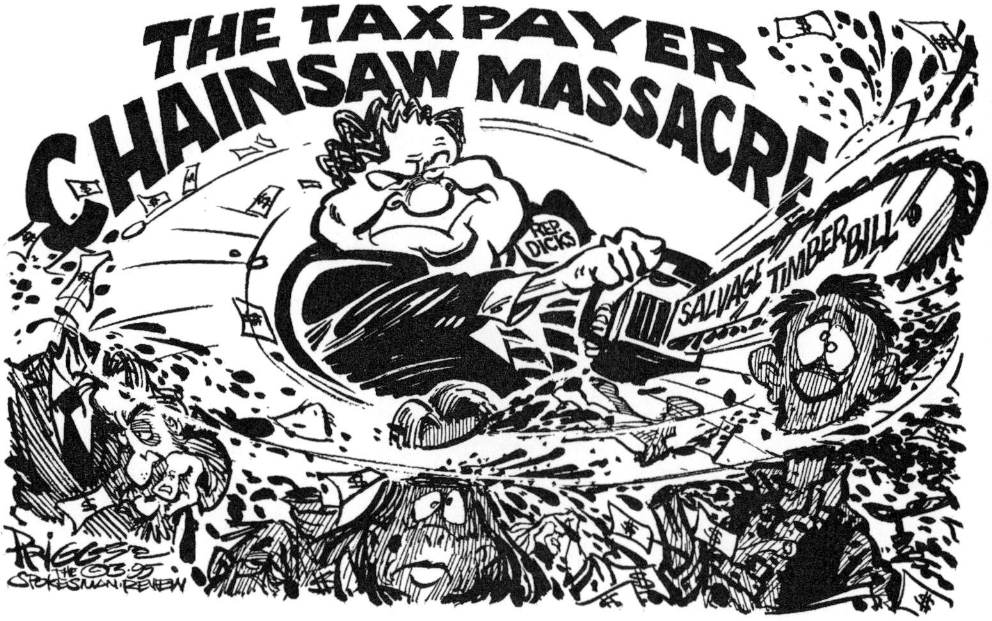
THE TAXPAYER
CHAINSAW MASSACRE
REP. DICKS
SALVAGE TIMBER BILL
PRIGGEE

MILT PRIGGEE
Courtesy Spokane Spokesman-Review

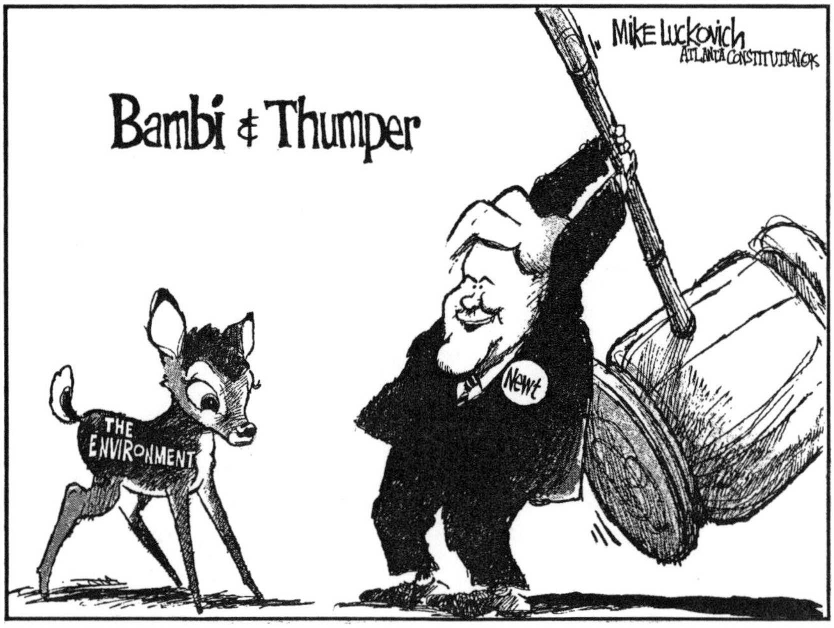
MIKE LUCKOVICH
Bambi & Thumper
THE ENVIRONMENT
Newt

MIKE LUCKOVICH
Courtesy Atlanta Constitution

JIMMY MARGULIES
Courtesy The Record (N.J.)/
North America Syndicate (by permission)

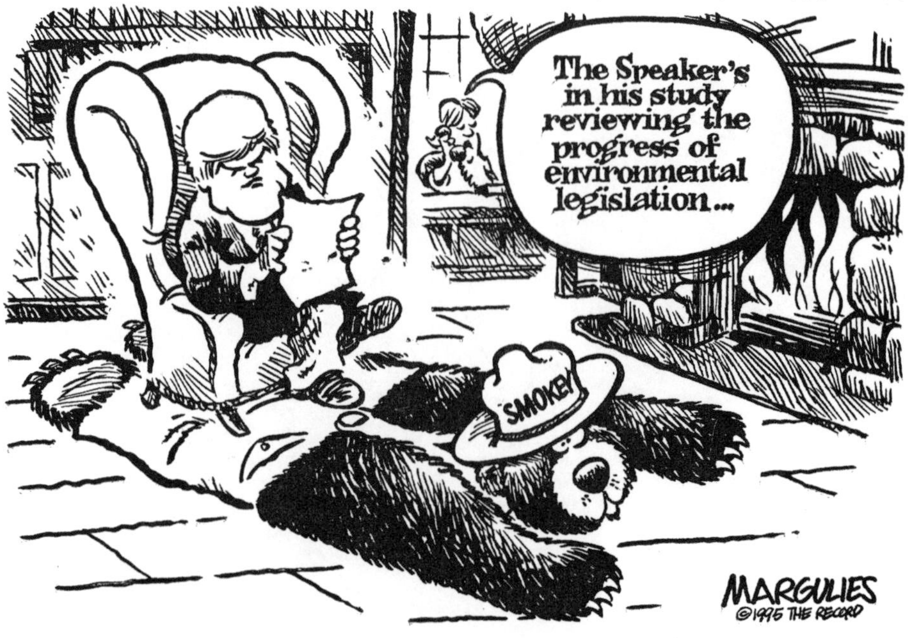
The Speaker's in his study reviewing the progress of environmental legislation...
SMOKEY
MARGULIES
©1995 THE RECORD

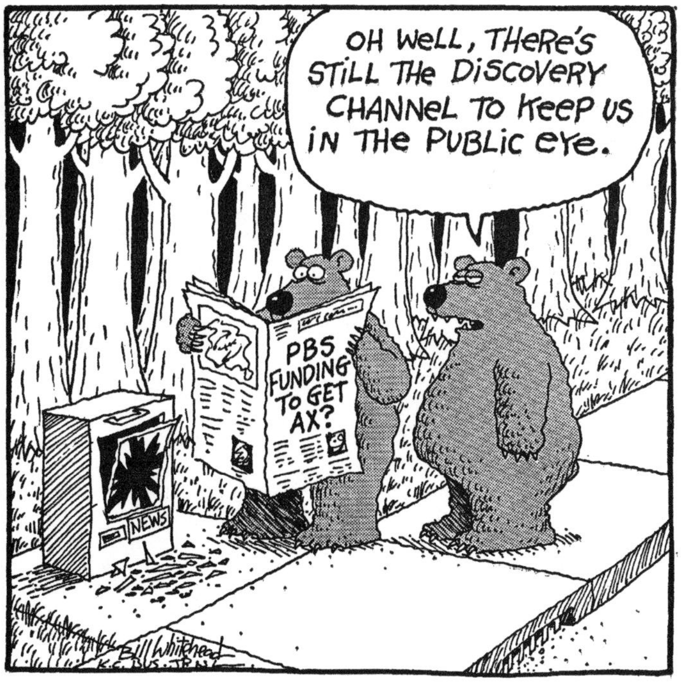
OH WELL, THERE'S STILL THE DISCOVERY CHANNEL TO KEEP US IN THE PUBLIC EYE.
PBS FUNDING TO GET AX?
NEWS

BILL WHITEHEAD
Courtesy Kansas City Business Journal

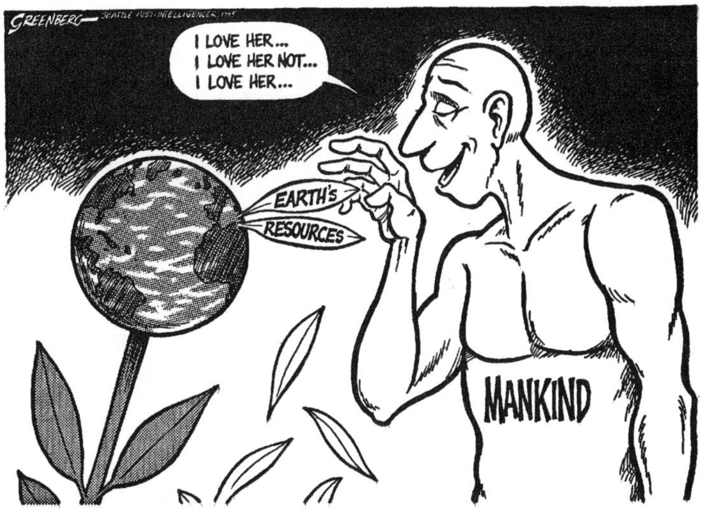
I LOVE HER...
I LOVE HER NOT...
I LOVE HER...
EARTH'S
RESOURCES
MANKIND

STEVE GREENBERG
Courtesy Seattle Post-Intelligencer

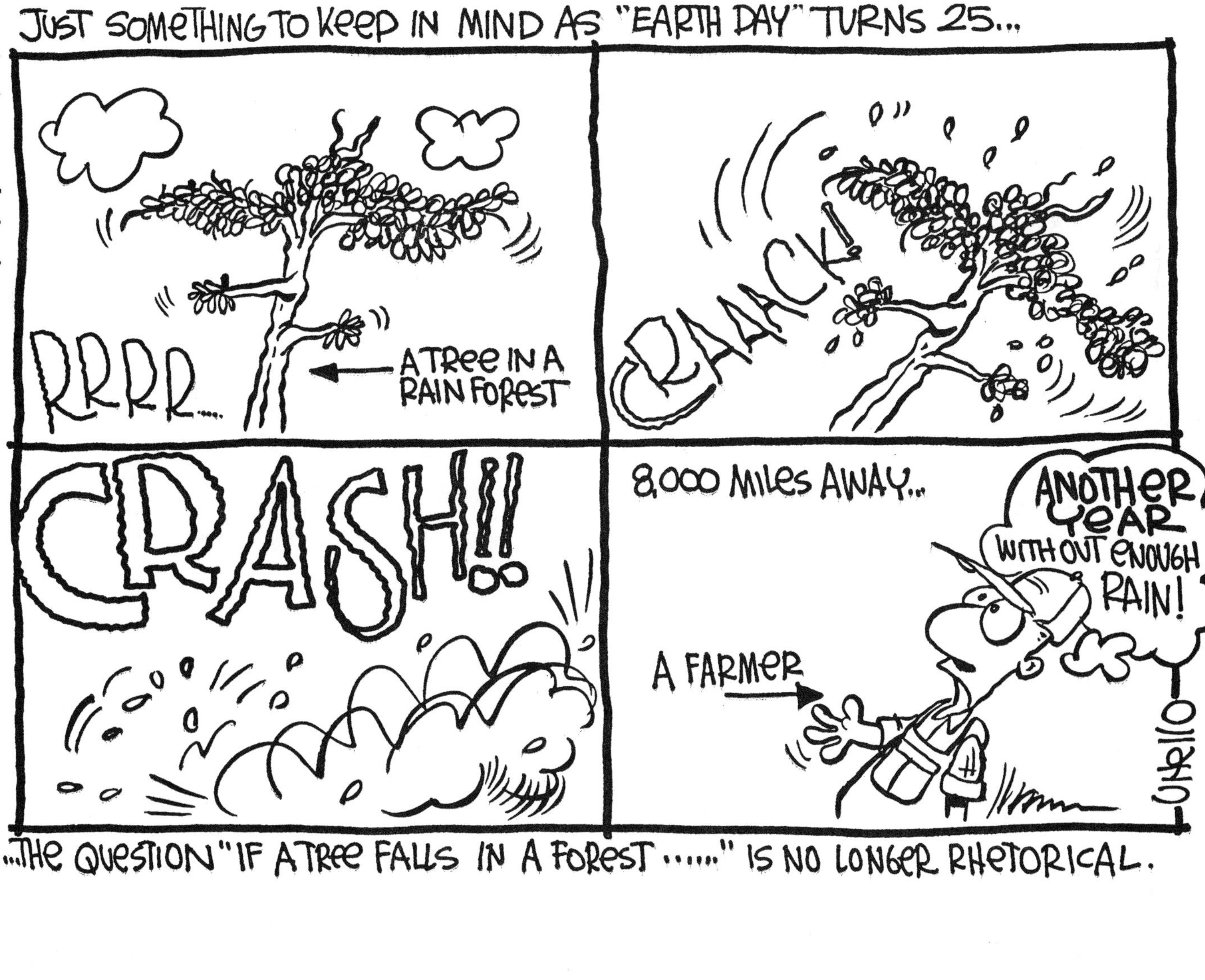
JUST SOMETHING TO KEEP IN MIND AS "EARTH DAY" TURNS 25...
RRRR....
A TREE IN A RAIN FOREST
CRAAACK!
CRASH!!
8,000 MILES AWAY...
ANOTHER YEAR WITH OUT ENOUGH RAIN!
A FARMER
...THE QUESTION "IF A TREE FALLS IN A FOREST ......" IS NO LONGER RHETORICAL.

ALAN VITELLO
Courtesy Daily Reporter-Herald (Colo.)

JERRY HOLBERT
Courtesy Boston Herald

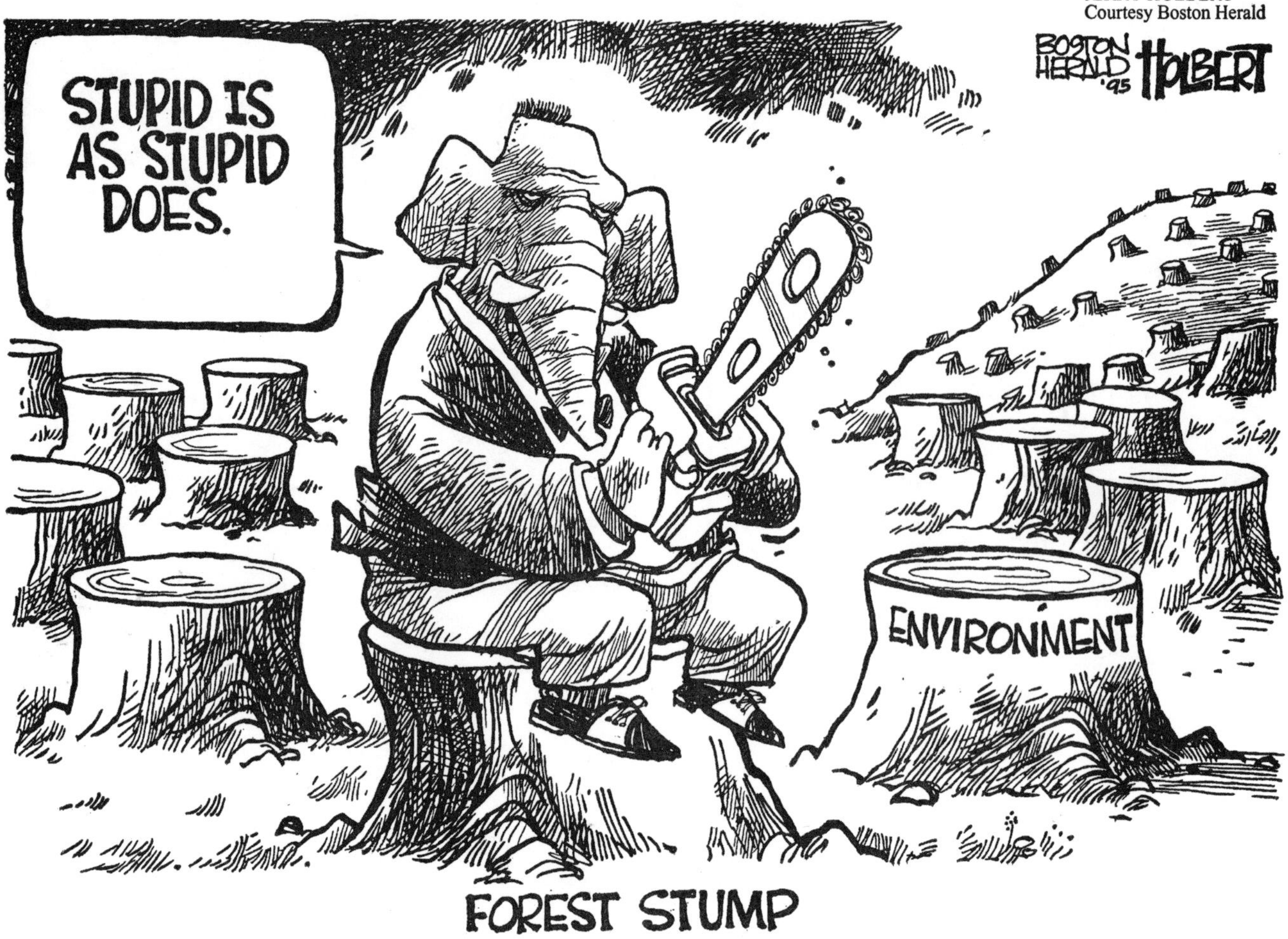
BOSTON HERALD '95 HOLBERT
STUPID IS AS STUPID DOES.
ENVIRONMENT
FOREST STUMP

KIRK ANDERSON
Courtesy Madison (Wis.) Capital Times

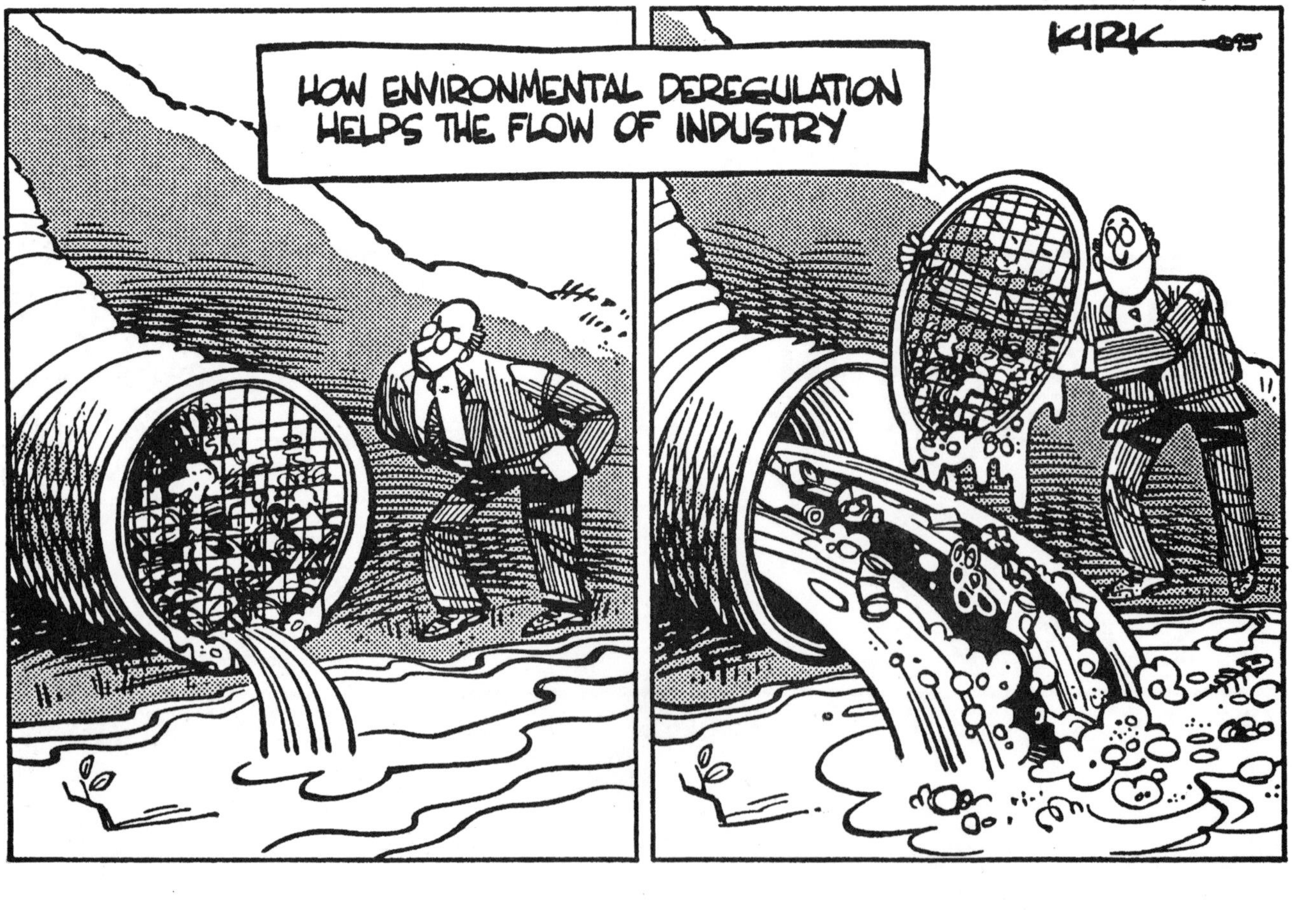
KIRK '95
HOW ENVIRONMENTAL DEREGULATION HELPS THE FLOW OF INDUSTRY

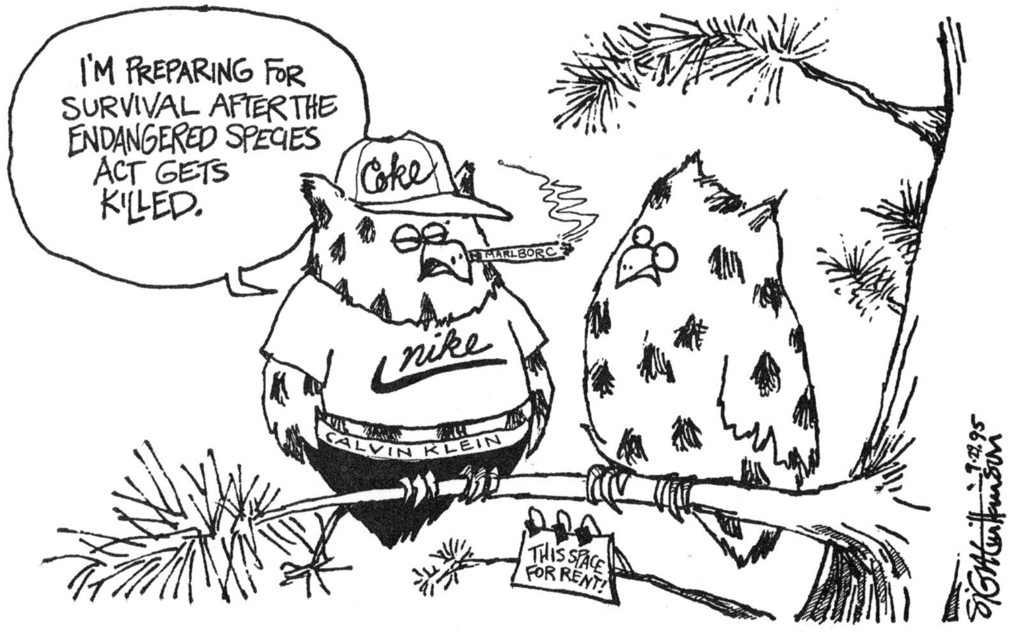
I'M PREPARING FOR SURVIVAL AFTER THE ENDANGERED SPECIES ACT GETS KILLED.
Coke
nike
CALVIN KLEIN
THIS SPACE FOR RENT!

SIGNE WILKINSON
Courtesy Philadelphia Daily News

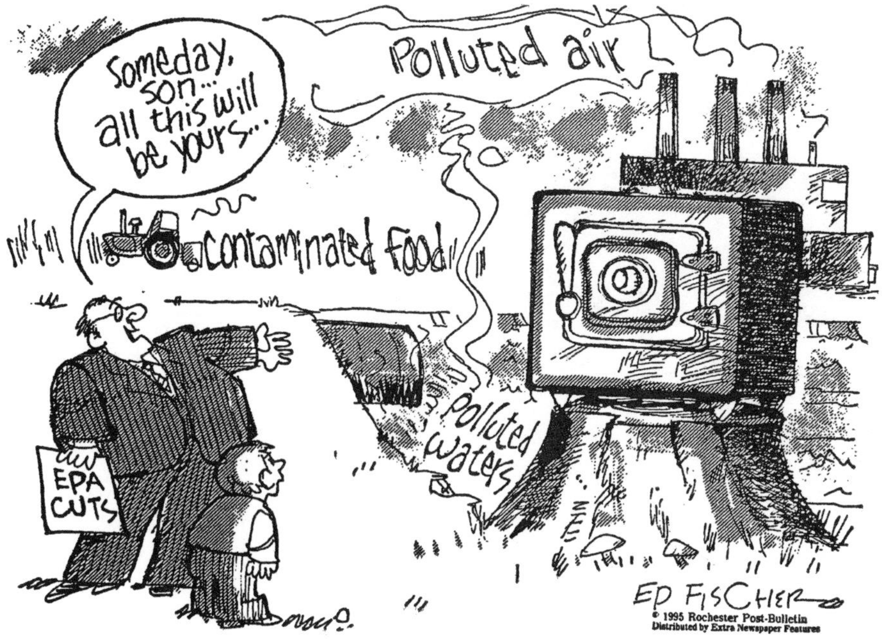
Someday, son... all this will be yours...
Polluted air
contaminated food
Polluted waters
EPA CUTS
ED FISCHER
© 1995 Rochester Post-Bulletin
Distributed by Extra Newspaper Features

ED FISCHER
Courtesy Rochester Post-Bulletin

JERRY BARNETT
Courtesy Indianapolis News

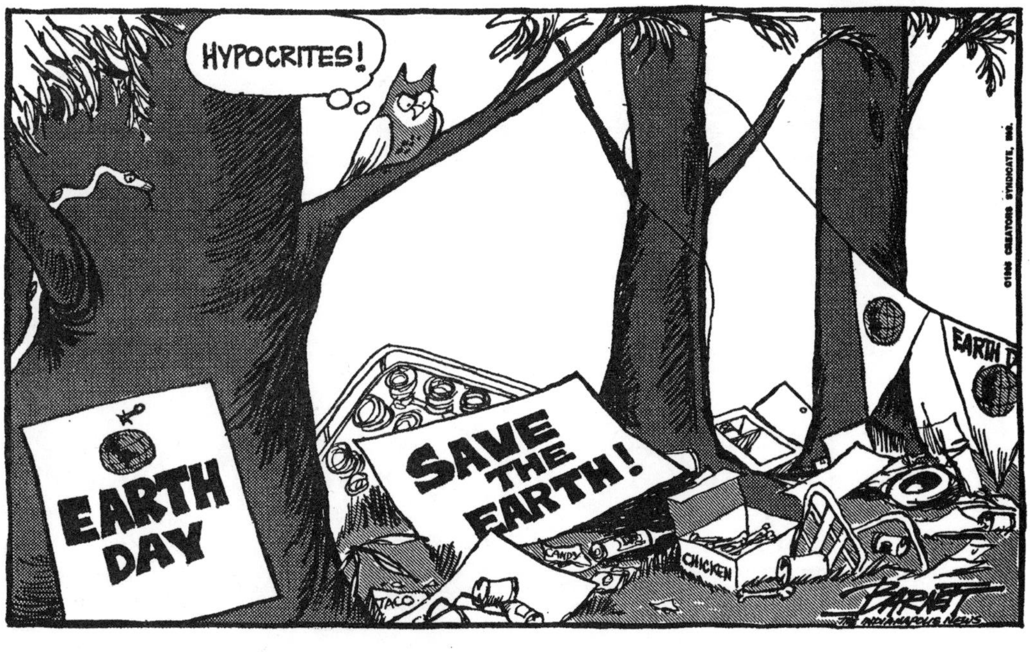
HYPOCRITES!
EARTH DAY
SAVE THE EARTH!
CANDY
CHICKEN
TACO
BARNETT

CHRIS OBRION
Courtesy Free Lance-Star (Va.)

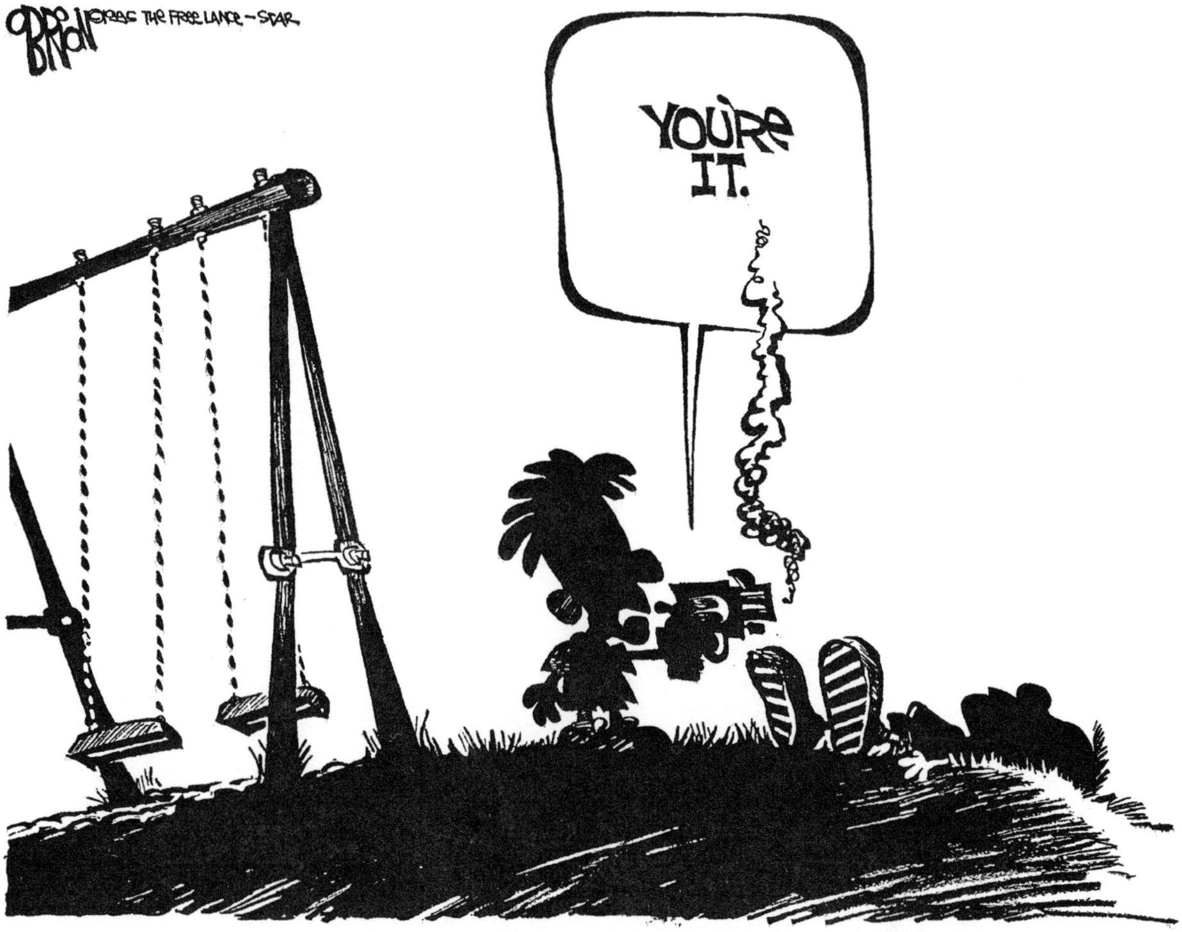
OBRION ©1985 THE FREE LANCE-STAR
YOU'RE IT.

BOB DORNFRIED
Courtesy Greenwich News

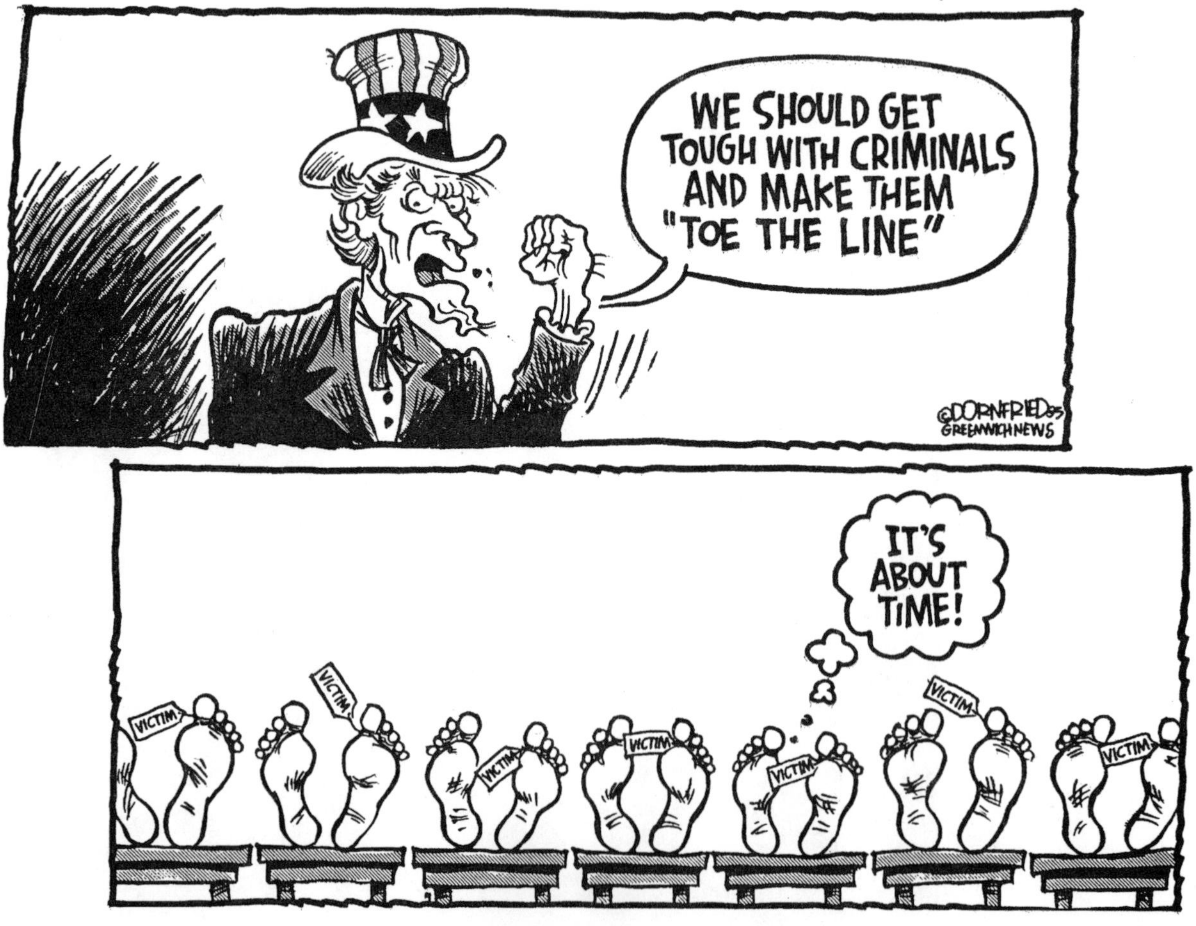
WE SHOULD GET TOUGH WITH CRIMINALS AND MAKE THEM "TOE THE LINE"
©DORNFRIED85 GREENWICH NEWS
IT'S ABOUT TIME!
VICTIM

Crime

Just after 9:00 A.M. on April 19, a deafening explosion ripped through the Oklahoma City Federal Building. Terrorism had reached America's heartland. A powerful bomb detonated just outside the building left unbelievable carnage, with 169 dead and more than 500 injured.

Accused of the crime were two army buddies, who are expected to face trial in 1996. It was speculated that the attack was a revenge act for the siege of the Branch Davidian compound near Waco, Texas, in 1993.

Time-Warner, under fire from political figures and newspapers across the U.S., decided profits from so-called "gangsta rap" weren't worth it. The company announced in October that it would sell its 50 percent stake in several leading labels for rappers because of the gutter-type and antipolice lyrics.

Someone called the Unabomber, who the FBI believes is responsible for sixteen bombings that killed three people and injured twenty-three others, became a published author. He promised to end his campaign of terrorism if his 35,000-word manifesto were published in several newspapers. The *New York Times* and the *Washington Post* reluctantly agreed to do so at the urging of the FBI.

Kids continued to kill kids during the year. The worst problem remained black-on-black crimes, black teens killing other black teens.

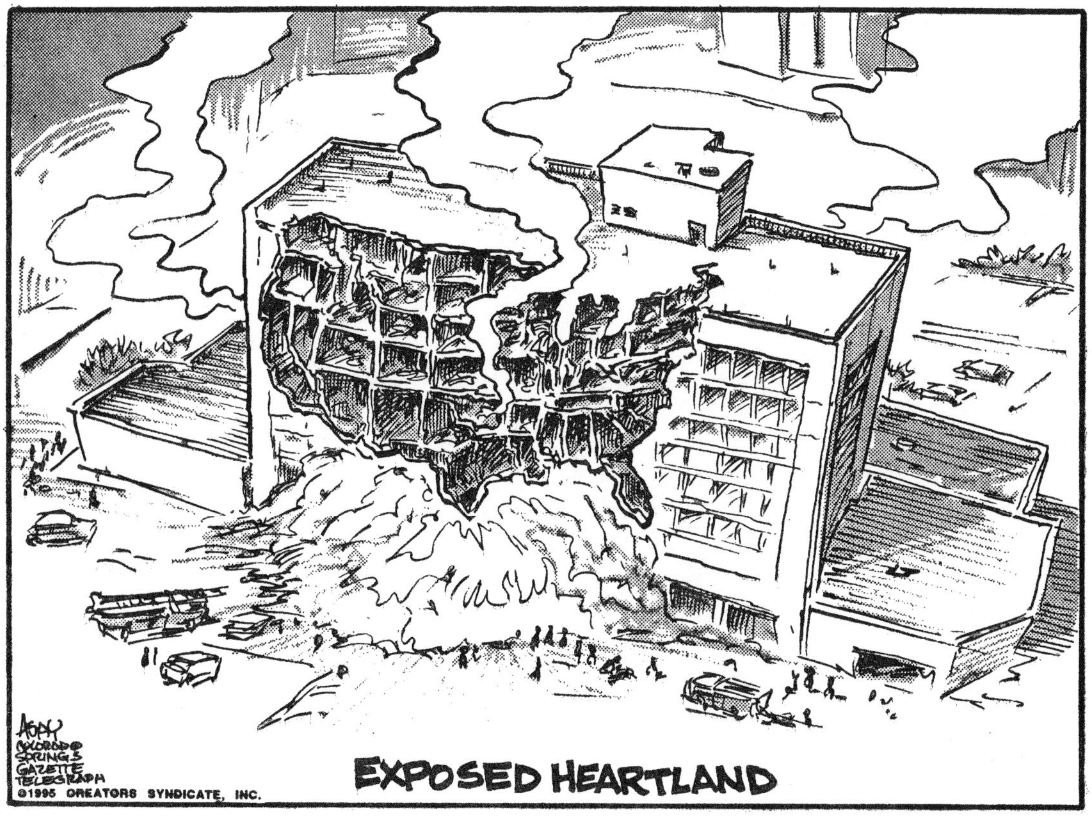
ASAY
COLORADO SPRINGS GAZETTE TELEGRAPH
©1995 CREATORS SYNDICATE, INC.
EXPOSED HEARTLAND

CHUCK ASAY
Courtesy Colorado Springs Gazette Telegraph

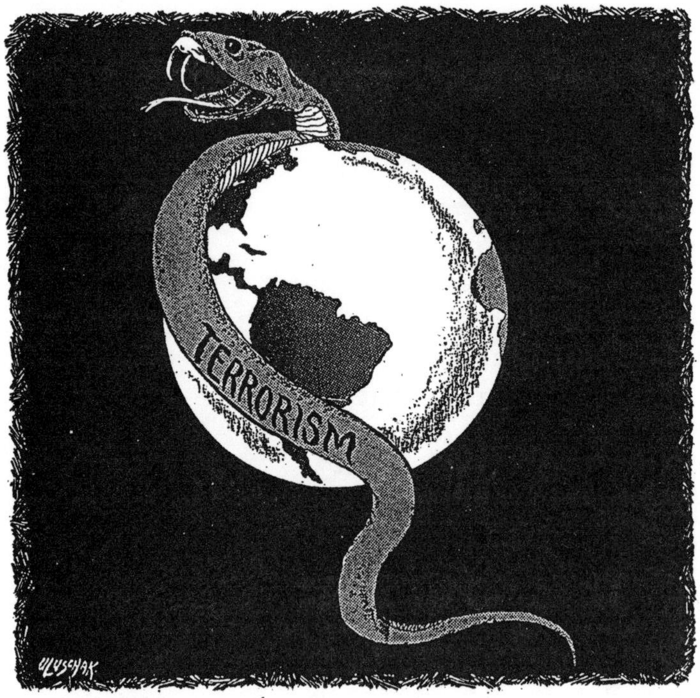
TERRORISM
ULUSCHAK

EDD ULUSCHAK
Courtesy The Sounder

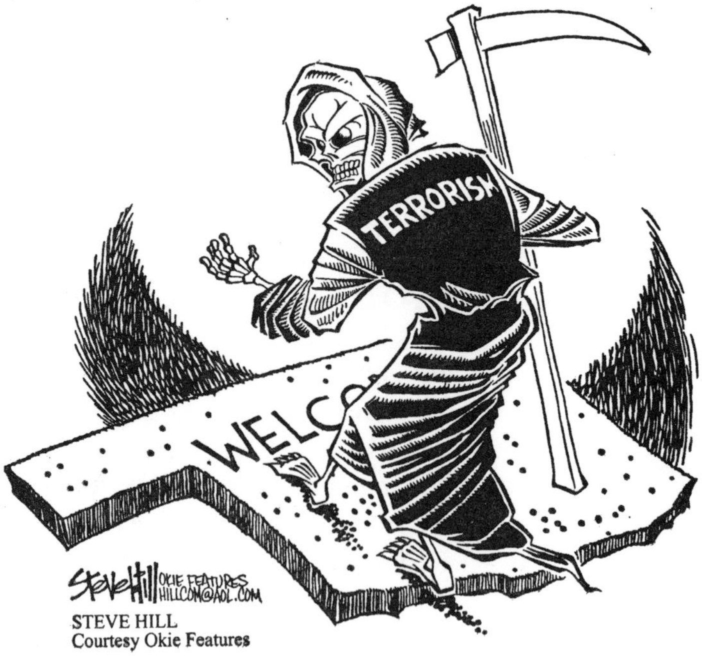
TERRORISM
WELCO
STEVE HILL OKIE FEATURES HILLCOM@AOL.COM

STEVE HILL
Courtesy Okie Features

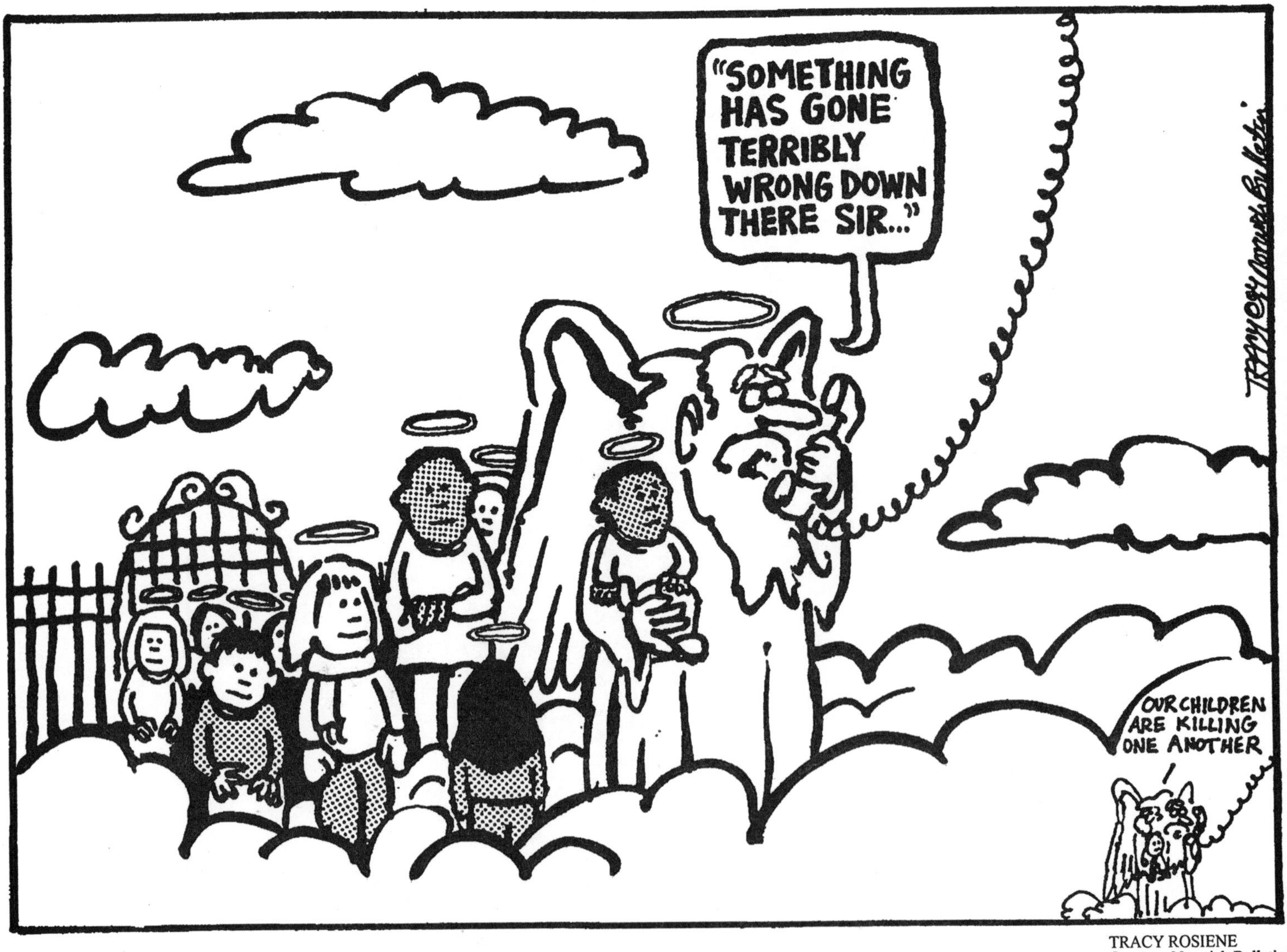
"SOMETHING HAS GONE TERRIBLY WRONG DOWN THERE SIR..."
OUR CHILDREN ARE KILLING ONE ANOTHER

TRACY ROSIENE
Courtesy Norwich Bulletin

CHIP BOK
Courtesy Akron Beacon Journal

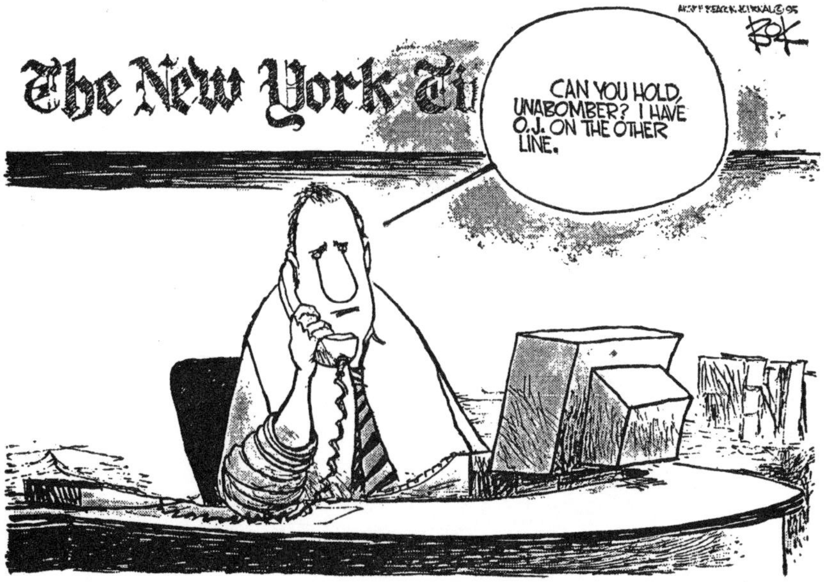
The New York Ti
CAN YOU HOLD, UNABOMBER? I HAVE O.J. ON THE OTHER LINE.

BOB LANG
Courtesy News-Sentinel (Ind.)

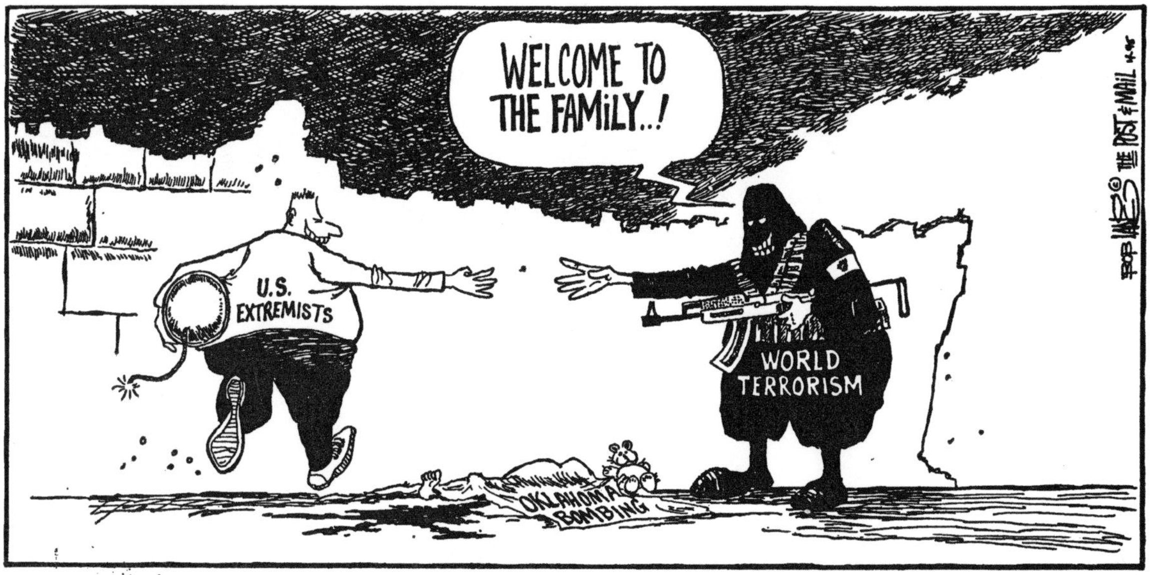
WELCOME TO THE FAMILY..!
U.S. EXTREMISTS
WORLD TERRORISM
OKLAHOMA BOMBING
THE POST & MAIL

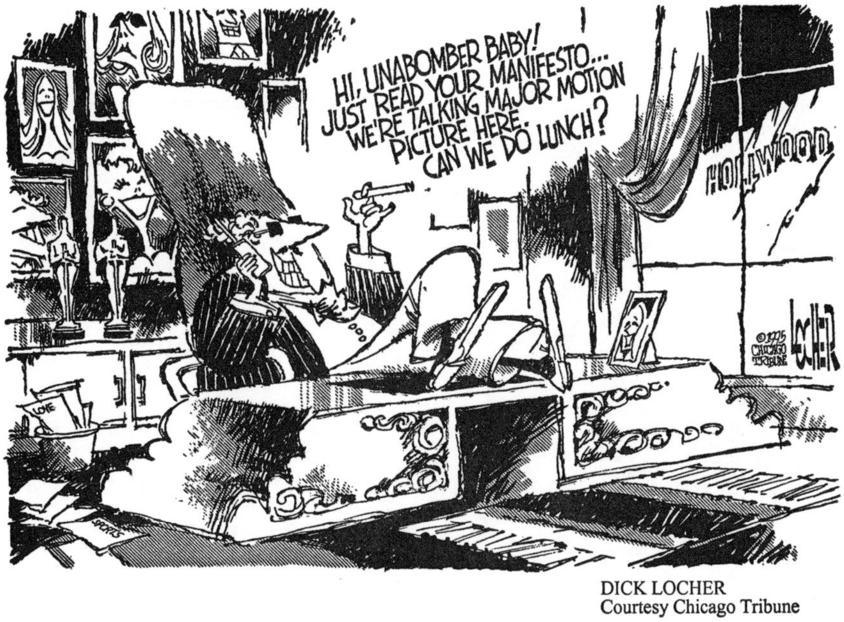
HI, UNABOMBER BABY! JUST READ YOUR MANIFESTO... WE'RE TALKING MAJOR MOTION PICTURE HERE. CAN WE DO LUNCH?
HOLLYWOOD
LOCHER

DICK LOCHER
Courtesy Chicago Tribune

BILL GARNER
Courtesy Washington Times

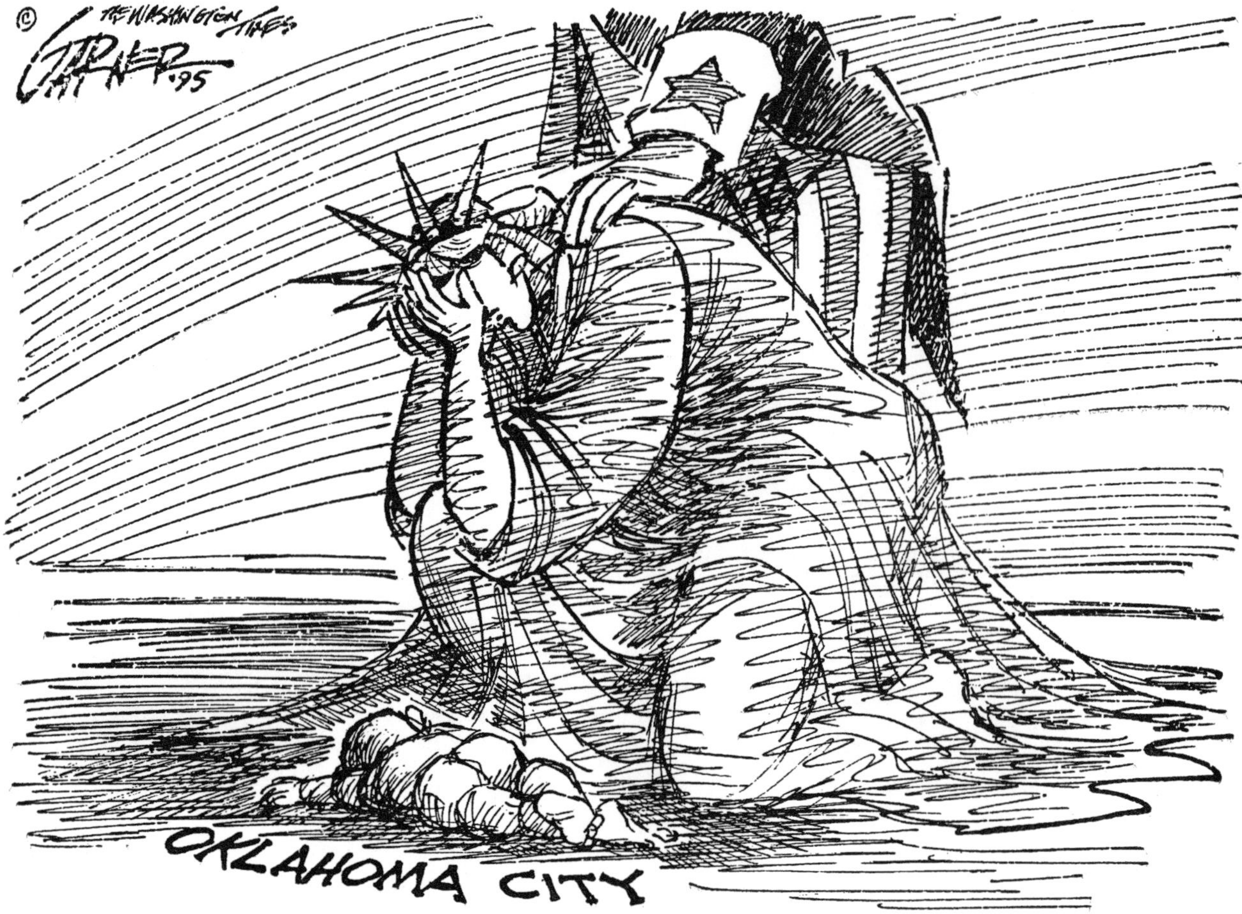
© THE WASHINGTON TIMES
GARNER '95
OKLAHOMA CITY

MICHAEL RAMIREZ
Courtesy Memphis Commercial Appeal

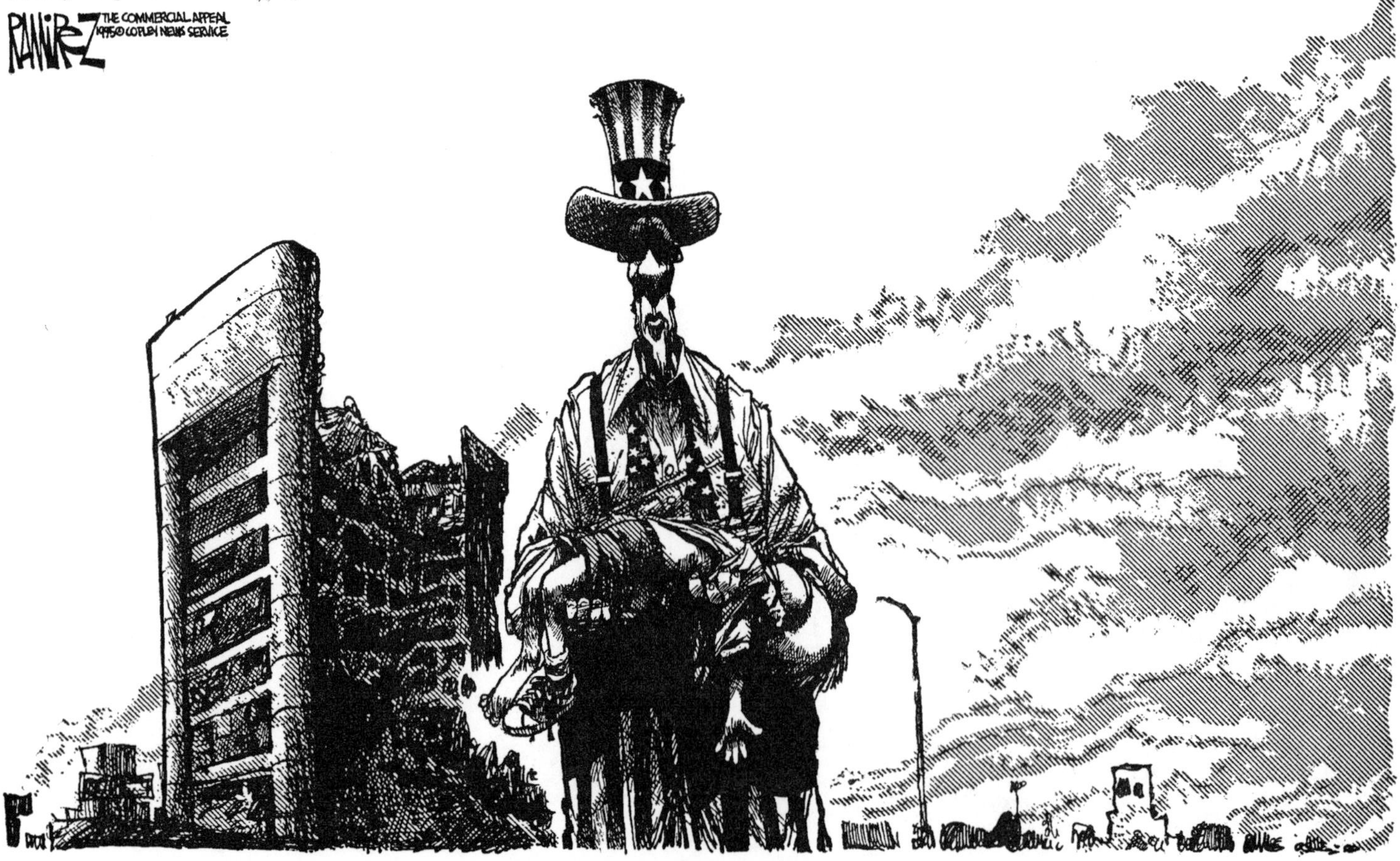
RAMIREZ THE COMMERCIAL APPEAL
1995 © COPLEY NEWS SERVICE

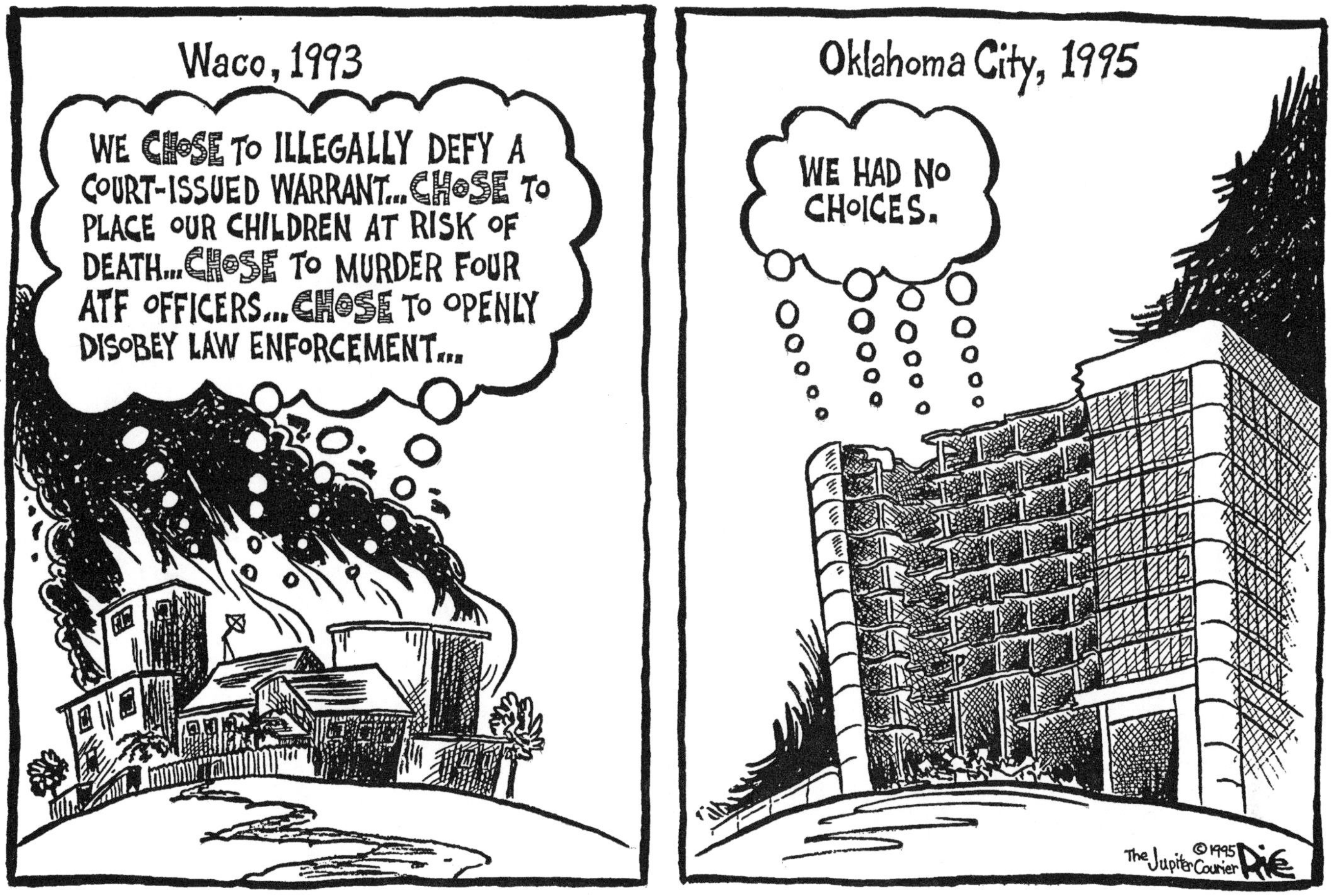
Waco, 1993
WE CHOSE TO ILLEGALLY DEFY A COURT-ISSUED WARRANT...CHOSE TO PLACE OUR CHILDREN AT RISK OF DEATH...CHOSE TO MURDER FOUR ATF OFFICERS...CHOSE TO OPENLY DISOBEY LAW ENFORCEMENT...
Oklahoma City, 1995
WE HAD NO CHOICES.
The Jupiter Courier ©1995 RICE

PATRICK RICE
Courtesy Jupiter Courier

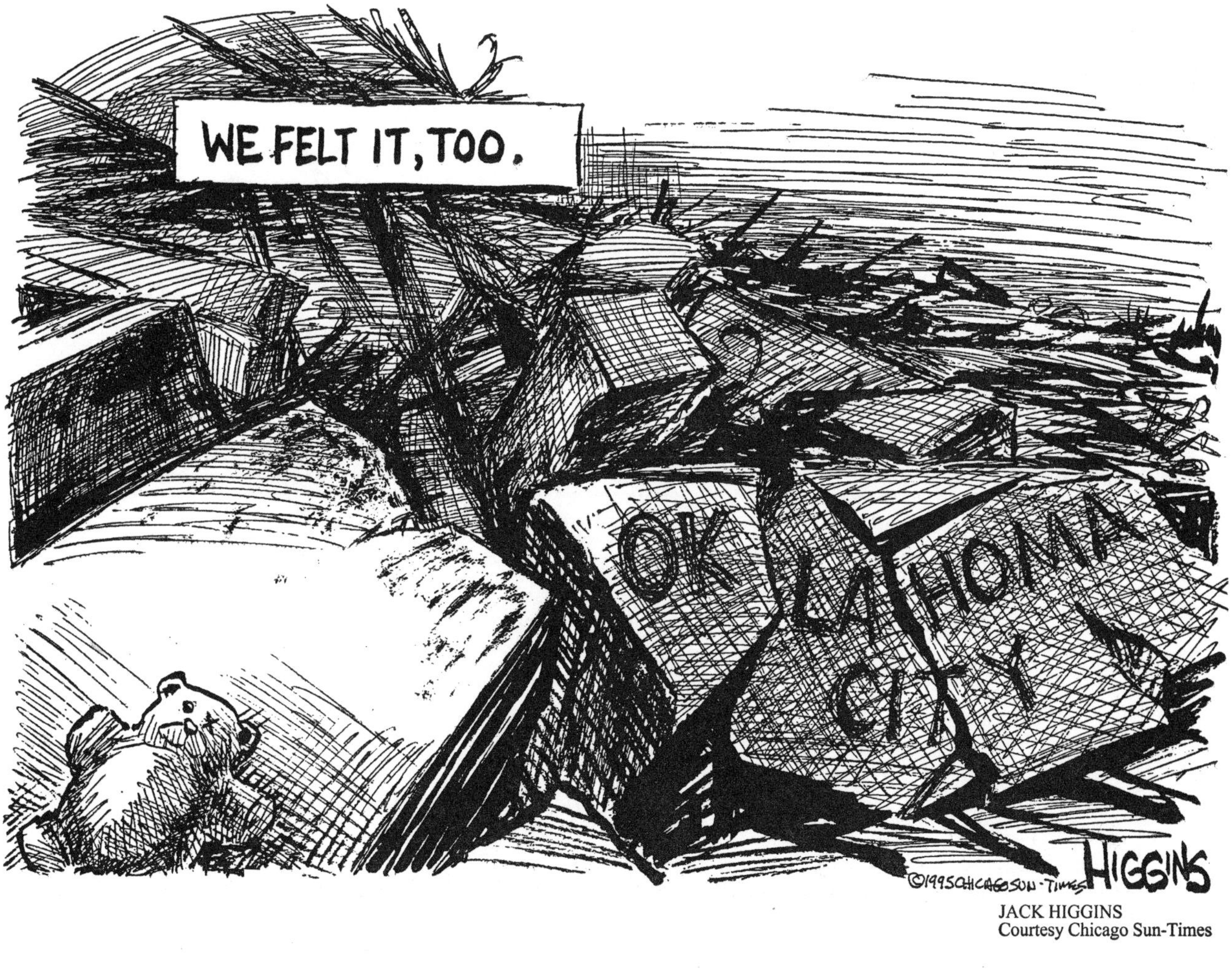
WE FELT IT, TOO.
OKLAHOMA CITY
©1995 CHICAGO SUN-TIMES HIGGINS

JACK HIGGINS
Courtesy Chicago Sun-Times

MARK CULLUM
Courtesy Birmingham News

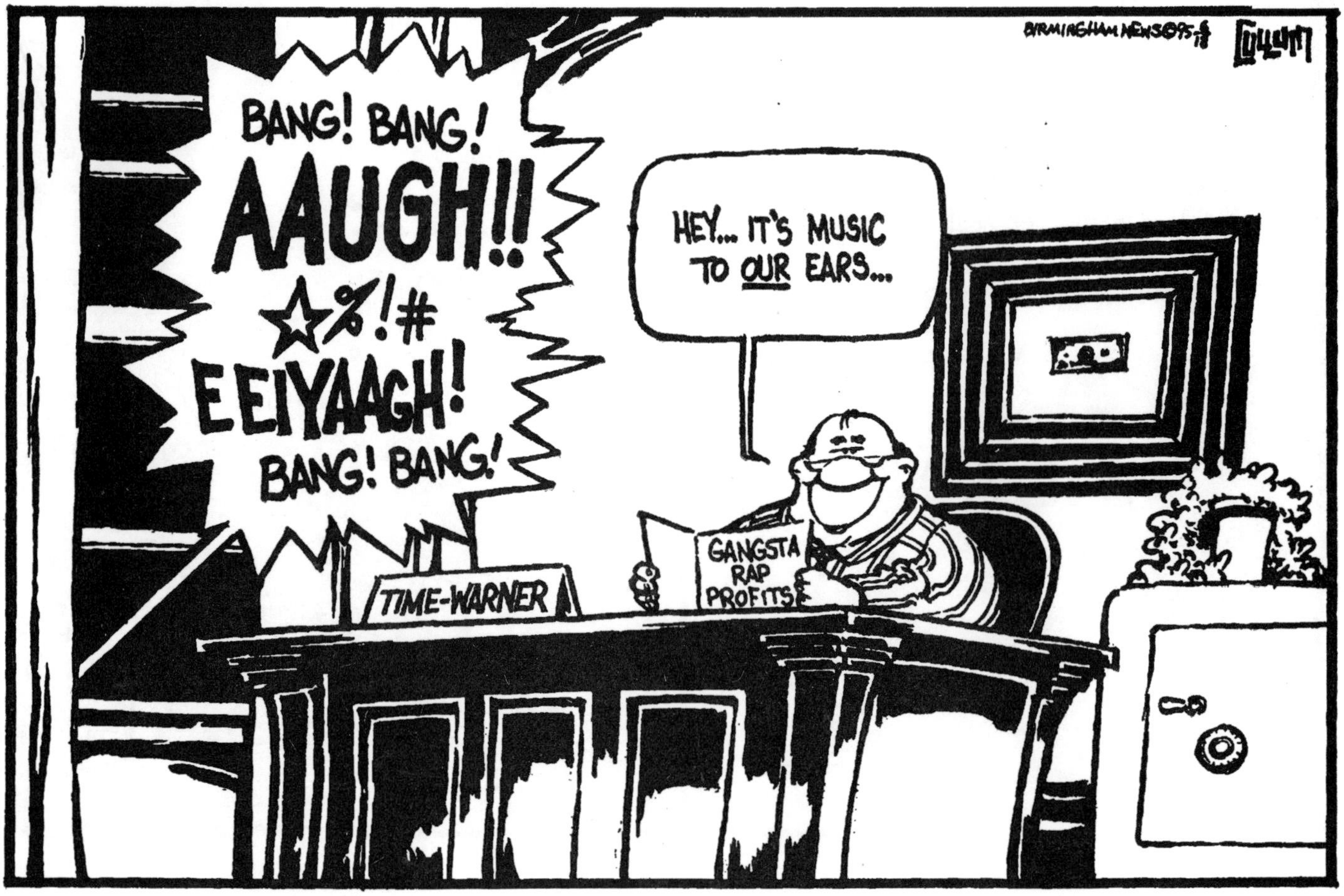

BIRMINGHAM NEWS©95
CULLUM
BANG! BANG!
AAUGH!!
☆%!#
EEIYAAGH!
BANG! BANG!
HEY... IT'S MUSIC TO OUR EARS...
TIME-WARNER
GANGSTA RAP PROFITS

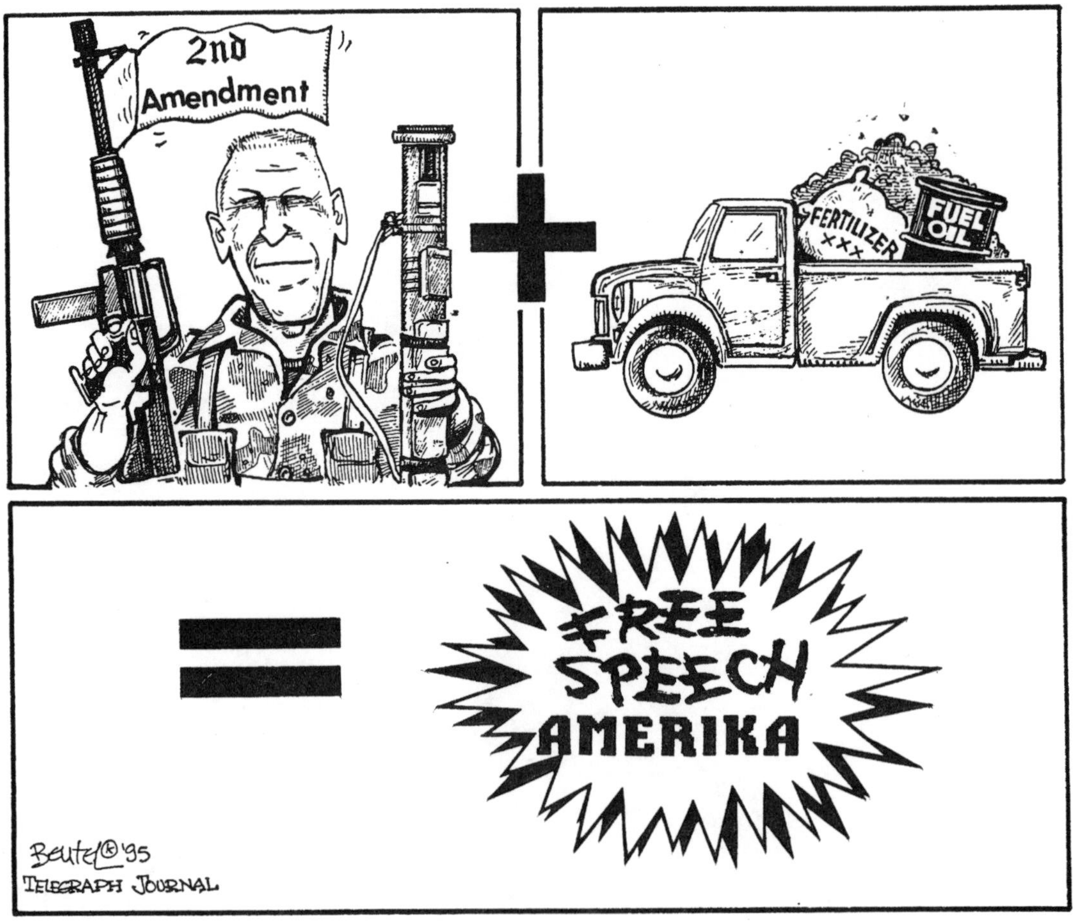

2nd Amendment
FERTILIZER
XXX
FUEL OIL
FREE SPEECH AMERIKA
Beutel©'95
TELEGRAPH JOURNAL

JOSH BEUTEL
Courtesy St. John Telegraph Journal

THE SEARCH GOES ON

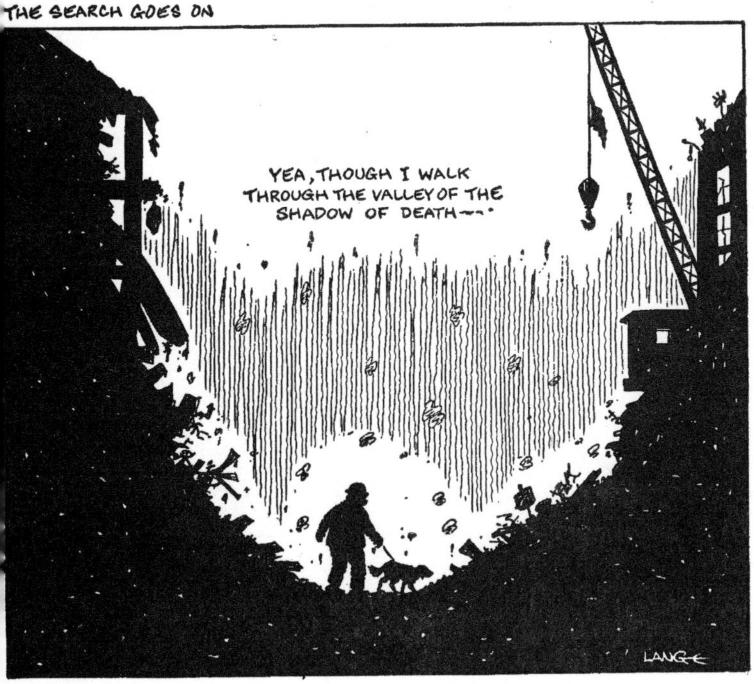
YEA, THOUGH I WALK THROUGH THE VALLEY OF THE SHADOW OF DEATH—...
LANGE

JIM LANGE
Courtesy Daily Oklahoman

STEVE KELLEY
Courtesy San Diego Union

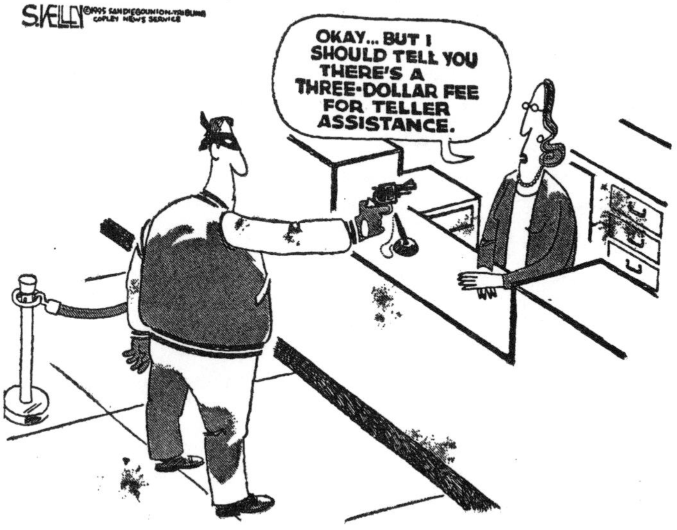
OKAY... BUT I SHOULD TELL YOU THERE'S A THREE-DOLLAR FEE FOR TELLER ASSISTANCE.

GARY MCCOY
Courtesy Suburban Journals

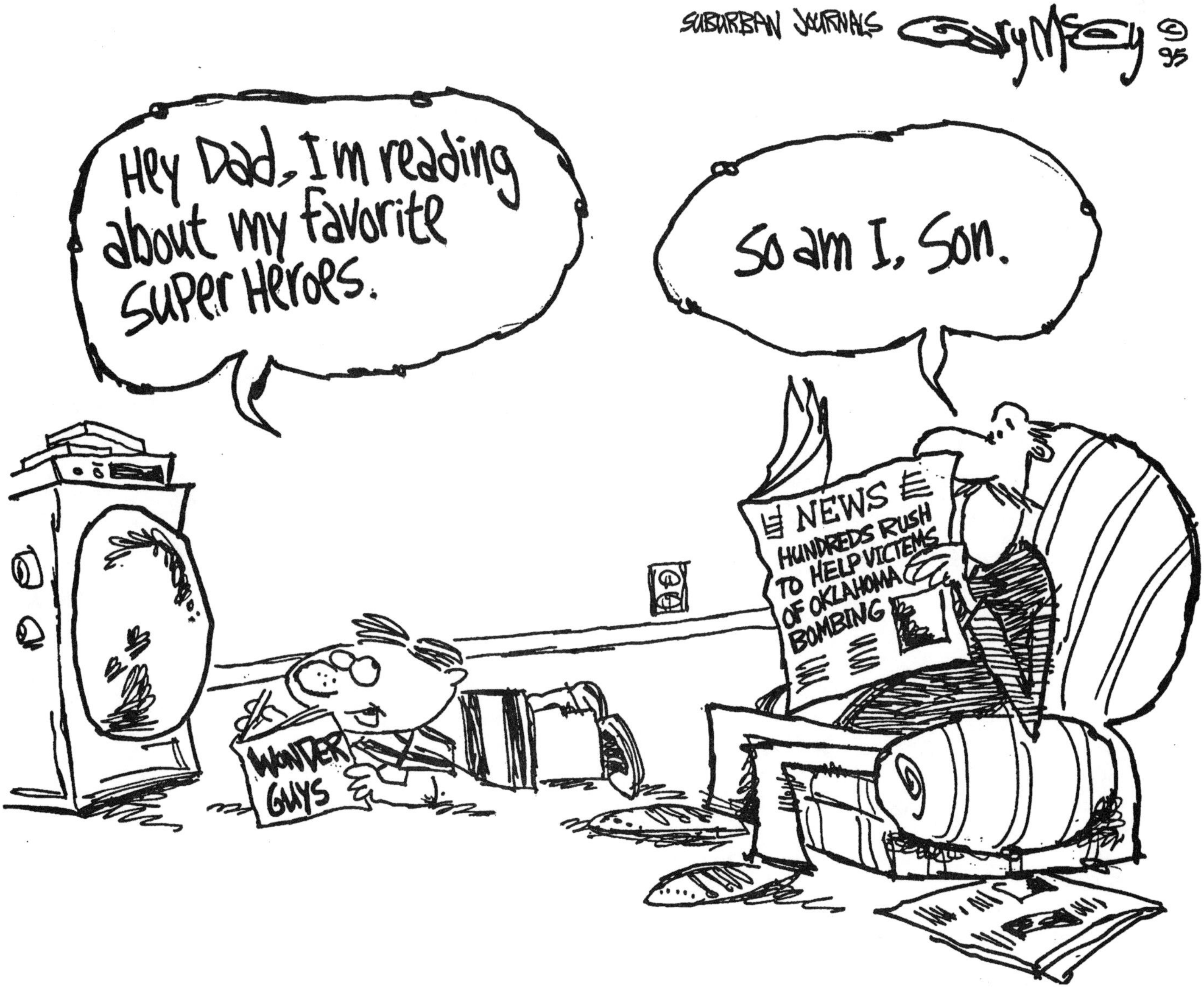
SUBURBAN JOURNALS Gary McCoy © 95
Hey Dad, I'm reading about my favorite Super Heroes.
So am I, Son.
NEWS
HUNDREDS RUSH TO HELP VICTEMS OF OKLAHOMA BOMBING
WONDER GUYS

DRAPER HILL
Courtesy Detroit News

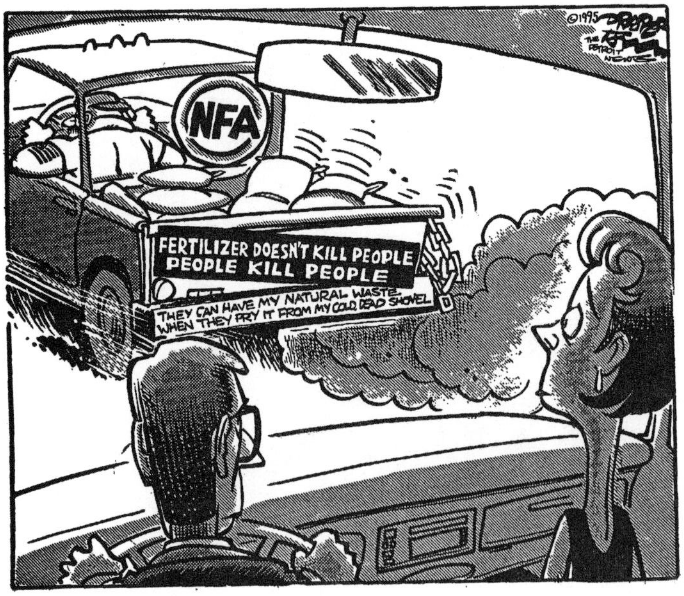
©1995 DRAPER
NFA
FERTILIZER DOESN'T KILL PEOPLE
PEOPLE KILL PEOPLE
THEY CAN HAVE MY NATURAL WASTE WHEN THEY PRY IT FROM MY COLD, DEAD SHOVEL

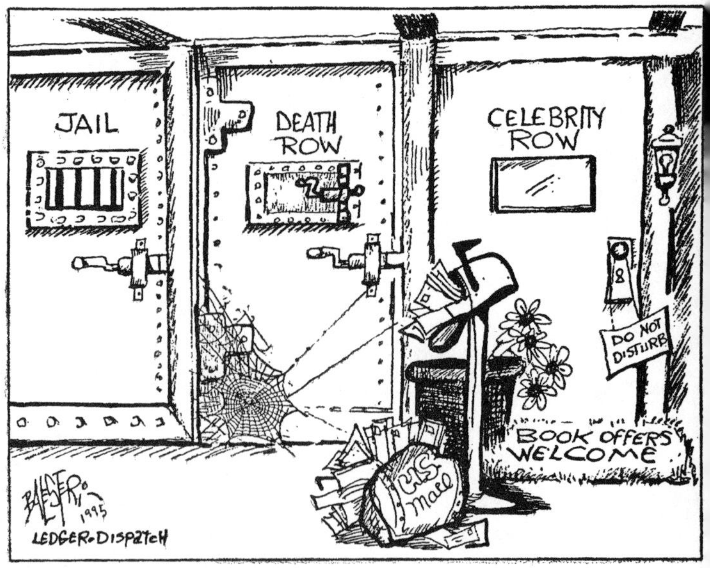
JAIL
DEATH ROW
CELEBRITY ROW
DO NOT DISTURB
BOOK OFFERS WELCOME
U.S. mail
BALESTERI 1995
LEDGER-DISPATCH

ANNETTE BALESTERI
Courtesy Antioch Daily Ledger (Calif.)

DOUGLAS REGALIA
Courtesy San Ramon Valley Times (Calif.)

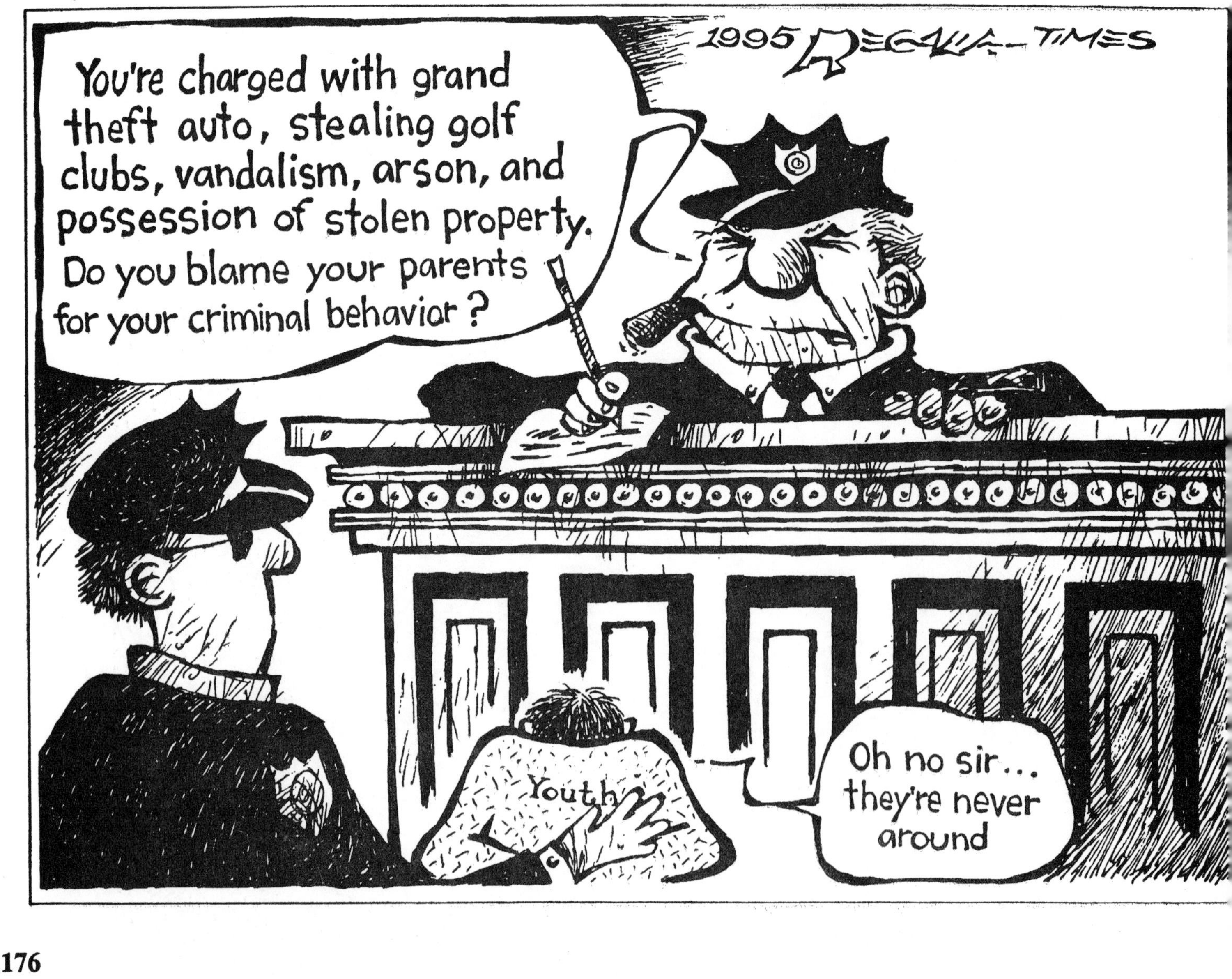
1995 REGALIA-TIMES
You're charged with grand theft auto, stealing golf clubs, vandalism, arson, and possession of stolen property. Do you blame your parents for your criminal behavior?
Youth
Oh no sir... they're never around

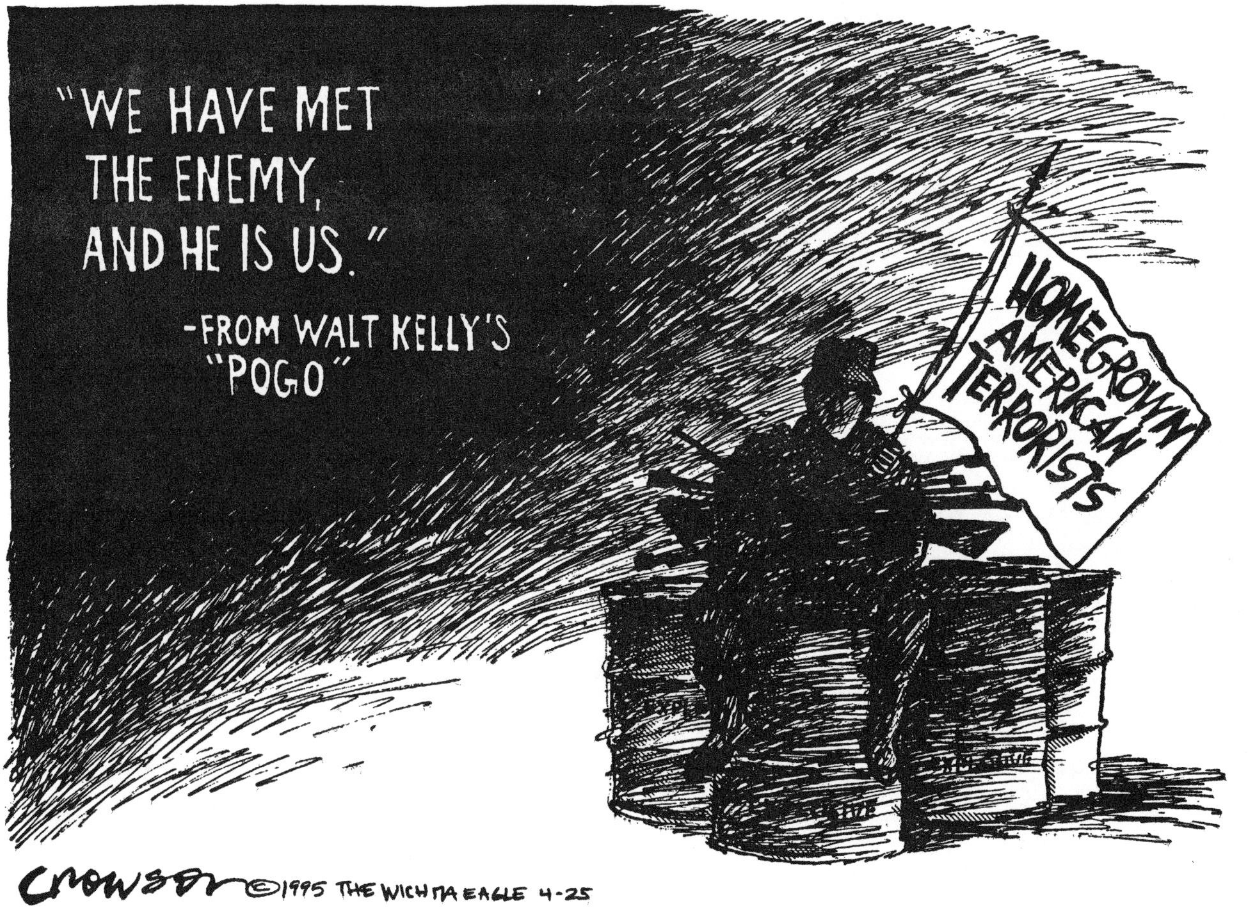
"WE HAVE MET
THE ENEMY,
AND HE IS US."
-FROM WALT KELLY'S
"POGO"
HOMEGROWN
AMERICAN
TERRORISTS
CROWSON ©1995 THE WICHITA EAGLE 4-25

RICHARD CROWSON
Courtesy Wichita Eagle

DALE STEPHANOS
Courtesy Boston Herald

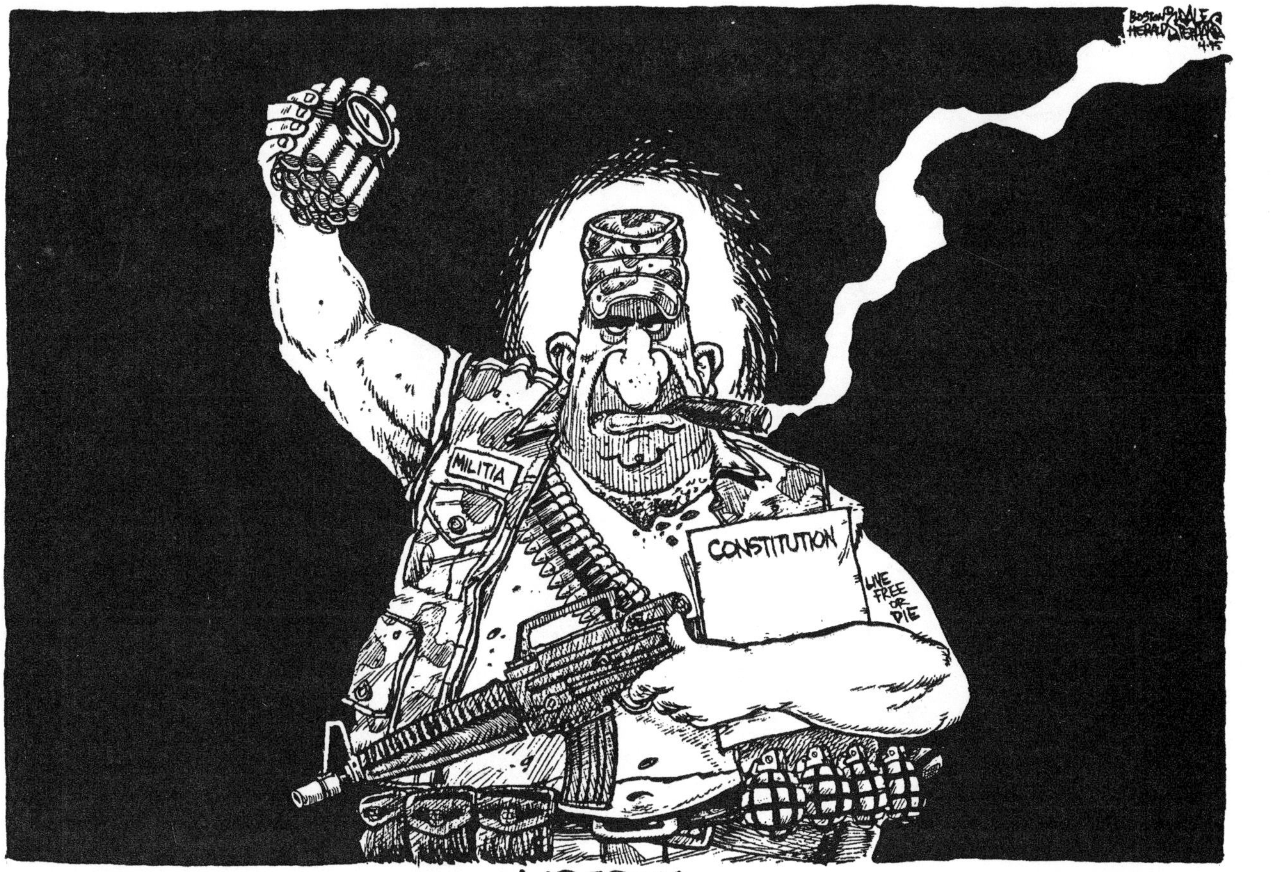
MILITIA
CONSTITUTION
LIVE FREE OR DIE
LIBERTY

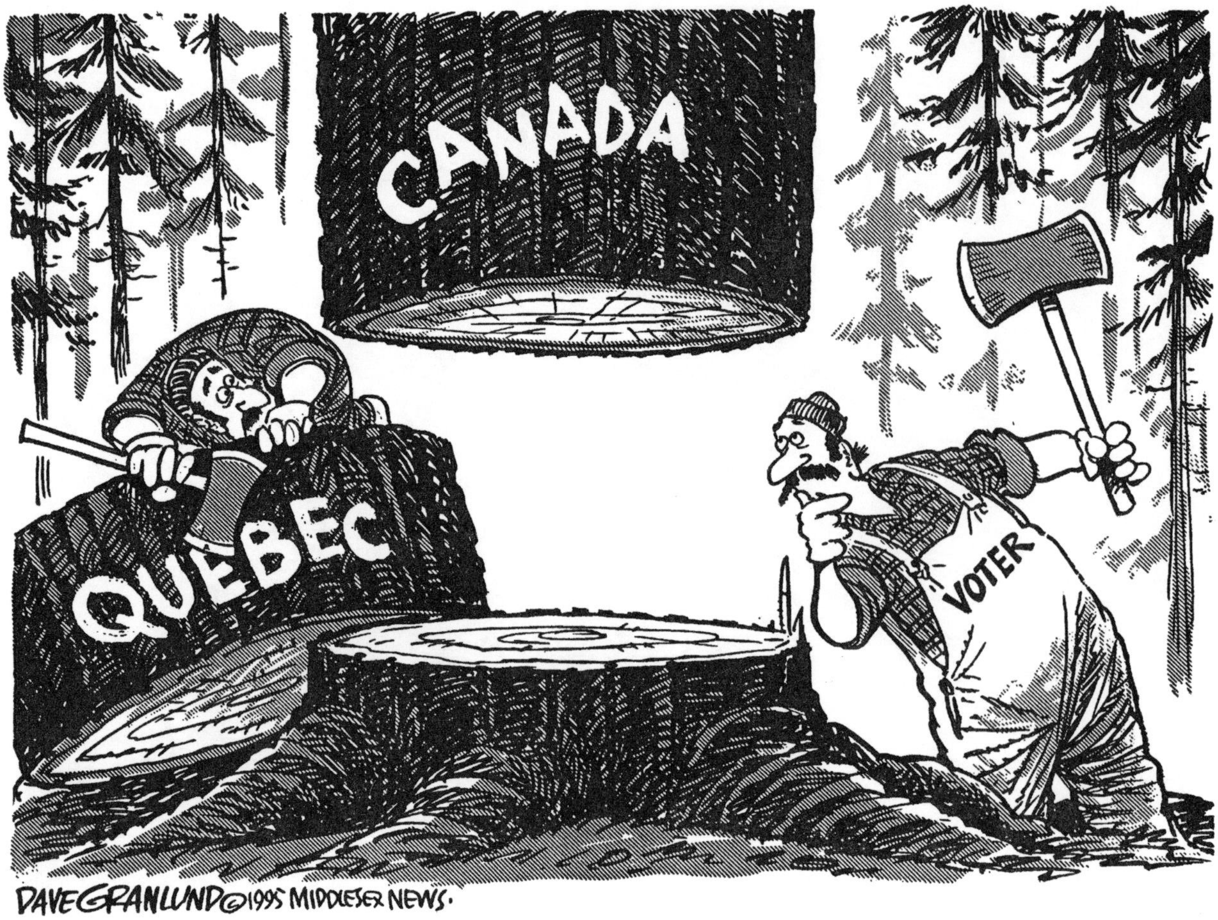
CANADA
QUEBEC
VOTER
DAVE GRANLUND ©1995 MIDDLESEX NEWS.

DAVID GRANLUND
Courtesy Middlesex News

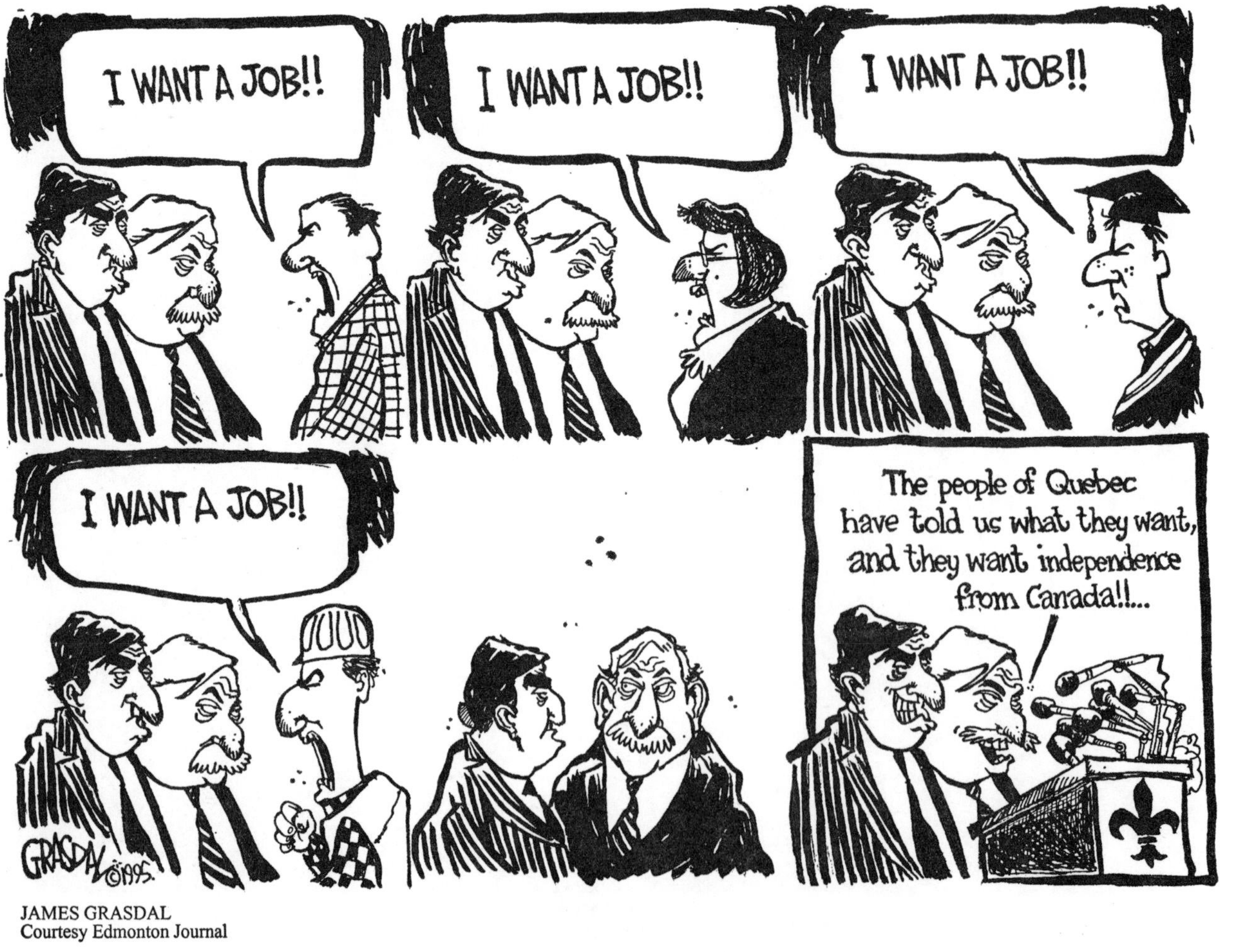
I WANT A JOB!!
I WANT A JOB!!
I WANT A JOB!!
I WANT A JOB!!
The people of Quebec have told us what they want, and they want independence from Canada!!...
GRASDAL ©1995.

JAMES GRASDAL
Courtesy Edmonton Journal

Canada

By the narrowest of margins—50.56 percent to 49.44 percent—the province of Quebec in a referendum on October 30 voted to remain a part of Canada. An earlier vote on independence in 1980 had been defeated 60 percent to 40 percent, so it was clear that separatists had gained strength. The vote obviously did not bode well for the future of a united Canada. Immediately after the vote was announced, the losers began calling for another ballot. Quebec has 7 million people, more than one-fourth of Canada's population, and 82 percent speak French.

Canada had its "O. J. of the North" trial, which attracted intensive news coverage for four months and heard eighty-six witnesses. A young suburbanite and his wife admitted to ghoulish criminal acts and were convicted.

The Canadian economy remained sluggish as more and more companies began downsizing. Canada's heavy public debt, which reached 65 percent of the gross domestic product, is among the highest among industrialized nations.

A Spanish trawler was impounded for fishing in Canadian waters, and trouble brewed with Alaskan fishermen.

The Canadian Football League title, the Grey Cup, was won by an American team, which left many citizens with red faces. But a nonpartisan study group nevertheless voted Canada the best place to live.

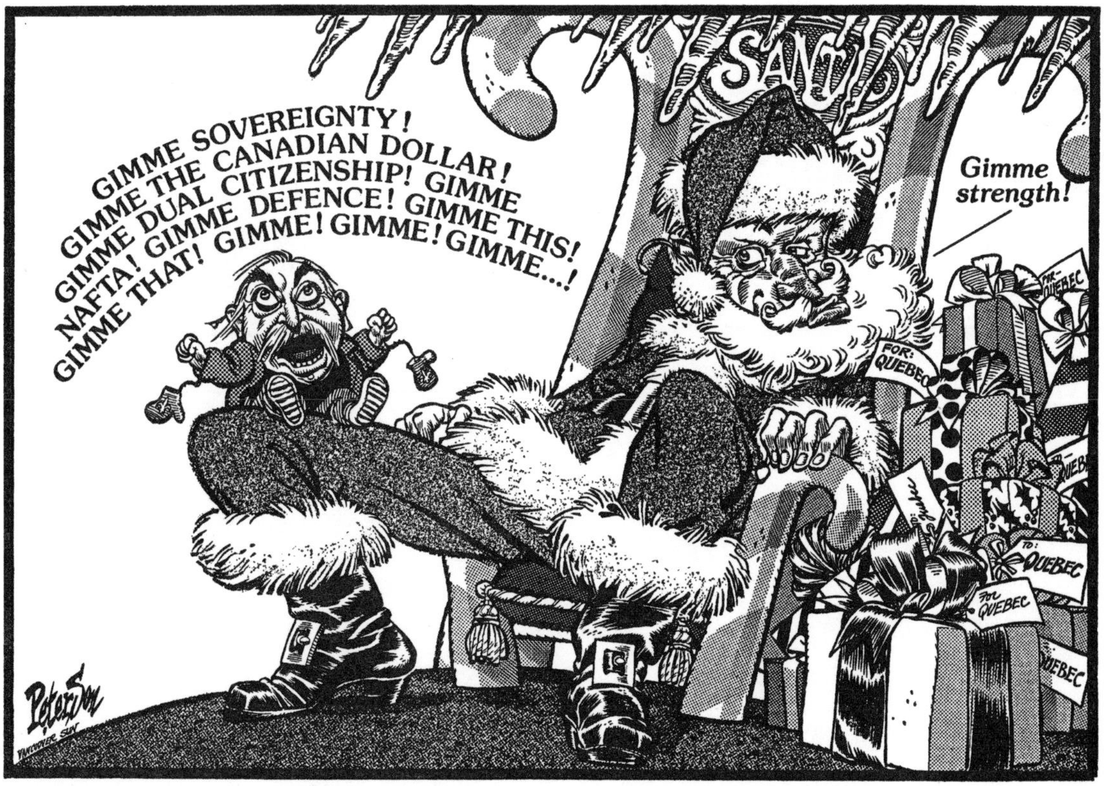
GIMME SOVEREIGNTY! GIMME THE CANADIAN DOLLAR! GIMME DUAL CITIZENSHIP! GIMME NAFTA! GIMME DEFENCE! GIMME THIS! GIMME THAT! GIMME! GIMME! GIMME...!
Gimme strength!
SANTA
FOR: QUEBEC
TO: QUEBEC
PETERSON

ROY PETERSON
Courtesy Vancouver Sun

JAMES GRASDAL
Courtesy Edmonton Journal

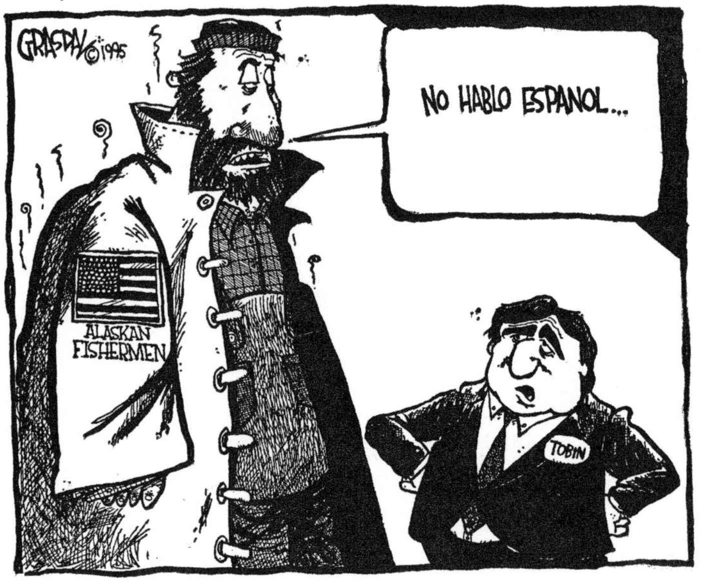
GRASDAL ©1995
NO HABLO ESPANOL...
ALASKAN FISHERMEN
TOBIN

EDD ULUSCHAK
Courtesy The Sounder

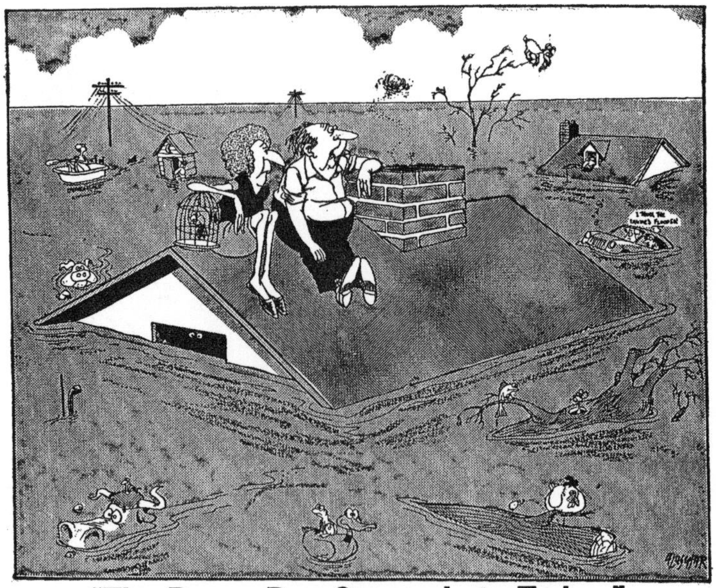

"The Paper Boy Seems Late Today."

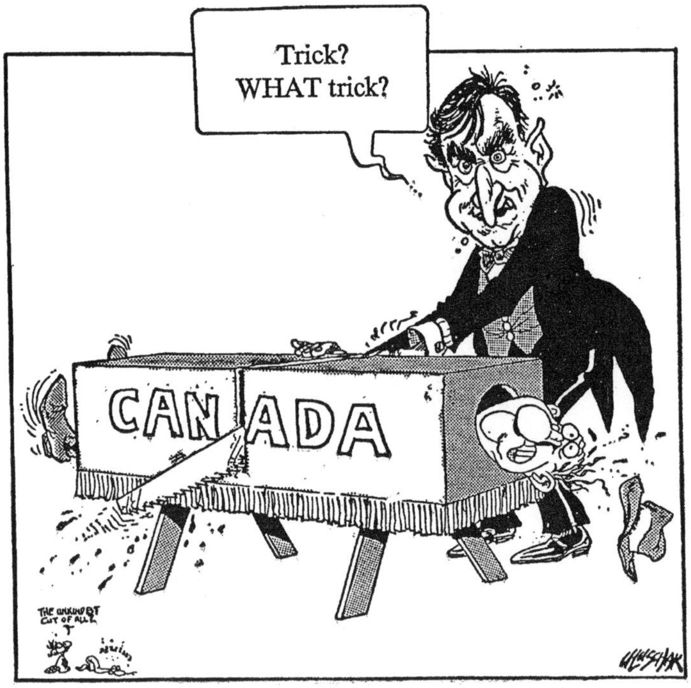
Trick?
WHAT trick?
CANADA
ULUSCHAK

EDD ULUSCHAK
Courtesy The Sounder

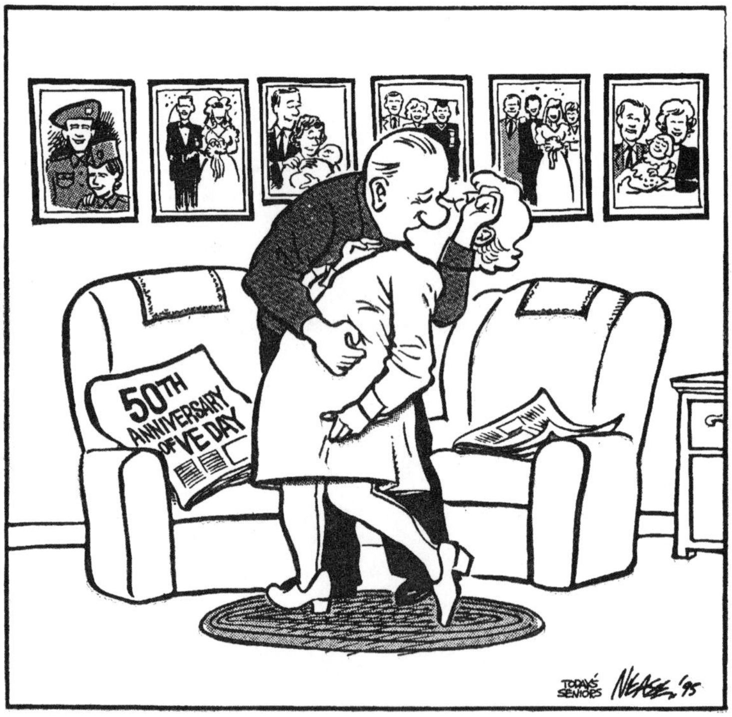
50TH ANNIVERSARY OF VE DAY
TODAY'S SENIORS
NEASE '95

STEPHEN NEASE
Courtesy Ottawa Citizen

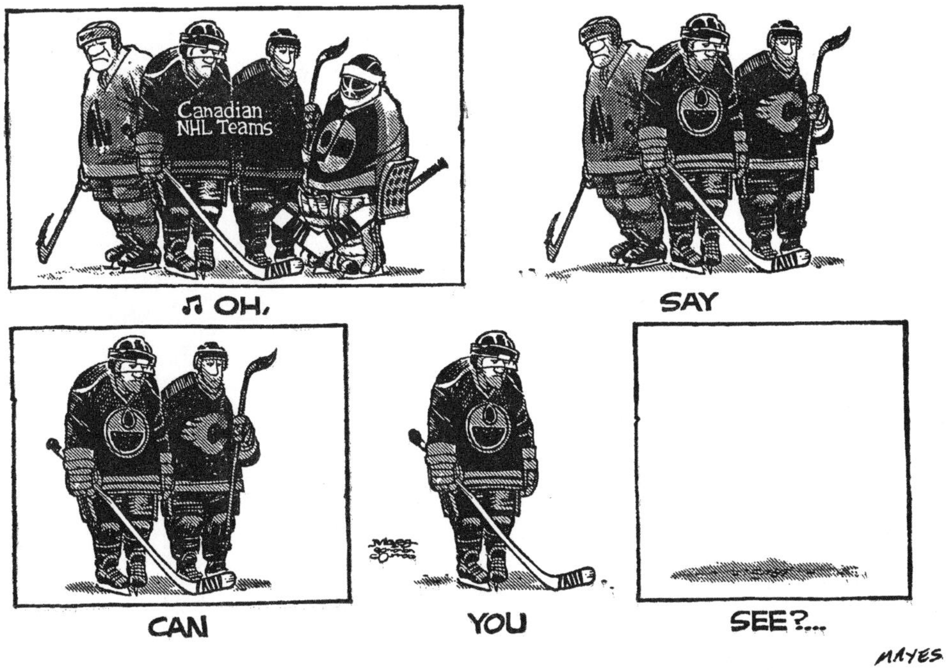

Canadian NHL Teams
♫ OH,
SAY
CAN
YOU
SEE?...
MAYES

MALCOLM MAYES
Courtesy Edmonton Journal

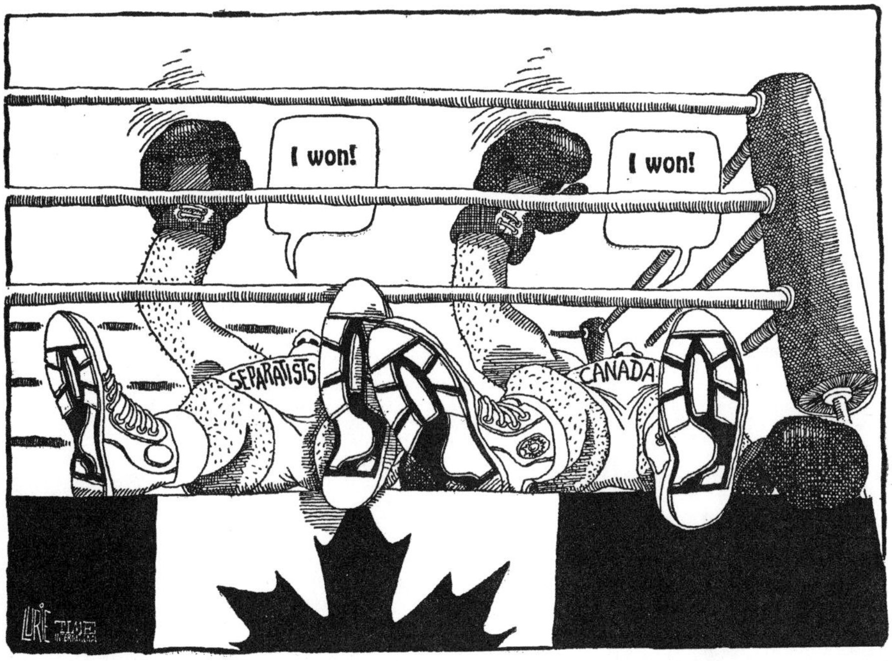

I won!
I won!
SEPARATISTS
CANADA
LURIE

RANAN LURIE
Courtesy Cartoonews International

JOE HOFFECKER
Courtesy Cincinnati Business Courier

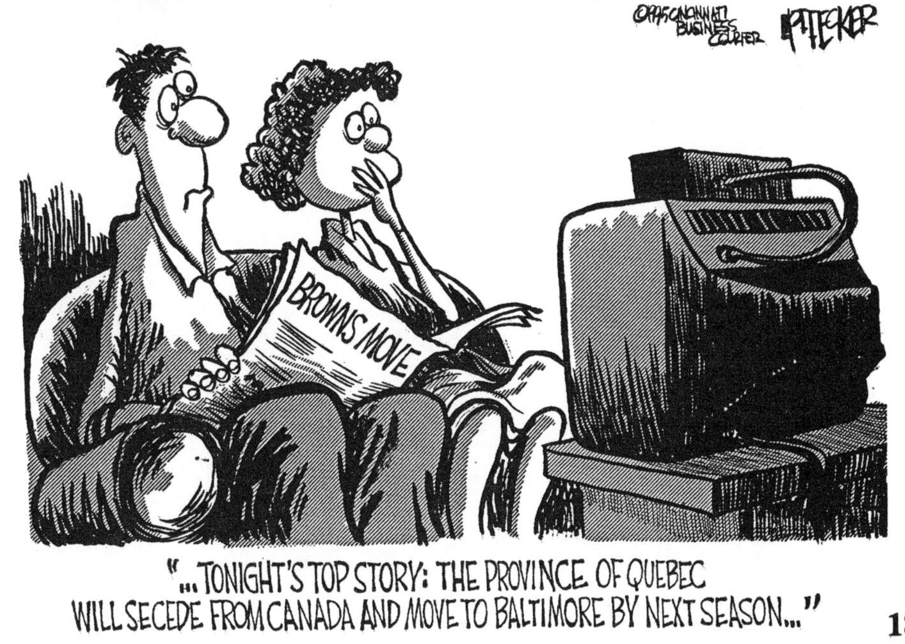

HOFFECKER
BROWNS MOVE

"...TONIGHT'S TOP STORY: THE PROVINCE OF QUEBEC WILL SECEDE FROM CANADA AND MOVE TO BALTIMORE BY NEXT SEASON..."

JAMES GRASDAL
Courtesy Edmonton Journal

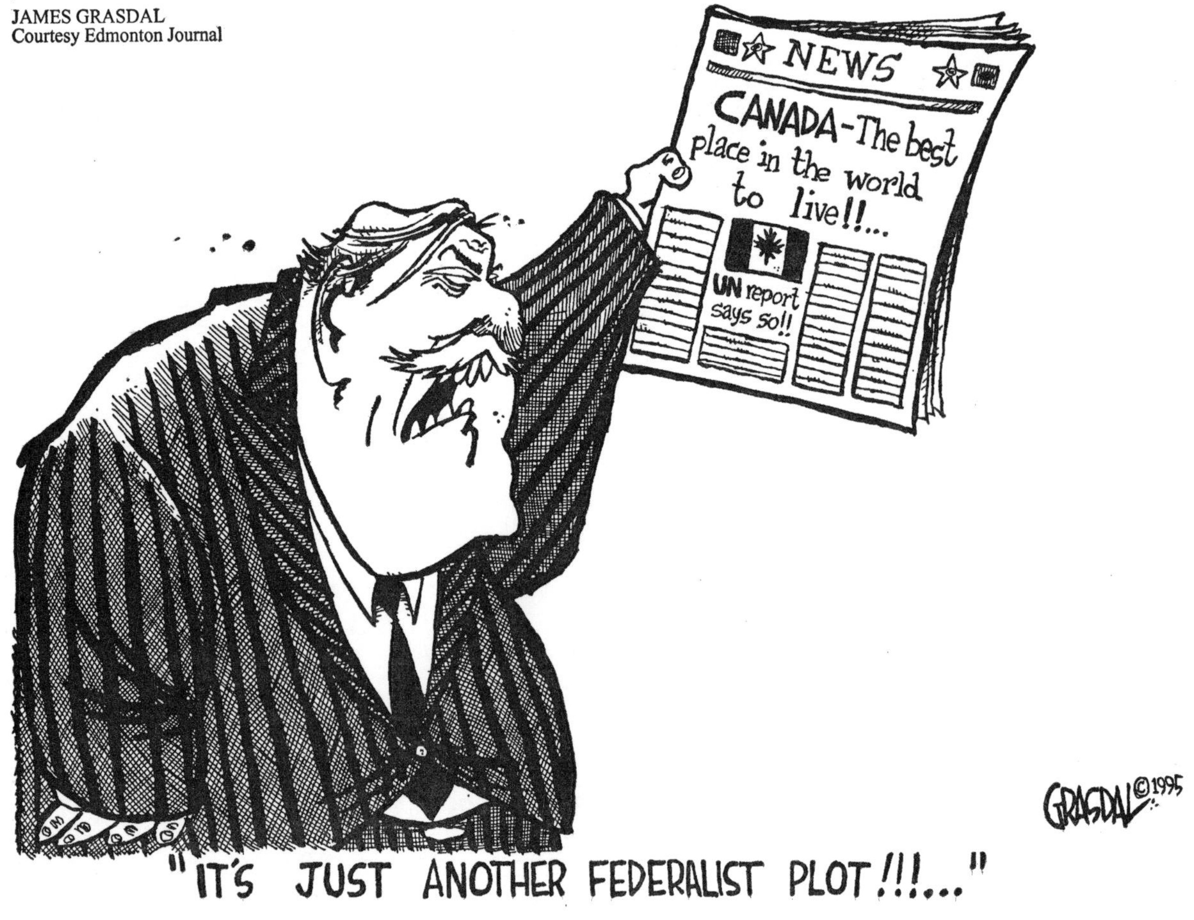
NEWS
CANADA-The best place in the world to live!!...
UN report says so!!
GRASDAL©1995
"IT'S JUST ANOTHER FEDERALIST PLOT!!!..."

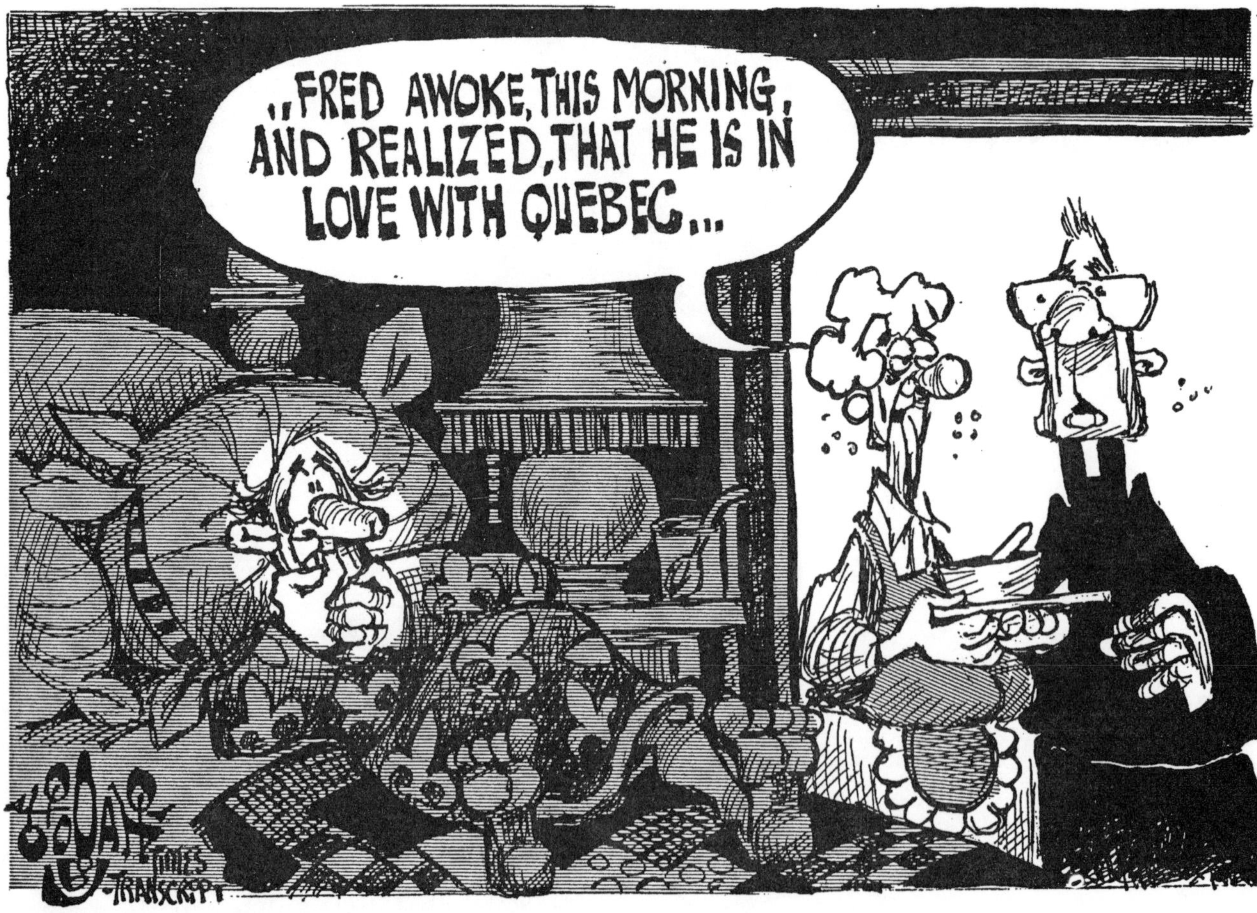
..FRED AWOKE, THIS MORNING, AND REALIZED, THAT HE IS IN LOVE WITH QUEBEC...
HOGAN TIMES-TRANSCRIPT

BILL HOGAN
Courtesy Times-Transcript (N. Bruns.)

PAUL SZEP
Courtesy Boston Globe

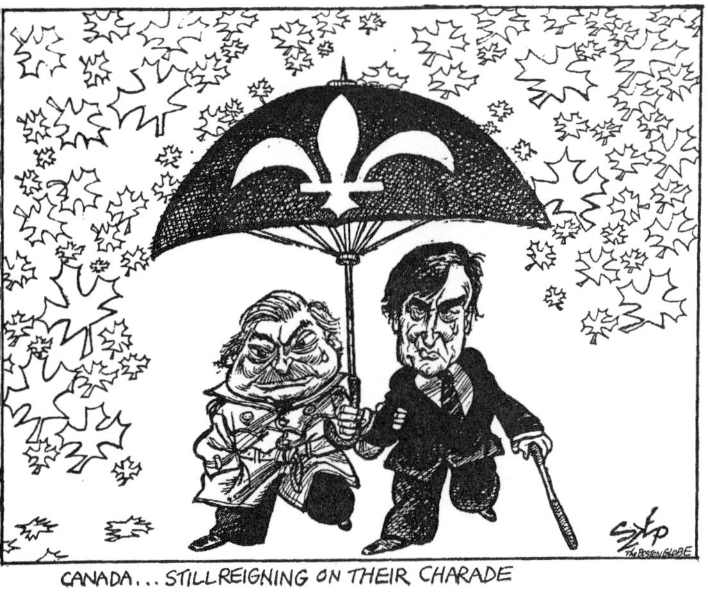
Szep
The Boston Globe

CANADA... STILL REIGNING ON THEIR CHARADE

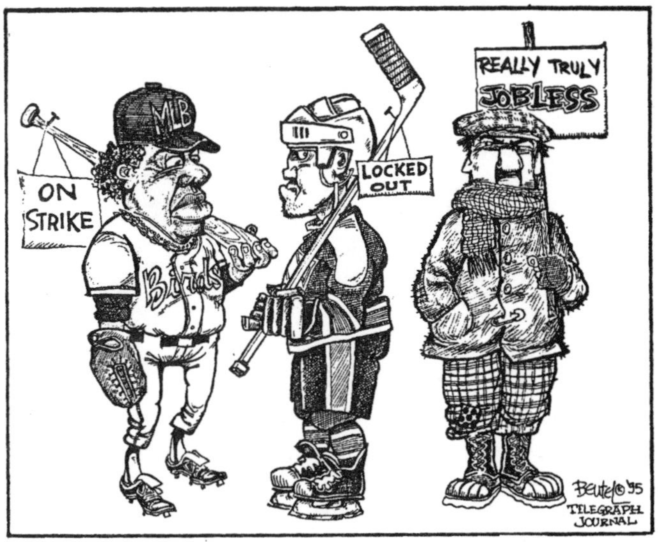
ON STRIKE
MLB
Birds
LOCKED OUT
REALLY TRULY JOBLESS
Beutel © '95
TELEGRAPH JOURNAL

JOSH BEUTEL
Courtesy St. John Telegraph Journal

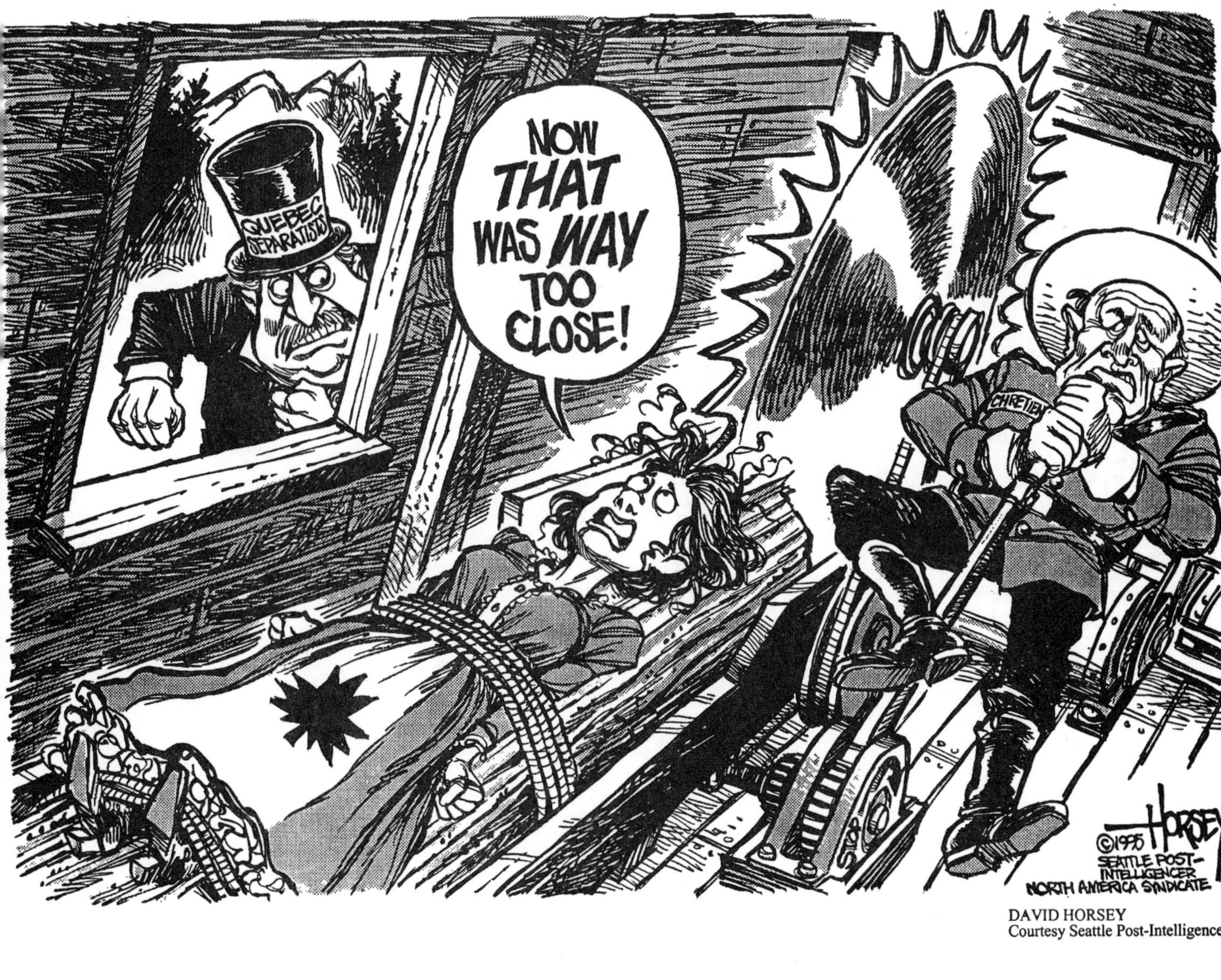
QUEBEC SEPARATISTS
NOW THAT WAS WAY TOO CLOSE!
CHRETIEN
STOP
©1995 HORSEY
SEATTLE POST-INTELLIGENCER
NORTH AMERICA SYNDICATE

DAVID HORSEY
Courtesy Seattle Post-Intelligencer

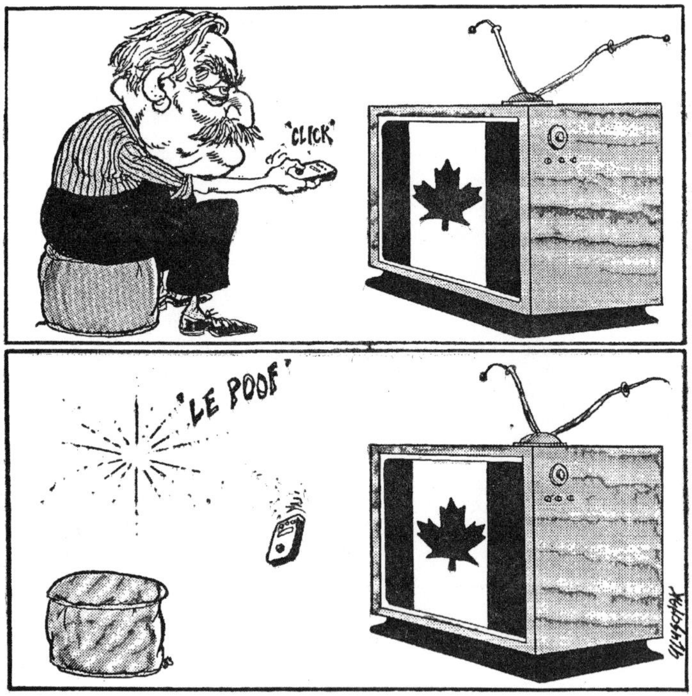
"CLICK"
'LE POOF'

EDD ULUSCHAK
Courtesy The Sounder

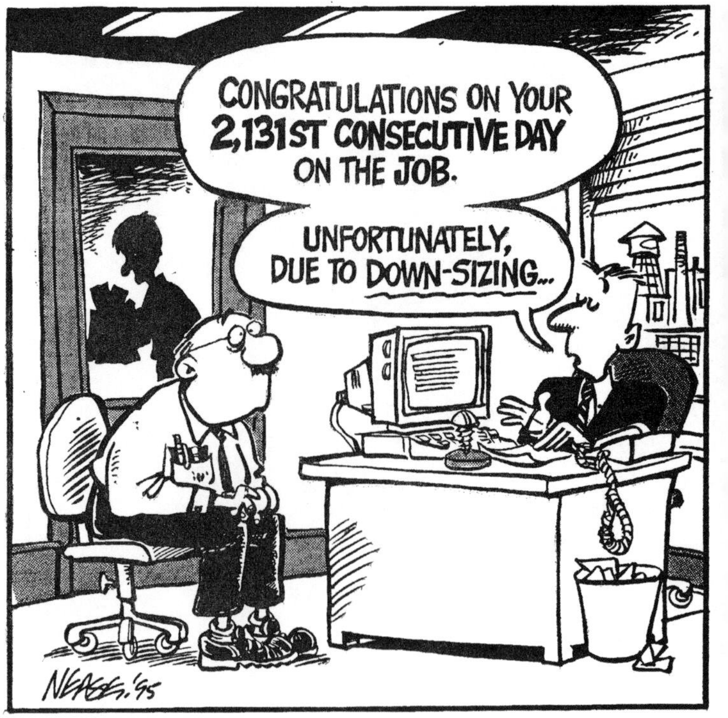
CONGRATULATIONS ON YOUR 2,131ST CONSECUTIVE DAY ON THE JOB.
UNFORTUNATELY, DUE TO DOWN-SIZING...

STEPHEN NEASE
Courtesy Victoria Times Colonist

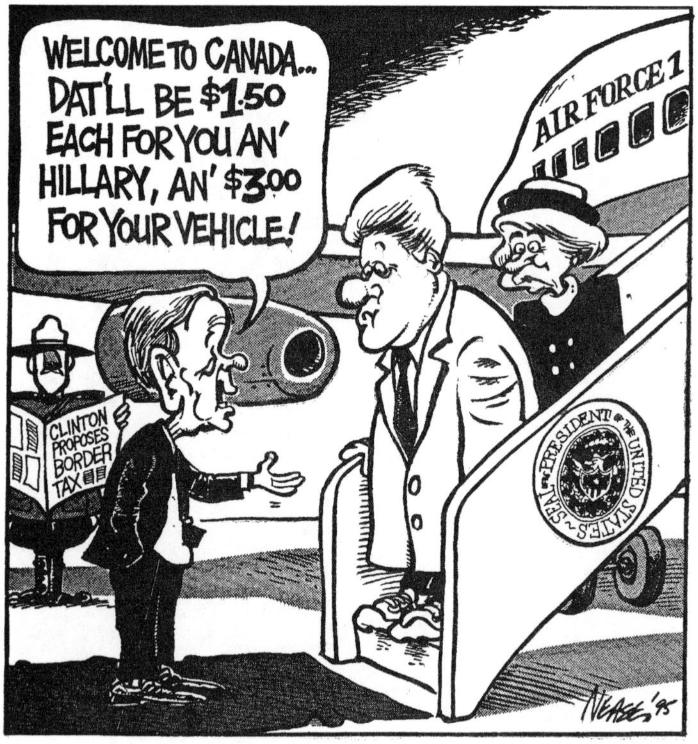
WELCOME TO CANADA... DAT'LL BE $1.50 EACH FOR YOU AN' HILLARY, AN' $3.00 FOR YOUR VEHICLE!
AIR FORCE 1
CLINTON PROPOSES BORDER TAX
SEAL OF THE PRESIDENT OF THE UNITED STATES

STEPHEN NEASE
Courtesy Victoria Times Colonist

BILL GARNER
Courtesy Washington Times

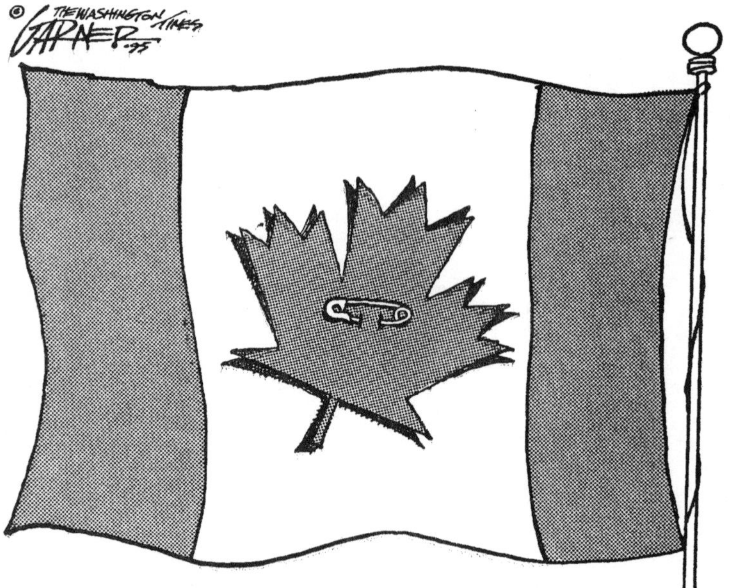

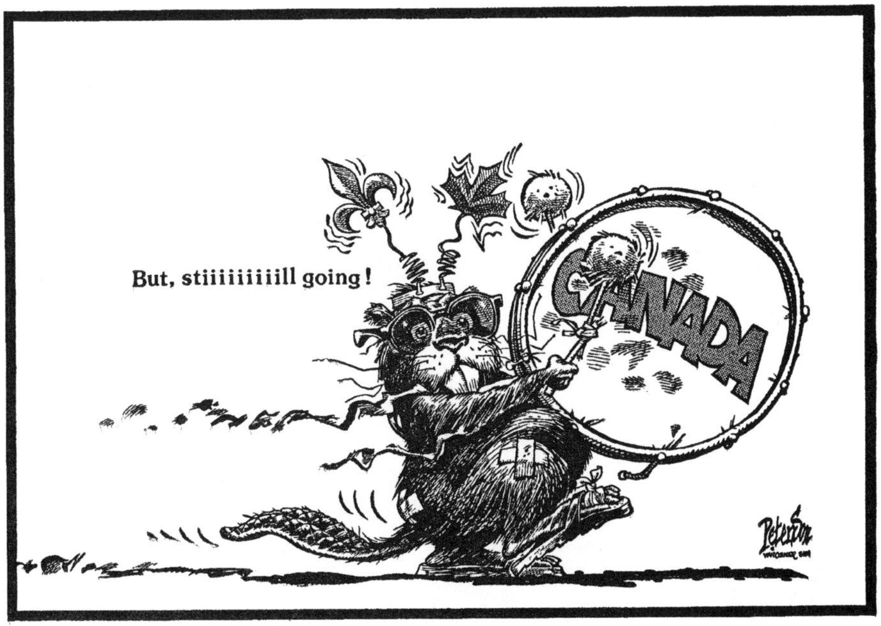
But, stiiiiiiiiill going!
CANADA

ROY PETERSON
Courtesy Vancouver Sun

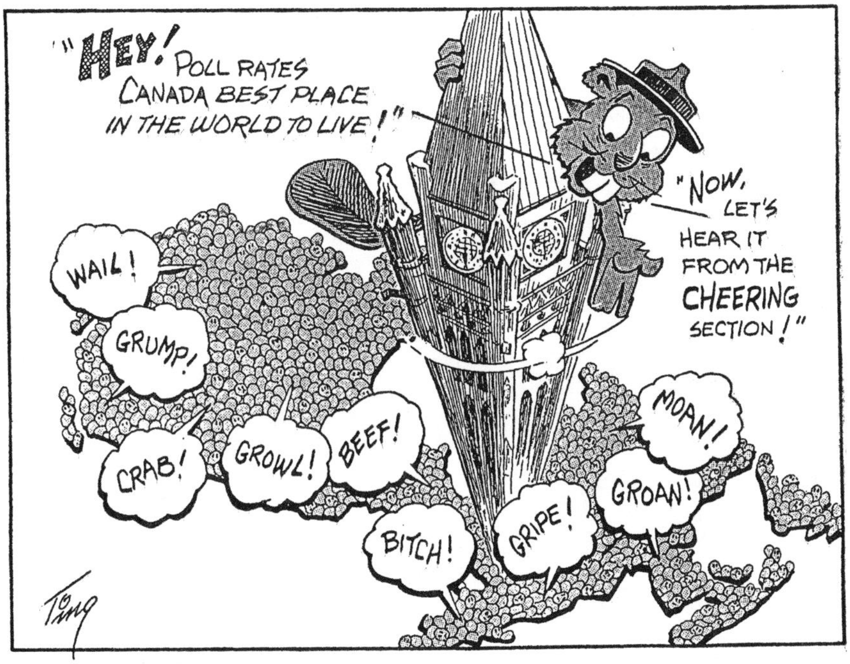
"HEY! POLL RATES CANADA BEST PLACE IN THE WORLD TO LIVE!"
"NOW, LET'S HEAR IT FROM THE CHEERING SECTION!"
WAIL!
GRUMP!
CRAB!
GROWL!
BEEF!
BITCH!
GRIPE!
GROAN!
MOAN!

MERLE R. TINGLEY
Courtesy Montreal Gazette

BILL HOGAN
Courtesy Times-Transcript (N. Bruns.)

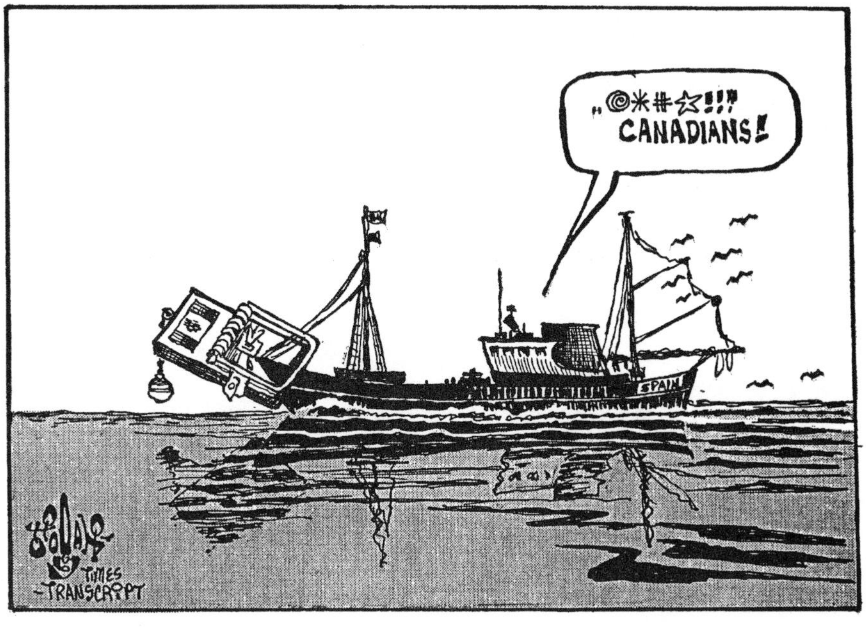
"@*#☆!!!"
CANADIANS!
SPAIN
TIMES -TRANSCRIPT

JIM MCCLOSKEY
Courtesy Staunton Daily News Leader

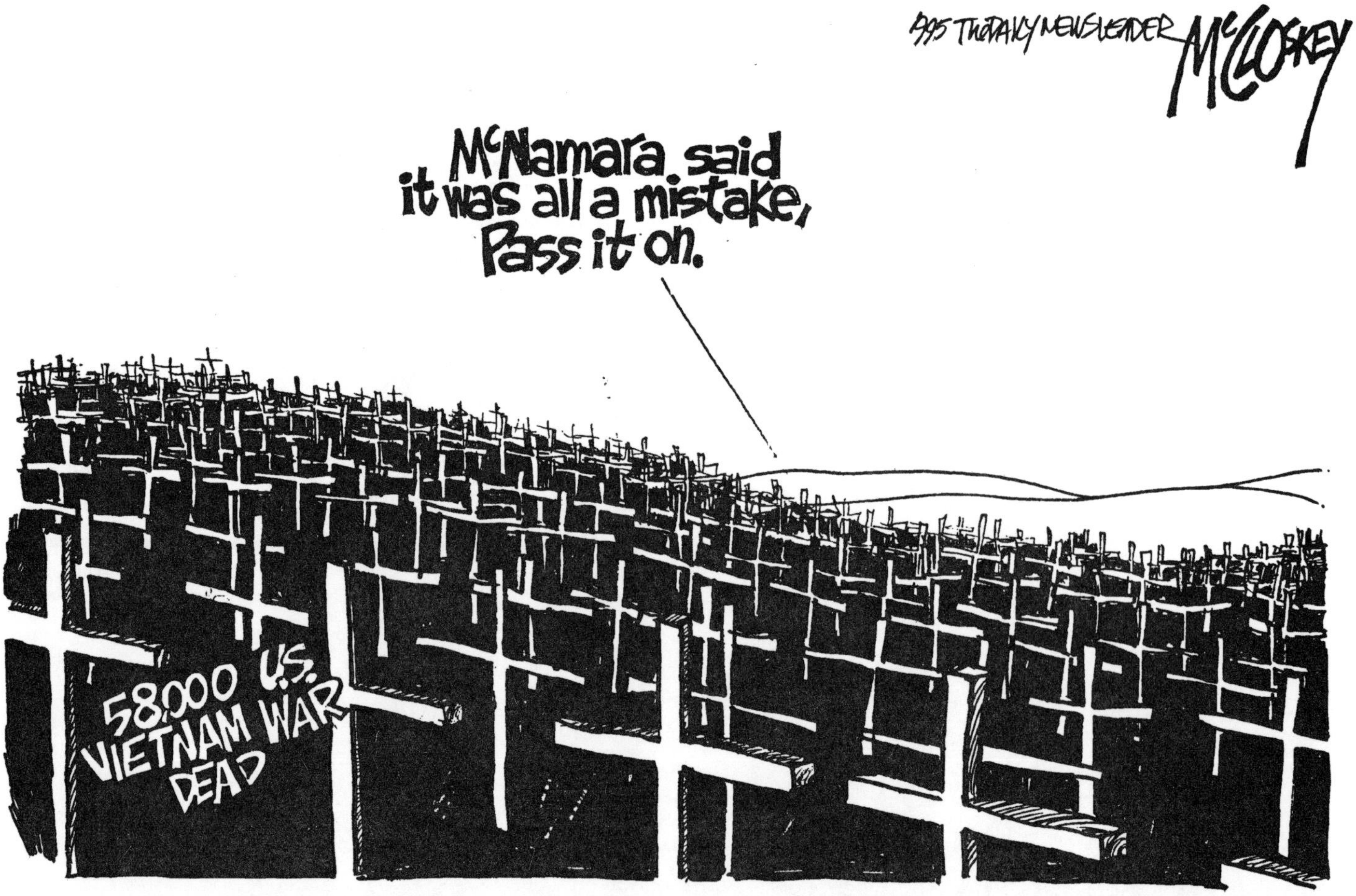
THE DAILY NEWS LEADER McCLOSKEY
McNamara said it was all a mistake, Pass it on.
58,000 U.S. VIETNAM WAR DEAD

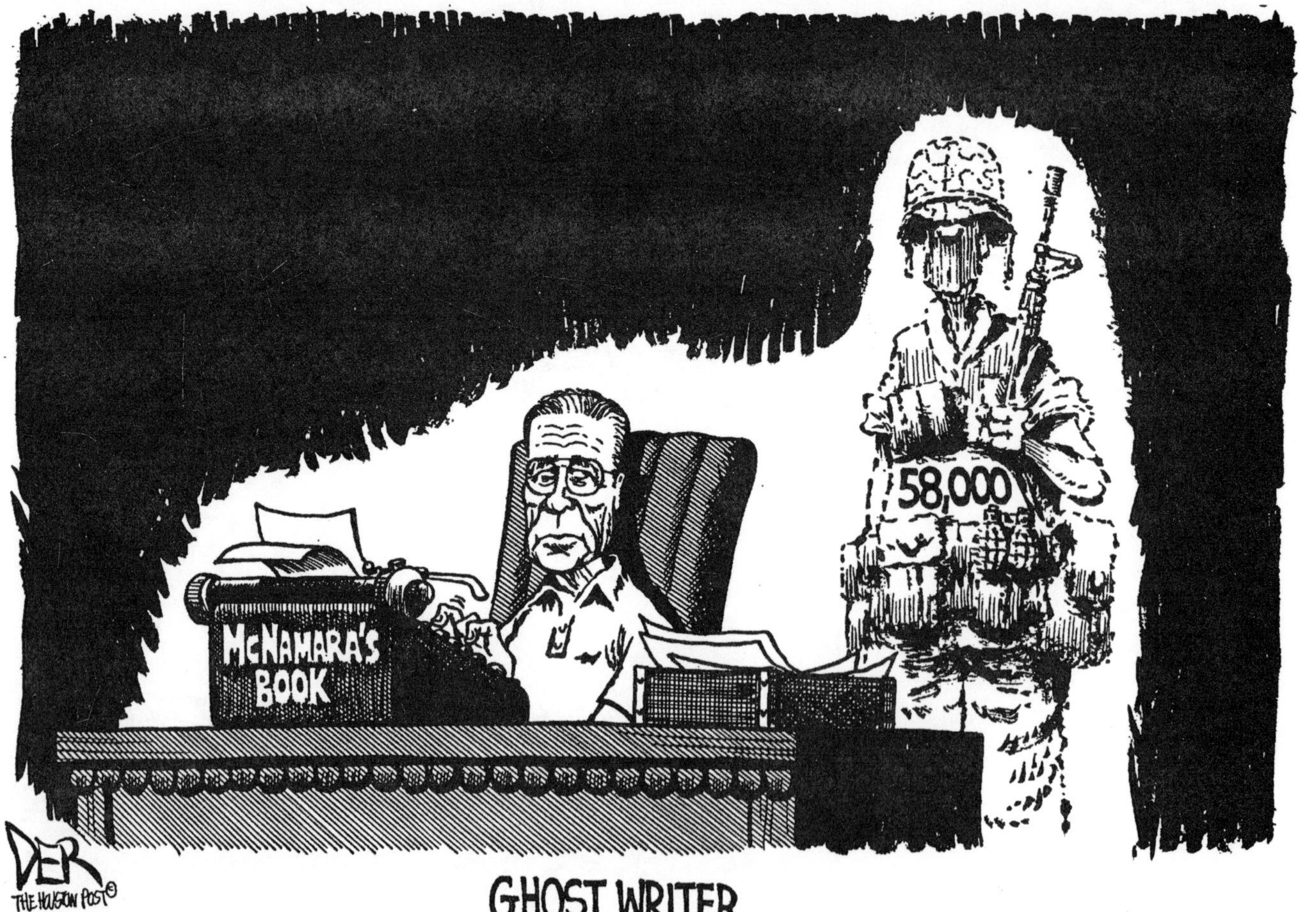
McNAMARA'S BOOK
58,000
DER
THE HOUSTON POST©

GHOST WRITER

LAMBERT DER
Courtesy Houston Post

...and Other Issues

Cartoonist Bill Watterson, creator of "Calvin and Hobbes," announced that he was retiring the popular comic strip featuring a six-year-old boy and his stuffed-tiger companion.

Celebrations marking the fiftieth anniversary of the end of World War II renewed controversy over using two atomic bombs on Japan to force a surrender. Veterans' organizations assailed President Clinton when he changed the designation of V-J Day, commemorating the victory over Japan, to simply End of the Pacific War. Robert S. McNamara, chief architect of American policy in the Vietnam War, declared that it had all been a mistake and he was sorry.

In a CBS television interview of Newt Gingrich's mother, Connie Chung asked her to "whisper in my ear" what the House speaker thought of Hillary Clinton. She did, using a word that rhymes with "witch," and it became front-page news. Shannon Faulkner, the first woman to win admission to The Citadel, an all-male military academy, quit after one week.

Israeli prime minister Yitzhak Rabin was assassinated in 1995. Other notables who died during the year included former U.S. chief justice Warren Burger, Mickey Mantle, Jonas Salk, Jerry Garcia of the rock group the Grateful Dead, Lana Turner, Ginger Rogers, and Dean Martin.

Calvin, Hobbes
to end Dec. 31
KANSAS CITY, Mo. — Calvin and Hobbes, the terrible tyke and his sidekick tiger, will be retired from the funny pages on Dec. 31.

WE DECIDED TO RETIRE WHILE THERE'S STILL SOCIAL SECURITY.

WITH APOLOGIES AND REGRETS DANIEL
©THE KNOXVILLE NEWS-SENTINEL

CHARLES DANIEL
Courtesy Knoxville News-Sentinel

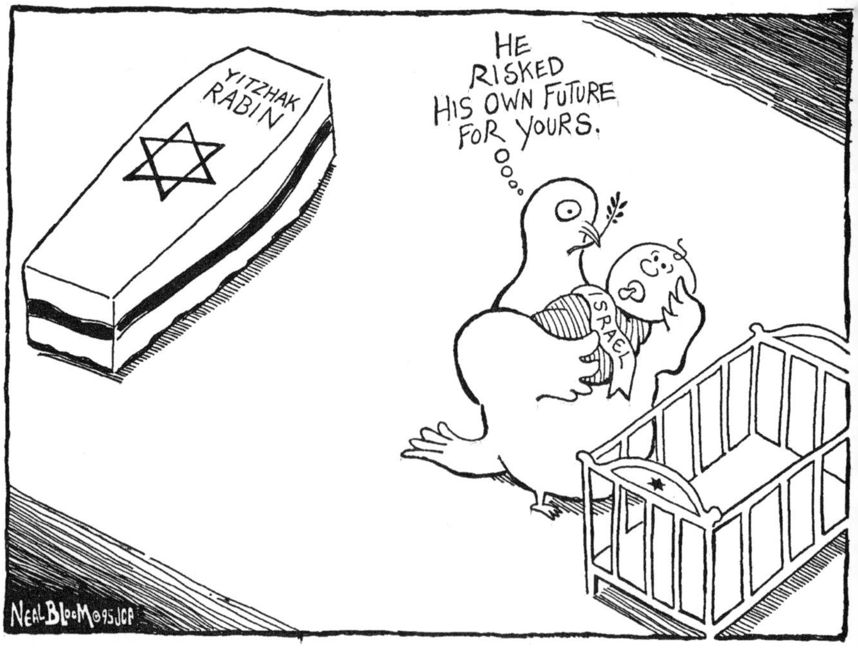
YITZHAK RABIN
HE RISKED HIS OWN FUTURE FOR YOURS.
ISRAEL
NEAL BLOOM ©95 JCP

NEAL BLOOM
Courtesy Jewish Cartoon Productions

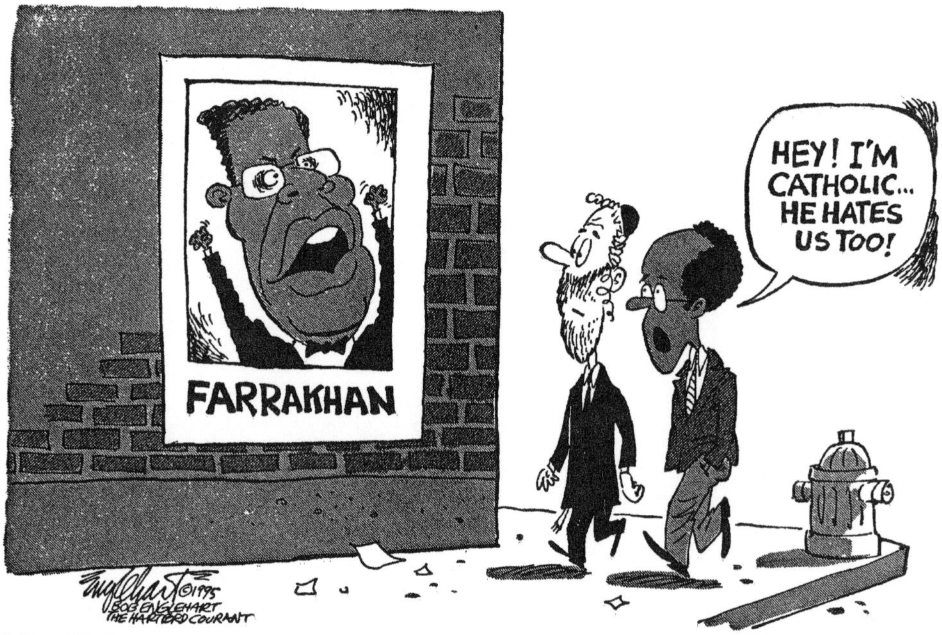
FARRAKHAN
HEY! I'M CATHOLIC... HE HATES US TOO!
©1995 BOB ENGLEHART THE HARTFORD COURANT

BOB ENGLEHART
Courtesy Hartford Courant

ROBERT ARIAIL
Courtesy The State (S.C.)

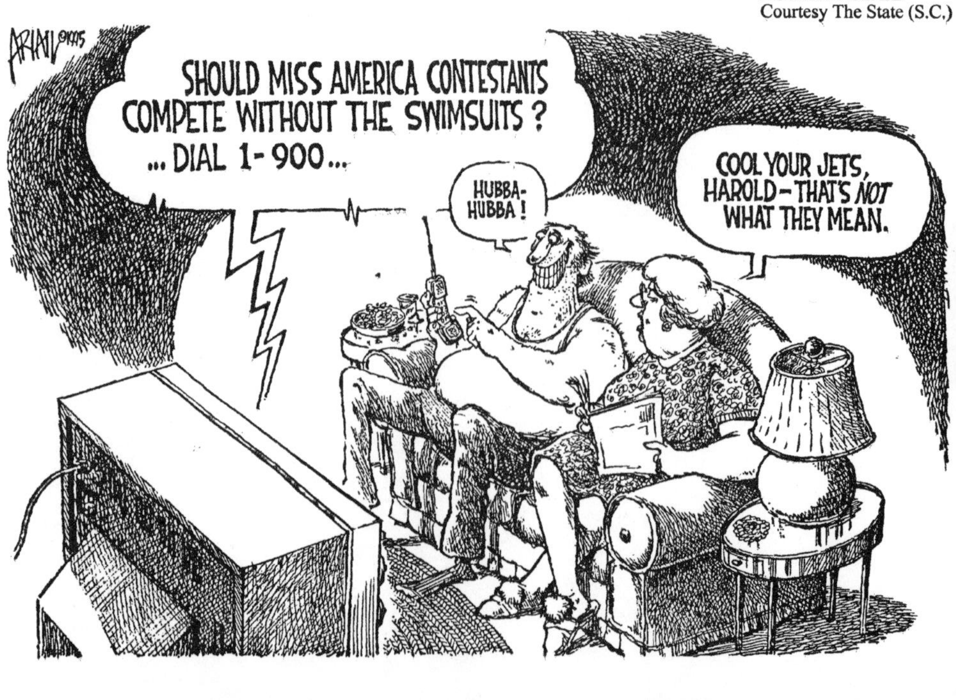
ARIAIL ©1995
SHOULD MISS AMERICA CONTESTANTS COMPETE WITHOUT THE SWIMSUITS? ... DIAL 1-900...
HUBBA-HUBBA!
COOL YOUR JETS, HAROLD—THAT'S NOT WHAT THEY MEAN.

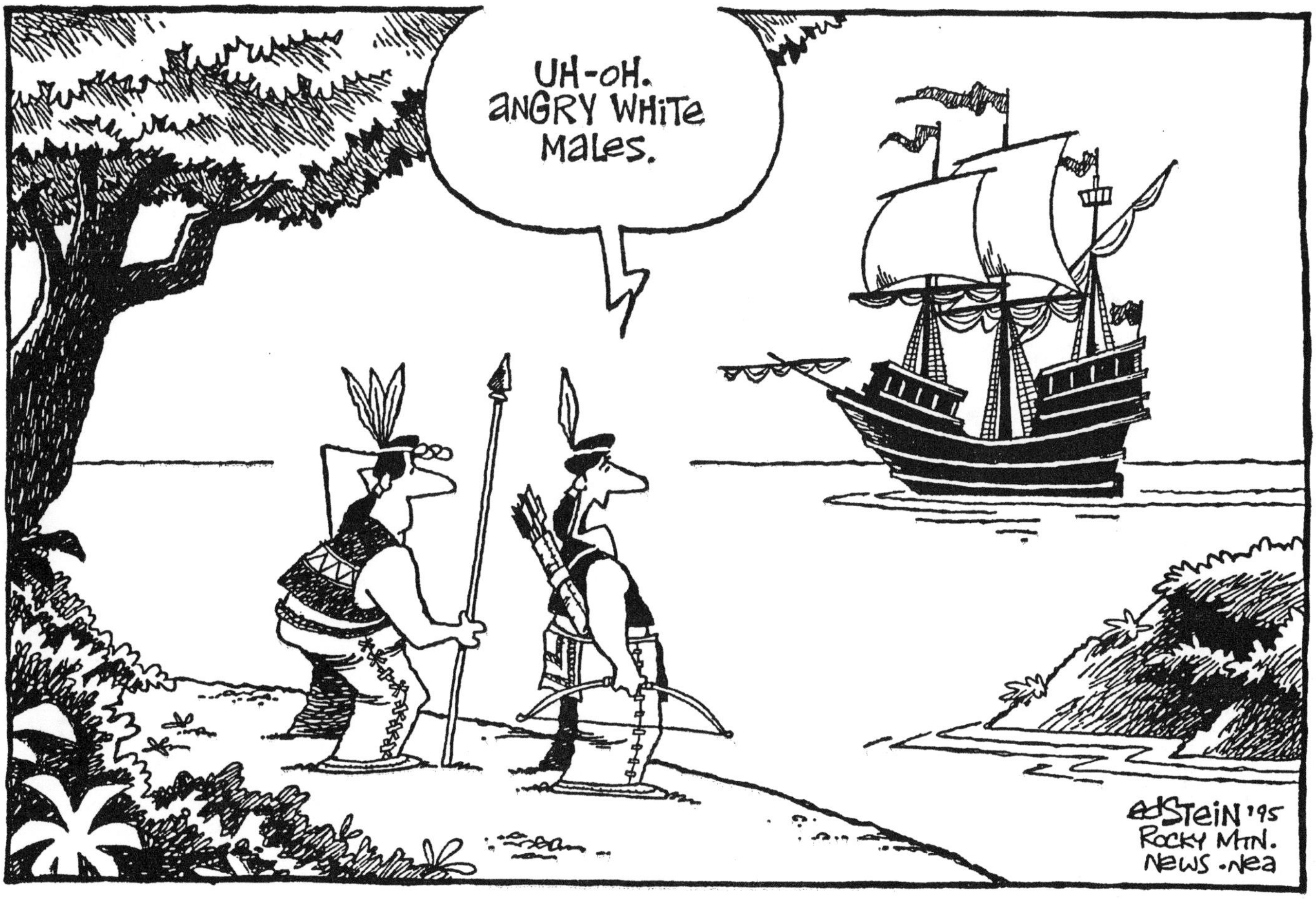
UH-OH.
ANGRY WHITE
MALES.
EDSTEIN '95
ROCKY MTN.
NEWS • NEA

ED STEIN
Courtesy Rocky Mountain News and NEA

LAMBERT DER
Courtesy Houston Post

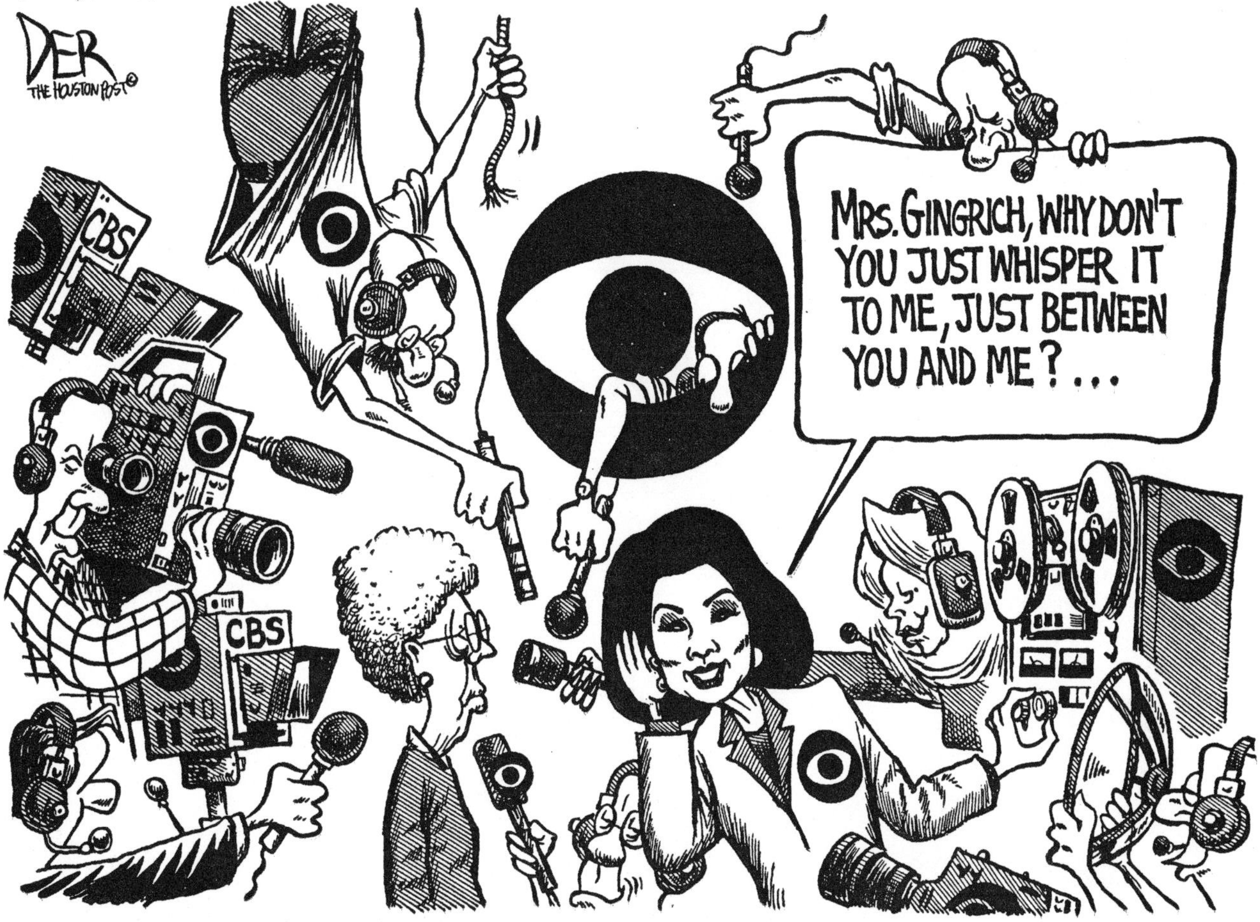
DER
THE HOUSTON POST ©
CBS
MRS. GINGRICH, WHY DON'T YOU JUST WHISPER IT TO ME, JUST BETWEEN YOU AND ME? ...
CBS

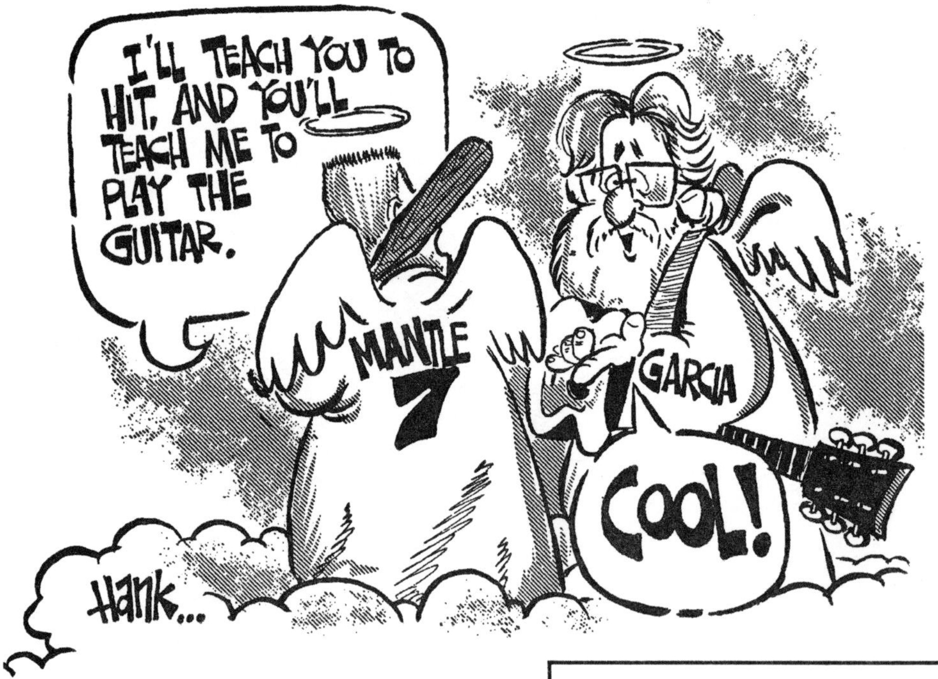
I'LL TEACH YOU TO HIT, AND YOU'LL TEACH ME TO PLAY THE GUITAR.
MANTLE
7
GARCIA
COOL!
Hank...

HANK MCCLURE
Courtesy Lawton Constitution

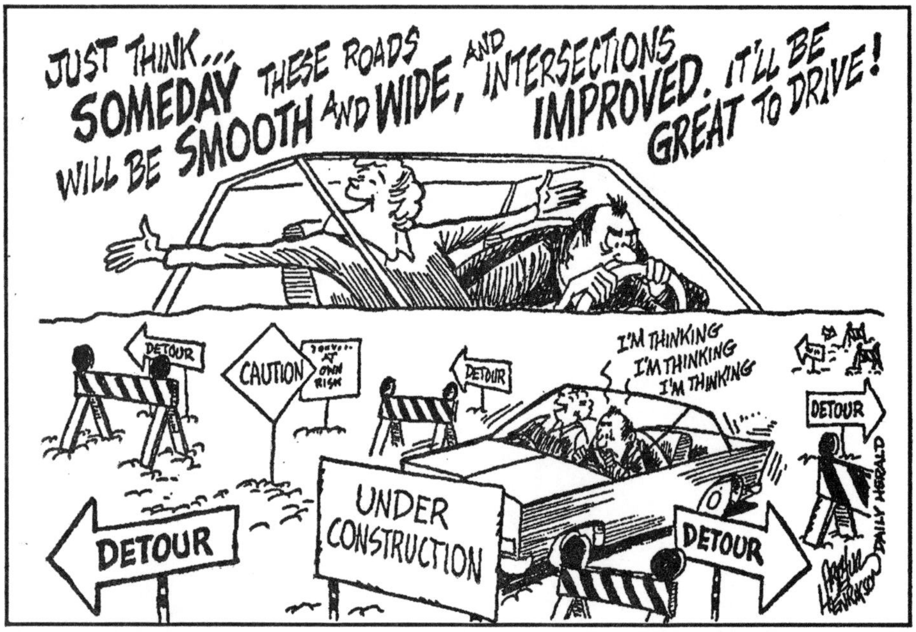
JUST THINK... SOMEDAY THESE ROADS WILL BE SMOOTH AND WIDE, AND INTERSECTIONS IMPROVED. IT'LL BE GREAT TO DRIVE!
DETOUR
CAUTION
DETOUR
I'M THINKING
I'M THINKING
I'M THINKING
DETOUR
UNDER CONSTRUCTION
DETOUR
DETOUR
DAILY HERALD

ART HENRIKSON
Courtesy Daily Herald (Ill.)

JOHN MARSHALL
Courtesy Binghampton Press and Sun-Bulletin

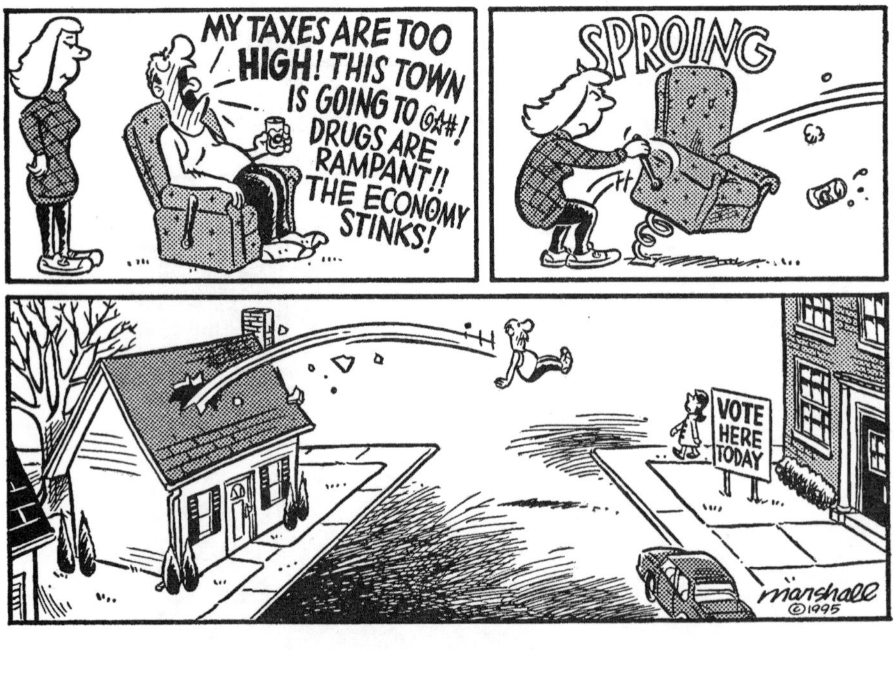
MY TAXES ARE TOO HIGH! THIS TOWN IS GOING TO @#! DRUGS ARE RAMPANT!! THE ECONOMY STINKS!
SPROING
VOTE HERE TODAY
marshall ©1995

S. C. RAWLS
Courtesy Rockdale Citizen

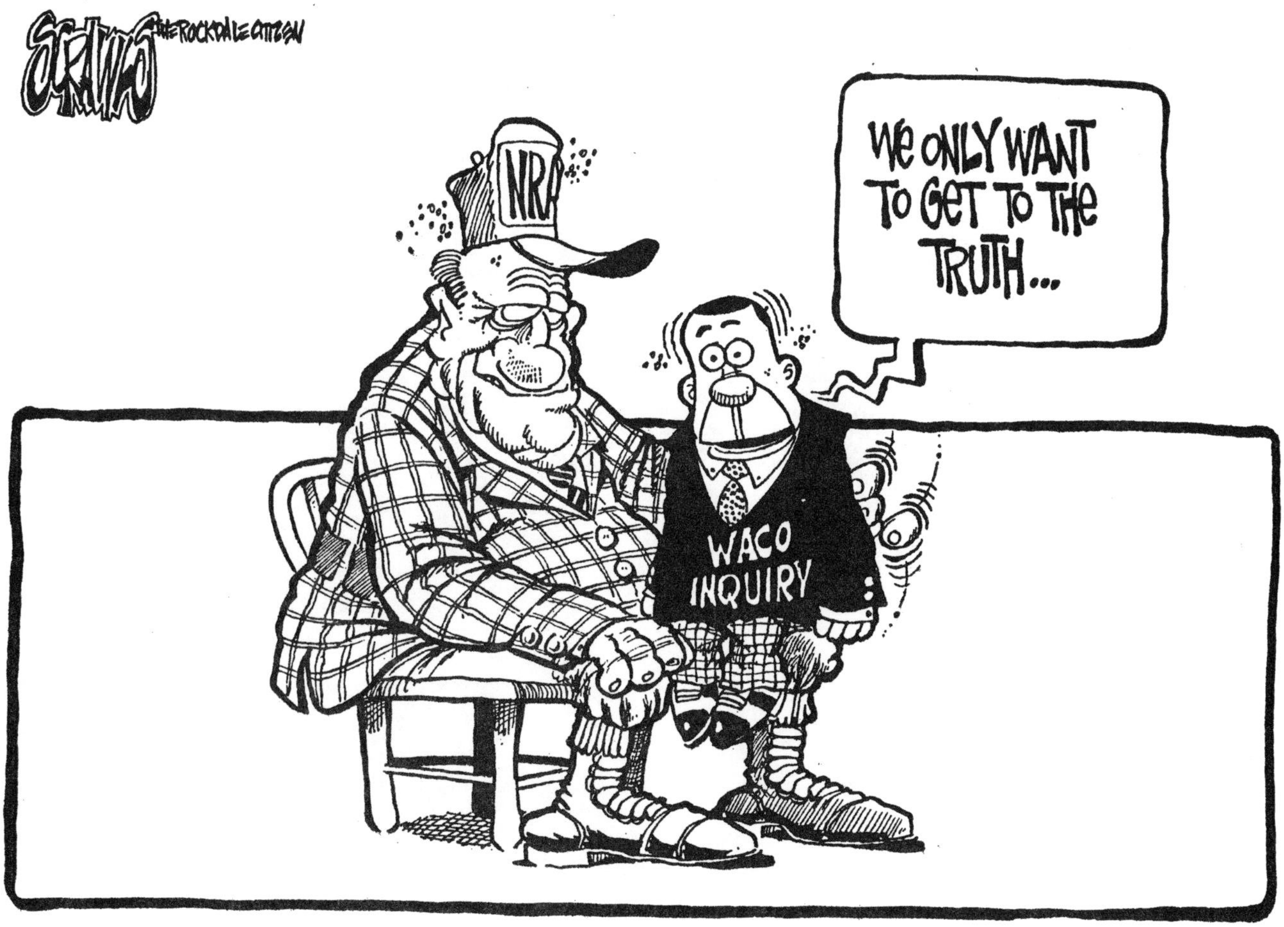
SCRAWLS THE ROCKDALE CITIZEN
WE ONLY WANT TO GET TO THE TRUTH...
NRA
WACO INQUIRY

KEN CATALINO
Courtesy Voice of the TImes

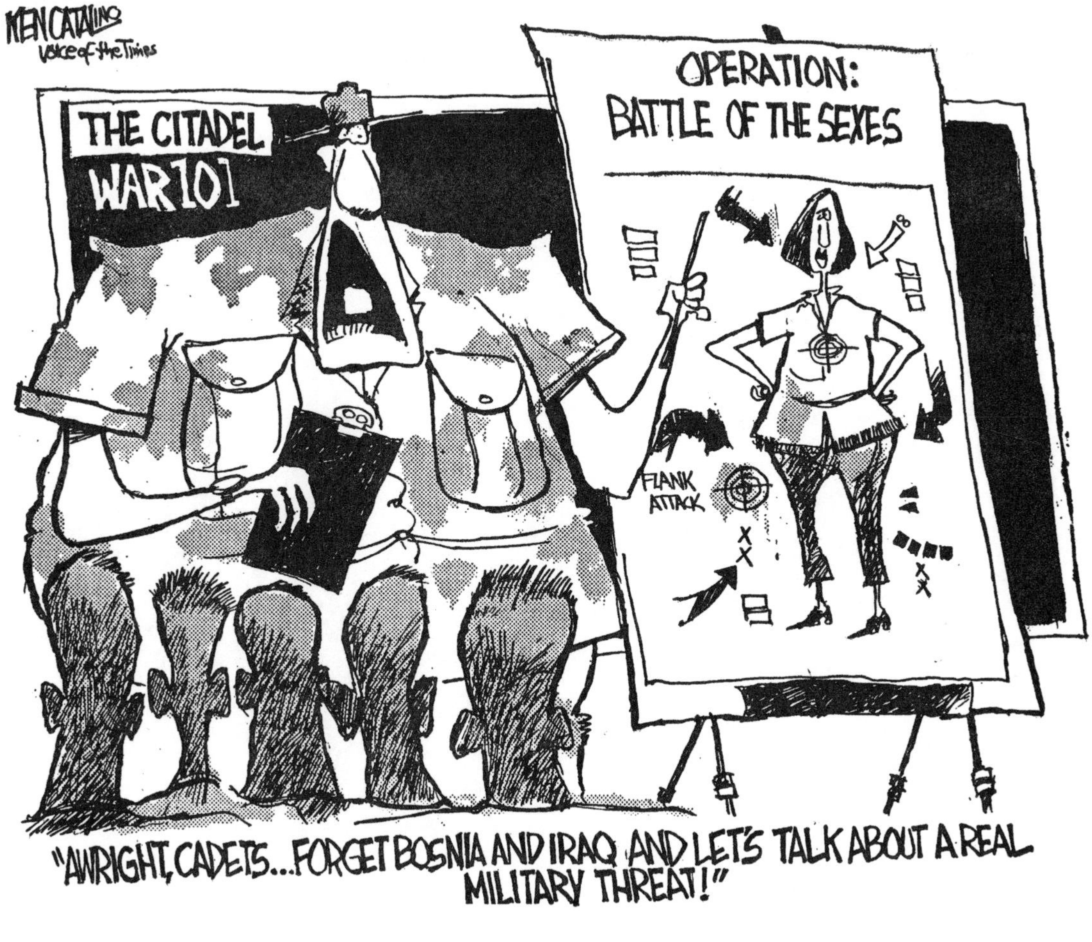
KEN CATALINO Voice of the Times
THE CITADEL
WAR 101
OPERATION: BATTLE OF THE SEXES
FLANK ATTACK
"AWRIGHT, CADETS...FORGET BOSNIA AND IRAQ AND LET'S TALK ABOUT A REAL MILITARY THREAT!"

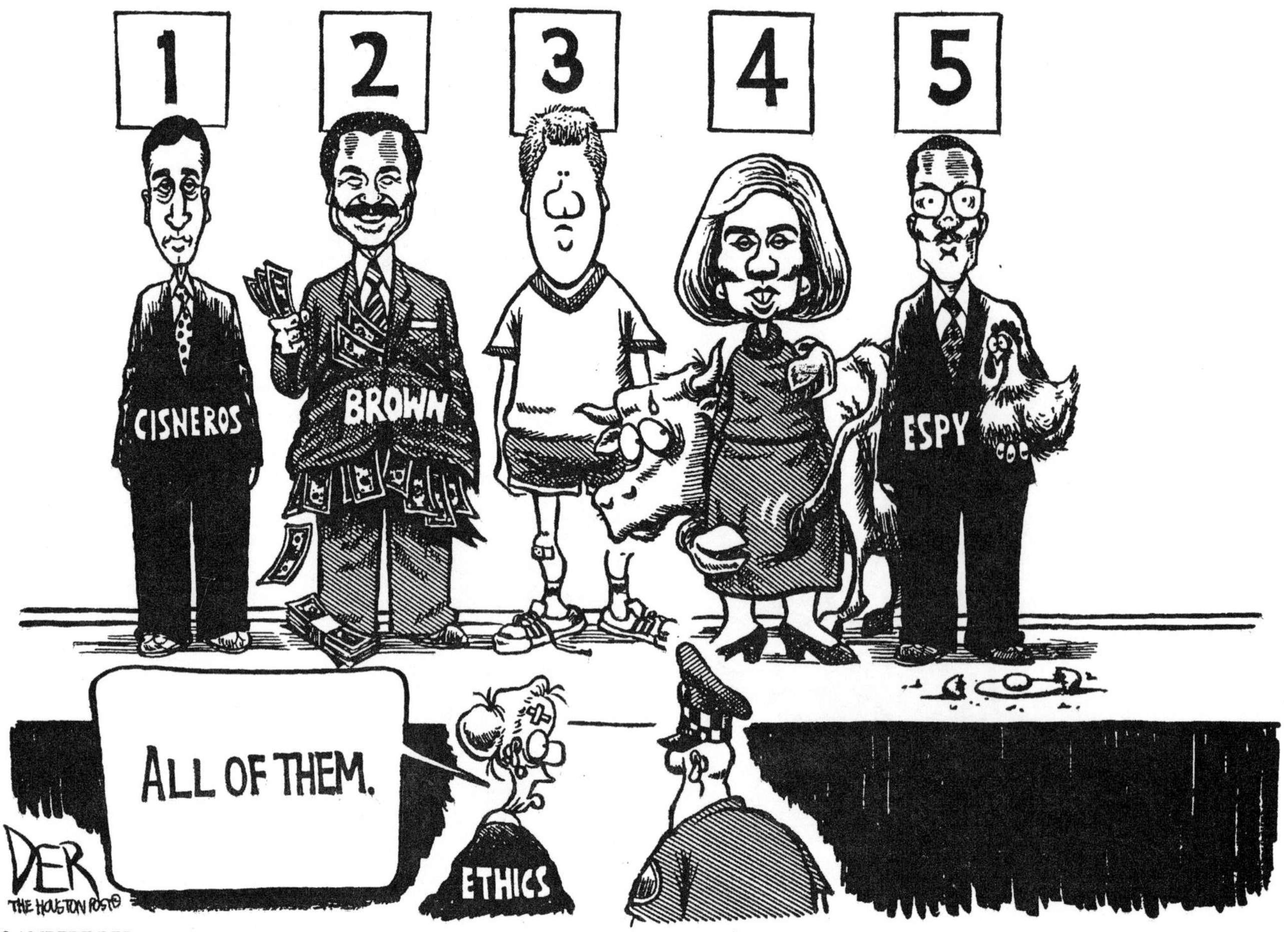
1
2
3
4
5
CISNEROS
BROWN
ESPY
ALL OF THEM.
ETHICS
DER
THE HOUSTON POST

LAMBERT DER
Courtesy Houston Post

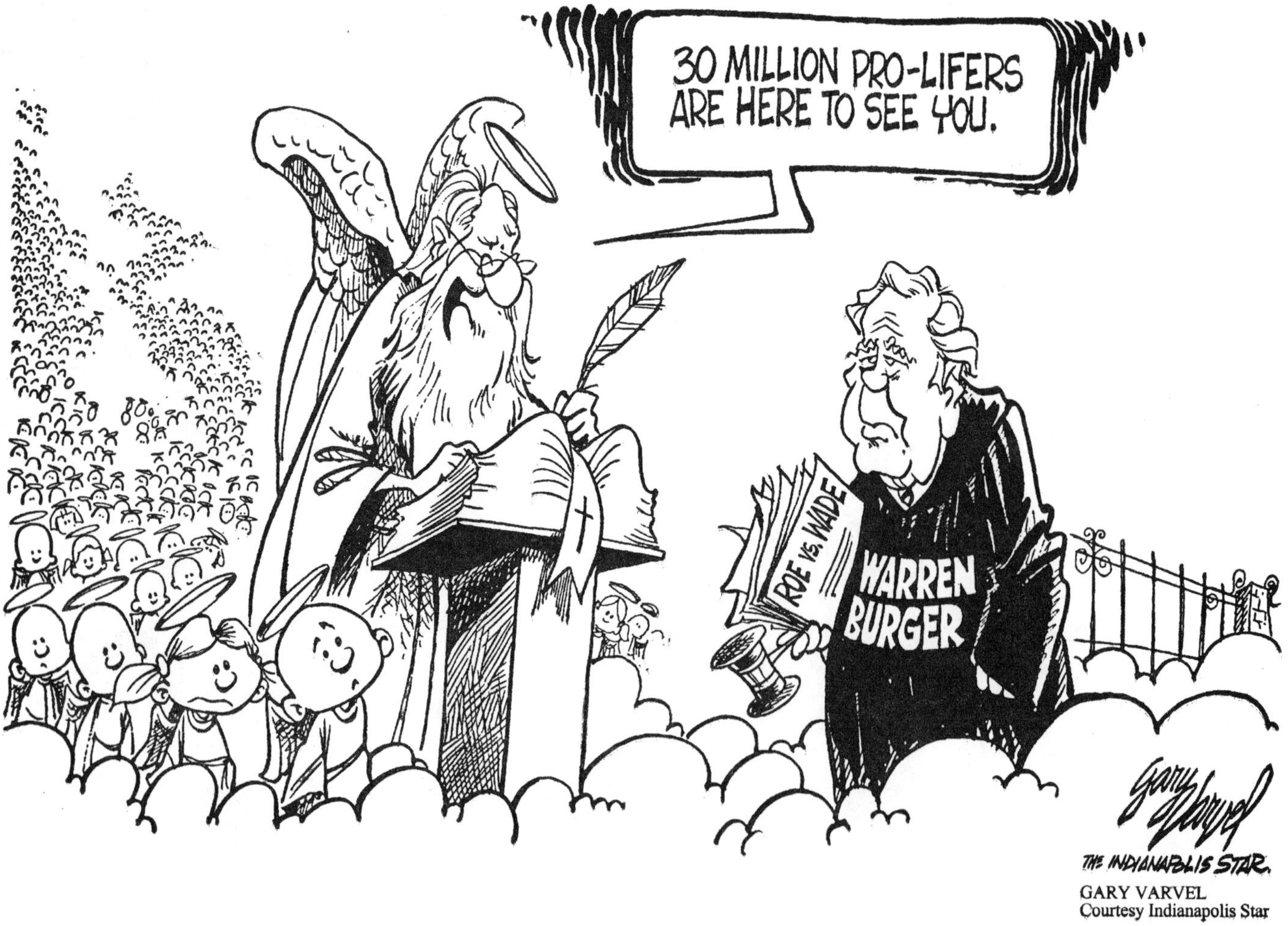
30 MILLION PRO-LIFERS ARE HERE TO SEE YOU.
ROE VS. WADE
WARREN BURGER
THE INDIANAPOLIS STAR

GARY VARVEL
Courtesy Indianapolis Star

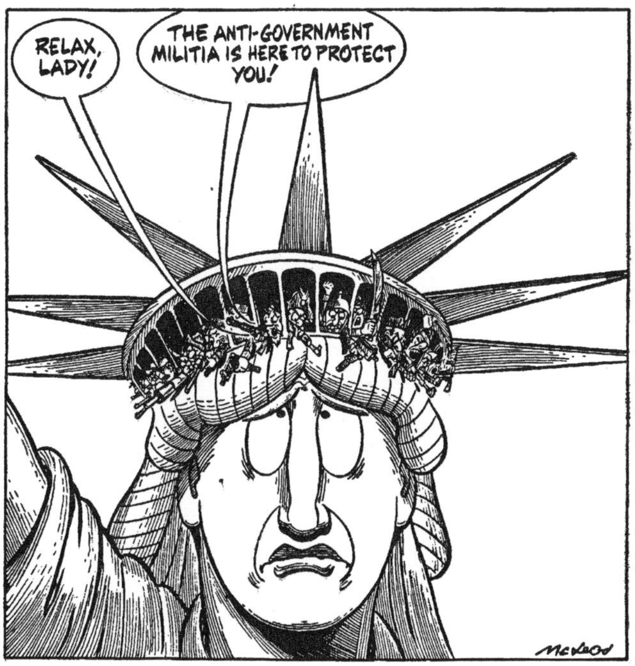
RELAX, LADY!
THE ANTI-GOVERNMENT MILITIA IS HERE TO PROTECT YOU!

JACK MCLEOD
Courtesy Army Times

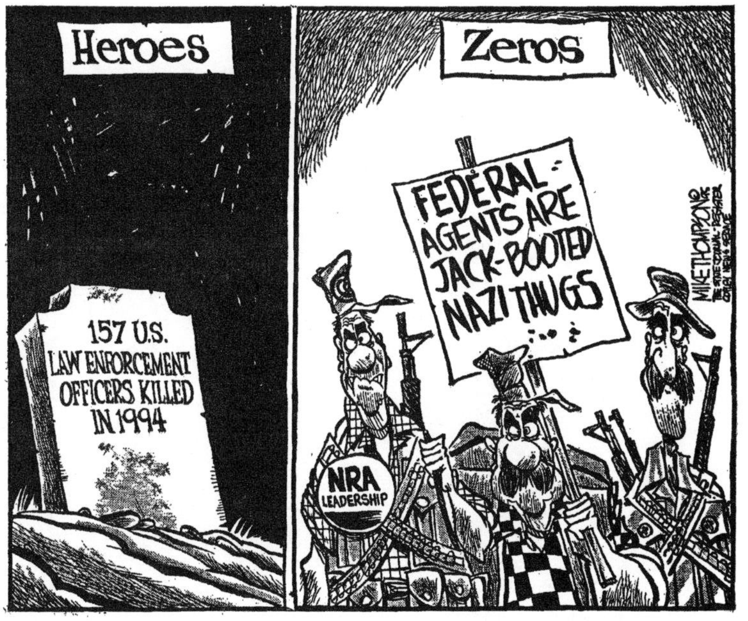
Heroes
Zeros
157 U.S. LAW ENFORCEMENT OFFICERS KILLED IN 1994
FEDERAL AGENTS ARE JACK-BOOTED NAZI THUGS
NRA LEADERSHIP

MIKE THOMPSON
Courtesy State Journal-Register (Ill.)

MIKE SMITH
Courtesy Las Vegas Sun

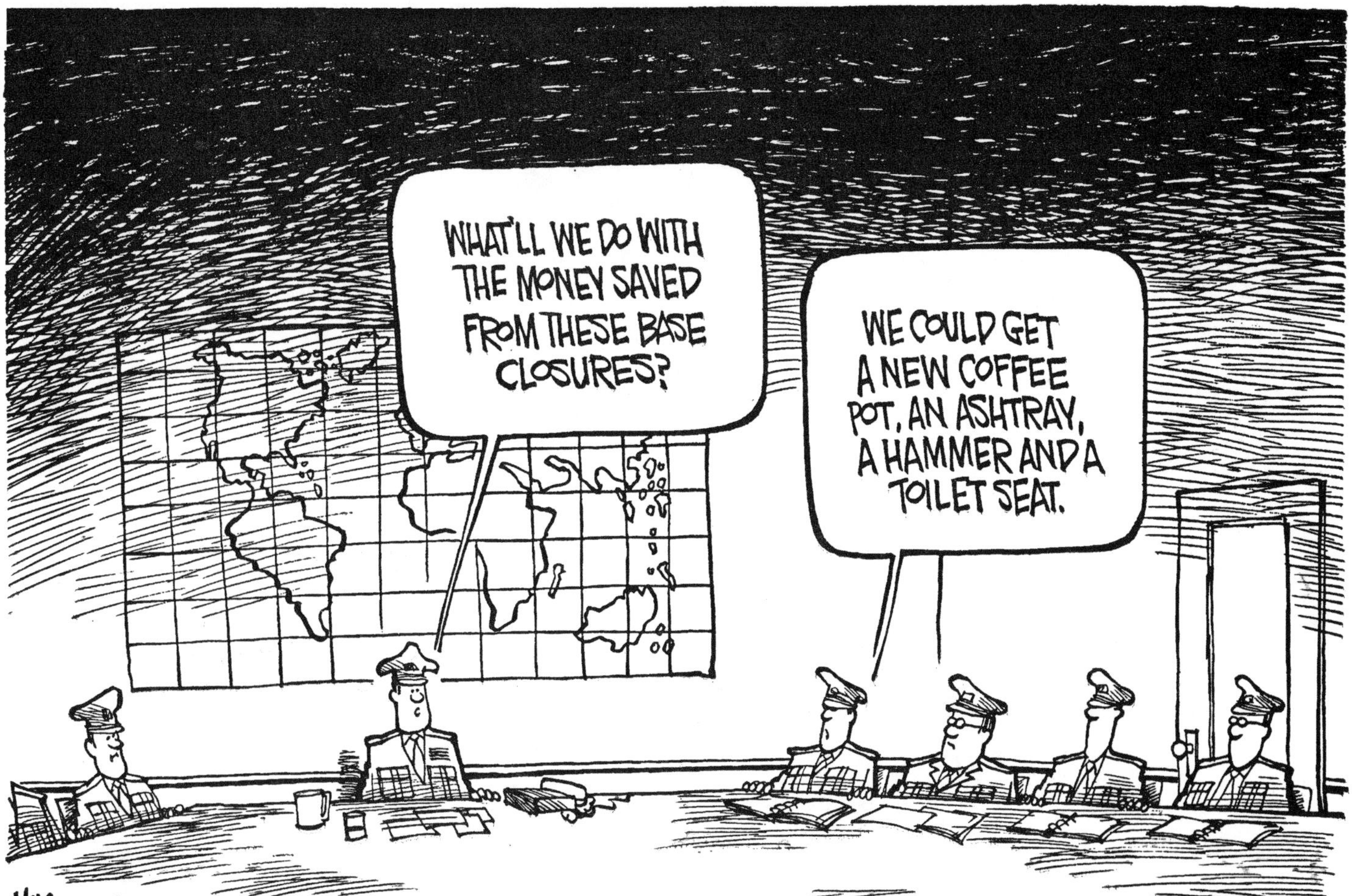
WHAT'LL WE DO WITH THE MONEY SAVED FROM THESE BASE CLOSURES?
WE COULD GET A NEW COFFEE POT, AN ASHTRAY, A HAMMER AND A TOILET SEAT.
MIKE SMITH

KIRK WALTERS
Courtesy Toledo Blade

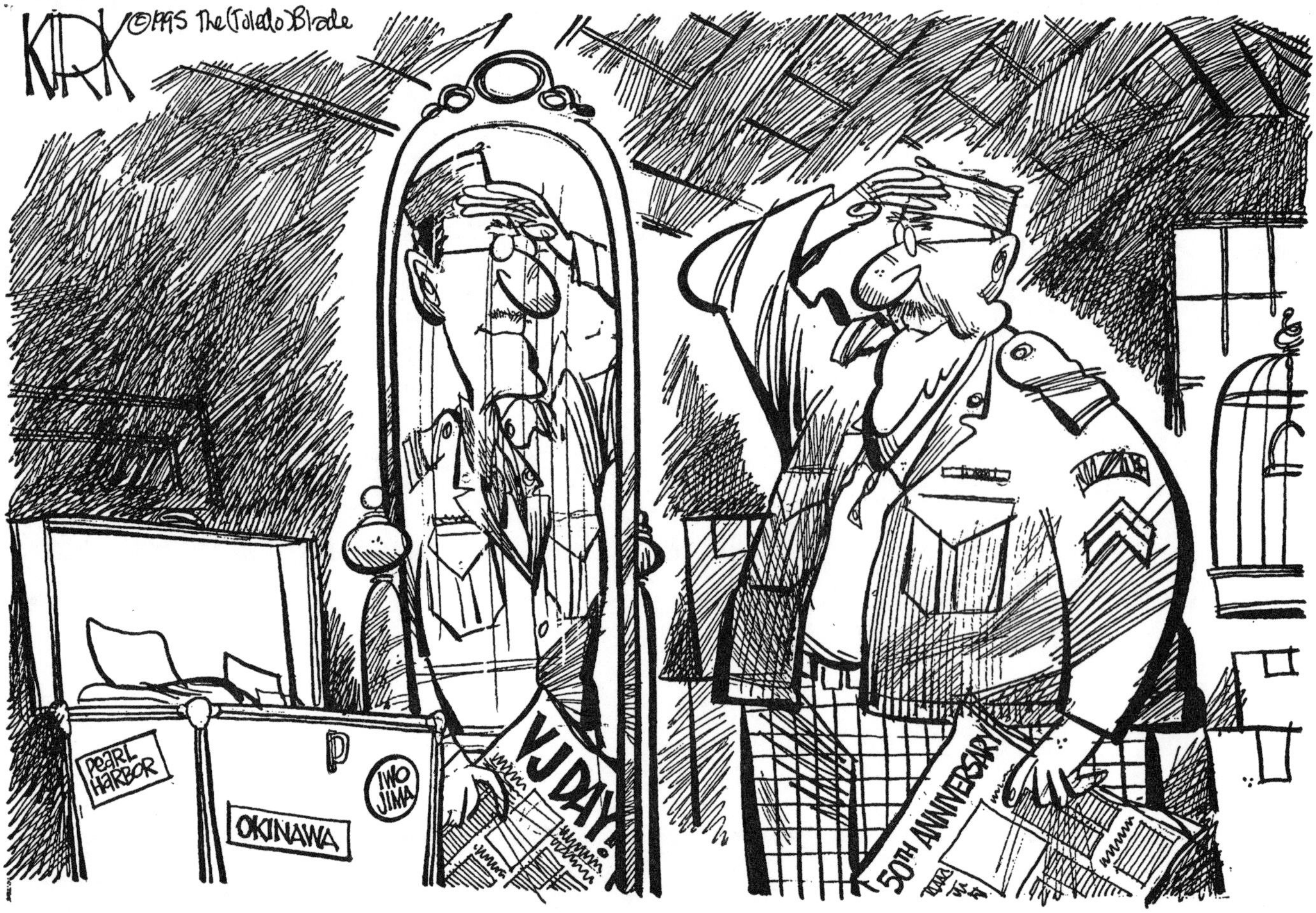
KIRK ©1995 The Toledo Blade
PEARL HARBOR
OKINAWA
IWO JIMA
VJ DAY!
50TH ANNIVERSARY

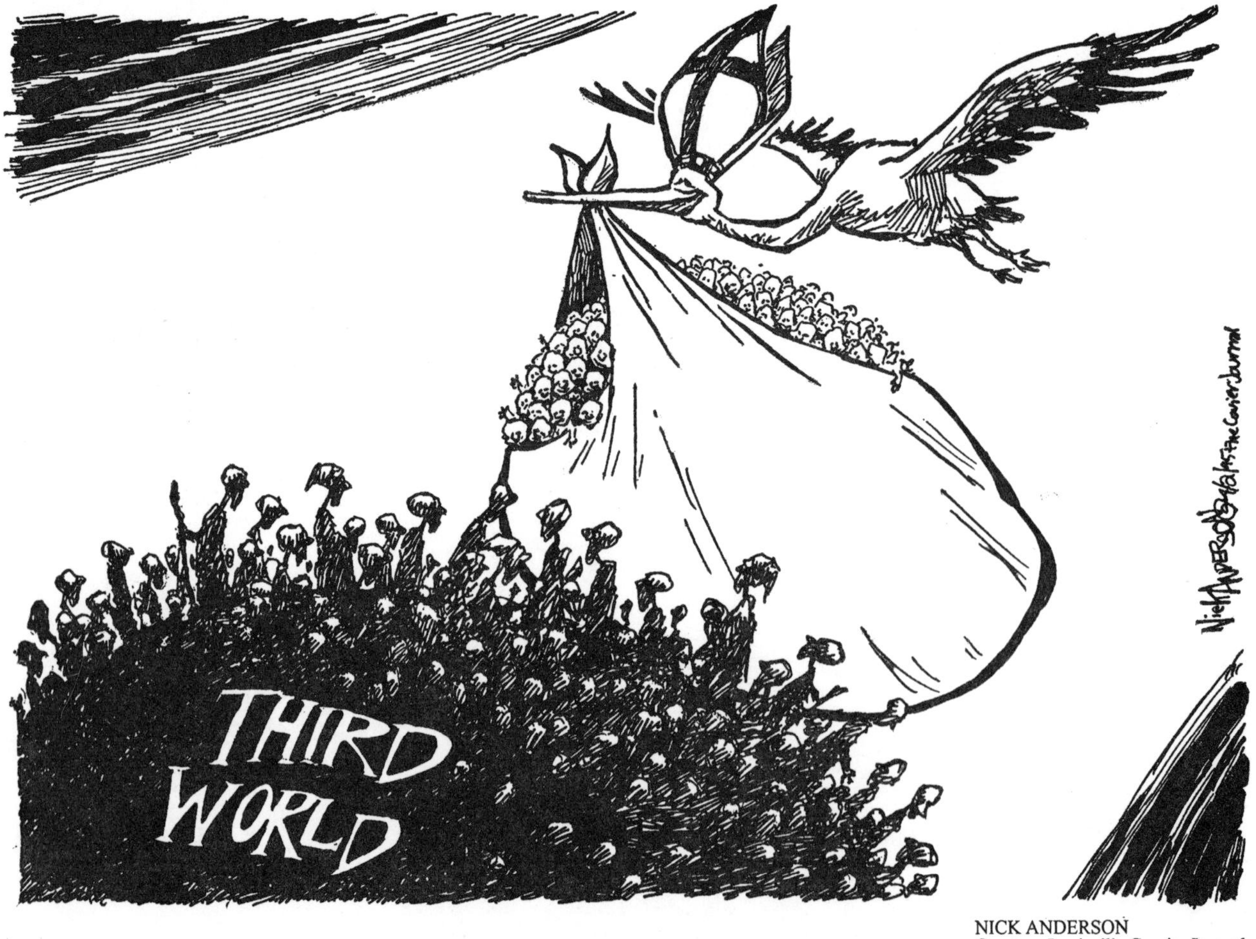
THIRD WORLD

NICK ANDERSON
Courtesy Louisville Courier Journal

JEFF KOTERBA
Courtesy Omaha World-Herald

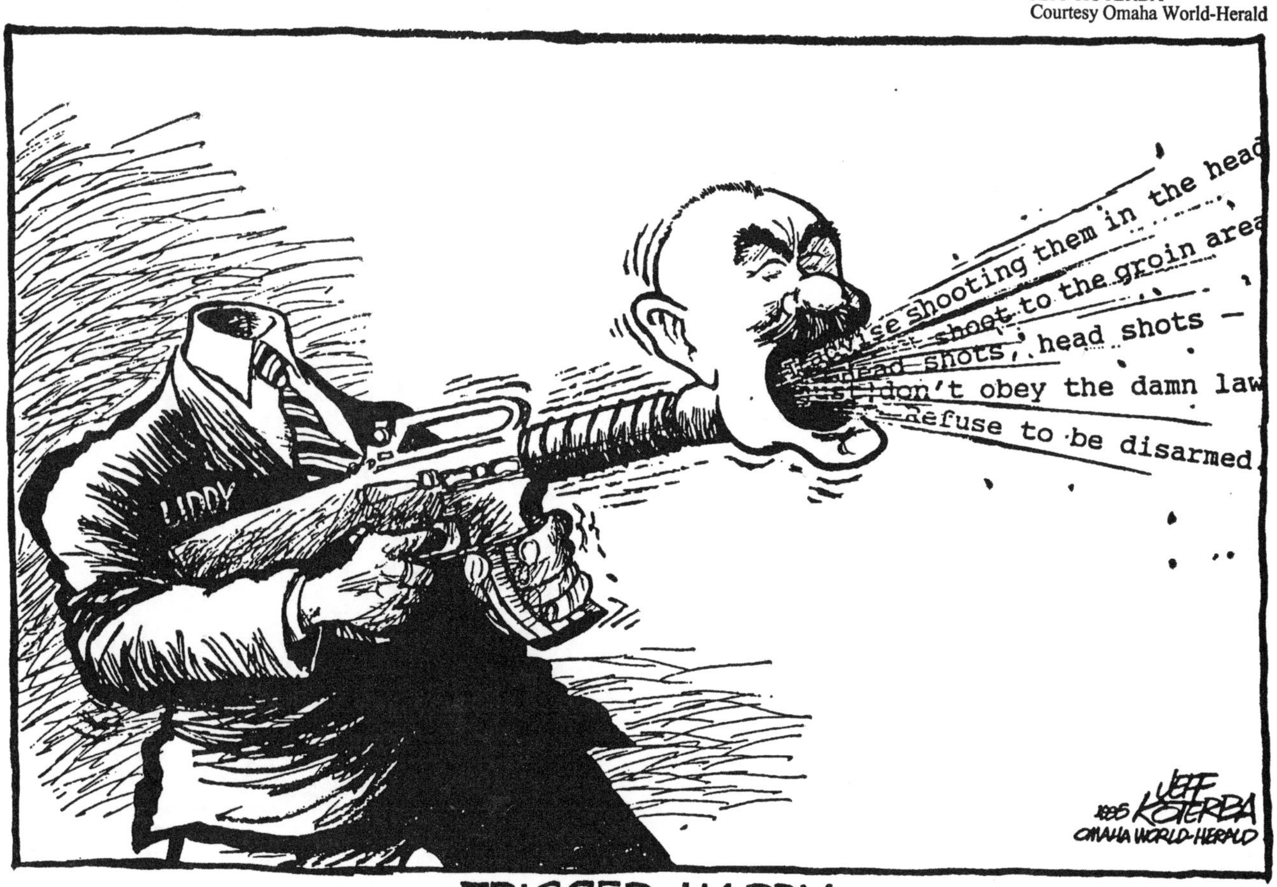
shooting them in the hea
shoot to the groin are
head shots, head shots –
don't obey the damn law
Refuse to be disarmed
LIDDY
JEFF KOTERBA 1995
OMAHA WORLD-HERALD

TRIGGER HAPPY

REX BABIN
Courtesy Albany Times Union

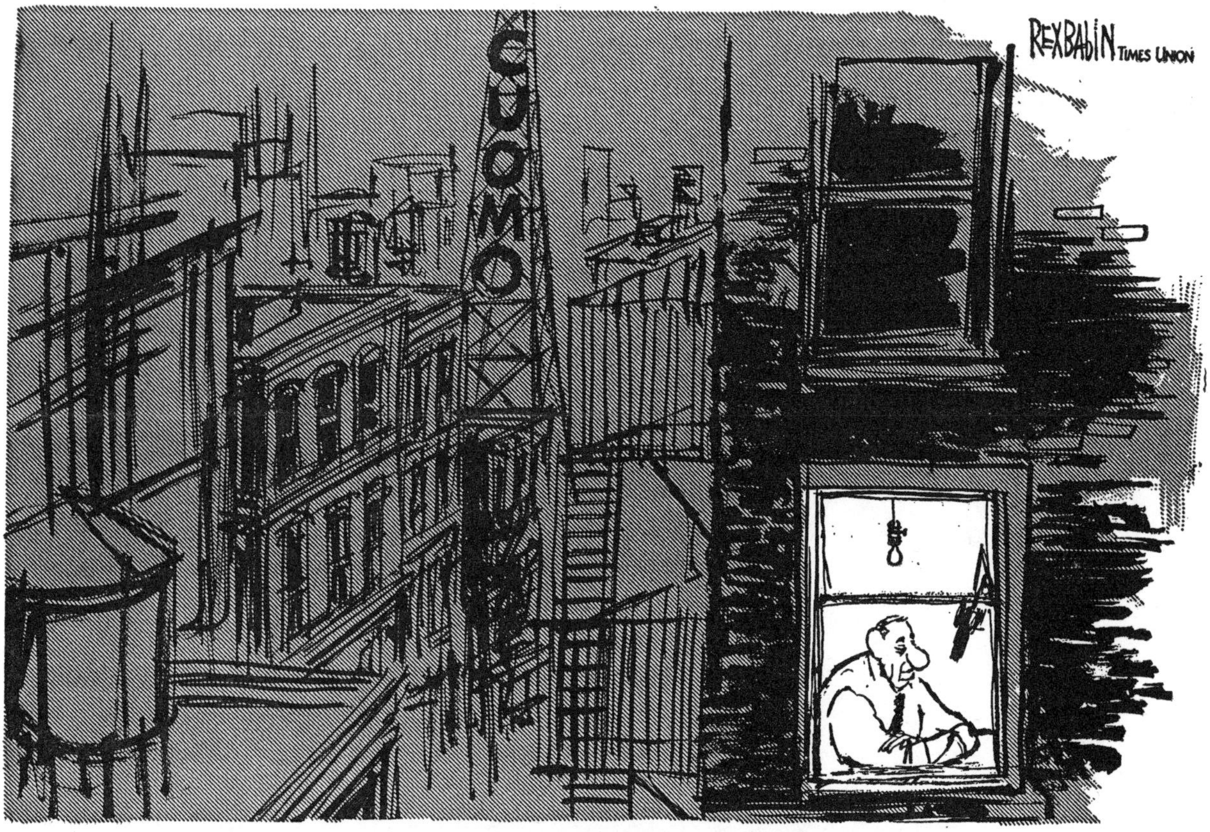
CUOMO
REXBABIN TIMES UNION

"THIS IS THE VOICE OF LIBERAL TALK RADIO SAYING, WE'VE GOT A LOT OF LINES OPEN... C'MON, I KNOW YOU'RE OUT THERE SOMEWHERE..."

NEIL GRAHAME
Courtesy Spencer Newspapers

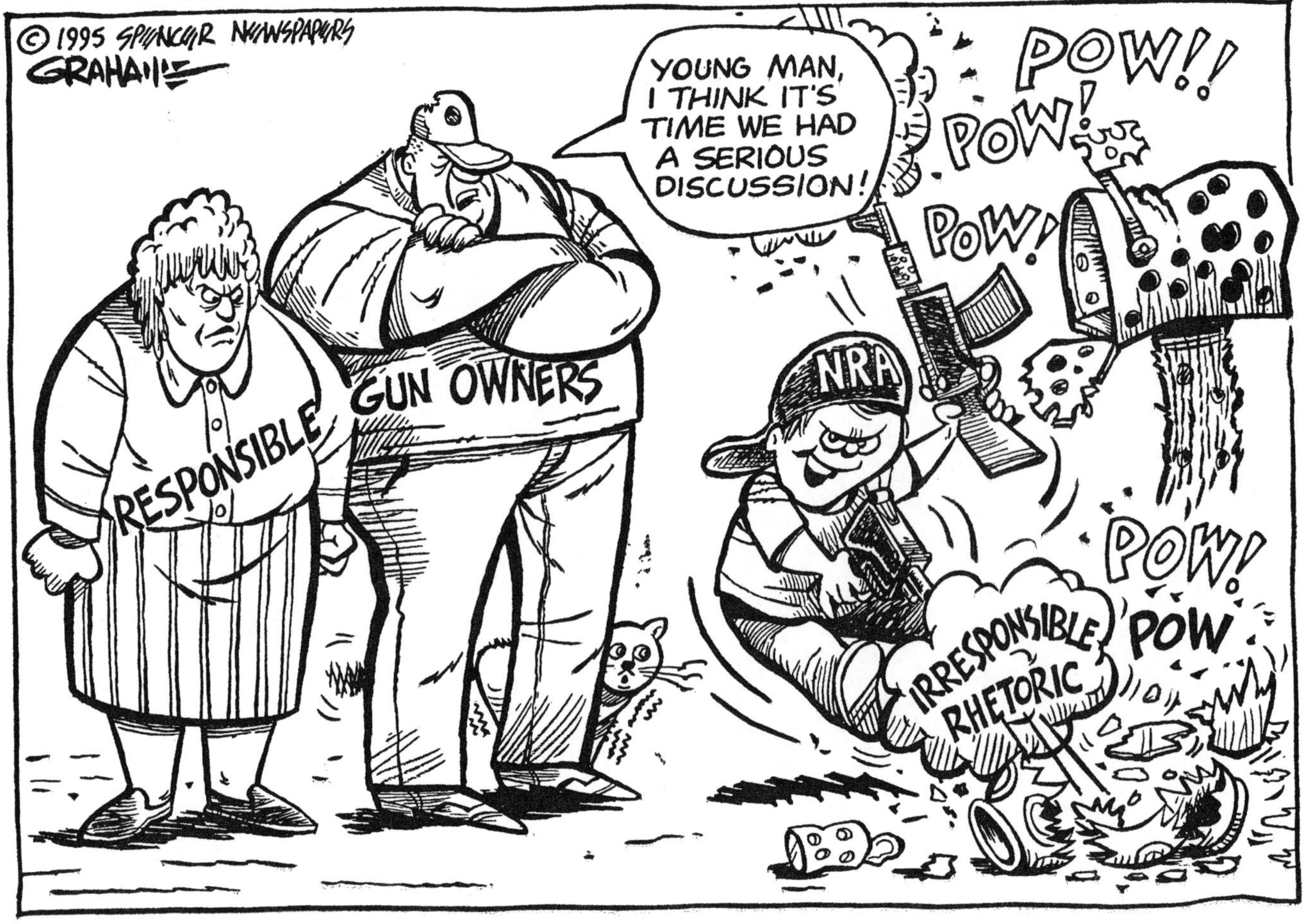

© 1995 SPENCER NEWSPAPERS
GRAHAME
YOUNG MAN, I THINK IT'S TIME WE HAD A SERIOUS DISCUSSION!
POW!!
POW!
POW!
POW!
POW
RESPONSIBLE
GUN OWNERS
NRA
IRRESPONSIBLE RHETORIC

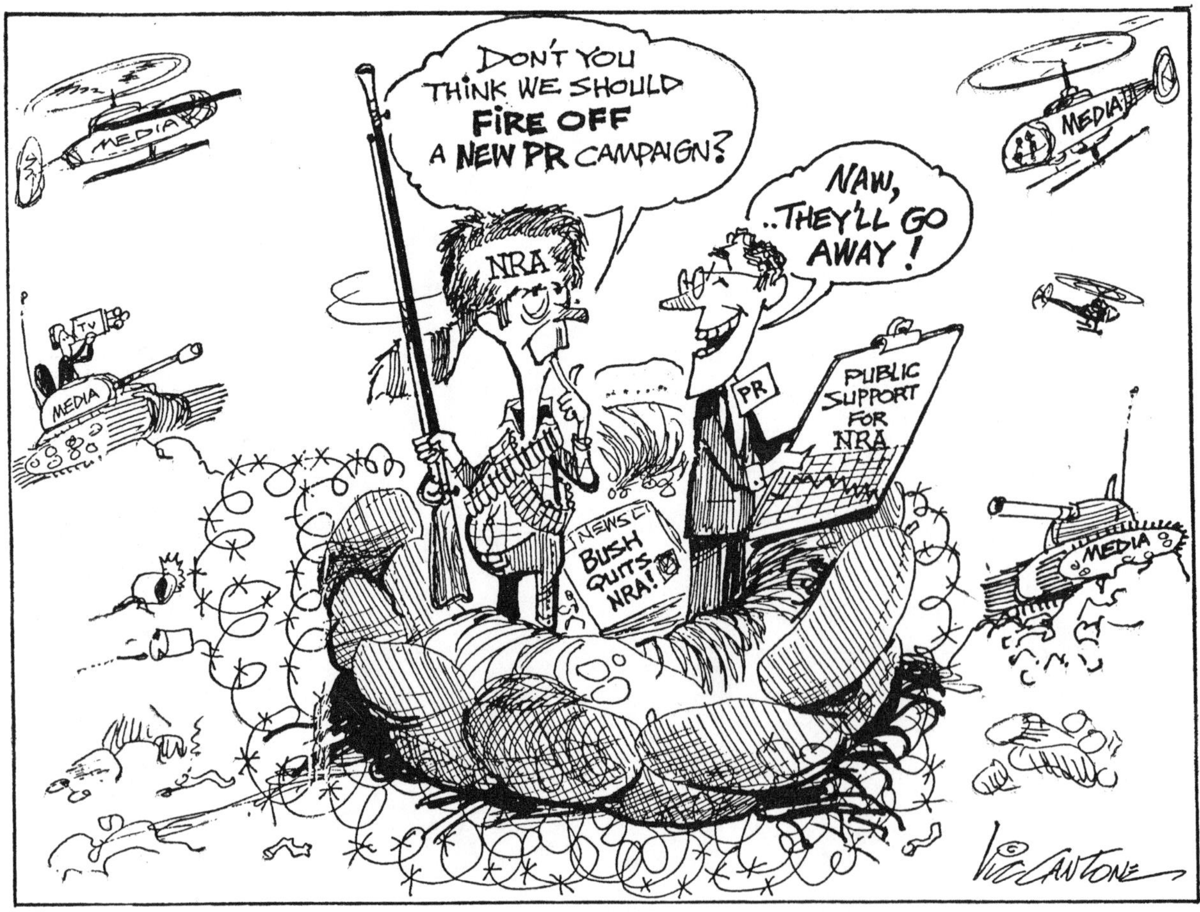

DON'T YOU THINK WE SHOULD FIRE OFF A NEW PR CAMPAIGN?
NAW, ..THEY'LL GO AWAY!
MEDIA
MEDIA
TV
MEDIA
MEDIA
NRA
PR
PUBLIC SUPPORT FOR NRA
NEWS
BUSH QUITS NRA!
VIC CANTONE

VIC CANTONE
Courtesy King Features/North American Syndicate

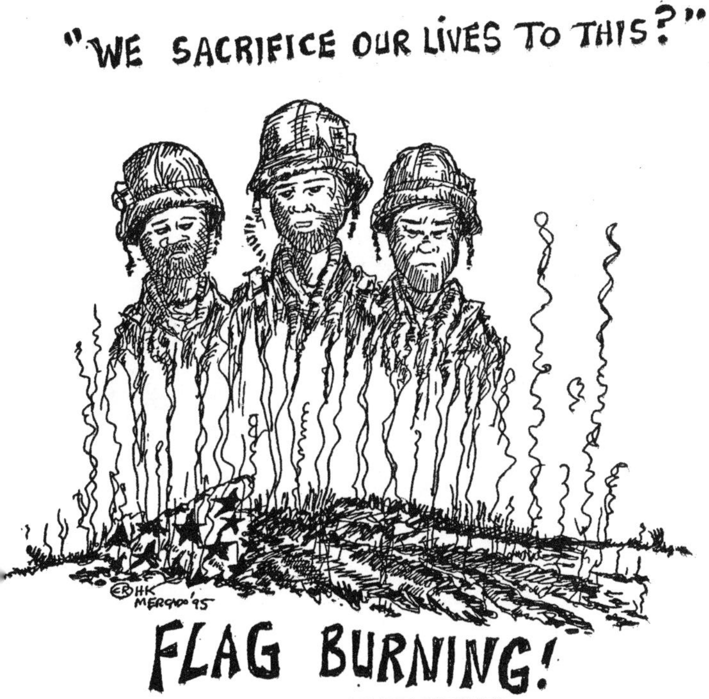
"WE SACRIFICE OUR LIVES TO THIS?"
FLAG BURNING!

JAMES MERCADO
Courtesy The Garden Island

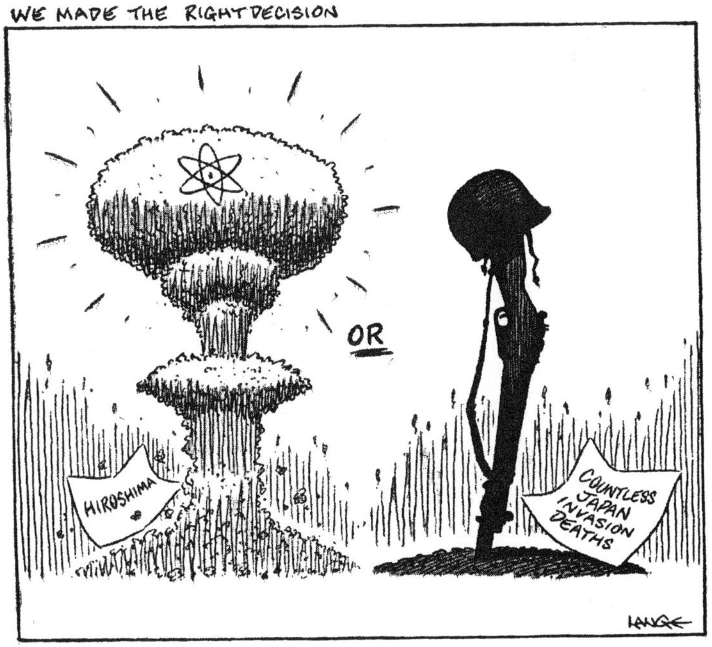
WE MADE THE RIGHT DECISION
HIROSHIMA
OR
COUNTLESS JAPAN INVASION DEATHS
LANGE

JIM LANGE
Courtesy Daily Oklahoman

DALE STEPHANOS
Courtesy USA Today

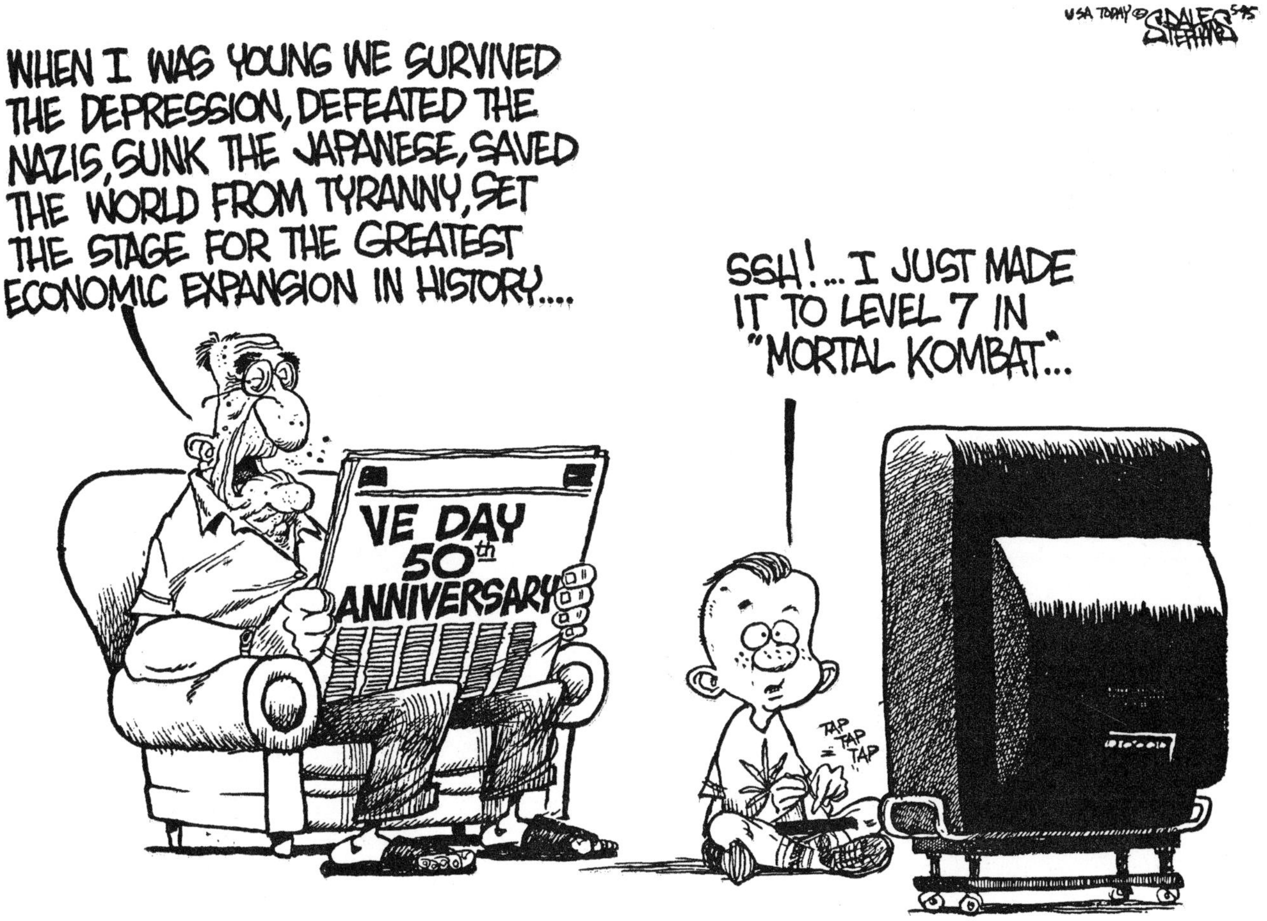
WHEN I WAS YOUNG WE SURVIVED THE DEPRESSION, DEFEATED THE NAZIS, SUNK THE JAPANESE, SAVED THE WORLD FROM TYRANNY, SET THE STAGE FOR THE GREATEST ECONOMIC EXPANSION IN HISTORY....
SSH!...I JUST MADE IT TO LEVEL 7 IN "MORTAL KOMBAT"...
VE DAY 50th ANNIVERSARY
TAP TAP TAP

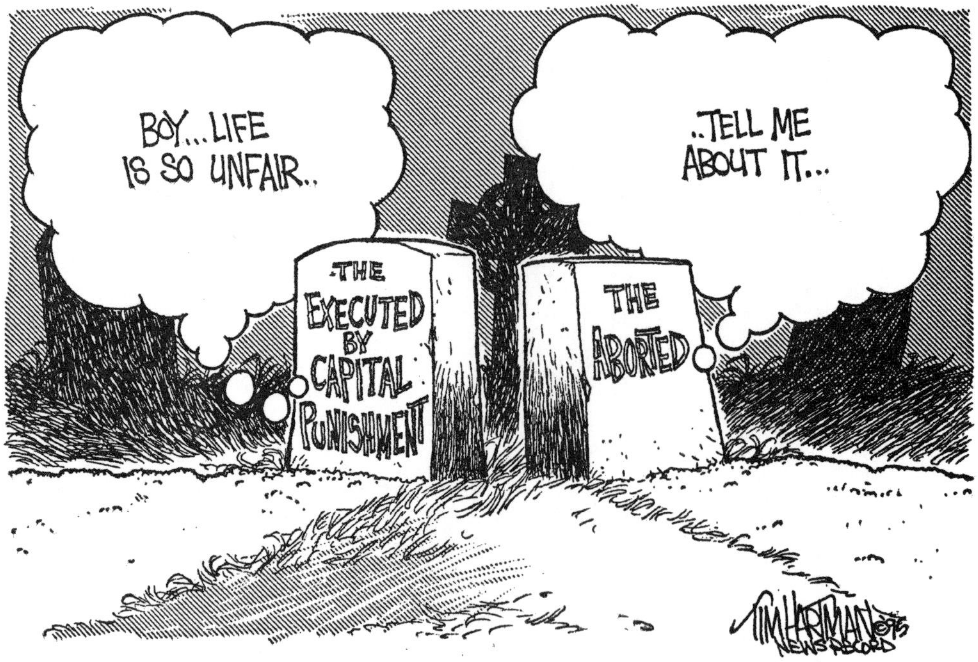
BOY... LIFE IS SO UNFAIR..
..TELL ME ABOUT IT...
THE EXECUTED BY CAPITAL PUNISHMENT
THE ABORTED
TIM HARTMAN ©95 NEWS RECORD

TIM HARTMAN
Courtesy North Hills News Record (Pa.)

JEFF KOTERBA
Courtesy Omaha World-Herald

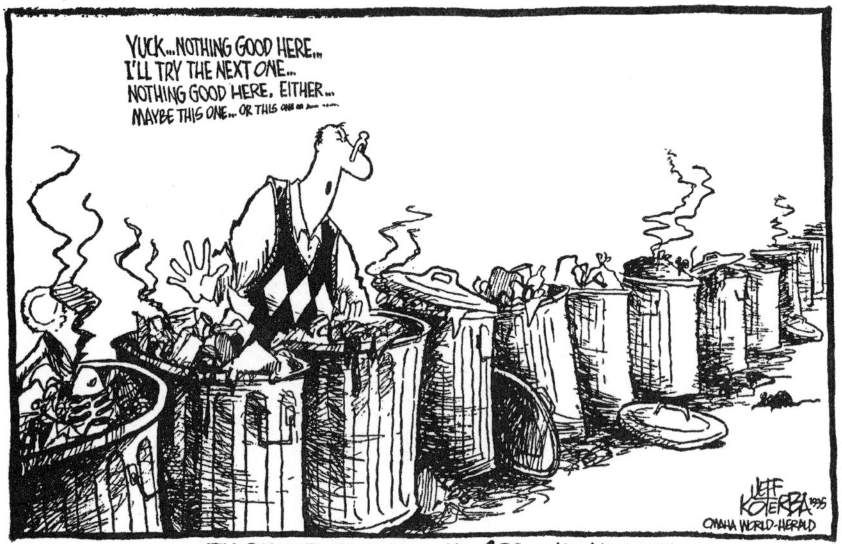
YUCK... NOTHING GOOD HERE...
I'LL TRY THE NEXT ONE...
NOTHING GOOD HERE, EITHER...
MAYBE THIS ONE... OR THIS
JEFF KOTERBA 1995
OMAHA WORLD-HERALD

TV CHANNEL SURFING in the '90s: AN ANALOGY

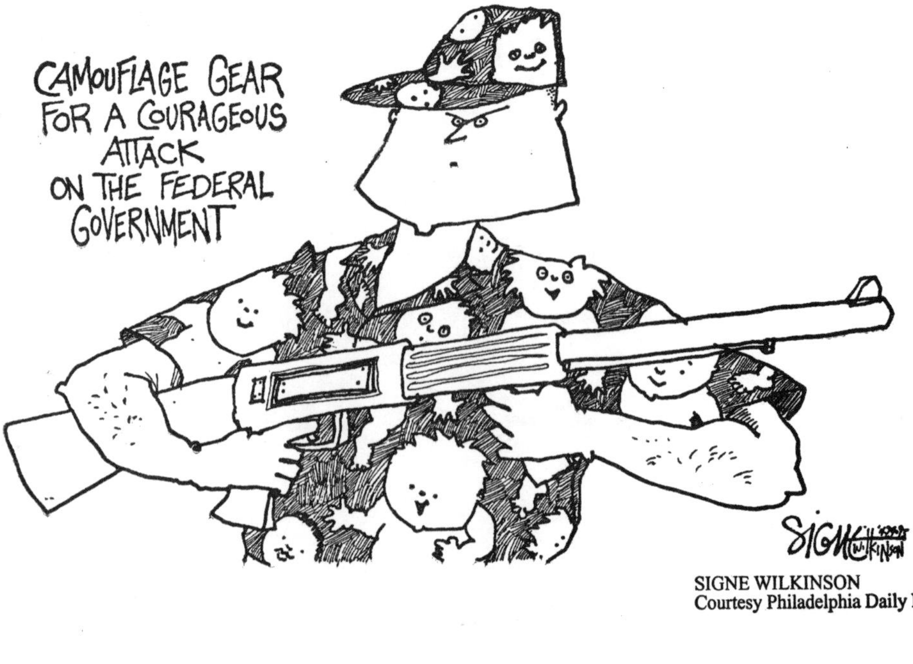
CAMOUFLAGE GEAR FOR A COURAGEOUS ATTACK ON THE FEDERAL GOVERNMENT
SIGNE WILKINSON

SIGNE WILKINSON
Courtesy Philadelphia Daily N

PAUL CONRAD
Courtesy Los Angeles Times

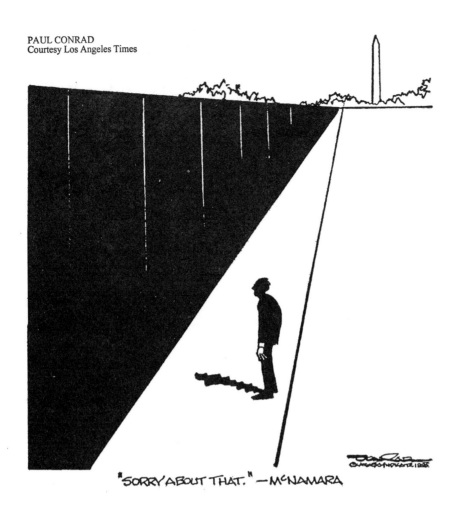

"SORRY ABOUT THAT." —McNAMARA

DON MARQUIS
Courtesy Chico News and Review

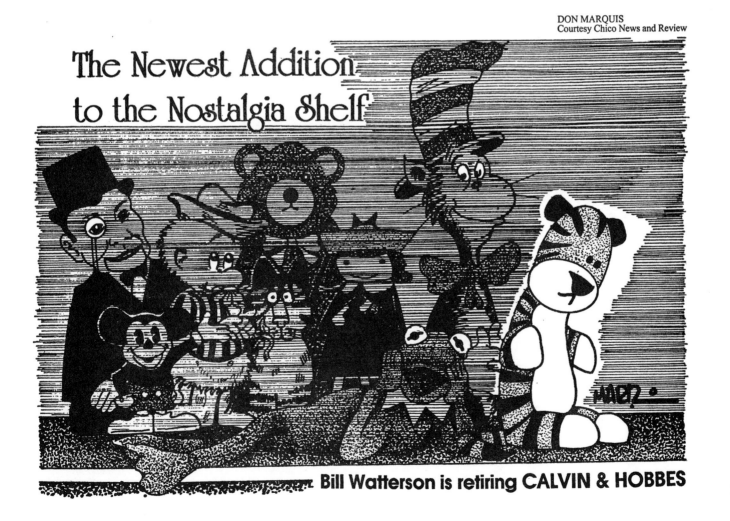

The Newest Addition to the Nostalgia Shelf

Bill Watterson is retiring CALVIN & HOBBES

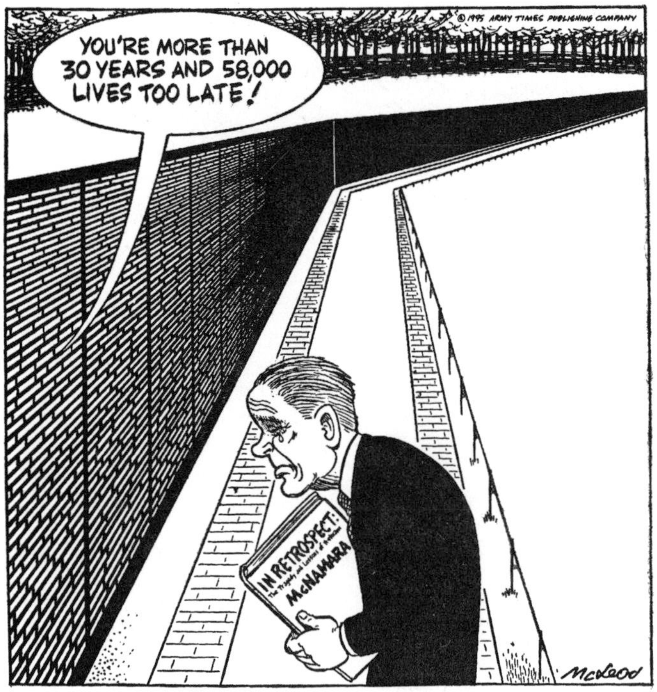
© 1995 ARMY TIMES PUBLISHING COMPANY
YOU'RE MORE THAN 30 YEARS AND 58,000 LIVES TOO LATE!
IN RETROSPECT:
McNAMARA
McLeod

JACK MCLEOD
Courtesy Army Times

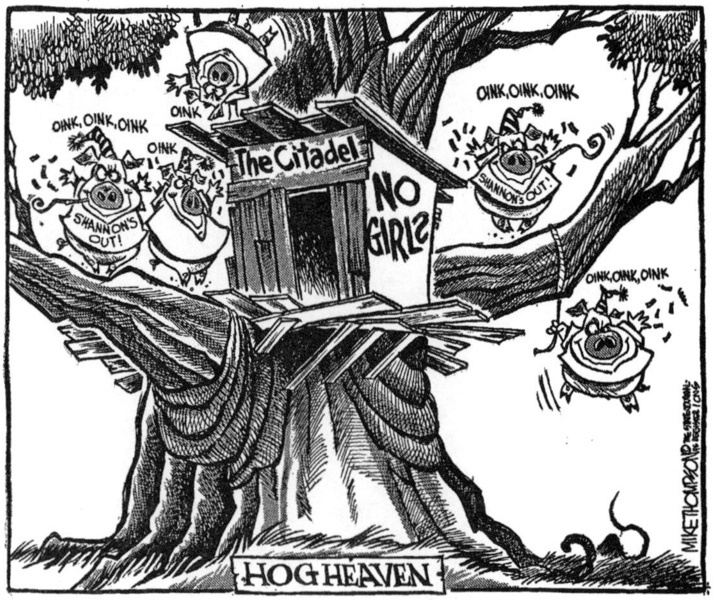
OINK
OINK, OINK, OINK
OINK
The Citadel
NO GIRLS
OINK, OINK, OINK
SHANNON'S OUT!
SHANNON'S OUT!
OINK, OINK, OINK
HOG HEAVEN
MIKE THOMPSON

MIKE THOMPSON
Courtesy State Journal-Register (Ill.)

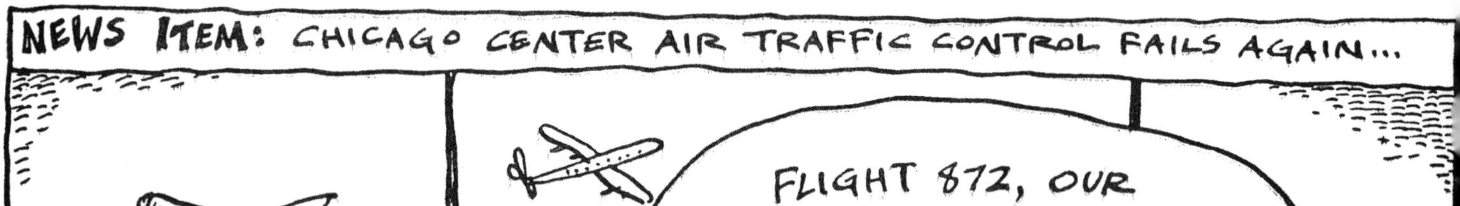
NEWS ITEM: CHICAGO CENTER AIR TRAFFIC CONTROL FAILS AGAIN...
FLIGHT 872, OUR COMPUTERS ARE DOWN, BUT DON'T WORRY, I'VE GOT YOU ON MY NINTENDO GAME BOY!
LARRY WRIGHT
©1995 THE DETROIT NEWS

LARRY WRIGHT
Courtesy Detroit News

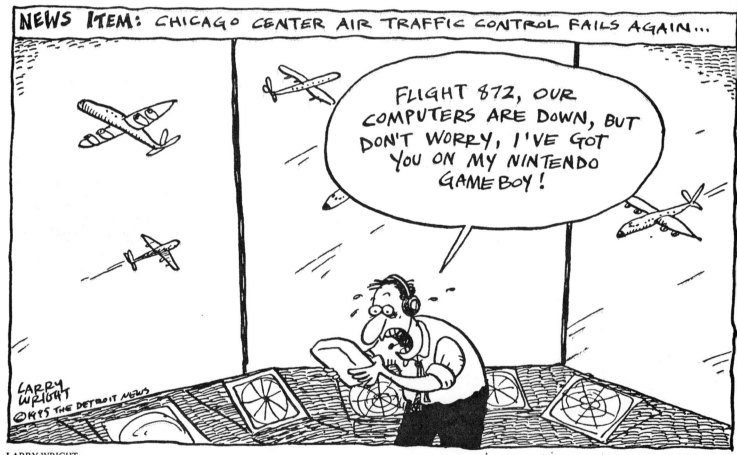

DANI AGUILA
Courtesy Filipino Reporter

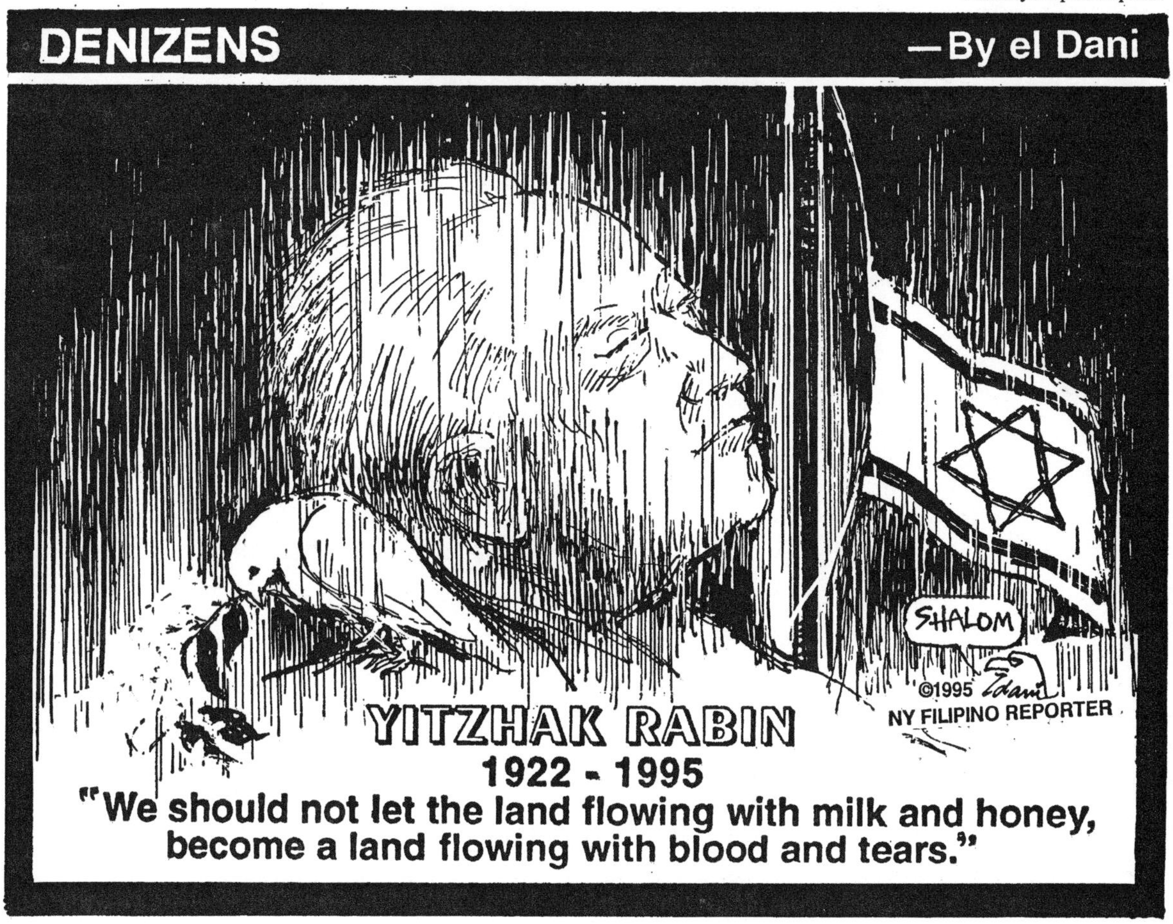
DENIZENS
—By el Dani
SHALOM
©1995 edani
NY FILIPINO REPORTER
YITZHAK RABIN
1922 - 1995
"We should not let the land flowing with milk and honey, become a land flowing with blood and tears."

JIM BORGMAN
Courtesy Cincinnati Enquirer

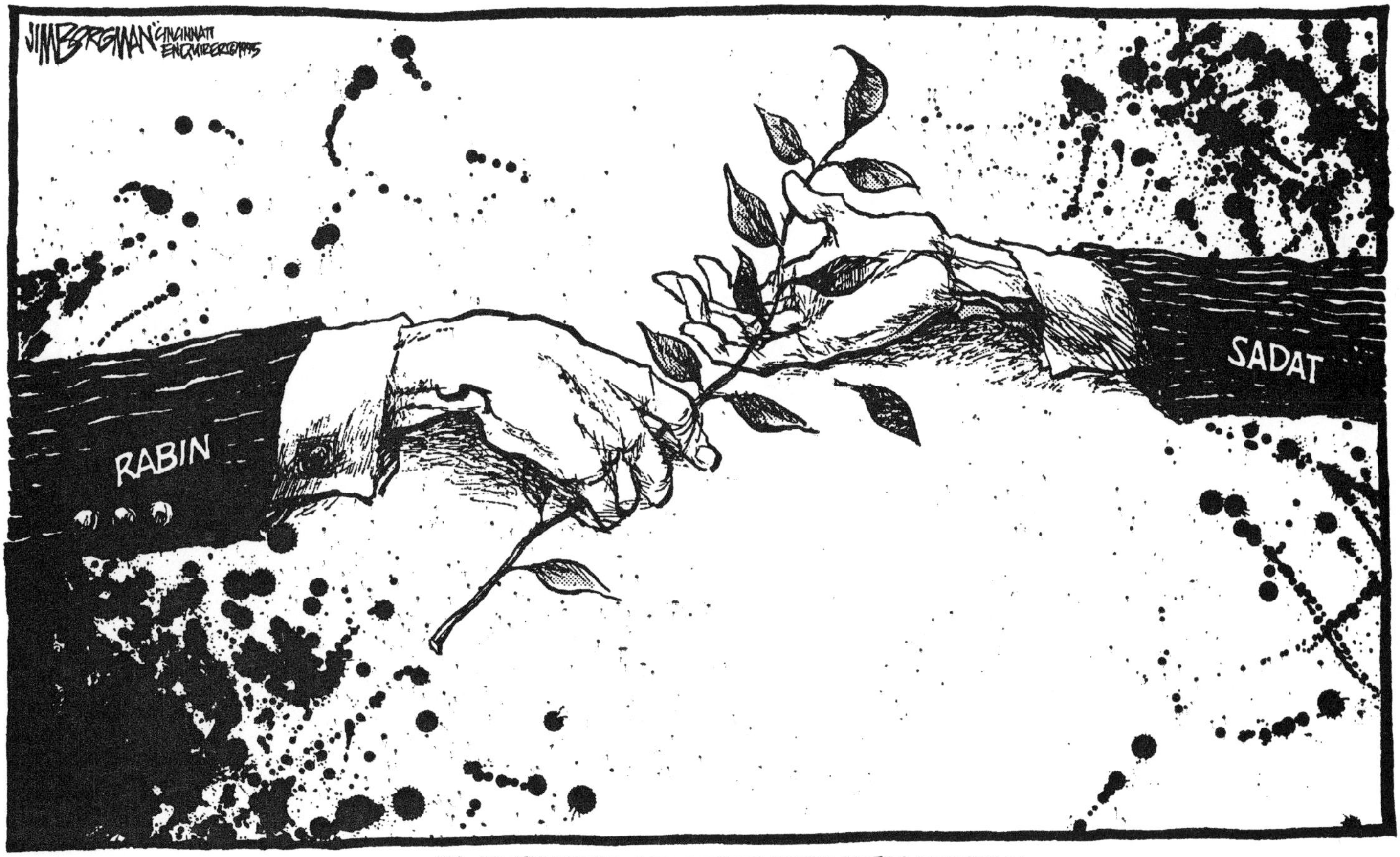
JIMBORGMAN CINCINNATI ENQUIRER©1995
RABIN
SADAT

BLOODIED ARE THE PEACEMAKERS

PAUL CONRAD
Courtesy Los Angeles Times

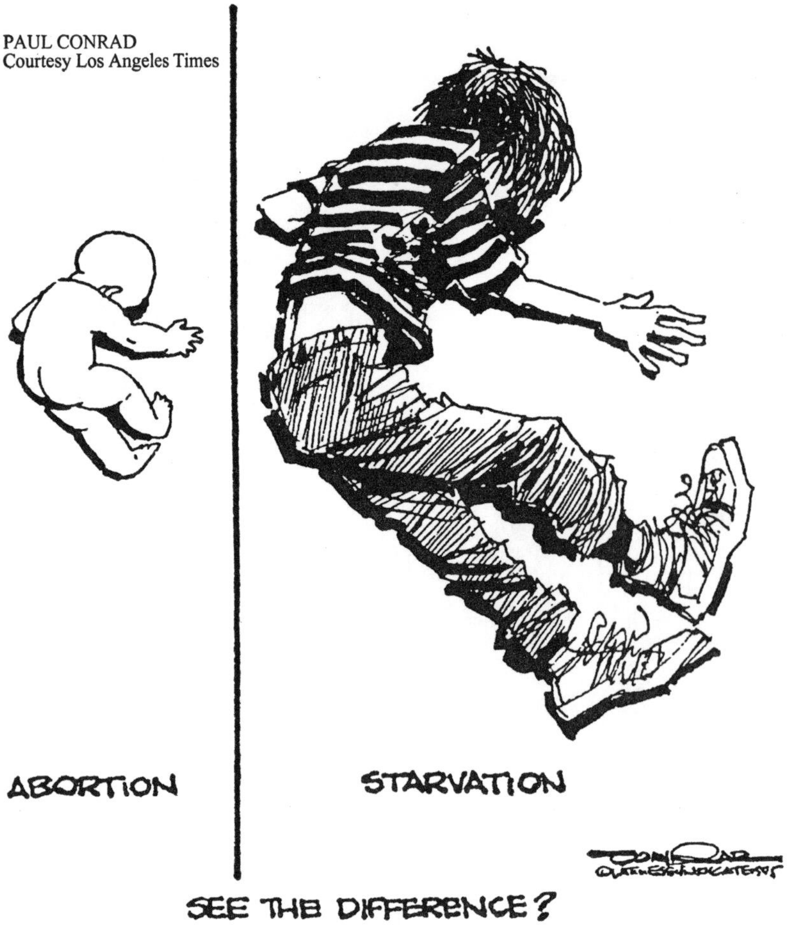

ABORTION
STARVATION
SEE THE DIFFERENCE?

JACK JURDEN
Courtesy Wilmington News Journal

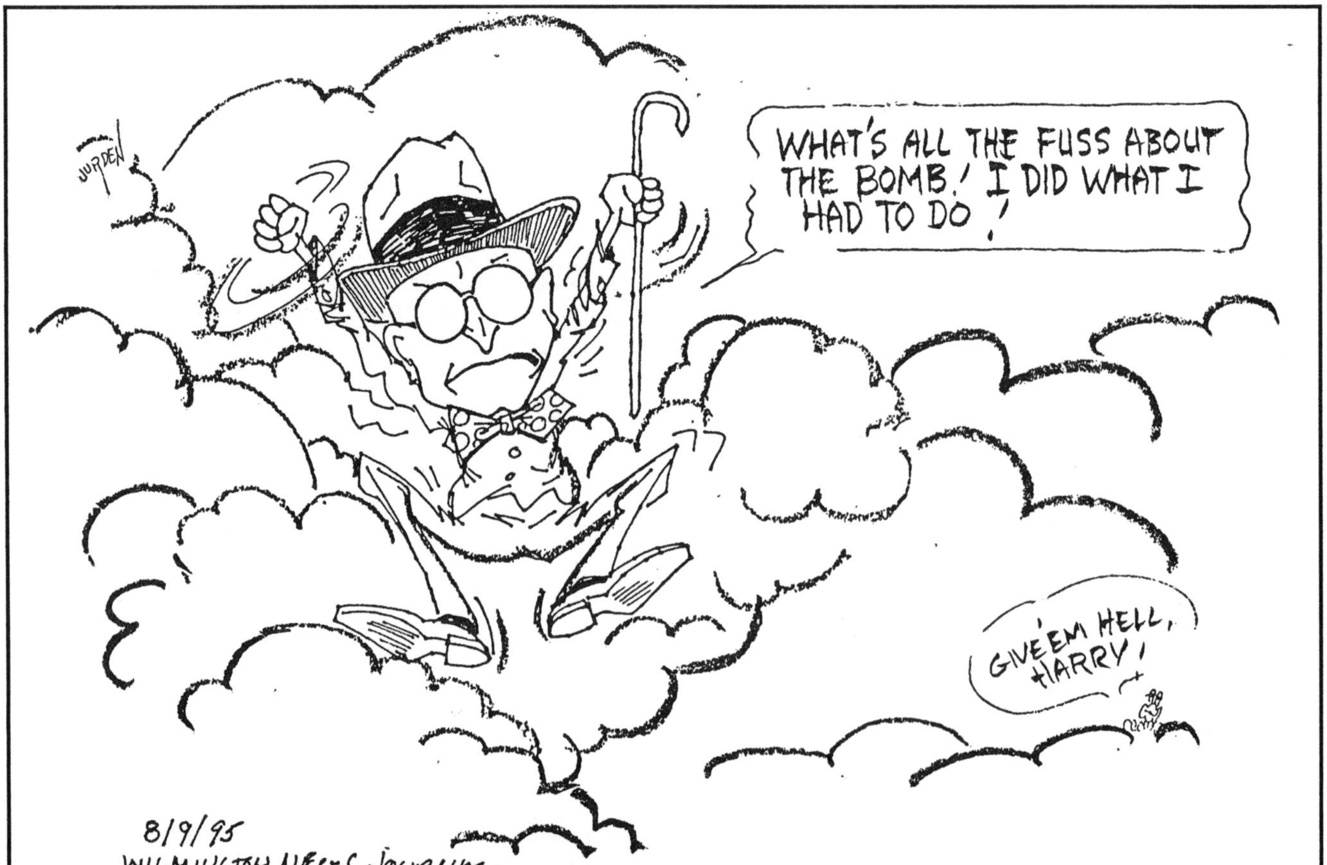

JURDEN
WHAT'S ALL THE FUSS ABOUT THE BOMB! I DID WHAT I HAD TO DO!
GIVE'EM HELL, HARRY!
8/9/95
WILMINGTON NEWS JOURNAL

Past Award Winners

NATIONAL HEADLINERS CLUB AWARD

1938—C. D. Batchelor, New York Daily News
1939—John Knott, Dallas News
1940—Herbert Block, NEA
1941—Charles H. Sykes, Philadelphia Evening Ledger
1942—Jerry Doyle, Philadelphia Record
1943—Vaughn Shoemaker, Chicago Daily News
1944—Roy Justus, Sioux City Journal
1945—F. O. Alexander, Philadelphia Bulletin
1946—Hank Barrow, Associated Press
1947—Cy Hungerford, Pittsburgh Post-Gazette
1948—Tom Little, Nashville Tennessean
1949—Bruce Russell, Los Angeles Times
1950—Dorman Smith, NEA
1951—C. G. Werner, Indianapolis Star
1952—John Fischetti, NEA
1953—James T. Berryman and
           Gib Crocket, Washington Star
1954—Scott Long, Minneapolis Tribune
1955—Leo Thiele, Los Angeles Mirror-News
1956—John Milt Morris, Associated Press
1957—Frank Miller, Des Moines Register
1958—Burris Jenkins, Jr., New York Journal-American
1959—Karl Hubenthal, Los Angeles Examiner
1960—Don Hesse, St. Louis Globe-Democrat
1961—L. D. Warren, Cincinnati Enquirer
1962—Franklin Morse, Los Angeles Mirror
1963—Charles Bissell, Nashville Tennessean
1964—Lou Grant, Oakland Tribune
1965—Merle R. Tingley, London (Ont.) Free Press
1966—Hugh Haynie, Louisville Courier-Journal
1967—Jim Berry, NEA
1968—Warren King, New York News
1969—Larry Barton, Toledo Blade
1970—Bill Crawford, NEA
1971—Ray Osrin, Cleveland Plain Dealer
1972—Jacob Burck, Chicago Sun-Times
1973—Ranan Lurie, New York Times
1974—Tom Darcy, Newsday
1975—Bill Sanders, Milwaukee Journal
1976—No award given
1977—Paul Szep, Boston Globe
1978—Dwane Powell, Raleigh News and Observer
1979—Pat Oliphant, Washington Star
1980—Don Wright, Miami News
1981—Bill Garner, Memphis Commercial Appeal
1982—Mike Peters, Dayton Daily News
1983—Doug Marlette, Charlotte Observer
1984—Steve Benson, Arizona Republic
1985—Bill Day, Detroit Free Press
1986—Mike Keefe, Denver Post
1987—Mike Peters, Dayton Daily News
1988—Doug Marlette, Charlotte Observer
1989—Walt Handelsman, Scranton Times
1990—Robert Ariail, The State
1991—Jim Borgman, Cincinnati Enquirer
1992—Mike Luckovich, Atlanta Constitution
1993—Walt Handelsman, New Orleans Times-Picayune
1994—Mike Peters, Dayton Daily News
1995—Rob Rogers, Pittsburgh Post-Gazette

PULITZER PRIZE

1922—Rollin Kirby, New York World
1923—No award given
1924—J. N. Darling, New York Herald Tribune
1925—Rollin Kirby, New York World
1926—D. R. Fitzpatrick, St. Louis Post-Dispatch
1927—Nelson Harding, Brooklyn Eagle
1928—Nelson Harding, Brooklyn Eagle
1929—Rollin Kirby, New York World
1930—Charles Macauley, Brooklyn Eagle
1931—Edmund Duffy, Baltimore Sun
1932—John T. McCutcheon, Chicago Tribune
1933—H. M. Talburt, Washington Daily News
1934—Edmund Duffy, Baltimore Sun
1935—Ross A. Lewis, Milwaukee Journal
1936—No award given
1937—C. D. Batchelor, New York Daily News
1938—Vaughn Shoemaker, Chicago Daily News
1939—Charles G. Werner, Daily Oklahoman
1940—Edmund Duffy, Baltimore Sun
1941—Jacob Burck, Chicago Times
1942—Herbert L. Block, NEA
1943—Jay N. Darling, New York Herald Tribune
1944—Clifford K. Berryman, Washington Star
1945—Bill Mauldin, United Features Syndicate
1946—Bruce Russell, Los Angeles Times
1947—Vaughn Shoemaker, Chicago Daily News
1948—Reuben L. ("Rube") Goldberg, New York Sun
1949—Lute Pease, Newark Evening News
1950—James T. Berryman, Washington Star
1951—Reginald W. Manning, Arizona Republic
1952—Fred L. Packer, New York Mirror
1953—Edward D. Kuekes, Cleveland Plain Dealer
1954—Herbert L. Block, Washington Post
1955—Daniel R. Fitzpatrick, St. Louis Post-Dispatch
1956—Robert York, Louisville Times
1957—Tom Little, Nashville Tennessean
1958—Bruce M. Shanks, Buffalo Evening News
1959—Bill Mauldin, St. Louis Post-Dispatch
1960—No award given
1961—Carey Orr, Chicago Tribune
1962—Edmund S. Valtman, Hartford Times

1963—Frank Miller, Des Moines Register
1964—Paul Conrad, Denver Post
1965—No award given
1966—Don Wright, Miami News
1967—Patrick B. Oliphant, Denver Post
1968—Eugene Gray Payne, Charlotte Observer
1969—John Fischetti, Chicago Daily News
1970—Thomas F. Darcy, Newsday
1971—Paul Conrad, Los Angeles Times
1972—Jeffrey K. MacNelly, Richmond News Leader
1973—No award given
1974—Paul Szep, Boston Globe
1975—Garry Trudeau, Universal Press Syndicate
1976—Tony Auth, Philadelphia Enquirer
1977—Paul Szep, Boston Globe
1978—Jeff MacNelly, Richmond News Leader
1979—Herbert Block, Washington Post
1980—Don Wright, Miami News
1981—Mike Peters, Dayton Daily News
1982—Ben Sargent, Austin American-Statesman
1983—Dick Locher, Chicago Tribune
1984—Paul Conrad, Los Angeles Times
1985—Jeff MacNelly, Chicago Tribune
1986—Jules Feiffer, Universal Press Syndicate
1987—Berke Breathed, Washington Post Writers Group
1988—Doug Marlette, Atlanta Constitution
1989—Jack Higgins, Chicago Sun-Times
1990—Tom Toles, Buffalo News
1991—Jim Borgman, Cincinnati Enquirer
1992—Signe Wilkinson, Philadelphia Daily News
1993—Steve Benson, Arizona Republic
1994—Michael Ramirez, Memphis Commercial Appeal
1995—Mike Luckovich, Atlanta Constitution

1962—Duncan Macpherson, Toronto Star
1963—Jan Kamienski, Winnipeg Tribune
1964—Ed McNally, Montreal Star
1965—Duncan Macpherson, Toronto Star
1966—Robert W. Chambers, Halifax Chronicle-Herald
1967—Raoul Hunter, Le Soleil, Quebec
1968—Roy Peterson, Vancouver Sun
1969—Edward Uluschak, Edmonton Journal
1970—Duncan Macpherson, Toronto Daily Star
1971—Yardley Jones, Toronto Star
1972—Duncan Macpherson, Toronto Star
1973—John Collins, Montreal Gazette
1974—Blaine, Hamilton Spectator
1975—Roy Peterson, Vancouver Sun
1976—Andy Donato, Toronto Sun
1977—Terry Mosher, Montreal Gazette
1978—Terry Mosher, Montreal Gazette
1979—Edd Uluschak, Edmonton Journal
1980—Vic Roschkov, Toronto Star
1981—Tom Innes, Calgary Herald
1982—Blaine, Hamilton Spectator
1983—Dale Cummings, Winnipeg Free Press
1984—Roy Peterson, Vancouver Sun
1985—Ed Franklin, Toronto Globe and Mail
1986—Brian Gable, Regina Leader Post
1987—Raffi Anderian, Ottawa Citizen
1988—Vance Rodewalt, Calgary Herald
1989—Cameron Cardow, Regina Leader-Post
1990—Roy Peterson, Vancouver Sun
1991—Guy Badeaux, Le Droit, Ottawa
1992—Bruce Mackinnon, Halifax Herald
1993—Bruce Mackinnon, Halifax Herald
1994—Roy Peterson, Vancouver Sun

NATIONAL NEWSPAPER AWARD / CANADA

1949—Jack Boothe, Toronto Globe and Mail
1950—James G. Reidford, Montreal Star
1951—Len Norris, Vancouver Sun
1952—Robert La Palme, Le Devoir, Montreal
1953—Robert W. Chambers, Halifax Chronicle-Herald
1954—John Collins, Montreal Gazette
1955—Merle R. Tingley, London Free Press
1956—James G. Reidford, Toronto Globe and Mail
1957—James G. Reidford, Toronto Globe and Mail
1958—Raoul Hunter, Le Soleil, Quebec
1959—Duncan Macpherson, Toronto Star
1960—Duncan Macpherson, Toronto Star
1961—Ed McNally, Montreal Star

FISCHETTI AWARD

1982—Lee Judge, Kansas City Times
1983—Bill DeOre, Dallas Morning News
1984—Tom Toles, Buffalo News
1985—Scott Willis, Dallas Times-Herald
1986—Doug Marlette, Charlotte Observer
1987—Dick Locher, Chicago Tribune
1988—Arthur Bok, Akron Beacon-Journal
1989—Lambert Der, Greenville News
1990—Jeff Stahler, Cincinnati Post
1991—Mike Keefe, Denver Post
1992—Doug Marlette, New York Newsday
1993—Bill Schorr, Kansas City Star
1994—John Deering, Arkansas Democrat-Gazette
1995—Stuart Carlson, Milwaukee Journal Sentinel

Index of Cartoonists

INDEX OF CARTOONISTS

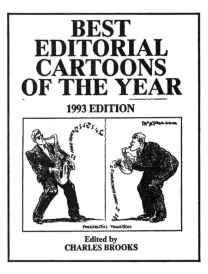

BEST EDITORIAL CARTOONS OF THE YEAR

1994 EDITION

Edited by
CHARLES BROOKS

COMPLETE YOUR CARTOON COLLECTION

BEST EDITORIAL CARTOONS OF THE YEAR

1993 EDITION

Edited by
CHARLES BROOKS

Previous editions of this timeless series are available for those wishing to update their collection of the most provocative moments of the past twenty years. In the early days the topics were the oil crisis, Richard Nixon's presidency, Watergate, and the Vietnam War. Over time the cartoonists and their subjects have changed along with presidential administrations. These days those subjects have been replaced by the Clinton Health Care Reform Bill, the Crime Bill, the NAFTA treaty results, the O. J. Simpson murder trial, and the United States' involvement in Haiti. But in the end, the wit and wisdom of the editorial cartoonists have prevailed. And on the pages of these op-ed galleries one can find memories and much more. from the

Select from the following supply of past editions

_____ 1972 Edition $18.95 hc	_____ 1981 Edition $14.95 pb	_____ 1988 Edition $14.95 pb
_____ 1974 Edition $18.95 hc	_____ 1982 Edition $14.95 pb	1989 Edition out of print
_____ 1975 Edition $18.95 hc	1983 Edition out of print	_____ 1990 Edition $14.95 pb
_____ 1976 Edition $18.95 hc	_____ 1984 Edition $14.95 pb	_____ 1991 Edition $14.95 pb
_____ 1977 Edition $18.95 hc	_____ 1985 Edition $14.95 pb	_____ 1992 Edition $14.95 pb
1978 Edition out of print	_____ 1986 Edition $14.95 pb	_____ 1993 Edition $14.95 pb
1979 Edition out of print	_____ 1987 Edition $14.95 pb	_____ 1994 Edition $14.95 pb
_____ 1980 Edition $18.95 hc	_____ Please add me to the list of standing orders for future editions.	

Please include $2.00 for 4th Class Postage and handling or $3.25 for UPS Ground Shipment plus $.75 for each additional copy ordered.*

Total enclosed: _____

NAME _____

ADDRESS_____

CITY _____ STATE _____ ZIP _____

Make checks payable to

PELICAN PUBLISHING COMPANY
P.O. Box 3110, Dept. 5BEC
Gretna, Louisiana 70054
CREDIT CARD ORDERS CALL 1-800-843-1724

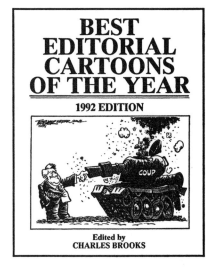

BEST EDITORIAL CARTOONS OF THE YEAR

1992 EDITION

Edited by
CHARLES BROOKS

* Jefferson Parish residents add 8¾% tax. All other Louisiana residents add 4% tax.